CRIMINAL LAW
FOR
PEACE OFFICERS

CRIMINAL LAW FOR PEACE OFFICERS

Jesse R. Pistole

RESTON PUBLISHING COMPANY, INC.
Reston, Virginia
A Prentice-Hall Company

Library of Congress Cataloging in Publication Data

Pistole, Jesse R
Criminal law for peace officers.

Includes index.
1. Criminal law–United States. 2. Criminal procedure–United States. 3. Police–United States –Handbooks, manuals, etc. I. Title.
KF9219.8.P65P5 345'.73'052 75-32420
ISBN 0-87909-163-0

10 9 8 7 6 5 4 3 2 1

Printed in the United States of America.

This book is dedicated to my wife, Alice, whose inspiration and assistance were indispensable in the preparation and production of this book.

Contents

Preface

The author recognizes the impossibility of compiling a text on criminal law that is equally applicable in all states, as the laws of the several states vary in comparison from slightly in some states to radically in others, and added to the differences in state laws are the inconsistencies of court interpretations. However, in the vast majority of cases the laws are either substantially the same or similar. Excerpts herein contained are selected to illustrate laws and court interpretations common to the majority of the states disregarding minor exceptions.

Included in this text are decisions of the United States Supreme Court, the federal circuit courts of appeal and the federal district courts. Also, a comprehensive selection of case law has been made of decisions of the state supreme courts and other courts of appeal. All court citations of authority include in the citation the year and the state in which the decision was made.

This text was prepared principally for peace officers and for students of police science or criminal jurisprudence who seek to become peace officers. Also, it is quite useful as a quick reference for prosecutors and criminal trial attorneys. May it fulfill your needs, whatever your field of endeavor.

Jesse R. Pistole

Acknowledgments

To all those who assisted or inspired me in the preparation of this text I express my gratitude, but especially to Mrs. Marie Sullivan, Snohomish County law librarian; Mrs. Janice (Armour) Lovell, Shoreline College; and Deputy Alan P. Healy, San Juan County, Washington, Sheriff's Office.

PART I

SOURCE, DEFINITION AND FUNCTION OF LAW

Chapter I

Fundamental Law

The Common Law

The rules of the common law of England is in full force and effect in all states (except Louisiana), unless abolished or modified by statute, or state or federal constitutions. *State v Egan,* 287 S 2d 1/Fla (1973); *Hook v Horner*, 517 P 2d 554/Id (1973).

The common law, like acts passed by a legislative body, is subject to change, modification or abrogation by that legislative body, as may be most conducive to the general welfare. *In re Davis*, 299 A 2d 856/Md (1973).

The legislature may validly abolish common law right or remedy prospectively without furnishing an adequate substitute (*Troy Hills Village Inc, v Fischler*, 301 A 2d 177/NJ–1973), but in the absence of a legislative enactment clearly intended to effectuate a change in the common law, the common law rules govern. *Tilbro Home Builders Inc v Leidel,* 344 NYS 2d 614/NY (1973).

Common law rules, which are court-made rules, can be changed by a court when the court is convinced that policies upon which the rules are based have lost their validity or when the rules are mistakenly conceived. *Spokane Methodist Homes Inc v Department of Labor and Industries,* 501 P 2d 589/Wn (1972).

The common law of England includes not only *lex non scripta* (unwritten law), but written statutes enacted by Parliament (*People v Baker*, 442 P 2d 675/Cal–1968), and that body of court decisions in the nonstatutory field to which the doctrine of *stare decisis* applies. *Windust v Dept of Labor & Industries,* 323 P 2d 241/Wn (1958).

Many states have, by legislative action, abolished the common law, but even though no such action has been taken, one may not be tried and convicted—either in local, state or federal court—unless there is in existence at the time an ordinance, regulation or statute commanding or forbidding the act. *In re Borzoz*, 510 P 2d 1017/Cal (1973).

International Law

International law takes precedence over state law where there is conflict (*State v Marley*, 509 P 2d 1095/Haw—1973), and other than that included in American treaties, it does not affect a state in its reasonable regulation of conduct within its territorial limits. *State v Marley, supra.*

When a ship enters the territorial limits of another country, it is subject to jurisdiction of the foreign soverign. *Mathews v Halford*, 374 FS 1003/La (1974).

A coastal state has the power to investigate crimes and arrest law violators where the crime occurred in international waters on a foreign vessel and the vessel docked within the territorial limits of that state and a request for assistance was made by the master of the vessel—here, a stabbing on a Liberian flag ship. *In re Chan Kam-Shu*, 477 F 2d 333/Fla (1973).

Congress has the power to enact laws which forbid the killing of one American citizen by another within diplomatic compounds on foreign soil. *United States v Erdos*, 474 F 2d 157/Va (1973).

Under the theory of objective territorial jurisdiction, the U.S. District Court could try defendant for forging, possessing and uttering, in Juarez, Mexico, social security checks drawn on the U.S. Treasury and stolen from U.S. mails, on the premise that such acts were designed to, and did, produce detrimental effects within the United States. *United States v Fernandez*, 496 F 2d 1294/Tex (1974).

Comity Agreements

"Comity" is the recognition which one nation extends within its own territory to legislative, executive or judicial acts of another; it is not a law but a rule of practice extended for convenience and expediency. *Somportex Limited v Philadelphia Chewing Gum Corp*, 453 F 2d 435/Pa (1971).

Under international law, comity is neither a matter of absolute obligation nor mere courtesy or good will; it is acts of governments having due regard for international duty and convenience, and for the rights of its own citizens or of other persons who are under the protection of its laws. *Sherif v Sherif*, 352 NYS 2d 781/NY (1974).

The Nature of Government

In its guarantee of a republican form of government, the U.S. Constitution defines the doctrine of "separation of powers"—the legislative power is the power to make, amend or repeal laws; the executive power is the power to enforce the laws; and the judicial power is the power to interpret and apply the laws in actual controversies. *Van Sickle v Shanahan*, 511 P 2d 223/Kan (1973).

Ministerial functions are inherent within all branches of government and are necessary methods for the implementation and accomplishment of the basic functions of each department. *Galloway v Tuesdell*, 422 P 2d 237/Nev (1967).

All substantive (statutory) law is either:

1. Definitive, when it defines words, phrases, intent of the legislature;
2. Permissive, when it permits an act or certain conduct and the methods by which it may be accomplished;
3. Prohibitive, when it forbids acts and conduct and prescribes a penalty for nonconformance; or
4. Mandatory, when it imposes a duty to act in the performance of some obligation.

The penal law of a state is the "general law." *People v Wilkerson*, 342 NYS 936/NY (1973).

The U.S. Constitution is a grant of power to the national state, which has no power not thus granted. State constitutions, however, are restrictions on the plenary powers of the states. *Caesar v Williams*, 371 P 2d 241/Id (1962).

Under state constitutions a state may do everything not prohibited thereby, while Congress, on the other hand, can do nothing unless authorized. *Joint Legislative Committee v Strain*, 268 S 2d 629/La (1972).

Self-Executing Provisions

A constitutional provision is said to be self-executing when it can be given effect without the aid of legislation and there is nothing to indicate that legislation is contemplated to render it operative. When there is manifest the intention that the provision should be immediately effective, ancillary legislation is unnecessary to the enjoyment of the right given. *Appeal of Crescent Precision Products Inc*, 516 P 2d 275/Ok (1973); *State ex rel Miller v Board of Education*, 511 P 2d 705/Kan (1973).

If a constitutional provision supplies the rule or means by which the right given may be enjoyed and protected or by which a duty imposed may be enforced without ancillary legislative enactment (*People v Western Airlines*, 268 P 2d 723/Cal–1954), such as the provision for a speedy and public trial (*Barker v Municipal Court*, 415 P 2d 809/Cal–1966), or the mandate that private property may not be taken by the state but by the payment of just compensation, then it requires no legislative enactment to arouse from dormancy. *State Highway Commission v Keneally*, 384 P 2d 770/Mont (1963).

Self-executing constitutional provisions are, in all respects, on equal footing with statutes as to their administrative effect and from the standpoint of enforcement, and the legislature is not authorized to enact any law in conflict therewith. *Roberts v Spray*, 223 P 2d 808/Az (1950).

Laws Amenable to Two Interpretations

If a constitutional amendment is susceptible to two constructions; one workable and one unworkable, the appellate court will assume that the legislature intended that construction which is workable and fair (*Hamilton v Autauga County*, 268 S 2d 30/Ala–1972). And it is also a fundamental principle that where there are two possible interpretations of a statute, one valid and the other invalid, the courts unanimously agree that validity of the statute is the preferred interpretation. *Ruble v Redden*, 517 P 2d 1124/Ok (1973).

Conflict of Provisions

As a rule, where a state law indicates a purpose to occupy an entire field, the field is preempted, and local laws are prohibited therein whether they duplicate, supplement or conflict therewith (*People v Wilkerson*, 342 NYS 2d 936/NY–1973). However, under the laws of some jurisdictions city ordinances may coexist with state statutes unless the ordinance is in conflict with state statute or with state or federal constitution in which case the city ordinance is preempted (*In re Black*, 304 NE 2d 394/Oh–1973). And where two constitutional provisions are in conflict the later enactment will prevail over the former. *Williams v Magma Copper Co*, 425 P 2d 138/Az (1967).

Ex Post Facto Laws

The U.S. Constitution and state constitutions as well forbid the enactment of *ex post facto* laws. This proscription means that a law cannot be given effect retroactively (*Hopt v Utah*, 110 US 574/1883). Further, an *ex post facto* law is one which, in its operation, not only makes an act criminal which was not criminal at the time of its commission, but also increases the punishment of a crime after its commission (*Wilensky v Fields*, 267 S 2d 1/Fla–1972). A statute must be considered *ex post facto* and thus unconstitutional if, after the commission of an act, it alters the situation to the disadvantage of the accused (*In re Jones*, 500 P 2d 690/Wyo–1972). But where the law required that a victim die within a year and a day for the act to be homicide, and the time span was increased to three years and a day after the fatal blow was inflicted and the victim lived 21 months before she died as a result of the blow, the trial of defendant for a felonious homicide was not barred by the *ex post facto* clause of the Constitution. *People v Snipe*, 102 CR 6/Cal (1972).

Prohibition against *ex post facto* laws applies only to laws affecting substantive rights and not to laws of a remedial or procedural nature (*Gregory v Flowers*, 290 NE 2d 181/Oh–1972).

When defendant sold stolen hubcaps in 1967, the law making the receiving of stolen property a felony if the property was worth more than $50 was applicable; the fact that the minimum value for felony receiving was changed to $100 in 1969 when the case was received was not relevant and to hold otherwise would be a violation of the *ex post facto* clause of the Constitution. *State v Hall*, 504 P 2d 534/Az (1972).

RIGHTS AND GUARANTEES UNDER THE CONSTITUTION

Rights in General

The right to earn a livelihood by following one's legitimate occupation is a right implicit in the Fourteenth Amendment to the U.S. Constitution (*Corey v City of Dallas*, 352 FS 977/Tex–1972), and that right cannot be taken away except under the police power of the state in paramount public interest for reasons of health, safety, morals and public welfare. *In re Aston Park Hospital Inc*, 193 SE 2d 729/NC (1973).

Forbidding of plaintiff to file for divorce on the ground that she had not attained a full year's residency in the state constituted a penalty and restricted her constitutionally protected right to travel, and a statutory residence requirement violated the equal protection clause. *Monroe v Monroe*, 289 NE 2d 915/Oh (1972).

Corporations do not have all the rights as individuals, but a corporation is a "person" within the meaning of equal protection and due process clauses. *Blawis v Bolin*, 358 FS 349/Az (1973).

An alien is a person within the constitutional guarantee of equal protection under the law (*Application of Griffiths*, 294 A 2d 281/Con–1972), and an alien who had entered the country illegally was entitled to seek recovery in the courts for work, labor and services performed pursuant to contract after his illegal entry. *Commercial Standard Fire & Marine Co v Galindo*, 484 SW 2d 635/Tex (1972).

Absent a statute to the contrary, a person may adopt any name he wishes to be known by as long as he does so consistently and without any intent to defraud (*Hardy v Hardy*, 306 A 2d 244/Md–1973). But here, it is the fraud and not the change of the name which is punishable. There is no known law to the author that denies an adult the right to change his name, and if one exists it is doubtful that it could survive the analytical scrutiny of an appellate court, nor is court or judicial sanction for such change necessary.

Individuals have a constitutional right to effect any mode of dress or grooming he so desires—including hair style—so long as he does not violate the rights of others, but there is no corresponding right to work any place he may desire while adorned in a hirsute style of his choice. *Schneider v Ohio Youth Commission*, 287 NE 2d 633/Oh (1972); *Keys v Continental Illinois Nat Bank & Trust Co*, 357 FS 376/Ill (1973).

A constitutional right may not be vicariously asserted (*State v Marley*, 509 P 2d 1095/Haw–1973), but must be asserted by one whose rights were violated. *Broadrick v Oklahoma*, 93 SC 2908 (1973).

To waive a constitutional right it must be shown (1) that the subject had knowledge of that right, and (2) he made a free decision to abandon the protection of that right. *People v Grimmett*, 202 NW 2d 278/Mich (1972).

Free Speech

The First and Fourteenth Amendments to the United States Constitution guarantee certain freedoms, *inter alia*, the freedom of speech, and to this end the California Supreme Court has declared:

- The First Amendment's guarantee of the right of freedom of speech necessarily embraces the right to receive it;
- The right of freedom of speech is a guarantee primarily intended to protect minority views;
- The right of freedom of speech includes the right to anonymity;
- Popularity of pronouncements is not a criterion for determining boundaries of free speech, and even erroneous statements are entitled to constitutional protection. *Huntley v Public Utilities Commission*, 442 P 2d 685/Cal (1968).

The First Amendment protects against state interference in the expression of ideas in a public place, of pronouncements which are unpopular as well as popular; it also protects the right to assemble peaceably in a public place in the interest and furtherance of pronouncements which are unpopular, as well as popular, including racist and anti-semitic views. *Socialist White People's Party v Ringers*, 473 F 2d 1010/Va (1973).

Restrictions on Free Speech

"Freedom of speech" under the First Amendment, has been held to include not only verbal speech but symbolic speech. But just as all verbal speech is not so protected, neither is all symbolic speech. One may not, under the protection of the First Amendment yell "fire" in a crowded theater when there is no fire, or utter obscenities in a public place to the annoyance of others; likewise, under the claim of protected symbolic speech, one cannot desecrate the United States Flag merely because he despises what it stands for (*Joyce v United States*, 454 F 2d 971/DC–1972), nor throw cherry bombs at firemen and policemen or at members of the ROTC merely because he abhors "the establishment". *United States v Mechanic*, 454 F 2d 849/Mc (1971).

Freedom of speech encompasses the right to receive information as well as the right to its expression (*Vail v Board of Education*, 354 FS 592/NH–1973), and denial of the corollary freedom to hear it would seriously discount the intended purpose and effect of the First Amendment (*Fritz v Gorton*, 517 P 2d 911/Wn–1974). But freedom of speech or obscene speech is not an absolute right (*State v Mayhew*, 288 S 2d 243/Fla–1973), nor a total right, for one may be held accountable for abuses of the privilege. *Gulf States Theaters Inc v Richardson*, 287 S 2d 480/La (1973).

The right of people to assemble peacefully and to make known their opinions and to petition for redress of their grievances does not permit them to congregate at any time or place or to communicate their viewpoint by whatever method they choose; free speech and peaceful assembly may not be exercised indiscriminately. *People v Barnett*, 287 NE 2d 247/Ill (1972).

Not all speech is within the protected area of the First Amendment (*Riley v United States*, 298 A 2d 228/DC–1972), and such speech as the wanton cursing or reviling, or the use of obscene or opprobrious expressions, are not a protected means of communication. *New Orleans v Lewis*, 269 S 2d 450/La (1972).

Expression may be limited when it constitutes fighting words, i.e., words likely to provoke violent reactions. *Kalembc v Turk*, 353 FS 1101/Oh (1973).

The federal antiriot statute which forbids interstate travel to incite riots and perform overt acts for any of the proscribed purposes does not infringe on an individual's constitutional right between states. *United States v Dellinger*, 472 F 2d 340/Ill (1972).

Where defendant affixed a black tape "peace symbol" to the American Flag and displayed it from his apartment window, he was in violation of the Flag antidesecration statute and not protected by the free speech clause. *State v Spence*, 506 P 2d 293/Wn (1973).

Prisoners in a mess hall and corridors in the performance of their duties do not have the unfettered right to freedom of speech and expression, and the curtailment of speech at certain times and in certain areas when necessary to insure safety and prison security is not unreasonable if such speech is otherwise allowed at more appropriate times. *Lamar v Coffield*, 353 FS 1081/Tex (1972).

Freedom of and Restrictions on the Press

A trial is a public event, and what transpires in a courtroom is public property, and those who see and hear what transpired during the trial may report it with impunity (*United States v Dickinson*, 465 F 2d 496/La–1972), and no court has the power to prohibit the news media from publishing the events of a trial. *Wood v Goodson*, 485 SW 2d 213/Ark (1972).

A trial judge has ample power to assure a fair trial for the accused in a criminal matter without suppressing the First Amendment rights of the news media in the reporting of criminal proceedings (*Miami Herald Pub Co v Rose*, 271 S 2d 483/Fla–1972), but the First Amendment right of the news media does not afford to a newsman the privilege to refuse to disclose confidential information relevant to a criminal prosecution. *United States v Liddy*, 354 FS 208/DC (1972).

The privilege, or seeming privilege, enjoyed by members of the news media has been reevaluated by the courts and in many instances has been declared to be nonexistent. Thus, the New Jersey courts have held that the First Amendment accords a newspaperman no privilege against appearing before a grand jury and identifying the source of his information, be that source a private person or a public official and notwithstanding that the information was given in confidence. *In re Bridge*, 295 A 2d 3/NJ (1972).

Religion

The First Amendment prohibits the making of a law proscribing the free exercise of religion (*Adams v Carlson*, 352 FS 882/Ill–1973), but a statute which forbade the manufacture of marijuana did not interfere with the free exercise of defendant's religious beliefs. *Gaskin v State*, 490 SW 2d 521/Ten (1973).

"Mandatory attendance of chapel" rule for cadets and midshipmen in the Army and Navy academies violated the "establishment" clause of the First Amendment. *Anderson v Laird*, 466 F 2d 283/DC (1972).

Maintenance of a "Ten Commandments" monument on publicly owned courthouse grounds at taxpayers' expense violated the establishment clause of the First Amendment and the "liberty" and "protection" clauses of the Fourteenth Amendment. *Anderson v Salt Lake City Corp*, 348 FS 1170/Ut (1972); *Lowe v City of Eugene*, 463 P 2d 360/Or (1969).

Privacy

The constitutional right to privacy protects citizens from invasion of privacy by agencies and units of government; this right does not protect citizens from invasion by private citizens (*Werley v State*, 271 S 2d 814/Fla–1973), but see *Galella v Onassis*, 353 FS 196/NY (1972), where a United States district court declared that a private photographer's alleged harassment of a public figure amounted to an unconstitutional invasion of privacy. Id.

An Air Force regulation providing for the discharge of pregnant officers did not deny one of liberty or property without due process, nor deny one to equal process or the right to privacy. *Struck v Secretary of Defense*, 460 F 2d 1372/Wn (1971).

What Are Not Rights

"All too often there are those who stoutly demand their rights while making a mockery of the legal process which assures them the rights which they are demanding." Here, appellant objects to the loyalty oath. *Fields v Askew*, 279 S 2d 822/Fla (1973).

In view of facts that the naked female breast is a symbol of sexuality but no such generalization can be made about the male chest, that the nature of the male and female breasts are different, an administrative rule against the use of topless waitresses on premises where liquor was sold did not offend against equal protection concepts. *Locker v Kirby*, 107 CR 446/Cal (1973).

Libel, like obscenity, is not protected by the First Amendment; thus, an injunction directed against libel is not unconstitutional. *Anderson v Dean*, 354 FS 639/Ga (1973).

Curfew ordinances forbidding that children below designated ages to loiter about the streets at night is not an unreasonable classification of age nor does it deny equal protection (*In re C*, 105 CR 113/Cal–1972). Nor is a statute unconstitutional which authorizes the juvenile court to certify any child over the age of 14 years to be tried in the criminal courts as an adult when in the sound discretion of the judge the interests of the child and the community will be better served thereby. *State v Jiminez*, 503 P 2d 315/NM (1972).

A child has no vested right in future child support, and an order extending payments for support beyond the age of majority is void. *Jungjohann v Jungjohann*, 516 P 2d 904/Kan (1973).

Each member of the general population possesses the right to choose the length or style of his or her hair as guaranteed by the Ninth Amendment, and persons included herein are policemen, lawyers and teachers. But personal freedoms are not absolute and must give way when outweighed by legitimate state interests. An order by the chief administrative officer of a police department limiting the hair length of officers so that there would be uniformity in standards of grooming was not unlike an order that all officers would wear black shoes or a certain style shirt. The importance of projecting a "neutral" image so as to be readily recognizable by the public in time of need is apparent. Grooming standards is a legitimate state interest, and the desire of a police officer for individuality in the selection of his hair style and length is outweighed by legitimate state interest. *Stradley v Andersen*, 349 FS 1120 (1972); affirmed 478 F 2d 188/Neb (1973).

One has the right to wear his hair and beard as he chooses, but one seeking unemployment relief must keep himself available for employment; where an automobile mechanic, because of long hair and beard, would be considered for employment by only ten to thirteen percent of employers, he thereby made himself ineligible for such aid. *Chambers v California Unemployment Ins Appeals Board*, 109 CR 413/Cal (1973).

A judicial or legislative interdiction against strikes by public employees does not constitute involuntary servitude nor an unwarranted impingement on one's constitutional rights, be they of free speech, assembly, due process or equal protection. *School Committee v Westerly Teachers' Assn*, 299 A 2d 441/RI (1973).

Crimes on Federal Enclaves

Whenever an act is committed or omitted and a prosecution therefor lies within the purview of the federal courts and there is no federal statute applicable thereto, but such act or omission is proscribed by state law, the state law is applicable. The federal statute reads:

> Whoever within or upon any of the places now existing or hereafter reserved or acquired as provided for in section 7 of this title is guilty of any act or omission which although not made punishable by any enactment of Congress, would be punishable if committed or omitted within the jurisdiction of the State, Territory, Possession or District in which such place is situated, by the laws thereof in force at the time of such act or omission, shall be guilty of a like offense and subject to a like punishment (Title 18, § 13, United States Code).

The United States Supreme Court in deciding the constitutionality of section 13, has declared the statute's purpose to be to conform the criminal law of federal enclaves to that of local law except in cases of specific federal crimes. *United States v Sharphack*, 355 US 286/Tex (1958).

Loyalty Oath

A statute requiring that prospective voters take a loyalty oath does not conflict with the Florida Constitution, nor with due process and equal protection clauses of the Federal Constitution. The Florida Supreme Court in so holding observed "Appellant is contending that his constitutional rights are denied by the requirement to subscribe to the oath which the very constitution he asserts, demands that he do, as a condition to the exercise of the right. Such an incongruous and inconsistent position can hardly support his contention of a denial of *his* 'constitutional rights.' " (Emphasis added). *Fields v Askew*, 279 S 2d 822/Fla (1973).

The oath required of candidates for public office that they will not advocate the overthrow, destruction or alteration of the constitutional form of government of the United States, or any individual state or political subdivision thereof by revolution, force or violence, does not proscribe free political exposition, and does not seek to contravene the Constitution. *Hughes v Kramer*, 511 P 1d 1344/Wn (1973).

Desecration of the American Flag

A statute making it a crime to place marks upon the American Flag, to use the Flag as an article of decoration, to mutilate, deface, defile or cast contempt upon the Flag or to place it upon the ground, is not unconstitutionally vague. *People v Sutherland*, 292 NE 2d 746/Ill (1973); *State v Kool*, 212 NW 2d 518/Ia (1973).

The spreading of the American Flag upon the ground and the placing of articles thereon was not a proper exercise of freedom of expression as contemplated under the First Amendment. *Cincinnati v Bunch*, 288 NE 2d 854/Oh (1971).

Where defendant had attached to his helmet an American flag containing 13 stars and 13 stripes and on which was superimposed the so-called "peace symbol," his conduct was in violation of the First Amendment. *City of Miami v Wolfenberger*, 265 S 2d 732/Fla (1972).

The burning of the United States Flag in a building located on a university campus and presumed to be an open forum for the free exchange of ideas, was not thererby purged of its criminal nature—that of knowingly casting contempt upon the Flag even though the ceremony was a symbolic protest against the Viet Nam conflict. *United States v Crosson*, 462 F 2d 96/Az (1972).

When Unconstitutionality May Be Asserted

Any person asserting the unconstitutionality of a statute assumes the burden of so proving by the production of facts essential to an adjudication on that issue (*United States v Canty*, 469 F 2d 114/DC–1972), and the courts recognize a duty to uphold rather than destroy an act until it is clearly shown to be unconstitutional (*Pruett v Delony*, 269 S 2d 109/Ala–1972). Where no clear threat to the constitutional rights of any person is presented, the courts are reluctant to reverse the wishes of the people or their elected representatives, especially when effective political checks exist by which to gauge popular will. *Alkire v Cashman*, 350 FS 360/Oh (1972).

The unconstitutionality of a statute may be asserted only by a litigant who is adversely affected thereby (*State v Mems*, 190 SE 2d 164/NC–1972), and one who raises the question of the constitutional rights of a class of people must be a member of that class (*Edelstein v Ferrell*, 295 A 2d 390/NJ–1972); where defendant was a male he could successfully challenge the systematic exclusion of women from the jury panel. *Mayfield v Steed*, 345 FS 806/Ark (1972).

Female plaintiffs who claimed to be of childbearing age had insufficient standing to challenge abortion laws, but pregnant females did have such standing. *Abele v Markle*, 452 F 2d 1121/Con (1971).

One who has asserted the unconstitutionality of a statute and who has failed to adequately support his assertion will not be heard to urge its possible unconstitutionality in other circumstances. *People v Parker*, 109 CR 354/Cal (1973).

Where defendant was convicted of soliciting sexual intercourse with a stranger for money, she could not attack the constitutionality of the statute on the ground that it prohibited one spouse from soliciting sexual intercourse from the other *(State v Willis,* 218 NW 2d 921/Ia–1974). And defendant, who was convicted of abducting a female under the age of eighteen years had no standing to attack the constitutionality of the statute on the grounds that it did not protect young men from abduction by women. *State v Sluder*, 521 P 2d 971/Wn (1974).

Defendant who was convicted of a crime punishable by death did not stand in position to challenge the constitutionality of the death penalty applicable thereto when he was not sentenced to death. *Hobbs v State*, 192 SE 2d 903/Ga (1972); *State v Duncan*, 193 SE 2d 65/NC (1972).

Although defendants were tried for the capital offense of rape, they were without standing to challenge the validity of the death sentence when the jury recommended, and the court imposed, life sentences. *State v Bynum*, 193 SE 2d 725/NC (1973).

Vague and Overbroad Statutes

To be consistent with due process, penal statutes or ordinances must contain ascertainable standards of guilt so that persons of reasonable understanding are not required to guess at their meaning. *Seattle v Drew*, 423 P 2d 522/Wn (1967).

Living under a rule of law entails various suppositions including the right of all persons to be informed as to what the state commands or forbids. *Papachristou v City of Jacksonville*, 92 SC 839/Fla (1972).

A statute which forbids or requires an act in terms so vague that men of common intelligence must necessarily guess at its meaning and differ as to its application violates the first essential of due process. *People v Barksdale*, 503 P 2d 257/Cal (1972).

A statute prohibiting the use of profane, vulgar and indecent language in a public place seeks to prohibit language which would necessarily incite a breach of the peace. As so construed, it is sufficiently explicit to withstand the test of vagueness and overbreadth and is sufficiently concise to inform one subject to its provisions on what conduct is prohibited. *State v Mayhew*, 288 S 2d 243/Fla (1973).

Constitutional Amendments

Generally, a constitutional amendment takes effect on the day it was ratified by the people (*Opinion of the Justices*, 287 NE 2d 910/Mas–1972), and unless a different intent is evident beyond reasonable question, an amendment operates prospectively only. *State ex rel Hall v Vaughn*, 483 SW 2d 396/Mo (1972).

Chapter II

Governmental Functions

EXECUTIVE BRANCH

In General

It is within the purview of the executive department of government to enforce all criminal laws; it is the duty of the legislative department to appropriate sufficient funds to enforce the laws which it has enacted, and it is the proper duty of the judiciary, in a constitutionally ideal sense, neither to enforce laws nor to appropriate money therefor, but to adjudicate. *Bradshaw v Ball*, 487 SW 2d 294/Ky (1972).

Although enforceable dictates of the courts must be executed by the executive arm of government, want of physical power to enforce its judgments does not prevent a court from deciding a justiciable issue. *Nixon v Sirica*, 487 F 2d 700/DC (1973).

The governor's commutation of the death penalty to life imprisonment was not an unconstitutional assumption of judicial power by the executive branch nor a denial of due process. *Stanley v State*, 490 SW 2d 828/Tex (1973).

Police Power

"Police power" does not refer to the authority and duty of a police officer nor necessarily to the authority of police in general. Police power is the power of a society to govern; it is the inherent power reserved to the state to subordinate individual rights to reasonable regulation in the interest of the general welfare. The state has the sovereign right and duty to protect its citizens—this is police power. *In re Quinn,* 110 CR 881/Cal (1973); *Barber Examining Board v Kuhn,* 312 A 2d 216/Md (1973).

Police power exists without express constitutional or statutorial declaration, and although not plenary, its only limitation is that it must tend reasonably to correct some evil or promote some interest of state and not violate constitutional mandate. *Reesman v State,* 445 P 2d 1004/Wn (1968).

The power reserved to the people, to be exercised by their representatives in the legislative branch of government, embraces the power of the state to preserve and promote the public good; it is concerned with whatever affects the peace, security, health, morals and general welfare of the community. *Ace Tire Co Inc v City of Waterville,* 302 A 2d 90/Me (1973).

The general rule is that if a legislative act will promote the welfare of the state, it is for a public purpose (*Tough v Ives,* 294 A 2d 67/Con–1972), and to this end it is within the state's police power to protect the public from disease and crime (*Boise Redevelopment Agency v Yick Kong Corp,* 499 P 2d 575/Id–1972); to devise reasonable schemes for the regulation of activities which affect health and safety of the public (*People ex rel Dunbar v Kogul,* 501 P 2d 738/Colo–1972); to enact laws to preserve a state's exhaustible resources. *Potomac Sand & Gravel Co v Governor of Maryland,* 293 A 2d 241/Md (1972).

The state has an indisputable right to protect citizens against riot and other unlawful forms of mob action (*State v Albers,* 303 A 2d 197/NH–1973), and the state as well as the federal government, under its inherent police power, in order to protect itself against sedition and treason, may take appropriate measures to guard against overthrow by force, violence, rebellion, or other illegal or unconstitutional means, and may proscribe participation by government employees in violent acts of criminal syndicalism. *Hughes v Kramer,* 511 P 2d 1344/Wn (1973).

In the exercise of its police power, each state has the right to enact laws to promote public health, safety, morals and welfare (*People v Drolet,* 105 CR 824/Cal–1973), and the courts do not sit as superlegislative bodies to determine the desirability or propriety of statutes enacted by the legislature. Id.

Such problems as traffic congestion, public disorder, littering, obstruction of free passage and related problems of public safety and convenience, are legitimate concerns of government. *Duchein v Lindsay,* 345 NYS 2d 53/NY (1973).

The state has the right under its police power to license, provide and regulate basic services to society such as police, fire, electricity, telephonic, sanitary, and legal and health services. *Garcia v Texas State Bd of Examiners,* 358 FS 1016/Tex (1973).

The state may, by any appropriate means, regulate any enterprise, trade, occupation or profession if reasonably necessary to protect health, welfare and morals. *Newman v Carson,* 280 S 2d 426/Fla (1973).

Although the implementation of a state statute permitted the California Department of Motor Vehicles to issue personalized license plates containing letters or a combination of letters and numbers, the Department could deny issuance of plates containing words which were offensive or in bad taste, in this case the issuance of a plate with the letter combination "E Z Lay" was denied. *Katz v Department of Motor Vehicles*, 108 CR 424/Cal (1973).

Children under the age of 18 years have no inherent right against criminal prosecution for crimes. The state has the power to award jurisdiction of all juveniles to the juvenile court or to make exception as to certain crimes or to decrease or increase the age of non-criminal liability, and declaring to be criminal, acts of aggravated rape perpetrated by any one over the age of 15 years does not offend due process nor equal protection clauses of the constitution. *Mason v Henderson*, 337 FS 35/La (1972).

Under its police power the state may enjoin its citizens from engaging in any activity which adversely affects safety, good order, morality, comfort or the welfare of the people (*Goldy v Gerber*, 377 P 2d 111/Colo–1962), but regulations which are arbitrary or capricious and which unreasonably restrict liberty without accomplishing the object of police power, are violations of the fundamental law. *Messerli v Monarch Memory Gardens Inc*, 397 P 2d 34/Id (1964).

Police power includes authority to destroy private property if such destruction is reasonably necessary to protect the public health and safety. *Miles v District of Columbia*, 354 FS 577/DC (1973).

LEGISLATIVE BRANCH

Power and Duty

The legislature's lawmaking power is supreme within its sphere of activity and is qualified only by the restrictions and limitations imposed by state and federal constitutions (*Application of County Courthouse Bldg Commission*, 403 P 2d 501/Ok–1965), and the judicial branch of government cannot question the wisdom of a decision made by the legislature in the proper performance of its lawmaking function. *Walker v Louisiana Expressway Authority*, 274 S 2d 716/La (1973).

The legislature cannot delegate its power to make law, which necessarily involves discretion as to what the law shall be (*Dixon v Zick*, 500 P 2d 130/Colo–1972), but it may allow an administrative agency to fill in the details of an enactment. *Fry Roofing Co v Dept of Health*, 499 P 2d 1176/Colo (1972).

The power of impeachment is exclusively a prerogative of the legislature—not the judiciary. *In re Mussman*, 289 A 2d 403/NH (1972).

Wisdom of Statutes

It is a cardinal rule that a legislative act is presumed valid and will not be declared unconstitutional unless it is patently invalid. *Florida Jai Alai Inc v Reclamation Dist*, 274 S 2d 522/Fla (1973).

It is not within the court's domain to concern itself as to whether a statute is wholesome and salutary in its operation, or whether it is harmful; the judiciary can interfere only when it clearly appears that a given act contravenes the basic law of the state. *Utility Services Authority v Corporation Commission*, 519 P 2d 919/Ok (1974).

The wisdom of the exercise of the legislative function in the selection of the means to promote the general welfare is not open to arbitrary inference or review by the judiciary (*Inganamort v Fort Lee*, 293 A 2d 720/NJ–1972). Thus, a statute may be unwise, impolitic or unjust, but the courts have no power to nullify it absent a clear constitutional violation. *Sanitary Landfill Authority v Hackensack*, 293 A 2d 426/NJ (1972).

Defining Crime and Fixing Punishment

It is the function of the legislative branch of government to define crimes and prescribe punishments, and such questions are for the judgment of the legislature alone, but the legislative authority remains ultimately circumscribed by the constitutional prohibition *against cruel* and unusual punishment; it is the task of the judicial branch of government to condemn any violation of that prohibition *(In re Lynch*, 503 P 2d 921/Cal–1972). However, it is a matter of legislative discretion as to what crimes will have felony status *(State v Miller*, 269 S 2d 829/La–1972), and the classification of a crime as a capital offense is a function of the legislature and not the judiciary. *Hudson v McAdory*, 268 S 2d 916/Mis (1972).

Amendment of Statutes

Questions of what is for the common good are in the first instance for the general assembly (legislative body) to determine, and the courts are not warranted in setting aside a statute unless it is clearly evasive or otherwise contrary to the Constitution. *City of Salem v Mackin*, 291 NE 2d 807/Ill (1972).

It is for the legislature alone to change law after its construction by the courts, and once the courts have determined legislative intent they have fulfilled their function; the courts cannot decide what the law ought to be; they can only construe and apply the law as enacted by the legislature. *Lampada v State Sand & Gravel Co*, 206 NW 2d 138/Wis (1973).

Whether the "Sunday Blue Laws" should be continued in force is a matter of legislative discretion, not judicial. *People v Star Supermarkets Inc*, 339 NYS 2d 262/NY (1972).

It is not within the power of the legislature to prescribe how courts will perform their function nor may the courts prescribe how the legislators or executive officers will perform their functions (*Holm v State*, 404 P 2d 740/Wyo–1965). Nor may the legislature interfere with or exercise any power properly belonging to the executive department. *State ex rel Warren v Nusbaum*, 208 NW 2d 780/Wis (1973).

The legislature cannot abdicate its lawmaking power nor transfer nor delegate such power to any other branch of government (*Miller v City of Tacoma*, 378 P 2d 464/Wn–1963), nor to an administrative board created by the legislature. *Isaacs v Oklahoma City*, 437 P 2d 229/certiorari denied 389 US 825 (1966).

The legislative branch of government may not confer jurisdiction on the courts to render advisory opinions (*S v D*, 93 SC 1146/Tex–1973), nor do the courts ordinarily render such opinions. *Rozenkovich v Kalamazoo Spring Corp*, 205 NW 2d 311/Mich (1973).

A statute providing for common law crimes cannot be considered repealed nor inoperative on the basis that there was no longer any necessity for the statute; a statute is not repealed by nonuse. *State v Egan*, 287 S 2d 1/Fla (1973).

JUDICIAL BRANCH

Ethics and Policy

It is the obligation of the judicial branch of government to enforce the Constitution against legislative and executive encroachment in our tripartite system of government. Also, in the exercise of this function there is an essential corollary principle that must be observed by the judicial branch—the principle of judicial restraint (*Orange County v Heim*, 106 CR 825/Cal–1973). To declare a statute unconstitutional is a judicial power to be delicately exercised. *Kohler v Barnes*, 301 A 2d 474/NJ (1973).

It is a well-established principle of American jurisprudence that courts have the inherent power to determine the constitutionality of a statute (*People v Simmons*, 337 NYS 2d 717/NY–1972), and "It . . . is the province and the duty of the judicial department to say what the law is"; and the law *is* what the Supreme Court says it is. *United States v Nixon*, 94 SC 3090/DC (1974).

All presumptions are in favor of the constitutionality of either a state statute or a city or county ordinance, and the burden of showing unconstitutionality is on the person who asserts it. *Towns v Kessler*, 293 NE 2d 761/Ill (1973).

It is the duty of the court, if it can be done, to construe a statute as valid, and where the statute contains words or provisions which are valid and others which are not, effect should be given to the valid words and provisions by separating them from the invalid ones. *Delorme v State*, 488 SW 2d 808/Tex (1973).

As a rule the courts will not inquire into the motives of the legislature in the passing of legislation, and a valid exercise of legislative or congressional powers will not be invalidated merely because of infirm motives. *Bulluck v Washington*, 468 F 2d 1096/DC (1972).

A court has no authority to declare sections of an ordinance unconstitutional which defendant was not charged with violating. *People v Wilkerson*, 342 NYS 2d 936/NY (1973).

Advisory Opinions

Often members of the legislature or general assembly will seek advisory opinions of courts of appeal—especially from state supreme courts, usually in areas of anticipated legislation. All courts of appeal are reluctant to render such opinions for such reasons as: the matter on which advice is sought may never be introduced for legislative vote, or if introduced it may be in amended form, or if voted upon it may be defeated. Also, if an opinion favorable to the anticipated legislation is rendered and the matter becomes law, the same court may feel compelled to later declare the matter unconstitutional because of some unforeseen circumstance brought out in appellate research. The vast majority of the courts of appeal will decline to render advisory opinions. *Reville v Reville*, 289 A 2d 695/Me (1972); *Speed v Moffat*, 477 SW 2d 391/Tex (1972); *Bucham v Leahy*, 287 A 2d 836/Vt (1972).

Under the U.S. Constitution, the federal courts are confined to the adjudication of live and existing controversies and may not render advisory opinions (*City of New York v Ruckelshaus*, 358 FS 669/DC–1973); to do so would be a usurpation of power granted to the legislature and thus a violation of the doctrine of separation of powers. *City of Mishawaka v Mahoney*, 297 NE 2d 858/Ind (1973).

Trial Courts

Each judicial district constitutes but a single court and where additional judges are assigned to that court, new courts are not thereby established, only new divisions are added to the existing court. *Piper v Olinde Hardware & Supply Co Inc*, 288 S 2d 626/La (1974).

Usually, a trial court should not rule on the constitutionality of a statute; enactment of statutes is the prerogative of the legislative body, and the test of their constitutionality is the prerogative of courts of appeal (*Chalmers v Chalmers*, 285 A 2d 77/NJ–1971). However, the California courts have ruled that both the superior and municipal courts have the power to rule a statute unconstitutional. *People v Lockheed Shipbuilding & Const Co*, 111 CR 106/Cal (1973).

Specific Judicial Powers

Only a judicial officer can issue a warrant (*Hawkins v State*, 203 SE 2d 622/Ga–1973). Exceptions to this rule exist, however, in the issuance of a warrant of extradition, which is issued by the governor, and in the issuance of a coroner's warrant. *Ault v Purcell*, 519 P 2d 1785/Or (1974).

The power to punish for contempt is inherent within the courts and the legislature cannot abridge nor destroy that power as it cannot take away power which it does not give. *Oregon State Bar v Lenske*, 407 P 2d 250/certiorari denied 384 US 943/Or (1965).

Courts have the inherent power to declare their decisions to be applied prospectively or retroactively. *Naramore v Colquitt*, 305 NE 2d 622/Ill (1973).

Stare Decisis

Trial courts are bound by decisions of the state supreme courts just as the district courts of appeal are bound by precedents set by the supreme courts (*State v Lott*, 286 S 2d 565/Fla–1973); however, the state courts of appeal are not bound by decisions of any federal court other than the Supreme Court. *People v Wilson*, 306 NE 2d 626/Ill (1973).

The state supreme courts are not bound by the divergent law established in other jurisdictions and each may establish its own precedent (*Fisher v Sears Roebuck & Co*, 214 NW 2d 85/SD–1974), provided that such precedent is not in contravention to the U.S. Constitution. Nor are the U.S. district courts in one circuit bound by the precedent set in another circuit. *Johnson v Associates Finance Inc*, 365 FS 1380/Ill (1973).

Grand Jury

Grand juries are arms of the courts and are inextricably bound up with them (*State v Digman*, 294 S 2d 325/Fla–1974). The grand jury initiates a criminal proceeding by returning an indictment, but may investigate other matters without returning an indictment. If evidence of a crime less than a felony is uncovered the evidence may be turned over to the prosecuting attorney, but the grand jury may not, absent statutory sanction, return an indictment for a misdemeanor (*United States v Reide*, 494 F 2d 644/NY–1974). Proceedings before a grand jury are *ex parte*, i.e., on the part of one party only. *Baxley v Strawbridge*, 296 S 2d 779/Ala (1974).

JURISDICTION

Defined

"Jurisdiction" is the right of a court to hear a matter in controversy and render a decision therein on its merits (*Lueders v Brewer*, 218 NW 2d 638/Ia–1974). It is of two types; jurisdiction over the subject matter and jurisdiction over the parties involved (*Com v Little*, 314 A 2d 270/Pa–1974). Unlike venue, jurisdiction cannot be conferred on another court or waived. *State v Baldwin*, 305 A 2d 555/Me (1973).

Jurisdiction of subject matter must derive from law, and consent of the parties is irrelevant (*State v Wiese*, 201 NW 2d 734/Ia–1972), and jurisdiction of a court to try a person for crime does not depend on how he came to be within the boundaries of that state. *State v Ulriksen*, 504 P 2d 232/Kan (1972).

Effect of Abduction of Defendant

Although evidence which was illegally obtained is constitutionally excluded under the Fourth Amendment, no such protection exists where the defendant is brought before the court illegally. The state of Illinois, among others, has ruled that the power of a court to try a person on a criminal charge is not impaired by the fact of an illegal arrest or even a forcible abduction (*People v Bradford*, 279 NE 2d 34/Ill–1971), and even though abducted from without the state and transported into the state in violation of extradition laws (*Watson v State*, 475 SW 2d 8/Mo–1972). When an arrestee is brought before the court by way of an illegal arrest, the only effect is the suppression of illegally obtained evidence. *MAP v Ryan*, 285 A 2d 310/DC (1971).

Assuming that defendant's claim that he was illegally arrested in the Panama Canal Zone and brought to the United States for trial was correct, there are no grounds for releasing him without trial, the rule being that a court has the power to try a person for crime although he has been brought before that court by forcible abduction. *United States v Vicars*, 467 F 2d 452/Tex (1972).

Subject Matter Jurisdiction

As a rule the lowest level of trial court does not have jurisdiction to hear and adjudicate felony matters; it may hold preliminary hearings in felony matters and may sit as the trial judge in all other matters (*State v Mays*, 204 NW 2d 862/Ia–1973). The lowest level of trial court is designated as: municipal, justice, district, traffic, police, family and others, depending on the preference or tradition of the jurisdiction; the highest level of trial court is usually designated as the superior court and the highest level of appellate court is the supreme court.

Juvenile Court Jurisdiction

The superior court has exclusive original jurisdiction in all proceedings and matters affecting incorrigible and delinquent juveniles under the age of 18 years, and judges of the juvenile court, which are necessarily judges of the superior court, may waive jurisdiction of a juvenile and remand the matter to the criminal court to there be tried as an adult. *State v Jiminez*, 509 P 2d 198/Az (1973).

The juvenile court may exercise its discretion in relinquishing jurisdiction over a juvenile when from the totality of the circumstances it appears that the child's age, maturity, experience and sophistication require prosecution under the general law, and it appears from the nature and seriousness of the child's conduct that he is a threat to the community, his conduct amounts to a violent and vicious crime and there is reasonable likelihood his future conduct will not be deterred by continued adjudication of his delinquency in the juvenile court. *State v ex rel T J H v Bills*, 495 SW 2d 722/Mo (1973).

As a rule, a juvenile court may in its discretion exercise or waive jurisdiction of a petition against a juvenile. The juvenile court judge, upon waiver of jurisdiction, must state his reasons for such waiver but he need not state his reasons for a refusal to waive, and a determination to retain jurisdiction is not reviewable on appeal. *State v Jump*, 309 NE 2d 148/Ind (1974).

Although a juvenile is presumed to be capable of committing crime if over the age of 14 (and in some states 12), the criminal courts are without jurisdiction unless jurisdiction is waived by the juvenile court. *Sherfield v State*, 511 P 2d 598/Ok (1973).

The juvenile court, as is the family court of New York, is civil in nature and does not have jurisdiction to convict a juvenile of a crime. *In re Pisello*, 293 NE 2d 228/Ind (1973); *In re White*, 334 NYS 2d 476/NY (1972).

Federal Jurisdiction

The jurisdiction of the United States district courts extends to all federal enclaves, all ships at sea flying the United States Flag, and over all acts denounced by the United States Congress.

In the absence of a controlling treaty provision or any assertion of authority by a foreign sovereign, it is the duty of the United States courts to interpret and apply the laws of the United States to acts committed by its citizens on vessels flying its flag. *United States v Reagan*, 453 F 2d 165/Oh (1971).

If a murder is committed on board an American vessel by one of the crew upon another crew member or upon a passenger or by one passenger upon another, while such vessel is lying in port within the jurisdiction of a foreign state, the offense is cognizable and punishable by the proper court of the United States as though it had been committed on board a vessel on the high seas. This is the doctrine of the law of nations and entirely conformable with the practice of modern nations. *United States v Reagan, supra.*

Where one embassy employee was killed by another, although on foreign soil but in the American Embassy compound, the United States district court had jurisdiction to try the homicide. *United States v Erdos*, 474 F 2d 157/Va (1973).

The federal jurisdiction over attempted aircraft piracy applies only when the aircraft is in flight, and where a female boarded a plane parked at an air terminal, attempted to seize the plane by piracy, then exited before the plane became airborne, the federal statute did not apply. *United States v Pliskow*, 354 FS 369/Mich (1973).

The fact that defendant was subject to prosecution in the federal court for mailing marijuana and peyote through the U.S. mails did not deprive the state of

New Mexico of jurisdiction for distributing controlled substances. *State v McHorse*, 517 P 2d 75/NM (1973).

VENUE

Defined

"Jurisdiction" refers to the power of the court to hear and decide issues on the merits, while "venue" refers to the geographical location in which the cause is to be heard. *Lueders v Brewer*, 218 NW 2d 638/Ia (1974).

Place of Trial

The place of the trial, absent a statute to the contrary, is in the county where the crime occurred (*Adams v Superior Court*, 104 CR 144/Cal–1972), and defendant does not have the right to choose which branch of a court will hear the case (*People v Jones*, 103 CR 475/Cal–1972). Nor does defendant, upon grant of motion for a change of venue, have the right to select the county in which his case is to be heard (*Gibson v State*, 300 A 2d 692/Md–1973), nor any particular district or court within the designated county. *Cherry v State*, 488 SW 2d 744/Tex (1972).

Crimes Committed Outside the State

A sovereign state may exercise jurisdiction over a matter only if committed in whole or in part within that state; no matter how close to a state's boundaries a criminal act may occur, if yet outside its boundaries it is without jurisdiction (*People v Kirby*, 201 NW 2d 355/Mich–1972). However, punishment of acts done outside a state is justified by the state if designed to produce or do produce detrimental effects within that state. (*Com v Bighum*, 307 A 2d 255/Pa–1973). Thus, where forgery was committed in Mexico under the theory of objective territorial jurisdiction, the United States District Court had the right to try defendant for possessing, forging and uttering, in Juarez, Mexico, social security checks drawn on the United States Treasury, in that such acts were designed to and did produce detrimental effects within the United States. *United States v Fernandez*, 496 F 2d 1294/Tex (1974).

Interstate Transportation of Stolen Property

Although the interstate transportation of stolen automobiles is triable under federal law, bringing stolen property into a state may be prosecuted in that state also. Thus, the courts of Utah may try one for grand larceny who stole a car in Texas and drove it into the state of Utah (*Conners v Turner*, 508 P 2d 1185/Ut–1973). Regardless of the nature of the property stolen, where the larceny was committed outside the state of Washington, it is not within the venue of that state, but under an appropriate statute (RCW 9.54.010), Washington does have venue over the transporting of stolen property into the state. *State v Ladely*, 509 P 2d 658/Wn (1973).

Crossing County Lines

In a prosecution for receiving stolen property venue is usually in the county in which the property was received or in any county through or into which the property was taken. *Holt v State*, 274 S 2d 356/Ala (1972).

In a prosecution for conspiracy, trial may be conducted in any county wherein an overt act was committed or where the substantive crime was committed in whole or in part. *Com v Tumolo*, 299 A 2d 15/Pa (1972).

Where two officers were kidnaped in Los Angeles County and one was assassinated in Kern County, the killing was the culmination of events commenced in Los Angeles County and was thus triable in Los Angeles County. *People v Powell*, 115 CR 109/Cal (1974).

Although kidnap and assault with intent to commit rape occurred on the same date and against the same victim, they occurred in different counties and there was no authority under which the prosecutor of either county could prosecute for both offenses at the same time. Therefore, the trial for assault with intent to commit rape in the second county, which followed an acquittal of kidnaping in the first county, was authorized and not barred under the double jeopardy clauses. *People v Joines*, 208 NW 2d 193/Mich (1973).

Pretrial Publicity

Usually pretrial publicity of a criminal case is sporadic and not by its nature prejudicial, and in such cases the trial court does not abuse discretion when it relies on a careful *voir dire* examination of the jury to ascertain whether community prejudice against the defendant has influenced any member of the jury panel (*Kable v State*, 299 A 2d 493/Md–1973). But extensive pretrial publicity which, *inter alia*, often referred to defendant as a twice-convicted rapist though both prior convictions had been set aside, and repeatedly referred to alleged communist affiliations of defense counsel, was of such a nature as to preclude the possibility of an impartial trial where practically all of the veniremen had read such articles despite sequestration of the jury during the trial. *Wansley v Miller*, 353 FS 42/Va (1973).

Change of Venue

A change of venue, that is, removal of the cause into another county for trial, is justified only upon a showing that the defendant cannot have a fair and impartial trial in the county where the crime was committed. It may be granted by motion of the defendant upon such showing and cannot otherwise be imposed upon the defendant. *Younger v Smith,* 106 CR 225/Cal (1973).

A presumption exists that defendant can have a fair and impartial trial in the county in which the crime was committed, and the person claiming otherwise assumes the responsibility of so proving. *Ellington v State,* 516 P 2d 287/Ok (1973).

The granting of a change of venue is within the sound discretion of the trial court and not a matter of right to the defendant, and the court's ruling will not be disturbed on appeal unless there appears clearly an abuse of discretion which prejudices the defendant. *State v Vendreson,* 506 P 2d 248/Az (1973).

A change of venue is a procedural safeguard employed by courts to help maximize the possibilities for a fair trial untainted by community bias and predisposition, and to this end in his discretion the trial judge should grant change of venue if an adequate showing of bias and prejudice has been made. *Burton v State,* 292 NE 2d 790/Ind (1973).

Where the court has granted a change of venue, there being nothing in the U.S. Constitution guaranteeing defendant the right to make a selection, the court and not the defendant will select the county in which the trial is to be held. *Whiteside v Superior Court,* 102 CR 381/Cal (1972).

The right of defendant to a change of venue is not of common law origin, and where it exists it is statutory. *State v Johnson,* 285 NE 2d 751/Oh (1972).

Change of venue is not the only cure for pretrial publicity adverse to the defendant, but when such publicity through the public news media creates the likelihood that defendant cannot have a fair and impartial trial within the venue of the crime, the cause should either be continued until the threat abates or a change of venue should be granted (*Corona v Superior Court,* 101 CR 411/Cal–1972). Although the Idaho Supreme Court has held that the trial court may not order a change of venue *sua sponte* (of its own motion), it would appear to be the better rule to allow such change when the reasons therefor are compelling but not requested by defendant, and the change would save the time and expense of a new trial (*State v Ash,* 493 P 2d 701/Id–1971). See *State v Valdez,* 495 P 2d 1079/NM (1972), where the later rule was followed. But mere publicity, even widespread publicity, is not of itself sufficient grounds for change of venue. *Gavin v State,* 259 S 2d 544/Fla (1972).

When two or more defendants are jointly tried and a change of venue is granted for one, unless the change prejudices one or more other defendants, venue is changed for all. *Banks v Superior Court,* 304 NW 2d 776/Ind (1973).

JUDICIAL NOTICE

Defined

"Judicial notice" is defined as cognizance taken by the court, usually by its own motion, of the existence and truth of certain facts having a bearing on the controversy at bar, but which, by their nature, are not properly the subject of testimony. Facts which may be judicially noticed are those which are universally regarded as established by common notoriety, such as international law and the laws of the nation and the state; historical events; the course of nature; geographic and astronomical features. The limits of judicial notice cannot be circumscribed nor defined with preciseness, but notoriety is usually the ultimate test of facts sought to be judicially noticed. *Black's Law Dictionary; Ashland Sav and Loan Assn v Aetna Ins Co*, 309 NE 293/Ill (1974).

The theory under which a court takes judicial notice of a fact is that the matter is so notorious that it will not be disputed. *Com v Barrett*, 296 NE 2d 712/Mas (1973).

Subjects of Proper Notice

The courts may take judicial notice of: the ordinary affairs of life; universal experiences of man; the qualities and properties of matter; well-known scientific facts; the meaning of words, phrases, and at times colloquialisms and slang expressions; well-known geological and physiological subdivisions; the laws and treaties of states and nations; the records of courts of record of the several states and of the United States; the nature and functions of the branches of government. *Corpus Juris Secundum*—Criminal Law § 331.

Courts are empowered to take judicial notice of state statutes (*Wyatt v State*, 270 S 2d 47/Fla—1972), but they usually may not take judicial notice of municipal ordinances (*Kansas City v Narron*, 493 SW 2d 394/Mo—1973), nor county ordinances (*State v Atlas*, 195 SE 2d 496/NC—1973), nor foreign law. *Kearney v Savannah Foods*, 350 FS 85/Ga (1972).

A court has taken judicial notice that the average normal breaking distance of an automobile traveling at 25 miles per hour is 91 feet (*McGraw v Corrin*, 303 A 2d 641/Del—1973); of highway fatalities (*Popp v Motor Vehicle Dept*, 508 P 2d 991/Kan—1973); that muscular dystrophy results in progressive disability (*Labrie v Labrie*, 305 A 2d 687/NH—1973); that the average reaction time of a driver is three-fourths of a second (*Casey v Standish*, 492 SW 2d 629/Tex (1973); and of the laws of physics. *Tanton v Zubkowicz*, 288 NE 2d 864/Oh (1971).

A court may take judicial notice of any scientific fact which may be ascertained by reference to a standard dictionary or which is of such general knowledge that it is known by any judicial officer. Thus, a trial court could properly take judicial notice of the fact that heroin is a narcotic drug and is habit-forming. *State v Brock*, 296 NE 2d 837/Oh (1973).

The court took judicial notice that an airport was located in a specified county (*State v Boyd*, 492 SW 2d 787/Mo—1973), that there were two district courts located in a named county. *McCrea v State*, 494 SW 2d 821/Tex (1973).

The court will take judicial notice that the polygraph is used extensively by the police and private agencies for investigative purposes (*State v McDavitt*,

297 A 2d 849/NJ–1972), that contraband is smuggled into custodial institutions. *Mathis v Superior Court*, 105 CR 126/Cal (1972).

When one is charged with a crime in which the sex of the perpetrator is an element, the court may take judicial notice thereof, but such notice is not necessarily conclusive of the issue. A claim of the contrary of the court's notice devolves upon the accused to rebut. *Sumpter v State*, 306 NE 2d 95/Ind (1974).

A court may take judicial notice that the period of human gestation is ten lunar months or 280 days. *SJB v SFS*, 504 SW 2d 233/Mo (1973).

Failure or refusal of the trial court to take judicial notice of a fact does not prevent the appellate court from taking such notice (*Wheeler v Aetna Casualty & Surety Co*, 298 NE 2d 329/Ill–1973). But see *People v Hambarian*, 107 CR 878/Cal (1973), where the California court held to the contrary.

PRESUMPTIONS

Conclusive Presumptions

Presumptions are of two kinds–rebuttable and conclusive. A presumption is rebuttable when it raises an assumption of law or fact which will stand until refuted by other evidence, and a presumption is nondiscretionary and binding; one which is discretionary is more properly an inference. Rebuttable presumptions are also called refutable, disputable and inconclusive. A conclusive presumption is one which the law requires; it must be accepted as fact and may not be refuted by the introduction of conflicting evidence. *Black's Law Dictionary*.

A conclusive presumption, also known as an irrebuttable or absolute presumption, is a rule of law setting forth the quantity of evidence requisite for the support of a particular averment which is not permitted to be refuted or attacked. *Paul v Los Angeles County Flood Control*, 112 CR 274/Cal (1974); *State v Warbritton*, 506 P 2d 1152/Kan (1973).

The legislature may enact rebuttable presumptions but cannot enact a conclusive presumption applicable in criminal matters. *O'Neal v State*, 498 P 2d 1232/Wyo (1972).

Some conclusive presumptions are:

- That a woman is able to bear children until the day she dies (*Betchard v Iverson*, 212 P 2d 783/Wn–1950);
- That one saw that which was visible to him had he looked (*Calvert v Seattle*, 162 P 2d 441/Wn–1945);
- Under the common law a child of less than seven years of age was presumed incapable of committing crime. *In re Davis*, 299 A 2d 856/Md (1973).

Legal Maxims

It is a universal maxim that ignorance of the law excuses no one. *Leschner v Department of Labor and Industries*, 185 P 2d 113/Wn (1947).

The law does not concern itself about little things. *Measday v Sweazea*, 438 P 2d 525/NM (1968).

The law does not require a futile act nor the impossible. *Minderman v Perry*, 437 P 2d 407/Az (1968).

Justice exists only where it can be effectively administered. *Amaya v Home Ice Fuel & Supply Co*, 379 P 2d 513/Cal (1963).

The wrong reason for a correct judicial ruling is not grounds for reversal. *Minderman v Perry, supra.*

When the reason for a rule disappears so should the rule. *Mancini v State*, 273 S 2d 371/Fla (1973).

One cannot do indirectly that which the law does not allow done directly. *Eschen v Roney*, 194 SE 2d 589/Ga (1972).

Disputable Presumptions

A presumption is an assumption of the fact that the law requires to be made from a group of facts or from another fact found or otherwise established in the action. Every rebuttable presumption is one either affecting the burden of proof, or affecting the burden of producing evidence. California Evidence Code §§ 600-01.

A presumption is not evidence, but takes the place of evidence, and it dissipates upon the introduction of evidence to the contrary and thus becomes an issue of fact. *State v Spry*, 207 NW 2d 504/SD (1973).

The effect of a presumption is merely to place the burden of producing evidence on the party against whom it operates. *Clayton v Burston*, 493 F 2d 429/Tex (1974).

"Presumption" Distinguished From "Inference"

The terms "presumption" and "inference" are often confused or used interchangeably. However, a true presumption is a conclusion which the law makes *mandatory* upon proof of required basic facts, while an inference is *permissible* based on the establishment of other facts. *State v Hansen*, 203 NW 2d 216/Ia (1972).

Although Illinois makes no distinction in the evidential value between presumptions and inferences *(Paulsen v Cochfield*, 278 Ill App 596), most states do so differentiate. That a presumption is not evidence but takes the place of evidence refers to a disputable presumption. *Hinds v John Hancock Mut Life Ins Co*, 155 A 2d 721/Me (1959).

A presumption may not be based on another presumption nor an inference on another inference. *Barkalow Bros Co v Floor-Brite Inc*, 198 NW 2d 329/Neb (1972).

Acts of the Legislature

Acts of the legislature or general assembly are presumptively constitutional. If a case can be decided without a determination of constitutionality, it should be so decided. All doubt as to a statute's validity must be resolved in favor of the act unless it is clearly incompatible with the constitution. *Redding v State*, 493 SW 2d 116/Ark (1973); *Plemmer v Matthewson*, 190 SE 2d 204/NC (1972).

A statute or ordinance is presumed to be constitutional (*Towns v Kessler*, 293 NE 2d 761/Ill–1973), and the one who assails a statute's constitutionality bears the heavy burden of so proving. *People v Lichtenwalter*, 520 P 2d 583/Colo (1974).

Foreign Law

Where no evidence of a foreign law is produced in a judicial proceeding, it will be presumed that it is the same as local law (*Glouer v Sink*, 195 SE 2d 443/Ga–1973); a Texas court will presume, in the absence of evidence to the contrary, that Mississippi law is the same as Texas law (*Utica Mutual Ins Co v Bennett*, 492 SW 2d 659/Tex–1973); Washington will presume, absent a contrary showing, that New York law is the same as that of Washington. *Copeland Planned Futures Inc v Obenchain*, 510 P 2d 654/Wn (1973).

Official Acts

The presumption of regularity supports official acts of public officers, and in the absence of clear evidence to the contrary, the courts will presume that they have properly discharged their official duties. *Carr v United States*, 347 FS 1390/NY (1972).

The law presumes:

- That a public officer properly discharges an official duty;
- That the law was obeyed;
- That the ordinary course of business was followed. *Carr v United States, supra.*

An officer is presumed to have acted legally in making an arrest until such time as the legality of the arrest is challenged. *Irwin v Dept of Motor Vehicles*, 517 P 2d 619/Wn (1974).

In a bench trial the trial judge is presumed to have considered only competent evidence at arriving at a verdict and such presumption may be rebutted only by an admission of the judge to the contrary. *People v West*, 311 NE 2d 237/Ill (1974).

Innocence

The accused is entitled to the presumption of innocence throughout all stages of the trial (*People v Licata*, 305 NE 2d 6/Ill–1973), and his refusal or failure to testify permits no adverse presumption against him. *State v Fisher*, 212 NW 2d 568/Neb (1973).

The presumption of innocence is not an ordinary evidentiary presumption and does not disappear when evidence to the contrary is received; it is overcome only by evidence sufficient to convince the trier of fact of defendant's guilt beyond a reasonable doubt (*United States v Cummings*, 468 F 2d 274/Nev–1972), and the law does not require that defendant establish his innocence. *People v Dennison*, 288 NE 2d 516/Ill (1972).

Placing the burden of proof on a defendant as to a fact peculiarly within his knowledge does not deny him the benefit of the presumption of innocence. *People v Felder*, 334 NYS 2d 992/NY (1972).

The accused carries no burden of proof in a criminal prosecution; the presumption of innocence precludes this necessity (*People v Compian*, 196 NW 2d 353/Mich–1972), but upon appeal from conviction defendant is presumed guilty. *McDonald v State*, 477 SW 2d 759/Ten (1971).

The compelling of defendant to wear prison clothing (any attire with either the word "jail" or "sheriff" stamped thereon) may deprive him of the presumption of innocence. *Bentley v Crist*, 469 F 2d 854/Mont (1972).

In a criminal trial all presumptions militate in favor of defendant's innocence (*State v Lee*, 488 SW 2d 272/Mo–1972). But after conviction the presumption of innocence and other protections afforded the accused dissipate and all presumptions then are in favor of the propriety of the proceedings and the judgement, and the burden of showing the contrary is on the petitioner. *Price v Turner*, 502 P 2d 121/Ut (1972).

The presumption of innocence is dispelled upon conviction, and presumption of guilt attaches notwithstanding defendant's appeal. *State v Grace*, 493 SW 2d 474/Ten (1973).

Sanity

A presumption of sanity of the defendant at the trial establishes this fact *prima facie* and relieves the state from proving sanity in the first instance in every case, but evidence of insanity presented by the defendant dispels the presumption of sanity and places on the state the burden of proving sanity, and the question then becomes a question to be decided by the trier of fact. *Hollander v State*, 296 NE 2d 449/Ind (1973); *State v Jacobs*, 205 NW 2d 662/Neb (1973).

Although a condition once determined to exist is presumed to continue until the contrary is established or unless neutralized by another presumption (*Mobil Oil Corp v Cook*, 494 SW 2d 925/Tex–1973), where the existent condition is insanity defendant may not avail himself of such presumption if after an adjudication of insanity he commits a homicide. For instance, after two previous adjudications of insanity and separate commitments to the state insane asylum, defendant, on a third occasion, was pronounced insane in a hearing held in the judge's chambers. He became enraged at the pronouncement and attempted to leave; the arresting officer who had brought him before the judge, attempted to prevent his departure but was shot and killed with a pistol which defendant was carrying. Upon his trial for murder defendant sought to establish his insanity by presumption. The court held: Though one may be laboring under partial insanity, if he understands the nature and character of his action and its consequences and if he knows that it is wrong and criminal and that if he does the act he will do wrong, insanity is not a defense. *People v Willard*, 89 P 124/Cal (1907).

At defendant's trial of the issue of fact he is presumed to be sane and that presumption may be so strong as to overcome abundant evidence to the contrary. *In re State v Johnson*, 409 P 2d 655/Wn (1965), the presumption of sanity prevailed over the testimony of defendant's psychiatrist to the insanity of defendant; in *People v Chamberlain*, 60 P 2d 299/Cal (1941), the presumption of defendant's sanity was so strong as to overcome the adverse testimony of three psychiatrists, two of whom were appointed by the state, and ten lay witnesses.

Miscellaneous Presumptions

Failure of a party to call a witness who is peculiarly within his power to summon raises the inference that his testimony would be adverse to that party (*United States v Blakemore*, 489 F 2d 193/Ky–1973). But no adverse presumption or inference may be drawn by defendant's failure to testify. *State v Fisher*, 212 NW 2d 568/Neb (1973).

A letter correctly addressed and properly mailed is presumed to have been delivered in the ordinary course of the mail, but to invoke this presumption the state must prove that the letter was properly mailed. *ITT Abrasive Products Co v Lewis*, 298 NE 2d 242/Ill (1973).

Under common law a child of the age of at least seven but less than fourteen was presumed incapable of committing crime. *In re Davis*, 299 A 2d 856/Md (1973).

A presumption exists that a man or a woman is capable of siring or having children as long as life lasts (*Lux v Lux*, 288 A 2d 701/RI–1972), and a child born during the course of a lawful marriage is presumed to be legitimate but this presumption may be rebutted by clear and convincing evidence that the husband could not have sired the child. *Gray v Richardson*, 340 FS 680/Oh (1972).

Contrary to popular belief there is no presumption that the defendant is of good character nor is there a presumption that he is of bad character. But the state may not introduce evidence of his bad character unless and until the defendant has presented evidence of his good character. *Mullins v United States*, 487 F 2d 581/Ia (1973).

Examples of such wide renown as to require no citation of authority are:

- Everyone knows the law;
- Every sane person intends the natural and probable consequences of his voluntary acts;
- A person not heard from for seven years is dead;
- A witness duly sworn gives truthful testimony;
- Persons obey the law;
- A person owns property over which he exercises ownership;
- At common law, children under the age of fourteen years could not commit crime. (This presumption exists in all states except that the maximum age may be modified by statute.)

Chapter III

Due Process

In General

Section One of the Fourteenth Amendment to the U.S. Constitution states in part, ". . . nor shall any State deprive any person of life, liberty, or property, without due process of law . . ." "Due process" is defined, *inter alia*, as a method used to advise a party of the nature of an action being brought against him (*Woodham v Northwestern Steel & Wire Co*, 390 F 2d 27/Fla–1968). It includes within its meaning all of the acts of the court, from the commencement of an action to its final adjudication; or, in a narrower sense, it is the manner through which a defendant is brought before the bar to answer to a complaint filed against him. "Service of process" includes two distinct but indispensable ends: the notification of the action to the defendant that he may defend himself, and the acquisition of jurisdiction over the defendant. *Executive Air Services Inc v Beech Aircraft Corp*, 254 FS 415/PR (1966).

The right of an arrestee to be brought without unnecessary delay before a magistrate does not, *per se*, impart a constitutional guarantee, and the rule laid down in *Mallory v United States*, 354 US 449 (1957) and *McNabb v United States*, 318 US 332 (1943) applies generally to federal courts and was not imposed on and, therefore, not necessarily binding on the state courts. *Brown v Justice's Court*, 428 P 2d 376/Nev (1967).

ACCUSATORY PLEADINGS

Complaints

A sworn complaint is a prerequisite to the commencement of a criminal prosecution, and it is irrelevant whether the information be used as a basis for the arrest or merely an accusatory pleading. *People v Coldiron*, 355 NYS 2d 518/NY (1974).

A complaint may be made on "information and belief" and need not be based on the personal knowledge of the affiant in a judicial proceeding against defendant. Also, information and belief may be a basis for the issuance of a warrant of arrest. *People v Burrill*, 214 NW 2d 823/Mich (1974).

Generally, any person who has reasonable grounds for believing that another has committed a crime may complain against the offender (*Ashton Co Inc v Jacobson*, 507 P 2d 983/Az–1973), but the state may, by statute, designate only certain described persons who may make a complaint. Id.

Indictments

An "indictment" is an accusation in writing found after lawful convocation and oath by the grand jury and presented to the court in which it was impanelled, charging that the person named therein is guilty of an act or an omission which by law is made criminal (*Black's Law Dictionary*). Since the superior court, only, has jurisdiction of felony cases, and since the grand jury must present its indictment in the court in which it was impanelled, the grand jury can return indictments only of crimes triable in the superior court, i.e., felonies.

Proceedings by indictment in all cases warranting serious punishment was the rule at common law and is required under the Fifth Amendment in certain types of crimes in federal courts; the rule of the state of Nevada (and most, if not all other states) is that felonies may be prosecuted by either an indictment or an information. *Cairns v Sheriff of Clark County*, 508 P 2d 1015/Nev (1973).

The requirement that a defendant be brought before the bar only by indictment found by a grand jury, unless waived, is purely statutory, and if not required by state statute it does not exist at the state level. However, in a federal court upon trial for an infamous or other high crime, the U.S. Constitution imposes such requirement. *Scales v Com*, 204 SE 2d 273/Va (1974).

Although the grand jury, as a rule, may return an indictment for felonies only, it may investigate other matters within its purview without returning an indictment. If evidence of misdemeanor, only, is adduced, such evidence may be turned over to the prosecuting attorney for the filing of a complaint. *United States v Reide*, 494 F 2d 644/NY (1974); *People v R*, 356 NYS 1006/NY (1974).

Inasmuch as the purpose of a grand jury proceeding and a preliminary hearing is to insure the existence of probable cause before an accused is brought to trial, the return of an indictment by the grand jury eliminates the necessity of holding a preliminary hearing. *United States v Mackey*, 474 F 2d 55/Md (1973); *Jenkins v State*, 305 A 2d 610/Del (1973).

When the name of the person responsible for a crime under investigation by the grand jury is unknown, the jury may nevertheless return an indictment charging him with the crime named therein; the perpetrator may be designated by a fictitious name, such as "John Doe," the indictment explaining that the perpetrator's name is unknown and the name in the indictment is fictitious. *Hubbard v State*, 313 NE 2d 346/Ind (1974).

The object of a bill of particulars is to supplement an otherwise sufficient indictment with additional details so as to advise the accused in greater detail of the nature of the charges against him (*People v Decker*, 311 NE 2d 228/Ill–1974), but a bill of particulars is not required as a rule. *Bright v State*, 293 S 2d 818/Mis (1974).

All jurisdictions are not in accord as to whether an indictment may rest on hearsay evidence. The federal circuit courts are not in agreement on this issue. The Fifth Circuit for the state of Georgia holds that an indictment may rest upon hearsay (*United States v Hodge*, 496 F 2d 87/Ga–1974), while the Seventh Circuit for Illinois holds that indictments based on hearsay are not improper (*United States v Annerino*, 495 F 2d 1159/Ill–1974). However, the states are in substantial agreement on the issue, Alabama holding that with the vast majority of the states an indictment may rest on hearsay. *State ex rel Baxley v Strawbridge*, 296 S 2d 779/Ala (1974).

Where the life of a grand jury is extended without authority of law, the jury reverts to a group of citizens without any special authority and an indictment found by such group is without legal efficacy. *McClure v Dutchess County*, 341 NYS 2d 855/NY (1973).

Informations

An "information" is a formal accusation of crime drawn up by the prosecuting attorney after a hearing before a committing magistrate wherein such magistrate has determined that there is sufficient evidence to establish the commission of a felony and that there is reasonable grounds to believe the defendant committed it. The information differs from the indictment only in its source as a result of a preliminary hearing as opposed to the grand jury. *Black's Law Dictionary*.

The fundamental purpose of the information is to inform the accused with reasonable certainty of the charge against him to thereby enable him to prepare his defense so as to effectively establish a bar to any future prosecution for the same offense. *State v Harig*, 218 NW 2d 884/Neb (1974); *State v Newhart*, 503 SW 2d 62/Mo (1973).

The due process clause does not require the states to observe the Fifth Amendment's provision for presentment or indictment by a grand jury (*Alexander v Louisiana,* 92 SC 1221/La–1972), and notwithstanding that the Fifth Amendment to the U.S. Constitution guarantees that "No person shall be held to answer for a capital, or otherwise infamous crime, unless on presentment or indictment of a grand jury . . .," defendant may be brought to bar by information.

Where the information named the county in which the crime occurred and the date on which it occurred, it was not fatally defective merely because it did not state the exact time and location of the crime. *State v Nixon,* 295 S 2d 121/Fla (1974).

PLEAS

In General

The purpose and necessity of arraignment is to fix the identity of the accused, to inform him of the nature of the charges against him, and to give him an opportunity to inform the court of his plea thereto. *Com v Jones,* 308 A 2d 598/Pa (1973).

The laws of the several states differ in the number and variety of pleas available to the defendant in a criminal case. In the state of Washington there are pleas of: (1) guilty, (2) not guilty, (3) former judgment of conviction or acquittal and (4) not guilty by reason of insanity (RCW 10.40.150). In California six pleas are available: (1) guilty, (2) not guilty, (3) not guilty by reason of insanity, (4) former conviction or acquittal, (5) once in jeopardy, and (6) *nolo contendere* (California Penal Code § 1016). When defendant pleads guilty no other plea conjunct thereto may be included but, as a rule, he may enter one or more of all other pleas available.

Defendant is not entitled, as a matter of right, to a plea of guilty; the court, upon good cause, may decline defendant's proffered plea of guilty and enter a plea of not guilty for him (*People v Selikoff,* 343 NYS 2d 387/NY–1973). A plea of guilty cannot stand if it lacks a factual basis and is not voluntary and accurate. *People v Alvarez,* 508 P 2d 1267/Colo (1973).

The acceptance of a plea of guilty to a lesser offense is discretionary (*United States v Melendrez,* 466 F 2d 861/Cal–1972) since there is no absolute right afforded defendant under any law to have his plea of guilty recorded (*Culbreath v Rundle,* 466 F 2d 730/Pa–1972); nor does defendant have the right to compel the acceptance of a plea of guilty to a lesser charge than that brought against him. *State v Ford,* 487 SW 2d 1/NC (1972).

Plea Bargaining

The state may properly encourage pleas of guilty either by being more lenient to those who plead guilty or by increasing the risk of punishment for those who choose to go to trial. *United States v Sepe*, 474 F 2d 784/Fla (1973).

Plea bargaining between the state's attorney and the defense attorney is now an acceptable and honorable practice (*Moulder v State*, 289 NE 2d 522/Ind–1972), but unsuccessful plea bargaining binds neither the state nor the defendant. *Hatfield v State*, 487 SW 2d 574/Mo (1972).

Unpleasant alternatives faced by defendant engaging in plea bargaining is not, *per se*, coercive. *Monsour v Cady*, 342 FS 353/Wis (1972).

Defendant must be assured that any plea bargain he enters into with the prosecuting attorney will be carried out according to the agreed terms. *State v Thomas*, 294 A 2d 57/NJ (1972).

Not Guilty Plea

In the absence of a plea of guilty or *nolo contendere*, a plea of not guilty must be entered and a trial on the issue of fact held, not simply an entry of verdict. *Duppins v State*, 302 A 2d 717/Md (1973).

When defendant stands mute in the face of an accusatory pleading at his arraignment, unless upon a special motion or demurrer, the court must enter a plea of not guilty on his behalf. Thus, where defendant refused to enter a plea after being requested to do so, the trial court properly entered a plea of not guilty. *Dickens v State*, 295 NE 2d 613/Ind (1973).

A plea of guilty must have been entered by defendant freely and voluntarily and with full knowledge of the consequences (*U.S. v Anderson*, 468 F 2d 440/La–1972), and where defendant pleads guilty and simultaneously asserts facts which would justify or excuse his act, his plea should be rejected. *Com v Slavik*, 297 A 2d 920/Pa (1972).

Where defendant has pleaded not guilty to the crime charged, the prosecutor may enter a *nolle prosequi*, thus declining to prosecute. In some states *nolle prosequi* rests solely within the discretion of the prosecuting attorney (*State ex rel Lodwick v Cottey*, 497 SW 2d 873/Mo–1973), while in other states such procedure rests within the discretion of the court. *People v Curtis*, 209 NW 2d 243/Mich (1973).

Guilty Plea

A plea of guilty when made in open court to a criminal charge is a formal admission of guilt and is the equivalent of a verdict of guilty (*In re Woods v Rhay*, 414 P 2d 601/Wn–1967), and being paramount to conviction, the acceptance of the plea must be based on a determination that the plea was voluntarily entered. *Thomas v State*, 306 NE 2d 136/Ind (1974).

A plea of guilty is not compelled or coerced and thus invalid under the Fifth Amendment if motivated by defendant's desire to accept the probability or certainty of a lesser penalty rather than face a wider range of possibilities extending from acquittal to conviction and after conviction a more severe penalty. *Com v Morrow*, 296 NE 2d 468/Mas (1973).

A valid plea of guilty waives all defenses known and unknown, and contention after plea by defendant that he was arrested without warrant, illegally detained for several days before arraignment, interrogated by police without advisement of constitutional rights, and that grand and petit jury panels were unconstitutionally drawn, was waived upon entry of his guilty plea. *Brown v Caldwell*, 190 SE 2d 52/Ga (1972).

When a defendant voluntarily and knowingly enters a plea of guilty he waives his right to a trial. Therefore, a subsequent motion for a new trial based on the grounds of newly discovered evidence is inappropriate. *United States v Forrest*, 356 FS 343/Mich (1973).

Nolo Contendere

A plea of *nolo contendere* (I will not contest it) has the same consequences as a guilty plea except that it cannot be used as an in-court admission in any subsequent judicial proceeding (*People v Tomlinson*, 213 NW 2d 803/Mich–1973). In other words, defendant stands convicted of the crime for which he is charged and is therefore subject to all consequences as follows a plea of guilty or a finding of guilt after trial. *Dower v Poston*, 351 NYS 2d 272/NY (1973).

A plea of *nolo contendere* stands on the same footing as a plea of guilty, thus empowering the judge to impose such sentence as may be authorized by law. *Marshall v State*, 197 SE 2d 161/Ga (1973).

A plea of "no contest" to a misdemeanor charge constitutes a stipulation that the judge may find defendant guilty or not guilty from an explanation of the circumstances, and it is not the legal equivalent of a *nolo contendere* found in federal rules (*State v Herman*, 286 NE 2d 296/Oh–1971). The essence of a no contest plea is that defendant cannot be heard in defense and any explanation offered by him acts only toward mitigation of penalty. Id.

Change of Plea

Before sentence the trial court may allow withdrawal of a plea of guilty for any fair and just reason, but this dispensation should not be as freely granted when the government has been prejudiced by reliance on a guilty plea. Denial of a motion to withdraw a guilty plea will be overturned upon a showing of an abuse of discretion by the trial court. *United States v Truglio*, 493 F 2d 574/W Va (1974).

RIGHTS OF DEFENDANT

Right to Counsel

In *Gideon v Wainwright*, 83 SC 792/Fla (1963), the Supreme Court ruled, "[I]n our adversary system of criminal justice, any person hailed into court, who is too poor to hire a lawyer, cannot be assured a fair trial unless counsel is provided for him." Since *Gideon* was convicted of a felony, it was assumed by many, if not most, members of the criminal justice system that an indigent defendant was entitled to *appointed* counsel only when being tried for a felony. In 1972, in *Argersinger v Hamlin*, 92 SC 2006/Fla (1972), as an extension of *Gideon*, the Supreme Court ruled that "... absent a knowing and intelligent waiver, no person may be imprisoned for any offense, whether classified as petty, misdemeanor, or felony unless he was represented by counsel at his trial ...."

The states are not necessarily bound by federal rules regarding defendant's right to counsel but may, upon their own initiative, impose stricter rules. *People v Green*, 214 NW 2d 891/Mich (1974).

Critical Stage

"Any critical stage of the proceeding" as refered to in *Gideon v Wainwright*, *supra*, and *Hamilton v Alabama*, 368 US 52 (1961), includes the preliminary hearing in felony cases as defendant's plea of guilty at the preliminary hearing may at some later time be used against him (*White v Maryland*, 373 US 59–1963). But where defendant was denied court-appointed counsel at his preliminary hearing wherein he had pleaded not guilty, the court ruled defendant could not have been prejudiced thereby. *Summers v Rhay*, 410 P 2d 608/Wn (1966).

Defendant's right to counsel attaches at or after the time that adversary judicial proceedings have been initiated against him; i.e., formal charge, preliminary hearing, indictment, information or arraignment. *State v Farrow*, 294 A 2d 873/NJ (1972).

Sentencing is a critical stage in a criminal proceeding and defendant is entitled to counsel, and if indigent, to appointed counsel, at time sentence is pronounced. *Gutierrez v Estelle*, 474 F 2d 899/Tex (1973).

An indigent defendant who has not waived his right to counsel is entitled to appointed counsel at a probation revocation hearing. *Ex parte Herrera*, 493 SW 2d 809/Tex (1973).

An indigent defendant has the right to appointed counsel but does not have the right to an appointed attorney of his choice. *People v Wilson*, 204 NW 2d 269/Mich (1972).

A defendant in a criminal case not only has the constitutional right to the assistance of counsel, but he has the correlative right to refuse the advice or interference of counsel and to present his own case; a court has no more right to force an attorney on the defendant than he has to deny the defendant's request for an attorney. *United States v Price*, 474 F 2d 1223/Cal (1973).

Defendant who declined to request counsel after being afforded a clear opportunity to do so, and who elected to proceed *in propria persona*, expressly waived his right to counsel. *People v Winfrey*, 199 NW 2d 663/Mich (1972).

Presence at Trial

Defendant is entitled to a fair trial under the Constitution but not a perfect trial (*Reid v Com*, 195 SE 2d 866/Va–1973). And he is entitled, as a matter of right, to be present during his trial up to the time of conviction and sentence, but he is not entitled to be present thereafter at special proceedings such as application for writs or when his case is argued on appeal. *Whipple v Smith*, 206 P 2d 510/Wn (1949).

Defendant has the right to be present in person during all stages of his trial, but he renounces this right if he engages in misconduct so disruptive and disrespectful that the trial cannot continue in his presence and he may be removed from the courtroom for the remainder of his trial (*Peters v State*, 516 P 2d 1372/Ok–1973). Also defendant's right to be present at all stages of his trial is a right which may be waived (*People v Meschino*, 294 NE 2d 712/Ill–1973), and a defendant who voluntarily absents himself during the course of his trial cannot be heard to complain that his rights were violated by a trial *in absentia*. *State v Myers*, 508 P 2d 1178/Ut (1973).

Right to Defend in Person and Testify

Defendant is guaranteed the right to appear both in person and with counsel in his own defense (*Bayless v United States*, 381 F 2d 67/Wn–1967); the right to defend *pro se* is a constitutional right and a court cannot deny defendant the right to defend himself merely because he lacks expertise and professional capabilities. *United States v Price*, 474 F 2d 1223/Cal (1973).

A defendant may testify or not at his trial; his failure to testify raises no presumption of guilt, does not disturb the presumption of innocence and cannot be commented on by the prosecutor (*Garner v State*, 500 P 2d 865/Ok–1972), and the decision of whether to testify is one personal to the defendant rather than his counsel. *People v Brown*, 294 NE 2d 285/Ill (1973).

Right to Silence

An arrestee has the right to remain silent upon arrest and the state may not usually offer testimony that he exercised that right except to impeach his later inconsistent statements or where alluded to by a witness under conditions that rendered the error harmless. *People v Kremko*, 218 NW 2d 122/Mich (1974).

Any words or conduct on the part of an arrestee which can be reasonably interpreted as a disinclination to discuss his crime with an officer, must be held to be an invocation of his right to silence under the Fifth Amendment (*People v Burton*, 491 P 2d 793/Cal–1971), but any statements volunteered by the arrestee are not affected by the *Miranda* decision and are admissible. *State v Kroupa*, 492 P 2d 750/Az (1972); *Miranda v Arizona*, 86 SC 1602/Az (1966).

The introduction of "admissions by silence," i.e., tacit admissions, during custodial periods for the purpose of proving guilt, violates defendant's privilege against self-incrimination (*State v Greer*, 492 P 2d 36/Az–1971). However, where arrestee, after being arrested and informed of his constitutional rights and he thereafter initiated a conversation in an attempt to exculpate himself, his admission by silence when confronted with a $100 bill which he had allegedly stolen was admissible. *State v O'Dell*, 492 P 2d 1160/Az (1972).

It has been previously held that once defendant invokes the Fifth Amendment right to remain silent that he cannot thereafter give information against interest (*People v Fioritto*, 441 P 2d 625/Cal–1968), but in this and other cases cited by the California court the defendant, after invoking his Fifth Amendment rights was requested by the police to waive those rights. Volunteered statements are not barred by the Fifth Amendment and defendant may change his mind due to his own psychological makeup and initiate conversation with officers wherein he makes admissions against interest (*State v Kroupa*, 492 P 2d 750/Az–1972). The more recent and prevalent rule is expressed by the Minnesota court wherein it observed that although defendant may exercise his constitutional right to remain silent, it is not improper for police to approach him after his initial refusal to cooperate and ask him to reconsider his exercise of the right to silence so long as such request is not in any manner compulsive or coercive. *State v O'Neill*, 216 NW 2d 822/Min (1974).

Line-ups

The Fifth Amendment to the U.S. Constitution states in part, ". . . No person . . . shall be compelled in a criminal case to be a witness against himself . . . ." This phrase has been held to be a guarantee against "testimonial incrimination," and neither defendant's voice at a line-up nor clothing, such as a raincoat and rainhat, identified as belonging to him are testimonial and constitutional protection does not apply. *King v Pinto*, 376 F 2d 593/NJ (1967).

Defendant has the right to have counsel present at a postindictment line-up for identification purposes (*People v Thomas*, 205 NW 2d 604/Mich–1973), but this right does not extend to preindictment line-ups. *State v Jenkins*, 494 SW 2d 14/Mo (1973); *Kirby v Illinois*, 406 US 682 (1972).

That defendant was required to participate in a line-up under circumstances which made him "stand out," or was required to recite certain designated phrases, is not a violation of the privilege against self-incrimination. *Powell v State*, 489 SW 2d 538/Ten (1972).

Show-ups

Although distinction is not always made between a "line-up" and a "show-up," there is a difference. A line-up requires that the witness view the suspect in line or in a group of several subjects, while a show-up is made by confronting a witness or victim with a single suspect and usually a short time after the commission of the crime.

There is no prohibition against a victim or witness viewing a suspect alone especially when such confrontation occurs a short time after the criminal act. *Payne v State*, 265 S 2d 192/Ala (1972).

Due process was not violated where defendant was pursued after a bank robbery and placed in confrontation of witnesses 15 minutes after the robbery despite claims of "suggestiveness" by appellant (*United States v Canty*, 469 F 2d 114/DC–1972); nor where police arrested a suspect in a robbery within an hour after the robbery and conducted a "one man show-up" by confronting victim with a single suspect was there created a substantial likelihood of irreparable misidentification since during the robbery, victim had had ample opportunity to observe the suspect. *United States ex rel Frasier v Henderson*, 464 F 2d 260/NY (1972).

When Right May Be Waived

The waiver of a constitutional right is traditionally defined as the intentional relinquishment of a *known* right (*State v Harper*, 205 NW 2d 1/Wis–1973). Any defendant, even a juvenile, may as a matter of law intelligently waive a constitutional right (*State v Roberts*, 274 S 2d 262/Fla–1973). Defendant may waive a constitutional right if (1) he has specific knowledge of its existence and (2) he abandons the protection of that right through intentional decision. Both elements must be present and if either is missing there can be no waiver and no finding of consent (*People v Grimmett*, 202 NW 2d 278/Mich–1972). But there can be no waiver of a right not known by the defendant to exist. *State v Atherton*, 410 P 2d 208/certiorari denied 384 US 1025/Or (1966).

RESTRICTIONS ON DEFENDANT'S RIGHTS

Arraignment

The federal rule of "arraignment without unreasonable delay," as declared in *Mallory* and *McNabb*, was not imposed on the several states and in the absence of a state statute requiring conformance to the federal rule, it has no application to prisoners held in state custody. *Mallory v United States*, 354 US 449 (1957); *McNabb v United States*, 318 US 332 (1943).

Self-Incrimination

Under the Fifth Amendment to the U.S. Constitution the defendant enjoys the right against self-incrimination. This right has been held to mean "testimonial" self-incrimination and does not protect defendant against a request by the prosecutor or the police to "don a stocking and [a] welder's cap"; wear a blouse; complete a handwriting exemplar; exhibit himself in various costumes; stand up and remove glasses; reveal tattoo marks on his arm; speak for voice identification. *Kessler v Cupp*, 502 P 2d 281/Or (1972).

The Fifth Amendment privilege against compulsory self-incrimination may be asserted in any proceeding—civil or criminal, administrative or judicial, investigatory or adjudicatory. *Kastigar v United States*, 92 SC 1653/Cal (1972).

Defendant is not privileged under the Fifth Amendment to refuse to answer incriminating questions when the statute of limitations on the crime thus revealed has expired. *Baker v Eisenstadt*, 456 F 2d 382/Mas (1972).

Nontestimonial Evidence

It is not a violation of due process to take blood from a corpse which may be needed or desired for evidence in court. Nor is it a violation of due process to withdraw blood from the veins of an unconscious person for the same reasons (*Zenith Transport v Bellingham Nat Bank*, 395 P 2d 498/Wn—1964), nor from the veins of a conscious person over his objections and against the advice of his attorney. *Schmerber v California*, 384 US 787 (1966).

Upon defendant denying, while on the witness stand under cross-examination, that he had "track marks" on his arms, he was asked by the solicitor, and required by the court, to take off his jacket and exhibit his arms to the jury. Such requirement is not in violation of the Fifth Amendment against self-incrimination. *State v Thomas*, 201 SE 2d 201/NC (1973).

Where defendant contended on appeal that his Fifth and Fourteenth Amendment rights were violated when he was required to repeat words purportedly uttered by the rapist, the court held the contention to be without merit. *State v Grierson*, 504 P 2d 1204/Id (1972); *United States v Wade*, 388 US 218 (1967).

When Counsel Not Required

Defendant is entitled to the assistance of counsel at all stages of a judicial proceeding but the competency of counsel will not be measured by his success in defense of his client but on the entire record. "Effective assistance of counsel" does not mean "successful assistance of counsel." *State v White*, 500 P 2d 1242/Wn (1972).

The "equal protection" clause of the Fourteenth Amendment does not require the state to furnish an indigent defendant with every luxury that a wealthy litigant might choose to purchase at his own expense. *Com v Britt*, 285 NE 2d 780/Mas (1972).

The Sixth Amendment does not guarantee the right of an accused to counsel at a photographic display conducted by government officers for the purpose of allowing a witness the opportunity to identify the offender in crime (*United States v Ash*, 93 SC 2568/DC–1973), and where a witness was given five photographs, the suspect's photograph being in the middle of the group, his selection of the suspect's photograph while sitting alone at a table did not violate the suspect's right to due process. *United States ex rel Johnson v Correctional Services*, 461 F 2d 956/NY (1972).

Defendant is not entitled to the services of an attorney at an on-the-scene identification (*State v Salcido*, 509 P 2d 1027/Az–1973), nor was counsel required during a jail search and physical examination where hair samples were taken. *State v Brierly*, 509 P 2d 203/Az (1973).

Defendant is not entitled to the presence of counsel while being given a breathalyzer test (*State v Driver*, 207 NW 2d 850/Wis–1973), nor while blood is being withdrawn to be used in a blood-alcohol analysis test. Id.

The Arrest

Advisement of constitutional rights applies only to government officers and their agents, not to private persons. Thus, a statement made by a patient who was being treated by a physician for a gun-shot wound sustained during apprehension was admissible (in the absence of a rule which declares such statement to be a privileged communication), and the rules set forth in *Escobedo* and *Miranda* do not apply. *Beecher v State*, 256 S 2d 154/Ala (1971).

The basic warnings required by the *Miranda* decision—that custodial interrogation be preceded by an advisement of defendant's right to counsel and the right against self-incrimination—are not violated unless evidence so obtained is introduced into evidence against defendant at his trial. *People v Wong*, 111 CR 314/Cal (1973).

The arrestee is not entitled to an attorney at the scene of arrest, for to await an attorney only to find that arrestee is innocent would allow the person responsible to escape. *State v Montgomery*, 504 P 2d 935/Az (1972).

Where one gives false testimony before a grand jury, he is not entitled to a *Miranda* warning, even though the proceedings have become "accusatory." *United States v McGinnis*, 344 FS 89/Tex (1972).

Fingerprints

There is no federal constitutional right not to be fingerprinted (*Snow v Oklahoma*, 489 F 2d 278–1973), and the privilege against self-incrimination does not protect against compulsion to submit to fingerprinting. *State v Jamerson*, 518 P 2d 779/NM (1974).

Handwriting Exemplars

The right against self-incrimination under the Fifth Amendment does not extend to guarantee against the production of incriminating physical evidence (*United States v Thompson*, 475 F 2d 1359/Tex–1973), which includes handwriting exemplars in a prosecution for forgery. *United States v Rogers*, 475 F 2d 82/Wis (1973).

Both handwriting and voice exemplars fall on the side of the line where no reasonable expectation of privacy exists and consequently are also outside the protection of the Fourth Amendment. Thus, where defendant refused or failed to comply with the court's order to furnish a handwriting exemplar, the jury could be appropriately instructed that they may infer that comparison of defendant's handwriting on the exemplar and the handwriting on the spurious application to purchase a firearm would have been adverse to the defendant and favorable to the government. *United States v Nix*, 465 F 2d 90/La (1972).

Selection of the Jury

Defendant is not entitled to constitutional guarantee to a jury consisting of members of a particular age or age group serving on the jury, and defendant's motion to quash the indictment because no juror was between the ages of 18 and 21 was properly denied (*Shadden v State*, 488 SW 2d 54/Ten–1972). Nor is defendant constitutionally entitled to a proportionate number of his own race on a jury which tries him or on a jury roll from which grand and petit jurors are selected. *Blyant v State*, 272 S 2d 286/Ala (1972).

Testimonial Incrimination by Others

Under the Fifth Amendment to the U.S. Constitution, defendant is protected against self-incrimination, but that provision does not protect him from incrimination by the testimony of another (*United States v Skolek*, 474 F 2d 582/Colo–1973); the privilege against self-incriminatin may be asserted only by the witness and not by another in his behalf (*Id.*), as constitutional rights may not be vicariously asserted. *State v Marley*, 509 P 2d 1095/Haw (1973).

Unequal Treatment of Defendants

It is not a requisite of equal protection or due process when one defendant is treated differently from another although charged with the identical offense (*State v Cousino*, 500 P 2d 1146/Az–1972); the fact that the state accepted pleas from some codefendants, granted immunity to others and prosecuted the remainder, did not violate the rights of those prosecuted and was constitutionally permissible. *United States v Dalton*, 465 F 2d 32/Tex (1972).

That defendant was the only one of 38 persons arrested in a drug raid did not amount to unequal enforcement prohibited by law. *Campion v State*, 500 P 2d 422/NM (1972).

Preliminary Hearing

As a prelude to trial, defendant is entitled to a preliminary hearing before a committing magistrate or to be indicted by a grand jury for the purpose of determining probable cause; or, he may waive the preliminary hearing, but he cannot waive indictment. *State v Foster*, 192 SE 2d 320/NC (1972).

Since the sole purpose of the preliminary hearing is to determine if a crime was committed and if there exists reasonable cause to believe defendant committed it (*People v Duncan*, 201 NW 2d 629/Mich–1972), the need for the preliminary hearing is obviated by the finding of an indictment by the grand jury, the indictment itself being based on probable cause. *Joy v Superior Court*, 298 A 2d 315/Del (1972).

The preliminary hearing is not a mini-trial of the issue of guilt, but is rather an investigation into the reasonableness of the basis for charge, and if it appears to the magistrate that there is reasonable cause to believe defendant committed the crime charged, it is his duty to hold the defendant to answer in a trial of the charge in the superior court. *Coleman v Burnett*, 427 F 2d 1187/DC (1973); *Myers v Com*, 298 NE 2d 819/Mas (1973).

The preliminary hearing is held to determine two issues: (1) is there reasonable cause to believe that a felony has been committed, and (2) is there reasonable cause to believe the accused committed it. Only if both issues are determined to the detriment of the accused will he be held to answer in a trial of the issue of fact (*Words and Phrases*, Volume 33 at 477-78). Since the guilt of the accused is not at issue, no jeopardy can attach as a result of a preliminary hearing. *State v Pietsch*, 508 P 2d 337/Az (1973).

"Sufficient cause," "reasonable cause," and "probable cause" are essentially the same and are defined to mean such a state of facts as would lead a man of ordinary caution and prudence to believe and entertain conscientiously a strong suspicion of the guilt of the accused *People v Uhlemann*, 503 P 2d 277/Cal (1972).

The *corpus delicti* must be proved independently of admissions and confessions made extrajudically by legal and credible evidence before defendant may be convicted of crime, and this rule is no less applicable at the preliminary examination except that defendant is not convicted at the preliminary hearing but merely held to answer (*State v Meyer*, 208 NW 2d 230/Mich–1973). But it is not necessary at the preliminary hearing that defendant's guilt be established beyond a reasonable doubt (*People v Maire*, 201 NW 2d 318/Mich–1972). The "beyond a reasonable doubt" concept operates at the trial, not at the preliminary hearing. *Com v Rose*, 297 A 2d 122/Pa (1972); *Bain v Sheriff of Clark County*, 504 P 2d 695/Nev (1972).

The preliminary hearing is a critical stage of a criminal proceeding and an indigent defendant is entitled to appointed counsel at such hearing. *Coleman v Alabama*, 399 US 1 (1970).

The finding of no probable cause at a preliminary hearing is not conclusive on the state's right subsequently to seek indictment for the dismissed charge. *People v Brown*, 306 NE 2d 561/Ill (1973).

Although defendant has the right to be present at the preliminary hearing, he waives such right when he engages in disruptive and obstreperous conduct, and where after being warned by the court that he would be removed from the courtroom if he continued his disorderly conduct, his ultimate removal did not deny him due process. *State v Kluck*, 217 NW 2d 202/Min (1974).

THE TRIAL

Speedy and Public

The issue of fact is heard before a jury, or by a judge upon waiver of a jury trial. If the trial be a "bench" or "court" trial, i.e., heard by a judge only, the judge resolves all issues of law and fact and passes on the credibility of witnesses and evidence. *City of St. Louis v Boos*, 503 SW 2d 133/Mo (1973); *People v Harper*, 305 NE 2d 680/Ill (1973).

The Sixth Amendment guarantees the accused a speedy and public trial, but nowhere in the Constitution is he guaranteed the right to a private trial. Secrecy in government, and particularly secret trials under our form of government, is abhorrent. *Avery v State*, 292 A 2d 728/Md (1973).

Although defendant is entitled to a speedy and public trial, where defendant's participation in a bank robbery was not discovered until nine months later, and there was a seven month delay between the filing of a complaint and the finding of an indictment (most of which time was attributable to defendant's resistance to extradition proceedings), absent a specific showing of predjudice, there was not a denial of a speedy trial nor due process. *Northern v United States*, 455 F 2d 427/Cal (1972).

Defendant should be unrestrained during his trial and usually should not be exposed to the jury while in chains or handcuffs, but this rule is not absolute where good and just cause exists to place defendant under proper restraint. *State v Kirk*, 510 SW 2d 196/Mo (1974).

It is inherently unfair to try defendant while he is dressed in jail clothing except that an intentional waiver of that right may be granted to defendant where he, upon advice of his counsel and as a defense tactic, chooses to appear in jail clothing to evoke sympathy. *Hollins v Beto*, 373 FS 1246/Tex (1974).

Presence of Defendant

As a rule a felony prisoner must be present during his trial, but when he is at liberty on bail and voluntarily absents himself from the trial after the trial has started, he waives the right to be present and the trial may proceed in his absence (*People v Colon*, 293 NE 2d 468/Ill–1973). But some jurisdictions will stay proceedings in defendant's absence.

Defendant has the constitutional right to conduct his trial *pro se* (for himself), but he waives that right when by his misconduct he makes it impossible for that right to be exercised. *State v Devecchio*, 519 P 2d 1137/Az (1974).

Before defendant may be permitted to waive his right to counsel, the trial court must determine that he is competent to represent himself. *People v Rhinehart*, 507 P 2d 642/Cal (1973).

It would be a violation of due process to put a defendant on trial on a criminal charge if he were not mentally competent to understand the nature of the charges against him and to assist in his own defense (*United States v Varner*, 467 F 2d 659/Ala–1972). Likewise, to convict the accused while he is legally incompetent violates due process. *Brown v State*, 485 SW 2d 424/Mo (1972).

Joint Trials

Generally, where two or more participants are indicted or otherwise charged together, they should be tried together. The granting of severance for one or more defendants so that he, or they, may be tried separately is within the sound discretion of the court (*People v Brooks*, 281 NE 2d 326/Ill–1972), and the only real justification for a granting of severance is upon a showing that defendant would be prejudiced by a joint trial (*Lowther v United States*, 455 F 2d 657/Colo–1972). To be granted severance defendant must demonstrate substantial prejudice from a joint trial, not merely a better chance at acquittal in a separate trial. *United States v Dornau*, 356 FS 1090/NY (1973).

Power and Duty of Trial Judge

The trial judge in a nonjury trial has the sole discretion in determining materiality and relevancy of evidence (*Orquist v Montgomery Ward*, 194 NW 2d 392/Mich–1961). He must exercise great care in his conduct and comments from the bench so that neither may be interpreted by the jury to be an expression of opinion on the facts or calculated to prejudice either party. *State v Allen*, 196 SE 2d 256/NC (1973).

The court has the power, which is discretionary, to exclude witnesses during a trial and to direct that each be examined out of the hearing of each other. *People v Jenkins*, 295 NE 2d 123/Ill (1973).

The power of a court to try a person for crime is not impaired by the fact that defendant was brought within the court's jurisdiction by means of forcible abduction (*Frisbie v Collins*, 342 US 519/Mich–1952), and where, on appeal, defendant argued that the New Mexico court was without jurisdiction to try him due to his arrest in Arizona and abduction into New Mexico without waiver of extradition, the New Mexico court held: "The law of New Mexico has long been to the contrary," citing *Frisbie, supra. State v Millican*, 501 P 2d 1076/NM (1972).

Jury Trial

Defendant's right to a trial by jury varies from state to state but only in cases of misdemeanor or petty offenses (*State v Sklor*, 317 A 2d 160/Me–1974). In all serious or felony offenses, and in any misdemeanor offense punishable by more than six months, defendant is entitled to a trial by jury. *Hoffman v Local No. 10*, 492 F 2d 929/Cal (1974).

Juries are not permitted to make special findings on their own initiative (*State v Robinson*, 523 P 2d 1192/Wn–1974), but mere surplusage may be disregarded if the intent of the jury is otherwise clear. *Peterson v State*, 508 SW 2d 844/Tex (1974).

In a trial by jury it is always the prerogative of the jury to fix guilt or innocence, but it is not within its purview to determine whether sentence is to be imposed, suspended or deferred; this decision rests with the court. *Miller v State*, 522 P 2d 642/Ok (1974).

A finding of guilty by eleven jurors after one of the original twelve had been excused because of illness was not a denial of due process where, at the outset of the trial, defendant had agreed to be tried by as few as ten jurors. *People v Chandler*, 289 NE 2d 67/Ill (1972).

The systematic exclusion of women from the jury panel deprived a male defendant of due process and could not be justified on the basis that many, if not all of those selected, could ask to be excused from the panel. *Mayfield v Steed*, 345 FS 806/Ark (1972).

A ruling that jurors should not take notes is discretionary to the trial court. Although cited here by appellant as error, the ruling was made upon the unanimous request of defendants (39 in number) and was opposed by the government. *United States v Murray*, 492 F 2d 178/Cal (1973).

As a rule, neither the jury as a whole (*United States v Johnson*, 495 F 2d 1097/Tex–1974), nor a single juror may impeach a verdict arrived at by diligent deliberation by disclosing deliberations or by subsequent affidavit. *People v Passero*, 357 NYS 2d 677/NY (1974).

Compulsion and Sequestration

Often the defendant, especially in a sex offense or a homicide, will move to sequester witnesses, presumably to prevent spectator witnesses from hearing another witness testify and thereby be influenced. The courts are in virtual unanimous agreement that the prosecutor is entitled to the presence of an arresting or investigating officer to assist in the presentation of his case. As a rule, if there are two arresting officers, upon motion of the prosecuting attorney, each may accompany and assist the prosecutor while the other is testifying. *McNeal v State*, 187 SE 2d 271/Ga (1972): *State v Neal*, 476 SW 2d 547/Mo (1972).

The incarceration of a material witness and paying him one dollar a day does not amount to the taking of one's property without just compensation; a witness so held is not entitled under the Constitution to any compensation. The giving of testimony in court under proper summons is the duty of every citizen, and that obligation persists no matter how financially burdensome it may be. The financial losses suffered during pretrial detention are an extension of the burdens borne by every witness who testifies. *Hurtado v United States*, 93 SC 1157 (1973).

A witness who testifies under compulsion, i.e., under subpoena, need not fear a future prosecution concerning any matter he revealed in the course of such testimony, but he may be prosecuted for perjury in the giving of false testimony or he may be found in contempt if he refuses to testify. *United States v Wilcox*, 450 F 2d 1131/Fla (1971); *People v Longo*, 327 NYS 2d 818/NY (1971).

Permitting an unsworn statement by defendant is within the court's discretion as is the permitting of counsel to ask defendant questions when he is not sworn (*Com v Haley*, 296 NE 2d 207/Mass–1973), (*Hilliard v State*, 195 SE 2d 772/Ga–1973). But defendant's unsworn statement is not evidence (*Walters v State*, 196 SE 2d 326/Ga–1973), nor is a question asked but unanswered evidence of any fact. *State v Anderson*, 195 SE 2d 561/NC (1973).

Directed Verdict

The jury must decide all issues of fact before it by the weighing of all the evidence, and when there is none the jury will not be permitted to speculate or to infer the existence of facts from mere possibilities (*Moran v Williams*, 313 A 2d 527/Md–1974). Therefore, when there is no evidence having probative force upon which the jury may make a finding, the movant is entitled to a directed verdict (*Le Noble v Weber et al*, 503 SW 2d 321/Tex–1973). The better practice is for the trial judge to announce to the jury that he is directing a verdict in favor of one of the parties and that such verdict will be entered on the record and then to discharge the jury. To require the jury to retire and formulate the verdict as directed is surplusage. *Moore v Standard Life & Acc Ins Co.*, 504 SW 2d 373/Ten (1972).

A denial of defendant's motion for a directed verdict of acquittal was reversible error where the uncontradicted testimony of a police officer placed defendant in police custody prior to the killing. *People v Moran*, 194 NW 2d 555/Mich (1971).

A motion for a directed verdict is proper only in a jury trial, and in a case tried without a jury a proper motion is for an involuntary dismissal. *Mills v Koscot Interplanetary Inc*, 187 SE 2d 372/NC (1972).

Res Judicata

"*Res judicata*" means a thing decided. More specifically, it means a matter decided by a judicial tribunal and that such decision will not be further disturbed by that tribunal.

Where the state did not appeal a court order suppressing evidence, although a statute provided for an appeal, the suppression was a final determination as to that court and thus *res judicata,* and the state could not thereafter use the evidence in a prosecution of defendants. *State v Swain,* 517 P 2d 684/Or (1974).

The dismissal of a cause after a preliminary hearing by the magistrate attaches no finality nor does it constitute jeopardy, and defendant may again be brought before the bar in a preliminary hearing or proceeded against by indictment. An exception exists, however, where after a full adversary hearing before a committing magistrate, the judge concludes that no crime was committed by the defendant. *People v Uhlemann,* 503 P 2d 277/Cal (1972).

APPEALS

In General

There is no right under the common law or under the U.S. Constitution to appeal; such right exists as a matter of grace and only to the extent allowed by statute (*Metron Steel Corp v Alby Mfg Inc,* 194 NW 2d 608/Wis–1972); (United *States v Rayburn,* 91 F 2d 162/Ia–1937). Most states, however, have provided means for appeal. Thus, in California every person convicted of crime has the right to have his conviction and sentence reviewed through appeal, and if he is indigent he has the right to prosecute his appeal through appointed counsel at no expense to himself; any right which exists for the benefit of defendant may be waived. *Com v Perrine,* 302 A 2d 432/Pa (1973); *Douglas v California,* 83 SC 814/Cal (1963).

When a criminal case goes before an appellate court for review in an appeal from conviction, it is first argued by the appellant and then by the government– the reverse of the procedure upon trial.

An appellate court usually reviews on appeal only those questions which were before the trial court upon which a ruling adverse to the defendant was made (*Chester v State,* 276 S 2d 76/Fla–1973). However, it will consider questions which are not raised at the trial whenever it is necessary to serve the ends of justice or prevent the denial of fundamental rights. *State v Marley,* 509 P 2d 1095/Haw (1973).

Constitutionality of Statutes

The enactment of laws and the fixing of penalties are matters exclusively within the power of the legislature, not the judiciary. Upon appeal the courts may not concern themselves with the wisdom or propriety of enactments; rather, the duties of courts are limited to a determination of whether an act contravenes a specific provision of the Constitution. *Lowe v State*, 298 NE 2d 421/Wis (1973).

The courts are under obligation to avoid ruling on the constitutionality of a statute if the questions raised on appeal can be adjudicated otherwise. *State v Liska*, 291 NE 2d 498/Oh (1971).

The fact that an inferior tribunal declares a statute unconstitutional does not divest the appellate court of jurisdiction to review the lower court's decision, and the appellate court may affirm the lower court's action or reinstate the statute to full efficacy. *People v Gebarowski*, 209 NW 2d 543/Mich (1973).

"Mootness" or a "moot question" is a question in controversy sought to be adjudicated in a court of law, but before a decision is rendered the question loses its character from some other cause and the controversy ceases to exist. Vol 27A, *Words and Phrases.*

A signed waiver of constitutional rights is not conclusive of that issue and the court of appeals may, *sua sponte*, review all evidence in the record pertaining to the waiver (*Dickerson v State*, 276 NE 2d 845/Ind–1972). Where a constitutional right is in issue, a waiver of that right cannot be presumed from a silent record. *Com v Norman*, 285 A 2d 523/Pa (1971).

When Taken

Although defendant may be granted a new trial for errors prejudicial to him committed in the course of his trial, he is not entitled to a declaration of mistrial and a new trial for errors committed which were prejudicial to the state. *State v Valentine*, 202 SE 2d 496/NC (1974).

Timely objection to questionable matters must be made during the process of the trial in order to preserve ground for review on appeal (*Franco v State*, 491 SW 2d 876/Tex–1973), and as a rule, issues raised for the first time on appeal will be ignored by the reviewing court (*Com v Debo*, 305 A 2d 21/Pa–1973). But an exception to this rule would be a claim of double jeopardy. *Muncy v State*, 505 SW 2d 925/Tex (1974).

When Denied

The state may not under any circumstances appeal from acquittal, even though erroneous; to allow appeal by the state would be a violation of the double jeopardy clause of the Fifth Amendment. *United States v Wilson*, 492 F 2d 1345/Pa (1974); *Carsey v City of Mansfield*, 310 NE 2d 263/Oh (1973).

As a rule, neither a motion granting a new trial (*Pate v Crescent Motors Exchange Inc*, 256 S 2d 471/La–1972), nor the denial of a motion for a new trial (*Newhouse v Upchurch*, 99 CR 436/Cal–1971) is appealable.

An order denying probation is not appealable (*Hinkle v State*, 278 S 2d 218/Ala–1973). Appeals may be taken on alleged errors, and denial of probation being discretionary to the trial court, is not an assignable error. *People v Polansky*, 287 NE 2d 747/Ill (1972).

An appeal cannot be taken by a fugitive from justice. *Com v Richards*, 296 NE 2d 506/Mas (1973).

Appeal From Inferior Court

In jurisdictions wherein courts designated as justice, district, municipal, police, and others which are not courts of record, an appeal from conviction therein must be heard anew in a higher court—usually the superior court and the forum in the lower court then becomes a nullity.

Where statute provides as a means for appeal from a district court to be a trial *de novo* in a superior court or a court of general jurisdiction, the right to appeal is absolute and appellant need not cite errors as a basis therefor. Nor may appellant seek appellate review of his conviction in the district court; the first forum is of no efficacy and the cause is treated as though it had been brought to the higher court in the first instance. *State v Keegan*, 296 A 2d 483/Me (1972); *Colten v Kentucky*, 407 US 113/Ky (1972).

The trial *de novo* is a two-edged sword in the two-tier criminal justice system. Defendant, after appeal from conviction of a misdemeanor in the lower court, and during his trial *de novo* in the superior court is protected against the introduction of any evidence accruing at the first forum in the lower court, and he is likewise denied the right to seek any benefits that may stem therefrom. *McClung v Weatherholtz*, 351 FS 5/Va (1972).

Upon appeal from conviction from a municipal or justice court, and the grant of a trial *de novo* in the superior court, defendant must be tried for the identical offense of which he was found guilty in the lower court. *Rossitto v State*, 287 A 2d 669/Del (1972).

Upon conviction in a trial *de novo* in the superior court, defendant may be sentenced to a greater sentence than that imposed in the lower court (*State v Turner*, 186 SE 2d 681/NC–1972), and the fact that defendant received a harsher sentence in a trial *de novo* than he had received after conviction in the lower court from which he appealed, is not error and does not chill defendant's right to appeal since the punishment prescribed for the crime was the same in either case. *State v Keegan*, 296 A 2d 483/Me (1972); *State v Martin*, 192 SE 2d 596/NC (1972).

Upon conviction in a district court, defendant has the right to prosecute an appeal devoid of fear and apprehension that the state will retaliate by substituting a more serious charge for the original thus subjecting him to an increased incarceration potential (*Blackledge v Perry*, 94 SC 2098/NC–1974), and a statute which provides for increased penalty after appeal from a district court to a superior court upon conviction in the superior court is unconstitutional. To hold otherwise would have a chilling effect on the exercise of a constitutional right.

Frivolous Appeals

Even though an appeal may appear frivolous, if it represents a legal question or raises a constitutional issue, the courts of appeal will entertain it. Thus, where defendant appealed from a conviction of the illegal possession of narcotics on the grounds that he was a narcotic addict and should be exempt from the law proscribing the possession of narcotics, his appeal was heard and ruled on—fortunately for society, adverse to the appellant. *Taylor v State*, 492 SW 2d 476/Tex (1973); *United States v Moore*, 486 F 2d 1139/DC (1973).

Defendant appealed from conviction of making obscene telephone calls, *inter alia*, on the ground that the court abused discretion in refusing to recess the proceeding in order that defendant may shave. The court, in denying relief, observed that defendant had cited no authority as a basis for his assignment of error, and in the absence of a citation of authority the court of appeal would not search books for authority to support a mere assertion. *Hall v State*, 498 P 2d 415/Ok (1972).

Defendant's conviction was sustained where he was convicted of possessing a firearm while serving a felony sentence in the state prison, his appeal urging a violation of his constitutional right to bear arms. *People v Wells*, 156 P 2d 979/Cal (1945).

Tort action would not lie where three minor children claimed damage by the wrongful birth of a fourth child (born after a vasectomy operation on the father), which allegedly detracted from their share of love and affection, as well as the reduction of their worldly interests and inheritance from one-third to one-fourth. *Arnoff v Snider*, 292 S 2d 418/Fla (1974).

Chapter IV

Crime and Punishment

"Crime" Defined

"Crime" or a "public offense" has been defined by the California Legislature as an act committed or omitted in violation of a law forbidding or commanding it and to which is annexed upon conviction either of the following punishments: (1) death, (2) imprisonment, (3) fine, (4) removal from office, and (5) disqualification to hold and enjoy any office or honor, trust or profit within the state. California Penal Code § 15.

In every crime or public offense there must exist a union or joint operation of act and intent or criminal negligence. *State v Wright*, 444 P 2d 676/Wn (1968).

The legislature has the power to define crimes and to specify appropriate punishments therefor (*Ledke v State*, 296 NE 2d 412/Ind–1973), and the courts should be reticent to redefine legislative intent to conform to their personal beliefs and concepts (*United States v Irick*, 369 FS 594/Tex–1974). Statutes are either: prohibitive, permissive, definitive or mandatory.

Statutory offenses are characterized as being either *mala in se* or *mala prohibita*. An act is *malum in se* if it is inherently and essentially wrong and injurious (such as rape, robbery, larceny, assault, arson). Those acts which do not fall within the category of *mala in se* but which are denounced by statute (such as traffic violations, use of drugs or narcotics, laws regarding permits or licenses), are *mala prohibita*. It is not the nature of the *mala prohibita* acts that make them wrong but statutory proscription. *State v Taylor*, 297 A 2d 216/NJ (1972).

A "tort," often defined as a civil wrong, may, and often does, result from the commission of crime. A tort is an act or a failure to act by one under obligation to act, which proximately causes damage to another person. A tort is an act against personal interest while a crime is an act against the interest of the state. *Black's Law Dictionary.*

"Felony" and "Misdemeanor" Distinguished

As a rule, under state law, a felony is any crime punishable by death or imprisonment in the state prison or penitentiary, and all other crimes are misdemeanors. Also, as a rule, no person may be sentenced upon conviction of a misdemeanor to a term in excess of one year. This does not mean, however, that one convicted of multiple misdemeanors may not be sentenced in the aggregate for a period in excess of one year where the court directs that the sentences run consecutively. *People v Washington,* 351 NYS 2d 259/NY (1953); *Lashley v State,* 180 S 717/Ala (1938).

Under federal law any crime punishable in excess of one year is a felony and if punishable for one year or less it is a misdemeanor. Title 18 USCA, § 1.

Crimes Must Be Described and Denounced

As a rule, no act, however reprehensible, is criminal unless specifically denounced by statute and a punishment prescribed therefor, and the rule at common law wherein the magistrate legislated and adjudicated to fit the act has no application today. In some states the common law, although a basis for substantive law, has been statutorily abolished while in other states, although not abolished, it merely serves as a guide or a supplement to the administration of law. *State v Hauck,* 209 NW 2d 580/Neb (1973).

In a criminal statute, the prohibited conduct must be defined with sufficient clarity to permit a citizen to know in advance from the written statute what act or omission is made criminal. *State v D'Amico,* 293 A 2d 304/RI (1972).

A criminal code provision that no conduct constitutes an offense unless it is described and proscribed in the code or some other statute, abolishes the common law and extra-code principles of accountability. *People v Kessler,* 296 NE 2d 631/Ill (1973).

Where a valid statute exists which defines and proscribes an act specifically, it should be employed in prosecutions rather than a statute which applies generally. *Jones v State,* 507 P 2d 1267/Ok (1973).

Crimes Categorized and Classified

All crimes recognized at common law were *mala in se.* Some are murder, larceny, kidnaping (*Black's Law Dictionary*); (*Wilson v State,* 303 A 2d 638/Del–1973). Further, crimes are classified generally into two types: felonies and misdemeanors. Felonies are sometimes further divided into two types: capital and noncapital or in degrees; misdemeanors are likewise further divided into high-grade misdemeanors, gross misdemeanors or infractions. As a rule under state law any crime punishable by death or imprisonment in a state prison or penitentiary is a felony; all other crimes are misdemeanors. Under federal law a "felony," as defined by Congress, is a crime punishable by imprisonment in excess of one year. *United States v Glasgow,* 478 F 2d 850/Min (1973).

Alternative Crimes

Under the laws of some states—California, Illinois and Nevada to name a few—a crime punishable in the alternative of imprisonment in the state penitentiary or by fine or imprisonment in a county or city jail, is a felony for purposes of arrest and trial, but if defendant is sentenced to a jail sentence or a fine only, the crime then, and for all purposes thereafter, is a misdemeanor. *People v Russell,* 99 CR 277/Cal (1971); *People v McGreal,* 278 NE 2d 504/Ill (1971); *Hernandez v State,* 519 P 2d 107/Nev (1974).

Abandonment of Crime

Once a crime is committed it cannot be "uncommitted" despite abandonment or change of heart, and where defendant telephoned a hospital registration desk, intending to play a joke on a friend, and told the person who answered, "There's a bomb going off in 15 minutes," her crime was complete. The fact that she approached the registration desk within a few moments and advised the clerk that she had made the call and that it was meant to be a joke, did not exculpate her as evacuation of the hospital had already started and was completed despite her revelation. *Cincinnati v Lattimore,* 288 NE 2d 334/Oh (1972).

Criminal Acts by Children

Under the common law a person between the ages of 7 and 14 presumptively could not commit crime, and unless amended or modified by statute, the common law still applies. *In the Interest of E P,* 291 S 2d 238/Fla (1974).

There exists in most if not all states statutes or rules establishing a rebuttable presumption in essential accordance with the common law rule, although the ages may vary, that children 7 years of age but less than 14 cannot, in the absence of clear proof that at the time they knew the act was wrong, commit crime. (*State v Taylor,* 512 P 2d 590/Az—1973). Also, children below the age of 7 years are conclusively presumed incapable of committing crime.

Delinquency and Juvenile Court Proceedings

A "delinquent act," defined as a crime, ceases to be a crime only for proceedings in the juvenile court at the resultant effects of the court's adjudication. *J E v State,* 194 SE 2d 288/Ga (1972).

A "delinquent" child is one who commits a violation of the law regardless of where the violation occurred and regardless of whether the act was made criminal under federal law, state statute of this or another state, or local ordinance. *J D D v State*, 268 S 2d 457/Fla (1972).

No criminal proceeding may be commenced against a juvenile until the juvenile court has waived jurisdiction pursuant to a waiver of jurisdiction hearing and the matter is transferred to the criminal court. *Jackson v State*, 300 A 2d 430/Md (1973).

A child faced with a possible waiver of jurisdiction by the juvenile court thus remanding him to the criminal court to stand trial in the manner of an adult, is entitled to a waiver of jurisdiction hearing and is entitled to counsel at that hearing. *Cox v United States*, 473 F 2d 334/NC (1973).

A proceeding in the juvenile court is not a trial for the purpose of punishment but for salvation (*S S v State*, 299 A 2d 560/Me–1973), and since procedure is civil in nature rather than criminal, the rules of criminal procedure are not applicable. *Lockamy v State*, 488 SW 2d 954/Tex (1973).

CORPUS DELICTI

Defined

The phrase "*corpus delicti*" is a Latin phrase meaning body of the crime, more specifically, the elements of the crime (*Black's Law Dictionary*). It is not necessarily a dead body as no crime is involved in natural, accidental or suicidal deaths, yet there is a dead body. Further, the dead body in a criminal homicide only serves to prove the *corpus delicti*: (1) the death of a human being and (2) a criminal agency causing death. All crimes, and only crimes, have a *corpus delicti.*

In general, the *corpus delicti* consists of proof, either direct or circumstantial that (1) a specifically described loss or injury occurred and (2) that it was occasioned by the criminal act or omission of another (*State v Summers*, 506 SW 2d 67/Mo–1974). It is the act which constitutes the substance of the crime, penally proscribed, and the criminal agency of a person in the accomplishment of that act. *State v Kennemore*, 295 NE 2d 680/Oh (1972).

How Established

The *corpus delicti* of a crime must be established independently of admissions and confessions, but once the *corpus delicti* is established, admissions and confessions, if voluntary, may be considered in determination of the issue of fact (*Tertrou v Sheriff of Clark County*, 509 P 2d 970/Nev–1973); (*Hopkins v State*, 296 NE 2d 151/Ind–1973). But it is not necessary antecedent to receiving an admission or a confession into evidence that the *corpus delicti* be proved beyond a reasonable doubt, only that it be established *prima facie*. Id.

It is a well-established rule that the *corpus delicti* must be established by evidence other than by confession of the accused, not only at defendant's trial but at his preliminary hearing as well. *People v Rendall*, 201 NW 2d 292/Mich (1972).

A statement which itself is an element of the offense may be admitted against defendant; excited utterances are admissible, and, in general, statements made before the crime was committed, contemporaneous thereto or shortly thereafter, are admissible to prove the *corpus delicti.* Id.

The identity of the perpetrator of crime is not an element of the *corpus delicti* of the crime with which he is charged. *Com v Palmer*, 292 A 2d 921/Pa (1972).

Criminal Homicide

Entertainers often refer to a corpse as the *corpus delicti*, thus spawning some of the misunderstanding of the phrase. A corpse or a dead human being is never a *corpus delicti*, and if death was accidental, suicidal or natural then the corpse is no portion of a *corpus delicti.*

To prove the *corpus delicti* in a homicide case the state must show that the person whose death is alleged is in fact dead, and that his death was caused by a criminal agency (*State v Coulter*, 506 P 2d 804/NM–1973); the *corpus delicti* in other crimes includes the fact of a specific loss or injury to one person and the criminality of another. *People v Randall*, 201 NW 2d 292/Mich (1972).

The *corpus delicti* of homicide was established where a hammer was found embedded in the head of deceased with the handle pointed backward and evidence showed that defendant was the only person in close enough proximity to deceased to have inflicted the fatal blow. *Hearns v State*, 261 S 2d 64/Ala (1972).

INTENT

Defined

"Criminal intent" is intent to commit crime; it is malice toward others as evidenced by an antisocial act. Further, it means an intent to cause pain, suffering or discomfort, or an intent to deprive another of his property by criminal means.

Intent is a state of mind; it is purpose, resolve, design or goal. For an act to be criminal there must exist in the mind of the perpetrator *mens rea*, that is, guilty intent, or the perpetrator must act with criminal negligence. Intent is of three kinds: general, specific and transferred.

A criminal offense can come about only through a joint operation of act and criminal intent or by criminal negligence. *People v Belcher*, 106 CR 807/Cal (1973).

Naked intent to commit crime, however opprobrious or diabolical, is not criminal (*Rosado v Martinez*, 369 FS 477/PR (1974); there must also be a forbidden act committed or omitted. *People v Rodriguez*, 8 CR 863/Cal (1960).

General Intent

"General intent" is synonymous with "presumed intent," and it is axiomatic that every sane person is presumed to intend the natural and probable consequences of his voluntary acts; therefore, when the criminal act is proved such act will be presumed to have been committed with criminal intent (*State v Decker*, 485 P 2d 171/Kan–1971). Thus, where one, in the commission of a wrongful act commits another wrong not intended by him, the unintended wrong is the natural and probable consequence of the wrongful act and the actor is liable (*People v Hickman*, 291 NE 2d 523/Ill–1973). And if he voluntarily commits an act which may result in the death of another human being, he is presumed to have intended that death result. *People v Williams*, 305 NE 2d 333/Ill (1973).

Although general intent can be presumed from the doing of an unlawful act, this rule has no application where a requisite element of the crime is specific intent such as assault with intent to commit murder. *Bishop v People*, 439 P 2d 342/Colo (1968).

Under the laws of some states the shooting of, or at, another with a firearm raises a presumption of intent to kill or maim (*State v Jordan*, 276 S 2d 277/La–1973), while in other states such act raises no presumption but merely presents a question to be resolved by the jury. *State v Bolden*, 494 SW 2d 61/Mo (1973).

Specific Intent

In crimes of "specific intent" an additional factor in certain crimes is added, and criminal statutes that use the words "willfully" or "intentionally", usually include the element of specific intent. *State v Jamison*, 517 P 2d 1241/Az (1974).

Specific intent is an essential ingredient of the crime of assault with intent to commit murder; that is, the state must prove that the actor actually committed an assault and that, at the time, he harbored an intent to kill his victim, which killing would have been murder if consummated. *Allison v State*, 274 S 2d 678/Mis (1973).

Intent to permanently deprive the owner of his property, a requisite of larceny, was established where evidence showed that defendant sold the property he was accused of stealing. *State v McClanahan*, 262 S 2d 499/La (1972).

Transferred Intent

Transferred intent is exemplified where a person entertains a preexisting design to accomplish a particular aim or goal, but because of some unforeseen and intervening circumstance another and unintended result is accomplished. Thus, where one with deliberate and premeditated malice attempts to kill one person, but my mistake or inadvertance kills another, his guilt is to be determined as though the fatal blow had caused the death of the person against whom it was directed. Here the law transfers his felonious intent from the object of his assault to the person actually killed. *People v Sutic*, 261 P 2d 241/Cal (1953); *State v Griego*, 294 P 2d 282/NM (1956).

It has long been accepted that if *A* unlawfully shoots at *B* intending to kill him, but instead, the bullet strikes *C*, then *A* has committed a criminal act as to *C*. In such instance the "malice follows the blow" and the criminal intent of *A* to harm *B* is transferred to *C*. However, if *A* had no criminal intent with respect to *B*, as where *A* is exercising the lawful right of self-defense, no criminal intent could exist as to *C*. *State v Pinkney*, 290 NE 2d 923/Oh (1972).

The fact that the homicidal act was directed against one other than the deceased does not relieve the slayer of criminal responsibility from assault against his intended victim plus the homicide, as it is the general rule that such a homicide partakes of the quality of the original act and the guilt of the perpetrator is exactly that which it would have been had the assault followed upon the intended victim. *State v Moffitt*, 431 P 2d 879/Kan (1967).

Proof of State of Mind

Defendant's conduct and demeanor a short time before a homicide have been held to be admissible to show state of mind at the time of the homicide (*Hicks v State*, 106 P 2d 136/Ok–1940). Where defendant had been drinking and quarreling with his wife and shortly thereafter he killed a third person, his conduct was admissible to show state of mind (*Jackson v State*, 179 P 2d 924/Ok–1947). In a prosecution of defendant for uxoricide (wife-killing), testimony of his threats to kill his wife ranging from eight months to two months before the homicide were admissible to show defendant's state of mind and malice toward deceased (*State v Russell*, 145 P 2d 1003/Ut–1944). Also, courts have held to be admissible evidence of threats made two years before the homicide, the remoteness going to weight rather than to competency. *People v Cartier*, 353 P 2d 53/Cal (1960).

Criminal Negligence

"Criminal negligence" is defined as a want of attention to the nature and consequences of an act which could be expected of a reasonable and prudent person [RCW 9.01.010 (1)]; it entails a failure to exercise that degree of care which a man of ordinary prudence would have exercised under the same circumstances. *Kimball v Palmer*, 80 F 240/Va (1897).

It is a general rule that contributory negligence is no defense to the commission of crime. *State v Pope*, 313 A 2d 84/Con (1972).

Intent As Affected by Intoxication

Intent in some form, that is, *mens rea*, a requisite of all crimes, is the rule of, and not the exception to, Anglo-American criminal jurisprudence (*Smith v California*, 80 S Ct 215–1959), and voluntary intoxication, as a rule, is no defense. The only exception occurs when a defendant, charged with a crime requiring specific intent, was so drunk that he was not able to formulate *mens rea*. *State v Gouer*, 298 A 2d 378/Md (1973).

Although intoxication can so diminish a person's mental capacity that he is unable to form a specific state of mind requisite of crime, even if it is sufficient to destroy volition, if done voluntarily it cannot excuse a criminal homicide. *People v Conley*, 411 P 2d 911/Cal (1966).

Knowledge

Proof of knowledge cannot usually be proved by direct evidence but must be inferred from other facts and circumstances known to defendant at the time he committed the crime (*State v Casey*, 300 A 2d 325/NH–1973). Fortunately, in proving knowledge, the state does not have to prove that certain facts were actually impressed within the mind of the subject as such proof is rarely available. It must prove, however, that the subject knew, or should have known, certain facts under the existing circumstances.

Evidence of collateral crimes is admissible where relevant as part of the *res gestae;* identity, *scienter*, intent, motive, system or malice, are relevant to rebut special defenses. *Murphy v State*, 294 S 2d 457/Ala (1974); *State v Pickering*, 217 NW 2d 877/ND (1974).

Where facts known to defendants were such that men of their ages, intelligence, and experience would have known that property was stolen, the trier of fact properly found that defendants possessed the requisite guilty knowledge and conviction of receiving stolen property was sustained. *State v Abraham*, 205 NW 2d 342/Neb (1973).

In a prosecution of defendant for possession of LSD with intent to distribute, it was permissible to show that a week prior he had sold marijuana and mescaline and thus was a dealer in drugs. *People v Wilkie*, 522 P 2d 727/Colo (1974).

MOTIVE

Defined

"Motive" is that elusive state of mind that impels to action or incites to reaction as opposed to instinct; motive is said to be reason or moving cause; it is that stimulation which tempts the mind to indulge in a particular act and is distinguishable from intent, which is purpose to use a particular means to effect a desired result. *State v Stevens,* 454 P 2d 945/Id (1969).

Motive is often confused with intent but the two are not synonymous. In a trial of the issue of fact proof of defendant's motive is always admissible, often helpful but never essential. Intent, on the other hand, is an essential element of all crime; it may be general or presumed intent, or it may be specific in which case it must be proved. But defendant may be convicted of a crime–general intent being presumed or specific intent being proved, absent proof of motive, or there appearing to be no logical or recognizable motive. When one does that which the law interdicts, or fails, refuses or neglects to do that which the laws commands, he will not be heard to urge in defense good motives or justifiable ends. *Smith v State,* 283 NE 2d 365/Ind (1972).

The Importance of Motive

Motive is not an essential element of a criminal offense and need not be proved in order to establish the commission of the offense. However, the prosecution may always introduce evidence of motive, if motive is known, as it is relevant as a circumstance tending to prove the commission of the crime. *Rodriquez v State,* 486 SW 2d 355/Tex (1972).

Although never essential to the issue of fact, motive may be important where the evidence, direct or circumstantial, fails to make out a satisfactory case (*State v Tuttle,* 118 P 2d 88/Az–1941), or, as held by the Oregon Supreme Court, "Though the existence of motive is not indispensable to a conviction, such proof is of 'great importance' in cases depending on circumstantial evidence." *State v Sack,* 300 P 2d 427/Or (1956).

Proof of motive is always permissible, in a criminal prosecution (*Lucy v State,* 269 S 2d 134/Ala–1972), and that defendant's motive for the commission of an illegal act is meritorious, does not render such motive a defense to the act. *Smith v State, supra.*

The state may prove prior acts of hostility toward deceased by the accused for the purpose of showing motive and malice. *Padgett v State,* 269 S 2d 147/Ala (1972).

That a peace bond had issued against defendant for threatening to kill deceased was properly admitted at defendant's trial to show motive and ill will of defendant. *Hill v State,* 286 S 2d 924/Ala (1973).

A leaflet which described guns as a basis of political power for the black man and which was found in a house where defendants were arrested for assault on peace officers, bore upon intent and motives of defendants and was properly admitted into evidence. *Bryant v State*, 272 S 2d 286/Ala (1972).

How Established

Motive may be established by the direct testimony of either the accused or other witnesses; it may be gleaned from the facts surrounding the case—from circumstantial evidence—or it may be ignored completely by the prosecuting agency. As a general rule, the fact that one other than the accused had a more compelling motive than the accused is inadmissible hearsay.

In proving motive the state may show that prior to the robbery defendant was penurious and in paying his rent by check the check was returned marked nonsufficient funds, but that shortly after the robbery he paid two months' rent in advance. *Thompson v United States*, 368 F 2d 318/Wn (1966).

Proof that defendant had been living far above his disclosed income is of great probative value in establishing motive for the commission of a crime for pecuniary gain (*United States v Falley*, 489 F 2d 33/NY—1973), and expensive trips, gambling or other instances of free spending and high living may be admissible in a prosecution for crimes with a motive of enrichment, and proof of defendant's prior impecunity is not necessary antecedent thereto. *United States v Kwitek*, 467 F 2d 1222/Wis (1972).

Financial Stress

Where defendant claimed he was motivated to commit robbery and burglary by dire financial circumstances of his family, his claim, even if true, would not justify nor excuse even an attempt to commit the crimes indicated. *Com v Schwartz*, 285 A 2d 154/Pa (1971).

Outstanding indebtedness of defendant who was insured was admissible to show his motive for arson, but motive alone will not support a conviction. *Mickelson v Homeland Ins Co of America*, 132 FS 670/Min (1955).

Motive for Murder

In a murder prosecution motive and prior conduct of defendant is as much a part of the substantive evidence to show premeditation as is the immediate reflective deliberation preceding the act itself (*State v Ross*, 353 P 2d 885/Wn—1960). The hostile relationship between the deceased mother and her accused son during the last several weeks prior to the homicide was admissible to show whether premeditation was present in the matricide. (*State v Davis*, 108 P 2d 641/Wn—1940). And in a marital homicide previous acts of ill treatment, assaults, jealousy, personal acts of violence, or threats of such conduct by a husband against his wife are admissible to show motive or malice. *Romero v People*, 460 P 2d 784/Colo (1969).

In a prosecution of defendant for murder by strychnine poisoning, a previous conviction of manslaughter was admissible where the strychnine victim had testified against defendant at defendant's manslaughter trial. *State v Pickering*, 217 NW 2d 877/SD (1974).

Where a note was found in the home of victim prior to the homicide which read "for a 25 bit whore," and a handwriting expert testified that it had been written by the defendant, it was relevant in defendant's prosecution to establish motive for murder. *State v Huson*, 440 P 2d 192/Wn (1968).

No Known Motive

The fact that no motive was shown, or even suggested, for the fire-bombing of a place of residence by defendant, did not preclude a conviction of first degree arson. (*Washington v State*, 276 S 2d 587/Ala–1973). And where the state's theory was that defendant killed the deceased without motive, it would not be allowed to prove collateral offenses committed by the defendant also without motive, as this would prove no issue in the instant case, but rather, that the accused was bad and committed crimes without motive. *Rodriquez v State*, 486 SW 2d 355/Tex (1972).

GUILT–HOW PROVED

Burden of Proof

In all prosecutions, without regard to the nature of a defense which the defendant may raise, the burden remains at all times with the state to establish the guilt of the defendant beyond a reasonable doubt. (*State v White*, 203 NW 2d 852/Min–1973). The burden of proof is always with the state and never shifts to the defendant. *State v General Motors Corp*, 296 NE 2d 317/Oh (1973).

Defendant is neither required nor allowed to prove his innocence, and any evidence of innocence is not usually admissible as innocence is presumed. Thus, evidence of the results of a lie detector test exculpating the defendant was properly excluded. *United States v Skeens*, 494 F 2d 1050/DC (1974).

Proof of Special Defenses

The burden of proving any special defense is upon the accused, and where he alleges that he was arrested or searched on an invalid warrant, he assumes the onus of proving in what respect the warrant was invalid (*Viadock v State*, 236 P 56/Ok–1925). That defendant must prove any special defense in his behalf does not mean that at this stage of the proceeding the burden of proof shifts to the defendant; the burden of proof is with the state always; only the burden of proceeding shifts to the defendant. *Crouse v State*, 263 P 681/Ok (1928).

Any affirmative defense claimed by defendant need not be proved beyond a reasonable doubt, but merely generate in the minds of the jury a reasonable doubt of his guilt (*Stowe v State*, 268 S 2d 45/Ala–1972). Although it may appear, in the case of an affirmative defense, that the burden of proof has shifted to the defendant, only the initiative or the burden of producing evidence has shifted (*State v Dragon*, 292 A 2d 826/Vt–1972). Also, the party who makes a motion in a judicial proceeding bears the burden of producing evidence in support thereof (*People v Manning*, 109 CR 531/Cal–1973), but the burden of a movant is not to be confused with the burden of proof. *Martin v State*, 300 NE 2d 128/Ind (1973).

Minimum Proof Requisite to Conviction

In a criminal prosecution the state must always prove two points: that the crime was actually committed and that it was committed by the defendant and none other, and both points must be proved beyond a reasonable doubt. *People v Jones*, 31 Cal 566 (1867).

The quantum of proof required in a delinquency hearing is the same as that required for conviction in a criminal proceeding. *People v Bynum*, 299 NE 2d 150/Ill (1973).

The degree of proof necessary in a parole or probation revocation hearing is less than that necessary to a conviction in the first instance. Proof beyond a reasonable doubt is not required, only that the hearing judge be "reasonably satisfied" that the terms of the release have been violated. *State v Wilhite*, 492 SW 2d 397/Mo (1973).

A plea of guilty voluntarily and knowingly entered is the equivalent of a confession to the charge and thus precludes the necessity of proof. *People v Ferguson*, 305 NE 2d 366/Ill (1973).

The Lie Detector

Lie detector testing has not yet attained scientific acceptance as a reliable and accurate means of ascertaining truth or deception, and in a criminal trial the state may not offer evidence to prove that defendant refused to take such test nor may defendant prove that he offered to submit to such test (*State v McDavitt*, 297 A 2d 849/NJ–1972); but the court observed deviations by the California and Iowa courts holding that defendant is bound by a stipulation of admissibility. The Arizona court has recently broadened the grounds of admissibility by holding that the art of lie detector testing has developed to a point that its results were probative enough to warrant admissibility upon stipulation. Id.

A United States district judge has ruled under Michigan law that "A [polygraph] test cannot be made without the full cooperation of the defendant. It seems clear, then, that if adequate warnings are given as to the possible use of the tests . . . the taking of the test itself is a waiver of the privilege [against self-incrimination]. It can be logically argued that privilege is not involved in the employment of the lie detector as a defendant may be required to put on a blouse for identification, give blood to determine alcoholic content, pose in a line-up, execute a handwriting exemplar, submit to fingerprinting, but with the polygraph there can be no compulsion." *United States v Ridling,* 350 FS 90/Mich (1972).

The results of polygraph tests are usually not admissible in any federal court and are admissible only in a few state courts, and then only after careful inquiry. The Supreme Court of Massachusetts has ruled that if defendant agrees in advance to submit to the polygraph test and that regardless of the outcome the results may be admitted into evidence, the trial judge, after searching inquiry into the qualifications of the examiner, the fitness of the defendant for such examination, and the methods utilized in conducting the test, may, in his discretion, allow the results admitted—not as binding or as conclusive, but to be considered along with other evidence. And since the results of a polygraph test are essentially testimonial in nature, it must be established that prior to the test defendant was advised of his constitutional rights. *Com v Juvenile (No 1),* 313 NE 2d 120/Mas (1974).

Prerequisite to widespread admissibility of the results of a polygraph test is its acceptance by the scientific community as a valid and reliable test of that which it purports to prove. *State v Melvin,* 319 A 2d 450/NJ (1974).

Relevancy

The general rule is that all relevant evidence is admissible to prove the fact at issue, to which there are some exceptions such as that which is hearsay, inflammatory or voluminous, but no evidence is admissible unless it is relevant. *State v Moore,* 278 S 2d 781/La (1972).

If relevant, the task of weighing possible unfair prejudice against probative value rests within the sound discretion of the trial judge (*United States v Fisher,* 455 F 2d 1101/NY–1972), and if the proffered evidence serves no purpose other than to inflame the minds of the jurors, its admission into evidence is reversible error. *United States v Bamberger,* 456 F 2d 1119/NJ (1972).

Hearsay

Hearsay is an out-of-court utterance offered into evidence to prove the truth of the matter asserted and is usually inadmissible. Rejection of hearsay is based on the grounds that there is no guarantee of its trustworthiness; the original speaker was not under oath, and the accused is denied the right to cross-examination. *Emmco Ins Co v Wallenius Caribbean Line,* 492 F 2d 508/Fla (1974).

A witness on the witness stand, except on rare occasion, may not testify as to what some third person saw, heard or said (*Beecher v State*, 256 S 2d 154/Alk–1971), but dying declarations are one of the few exceptions to the hearsay rule. *State v Ellis*, 297 A 2d 91/Me (1972).

Unless hearsay evidence is objected to at the time it is offered, it remains in evidence and is entitled to consideration by the trier of fact; an objection, if made for the first time on appeal, comes too late (*People v Riles*, 295 NE 2d 234/Ill–1973). Hearsay is evidence that is perceived by one party but offered into evidence by another party as fact (*Ruden v Hansen*, 206 NW 2d 713/Ia–1973); thus, *A* perceives things through his senses; he tells *B* what he has perceived; *B* offers what *A* has told him into evidence by way of testimony, and for the purpose of establishing its verity.

The *res gestae* exception to the hearsay rule allows into evidence statements uttered under stress of excitement produced by a startling event and made before the declarant has had time or the opportunity to reflect or contrive. *United States v Lehmen*, 468 F 2d 93/Ill (1972).

Evidence obtained from one in a hypnotic trance, whether obtained from one testifying as a witness or whether from another's revelation of that which the subject said, is inadmissible in a criminal prosecution. *Greenfield v Com*, 204 SE 2d 414/Va (1974).

The results of a lie detector test are not admissible on behalf of defendant to establish his innocence, as such evidence is self-serving and hearsay (*People v Gargano*, 295 NE 2d 342/Ill–1973). Nor are the results of a truth serum test admissible. *Cherry v State*, 518 P 2d 324/Ok (1974).

Res Gestae

Acts done, declarations made and objects used before, during and after the occurrence of the principal fact, which are so closely connected therewith as to be a part thereof, are admissible under the *res gestae* rule. *State v Platz*, 519 P 2d 1097/Kan (1974).

The purpose of the introduction of testimony under the *res gestae* rule permitting introduction of acts, declarations, and demeanor of defendant before or after the offense, is to shed some light on the issues and to help the jury determine cause, motivation, or other circumstances which may have played a part in bringing on the transaction or in explaining it retrospectively. *Claridy v State*, 270 S 2d 685/Ala (1972).

The *res gestae* exception to the hearsay rule includes four distinct types of conditions: excited utterances, declarations of present sense impressions, declarations as to state of mind, and declarations as to body conditions. *State v Newman*, 513 P 2d 258/Mont (1973).

NONTESTIMONIAL PROOF

Prior Crimes

Evidence of other crimes are admissible against defendant if they tend to prove the fact at issue, and it is immaterial whether the prior crime was committed prior to or subsequent to the crime for which defendant is at bar. *State v Capitan*, 494 P 2d 443/Or (1972).

Other crimes are admissible when relevant to (1) prove identity, (2) show a common scheme or design, (3) show knowledge, (4) prove intent, motive or pattern, (5) show absence of mistake, (6) show a system of general pattern of criminality, (7) disprove alibi, (8) disprove entrapment, or (9) as a part of the *res gestae* (*Marion v State*, 287 S 2d 419/Fla–1974). They are also admissible to impeach a witness, or to place defendant in the proximity of the scene at the time of the crime. *People v Manzella*, 306 NE 2d 16/Ill (1973).

If evidence of other crimes committed by defendant does not tend to prove the fact at issue, it is irrelevant and its admission constitutes reversible error (*Marion v State*, 287 S 2d 419/Fla–1974), but evidence of other crimes is admissible if relevant and if it shows other than mere propensity or predisposition of defendant to commit crime. *United States v Williams*, 367 FS 768/Pa (1973).

Prior Acts and Conditions

The state, in a homicide prosecution, may show prior acts of hostility by the accused toward victim for the purpose of showing motive and malice. *Padgett v State*, 269 S 2d 147/Ala (1972).

As a rule, remoteness of prior acts does not affect admissibility of the act, but goes rather, to its weight. Thus in a prosecution of defendant for uxoricide, testimony of deceased wife's friend that about four years prior to the homicide she had observed bruises on the body of defendant's wife and that defendant had admitted mistreating his wife, was admissible to show defendant's state of mind concerning his wife. *Smith v State*, 502 SW 2d 814/Tex (1973).

Testimony relating to sexual advances made by defendant toward deceased cell mate a day or two prior to the killing was admissible against defendant in a murder prosecution. *Anderson v State*, 479 SW 2d 57/Tex (1972).

Testimony by the father and mother of the deceased that they had overheard conversations in which defendant had threatened to kill deceased was properly admitted into evidence to show motive and malice. *Hill v State*, 286 S 2d 924/Ala (1973).

Evidence of defendant's financial obligations and pending lawsuits against him was relevant in a prosecution of defendant for felonious burning and the presentation of a false insurance claim. *State v Harrell*, 201 SE 2d 716/NC (1974).

Body Substances

Body substances, such as breath, blood or urine, may be taken from one *who is under arrest* for driving while intoxicated, to be analyzed for alcoholic content and to be used against the driver in a criminal prosecution.

A urinalysis may be classified as a test for real or physical evidence not dissimilar to the breathalyzer or blood test, and such test may be utilized over the objection by the defendant that their use is a violation of his privilege against self-incrimination. *Ewing v State*, 310 NE 2d 571/Ind (1974).

Where defendant, under arrest for driving while intoxicated, refuses to submit to a chemical test for blood alcohol content, such refusal in some jurisdictions is inadmissible against him in a prosecution for that offense (*State v Schlinger*, 216 NW 2d 835/Min–1974); (*People v Boyd*, 309 NE 2d 29/Ill–1974); but see *State v Jensen*, 216 NW 2d 369/Ia (1974), where the Iowa court ruled to the contrary, holding that refusal to submit to a test where proper procedure is followed is admissible against defendant.

The taking of a sample of defendant's blood, even if by force, does not violate defendant's right under the Fifth Amendment against self-incrimination. *Brattain v Herron*, 309 NE 2d 150/Ind (1974).

Consciousness of Guilt

Admissible against defendant as tending to show a consciousness of guilt are: an act designed to prevent arrest (*People v Wong*, 111 CR 314/Cal–1973); attempt by arrestee to evade arrest and acts of concealment; (*Sotka v State*, 503 SW 2d 212/Ten–1972); attempt by defendant to suborn a witness into testifying falsely (*State v Reuschel*, 312 A 2d 739/Vt–1973); escape, attempt to escape or flight (*Johnson v State*, 312 A 2d 630/Del–1973); false statements in an attempt to exculpate himself (*Andrews v Knowlton*, 367 FS 1263/NY–1973); attempt to suppress, destroy or conceal evidence. *Sotka v State, supra.*

Flight from the scene of the crime is relevant as tending to show a consciousness of guilt (*State v Lane*, 292 S 2d 711/La–1974), but absence of flight, on the other hand, is not admissible as evidence of innocence, for innocence is presumed and defendant is neither required nor allowed to prove innocence. *Adams v State*, 203 SE 2d 318/Ga (1974).

"Flight" is considered to exist, as opposed to mere departure, when the accused departs from the vicinity of the crime under circumstances which indicate a sense of fear or guilt or an attempt to avoid arrest, even before the accused has been suspected of crime. *Williams v State*, 268 S 2d 566/Fla (1972).

Where, after being accused of theft, defendant paid the owner for his property still maintaining his innocence, payment raised a substantial inference of his guilt. *Shelton v Com*, 484 SW 2d 95/Ky (1971).

Acts showing a consciousness of guilt are admissible against defendant as evidence of guilt, but he may explain them should he choose to testify. *Machado v State*, 494 SW 2d 859/Tex (1973).

Examples

Prior crimes which have been held to be admissible in a subsequent prosecution are: prior conviction of defendant for beating deceased with a hammer where he was on trial for the murder of deceased with a hammer (*State v Fulcher*, 201 SE 2d 233/NC–1973); a prior conviction of robbery in a prosecution for murder and aggravated battery (*People v Ligon*, 305 NE 2d 212/Ill–1973); evidence of prior robberies in a subsequent prosecution of robbery (*Cobb v State*, 503 SW 2d 249/Tex–1973); prior threats of death and destruction issued by telephone where defendant was under a similar charge at bar (*United States v Cox*, 487 F 2d 634/Tex–1973); prior conviction for the same or a similar offense in a prosecution for the sale of dangerous drugs (*People v Foster*, 111 CR 666/Cal–1974); previous conviction for theft and sale of a stolen motor vehicle in a prosecution for felony theft. *Barnes v State*, 503 SW 2d 267/Tex (1974).

In a prosecution for assaulting an officer with a firearm, evidence that showed defendant had shortly before been operating a motor vehicle while intoxicated was admissible to prove that the officer was acting in line of duty and that defendant was in lawful custody at the time of the assault. *State v Powell*, 198 SE 2d 70/NC (1973).

A mother's testimony to the father's physical punishment of a child on days previous to the day the child died was relevant in a prosecution of the father for manslaughter. *Walter v State*, 272 S 2d 180/Fla (1973).

Where defendant was arrested when he attempted to make a purchase with a stolen traveler's check, other stolen checks found in his room in a subsequent search were admissible against him for the limited purpose of showing intent. *United States v Restrepo*, 417 F 2d 927/Fla (1969).

Permitting a witness to testify that she had cashed about 40 government checks for defendant did not constitute error in a prosecution for uttering forged treasury checks even though defendant was charged in the indictment with only four counts of forgery. *United States v Harden*, 469 F 2d 65/Fla (1972).

Miscellaneous Exemplars

A voice exemplar is nontestimonial and admissible against defendant and does not fall within the ambit of the Fifth Amendment against self-incrimination. *United States v Herrmann*, 371 FS 343/Wis (1974).

Fingerprints are not within the area of constitutional protection against self-incrimination and specimens taken at the time of defendant's arrest are admissible against him. *Campbell v State*, 493 P 2d 1126/Ok (1972).

Handwriting exemplars are not protected by the Fifth Amendment privilege against compulsory self-incrimination. *People v Redock,* 300 NE 2d 31/Ill (1973).

TESTIMONIAL PROOF

Admissions

The *corpus delicti* must be established independently of any extra-judicial admission or confession (*State v Goranson,* 408 P 2d 7–1965), and no element thereof may be established by a presumption (*People v Miller,* 2 Cal 2d 527–1934).

A *prima facie* showing of the *corpus delicti* is all that is required before a defendant's extrajudicial statements, admissions or confession, may be received into evidence. *People v Cantrell,* 504 P 2d 1256/Cal (1973).

"Prima facie" means at first sight, at first appearance, on the face of it. It refers to a fact presumed to be established until rebutted. *Black's Law Dictionary.*

Where, upon looking into a satchel in the back seat of defendants' automobile which both defendants had disclaimed and seeing what he thought to be "thousands of bags of heroin," the officer exclaimed, "Holy cow," whereupon one of defendants remarked, "You don't have shit, this is an illegal search and seizure," such statement was admissible to prove knowledge of the nature of the substance. *People v Cameron,* 342 NYS 2d 773/NY (1973).

Admissions or declarations against interest are admissible against defendant as an exception to the hearsay rule on the theory that it can be reasoned that one would not make a false statement knowing it was against his penal interests. *Shamrock Hilton Hotel v Caranas,* 488 SW 2d 151/Tex (1972).

Confessions

As a rule, a confession or an admission is not admissible until the *corpus delicti* of the crime has been established by independent evidence (*State v Pineda,* 519 P 2d 41/Az–1974), but the court in its sound discretion may permit the reverse order though still contingent upon establishing the *corpus delicti* independently. *Ballard v State,* 309 NE 2d 817/Ind (1974).

It has long been the rule in the federal courts that a confession obtained by force or coercion violates due process. A confession, to be admissible, must be obtained under circumstances which assure the court that it was made by the defendant through the exercise of freedom of choice and volition. Confessions of bygone days which were held to have been "freely and voluntarily given," would not necessarily withstand the rigorous tests of today.

In 1964 in *Escobedo v Illinois,* 378 US 478 (1964), the United States Supreme Court imposed one of its most significant restrictions on the state courts by reversing conviction based on defendant's confession obtained while defendant's retained attorney waited for an audience with his client. *Escobedo* was further enlarged in *Miranda v Arizona,* 386 US 436 (1966) and is considered by many authorities to have superseded *Escobedo.* In *Miranda* the court held that when defendant was deprived of his liberty in any significant way, prior to any questioning he must be advised of his right to counsel—retained or appointed—to silence and to the use against him of any information he may give.

A confession may not be admitted into evidence until the state shows to the satisfaction of the court that the confession was made freely and voluntarily (*Sheppard v State,* 275 S 2d 353/Ala–1973), and after advisement of defendant's constitutional rights to silence and to an attorney (*State v Easthope,* 510 P 2d 933/Ut–1973). If any inducement of profit or benefit is extended, or if hope is engendered or encouraged in the mind of the defendant that his sentence will be lightened or ameliorated if he confesses, his confession will be thereby contaminated. *Wallace v State,* 275 S 2d 634/Ala (1973).

Whenever the accused offers testimony that his confession was induced by violence, threats, coercion or offers of reward, the burden is on the state to refute such claims and establish the voluntariness of the confession (*Smith v State,* 494 SW 2d 489/Ark–1973), but statements made by one who voluntarily goes to a police station and informs police of his part in a crime are admissible even though the speaker is not advised of his rights under *Miranda. State v Carlson,* 192 NW 2d 820/Min (1971).

Any extrajudicial confession is presumed to be involuntary and is *prima facie* inadmissible, thus placing the onus of proof of voluntariness of the confession on the prosecution. *Wallace v State, supra.*

The rule that defendant's confession alone will not support a conviction unless the *corpus delicti* is first established independently, refers to an extrajudicial confession (*People v Applegate,* 509 P 2d 1238/Colo–1973); a judicial, or in-court confession, uncorroborated, will sustain conviction. *Heredia v State,* 493 SW 2d 238/Tex (1973).

Spontaneous Declarations

Just as dying declarations are deemed trustworthy because of the truth-compelling force of the circumstances in which the declarant knows himself to be, so spontaneous statements are deemed trustworthy because the impact of shock or terror it precipitates destroys will and capacity to fabricate. *State v Ellis,* 297 A 2d 91/Me (1972).

As a rule the response of victim in answer to a question is not admissible under the *res gestae* rule, but where the victim of a shooting lay in his driveway mortally wounded, and his response to a neighbor's question of "Who done it?"

was "Eunice done it," his statement was held to be admissible (*Williams v State*, 279 S 2d 478/Ala–1973). Also see similar case in *State v Carraturo*, 308 A 2d 828/RI (1973), and *People v Alexander*, 298 NE 2d 355/Ill (1973), where victim's response to questions a few minutes after being raped was likewise held to be admissible as spontaneous declarations.

Victim's statement "Jimmie, that whore shot me and I am hurt," to a bystander was admissible in a murder prosecution under the *res gestae* rule of spontaneous declarations. *People v Burchette*, 281 NE 2d 773/Ill (1972).

A dying declaration is admissible in a homicide prosecution if (1) the declarant's statement relates to the cause of his dying condition; (2) he is aware that death is imminent (*State v Brown*, 202 NW 2d 591/Neb–1972) and, of course, (3) declarant dies. The declaration is admissible only after it is shown that it was made *in extremis*, that is, under a sense of impending death—all hope of recovery having fled—and that the declaration related to his fatal injury. That decedent lived 15 days after making the declaration did not affect its admissibility. *Whitson v State*, 495 SW 2d 944/Tex (1973).

If there is a glimmer of hope of recovery in the mind of declarant, his statement is not admissible as a dying declaration. *Kidd v State*, 258 S 2d 423/Mis (1972).

Corroboration

"Proof" sometimes includes testimony plus "corroboration." Where the only direct evidence of the guilt of defendant is the testimony of an accomplice, as a rule, the accomplice's testimony must be corroborated. Corroboration of an accomplice means evidence independent of the testimony of the accomplice, tending to prove facts connecting defendant with the commission of the offense charged (*Words and Phrases*, 9A at 554); or in a prosecution for a sex offense committed in jurisdictions which require corroboration of the prosecutrix, corroboration means evidence which does not emanate from the mouth of the prosecutrix, but such other independent evidence which adds to, strengthens, confirms or reinforces her testimony. *Words and Phrases*, 9A at 562.

The granting of immunity to a witness accomplice does not enshroud him with an aura of innocence nor shield him from prosecution for crimes inquired into. It does, however, prohibit the use of his testimony against him and this necessarily includes other evidence gained indirectly as a result of his testimony. *United States v First Western State Bank*, 491 F 2d 780/ND (1974).

Corroboration of the testimony of an admitted heroin addict who was not the accomplice of defendant was not necessary to a conviction where he testified that by the effect of a substance sold to him by defendant he knew it to be heroin. *Howard v State*, 496 P 2d 657/Alk (1972).

CONVICTION

In General

"Conviction" refers to (1) a plea of guilty, (2) a verdict of guilty by a jury, or (3) a verdict of guilty by a judge sitting without a jury. *Reed v State*, 295 A 2d 657/Me (1972).

As a rule, all matters of law are resolved by the court and all matters of fact, when a jury is sitting are resolved by the jury. An exception to this rule may exist by statutory provision. For instance, under California law a single exception exists: There, in a prosecution for libel, the jury may decide both law and fact. *California Penal Code*, § 251.

In a criminal prosecution defendant does not have the burden of proving his innocence beyond a reasonable doubt, as innocence is presumed. Rather, the government has the burden of proving defendant's guilt beyond a reasonable doubt. *United States v Dillet*, 265 FS 980/NY (1966).

In most states in a trial by jury a unanimous verdict is essential to conviction. *Brown v State*, 508 SW 2d 91/Tex (1974).

Upon return of a verdict of guilty the defendant has the right to poll the jury to determine if the verdict was that of each individual juror (*Shouse v State*, 203 SE 2d 537/Ga–1974), but the right to poll a jury expires upon discharge of the jury and cannot thereafter be exercised. *Clements v State*, 291 S 2d 748/Ala (1974).

Lesser Conviction

A finding of guilty on a lesser included offense is in effect an acquittal of the greater offense, and upon a successful appeal from conviction of the lesser offense—a new trial being granted—defendant cannot be convicted of any crime more serious than that for which he was first convicted. *People v Doolittle*, 99 CR 810/Cal (1972).

A plea of guilty to voluntary manslaughter by one accused of murder, was in effect an acquittal of the murder charge and a further prosecution for murder was barred even though the manslaughter conviction was set aside and the case was remanded for retrial (*People v Dugan*, 305 NE 2d 308/Ill–1973). Also, where defendant was convicted of second degree murder at the first trial, such was the permissible limit on retrial, and proof of felony-murder would be impermissible at retrial as felony-murder can only be first degree murder. *People v Clayton*, 350 NYS 2d 495/NY (1973); *Robinson v Neil*, 366 FS 924/Ten (1973).

Defendant cannot be convicted of murder under the felony-murder rule, i.e., a killing in the commission of robbery, and also of the robbery where the armed robbery was an integral part of the felony-murder (*State v Hubbard*, 303

A 2d 87/NJ–1973). Robbery wherein a human being is killed, becomes a lesser included offense of the felony-murder and merges with the greater crime of murder. Id.

Multiple Convictions—Single Impulse

Where defendant pled guilty to a charge of aggravated battery, a subsequent charge of murder could be properly brought against him when his victim died. *State v Hayden*, 267 S 2d 551/La (1972).

Where serious injury was inflicted upon the victim of robbery, defendant could be convicted of both the robbery with a dangerous weapon and gross assault with a deadly weapon with intent to kill. *State v Kinsey*, 193 SE 2d 430/NC (1972).

Where force and violence inflicted upon a rape victim occurred after the rape and was separate and distinct from the force and violence employed in accomplishing the rape, an additional conviction of aggravated battery was justified. *People v Johnson*, 289 NE 2d 722/Ill (1972).

Juvenile Proceedings

The juvenile court, at its discretion, may exercise or waive jurisdiction over a juvenile who has committed crime (*State v Jump*, 309 NE 2d 148/Ind–1974). If it waives jurisdiction it usually must state the grounds therefor, but it need not state grounds for refusing to waive jurisdiction. Id.

The juvenile court is civil, not criminal, and, although based on criminal acts, an adjudication of delinquency therein is not a "conviction" of crime (*KMS v State*, 200 SE 2d 916/Ga–1973); unless specifically provided by statute, the juvenile court cannot find a juvenile guilty of crime. Id.

Acquittal

A verdict of acquittal does not establish a status of innocence; there may be a murder committed in fact and still the state may not be able to establish murder by legal evidence for the purpose of imposing penalty. *People v Jones*, 518 P 2d 819/Colo (1974).

The fact that a jury acquitted defendant of ten of the eleven counts of mail fraud, convicting him of the eleventh only, was not irrational, as the jury may have been exercising its historic power of leniety. *United States v Reicin*, 497 F 2d 563/Ill (1974).

Conviction or acquittal of a lower degree of any offense included in the crime charged is a bar to a subsequent prosecution for the higher crime. *State v Sullivan*, 215 NW 491/Ia (1974).

LESSER INCLUDED OFFENSES

In General

Lesser offenses are those necessarily included in greater offenses. When in the commission of an offense another lesser offense is always committed, the lesser offense is a necessarily included offense. *Geitner v State*, 207 NW 2d 837/Wis (1973).

A single act may be an offense in violation of two statutes, and if each statute requires proof not required in the *corpus delicti* of the other, acquittal or conviction under one does not exempt defendant from prosecution and conviction under the other. *United States v Tonarelli*, 371 FS 891/PR (1973).

The test as to whether a defendant may be convicted of two or more crimes is dependent upon whether a second or subsequent crime requires proof of additional facts. *People v Compain*, 196 NW 2d 353/Mich (1972).

If one crime is a lesser included offense of the greater, defendant cannot be convicted of both; if the same act constitutes two offenses, neither being a lesser included offense of the other, they constitute multiple offenses and defendant may be convicted of either or both. *Geitner v State*, 207 NW 2d 837/Wis (1973).

When Not Tenable

Defendant may be convicted of any lesser included offense if supported by evidence. If the trial be by jury, the court must instruct the jury on the lesser offense. However, the jury is not, in all cases, entitled to an instruction on a lesser offense for evidence may warrant the instruction that the defendant is either guilty of the crime charged or not guilty. *Green v United States*, 218 F 2d 856/DC (1955).

In a prosecution for assault with a deadly weapon the jury was not entitled to an instruction that battery was a necessarily included offense, and to so instruct would be error (*People v Mueller*, 305 P 2d 178/Cal–1957). Where defendant was charged with grand theft in the stealing of sheep, petty theft was not a necessarily included offense and defendant was either guilty of grand theft or not guilty (*People v Piazza*, 252 P 2d 947/Cal–1953). As a rule, the theft of sheep and most other domestic livestock is grand theft regardless of the value of the animal.

Where evidence at the trial of defendant showed that the killing was committed during the course of an armed robbery, defendant was not entitled to an instruction on manslaughter as the defendant was guilty of first degree murder or not guilty. *Conroy v State*, 202 SE 2d 398/Ga (1973).

Effect of Lesser Conviction

When the trier of facts finds defendant guilty of a lesser degree of the offense charged, or of a lesser included offense, there is an implied acquittal of the greater offense (*People v Serrato*, 512 P 2d 289/Cal–1973), and where defendant was tried for murder and found guilty of voluntary manslaughter, there was an implied acquittal of the murder charge. *People v Thompson*, 297 NE 2d 592/Ill (1973).

Where defendant is charged and tried for aggravated battery and convicted of a lesser offense of battery, the lesser conviction is in effect an acquittal of the offense charged and to again try defendant on the original charge would amount to double jeopardy. *State v Gunzelman*, 502 P 2d 705/Kan (1972).

In a prosecution for rape, the finding of defendant guilty of assault with intent to commit rape was not defective on the ground that rape was actually committed. *State v Banks*, 213 NW 2d 483/Ia (1973).

Included Offenses

Where two crimes arise out of identical conduct, the more serious crime includes the lesser (*People v Steen*, 292 NE 2d 513/Ill–1972), and where defendant was charged with fondling a boy's penis and committing fellatio thereon, a proper charge was indecent liberties with a greater punishment which included the lesser offense of gross indecency. *People v Verberg*, 205 NW 2d 315/Mich (1973).

Assault is a necessarily included offense of battery but battery is not a lesser included offense of felonious assault. *People v Parker*, 213 NW 2d 576/Mich (1973).

Indecent liberties is a lesser included offense of rape, but where both counts are based on the same act, defendant could not be convicted of both offenses. *People v Lilly*, 309 NE 2d 1/Ill (1974).

Under an indictment charging murder where defendant was convicted of manslaughter and a new trial was ordered, defendant could be neither tried for nor convicted of murder. *People v Gilmore*, 4 Cal 376 (1894).

PUNISHMENT

Purpose of Punishment

The primary function of criminal law and criminal jurisprudence is to protect individuals and society in general from the depredations of the criminally disposed (*State v Etchison*, 195 NW 2d 498/Neb–1972). The *deterrent effect* on others is a relevant consideration in imposing sentence (*State v Patzer*, 493 P 2d 1389/Or–1972), and punishment *is* a deterrent to the criminally inclined; it is a truism that the greater the risk of being caught and punished the greater the deterrent.

The primary purpose of a system of criminal law is to inhibit antisocial conduct by the imposition of appropriate punishment, and to achieve that purpose attention must be focused on the intent and conduct of the perpetrator rather than the result of his act. *Thessen v State*, 508 P 2d 1192/Alk (1973).

Who Are Punishable

Except when exempted by statute, all persons are liable to punishment by the individual states who:

1. Commit any crime in whole or in part within the boundaries of a state;
2. Being outside the state advise, encourage or counsel the commission of crime within the state;
3. Commit any crime without the state which would be larceny if committed within the state and afterward bring any of the stolen property into the state;
4. Kidnap or abduct any person without the state and afterward take the victim into the state.

Provision of Punishment

It is the prerogative of the legislature (or the Congress), and not the judiciary, to determine and assess penalties for violations of laws; what constitutes adequate penalty is a matter of legislative judgment and discretion, and the courts will not usually interfere unless the penalty prescribed is determined to be clearly and manifestly cruel and unusual. *State v Smith*, 446 P 2d 571/Wn (1968); *Furman v Georgia*, 92 S Ct 2726 (1972).

Trends in Penology

The post-war trend in the philosophy of punishment is a deemphasis on punishment and an accent on rehabilitation. Even a cold-blooded killer is "rehabilitated" with a view toward his ultimate release to again enjoy freedom and the pursuit of happiness; yet his victim, blameless morally and legally, is forever dead.

Retribution is not the dominant objective of criminal law; reformation and rehabilitation of offenders are also important goals of criminal jurisprudence. *In re Lamb*, 296 NE 2d 280/Oh (1973).

Punishment, as a deterrent to crime, includes:

1. Death
2. Imprisonment
3. Fine
4. Removal from and disqualification to thereafter hold public office

5. Asexualization
6. Performance of certain tasks as directed by the court in lieu of fine or incarceration.

Pertinent Issues in Sentencing

In imposing sentence the trial courts may and should take into consideration the defendant's criminal history, if any (*Crow v State*, 492 SW 2d 40/Mo–1973), and it was not error for the court to take into consideration at the time of sentencing, defendant's prior arrest and his juvenile record. *State v Camel*, 510 P 2d 576/Or (1973).

Where a judge erroneously sentences defendant to a sentence lesser than prescribed by law, it is proper to correct the sentence by a *nunc pro tunc* (now for then) order, that is, an order with retroactive effect. *People v Coffman*, 206 NW 2d 795/Mich (1973).

A statute which prohibits suspension of sentence upon conviction of distributing marijuana is not unconstitutional on the grounds that the power to suspend sentence is exclusively that of the trial court. *Delaney v State*, 507 P 2d 564/Ok (1973).

Defendant may not be punished because he has, in good faith, exercised his right to plead not guilty and stand trial and his efforts prove unsuccessful; it is improper to impose a more severe sentence because he has done so (*United States v Floyd*, 477 F 2d 217/Ok–1973). However, it is permissible in a trial *de novo* in the superior court, after an appeal from conviction in a justice or municipal court, to impose a greater sentence than was imposed in the lower court. *State v Toler*, 196 SE 2d 295/NC (1973).

Under the state laws providing for indeterminate sentencing, defendant, after sentence by the court and before actual sentence is fixed by the state parole board within the indeterminate limits, is deemed to be serving the maximum prescribed for the crime of which he was convicted, and he has no vested right to a determination of a less than maximum sentence, nor to parole. *Dorado v Kerr*, 454 F 2d 892/Cal (1972).

The question of whether multiple sentences shall run concurrently or consecutively is a matter within the discretion of the trial court. *Delacey v Com*, 494 SW 735/Ky (1973).

Cruel and Unusual Punishment

A statute declaring a crime to be punishable by death or life imprisonment, leaving discretion to either a judge or jury to set the penalty, is cruel and unusual in violation of the U.S. Constitution and cannot be carried out. *State v Watkins*, 194 SE 2d 800/NC (1973); *Furman v Georgia*, 408 US (1972).

A showing of prejudice at the time of sentence requires that sentence be adjusted to conform to law (*State v Moreno*, 508 P 2d 730/Az–1973), and where the judge sentenced defendant to the state penitentiary "at hard labor," hard labor was mere surplusage and had no effect on the sentence. *Rodgers v State*, 510 P 2d 992/Ok (1973).

A law which punishes a status or condition is violative of the U.S. Constitution which denounces cruel and unusual punishment. For example, narcotic addiction, as proscribed under California law was a "status" or "condition," and could not stand. *Robinson v California*, 370 US 660 (1962).

What Is Not Cruel and Unusual

Where defendant was convicted of kidnaping after a previous conviction of rape, his sentence of 300 years, reviewed on appeal, was held not to be excessive. *Futerll v State*, 501 P 2d 901/Ok (1972).

Where a convicted felon is placed on probation and as a condition of probation he is required to obey all laws, such condition does not, under the Constitution, inflict cruel and unusual punishment. *Jennings v State*, 511 P 2d 1048/Nev (1973).

Where defendants were 14 and 15 years of age when they were indicted for murder and deviate sexual assault, their sentences of 75 to 90 years for murder and 13 to 14 years for deviate sexual assault was not excessive in view of the viciousness and brutality of their crimes and their past records of crime. *People v Sprinkle*, 307 NE 2d 161/Ill (1974).

The prosecution, conviction and punishment of a narcotic addict for the possession of drugs and narcotic paraphernalia does not constitute cruel and unusual punishment. *Skinner v State*, 293 A 2d 828/Md (1972).

The fact that defendant's accomplices received lighter sentences than defendant whose claimed participation was lesser did not establish that defendant was unduly punished. *Williams v State*, 255 S 2d 58/Ala (1972).

The Death Penalty

The Supreme Court has existed since 1789, yet did not deem the death penalty to be cruel and unusual until 1972, when in June, in *Furman v Georgia*, 92 S Ct 2726, it abolished the death penalty by a 5-4 decision. Many of the states have drawn up new statutes employing the death penalty. Hopefully, under newly drawn statutes, the court will recognize the need to protect the rights of society as a whole as more compelling than to protect the individual rights of the killer.

Capital punishment is not *per se*, violative of constitutional guarantees against "cruel" or "cruel and unusual" punishment, and retention or abolition of this form of punishment is for the people of the state speaking through their chosen representatives to decide (*State v Dickerson*, 298 A 2d 261/Del–1973). Accordingly, we hold that, uniformly applied, the mandatory death provision of the murder statute, standing alone, will not constitute "cruel" or "cruel and unusual" punishment in violation of the constitutional guarantees. Id.

Upon the trial of any defendant charged with a capital crime, the trial judge may not instruct the jury that it may add to its verdict a recommendation of life imprisonment. Rather, he should instruct the jury under what circumstances a verdict of guilty or not guilty should be returned, and upon the return of a verdict of guilty the court has no alternative but to sentence defendant to death. *State v Waddell*, 194 SE 2d 19/NC (1973).

A statute which provides that the death penalty be imposed upon an inmate who kills a prison guard is constitutional and the fact that it classifies certain victims does not deny due process. *Jefferson v Com*, 204 SE 2d 258/Va (1974).

Where the victim was kidnaped, raped and severely beaten by three assailants, the imposition of the death penalty was proper as to appellant. *Eberheart v State*, 206 SE 2d 12/Ga (1974).

Unconventional Punishment

Revocation of license under an implied consent statute is not punishment for a crime, and such statute does not offend against the U.S. Constitution in its prohibition against a bill of attainder. *Daly v State Department of Highways*, 207 NW 2d 541/Min (1973).

As to whether removal of a public official from office constitutes punishment is a matter of legislative discretion. Under the Illinois law the removal from office of a public official upon conviction of an infamous crime is not punishment but simply a consequence of a condition imposed on public officials in furtherance of the public interest (*Taborski v Illinois Appellate Court*, 278 NE 2d 796/Ill (1972). But under California law the removal from public office is one of five punishments imposed upon conviction of crime. California Penal Code, § 15.

Although often not specifically designated as a punishment, some states provide, as an addition to any punishment which may be prescribed, that the court may order an operation for the prevention of procreation. This operation is usually prescribed for sexual psychopaths, the criminally insane, habitual criminals, and people who committed forcible rape or sodomy and some sex offenses against children. RCW 9.92.100; California Penal Code §§ 645, 2670.

Defendant is not entitled, as a matter of right, to credit on his sentence for time spent in jail pending imposition of sentence, but such time may, in the discretion of the court, be given due consideration. *State v Lerma*, 495 P 2d 880/Az (1972).

PARDON

Executive Authority

The governor, by virtue of his office, may grant pardons but is without specific authority to grant parole. However, under Texas law the courts have held that the power to grant pardons includes the power to grant paroles, which are classified as "conditional pardons." *Clifford v Beto*, 464 F 2d 1191/Tex (1972).

The governor has the exclusive power to grant reprieves, commutations and pardons after conviction, and his action is nonappealable. *Dunvar v District Court*, 502 P 2d 420/Colo (1972).

The power vested in the governor to grant full and unconditional pardons is exclusive of the prison board as each acts independently of the other (*Ex Parte Costello*, 157 P 2d 713/Wn–1945), and the courts are without power to review an executive pardon. *Bishop v United States*, 223 F 2d 582/DC (1955).

Effect of Pardon

In some jurisdictions the effect of executive pardon is to completely free the offender from control of the state and relieve him of all legal disabilities resulting therefrom, while in others the courts hold that a conviction is not wiped out by pardon, as a pardon by the executive power does not blot out the solemn act of the judicial branch of government. Thus, one pardoned after a felony conviction may, nevertheless, be subject to increased punishment for a subsequent conviction under an habitual criminal act. *Jeremiah v State*, 504 P 2d 442/Ok (1972).

Amnesty

"Amnesty" is the exercise of sovereign power by which immunity to prosecution is granted by nullifying the offense committed by a group or class of people or a single person, and is provided for by the Congress or by a legislative body. Neither the prosecutor nor the courts may grant amnesty. *State v Frazier*, 185 SE 2d 652/NC (1972).

PAROLE

Defined

"Parole" is the conditional release of a prisoner from the confines of the prison prior to the expiration date of his sentence. The conditions of his release may be many and varied depending on the nature of the offense for which he was convicted and his background as a prisoner. One condition which is common to all such releases is the continued supervision of the prisoner; a person on parole is a prisoner at large. *Mileham v Bd of Prison Terms and Paroles,* 520 P 2d 840/Az (1974).

A parolee or probationer is in legal custody even though at liberty, and custody continues throughout the period of probation or parole and by its nature entails a degree of supervision. *People v Adams,* 336 NYS 2d 533/NY (1972).

The Purpose of Parole

The object of the parole board is to determine the optimum release date for each prisoner giving full consideration to the nature of the offense, degree of risk, release plans, extent of rehabilitation and the subject's potential for living within acceptable norms of society. *Alvarez v Turner,* 422 F 2d 214/Ut (1970).

The purpose of parole is to permit deserving prisoners to leave the prison before the expiration of their terms so they may serve the balance of their sentence while living in the community in comparative freedom. *Woods v Steiner,* 207 FS 945/Md (1962).

Restrictions on Parole Boards

The authority of the parole board is limited to shortening the duration of confinement fixed by the court, but when the board attempts to enlarge or extend the term fixed by the court's commitment it exceeds its authority as such extension of time would contravene the Constitution by imposing punishment without due process. *Wyback v Board of Prison Terms and Paroles,* 203 P 2d 1083/Wn (1949).

As a rule the board of prison terms and paroles, or its equivalent by whatever name, has the power to return a prisoner to the confines of the institution at its discretion for violation of the terms of parole at any time prior to the expiration of the maximum term of imprisonment. *Eskridge v Rhay,* 364 P 2d 819/Wn (1961).

Parolee's parole may be revoked for criminal acts committed while on parole even though acquitted for those acts in a criminal proceeding. *Standlee v Smith,* 518 P 2d 721/Wn (1974).

The courts are without power to grant paroles or to determine a prisoner's eligibility therefor. (*Brest v Ciccone,* 371 F 2d 981/Mo–1967), or to review an executive pardon. *Bishop v United States,* 223 F 2d 582/DC (1955).

Parole—A Matter of Grace

The state is not required to provide laws or rules whereby prisoners may be released from prison on parole (*Bradford v Weinstein,* 357 FS 1127/NC–1973), but a prisoner having accepted parole is bound by the express terms and conditions of his release. *Sheppard v State ex rel Eyman,* 500 P 2d 639/Az (1972); *Clifton v Beto,* 298 FS 1384/Tex (1968).

The granting of parole by the United States Parole Board is not a matter of right but a matter of legislative grace (*Godoy v United States*, 345 FS 1292/Cal–1972), nor is parole at the state level a matter of right. Parole is a matter of grace whether extended at the state level or at the federal level. *Witt v State ex rel Eyman*, 500 P 2d 905/Az (1972).

Probationers and parolees are entitled, as are freemen, to constitutional protection against *unreasonable* searches and seizures, but what is reasonable in the case of a "free citizen" is not the same as in the case of a person in legal custody and under continuing supervision. *People v Adams*, 336 NYS 2d 533/NY (1972).

Revocation Hearing–Right to Counsel

An indigent parolee is entitled to appointed counsel at both the preliminary and the formal parole revocation hearings. He is also entitled to (1) written notice of alleged parole violatons; (2) disclosure of evidence; (3) opportunity to be heard in person, to present witnesses and documentary evidence; (4) confront and cross-examine witnesses; (5) a neutral and detached hearing body; and (6) a written statement as to reasons for revocation. *Morrissey v Brewer*, 92 SC 2593/Ky (1972).

The hearing on the revocation of conditional parole is not a criminal proceeding, but administrative in nature. *Russell v Douthitt*, 291 NE 2d 361/Ind (1973).

Time Spent on Parole–Effect of

The federal courts have repeatedly held that the statutes denying to a prisoner while on parole "time served" status are constitutional. Consequently, a prisoner who is awarded parole ceases to serve his sentence from the date of his conditional release, and if at any time thereafter he violates the terms of his parole he may be returned to prison to serve the remainder of his sentence without credit for time spent on parole (*Dolan v Swope*, 138 F 2d 301/Ind–1943), and any good time which had accrued prior to his parole may be revoked. *Oliver v Alldredge*, 339 FS 912/Ten (1972); *Starnes v Connett*, 464 F 2d 524/Tex (1972).

PROBATION

Defined

The basic difference between "probation" and "parole" is that probation is a result of judicial action taken by the court before the prison door is closed, whereas parole results from executive or administrative action taken after commencement of sentence, but in the absence of a statute to the contrary both follow in the wake of conviction and sentence. *State v Wright*, 202 NW 2d 72/Ia (1972).

The primary objective of probation is the protection of society through rehabitation of the offender (*United States v Allen*, 349 FS 749/Cal–1972). Probation is not a sentence to punishment but a suspension of sentence. *People v Boucher*, 295 NE 2d 334/Ill (1973).

Factors in Revocation

At defendant's trial the state must prove its case beyond a reasonable doubt, but at a probation revocation hearing, being civil in nature, violative conduct of the probationer need be proved by a preponderance of evidence, only. *State v Pietsch*, 508 P 2d 337/Az (1973); *People v Perkins*, 297 NE 2d 15/Ill (1973).

Neither commission of a crime nor subsequent conviction of crime is a prerequisite to a revocation of probation (*Barnes v State*, 494 SW 2d 711/Ark–1973). Failure to report to a probation officer pursuant to the terms of probation (*Isabell v State*, 494 SW 2d 572/Tex–1973), or deceit, untruthfulness and deception, are grounds for revocation (*State v Lintz*, 509 P 2d 13/Mont–1973), and any court which grants probation has the inherent power to revoke it. *State v Reisch*, 491 P 2d 1254/Wyo (1971).

Chapter V

Defenses

In General

A person pleading an affirmative defense assumes the burden of proving that defense by a preponderance of evidence (*Crescent Corp v Toca*, 271 S 2d 53/La–1972), and contributory negligence is not a defense to a criminal charge. *State v Betts*, 519 P 2d 655/Kan (1974).

When a person commits an act proscribed by law or fails to perform an act prescribed by law, he is criminally responsible unless his act was justifiable or excusable under a recognized defense. The major defenses to criminal prosecution are:

- Alibi
- Compulsion
- Consent
- Entrapment
- Former jeopardy
- Incapacity
- Insanity or mental irresponsibility
- Intoxication
- Self-defense
- Statute of limitations
- Unconsciousness

Among affirmative defenses are self-defense, duress, insanity and intoxication. Affirmative defenses must be proved by the defendant not beyond a reasonable doubt but by a preponderance of the evidence. *State v Poole*, 294 NE 2d 888/Oh (1973).

One compelled to testify by a grant of immunity after invoking the Fifth Amendment privilege against self-incrimination, is constitutionally entitled to protection from "use plus derivative use" of his testimony (*United States v Filiberti*, 366 FS 1062/DC–1973). This means that if a person testifying as to one criminal transaction discloses, in the course of his testimony, facts which link him to separate and independent criminal transactions, the immunity applies to both transactions (*Hough v Popper*, 287 S 2d 282/Fla–1973). However, defendant may be tried for the separate and independent crime but evidence revealed under subpoena at the trial may not be used against him. Id.

The defense of necessity exonerates one who committed the crime under the pressure of circumstances wherein the harm that would have resulted from compliance with the law significantly exceeds the harm actually resulting from defendant's violation of that law. But necessity does not apply when there is a third alternative available to defendant which does not involve a violation of the law. *State v Marley*, 509 P 2d 1095/Haw (1973).

A mistake of law may excuse an act if it resulted from a good-faith reliance upon a court order or upon the legal advice of an executive officer charged with enforcing or interpreting a law; but if the object crime was a *malum in se* crime, mistake of law is not a defense. *United States v Erlichman*, 376 FS 29/DC (1974).

Acts clearly defined and proscribed and within the letter and the spirit of the law cannot be successfully defended on the grounds of desuetude nor because no attempt had been previously made to enforce them. *Everhart v People*, 130 P 1076/Colo (1913).

Restoration or restitution to the owner or victim of larceny does not expurgate the larceny, and the taker is still criminally liable. *People v Roans*, 313 NE 2d 184/Ill (1974).

That defendant did not know the age of the prosecutrix is no defense in a prosecution for contributing to the delinquency of a minor. *Jung v State*, 201 NW 58/Wis (1972).

ALIBI

Defined

An "alibi" is evidence offered in rebuttal of the state's case and literally means "elsewhere." To be effective it must show that the accused was at another place so far removed from the scene of the crime that he could not, with ordinary exertion, have reached the scene and participated in the crime. *Azbill v State*, 172 P 658/Az (1918).

Alibi as a defense involves the impossibility of the presence of the accused at the scene of the crime at the time of its commission; alibi should be established to the reasonable satisfaction of the jury and need not be established beyond a reasonable doubt. *Trimble v State*, 191 SE 2d 857/Ga (1972).

The defense of alibi raises no issue that the crime charged did not occur, only that the defendant could not have been involved, *United States v Spoonhunter*, 476 F 2d 1050/Wyo (1973).

How Proved

The function of evidence relating to alibi is not to establish a defense nor to prove any point in the proceeding, but merely to raise a reasonable doubt of the presence of the defendant at the scene of the crime. *State v Skinner*, 503 P 2d 168/Kan (1972).

A defendant who asserts alibi does not have to prove that he was not at the scene; to so assert establishes *prima facie* that defendant was not at the scene, and the state must prove that defendant was at the scene. *Com v Pierce*, 288 A 2d 807/Pa (1972).

The trier of fact, whether court or jury, is not obligated to believe alibi witnesses offered by defendant over positive identification of the accused, even though alibi witnesses outnumber the identification witnesses. *People v Jackson*, 295 NE 2d 462/Ill (1973).

Instruction to the Jury

Instruction to the jury that "alibi as a defense should be established to the reasonable satisfaction of the jury," did not shift the burden of proof to the defendant, nor did such instruction relieve the state of the onus of proving guilt beyond a reasonable doubt. *Trimble v State*, 191 SE 2d 857/Ga (1972).

The testimony of defendant's wife placing defendant 180 miles away from the scene 10 hours prior to the commission of the crime was properly refused as immaterial. *Hafer v People*, 492 P 2d 847/Colo (1972).

Where defendant is prosecuted with others on the theory that all conspired together to commit the crime, and there is testimony to this point, alibi is not a tenable defense. *State v Skinner*, 503 P 2d 168/Kan (1972).

COMPULSION

Defined

"Compulsion" is a defense to a criminal charge when the act and threats were sufficient to show that defendant's life was in "present and immediate" danger (*People v Sanders*, 256 P 251/Cal–1927), and threats of future violence constitute no defense under the defense of compulsion (*State v Weston*, 219 P 180/Or–1923). Threats of a future prosecution for a past larceny–not being threats of present, imminent and impending bodily harm–does not present sufficient compulsion to excuse the crime of embezzlement (*State v Patterson*,

241 P 977/Or–1925); (*People v Lo Cicero*, 459 P 2d 241/Cal–1969). But even if the threats or menaces are of immediate death or great bodily injury and there is reason to believe such threats will be executed upon defendant's refusal to cooperate, such threats will not excuse the commission of murder or robbery wherein a human being is killed. *State v Moretti*, 120 P 102/Wn (1912).

To establish the defense of compulsion there must be a threat of imminent death or great bodily injury, and a threat to be carried out at some future time is no defense. *State v Milum*, 516 P 2d 984/Kan (1973).

Permissible Limits of Defensible Coercion

As a rule one who commits an act denounced as criminal under coercion or duress of a coparticipant, in order to avail himself of the defense of compulsion, must have participated under threats or menaces sufficient to create in the mind of an ordinarily prudent man a reasonable apprehension of death or great bodily injury if he refused. This defense, however, is not tenable in the crime of murder or in the commission of an act imminently dangerous to life from which act death results. *Black's Law Dictionary*.

Coercion of Wife

At common law a married woman who committed a misdemeanor under the threats, command or coercion of her husband was presumed to have acted under compulsion and was not criminally responsible. Many of the states still abide by this rule. The fact that the wife is without fault, however, would not prevent a prosecution of her husband as a principal for advising, encouraging or counseling the commission of crime under the concept of principality in crime. California Penal Code, § 26.

CONSENT

Defined

"Consent" in law means a voluntary agreement by one who is competent to do something or to refrain from doing an act proposed by another. Consent differs from assent which means passivity or submission. *People v Dong Pok Yip*, 127 P 1031/Cal (1912); *Perryman v State*, 12 SE 2d 388/Ga (1940).

Consent is at times a complete defense to crime where the consentor is competent to give consent and consent is freely given. Some examples would be rape by force, battery, larceny. It must be remembered, however, that once the act is committed under criminal circumstances subsequent forgiveness or ratification will not negate the criminal character of the act as a crime is always an act against the state. *State v Camp*, 430 P 2d 187/Wn (1967).

Competency of Consent

Although the victim consented to a hypodermic injection from which she lapsed into unconsciousness, the defendant physician's act of thereafter removing her clothing and getting on top of her constituted an assault and battery and the defense of consent was not tenable. *Avery v State*, 292 A 2d 728/Md (1972).

Consent is not a defense to a charge of aggravated battery irrespective of the fact that victim produced a pistol, gave it to defendant and said, "Go ahead and shoot me if you want to," and she did. *State v Fransua*, 510 P 2d 106/NM (1973).

The actions of an undercover police officer while lying on the front seat of a rented automobile feigning intoxication, in turning over so as to expose his pocket containing money in a clip, did not amount to consent to its taking. *Odom v Sheriff*, 497 P 2d 906/Nev (1972).

ENTRAPMENT

Defined

The United States Supreme Court has defined entrapment as follows:

> The government agents must manufacture the crime; the criminal design must originate with the government agent; the defendant must be an innocent person. The government agent must implant in the mind of the innocent defendant the disposition to commit the offense; the government agent must induce the commission of the crime in order that the defendant may be prosecuted; the government agent must tempt innocent persons into violations; the government agent must use enticement and guile . . . the fact that the government agents "merely afford opportunities or facilities for the commission of the offense does not" constitute entrapment. Entrapment occurs only when the criminal conduct was "the product or the *creative* activity" of law enforcement officials. *Sherman v United States*, 356 US 369 (1968).

The allegation of entrapment presents two issues of fact: (1) was there inducement by a government officer or agent, and (2) was the accused ready and willing to commit the crime charged without persuasion. *United States v Jones*, 473 F 2d 293/Ala (1973).

The accused can rely on the defense of entrapment when he is induced to commit a crime which he had no previous disposition to commit, but he cannot rely on this defense when he conceived the criminal purpose and was merely afforded an opportunity by law enforcement officers to commit the crime. *State v Houpt*, 504 P 2d 570/Kan (1972); *Johnson v United States*, 317 F 2d 127/DC (1963).

The rules of entrapment apply not only to law enforcement officers, but also apply with equal force to "agents" or "informers" acting under instructions from police (*Riddle v State*, 373 P 2d 732/Ok–1962); but where one is induced to commit crime, not by law enforcement officers or their agents but by confederates, there is no entrapment. *People v Miller*, 276 P 2d 846/Cal (1954).

Entrapment does not purge the actor of criminal intent nor the act of its criminal nature but grants immunity from conviction of acts concededly committed. *State v Walker*, 521 P 2d 215/Wn (1974).

The Nature of Entrapment

Entrapment is an affirmative defense in the nature of confession and avoidance, i.e., defendant must admit committing acts charged, but in avoidance, seek relief from guilt on the ground that the criminal intent was implanted by a government agent in his otherwise innocent mind by suggestion or solicitation. *State v Fitzgibbon*, 507 P 2d 313/Kan (1973); *Crosby v State*, 295 A 2d 708/Del (1972).

The law does not frown on the entrapment of a criminal, but condemns the seduction of innocent persons into a criminal act by its police officers (*People v Finn*, 288 P 2d 281/Cal–1955). A violation of the law under the guise of attempting to enforce that law is not only illegal, but anarchy. *Crawford v Ferguson*, 115 P 258/Ok (1911).

The courts are in unanimous agreement that entrapment is a question of fact to be decided by the jury when there is a conflict in the evidence or the evidence is disputed, but when the evidence is undisputed and there is no conflict the point becomes a matter of law to be resolved by the court. *Riddle v State*, 373 P 2d 832/Ok (1962).

The defense of entrapment, if not properly asserted by defendant at his trial, cannot be raised for the first time on appeal. *People v Pijal*, 109 CR 230/Cal (1973).

Trap vs Entrapment

In assessing entrapment, a line must be drawn between a trap for the unwary innocent and a trap for the unwary criminal. The defense of entrapment does not attach where one is ready to commit the offense given but the opportunity. *State v Thurston*, 413 P 2d 764/Az (1966).

An officer may, when acting in good faith and with a view to detecting crime, make use of deception, trickery or artifice, without entrapping a criminal suspect (*Robinson v State*, 507 P 2d 1296/Ok–1973). He may make use of paid informers, undercover agents and deceitful practices; he may even join a conspiracy in the investigation and obtaining of evidence in such crimes as prostitution, homosexuality, liquor sales, narcotic sales and gambling. *State v Emerson*, 517 P 2d 245/Wn (1973).

Where customs officers removed a metal container from a package addressed to defendant, removed part of the contents—cocaine—and replaced it with powder, then left a "notice of attempt to deliver mail" at the addressee's hotel, there was no entrapment when defendant called for and accepted the package containing cocaine. *United States v Doe,* 472 F 2d 982/Con (1973).

The defense of entrapment was not tenable where, after the offense was committed, defendant was tricked into making incriminating statements over the telephone while the conversation was being monitored by government agents. *United States v Howell,* 470 F 2d 1064/Cal (1972).

An undercover officer, under Ohio law, may, with impunity, smoke, sell or deliver marijuana to give credence and validity to his appearance when the sole purpose of his conduct is to ferret out illegal drug trade and to bring those involved before the bar of justice. *State v Rowan,* 288 NE 2d 829/Oh (1972).

Entrapment Assumes Crime Committed

Although the doctrine of entrapment may be asserted along with a plea of not guilty, the defense of entrapment is not tenable where defendant denies he committed the act on which the charge is predicated. Where defendant testified that the tablets he delivered to an undercover agent were aspirin, he, in effect, denied the unlawful sale of hallucinogenic drugs (*State v Bruno,* 204 NW 2d 879/Ia—1973); therefore, the defense of entrapment was not available to him. *United States v Cunningham,* 349 FS 1115/Fla (1972).

Where neither of two defendants admitted to the possession of cocaine with intent to distribute, neither was entitled to the defense of entrapment. *United States v Daras,* 462 F 2d 1361/Cal (1972).

Opportunity vs Incitement

There is no inciting of crime where one is in the contraband business; he is not incited to engage in that business when a person comes to him with funds and seeks to buy that which the contraband dealer is selling—in the instant case, narcotics. *Ex Parte Pickerill,* 44 FS 741/Tex (1942).

Where two police officers obtained a key, unlocked a shop in a shopping center and defendant, another officer, in finding the shop unlocked, entered and removed articles of property therefrom of his own volition and motives, he is not entrapped and not entitled to that defense in a prosecution for storehouse breaking. *Green v Com,* 488 SW 2d 339/Ky (1972).

Where evidence showed that defendant had 20 tablets containing LSD in his possession for two months and sold them to an agent of the Bureau of Narcotics, the jury could infer that defendant's intent to sell originated in his mind and not in the mind of the agent. *People v Moran,* 463 P 2d 763/Cal (1970).

Where defendant was willing and anxious to sell LSD in wholesale lots and was given the opportunity by a man who did not reveal his identity as an undercover officer, the defense of entrapment was not tenable. *Dumon v Com*, 488 SW 2d 343/Ky (1972).

Solicitation by Officers

There was no entrapment where a narcotics officer, in company with an informant, solicited defendant by telephone to deliver to them at a named location ten capsules of heroin. Defendant, in company with a female, kept the appointment but appeared reluctant to deliver the heroin after receiving $24 from the officer. However, after some discussion the heroin was delivered allegedly because the informant stated several times, "I'm sick, I'm real sick." *People v Ramos*, 303 P 2d 783/Cal (1956).

Where defendant—a hitchhiker—was picked up by two undercover officers and one of the officers asked where he might procure some marijuana, which drew a negative response, followed by volunteered information that he possessed peyote which he would sell, there was no entrapment. *United States v Hodas*, 467 F 2d 211/Az (1972).

Solicitation by Police Agent

The solicitation and use by police of a minor to purchase liquor from defendant would not give rise to the defense of entrapment. The police, through the medium of the minor, merely created an opportunity for the defendant to commit a crime which he was predisposed to commit. *Village of Spring Lake v Gardner*, 196 NW 2d 5/Mich (1972).

Where an officer sent two prisoners into an establishment to purchase illegal liquor, the intent to "sell" illegal liquor did not originate in the mind of the officer but in the mind of the defendant. Nor was the officer obliged to advise defendant of her constitutional rights outlined in *Miranda v Arizona*, 384 US 436 (1966), as she was not in the act of confessing to crime but in the act of committing it. *State v Kelly*, 268 S 2d 650/La (1972).

That a probation officer gave a minor some money and told him to buy a bottle of whiskey at defendant's bar, did not amount to entrapment in the absence of a deception as to purchaser's age. *State v Parr*, 283 P 2d 1086/Mont (1955).

Enticement by Private Person

Ordinarily, the defense of entrapment does not extend to acts of inducement perpetrated by a private citizen who is not a peace officer (*State v Farmer*, 510 P 2d 180/Kan—1973). Thus, defendant had no standing to claim entrapment when all his dealings were with his coprincipal and he had had no contact with a government officer or agent. *United States v Dodson*, 481 F 2d 656/Ga (1973).

Effect of Officer Participation

Infiltration of drug rings by undercover narcotics officers and limited participation in unlawful practices of such rings are a recognized and permissible means of apprehension, and thus the supplying of some item of value by the officer which the drug ring requires—here, phenyl-2-propanone, a drug ingredient—does not violate fundamental fairness and is not shocking to a universal sense of justice. *United States v Russell,* 93 SC 1637/Wn (1973).

The fact that the person recruited pursuant to a conspiracy to carry drugs to New York was an undercover agent, would not support the defense of entrapment in view of defendant's predisposition to commit the crimes for which he was charged. *United States v Barbera,* 486 F 2d 333/NY (1973).

Where defendant contended for the first time on appeal that an undercover officer's availability when solicited to engage in an act of sodomy, coupled with his communicating gestures and conversation, including concealment of the fact that he was a vice officer, amounted to entrapment as a matter of law, his contention was without merit. *Riley v United States,* 298 A 2d 288/DC (1972).

Where the Suspect Is a Prostitute

An interesting point of entrapment is evidenced in the difference in the application of the concept of entrapment when the offense is prostitution. Under the ordinary rules of entrapment an officer or his agent may not induce another to commit a crime which he had no intention of committing and then prosecute him for that crime (*State v McDonald,* 289 NE 2d 583/Ok–1972); but an officer may actually solicit another to commit crime which he is ready and willing to commit should the opportunity arise if the crime solicited involves the illegal sale of narcotics, alcohol or the accepting of an off-track bet on a horse race (*United States v Hill,* 469 F 2d 673/Oh–1972). Admittedly, a fundamental difference exists in the "commodity" involved, where one is tangible and the other is in the manner of a personal service. As a rule, the courts hold that a suspected prostitute, or even a known prostitute, may not be solicited by an officer or his agent to engage in an act of prostitution even though the subject is ready and willing; for a successful prosecution the officer may do no more than present himself as a prospective "customer" and await an offer upon the initiative of the prostitute.

Where an officer in plainclothes greeted defendant in the early morning hours where she was walking and she responded by asking him if he wanted a date and when he responded affirmatively, she asked him how much money he had; when he answered that he had $24, she got into his car and asked him what he wanted and he answered, "BJ," which meant oral sodomy, to which she answered "OK," there was no entrapment as the officer merely afforded defendant an opportunity to do that which she was ready to do should the opportunity arise. *State v Williams*, 503 P 2d 1254/Or (1972).

Where federal narcotics agents supplied defendant with a chemical essential to the manufacture of methamphetamine, such chemical being indispensable to the delivery or sale of the drug, there was an intolerable degree of governmental participation in the criminal enterprise to the extent of precluding conviction, even though defendant was predisposed to commit the crime. *United States v Russell*, 459 F 2d 671/Wn (1972).

When a government agent furnishes contraband to defendant a case for entrapment is established. *United States v Harruff*, 352 FS 224/Mich (1972).

INCAPACITY

Feeblemindedness Defined

Medical science recognizes three stages of "feeblemindedness": idiocy, imbecility and moronism. These stages are loosely defined as follows:

- *Idiot*—incapable of learning and understanding or performing the simplest of motor skills; a complete lack of coordination; has a mental development of less than one year.
- *Imbecile*—may learn to communicate with others; able to perform simple motor skills under supervision but unable to earn a living or take his place in society; has a mental development of about one to seven years.
- *Moron*—the mildest degree of mental deficiency; is usually trainable; may be able to earn a living, but if a low-grade moron must be closely supervised; has a mental capacity of about seven to twelve years.

"Amentia" and "Dementia" Distinguished

Feeblemindedness differs from insanity in that the former characterizes a retarded development or a lack of full development of the mind, whereas insanity is the result of mental disease and usually attacks and distorts a fully developed mind which may, during lucid intervals, be restored to full potential. *In re Hendrickson*, 123 P 2d 322/Wn (1942).

A feebleminded person is a mental dwarf who has never enjoyed normal mentality; an insane person is one whose mind has once been normal but has deteriorated due to injury or disease (*In re Hendrickson, supra*); and senile dementia is that weakness and diminution of the mental faculties which occurs in extreme old age. It sets in gradually and progresses in character and nature; it is a form of insanity in the aged which reduces the person afflicted to second childhood. *In re Dennison's Estate*, 162 P 2d 245/Wn (1945).

Legal Responsibility

An idiot is a person destitute of mind at birth or possessing a mind so weak and feeble from birth as to render him incapable of knowing right from wrong, or knowing right from wrong, he has not, by reason of such mental condition, the willpower to resist. *Singleton v State*, 522 P 2d 1221/Nev (1973).

The California Supreme Court has held that imbecility is not a defense to a criminal charge unless it is of such a pronounced nature as to deprive the actor of the power to distinguish between right and wrong (*People v Keyes*, 175 P 6/Cal–1918). Likewise, the Washington Supreme Court has held that one with the mental capacity of a nine-year-old is not without mental capacity and moral freedom to commit homicide as a matter of law. *State v Schafer*, 286 P 833/Wn (1930).

Where defendant had the mental and moral age of one less than 14 years, her criminal responsibility for the act of assault with caustic chemicals was not altered thereby. *People v Day*, 248 P 250/Cal (1926).

At common law idiocy was a defense to crime but unless specifically exempted by statute, neither inbecility or moronism is a defense.

Impossibility—Legal vs Physical

Impossibility embraces the elements of "legal" incapacity and "physical" incapacity. As a rule where incapacity results from a legal obstacle, one committing or attempting to commit the act has a defense; conversely, when incapacity is occasioned by some physical barrier or the absence of a physical object, the accused has no defense. An exception to the legal incapacity rule is illustrated in *State v Martin*, 194 SE 2d 60/NC (1973), wherein defendant and a friend, after consuming an unknown quantity of alcohol, went to defendant's home where he restrained his wife while his friend had an act of sexual intercourse with her. Both friend and husband were convicted of rape, and in affirming conviction the court observed: "Just as a woman is *physically* incapable of raping another woman . . . so a husband is *legally* incapable of raping his wife . . . ." Yet each may be convicted of rape. Although the wife has given her body to her husband in marriage, she is not under the vows of marriage to be by him prostituted to another. Id.

There can be no conviction of a crime which is legally impossible to commit, i.e., the act must be defined and proscribed by statute or ordinance, and it logically follows that there can be no conviction of an attempt to commit a crime which cannot be legally committed. *United States v Berrigan*, 482 F 2d 171/Pa (1973).

From the standpoint of attempt to commit crime, "legal impossibility" denotes conduct wherein the goal of the actor is not criminal, although he believes it to be; "factual impossibility" denotes conduct wherein the object is proscribed by law, but circumstances unknown to the actor prevent him from accomplishing his purpose; "inherent impossibility" results when the means employed are totally ineffective in bringing about the desired result. *United States v Heng Awkak Roman*, 356 FS 434/NY (1973).

Infancy—Legal Responsibility

Under the Arizona and California law, which follows the common law, children seven years of age but less than fourteen are rebuttably presumed to be incapable of crime, but this presumption may be refuted by clear proof that at the time of the crime the child knew of its wrongfulness; and children under the age of seven years are conclusively presumed to be unable to commit crime (*State v Taylor*, 512 P 2d 590/Az–1973); California Penal Code, § 26. All states adhere essentially to this rule, but the age of incapacity may vary slightly in some states.

FORMER JEOPARDY

Defined

The "double jeopardy" provision of the Constitution is designed to protect individuals from a second or subsequent trial for the same offense, and this safeguard is not limited to retrial of the question of guilt, but also to resentencing for the same offense *(Chandler v United States*, 468 F 2d 834/Tex–1972); defendant has suffered double jeopardy when he is either tried twice or punished twice for the same crime. *State v Carlisle*, 201 SE 2d 704/NC (1974).

For the purpose of prohibition against double jeopardy, a court proceeding which may result in incarceration places the person–adult or juvenile–in jeopardy. *Fain v Duff*, 488 F 2d 218/Fla (1973).

For a plea or defense of former jeopardy to avail, it must appear that the defendant was actually acquitted or convicted in a former trial on the merits of the crime for which he is again sought to be tried. *Bounds v State*, 271 S 2d 435/Mis (1973).

Purpose of Double Jeopardy Clause

The purpose of constitutional prohibition against double jeopardy is to prevent the government from making repeated attempts to convict an individual for an alleged offense thereby subjecting him to embarrassment, expense and the ordeal of living in fear and in a state of continuing anxiety of ultimate conviction though he may be innocent of wrongdoing. *United States v Tinney*, 473 F 2d 1085/Pa (1973).

The principle of double jeopardy requires the prosecutor to bring, in a single proceeding, all known charges against a defendant arising from "a single criminal episode," thus preventing repeated attempts to convict one accused of crime through a series of prosecutions. *Com v Campana,* 304 A 2d 432/Pa (1973).

Prerequisite of Jeopardy

Before double jeopardy can attach the following conditions must exist: (1) defendant must be on trial before a court of competent jurisdiction; (2) the indictment, information or complaint must be of sufficient efficacy to sustain conviction; (3) the jury must have been unnecessarily discharged; and (4) the jury must have been so discharged without consent of the defendant. *Sussman v District Court,* 455 P 2d 724/Ok (1969).

When Jeopardy Attaches

Generally, jeopardy attaches when defendant has been brought before the bar on a valid indictment or information in a court of competent jurisdiction, when he has been arraigned and has pleaded and when the jury has been impaneled and sworn (*Maes v Denver,* 503 P 2d 621/Colo–1972). But under New York law jeopardy does not attach at this precise point but upon the swearing of the first witness. *People v Scott,* 337 NYS 2d 640/NY (1972).

The precise moment when jeopardy attaches varies only slightly and somewhere between the two following extremes: in Maryland jeopardy attaches in a jury trial when the jury has been sworn to try the case (*Blondes v State,* 314 A 2d 746/Md–1974), and in Arizona jeopardy attaches when the jury has been impaneled and sworn and the proceedings commence. *City of Tucson v Valencia,* 517 P 2d 106/Az (1973).

Prior Administrative Punishment

Although escape from a penal institution constitutes both a criminal offense and a violation of prison rules punishable, *inter alia,* under prison administrative rules by the revocation of good time, double jeopardy is not involved and the escapee may be prosecuted, convicted and punished for the escape in addition to any administrative punishment. *People v Bachman,* 213 NW 2d 800/Mich (1973); *United States v Williamson,* 469 F 2d 88/Tex (1972).

Indictment–Effect of Dismissal

The dismissal of an indictment at the request of the government prior to commencement of the trial, does not bar a subsequent prosecution for criminal acts described in that indictment as defendant has never been in jeopardy (*De Marrias v United States,* 487 F 2d 19/SD–1973). Nor would dismissal of a previous indictment charging a single crime, e.g., that of bank robbery, prevent reindictment on the bank robbery plus conspiracy and interstate transportation of stolen money. *United States v Davis,* 487 F 2d 112/Tex (1973).

A magistrate's order dismissing a felony complaint is not a bar to a subsequent prosecution for the same offense either by the filing of a subsequent complaint or by the seeking of a grand jury indictment. *People v Uhlemann*, 511 P 2d 609/Cal (1973).

The law proscribes two trials on identical charges, not two indictments on the same charge. *Delph v Slayton*, 343 FS 449/Va (1972).

Preliminary Hearing–Effect of Dismissal at

The preliminary hearing is not a proceeding in which jeopardy attaches (*State v Pietsch*, 508 P 2d 337/Az–1973), and an indictment which followed dismissal of defendant at the preliminary hearing in the municipal court was proper. *State v Tolson*, 296 NE 2d 705/Oh (1973).

Neither a preliminary hearing nor a hearing on a motion to suppress evidence during which hearing testimony from both sides was heard, places defendant in jeopardy as the court is not deciding guilt or innocence at either hearing. *United States v Hill*, 473 F 2d 759/Cal (1972).

Effect of *Nolle Prosequi*

It is the general rule that a *nolle prosequi* (a dismissal of a criminal charge), if made before the jury is impaneled and sworn, is not a bar to a subsequent prosecution for the same offense. *State v Fields*, 487 SW 2d 560/Mo (1972).

The actions of the solicitor (prosecuting attorney) may bar future prosecution where he enters a *nolle prosequi* after the proceeding has commenced, but a mere dismissal upon motion of the solicitor where jeopardy has not attached is not a bar. *State v Frazier*, 185 SE 2d 652/NC (1972); *People v Krum*, 328 NYS 2d 167/NY (1972).

Single Act or Impulse–Multiple Crimes

A single act may be a violation of two statutes and if each statute requires proof of a fact that the other does not, acquittal or conviction under one statute will not bar prosecution and conviction under the other (*United States v Tonarelli*, 371 FS 891/PR–1973). Thus, where defendant was tried and convicted for speeding, his subsequent trial and conviction for driving while intoxicated was not double jeopardy, even though both offenses occurred simultaneously. *Grant v State*, 505 SW 2d 279/Tex (1974).

Since larceny and burglary are two separate and distinct offenses in most jurisdictions, defendant could be convicted of burglary and subsequently tried on a separate charge and convicted of a larceny committed during that burglary; the second proceeding is not double jeopardy (*Garcia v Veto*, 348 FS 884/Tex–1972). The prosecution of one for conspiracy and a substantive offense committed in furtherance of that conspiracy is not double jeopardy

(*Ottomano v United States*, 468 F 2d 269/Mas–1972); defendant's conviction for gambling under state law did not operate as once in jeopardy so as to bar prosecution under federal law for transmitting wagering information and conspiracy to commit such offense. *United States v Barone*, 467 F 2d 247/NY (1972).

Where defendant is convicted of an assault, battery or aggravated assault and is serving time therefor, and subsequent to his conviction the victim dies, defendant then may be tried for felonious homicide and the defense of double jeopardy is not tenable. *Culberson v Wainwright*, 453 F 2d 1219/Fla (1972).

Defendant could be convicted of both kidnap and rape of the same victim without offending against the concept of double jeopardy. *Futerll v State*, 501 P 2d 901/Ok (1972).

Single Act—State and Federal Violations

An act denounced by both state and federal sovereignties is an offense against the peace and dignity of each sovereign and may be punished by each (*United States v Jackson*, 470 F 2d 684/Fla–1972), and where defendant was tried and convicted in the state court for altering and uttering a United States Treasury check, the double jeopardy clause did not prevent his subsequent prosecution and conviction in a federal court for the same offense. Id.

Where a federal indictment charged defendant with assault of a special agent who was performing his official duties and when defendant was acquitted, he could not claim double jeopardy as a defense in a subsequent prosecution under state law for assault with a deadly weapon and robbery of a special agent and robbery of a volunteer police worker. *People v Belcher*, 106 CR 807/Cal (1973).

On the other hand, where defendant, after a robbery wherein he took a bank manager hostage, was allowed to plead guilty in a federal court to forced accompaniment, his subsequent trial in a state court for kidnaping of the same hostage in the same robbery—kidnaping being essentially synonymous with forced accompaniment—was forbidden by the double jeopardy clause. *Brighenti v Judges*, 343 NYS 2d 123/NY (1973).

Mistrial—Consent or Manifest Necessity

No jeopardy attaches where a mistrial has been declared and there was legal necessity therefor; where legal necessity typically arises from an inability of jurors to agree, commonly referred to as a "hung jury"; or where there is illness, death or absence of the judge or a juror, or unexcused absence of the defendant when his presence is required. *Curry v Superior Court*, 470 P 2d 345/Cal (1970).

The genuine inability of a jury to agree on a verdict constitutes manifest necessity warranting a declaration of a mistrial, and defendant is purged from jeopardy and may again be tried (*United States v Goldstein*, 479 F 2d

1061/NY–1973). The fact that two previous trials resulted in deadlocked juries did not warrant dismissal on the ground that further prosecution would violate the double jeopardy clause of the Fifth Amendment to the U.S. Constitution. *United States v Castellanos*, 478 F 2d 749/NY (1973).

Where the jury reported a hopeless deadlock after three days of deliberation, and three of the jurors required medical attention, the court properly declared a mistrial for reasons of "manifest necessity," and a second trial was not barred by constitutional provision against double jeopardy. *Com v Brown*, 301 A 2d 876/Pa (1973).

A declaration of mistrial at defendant's instance is normally a sufficient indicant of his consent to the discharge of the jury and a bar to a later recourse of "once in jeopardy" (*People v Hathcock*, 502 P 2d 476/Cal–1973). Double jeopardy is not a defense and cannot be maintained where defendant has consented to the prior discharge of the jury. Id.

Where a mistrial was declared due to failure to properly swear in the jury and the error was discovered before the rendering of a verdict, jeopardy had not attached and defendant could properly be tried a second time (*Bounds v State*, 271 S 2d 435/Mis–1973). Nor did jeopardy attach where the jury was dismissed before it was sworn. *United States v Whitman*, 480 F 2d 1028/Ten (1973).

Jeopardy–Habitual Criminal Act

The recidivist principle of additional or extended sentences for habitual criminals does not constitute double jeopardy (*Wilson v Slayton*, 470 F 2d 986/Va–1972). Double jeopardy, therefore, is not properly an issue in a sentence under a habitual criminal act (*Marsh v State*, 468 P 2d 800/Ok–1970); nor in a prosecution for attempted escape from a state institution while a defendant is under sentence and after administrative punishment by prison officials (*State v Bowling*, 459 P 2d 454/Or–1969); nor in a prosecution, along with revocation of probation, for a crime committed by defendant while on probation. *State v Montgomery*, 474 P 2d 780/Or (1970).

Retrial–When Permissible

There is no constitutional limit on the number of times a defendant may be tried following mistrial, reversal or deadlocked jury. In *United States v Persico*, 425 F 2d 1375/NY (1970), the Second Circuit Court upheld a fifth trial and conviction of three defendants after two appellate reversals, one deadlocked jury and one mistrial, and upheld a fourth defendant's conviction after two deadlocked juries and two reversals. Id.

The provision forbidding double jeopardy does not prevent a retrial under any and all circumstances; two situations exist wherein a second trial is permitted: (1) manifest necessity and (2) consent of the defendant to mistrial. *People v Grimmett*, 202 NW 2d 278/Mich (1972).

Manifest necessity is difficult to define precisely but examples are the failure of the jury to reach verdict and misconduct by a member of the jury, there being no previous agreement to try the case with a lesser number of jurors. *People v Grimmett, supra.*

Trial *de Novo*

Where the method of appeal from a municipal or justice court is a trial *de novo* in the superior court, the appeal has the effect of setting aside and nullifying the conviction in the lower court the net effect of which is advantageous to the defendant—that he is given two opportunities to seek acquittal without being subjected to double jeopardy. *State v Fields,* 487 SW 2d 560/Mo (1972).

Where defendant who was convicted of a misdemeanor in a state district (justice) court appealed, he was entitled to a trial *de novo* in the superior court and the first forum was a nullity; notwithstanding that under renewed investigation the prosecutor discovered evidence that the crime was actually a felony, he could not proceed against defendant for the felony—only for the misdemeanor of which he was originally convicted. *Blackledge v Perry,* 94 SC 2098/NC (1974).

Reversal—Effect of

The double jeopardy clause does not bar reprosecution after reversal on appeal (*O'Clair v United States,* 470 F 2d 1199/Me—1972), and except when the appellate court expressly orders the discharge of appellant, the reversal of conviction does not bar a second prosecution for the same offense, jeopardy being expunged. *United States v Cioffi,* 487 F 2d 492/NY (1973); *State v Sanders,* 516 P 2d 372/Mont (1973).

Lesser Conviction—Effect of

Implicit in a court's acceptance of a plea to a lesser included offense is a determination that the right to prosecute defendant on the more serious offense has been relinquished, and the effect of the entire transaction, for double jeopardy purposes, is the equivalent of a jury's refusal to convict on the more serious charge. *Rivers v Lucas,* 477 F 2d 199/Mich (1973).

Where defendant was charged with aggravated battery and was convicted of a lesser included offense of battery (*State v Gunzelman,* 502 P 2d 705/Kan—1972), or where defendant was tried for driving a vehicle while under the influence of alcohol and was convicted of the lesser offense of impaired driving, he could not thereafter be tried on the original offense. *Buck v City of Danville,* 192 SE 2d 758/Va (1972).

Acquittal

Once having been tried for a criminal offense and acquitted therefor, defendant cannot again be held to answer for the same offense, even though acquittal was occasioned by errors of the trial judge. *People v Webb*, 38 Cal 467 (1869).

The fact that two previous trials resulted in deadlocked juries did not warrant dismissal on the ground that further prosecution would violate the double jeopardy clause of the U.S. Constitution (*United States v Castellanos*, 478 F 2d 749/NY–1973). But a judgment of acquittal, whether resulting from a jury verdict or ordered by the court, and whether correctly arrived at, terminates the prosecution and the supreme court cannot reverse a trial court's order of acquittal.

Where the trial court grants a motion for acquittal, even after a verdict finding defendant guilty, such order amounts to *res judicata* and is thus final and not appealable by the state. *State v Gustin*, 510 P 2d 1290/Kan (1973).

Adjudication of Delinquency

Where a minor was convicted and fined in the criminal court of one jurisdiction for a traffic violation, her adjudication of "traffic offender" in the juvenile court of another jurisdiction was improper and had to be set aside. *In Interest of SJY*, 273 S 2d 430/Fla (1973).

A juvenile, pursuant to a petition alleging rape and who is adjudicated a delinquent as a result of such petition, may not thereafter be tried for that rape in the criminal courts, since an adjudication of delinquency in a juvenile court is the equivalent of a conviction for the purpose of former jeopardy. *Faire v Duff*, 488 F 2d 218/Fla (1973).

Guilty Verdict and Equivalent

A plea of guilty is the equivalent of a conviction, and one who has previously pleaded guilty to a criminal charge may not thereafter be tried for that offense. *Gonzalez v Municipal Court*, 108 CR 612/Cal (1973).

INSANITY

Present Insanity

Sanity at the time of the crime and mental competency at the time of the trial present two entirely different questions (*Swisher v United States*, 354 F 2d 472/Mo–1966); further, a person may not be competent to stand trial due to psychosis or other mental disease and yet competent to testify at his sanity hearing. *State v Myers*, 494 P 2d 1015/Wn (1972).

It is fundamental that an insane person cannot plead to an arraignment, be subjected to trial, after conviction be adjudged to punishment, or after judgment undergo punishment. The perpetrator of crime, however, is not excused of his crime because he is presently insane; any proceeding then pending is merely stayed until defendant's sanity is restored. *Forthoffer v Swope*, 103 F 2d 707/Wn (1939).

One who is found to possess a sociopathic personality and to be suffering from psychological and social disturbances, is not necessarily incompetent to stand trial. *People v Jackson*, 297 NE 2d 195/Ill (1973).

Psychiatric Test and Sanity Hearing

The court has the power to order a psychiatric examination of defendant, but such examination is not mandatory when requested by the defendant, even if there is a question as to his sanity. Such examination is within the sound discretion of the court. *Taylor v State*, 192 SE 2d 249/Ga (1972).

A hearing to determine defendant's competency to stand trial is a preliminary civil proceeding at which the competency of the accused is determined by a preponderance of the evidence (*People v Cole*, 296 NW 2d 773/Ill–1973), and such hearing must be ordered *sua sponte* (of the court's own motion) if the evidence raises a bona fide doubt as to defendant's competency to stand trial. *Russell v State*, 494 SW 2d 30/Mo (1973).

Competency—Factors Not Affecting

To be competent to stand trial defendant's memory and intellect, which are crucial to the construction and presentation of his defense, must be substantially unimpaired by mental disorder (*Hansford v United States*, 365 F 2d 920/DC–1966), but the mere fact that defendant is suffering from a mental disease does not preclude criminal action against him, for he may be so afflicted and yet have a rational and factual understanding of court proceedings and be able to consult with and assist his counsel in his defense. *Lee v Alabama*, 406 F 2d 466/Ala (1968).

The fact that defendant had been committed to a state hospital for emergency mental treatment, or was illiterate or had a drinking problem, was not alone of sufficient magnitude to raise a bona fide doubt of his competency to stand trial. *People v Shaw*, 286 NE 2d 107/Ill (1972).

Procedure When Incompetency Determined

If at any time while criminal proceedings are pending, facts are brought to the attention of the court, either from the court's observation or upon advisement of counsel, that defendant is or may be presently incompetent to cooperate with counsel in his defense, the proceeding should be suspended and the issue of present insanity resolved *(State v Cortez*, 218 NW 2d 217/Neb–1974). But a pretrial determination of sanity is not required upon a bare suggestion of insanity unless it appears to the court that there is a bona fide doubt as to defendant's sanity. *Grissom v Wainwright*, 494 F 2d 30/Fla (1974).

When defendant has been ordered committed due to present insanity, the court may upon receipt of a certification of incompetency from the hospital superintendent commit the accused to a mental hospital for care and treatment, and upon a certification of restoration of competency, the court may proceed with the trial. In case there is an object interposed by either party after receipt of certification, such objections will be disposed of before commitment or trial as the case may be. *Whalem v United States*, 346 F 2d 812/DC (1965).

PAST INSANITY

In General

The term "criminal insanity" is synonymous with the term "mental irresponsibility" *(State v Welsh*, 508 P 2d 1041/Wn–1973), and the *M'Naghten* test is the applicable test for insanity as a defense in a criminal proceeding. Id; *Queen v M'Naghten*, 10 Clark & Finney, 200 Eng Rpts 718 (1843).

The label assigned by a psychiatrist to a mental condition does not control the standard to be applied in determining the legal responsibility of the subject. *United States v Kohlman*, 469 F 2d 247/NY (1972).

The policy underlying the distinction between treatment for the mentally irresponsible lawbreaker who is sent to a mental hospital, and punishment for the mentally responsible lawbreaker who is confined in a prison is that (1) it is both wrong and foolish to punish one who is not to blame and whose behavior punishment cannot correct, and (2) the security of the community may be more effectively protected by hospitalization than by imprisonment. *Williams v United States*, 250 F 2d 19/DC (1955).

Evidence of mental disease is not a justification for the mitigation of an offense nor for the reduction of the degree of a crime committed, but a complete defense. *State v Sturdivan*, 497 SW 2d 139/Mo (1973); *Parks v Denver*, 503 P 2d 1029/Colo (1972).

Order of Proof

The state may not offer evidence of defendant's sanity before it becomes an issue, and the state's introduction of testimonial evidence of defendant's sanity over his objection and before his sanity was put at issue, was reversible error *(People v Plummer*, 195 NW 2d 328/Mich–1972). The reason for this rule is that sanity in a criminal proceeding is, in the first instance, presumed, and to offer evidence to prove a presumption is irrelevant. *Cook v State*, 271 S 2d 232/Fla (1973).

Defendant Must Prove

The defense of insanity or mental irresponsibility is an affirmative defense which the one so claiming must prove, and the state is under no obligation to introduce evidence of defendant's sanity, thus relying on the presumption of sanity. *State v Myers*, 494 P 2d 574/Id (1972).

Prior periods of insanity are admissible to establish the defense of insanity; defendant's insanity at the time of the trial is admissible to prove insanity at the time of the crime. *People v Mallette*, 102 P 2d 1084/Cal (1940).

Testimony of a lay witness on the issue of insanity requires a predicate. This means simply that the witness must have been acquainted with the subject over a sufficient period of time to afford an opportunity for frequent observation. *Williams v State*, 279 S 2d 478/Ala (1973).

In a prosecution for murder where the defendant pleads not guilty by reason of insanity, he is presumed sane and it devolves upon him to establish his sanity by a preponderance of evidence or at least to cast a reasonable doubt on his sanity (*High v State*, 401 P 2d 189/Ok–1965), and this rule applies even though defendant has been previously committed to a mental institution for treatment of a disordered mind. *State v Hawkins*, 425 P 2d 390/certiorari denied 390 US 912/Wn (1967).

Sanity Presumed

The presumption of sanity reigns at defendant's trial, but only until the issue of insanity is raised; at this juncture the presumption fades and the state must either produce evidence of defendant's sanity or it may rely on the presumption of sanity to overcome evidence of insanity. *United States v Milne*, 487 F 2d 1232/Fla (1973); *People v Chamberlain*, 60 P 2d 299/Cal (1936).

The presumption of sanity is a legal presumption and of sufficient force to establish the sanity of the defendant *prima facie*, the purpose being to obviate the necessity for the state to establish sanity in all cases. *Young v State*, 280/NE 2d 595/Ind (1972).

The presumption of sanity may be of sufficient force to negate abundant evidence to the contrary, as in the case of *People v Chamberlain, supra*, wherein ten lay witnesses testified to defendant's insanity, followed by three psychiatrists—two of whom were appointed by the state, who also testified to defendant's insanity—but all testimony was rejected by the jury and defendant's adjudication of sanity was upheld by the California Supreme Court. The jury is under no obligation to accept the testimony of a witness, even an expert witness. Id.

Defendant, on trial for the murder of her husband by shooting, was found sane and thus responsible, notwithstanding testimony by a psychiatrist as to her insanity, the presumption of sanity being of sufficient force to overcome positive evidence to the contrary (*Bowker v State*, 373 P 2d 500/Alk–1962). Also, evidence of the manner in which a murder plan was conceived and executed supported a guilty verdict notwithstanding the testimony of two alienists to defendant's insanity. *State v Holt*, 449 P 2d 119/Ut (1969).

Where insanity is a defense and not a plea, defendant's presumption of sanity retains its vitality until some evidence to the contrary is presented (*People v Johnson*, 503 P 2d 1019/Colo–1972), and the presumption vanishes only when there is offered testimony as to defendant's insanity sufficient to create a reasonable doubt as to his sanity. Unless the state overcomes such evidence, defendant is entitled to an acquittal. *Cook v State*, 271 S 2d 232/Fla (1973).

As a rule, where a plea of both not guilty and not guilty by reason of insanity are available to defendant, the issue of guilt is decided first, and during this controversy defendant is conclusively presumed to be sane. Only after a finding of guilty is the issue of insanity heard since a finding of not guilty on the issue of fact terminates the controversy. *People v Smith*, 108 CR 698/Cal (1973).

Some types of insanity are characterized by "periods of light," also referred to as rational intervals or lucid intervals, and when it is shown that a person so afflicted committed a criminal act a presumption arises that he committed the crime during one of those intervals. *McConnell v People*, 402 P 2d 75/Colo (1965).

Test of Insanity

"Every sane person is responsible for his voluntary acts" *(State v Mays*, 395 P 2d 758/Wn–1964). Further, if a person has the capability of distinguishing between right and wrong and knows the nature and moral quality of his voluntary acts, he is deemed sane under the *M'Naghten* rule. The rule of sanity set forth in *Queen v M'Naghten*, 10 Clark & Finney, 200 Eng Rpts 718 (1843), in England, is the rule of sanity which is still followed by the vast majority of the states. *State v Reece*, 486 P 2d 1088/Wn (1971).

The court's instruction to the jury on the subject of insanity based on the "right and wrong" test (*Queen v M'Naghten supra,*) in a prosecution for murder was proper despite defendant's claim that a more recent test of insanity (*Durham v United States*, 214 F 2d 862/DC–1964) should be adopted. *French v State*, 416 P 2d 171/Ok (1966).

Psychiatric Examination

Defendant is not entitled, as a matter of right, to a suspension of a criminal proceeding to undergo psychiatric examination merely because he demands it, as such examination is largely within the discretion of the trial court; unless there is some evidence of mental disorder such request will not usually be granted. *Crawn v United States,* 254 FS 669/Pa (1966).

Under Florida law, one who relies on the defense of insanity must cooperate with court-appointed experts by answering questions propounded to him, or in alternative be precluded from offering his independent expert testimony on the subject. *McMunn v State,* 264 S 2d 868/Fla (1972).

Where defendant has pleaded not guilty by reason of insanity, and has submitted to a psychiatric examination by a psychiatrist of his own choosing who has offered testimony in his behalf as to the results thereof, the state then must prove legal sanity, and in order to do so the court may require the defendant to submit to a psychiatric examination by a court-appointed alienist. The purpose and result of his examination are not to compel incriminating evidence from the mouth of defendant as to whether he committed the crime charged, but whether he possessed the requisite mental capacity to be criminally responsible therefor *(United States v Albright,* 388 F 2d 719/W Va–1968). The right to silence under the Fifth Amendment does not entitle defendant to remain silent in the face of a psychiatric examination where his defense to murder is mental irresponsibility. *State v Huson,* 440 P 2d 192/Wn (1968).

The jury is not bound by the findings of a psychiatrist. Thus, where defendant was examined by eleven alienists and only three were of the opinion that the homicide was the product of a diseased or defective mind, there was insufficient evidence, as a matter of law, to raise a reasonable doubt of insanity and the conflict in the psychiatric testimony became an issue to be resolved by the jury. *Williams v United States,* 312 F 2d 862/DC (1962).

Mental Aberrations Not Necessarily Insanity

An adjudication of insanity in another state two and one-half years previously does not raise the issue of insanity, and a commitment to a mental hospital for treatment is not an adjudication of insanity. Nor does it foreclose the presumption of sanity, nor alter defendant's burden to prove the defense of insanity, nor place upon the state the burden of proving the restoration of sanity. *State v Hawkins,* 425 P 2d 390/Wn (1967).

A state of insanity induced by the voluntary ingestion of drugs, narcotics or alcohol, does not relieve the defendant of criminal responsibility; to hold otherwise would give license to the criminal. *State v Bower,* 440 P 2d 167/Wn (1968).

One may be mentally disordered to a degree less than insanity and still be capable of premediating an act and entertaining intent to commit crime (*Singleton v State,* 522 P 2d 1221/Nev–1974), and merely because one is classified as paranoid schizophrenic does not, standing alone, exempt him from criminal responsibility for his intentional acts. *State v Potter,* 204 SE 2d 649/NC (1974).

Amnesia of defendant at the time of the trial concerning events at the time of the crime should not, in and of itself, preclude the state from relying, with respect to any insanity defense, on the proposition that most men are sane and responsible for their acts. *United States ex rel Parson v Anderson,* 354 FS 1060/Del (1972).

Sexual Psychopathy

Where defendant is tried as a mentally disordered sex offender before a jury, the sole question before the jury is to determine whether defendant is a mentally disordered sex offender, and it is not within its province to recommend treatment or any other disposition. *People v Allen,* 106 CR 43/Cal (1973).

In order to obtain release from commitment as a sexually dangerous person, the defendant must prove by a preponderance of evidence that he is no longer sexually dangerous. *People v Beksel,* 294 NE 2d 111/Ill (1973).

Diminished Capacity

The *Durham* rule by which an accused is not criminally responsible for his criminal acts if his unlawful act was the product of a mental disease or defect, is not approved in West Virginia since it is subject to misinterpretation as it prescribes a test which is too diagnostic and tends to confuse the jury. *State v Grimm,* 195 SE 2d 637/W Va (1973); *Durham v United States,* 214 F 2d 862/DC (1954).

In states holding to the rule of "diminished mental capacity" (here California), a mental aberration not amounting to legal insanity still may negate the existence of a particular mental state which is an element of the crime charged. The rule of diminished capacity is not a subject of fundamental constitutional error. *In re Walker,* 104 CR 668/Cal (1972).

Finding of Insanity—Effect of

Where defendant is found not guilty by reason of insanity at the time the act was committed, such insanity is presumed to continue thereafter *(Fortune v Reshetylo,* 294 NE 2d 880/Oh—1973), and it is the duty of the trial court to commit defendant to the mental hospital for a hearing to determine if he is entitled to a release; in that hearing defendant has the burden of proving by a preponderance of evidence that he is not likely to injure himself or others due to his mental illness if he is released from custody. *United States v Brawner,* 471 F 2d 969/DC (1972).

One found not guilty by reason of insanity and committed to an institution for the insane, may not be released from such institution unless and until the superintendent of the hospital certifies that the patient has recovered his sanity and thus, in his opinion, in the reasonably foreseeable future the patient will not present a danger to himself or to others. *Robertson v Cameron*, 224 FS 60/DC (1963).

One who conspires with or aids and abets another in the commission of homicide is none the less guilty and not exempt from prosecution for second degree murder because of his principal's insanity at the time of the killing; to hold otherwise would permit the use of insane persons as an agent of destruction. *Babcock v State*, 485 SW 2d 85/Mo (1972).

Irresistible Impulse

The test of criminal responsibility is the ability of the accused at the time he committed the act to realize and appreciate the nature and quality thereof—his ability to distinguish between right and wrong. The doctrine of "irresistible impulse" does not constitute a test of criminal responsibility. *State v Humphry*, 196 SE 2d 516/NC (1973).

Irresistible impulse is not a defense to crime unless the condition meets the test of insanity or mental irresponsibility. If a person is conscious of, knows and appreciates the nature and wrongfulness of his act, he does the act at his peril (*State v Iverson*, 289 P 2d 60/Id–1955). The California Supreme Court has said of irresistible impulse: "We do not know if the impulse was irresistible, only that it was not resisted." *People v Nash*, 52 Cal 2d 36 (1959); *Sollars v State*, 316 P 2d 917/Nev (1957).

Neither uncontrollable nor irresistible impulse, nor emotional nor moral insanity is a defense. *People v Trebilcox*, 86 P 684/Cal (1906).

INTOXICATION

In General

"Intoxication" refers to impaired mental and physical condition caused by alcohol, which is in fact a drug, or by some other drug (*State v Zemora*, 491 P 2d 1342/Wn–1971), and voluntary intoxication from the ingestion of alcohol or drugs will not absolve defendant from criminal responsibility. *State v Bellue*, 194 SE 2d 193/SC (1973).

The question of whether intoxication and premediation can coexist depends upon the degree of drunkenness and its effect on the mind and passions of the subject. *State v Bunn*, 196 SE 2d 777/NC (1973).

Some states hold that voluntary intoxication is neither an excuse nor a mitigating circumstance for the commission of crime. Thus, in Maine the courts have held that one who intentionally kills a human being will gain no aid, for purposes of reducing the severity of the penalty from murder to manslaughter, from the fact that his condition was affected or may have been affected by his voluntary consumption of alcohol (*State v Rollins*, 294 A 2d 914/Me–1972).

And under Missouri law, voluntary intoxication not only is not a defense to a criminal prosecution, but cannot even be introduced on behalf of defendant in a prosecution of a crime of specific intent. *State v Richardson*, 495 SW 2d 435/Mo–1973). But see *People v Velasquez*, 105 CR 181 (1972), wherein the California court declared that an assault with intent to commit murder is a crime requiring specific intent and such element can be negated by proof of inability to form the required intent due to voluntary intoxication.

Involuntary Intoxication

Involuntary intoxication is a rare phenomenon and cannot exist where the subject knows what he is drinking and drinks it voluntarily without being subjected to force, intimidation or coercion. *State v Bunn*, 196 SE 2d 777/NC (1973).

Intoxication—whether the result of drugs, narcotics or alcohol—to be a defense must be either involuntarily produced and render the actor incapable of distinguishing between right and wrong, or a condition which negates the existence of a state of mind essential to the *corpus delicti* of the crime (*Gibson v State*, 197 NW 2d 813/Wis–1972). It must be sufficient to affect the actor's reason to the extent of depriving him of understanding and appreciation of the nature and consequences of his act, and the inducement must have amounted to force or fraud. *Burrows v State*, 297 P 1029/Az (1931).

Where the accused is caused to become intoxicated without his consent through force or fraud exerted upon him by another, his condition is that of involuntary drunkenness and a criminal act committed by him while in such a state may be defended by any justifiable means. *Easter v District of Columbia*, 209 A 2d 625 (1965).

A crime committed while in a state of involuntary intoxication induced by the administration of a drug by an unskilled physician would ordinarily be defensible. *Saldiveri v State*, 143 A 2d 70/Md (1958).

Intoxication As Bearing on Intent

The defense of intoxication is not available to one who is charged with indecent liberties as specific intent is not an element of indecent liberties (*State v Haywood*, 466 P 2d 859/Wn–1970). But under a statute which forbids the commission of a lewd act upon the person of a child *with intent* to arouse the passion of either the child or the actor, intoxication of the perpetrator may be considered by the jury as affecting intent. *State v Johnson*, 261 P 2d 638/Id (1953).

Temporary insanity resulting from the use of intoxicants may be sufficient to deprive the accused of the capacity to entertain the specific intent essential to the commission of a particular offense. Drunkenness does not excuse a crime but it may preclude the existence of a mental condition essential to a particular crime or degree of crime (*Bieller v State*, 275 S 2d 97/Mis–1973), and then only when the actor is so intoxicated as to render him incapable of forming the required specific intent. *Parsons v State*, 304 NE 2d 802/Ind (1973).

Intoxication in the Commission of Homicide

Evidence of intoxication is admissible in a homicide prosecution to show the absence of a premeditated design to kill and for the purpose of showing whether the killing was murder or manslaughter; and intoxication which will reduce homicide from murder to manslaughter must be of such a nature as to render the defendant incapable of forming a design to effect death. *Sharp v State*, 407 P 2d 593/Ok (1965).

Where two close personal friends of long-standing had been drinking together and in sufficient quantities so as to become embroiled in a bitter argument as to the proprietorship of a partial bottle of beer, and thereupon engaged in combat, and appellant after being knocked down by decedent, went into his house, obtained a 22 caliber rifle, returned and fatally shot decedent, the court observed in reducing conviction from first degree murder to manslaughter: "While voluntary intoxication is no excuse for his act, it is to be taken into consideration in determining the existence or nonexistence . . . of malice aforethought which distinguishes murder from voluntary manslaughter." *State v Sprouse*, 118 P 2d 378/Id (1941).

Failure of the court to instruct the jury on the effect of voluntary intoxication on intent, in a prosecution for murder where there is ample evidence of intoxication, is reversible error (*State v Huson*, 331 P 2d 1092/Az–1958). But the mere fact of drinking by defendant prior to the crime, where there is no evidence of intoxication, does not require special instruction and it is not error to decline such tendered instruction. *People v Turville*, 335 P 2d 678/Cal (1959).

Larceny and Robbery

In the crimes of larceny and robbery, being crimes of specific intent, intoxication may be a defense. Thus, if defendant, at the time of the alleged armed robbery, is so inebriated that he possesses no reason or understanding and is incapable of entertaining the design to take and permanently convert the property of another to his own use—a requisite element of robbery—such condition would constitute a defense (*State v Gover*, 298 A 2d 378/Md–1973). However, if a criminal conceives his deed in comparative sobriety and then drinks to bolster his courage or to prepare a defense if captured, he "can gain no more than a headache." Id.

Alcoholism As a Status

The state may not punish a "status" such as addictive alcoholism but it may punish acts and conduct related thereto, and one who is intoxicated, that is, "sprawled across a public sidewalk late at night," is not guilty of a status but an act of conduct. *Seattle v Hill*, 435 P 2d 692/certiorari denied 393 US 872/Wn (1967).

Chronic alcoholism is not a defense except that the jury may consider such condition in weighing intent and motive (*Seattle v Hill, supra)*, and one who voluntarily drinks himself into a state of unconsciousness intends whatever foreseeable consequences or inevitable results of such intoxication and that intent may be sufficient to support a conviction for second degree murder. *Watkins v People*, 408 P 2d 425/Colo (1965).

Ignorance or Mistake of Law

Generally, ignorance of the common or statutory law affords no exemption from prosecution (*Aarco American Inc v Baylor*, 309 NE 2d 380/Ill–1974). However, "mistake of law" is often a defense to a *malum prohibitum* crime requiring specific intent–such as those created by federal tax laws–but is not a defense to *malum prohibitum* crimes. *United States v Erlichman*, 376 FS 29/DC (1974).

Reasonable mistake of law may be a complete defense to a criminal charge when the mistake of law negates a mental state which must be shown to establish a material element of the crime. *State v Marley*, 509 P 2d 1095/Haw (1973).

Ignorance or Mistake of Fact

Reasonable ignorance of a fact is a defense to a criminal prosecution but unreasonable ignorance is not. *State v Henderson*, 296 S 2d 805/La (1974).

Ignorance of facts may excuse the commission of crime, where such ignorance makes the act itself involuntary. Where one does an act in violation of a criminal statute, he may show that he was ignorant of facts that would make his acts criminal. Such ignorance, entertained in good faith and on reasonable grounds, will usually excuse crime. *State v General Motors Corp*, 296 NE 2d 317/Oh (1973).

Ignorance or mistake of fact is no defense to a violation of an existing law. Defendant will not be heard to urge that he did not know of the existence of the law he violated. *People v Famalett*, 346 NYS 2d 957/NY (1973).

SELF-DEFENSE

In General

"Self-defense" is a right in law of one to repel force with force even to the extent of taking life, in defense of his person, property or habitation, or of a member of his family, against one who manifests an intent, endeavor or attempt, by violence or surprise, to commit a felony upon any of the aforementioned. An essential element of self-defense is that the defendant provoke no difficulty, and there must be an impending peril without convenient or reasonable avenue of escape. *Black's Law Dictionary.*

The term "self-defense" is usually employed in reference to defending against attack to the point of killing the assailant. This defense is also available in lesser assaults to the extent that a person may fight to protect himself from bodily harm or offensive physical contact. *State v Beaver*, 188 SE 2d 576/NC (1972); *Com v Presogna*, 292 A 2d 476/Pa (1972).

The right to take a human life in self-defense is not to be tested by the honesty or good faith of the accused, but whether reasonable grounds exist for such belief (*Hood v State*, 106 P 2d 271/Ok–1940), and threats alone, unaccompanied by any act which induces such belief, will not justify homicide in self-defense (*People v Lucas*, 324 P 2d 933/Cal–1958). However, where the peril is swift and imminent and the necessity for action is immediate, the law does not weigh the assailant's conduct on scales too delicately balanced even though it may appear later that other less deadly avenues of defense were open to the assailant. *People v Dawson*, 198 P 2d 338/Cal (1948).

The theory of self-defense is compatible to and consistent with the crime of voluntary manslaughter (*People v Kendricks*, 283 NE 2d 273/Ill–1972), and involves a claim that life was taken by an intentional affirmative act and presupposes an intention to kill or, at least, to cause great bodily injury; but self-defense is inconsistent with the crime of involuntary manslaughter. *People v Mitchell*, 299 NE 2d 472/Ill (1973); *State v Sherrill*, 496 SW 2d 321/Mo (1973).

Self-defense will lie where the defendant is free from fault in bringing on the fatal difficulty and when there was present an impending peril to life or danger of great bodily harm, either real or so apparent as to impress on the mind of a reasonable person a belief of the existing necessity to take the life of his adversary. But before he may take the life of another in lawful self-defense, under Alabama law, he must flee or retreat if by retreating he could secure his safety (*Griffin v State*, 273 S 2d 478/Ala–1972). The requirement that defendant retreat or flee before he may exercise the right of self-defense, is not the law of most states. Even though the law of self-defense in Alabama requires one to retreat or flee before striking in self-defense, the Alabama court observes that one assaulted need not retreat from his own home. Also see *Com v Daniels*, 301 A 2d 841/Pa (1973), wherein the Pennsylvania court held similarly.

It was the rule at common law, and is the law of most states, that:

> A man may repel force by force in defense of his person, habitation or property against one who manifestly intends or endeavors by violence and surprise to commit a known felony, such as murder, rape, robbery, arson, burglary and the like, upon either. In these cases he is not obliged to retreat, *but may pursue* his adversary until he has secured himself from all danger; and if he kills him in so doing, it is called justifiable self-defense (emphasis added). *State v Phillips*, 109 P 1047/Wn (1910).

To justify the taking of a life in self-defense, the danger of death or great bodily injury may be either real or apparent but must be imminent. *Collier v State*, 275 S 2d 364/Ala (1973).

Even a trespasser does not lose the right of self-defense and when confronted with imminent danger of death or great bodily injury he need not dive for cover but may defend and, if necessary, may take the life of his assailant. And the fact of trespass plus the fact of carrying a weapon without permit, neither singly nor in combination, deprives one of the right of self-defense. *People v Dillard*, 284 NE 2d 490/Ill (1972).

One who pleads self-defense is not allowed to be the sole judge of the necessity to strike in self-defense and he strikes at his own peril of being able to convince a jury that a killing was in *necessary* self-defense. *State v Washington*, 193 SE 2d 509/SC (1972).

Amount of Force Permitted

The doctrine of self-defense will apply where one repels an assault with force slightly disproportionate to that used by his assailant, but he may not resort to a marked excess of force under the protective doctrine of self-defense and use a deadly weapon to repel a simple assault *(State v Brooks*, 19 P 2d 924/Wn–1933). A claim of self-defense is not necessarily negated because the accused, in reacting to an assault under heat of passion, used more force than would have appeared necessary to a calmer mind. *Perry v United States*, 422 F 2d 697/DC (1969).

Where one reasonably believes he is threatened with bodily harm, he may use whatever force appears reasonable and necessary to protect himself against the threatened injury. Each case must be decided on its own merits, such as the relative size, age and strength of the parties, their reputations for violence, which person was the aggressor, the degree of harm reasonably feared, the presence or absence of weapons. *Brasseaux v Girouard*, 269 S 2d 590/La (1972).

When the disparity in age, strength or physical condition is at considerable variance, and the weaker employs a deadly weapon in an affray against his stronger and younger adversary, such circumstances may warrant an instruction to the jury that the use of a weapon by the weaker may be justified. *State v Blacksten*, 387 P 2d 467/Id (1963).

The standard of force allowable is the same in the prevention of a felony as it is in self-defense. *Kittrell v State*, 279 S 2d 426/Ala (1973).

One acting in defense of habitation against burglary or other felony of surprise or violence may use all necessary force—even deadly force—and under California law the setting of a spring gun which, when triggered by two burglars injured one of the two who were attempting to burglarize the basement of a building, did not amount to excessive force as a matter of law since the force employed was no greater than the victim could have used in person. *People v Ceballos*, 108 CR 536/Cal (1973); however, the mere setting of a spring gun in some states is illegal.

In Defense of a Third Person

One is privileged to defend a third person from harm if under the same conditions and by the same means as he might defend himself, if he reasonablly believes the circumstances are such as to give the third person the privilege of self-defense, if his intervention is necessary and if the third person is a member of his immediate family or a person whom he is under legal or social duty to protect. *Carter v State,* 507 P 2d 932/Ok (1973).

A private citizen has the right to go to the defense of another if he has a well-grounded belief that a felonious assault is about to be committed upon him; under such circumstances the private citizen has not only the right but the duty to interfere in the prevention of the imminent crime. *State v Graves,* 196 SE 2d 582/NC (1973).

Where Third Person Is Injured or Killed

Generally, if a person acts in lawful self-defense and accidentally kills another, the killing is excusable (*People v Adams,* 291 NE 2d 54/Ill–1972). Also, if a person is acting in necessary self-defense and he unintentionally injures a third person, such injury does not constitute an assault and battery. *State v Castillo,* 457 P 2d 618/Ut(1969).

Character and Reputation of Decedent

When self-defense is invoked, proof of the character of the person injured or killed—such as that he was powerful, dangerous, quarrelsome or violent—*if known to his assailant,* may be admitted into evidence as tending to establish the assailant's apprehension and the reasonableness of that apprehension, and such evidence may be offered into evidence by one other than defendant (*Com v Edmonds,* 313 NE 2d 429/Mas–1974). Also admissible in defense of the accused is the character and reputation of the decedent for violence; again, it must be shown that the accused was aware of decedent's reputation prior to the fatal blow (*Randazzo v Follette,* 282 FS 2/NY–1968); *Kilgore v State,* 271 S 2d 148/Fla–1972).

Former acts and threats of violence by the deceased directed toward the defendant are properly admitted in a homicide prosecution in which self-defense was claimed by defendant (*State v Blocker,* 505 P 2d 1099/Kan–1973), but the character and reputation of deceased for violence and turbulance cannot be proved by specific acts of violence against one other than the defendant. *State v Nelson,* 484 SW 2d 306/Mo (1972).

Resisting Arrest

An increasing number of jurisdictions are adopting the principal that one may not resist an arrest—even an unlawful arrest—if he knows, or by the exercise of reasonable care he should have known, he was being arrested by a peace officer in the performance of his duties. See *Model Penal Code* § 3.04 (2) (i).

Under New Jersey law a citizen may not resist an unlawful arrest if the person arresting is known to the defendant to be a police officer, nor may a third person interfere with such arrest. *State v Madden*, 294 A 2d 609/NJ (1972).

A law which allows one to resist an unlawful search by a peace officer, does not permit resistance to the point of killing an officer to prevent trespass; self-defense or defense of habitation did not lie where defendant killed an investigator of the Department of Internal Revenue under a claim of illegal search. *Arwood v United States*, 134 F 2d 1007/Ten (1973).

In the absence of a controlling statute. if one is subjected to an unlawful arrest he may employ any reasonable means, including force, to resist that arrest and to perfect his escape. *Kraft v State*, 305 A 2d 489/Md (1973).

The right to defend against the unlawful deprivation of liberty is but a part of or an extension of the law of self-defense, and in judging that right the jury members must view the situation from the standpoint of the defendant and not from their own secure positions in the jury box. *Forbau v State*, 492 SW 2d 516/Tex (1973).

Duty Toward Retreat

The states differ in the application of the rule of self-defense. In some states one claiming self-defense must show not only that decedent was the aggressor, but that he himself exerted all reasonable means within his power—including retreat if retreat was practicable—to avoid the fatal encounter; if in that respect he acted without due care, his act is manslaughter and not justifiable homicide. *Burton v State*, 495 SW 2d 841/Ark (1973); *State v Sherrill*, 496 SW 2d 321/Mo (1973).

The "retreat to the wall" doctrine, a necessary ingredient of self-defense at common law, exists only in a few states, having been abrogated by statute to permit a more modern doctrine of "stand his ground" and meet force with force; Pennsylvania is one of the few remaining states adhering to the common law rule (*Com v Persogna*, 292 A 2d 476/Pa—1972). However, the "retreat to the wall" doctrine is not the rule when one is attacked in his own home (*Com v Edwards*, 292 A 2d 361/Pa—1972), unless both parties live in the same house, *Com v Walker*, 288 A 2d 741/Pa (1972).

Self-defense is not tenable unless (1) the accused was without fault, i.e., he must not be the aggressor; (2) the accused must have appeared to be in danger of death or great bodily injury; (3) his only recourse lay in repelling the attack by physical force, and (4) that there was no avenue open through which the actor could retreat, a fourth dimension present in a few states, here Michigan (*People v Bright*, 213 NW 2d 279/Mich—1973). But under California and Illinois laws (and the majority of the states), the courts have ruled that as long as a person is at a place where he has a legal right to be at the time of the fatal confrontation, he is not required to retreat but may stand his ground. *People v Bailey*, 304 NE 2d 668/Ill (1963).

In jurisdictions holding to the doctrine of "stand his ground," one assailed may not only stand his ground and meet force with force, but may under some circumstances *pursue* his assailant and use deadly force upon him with justification. *Johnson v State*, 503 SW 2d 788/Tex (1974).

Burden of Proof

When the accused claims and offers evidence to support a claim of self-defense, the burden is then upon the state to prove beyond a reasonable doubt that the accused did not act in self-defense. *State v Vick*, 205 NW 2d 727/Ia (1973).

Although some jurisdictions hold that self-defense is an affirmative defense and must be proved by defendant by a preponderance of evidence (*Com v Carbonetto*, 314 A 2d 304/Pa–1974), the better rule appears to be reflected by the Alabama rule that there is no burden on the defendant to prove self-defense; once the issue is raised the prosecution must prove beyond a reasonable doubt that defendant did not act in self-defense. *Hill v State*, 286 S 2d 924/Ala (1973).

Self-defense was a valid claim where defendant, who was sitting on the front fender of his automobile, was attacked by a disorderly group of men and women whereupon he retrieved a pistol from the floor of his automobile and fired on his attackers while backing away (*Wilson v United States*, 198 F 2d 299/DC–1952). And where a 58-year-old custodian, partially disabled, was informed that two burglars were in the building, and while crawling through a chicken-wire fence to investigate he was approached by an unknown man "in an attitude of attack" who failed to stop on command, he was warranted in the conclusion that his life was in danger which justified the use of deadly force in self-defense. *People v Dawson*, 198 P 2d 338/Cal (1948).

Where plaintiff, a large man, went upon defendant's parking lot and verbally abused defendant, a small man, and advanced upon defendant when ordered to leave, defendant's act of firing a shotgun into the ground and wounding plaintiff on the foot was held to be lawful self-defense (*Silas v Bowen*, 277 FS 314/SC–1967). And where an off-duty bartender engaged a working employee in an argument and was told by the manager to stop quarreling and go home, and he advised the manager that he would do as he pleased which included blowing the manager's brains out, whereupon he fired a shot at him, the manager was justified in killing the bartender. *Burdon v Wood*, 142 F 2d 303/Ind (1944).

Bare Fear

Fear alone is not legal justification for killing in self-defense; there must be, in addition to defendant's perception of the situation, circumstances which would excite the fears of a reasonable man and the criterion which is applicable is objective, not subjective, in evaluating the defendant's state of mind *(State v Rodriquez,* 460 P 2d 711/Id–1969). Nor is real danger the criterion for assessing probable cause for killing in self-defense, the rule being that when it appears to the reasonable man, and when there are reasonable grounds for belief that his life is in danger, he may act on appearances alone, even though it turns out that no such danger existed. *People v La Voie,* 395 P 2d 1001/Colo (1964).

When Self-Defense Not Tenable

Where defendant testified that decedent husband had been drinking and she feared for her life, evidence that decedent after being shot once fell face-down on the floor and defendant then fired three more shots into his prostrate body from his back, warranted a finding that the homicide was not committed in self-defense, thus justifying conviction of second degree murder. *State v Hassman,* 422 P 2d 699/Az (1967).

Defendant's defense failed where he pleaded self-defense to a murder charge and evidence showed that deceased's body contained 50 stab wounds and that defendant had attempted to destroy all evidence of the killing to avoid arrest. *State v Barrett,* 290 A 2d 14/Vt (1972).

The court was not obliged to instruct the jury in self-defense in a homicide prosecution where the defendant testified that he did not shoot the deceased *(Furlow v State,* 475 SW 2d 524/Ark–1972). Likewise, where defendant requested that the court instruct the jury on both self-defense and accident, the court properly refused on the grounds that they are inconsistent defenses when offered in defense of one acting alone. *State v Brown,* 502 SW 2d 295/Mo (1973).

One who is in the act of committing a robbery cannot exercise the right of self-defense against an attack of the victim of the robbery. *State v Wilson,* 174 P 2d 533/Wn (1946).

Where the danger of attack is at a future time or against one who is not present at the time of the killing, self-defense will not lie. Defendant was not entitled to have the jury instructed on self-defense where he committed a homicide allegedly to prevent deceased from carrying out a threat to commit an act of sex-perversion on a female known to both parties but not present at the time. *People v Griego,* 288 P 2d 175/Cal (1955).

Mutual Combat

When two persons voluntarily engage in mutual combat, neither participant may take the life of the other under the doctrine of self-defense unless and until he withdraws or endeavors in good faith to withdraw and this fact is brought home to his adversary. *State v Graham,* 196 SE 2d 495/SC (1973).

It is "mutual combat," or combat entered into voluntarily–and not "mortal combat"—from which one must endeavor to withdraw before taking the life of another (*People v Hatchett*, 146 P 2d 469/Cal—1944); where defendant without real or apparent necessity voluntarily enters into mutual combat with another in which he takes the life of his adversary, such killing will not be in self-defense but murder or manslaughter according to the circumstances and nature of the combat. *Freeman v State*, 262 P 2d 713/Ok (1953).

The "Aggressor" Rule

Persons seeking to avail themselves of the affirmative defense of justifiable use of force must not be aggressors. *People v Oliver*, 296 NE 2d 70/Ill (1973).

If one person provokes a conflict with another and thereafter withdraws in good faith and informs his adversary by words or actions of his desire to end the conflict, and he is thereafter beset and pursued, he is justified in using deadly force to secure himself from imminent danger of death or serious bodily injury. *State v Haakenson*, 213 NW 2d 394/ND (1973).

Self-defense is not available to one who seeks a quarrel with a design to force a deadly issue and through his fraud or contrivance to create a real or apparent necessity to kill. *People v Campanella*, 103 P 2d 193/Cal (1940).

When the danger has passed and the attacker has withdrawn, the assailed is not justified in pursuing and killing his attacker (*People v Keys*, 145 P 2d 589/Cal—1944); where deceased by his aggressive acts brought the difficulty upon himself but then in good faith withdrew therefrom and fled, and the accused then pursued, overtook and inflicted a fatal wound upon deceased, the assailant-victim relationship is reversed and the original victim thus becomes the aggressor and self-defense is not available to him. *State v Randall*, 385 P 2d 709/Az (1963).

Danger Past

In order to establish a valid claim of self-defense, defendant must prove not only that he believed he was in imminent danger of death or great bodily injury, but also that such belief was reasonable under prevailing circumstances (*Day v State*, 201 NW 2d 42/Wis—1972); the employment of violence upon an assailant after he is disarmed or helpless and all danger is clearly past, does not amount to self-defense. *Gil v State*, 266 S 2d 43/Fla (1972).

Even though defendant has been subjected to assault by the decedent and a companion, the force used must be reasonable. Also, the force used must be to protect one from imminent death or great bodily injury—not in a spirit of retaliation or revenge. Where defendant, after being attacked by the decedent and another, went to his automobile, removed a shotgun from under the seat, and returned to his assailants, the danger had past and his advantage by being armed against unarmed assailants precluded the further use of force, especially deadly force. *People v Martinez*, 283 NE 2d 268/Ill (1972).

Not a Mitigating Circumstance

Self-defense, when established, does not militate toward mitigation or reduction of the degree of an assault but constitutes a complete justification (*State v Rodriquez*, 152 P 2d 970/Wn–1944), and a finding that defendant acted in lawful self-defense is a bar to recovery as a person acting in lawful self-defense can neither be punished criminally for assault nor held responsible in a civil action. *Silas v Bowen*, 277 FS 314/SC (1967).

STATUTE OF LIMITATIONS

In General

As a rule, there is no limitation within which a prosecution for murder must be commenced; the limitation of felonies is three years and misdemeanors, or crimes less than a felony by whatever designation, have a limitation of one year.

The "statute of limitations" is based on the theory that, even if one has a just cause, it is unjust not to put the adversary on notice to defend within the period of limitation and that the right to be free of stale claims prevails over the right to prosecute the offender. *Twitchco Inc v United States*, 348 FS 330/Ala (1972).

The statute begins to run at the time the crime is committed, not necessarily on the date of discovery (*Sautter v Contractors' State License Bd*, 268 P 2d 139/Cal–1954), but where the crime charged is conspiracy, time is computed from the date of the last overt act (*People v Crosby*, 375 P 2d 839/Cal–1962); or where an offense is one of a continuing nature–here, failure to provide for minor children–evidence is not limited to the date charged nor to the limitation period specified in the statute. *Day v State*, 481 P 2d 807/Ok (1971).

The Common Law on Limitations

The rule of prosecution for a criminal act at common law knew no limits and prosecution could be commenced at any time after the discovery of the crime. Therefore, unless a limitation is imposed by state statute the common law applies and there is no limitation on any criminal action. *Bush v International Alliance*, 130 P 2d 788/Cal (1943).

In North Carolina there is no statute limiting the time within which an action must be commenced in a prosecution for a felony; therefore the common law applies, and action may be commenced at any time after discovery, except that defendant is entitled to a speedy trial. *State v Harden*, 201 SE 2d 74/SC (1973).

How Time Is Computed

In computing lapsed time under the statute of limitations, the day on which the crime was committed shall not be reckoned. In *State v Levesque*, 106 P 2d 309/Wn (1940), defendant was charged with endangering life and property by the use of explosives, a felony, on Feb. 20, 1939, though the crime allegedly had been committed on Feb. 20, 1936.

The Tolling of the Statute

It is a settled rule of criminal law in the courts of the United States that the statute of limitations does not run in favor of fugitives from justice. A "fugitive from justice" under federal interpretation is a person who, having committed crime, flees from the jurisdiction of the court where the crime was committed or departs from his usual place of abode and conceals himself within the district. *Forthoffer v Swope*, 103 F 2d 707/Wn (1939).

The statute is tolled by the commencement of action and if action is commenced within the limitation the path is open for a successful prosecution. An action is "commenced" when an indictment is found and filed with the clerk of the court, or, in cases triable otherwise than by indictment, when a complaint is filed. Where a kidnaping prosecution was commenced by information within the period permitted by the statute of limitations and was never dismissed, the statute was tolled and the state was not limited to the three year period provided in the statute. *State v Miller*, 458 P 2d 1017/Or (1969); *Mascarenas v State*, 458 P 2d 789/NM (1969).

When defendant voluntarily leaves the state of jurisdiction after the commission of crime, he becomes a fugitive from justice and the statute is tolled during his absence from the state (*People v Snowden*, 308 P 2d 815/Cal–1957). Also see *People v Levine*, 250 P 2d 645/Cal (1952), where an information was filed after six years and three months, five years and ten months of which time defendant was absent from the state. Id; *Com v Cardonick*, 292 A 2d 402/Pa (1972).

Effect of a Lesser Conviction

If an information charging murder is filed more than three years after the commission of the crime, the statute of limitations would bar a conviction for manslaughter where the limitation in a prosecution for manslaughter is three years (*In re McCartney*, 415 P 2d 782/Cal–1966); the same rule would apply in a prosecution for a felony not barred, wherein defendant is convicted for a lesser included offense—a misdemeanor—which is barred. An example would be prosecution for felonious assault, a felony, which results in conviction of battery, a misdemeanor; the conviction cannot stand. *Chaifetz v United States*, 288 F 2d 133/DC (1960).

Continuing Offenses

The statute of limitations for false imprisonment, in the absence of a contrary statute, does not commence until the final termination of the imprisonment. *Kirwan v State*, 320 A 2d 837/Con (1974).

The termination date, not the starting date of the commission of a crime continuous in nature, is the date used in the computation of the statute of limitations. *People v Lofton*, 340 NYS 2d 984/NY (1973).

Conspiracy is a continuing offense for purposes of the statute of limitations (*Com v Cardonick*, 292 A 2d 402/Pa–1972), and the statute of limitations begins to run on the date of the last overt act. *United States v Boyle*, 338 FS 1028/DC (1972).

The statute of limitations for receiving stolen property commences to run at the time the property is received with knowledge of its status. *State v Ladely*, 509 P 2d 658/Wn (1973).

UNCONSCIOUSNESS

Defined

"Unconsciousness" is a state of mind of a person of sound mind suffering from some agency which deprives him of awareness of his act. The agency may have been induced by either the voluntary or the involuntary act of the person affected or of another, or by accident. *Greenfield v Com*, 204 SE 2d 414/Va (1974).

"Unconscious act" within the statutory meaning is an act committed by a person who, because of somnambulism, a blow on the head or some similar cause, is not conscious of his act and thus not responsible (*People v Sedeno*, 518 P 2d 913/Cal–1974). Unconsciousness, when not voluntarily induced, is a complete defense to a criminal charge. Id.

Unconsciousness, as a defense to a criminal prosecution, includes not only a state of coma or immobility, but also the condition in which the subject acts without awareness (*People v Heffington*, 107 CR 859/Cal–1973). But where defendant charged with assault with a deadly weapon was aware of her acts, she was not entitled to the defense of unconsciousness; if unaware and her condition was brought about by the voluntary ingestion of drugs, she was likewise not entitled to the defense of unconsciousness. *People v Kelly*, 516 P 2d 875/Cal (1973).

Complete Defense

Unconsciousness, if not self-induced, is a complete defense—even to a criminal homicide; but if self-induced, unconsciousness goes only to the grade of the offense and is not a complete defense. *Greenfield v Com*, 204 SE 2d 414/Va (1974).

A defendant charged with murder and assault with intent to commit murder, would not be guilty of manslaughter or any other crime if he acted while wholly unconscious. *People v Danielly*, 202 P 2d 18/Cal (1949).

Effect When Self-Induced

Unconsciousness caused by voluntary intoxication is no defense to a crime in which specific intent is not an element, and since assault with a deadly weapon does not require specific intent, unconsciousness from voluntary intoxication would not be a defense. *People v Kelly, supra.*

The jury are the triers of fact and may reject any part of, all or none of the testimony or evidence offered by any witness. And where evidence showed that defendant was the only person in the room with deceased, owned the gun which killed her, and a witness testified that defendant was heard to cry out after the shooting, "Oh my God, I killed her . . .", the testimony of defendant that he was unconscious from the use of drugs at the time was rejected by the jury and a conviction of second degree murder was awarded. *State v Caruthers*, 495 P 2d 1319/Az (1972).

Chapter VI

Inchoate Offenses

ATTEMPTS

Defined

Attempts to commit crime have three elements: (1) intent to commit a specific crime, (2) an overt act done toward its commission, and (3) failure to consummate the intended crime. *Hall v State*, 490 SW 2d 495/Ten (1973).

An attempt to commit crime is an act done with intent actually to commit such crime; it goes beyond mere preparation; it is an act which would apparently result in consummation in the usual and natural course of events if permitted to reach fruition (*State v Thyfault*, 297 A 2d 873/NJ–1972). There must exist in the mind of the actor specific intent to commit a particular crime and a direct ineffectual act done toward its commission. *People v Ceballos*, 108 CR 536/Cal (1973).

Since an attempt is intent plus an overt act toward the commission of crime, the goal or purpose sought to be accomplished must be criminal; if it is not, then the attempt is not criminal. *United States v Berrigan*, 482 F 2d 171/Pa (1973).

Intent Alone

Intent alone, however diabolical or reprehensible, is not punishable. There must be, in addition to the evil design, an overt act committed toward the object crime which, under ordinary circumstances, would have resulted in the completed crime had not the hand of the perpetrator been interrupted or stayed.

Once the perpetrator has gone beyond acts of preparation to the extent that the objective is beginning to be accomplished, he cannot thereafter escape criminal responsibility by abandonment of his attempt. *State v Goddard*, 447 P 2d 180/Wn (1968).

The solicitation alone of one to commit crime does not amount to an attempt, but the hiring of another for the purpose of committing a specific crime amounts to the consummation of a contract and goes beyond the sphere of solicitation, evincing intent plus an overt act toward the object crime. *State v Gay*, 486 P 2d 341/Wn (1971).

Acts of Preparation

The law recognizes a difference between acts of preparation and overt acts. Acts of preparation consist of such details as assembling the necessary tools or persons, or laying the necessary plans that are preliminary to the overt act. Intent, plus acts of preparation only, is not criminal. An exception to this rule, however, exists under the statutes of some states. Where, by statute, the crime of attempted arson is denounced separate and distinct from other attempts, it will be noted that acts of preparation plus intent to commit arson perfect the crime of attempted arson. Cal PC § 451a; RCW § 9.09.060.

Intent to commit rape plus acts of preparation does not constitute an attempt. Thus, where appellant was the last of several accomplices to take a female aside in his automobile for an act of sexual intercourse—the female being of unsound mind and incompetent to consent—and was frightened during preliminaries to the sex act by a passing police car to the extent that he could not accomplish erection even with the assistance of the female who voluntarily rendered artificial manipulation, there was no attempt rape and appellant's conviction for attempt rape could not stand on appeal as he had progressed no further than intent plus acts of preparation. *State v Meyer*, 226 P 2d 204/Wn (1951).

Under the laws of most states, the crime of rape requires a female victim, and an attempt to force an act of sexual intercourse upon a man dressed in women's clothing, believed by the accused to be female, does not constitute an attempt rape. *People v Fratiano*, 282 P 2d 1002/Cal (1955).

Although the crime attempted may be a legal impossibility, it does not necessarily follow that one attempting such an act is without the pale of the law, for his act may constitute a crime not anticipated or intended.

Physical Impossibility

The defense of impossibility means "legal impossibility" wherein the conduct of the actor is not criminal but he believes it to be; "factual impossibility" denotes conduct wherein the objective is prohibited by criminal law but circumstances unknown to the actor intervene to prevent accomplishment. Thus, where defendant arranged with a police informer to bring heroin into the United States, and he thereafter showed one of them soap powder, after which he placed it into a locker, defendant's failure to possess heroin for sale was factual, his object and intent criminal; therefore the defense of impossibility was untenable. *United States v Awak Roman,* 356 FS 434/NY (1973).

"Present ability" to complete the crime attempted was not an element in a prosecution of defendant for attempt to commit murder by placing a time bomb on an airplane on which his wife and children were planning to embark, and the court correctly stated the law in its instruction to the jury that it was immaterial whether the crime attempted was impossible to commit by the means used as long as it appeared possible in the mind of the accused. *People v Grant,* 233 P 2d 660/Cal (1951).

Where defendant, who accosted two young girls in a wooded area, declared his intention to rape them, ordered them to disrobe and lie down and assume a position designed to facilitate sexual conversation, then lay on top of one making movements characteristic of sexual intercourse, his acts and conduct amounted to attempt rape notwithstanding his futile attempt to coax erection. *State v Nicholson,* 463 P 2d 633/Wn (1969).

Abandonment of Purpose

The crime of attempt rape is committed if at any moment during the struggle between the accused and the female, the accused formed the intent to use such force as was necessary to gratify his concupiscence against the will of the female (*People v Stewart,* 240 P 2d 704/Cal–1952) and abandonment of purpose, once the defendant has gone sufficiently far in his pursuit to constitute an attempt to commit rape, is immaterial as defendant cannot thereby escape criminal responsibility. *People v House,* 320 P 2d 542/Cal (1958).

That defendant abandoned his attempt to rape prosecutrix only after she told him she had gonorrhea or was menstruating does not exculpate him and does not prevent a finding of attempt rape. *People v Welch.* 501 P 2d 225/Cal (1972); *People v Westmire,* 162 P 2d 988/Cal (1945).

Where defendant approached the teller of a savings and loan association, presented a hand-printed note which read, "This is a hold-up" and at that time another teller approached who defendant recognized as his sister's neighbor, whereupon defendant took back the note and said, "I was just kidding," and left the building, there was ample evidence to support a conviction of attempt robbery. Intent to rob, putting of the teller in fear and presenting the note constituted proof of intent plus a direct ineffectual act toward the commission of robbery, which act was interrupted or stayed due to some unforeseen circumstance. *State v Hoover,* 187 SE 2d 453/NC (1972).

The crime of attempted burglary was complete when perpetrator broke the lock on the door of a tavern and opened it, and his alleged change of heart followed by his closing of the door and leaving the scene did not purge him of criminal responsibility; once a crime is consummated it cannot be "uncommitted." *Marones v State*, 213 NW 2d 31/Wis (1973).

Effect When Crime Actually Completed

An attempt to commit crime is specifically defined as an offense included in the completed crime; thus, in the absence of an intervening statute, one may be convicted of an attempt though he consummated the crime. *State v Rowe*, 376 P 2d 446/Wn (1962).

A conviction of attempted incest was sustained where the evidence was not clear whether the act of sexual commerce was attempted only, or was consummated, and a verdict of guilty of the attempt was valid though the crime was completed or abandoned. *State v McGilvery*, 55 P 115/Wn (1898).

Assault to Commit Crime Includes Attempt

Assault with intent to commit crime necessarily embraces an attempt to commit the crime intended. Where defendant went into victim's bedroom not wearing trousers, climbed upon victim and held her hands threatening to choke her and left the room after she called for help, it could be inferred that his intent was to commit rape and his conviction for attempt rape was sustained. *State v La Vine*, 411 P 2d 436/Wn (1966).

Assault with intent to commit murder is one form of attempted murder. *People v Heffington*, 107 CR 859/Cal (1973).

Examples

The crime of attempt to commit murder does not necessarily include the offense of assault with intent to commit murder, as there may be an attempt without an assault. *Graves v Young*, 420 P 2d 618/Nev (1966).

Attempt to commit murder was proved where evidence showed that defendant, intent on murder, armed himself with a deadly weapon, went to victim's house and attempted a forcible entry but was prevented from carrying out his intent when his intended victim shot him. *Peyton v State*, 286 S 2d 817/Mis (1973).

Defendant's act of forcing victim at gun point into a waiting vehicle with declared intent of killing victim as soon as he could be speeded to an appropriate destination, amounted to attempted murder although thwarted when victim seized the gun and disarmed defendant. *Com v Clopton*, 289 A 2d 455/Pa (1972).

Where suspect approached prosecutrix who was wearing shorts and a halter and ripped away the halter saying, "Let me see what you have," and when prosecutrix fell to the ground he pulled outward on the waist of her shorts, slapped her and told her to shut up, his acts warranted a finding of attempted rape even though the attack occurred in a public park in midafternoon and in the presence of seven children. *People v Hornbuckle,* 287 NE 2d 294/Ill (1972).

Defendant's conviction of attempt to commit armed robbery was affirmed where evidence showed that one of his companions entered a liquor store, pulled a gun on the manager and told him to lie down on the floor behind the counter, but fled when a witness walked into the store, saw the gun and started screaming. *State v Paul,* 495 P 2d 797/NM (1972).

The pulling of a child into an automobile against his will, allaying the child's fears and starting the motor, constituted attempted kidnap. *People v Loignon,* 325 P 2d 541/Cal (1958).

Where defendant was observed by a witness to try the doorknob on a side door of a garage, then shove the door with his shoulder and try to lift it into its overhead track, plus his admission that he tried to enter the garage, was sufficient evidence of attempt entry to warrant conviction of attempt burglary. *People v Binder,* 310 NE 2d 661/Ill (1974).

Defendant was convicted for attempt larceny by false pretenses where he represented that a prescribed ointment was effective as a treatment for internal cancer, and such representations were made either falsely or with a reckless disregard for their verity in an attempt to obtain money from his victim. *People v Ryan,* 230 P 2d 359/Cal (1951).

Attempt to obtain narcotic drugs was sustained where defendant, by fraud and deceit, acting in consort with an accomplice, telephoned a narcotic prescription to a drugstore, giving his name as that of a well-known physician, and later attempted to fill the prescription (*State v Denny,* 418 P 2d 468/Wn–1966). Also, where defendant, a deputy sheriff, solicited a "large quantity of heroin" from a fellow deputy assigned to the narcotics detail and the narcotics officer reported the solicitation to his superiors who instructed him to feign complicity and make delivery as planned, but to substitute talcum powder for heroin, and defenant was arrested in the act of placing the talcum powder in his locker–having completed an overt act with the requisite specific intent to possess heroin–the attempt was complete. *People v Siu,* 271 P 2d 515/Cal (1954).

Where evidence showed that defendant had threatened to kill several members of a household and thereafter mailed poisoned candy to one of the members, a conviction of attempted murder of all members was sustained even though the candy was addressed to only one member. *People v Gaither,* 343 P 2d 799/Cal (1959).

COMPOUNDING

As a rule, no person except a public officer is under any legal obligation to report a crime, or cooperate or assist in any investigation thereof, or volunteer his services as a witness. If subpoenaed as a witness, however, the subject must testify unless otherwise excused, or face an assessment of contempt. There is a legal difference in merely failing or declining to assist in the investigating and reporting of crime, and in the acceptance of a thing of value for such failure or refusal.

Compounding is defined as follows:

> Every person who, having knowledge of the actual commission of a crime, takes money or the property of another, or any gratuity or reward, or any engagement, or promise thereof, upon any agreement or understanding to compound or conceal such crime, or to abstain from any prosecution thereof, or to withhold any evidence thereof, except in the cases provided for by law, in which crimes may be compromised by leave of the court . . . . [is guilty of compounding]. *California Penal Code,* § *153.*

Crimes which may not be compromised are those committed:

1. By or upon an officer while in the execution of the duties of his office;
2. Riotously;
3. With intent to commit a felony (*California Penal Code,* § 1377; *Revised Code of Washington,* § 10.22.010).

All crimes not falling within any of the aforementioned categories may be compromised but only "with leave of the court."

In cases where compromise is permitted and desired, the injured party must appear in the court where the cause is pending at any time before final judgment is rendered and acknowledge in writing that he has received satisfaction for the injury. The court then may, in its discretion, upon payment of costs incurred, order all proceedings in the matter discontinued and the defendant discharged. The court must then enter into the minutes the reason for such discharge. Such order is a bar to any future prosecution for the same offense. RCW 10.22.020.

CONSPIRACY

In General

"Conspiracy" is a criminal partnership, differing from the partnership recognized by law as a legal method of transacting business, in that the conspiracy has as its object the doing of one or more of the unlawful acts listed in the conspiracy statute. It follows that a legal association of individuals engaged in a lawful enterprise may become a criminal conspiracy by including in its objects an act denounced by law, or by an agreement to accomplish one of its lawful objects or purposes by an unlawful act.[1]

Conspiracy at common law consisted essentially of an agreement between two or more persons to commit some crime, and an overt act was not an element of the *corpus delicti* (*Hyde v United States*, 225 US 347/DC–1912). To date many of the states have added the overt act as an element of the *corpus delicti* and in those states the agreement alone is not criminal.

To establish conspiracy, the government must show that two or more persons conspired to commit a crime and at least one of the conspirators did some act in furtherance of the conspiracy, but a formal agreement is not necessary. *United States v Hopkins*, 354 FS 634/DC (1973).

The essence of conspiracy is an evil design and a corrupt agreement to commit an unlawful act, and it is the evil intent which makes the combination criminally indictable (*People v Marsh*, 376 P 2d 300/Cal–1962). Thus, if the completed action which was agreed upon would not amount to kidnaping, then the agreement could not be conspiracy to kidnap. *State v Davis*, 294 P 2d 934/Wn (1956).

If the illegal object of a conspiracy is accomplished, the conspiracy and the substantive offense may be separately prosecuted and punished. *Williams v Superior Court*, 106 CR 89/Cal (1973).

Conviction of conspiracy may be sustained whether or not the substantive offense was committed, and the state need not show one in a prosecution for the other; nor need the state show that each conspirator knew all of the details of, nor all parties to, the conspiracy. But the state must show that each conspirator knew the purpose of the conspiracy. *Twitchell v United States*, 313 F 2d 425/Wn (1963).

Usually an actionable conspiracy must be an agreement to commit a crime within the state, but under the laws of some states, here Indiana, the object crime may be one to be committed outside the state. *Samuels v State*, 308 NE 2d 879/Ind (1974).

The Agreement

To sustain conviction for conspiracy the state must prove that defendant entered into an agreement which included a specific intent to commit a particular crime (*People v Smith*, 409 P 2d 222/Cal–1966); it is not necessary to establish an express agreement in order to find a conspiracy, and it is sufficient that a concert of action is contemplated and that defendants conform to the arrangement. *United States v Paramount Pictures*, 334 US 131 (1948).

---

[1] Charles W. Fricke and Arthur R. Alarcon, *California Criminal Law*, 10th edition (Los Angeles: Legal Book Corp., 1970).

To be criminal, there must be an agreement between two or more persons to commit some act denounced by the conspiracy statute, but a good-faith agreement between two or more persons who collaborate to convict another of crime does not constitute guilt of criminal conspiracy unless they employ unlawful means in the pursuit of their objective. *State v Brent,* 183 P 2d 495/reversed on other grounds and reproduced in 191 P 2d 682/Wn (1948).

The common law rule on conspiracy did not include criminal agreements between husband and wife unless there was a third person in the agreement, but this rule was abrogated in *United States v Dege,* 364 US 61 (1960), the court holding that husband and wife, without a third party, may be convicted of conspiracy. Some states had already abandoned the rule before *Dege* and since that decision several others have adopted the rule. *People v Pierce,* 395 P 2d 893/Cal (1966).

Nature of the Offense

Conspiracy is an inchoate offense and distinct from the object crime; it requires proof of both an agreement to do some unlawful act and some act done by any member in pursuance of the common design. *United States v Harvey,* 464 F 2d 1286/Fla (1972).

Each conspirator is responsible for the acts of his coconspirators committed pursuant to and in furtherance of the conspiracy whether or not he is aware of the performance of those acts or the existence of the actors (*United States v Murray,* 492 F 2d 178/Cal–1973), but acts and declarations of one conspirator are not admissible against a coconspirator until his participation in the conspiracy has been established by other independent evidence. *United States v Cerone,* 452 F 2d 274/Ill (1971); *Honchell v State,* 257 S 2d 889/Fla (1971).

Where three defendants conspired to commit robbery, evidence of two attempted robberies and a gun battle with police by two of the conspirators was admissible against a third conspirator in a charge of conspiracy to commit robbery although he was in custody at the time of the two attempts. *State v Witherspoon,* 292 S 2d 499/La (1974).

A statute which proscribes conspiracy to commit a misdemeanor and makes no distinction between misdemeanors denounced by state statute and city ordinance, would be criminal conspiracy if the object crime was forbidden by either statute or ordinance. *People v Malotte,* 292 P 2d 517/Cal (1956).

Conspiracy is a single crime whether it contemplates as its object one crime or multiple crimes, and one may be guilty of conspiracy and innocent of any substantive offense. *United States v Magliano,* 336 F 2d 817/Md (1964).

Conspiracy is a continuing crime and deemed to have been committed on the date of the last overt act. *State v Carroll,* 500 P 2d 115/Wn (1972).

One person cannot conspire with himself, an essential element being a combination of two or more persons (*Harrington v Richeson,* 245 P 2d

191/Wn–1952). And where there are only two parties thereto, and one is a government agent whose intent is to frustrate the conspiracy or uncover evidence thereof, there is no conspiracy. *Sears v United States*, 343 F 2d 139/Ga (1965).

The resigning or the adding of a member to an existing conspiracy does not necessarily mean that a new conspiracy is formed as the existing conspiracy may not be affected thereby. *United States v Cox*, 462 F 2d 1293/Mo (1972).

Conviction or acquittal of an attempt to commit crime does not bar subsequent prosecution for conspiracy to commit that crime, nor does conviction or acquittal of conspiracy to commit the crime affect a subsequent prosecution for the substantive offense or an attempt. *United States v General Electric Co*, 80 FS 989 (1948).

Distinct From Substantive Offense

If there is no statute merging the conspiracy with the object crime, a conviction for both the conspiracy and the object crime will lie and the imposition of consecutive sentences may be properly sustained on appeal (*Hill v United States*, 306 F 2d 245/Wn–1969). Where four defendants conspired to commit robbery it was held to be error to regard conspiracy as a lesser included offense (*State v McNeil*, 296 P 555/Wn–1931). And in *Clermont v United States*, 432 F 2d 1215/Wn (1970), defendant's conviction was sustained for conspiracy to commit burglary and larceny and for the substantive offenses also.

"Conspiracy" Distinguished From "Aiding and Abetting"

Conspiracy is not synonymous with aiding and abetting or participating; conspiracy implies an agreement to commit crime, while aiding and abetting requires actual participation in the commission of the substantive offense. *People v Malotte*, 292 P 2d 517/appeal dismissed 352 US 805/Cal (1956).

One does not become a party to a conspiracy merely by aiding and abetting it unless he knows of the conspiracy. *State v Dressell*, 513 P 2d 187/NM (1973).

Where each defendant intentionally aided the perpetrator in the commission of rape, during the course of which the victim was killed, all participants may be found guilty of first degree murder under the felony-murder rule. *People v Streiff*, 342 NYS 2d 543/NY (1973).

The Object Crime

In a prosecution for conspiracy, the state must prove an object crime which may be either a felony or a misdemeanor (*Williams v Superior Court*, 106 CR 89/Cal–1973). And if a conspiracy has more than one object, all object crimes need not be charged as one is sufficient. *United States v Grizaffi*, 471 F 2d 69/Ill (1972).

Where an indictment alleged conspiracy only, and the object of the conspiracy was the commission of several distinct substantive offenses, the state proved its case when it showed that the conspirators intended to commit one of the offenses. *People v Hess,* 234 P 2d 65/appeal dismissed 342 US 880/Cal (1951); *United States v Grizaffi.* Id.

Where the object crime is one divided into degrees, it is not essential to a successful prosecution that the allegation charge the degree of the object crime, here robbery (*People v Klinkenberg,* 204 P 2d 47/Cal–1949), but a conspiracy to commit murder can only be a conspiracy to commit murder in the first degree because of the presence of premeditation (*People v Kynette,* 104 P 2d 794/Cal–1940). Likewise there can be no conspiracy to commit manslaughter.

In the prosecution of a coconspirator for a substantive offense that occurred as a direct or indirect result of the conspiracy, the state may prove the conspiracy even though not charged in the accusatory pleading. *State v Madden,* 294 A 2d 609/NJ (1972).

The Overt Act

Conspiracy under federal law (Title 18, United States Code) includes as a part of the *corpus delicti* an overt act; in other words, the plan or scheme alone is not criminal (*Fiswick v United States,* 329 US 211–1946). Since no overt act was necessary to the perfection of conspiracy at common law, the common law rule applies unless it has been amended by statute to include an overt act as an element (*State v Ferguson,* 70 SE 2d 355/certiorari denied 344 US 830/SC–1952). The federal statute requiring that an act be done to effect the objects of the conspiracy presents an opportunity, between the agreement and the overt act, for one or all of the conspirators to abandon their evil design and thus escape the pale of the law. *United States v Britton,* 108 US 199 (1892).

The United States District Court has observed, "The law of conspiracy–in this country, not in the old country, from which we got it . . . has the element of requiring the commission of overt acts. When we transplanted the law of conspiracy in this country we added that feature to it." *United States v Belisle,* 107 FS 283/Wn (1951).

The word "overt" means visible, observable, open to view; but when used in connection with conspiracy, the "overt act" does not necessarily mean an observable act, for an act may be properly classed as overt although done covertly and secretly.

The overt act is important in demonstrating more than a subjective mental intent to commit crime on the part of the conspirators (*United States v Small,* 472 F 2d 818/Pa–1972). Overt acts need not of themselves be criminal, and an overt act standing alone may be an entirely innocent act (*People v Robinson,* 271 P 2d 865/Cal–1964); nor is it necessary that the overt act amount to an attempt to commit the object crime. *People v Shaw,* 252 P 2d 670/Cal (1963).

Manner of Withdrawal

Under the "abandonment" or "withdrawal" doctrine as it relates to conspiracy, one is not punishable as a member if he withdraws before an overt act is committed (*United States v Heckman*, 479 F 2d 726/Pa–1973), and provided his intent to withdraw is communicated to his coconspirators in sufficient time to afford them a like opportunity to withdraw. *Com v Griffey*, 307 A 2d 283/Pa (1973).

Once a conspirator has manifested his membership in a conspiracy and advises, counsels and encourages the commission of crime, he cannot escape criminal responsibility by quietly withdrawing therefrom nor by remaining away from the scene of the object crime or a collateral crime. *People v Madsen*, 270 P 2d 237/Cal (1928).

Responsibility of New Members

Any party coming into a conspiracy at any point during the life of the conspiracy with knowledge, is regarded as a party to all acts done by any of the other parties then or afterward, in furtherance of the common design. *United States v Olmstead*, 5 F 2d 712/Wn (1923); *United States v Thomas*, 468 F 2d 422/Ok (1972).

One who joins a conspiracy after it becomes operative is not criminally liable for substantive crimes committed by others before his joining (*People v Weise*, 327 P 2d 888/Cal–1959), and an instruction to the jury which indicates that a coconspirator could be held criminally liable for a substantive offense committed prior to his joining is error but not prejudicial error where there is no evidence of a substantive offense having been committed. *People v Kefry*, 332 P 2d 848/Cal (1958).

Collateral Crimes

As a rule, coconspirators are not criminally responsible for collateral crimes which are not a part of the common design and have no tendency toward the promotion of the conspiracy and are not a probable result of the common design, but the existence of a conspiracy between two or more persons renders each member guilty of any crime committed by any member if the crime committed was in furtherance of the common design. *State v Howard*, 485 P 2d 439/Or (1971).

When a conspiracy to commit an offense of a certain class is shown, each conspirator is deemed to be criminally responsible for each and every collateral crime committed by any of the coconspirators in furtherance of the conspiracy. *People v Murphy*, 200 P 484/Cal (1921).

If two or more persons enter into a conspiracy to commit arson and one of the coconspirators is killed, the surviving members are all guilty of first degree murder, and this rule applies even to members who were not present at the time of the object crime was committed. *State v Morran,* 306 P 2d 679/Mont (1957).

A party to a conspiracy is liable as a principal for all offenses committed in furtherance of the conspiracy while he is a member. *United States v Apollo,* 476 F 2d 156/Tex (1973).

How Proved

To constitute conspiracy the state must prove (1) that the conspirators were physically present within the state when the agreement was made; (2) that the object crime was one to be committed within the state, and where an overt act is an essential element of the *corpus delicti,* (3) that at least one overt act was committed within the state. If any element was consummated without the state there is no conspiracy. *People v Buffum,* 256 P 2d 317/Cal (1953).

Direct testimony to a conspiracy is not necessary to sustain conviction as the crime is usually covert and thus may be established by inference from facts proved (*Palmer v People,* 424 P 2d 776/Colo–1967). Nor is it necessary to show a meeting or a formal agreement in words or in writing between coconspirators (*Stewart v People,* 419 P 2d 650/Colo–1966). Existence of the agreement or assent of minds necessary to constitute conspiracy was justified where defendants pursued the same object, often by the same means, each performing a part so as to accomplish the same object (*Abeyta v People,* 400 P 2d 431/Colo–1965). A conspiracy may be proved whether or not pleaded and is helpful in establishing motive and intent. *People v Andrus,* 324 P 2d 617/Cal (1958).

An out-of-court declaration made by one coconspirator is admissible against all other coconspirators (*United States v Kenny,* 462 F 2d 1205/NJ–1972), but such statement must have been made during the life of the conspiracy and in furtherance thereof (*People v Sailing,* 500 P 2d 610/Cal–1972). Such statements are admissible as an exception to the hearsay rule. *United States v Yow,* 465 F 2d 1328/Neb (1972).

The government cannot sustain conviction for conspiracy by charging a conspiracy to commit one crime and proving a conspiracy to commit another. However, proof of a conspiracy to commit other crimes not named in the indictment is not cause for reversal provided the government proves the conspiracy charged in the indictment (*Kepl v United States,* 299 F 590/Wn (1924).

It is not necessary that two or more conspirators be charged; one person may properly be charged. *Stefano v Langston,* 274 S 2d 533/Fla (1973).

When Terminated

Even though the object crime has been committed, the conspiracy is not necessarily terminated but continues in effect until the aims of the conspirators have been achieved, and conspiracy to commit kidnap for ransom continues until the ransom money is paid (*Goldsmith v Sheriff*, 454 P 2d 86/Nev–1969); or when the object crime is one of a nature necessitating escape from the scene to avoid detection or capture, the conspiracy continues until conspirators reach a place of temporary sanctuary. *Johnson v State*, 482 SW 2d 600/Ark (1972).

Where the object of the conspiracy is to make a profit by illegal means, such conspiracy is not at end until the fruits of the crime have been disposed of. *United States v Iacovetti*, 466 F 2d 1147/Fla (1972).

Effect of Acquittal

Conspiracy requires a plurality of actors and an acquittal of one of two conspirators *in a joint trial* is, in effect, an acquittal of the second also (*Lubin v United States*, 313 F 2d 419/Cal–1963). And where three conspirators are jointly tried and the state fails to prove the guilt of two, the third must be acquitted. But this rule does not apply where the indictment charges conspiracy with unknown persons as well as with known persons and where the alleged coconspirators are referred to but not joined as defendants. *State v Collins*, 293 A 2d 235/NJ (1972).

The acquittal of one of two defendants *tried separately* does not require a dismissal of action or a reversal of conviction as to the second defendant. *People v Mayes*, 177 P 2d 590/certiorari denied 333 US 852/Cal (1947).

Where the indictment alleged that defendant with three other named codefendants were the sole perpetrators of a conspiracy, and three codefendants were acquitted, the fourth defendant's conviction could not stand (*Romontio v United States*, 400 F 2d 618/Ok–1968). But where several codefendants were charged, some were acquitted, and two more were granted severance—one of whom was granted a *nolle prosequi*—appellant was not entitled to reversal as one of the two who was granted severance had not yet been tried. *United States v Shipp*, 359 F 2d 185/Ten (1966).

Where appellant and three codefendants were charged with burglary and conspiracy to commit burglary, their acquittal of the substantive offense of burglary did not require an acquittal of conspiracy also. *Hughes v People*, 487 P 2d 810/Colo (1971).

Examples

Evidence which showed that defendant recruited women and trained them in the art of "flimflam," which consisted of inducing elderly persons to withdraw money from their bank accounts after which they would be deceived and defrauded of the money, supported a conviction of conspiracy. *Parker v State*, 201 SE 2d 329/Ga (1973).

An agreement among public officials to refrain from performing their duties of office by not enforcing criminal laws of the state is an "obstruction of justice" and an indictable offense under the common law, and this subsection of the conspiracy statute is not vague and uncertain so as to offend under the Constitution. *State v Erwin*, 120 P 2d 285/Ut (1941).

Evidence that defendant arranged to have an "automobile accident" to delay his extradition, was properly admitted in a trial for conspiracy to obstruct justice. *People v Rosoto*, 373 P 2d 867/Cal (1962).

Not Actionable Civilly

There is no such proceeding as a civil action for conspiracy (*Tovre Land & Cattle Co v Lesmeyer*, 412 P 2d 47/Az–1966); the gist of a civil action arising out of a conspiracy is not for the conspiracy *per se*, but for the damages resulting from the objects of the conspiracy. *Aldabe v Adams*, 402 P 2d 34/Nev (1965); *Barber's Super Markets v Stryker*, 500 P 2d 1304/NM (1972).

Both perjury and conspiracy to commit perjury are public offenses but neither is actionable in a civil proceeding, and in the absence of a statute to the contrary no action will lie to recover damages for perjury or conspiracy to commit perjury. *W G Platts Inc v Platts* 438 P 2d 687/Wn (1968).

ACCOMPLICES

Defined

The word "accomplice" means guilty associate, coconspirator or coprincipal in the commission of crime but does not include accessory after the fact. In a prosecution of multiple defendants for the same offense the word "accomplice" is not usually employed unless one or more of the coprincipals give testimony either for the state or for the remaining codefendants. To be an accomplice one must also be a principal in the crime in which he gives testimony and thus subject to prosecution for that offense. *State v Kasai*, 495 P 2d 1265/Ut (1972).

The "Accomplice" Rule

The "accomplice rule" means that ". . . one who testifies while he is faced with criminal charges may be influenced to testify falsely by the hope of leniency, and ordinarily the defendant, upon request, is entitled to have the jury, so advised by an appropriate charge . . ." (*State v Mangrella*, 207 A 2d 175/NJ–1965). "Charge," as here used, means instruction.

All states do not abide by the accomplice rule. Often the testimony of an accomplice is the only character of evidence that the state can produce, and if the rule were otherwise, many criminals would go unpunished (*State v Harding*, 161 Wn 379/1931). Although an accomplice's testimony need not be corroborated to sustain conviction in some jurisdictions, if the only evidence is the testimony of an accomplice, the court must instruct the jury that the witness' testimony must be viewed with caution and careful consideration, but if there exists sufficient corroboration to connect defendant with the commission of the offense then the cautionary instruction need not be given. *State v Bixby*, 177 P 2d 689/Wn (1947).

Who Are Accomplices

An "accomplice" or an "accomplice witness" is one who could have been charged with the same offense as the person against whom he testified, either as a principal or an accessory before the fact *(Government of Virgin Islands v Torres*, 476 F 2d 486/VI–1973). He is one who knowingly, voluntarily, and with common intent with the principal offender, unites with him in the commission of the crime; an exception may be a child of tender years, in which case the test would turn on whether the child could be indicted and tried for the same offense as the defendant. *Marshall v State*, 497 SW 2d 761/Ten (1973); *Johnson v State*, 502 SW 2d 761/Tex (1973).

A conspirator is the accomplice of his coconspirator in a prosecution for either the conspiracy or the crime committed pursuant to the conspiracy. *People v Doble*, 265 P 184/Cal (1928).

Corroboration

In some jurisdictions today, as was the case under the common law, the testimony of an accomplice alone, if believed by the jury, is sufficient for conviction. Such is the case under federal law (*United States v Castro*, 476 F 2d 750/Cal–1973); *(United States v Ross*, 477 F 2d 551/Mich–1973), and unless abridged by statute, the common law rule prevails.

In Pennsylvania the uncorroborated testimony of an accomplice is sufficient evidence for a conviction; therefore it would be inconsistent to hold that information supplied by a confessed accomplice is an insufficient basis for a probable cause arrest (*Com v Bradley*, 295 A 2d 842/Pa–1972). But in Oklahoma the courts have held that the testimony of an accomplice is not worthy of belief, and in the absence of other evidence against defendant tending to connect him in the commission of the offense, he is entitled to an acquittal. *Kirby v State*, 505 P 2d 504/Ok (1973).

Evidence corroborating the testimony of an accomplice need not be sufficient standing alone to sustain conviction *(King v State*, 494 SE 2d 476/Ark–1973). The corroboration must come from some source other than the testimony of the accomplice but it may *not* come from the testimony of a second accomplice. *People v Randono*, 108 CR 326/Cal (1973).

Slight evidence, circumstantial or direct, from an extraneous source identifying the accused as a participant in the criminal act is sufficient corroboration of an accomplice to support a verdict. *Hutchins v State*, 194 SE 2d 442/Ga (1972).

Who Are Not Accomplices

An accessory after the fact is not an accomplice (*Pennington v State*, 478 SW 2d 892/Ten–1971); (*Alvarez v State*, 478 SW 2d 450/Tex–1972), nor a child under the age of consent who is a victim of child molestation (*Young v State*, 186 SE 2d 805/Ga–1971); *State v Goff*, 195 NW 2d 521/SD (1972).

The giver of a bribe is not the accomplice of the receiver; the receiver or disposer of stolen property is not the accomplice of the thief who stole the property; a police informer who was recruited by police to purchase narcotics is exempt from prosecution therefor and is not the accomplice of the seller; a sixteen-year-old prostitute who gave her earnings as a prostitute to her pimp is not an accomplice to defendant in a prosecution for pimping and statutory rape; a person knowingly harboring and concealing a felon after the commission of crime is an accessory and not an accomplice; a narcotics officer who, pursuant to undercover assignment, purchased a marijuana cigarette, accompanied a group to a house and there "puffed" on the cigarette is not the accomplice of defendants as feigned complicity is not complicity within the law relating to accomplices. Vol 1A *Words and Phrases*, at pp. 14-16.

The purchaser or user of heroin is not the accomplice of the seller, in a prosecution of defendant for the sale of heroin, and if believed by the trier of fact when he testifies that by the effect of a substance purchased from the seller he knew it to be heroin, conviction will lie. *Howard v State*, 496 P 2d 657/Alk (1972).

Feigned Complicity

One who feigns complicity in a crime in order to secure evidence to prosecute the offender is not required to take an officer into his confidence to avoid imputation of criminal intent. *People v Emmons*, 95 P 1032/Cal (1908).

A government agent who purchases heroin from a dealer in order to secure evidence is not subject to prosecution and is not an accomplice of the dealer (*Howard v State*, 496 P 2d 657/Alk–1972), nor is an undercover aide of police an accomplice within the meaning of the rule requiring testimonial corroboration. *Guerrero v State*, 507 SW 2d 765/Tex (1974).

Coercive Sodomy

In a prosecution for sodomy where one participates in the act under threats of immediate and great bodily harm, he is not an accomplice in the act and his testimony need not be corroborated. *Sier v State*, 517 P 2d 803/Ok (1973).

The question of whether a twelve-year-old boy was an accomplice to an act of fellatio committed upon him thus necessitating corroboration to sustain conviction was a question for the jury; here, the jury viewed the boy as the victim of a sexually perverse act, on whose testimony alone defendant could legally be convicted. *State v Taylor*, 512 P 2d 590/Az (1973).

If resistance to an act of sodomy was prevented by threats or other coercive conduct, then the act was not done voluntarily although the party seemingly assented. "Consent" differs materially from "assent." The former implies some positive action and always involves submission; the latter means passivity or submission but without consent. Therefore, one forced or coerced into an act of sodomy, although seemingly assenting, is not an accomplice and defendant may be convicted on victim's uncorroborated testimony. *Perryman v State*, 12 SE 2d 388/Ga (1940).

Victim of Incest

Where defendant was charged with incest with his 15-year-old daughter, her uncorroborated testimony would be insufficient evidence to sustain conviction if she were a willing participant under Tennessee law (*Henley v State*, 489 SW 2d 53/Ten–1972). In most states, however, the age of consent is 18 and extramarital sex relations with a female is either statutory rape or carnal knowledge, even though the female is a willing participant. And if the participants are closely related by consanguinity, the crime is incest. Traditionally, the female has been viewed as the victim although her male coparticipant may also be under the age of 18 years.

Where prosecutrix, the 13-year-old daughter of defendant, testified that she had sexual relations with her father under the inducement of hamburgers, groceries and other favors, and there was no evidence that force or coercion was used, the prosecutrix, under Texas law, was an accomplice in defendant's prosecution for incest and defendant could not be convicted on her uncorroborated testimony. *Bolin v State*, 505 SW 2d 912/Tex (1973).

Competency and Immunity of Witnesses

A witness immunity act, which provides for the immunity of a witness who testifies for the state, amounts to a promise that the witness will testify as he has indicated and if he testifies contrary to previous statements he is entitled to no immunity. *People v Brunner*, 108 CR 501/Cal (1973).

The fact that an accomplice hopes or expects that he will ameliorate his position and receive a lighter sentence in exchange for his testimony against a coprincipal does not disqualify him (*People v Taylor*, 207 NW 2d 899/Mich–1973). Under a particular state law, defendant may be convicted solely upon the testimony of an accomplice, or under the alternative rule that the testimony of an accomplice be corroborated by such other evidence as tends to connect defendant with the commission of the offense, an accomplice is a competent witness. *Martin v State*, 279 NE 2d 189/Ind (1972).

Where different inferences may be drawn from the evidence, the jury may decide whether the state's witness is an accomplice; if there is no conflict in the evidence, the question is one of law for the court to decide, and whether or not the accomplice is corroborated by other evidence is one of fact for the jury. *State v Fitzgerald*, 513 P 2d 817/Or (1973).

ACCESSORY

"After the Fact" and "Before the Fact" Distinguished

"Accessory before the fact" and "accessory after the fact" state separate and distinct crimes. In most jurisdictions an accessory after the fact cannot be charged as a principal while accessory before the fact is a principal. *State v Wyatt,* 192 SE 2d 683/NC (1972).

The offense of accessory before the fact involves counseling, hiring or otherwise procuring, which goes beyond mere acquiescence, but does not require physical participation. *Com v Morrow,* 296 NE 2d 468/Mas (1973).

"After the Fact" Defined

An accessory after the fact is one who after a felony has been committed, knowingly harbors or conceals or renders personal assistance to such felon, or in any manner aids him to evade arrest or escape punishment. *State v Williams,* 193 SE 2d 452/NC (1972).

American Jurisprudence defines accessories as follows:

> At common law, an accessory after the fact is one who, knowing that a felony had been committed by another, receives, relieves, comforts, or assists the felon, or in any manner aids him to escape arrest or punishment. This is similar to statutory definitions. Mere failure to reveal knowledge that a person had committed a felony did not make one an accessory after the fact at common law; but the rule may be made otherwise by statute. Accessories After The Fact, 21 *Am Jur 2d* § 126.

"After the commission of a felony," as used in the definition of accessories, has been defined as "any felony," including those committed outside the state of venue. *Goldsmith v Cheney,* 468 P 2d 813/Wyo (1970).

The gist of the crime of accessory after the fact lies essentially in the obstruction of justice by rendering assistance to the principal in order to hinder or prevent the arrest of the offender after he has committed the crime. The very definition of the crime also requires that the felony not be in progress at the time the assistance is rendered as such assistance would make the party a principal rather than an accessory. *United States v Barlow,* 470 F 2d 1245/DC (1972).

"Before the Fact" Defined

Accessory may be designated as two different types of participation in crime. In some states the degrees of principality, i.e., principals of the first and second degrees and accessories before the fact, have been abrogated and included in one designation—that simply of principals. In Kansas principals of the second degree and accessories before the fact are guilty of the crime charged and to the same extent as a principal of the first degree (*State v Ridge*, 491 P 2d 900/Kan–1971). North Carolina, among others, holds that an accessory before the fact is one who, although absent at the time and place of the crime, procured, counseled, commanded or encouraged its commission. *State v Wyatt*, 192 SE 2d 683/NC (1972).

Where Efforts Are Ineffectual

An accessory's act is criminal because it is calculated to frustrate the administration of justice, and where there is proof of an overt act plus an unlawful intent to conceal the perpetrator in crime, there is sufficient evidence of the crime of accessory and it is immaterial that defendant's act did not, in fact, frustrate the police investigation or their efforts to arrest. *State v Clifford*, 495 P 2d 49/Or (1972).

It is not essential to the crime of accessory that assistance be rendered personally to the principal, as assistance furnished through an intermediary will constitute the offense. Nor is it necessary that the one assisted shall have escaped or evaded capture, but only that the actor did some positive, affirmative act intended to aid the principal to escape arrest, trial or punishment. One who knowingly warns the principal of the approach of officers when the principal is in hiding or concealment, or who keeps the felon secreted and loans him money or who lodges, gives refuge or shelter to a felon, is guilty of the crime of accessory. Vol 22 *Corpus Juris Secundum*, § 95.

Examples

Defendant was convicted of accessory to murder where the evidence showed that he knowingly aided the murderer in the disposal of the body by burial; and the murderer, having aided and abetted the accessory thus became an accessory to the murder he committed. *People v Wallin*, 197 P 2d 734/Cal (1949).

Where evidence showed that defendant lied when asked by detectives whether he had seen a named felon, there was sufficient "concealment" or "aid" to warrant submission of the cause to the jury and to sustain conviction as an accessory to such felony. *State v Clifford*, 491 P 2d 1195/Or (1971).

Where defendant told hospital authorities that a child had sustained fatal injuries in a fall though she knew the child had been murdered, she inculpated herself as an accessory after the fact to murder. *Prine v State*, 509 SW 2d 617/Tex (1974).

Mere passive failure to disclose the commission of a crime does not make a person an accessory after the fact (*Satterfield v State*, 483 SW 2d 171/Ark–1972). Nor was evidence that defendant lied when asked by police whether he had seen a named felon of itself sufficient to support a verdict of guilty of accessory. The state must also prove defendant's knowledge of the felony. *State v Clifford, supra.*

Criminal Responsibility

The responsibility of an accessory after the fact is measured by the nature of the felony committed by the principal and not by the punishment imposed on the principal. In most jurisdictions there can be no accessory after the fact to a misdemeanor (*State v Clifford, supra*), but unless the designation of accessory before the fact has been abolished there may be an accessory *before* the fact to any crime.

To convict of the crime of accessory there must be sufficient evidence to establish that there was, in fact, a principal guilty of the crime, although it is inconsequential whether or not the principal was ever charged. *Britto v People*, 497 P 2d 325/Colo (1972).

PRINCIPALS

Defined

All persons concerned with the commission of a crime—whether they directly commit the act constituting the offense, or aid and abet in its commission—are responsible as "principals" if it can be said they acted in furtherance of the common design. *Hall v State*, 503 P 2d 229/Ok (1972).

At common law the actual perpetrator of the crime was a principal in the first degree; one who was present and actively aided and abetted in the commission of the crime was a principal in the second degree; and one who, although absent at the time the crime was committed, had procured, counseled or commanded another to commit crime was an accessory before the fact. *People v Ah Gee*, 174 P 371/Cal (1918).

Most jurisdictions by statute have abrogated the distinction between accessory before the fact and principal, and treat all persons concerned in the commission of crime as principals, whether they directly commit the proscribed act, or aid and abet in its commission, or counsel, encourage or advise another in its commission. *Wilson v State*, 306 P 2d 717/Ok (1957).

To "aid" only, does not imply guilty knowledge of the wrongful purpose of the perpetrator, but to "abet" does so imply, and includes counsel and encouragement in the commission of the crime. *State v Hinkley*, 325 P 2d 889/Wn (1958).

Participants in the commission of misdemeanors are principals, and the grade of the object crime has no bearing on one's principality. *State v Sears*, 296 A 2d 218/Vt (1972).

Acts Constituting Principality

To sustain conviction for aiding and abetting there must be evidence that the accused knowingly associated himself in some way with the criminal venture, that he participated in it as something he wished to bring about and sought by his actions to make it succeed (*United States v Barlow*, 470 F 2d 1245/DC–1972). But it is not material to consider the amount of advice or encouragement rendered if the net result was to induce the commission of crime. *People v Wright*, 205 NW 2d 62/Mich (1972).

The advice or encouragement which will render one an accessory before the fact may be acts or words, but whatever means of communication are employed they must have been used to encourage and abet the crime. *State v Alvarez*, 202 NW 2d 600/Neb (1972).

To share the guilt with the principal by aiding and abetting, one must share the criminal intent with the principal; there must be a community of purpose in the unlawful undertaking. Aiding and abetting may be shown by evidence of acts, conduct, words, signs or any means sufficient to incite, encourage or instigate the commission of the offense. *State v Atwood*, 492 P 2d 1279/NM (1972).

One who solicits another to commit crime which is thereby committed, is a principal. *People v Harper*, 156 P 2d 249/Cal (1945).

When Abettor's Role Is Small

Where one aided and abetted in the commission of a crime it is no defense that his role therein was small and his participation slight, nor would such participation be a mitigating circumstance. One is either guilty of the crime charged as a principal, or not guilty. Thus, one who played a small part in larceny or burglary is just as guilty in the eyes of the law by aiding and abetting as who played a major role or was the ringleader. *Dawson v Peyton*, 246 FS 444/affirmed 359 F 2d 149/Va (1965).

Where evidence showed that appellant and others committed a robbery and appellant's only participation was to secure a gun and four cartridges to be used in the robbery, she was deemed to have assumed criminal responsibility for the natural and probable consequences for the undertaking including kidnaping, although no kidnaping was contemplated (*People v Simpson*, 152 P 2d 339/Cal–1944). And where defendant's only participation in a bank robbery was to meet his two coprincipals after the robbery as per prearrangement for the purpose of facilitating their escape, he was guilty of robbery by aiding and abetting and not of the crime of accessory. *United States v Burkeen*, 350 F 2d 261/Ten (1965).

Driver of Getaway Car

One who remains in an automobile and enables or assists others who do the actual robbing to make a successful getaway, is as much a principal as though he were present and assisting in the taking of property (*People v Dills*, 340 P 2d 273/Cal–1959). Where one of three robbers remained in the getaway car while the other two committed a robbery wherein one of the two robbers was killed by the victim's wife, both of the surviving robbers were guilty of robbery and statutory first degree murder notwithstanding that the driver of the getaway car fled when the shooting started, leaving the other surviving robber to his own device. *Taylor v Superior Court*, 477 P 2d 131/Cal (1970).

Where defendant drove the getaway car but did not enter the premises where a beating and murder was committed, his participation was nevertheless sufficient to warrant conviction of first degree murder with a penalty of death by electrocution; however, the penalty was mitigated to life imprisonment on appeal. *Lewis v State*, 415 P 2d 399/Ok (1967).

Acting As a Lookout

Acting as a "lookout" for a coprincipal constitutes aiding and abetting and thus seals one's complicity in the crime (*State v Naples*, 319 P 2d 1096/Wn–1958. Where defendant was asked by a confederate to watch out for police while he robbed a taxicab driver and defendant complied, he was guilty of robbery and murder committed in the course thereof even though he did not intend nor anticipate the taking of life. *People v Murphy*, 308 NE 2d 235/Ill (1974).

Conviction of first degree murder was sustained against defendant where his only participation in the crime was to act as a lookout for his coparticipant who entered an attic with the victim allegedly to engage in an act of sex perversion, but when the victim removed his clothing in apparent preparation for the act, defendant "commenced cutting," fatally wounding victim. *State v Rivenburgh*, 355 P 2d 689/Certiorari denied 368 US 922/Ut (1960).

For a conviction of an accomplice of aiding and abetting rape, it is not necessary that he personally accomplish penetration. Where defendant acted as a lookout, although he did not otherwise participate, he did render aid and generally encourage the rape which furnished sound factual basis for his conviction. *Com v Morrow*, 296 NE 468/Mas (1963).

Aiding and Abetting Rape

There are some crimes which cannot be committed by a particular person or class of persons when acting alone and unaided, but which can be committed when acting in concert with another. Thus, a husband cannot commit rape upon his wife, nor can one woman commit rape upon another when acting alone. But a husband may be convicted of the rape of his wife where he aids and abets another in the commission of an act of forcible sexual intercourse upon his wife against her will and without her consent (*State v Blockwell*, 407 P 2d 617/Or–1962); (*Cody v State*, 376 P 2d 625/Ok–1962), and the acquittal of defendant who actually ravished a female would not foreclose conviction of her husband who held her while she was sexually assaulted (*Rozell v State*, 502 SW 2d 16/Tex–1973). Similarly, a mother may be convicted of the rape of her daughter where she aids and abets the principal perpetrator. *People v Haywood*, 280 P 2d 180/Cal (1955).

Defendant's participation, which consisted of encouraging two minors to disrobe and engage in an act of sexual intercourse while he photographed their activity, warranted his conviction of statutory rape as a principal. *People v Lewis*, 248 P 2d 461/Cal (1952).

Where defendant, with knowledge that a female was unmarried and under the age of eighteen years, procured a room for her and a male companion, knowing the room was to be used for an act of sexual intercourse, he was guilty of statutory rape notwithstanding that the principal was never tried, instead testifying against his aider and abettor as a witness for the state. *People v Wood*, 205 P 698/Cal (1922).

Presence at Scene

Where presence, actual or constructive, is an element to second degree principality, the actual distance of the principal from the scene of the crime is not always material to "constructive" presence (*State v Wiggins*, 192 SE 2d 680/NC–1972). The fact that defendant was not physically present at a bank robbery did not preclude his conviction as an aider and abettor of the offense of aggravated bank robbery by assaulting or jeopardizing lives. *United States v Waters*, 461 F 2d 248/Kan (1972).

For one to be guilty of aiding and abetting by his presence at the scene of the crime, he must be ready to assist by physical aid or counsel or the very fact of his presence must assist. *State v Broxton*, 516 P 2d 771/Wn (1973).

Where defendant has present and actively participating in a jail break during which activity a jailor was cut, he was a principal in the offense of malicious cutting although neither he nor his knife did the cutting. *Smith v Com*, 473 SW 2d 829/Ky (1971).

The mere witnessing of a crime without intervention does not make one a party thereto unless it was his duty to interfere or unless his noninterference was designed to and did operate as an encouragement or protection to the perpetrator (*State v Haines*, 192 SE 2d 879/W Va–1972). Nor does mere association with one who perpetrates an unlawful act render him *particeps criminis* so long as his acts are innocent. *State v Clifton*, 290 NE 2d 921/Oh (1972).

In the absence of evidence that defendant assisted, advised or encouraged the principal in any way, a conviction could not stand where defendant's only participation was to accompany the principal to the building where a rape occurred but he was not present in the room at the time of the alleged act (*State v Spillman*, 468 P 2d 376/Az–1970); but absence from the scene at the time of the crime will not assure acquittal since defendant may be guilty by counseling, advising or encouraging. *Nichols v Vance*, 293 FS 680/Tex (1968).

Examples

Where several persons participate in a robbery, it is immaterial which one takes the property as all are equally guilty of robbery (*Gibson v State*, 268 S 2d 49/Ala–1972), and likewise, where one suspect holds a knife to victim's throat while the other removes his wallet, it is immaterial who held the knife as each is equally guilty of armed robbery. *Shows v State*, 267 S 2d 811/Mis (1972).

Defendant was properly convicted as a principal where he was proved to have furnished at least 20 sets of false identification used to facilitate the passing of forged government bonds (*United States v Calaboro*, 467 F 2d 97/NY–1972). Likewise, defendant was convicted of forgery where he "vouched" for another who uttered a forged United States Treasury check, knowing the endorsement on the check was a forgery. *United States v Kane*, 322 F 2d 787/NY (1963).

One aiding a bookmaker in contacting his patrons as proprietor of a telephonic relay spot makes him a principal to the crime of bookmaking (*People v Allen*, 248 P 2d 474/Cal–1941), and a "lay-off" man with whom the bookie rebets all or part of his customers' bets at higher odds than he gives his customers, is a principal in an illegal bookmaking scheme. *People v Oreck*, 168 P 2d 186/Cal (1946).

One does not have to share in the proceeds from a crime to be guilty of that crime. *United States v Powers*, 467 F 2d 1089/Ill (1972).

Minimum Essential Proof

The federal appellate court for Washington, D.C., has ruled–and holds with the majority of jurisdictions–that in order to convict an aider and abettor, all that is necessary antecedent thereto is proof that the crime was committed by someone; it is not necessary that the principal be tried and convicted or even identified (*United States v Clearfield*, 358 FS 564/DC–1973); and the fact that the perpetrator was allowed to plead guilty to a lesser offense would not preclude defendant's conviction as an accessory before the fact (*Combs v State*, 295 NE 2d 366/Ind–1973). However, under North Carolina law, which illustrates the minority holding, conviction of an aider and abettor cannot stand unless the principal perpetrator was tried and convicted. *State v Spencer*, 197 SE 2d 232/NC (1973).

PART II

ARREST, SEARCH AND SEIZURE

Chapter VII

Arrest

ARRESTS BY OFFICERS

Defined

There are two common views of "arrest"; one is that it is the lawful taking of a person into custody in order that he may be forthcoming to answer for the commission of an alleged crime; the other view is that an arrest is any act that indicates an intention to take a person into custody and that subjects him to the actual control and will of the person making the arrest. Thus, a deprivation or restraint of a person's liberty, whether or not it culminates in criminal charges being filed, is an arrest (*Miles v Com*, 304 A 2d 704/Pa–1973). Arrest signifies restraint of the person depriving him of his own will and liberty (*People v PAJ Theater Corp*, 339 NYS 2d 152/NY–1972). For an arrest to be lawful the officer must have arrested under the authority of a warrant or have had reasonable or probable cause to believe the person arrested had committed or was committing a crime. *State v Glick*, 201 NW 2d 867/SD (1972).

An arrest involves three elements: (1) authority to arrest; (2) assertion of that authority with intention to effect arrest, and (3) restraint of the person to be arrested. A conversation between a police officer and a citizen is not a restraint of liberty nor is one under arrest when commanded by a police officer to stop. *People v Colon*, 293 NE 2d 468/Ill (1973).

To arrest is of greater consequence than to "stop and frisk," and must be more narrowly circumscribed lest an innocent error be inflated into a major disturbance. *People v Curtis*, 450 P 2d 33/Cal (1969).

A presumption as to the legality of an arrest by an officer exists unless and until challenged; then the presumption is removed and the state must justify the arrest. *Irwin v Dept of Motor Vehicles*, 517 P 2d 619/Wn (1974).

How Made

To constitute an arrest there must be an actual or constructive detention with intention to do so and understood to be so by the person restrained. The arrest need not be preceded by formal words nor followed by stationhouse booking; any restraint, however slight, upon the personal liberty of another to go and come as he chooses is an arrest. *United States v Jones*, 352 FS 369/Ga (1972).

When making an arrest without a warrant, in order to foreclose the possibility of an action for false imprisonment, an officer should inform an arrestee of his authority to arrest and the reason therefor unless the arrestee is then engaged in the commission of a crime (*Beard v Stevens*, 372 F 2d 685/Ala–1967). But a failure by an officer to inform an arrestee of the reason for arrest did not vitiate an otherwise valid felony arrest when the arrestee knew the person arresting was an officer acting in his official capacity (*Wafers v State*, 444 P 2d 825/Ok–1968); nor is an otherwise legal arrest nullified merely because an officer indicates another and improper cause for the arrest. *State v Cloman*, 456 P 2d 67/Or (1969).

An officer is not required to inform an arrestee who is arrested in the commission of a crime why he has been arrested, such as where arrestee stepped into the street close to a police cruiser car in which two officers were riding and through a megaphone shouted, "Pig. White Pig. Sooey, sooey," which act, under Florida law, amounted to verbally abusing a police officer in line of duty (*City of St Petersburg v Waller*, 261 S 2d 151/Fla–1972). Nor are officers required to inform arrestee of the reason for arrest when in flight from the scene immediately after the commission of crime. *State v Anknev*, 195 NW 2d 547/ND (1972).

The validity of an arrest does not depend on words used by the arresting officer as no particular words need be spoken; furthermore, no word need be spoken when the arresting person's intent is obvious. *Taylor v State*, 313 NE 2d 92/Ind (1974).

When Made

Although a peace officer's powers of arrest are not identical in all states, they generally conform to those prescribed by the California Penal Code. They are:

> A peace officer may make an arrest in obedience to a warrant, or may, without a warrant, arrest a person:
>
> 1. Whenever he has reasonable cause to believe that the person to be arrested has committed a public offense in his presence.

2. When a person arrested has committed a felony, although not in his presence.
3. Whenever he has reasonable cause to believe that the person to be arrested has committed a felony, whether or not a felony has in fact been committed. California Penal Code, § 836.

An officer may arrest any person without a warrant, on any day and at any time, for any public offense committed in his presence. And in all cases of attempted legal arrest an officer is under a duty to act aggressively and go forward in perfecting the arrest; he may repel force with force and need not retreat nor desist. *Weeks v State*, 274 S 2d 646/Ala (1973).

An arrest may occur although the word "arrest" is not used by the officer, and where the arresting officer saw the suspect of a recent rape jump over a fence and start across a yard and the officer drew his pistol and ordered the suspect to halt, whereupon suspect halted and returned to the sidewalk, he was under legal arrest. It is actual restraint or consent to restraint that constitutes an arrest. *McDonald v State*, 491 SW 2d 36/Ark (1973).

A difference exists between an arrest and a "taking into custody," the difference being that an arrest properly made is for the violation of some law and contemplates charging the arrestee with the crime committed, while a mere taking into custody may be protective only, and may contemplate no criminal charge. *State v Hough*, 515 P 2d 613/Mont (1973).

For the purpose of determining arrest, defendant was arrested when taken into custody, told to place his hands on top of a vehicle and searched, not after narcotics was found on his person and he was told formally that he was under arrest. *State v Hutton*, 505 P 2d 263/Az (1973).

The mere "curbing" of a car does not constitute an arrest of the driver; there must be authority to arrest, assertion of that authority and restraint of the person to be arrested. *People v Colon*, 293 NE 2d 468/Ill (1973).

Some states have enacted legislation authorizing the arrest of a person by a peace officer when there is reasonable cause to believe he has committed, is committing or *about to commit* a felony. Also, some appellate courts have upheld on appeal an arrest of one believed "about to commit" a felony, although not supported by legislation. It is reasonable to assume that such an arrest would be upheld in all cases especially a felony endangering life or property. *State v Johnson*, 201 SE 2d 309/W Va (1973); *State v Baxter*, 413 P 2d 638/Wn (1966); *Dotson v State*, 389 P 2d 77/Nev (1964); *People v Dallen*, 132 P 1064/Cal (1913).

"In His Presence" Defined

An officer, without a warrant, may arrest one who commits a misdemeanor in his presence; further, he may arrest if he has reasonable cause to believe that a misdemeanor has been or is being committed in his presence if circumstances are such as to induce such belief in the mind of a reasonable person (*People v Dixon*, 205 NW 2d 852/Mich–1973). Thus, where officers saw defendant standing beside another who broke a window to a clothing store and who left the scene as officers cruised by, and about 15 minutes later both subjects were seen together in a restaurant, officers had reasonable grounds to believe that the second subject had aided and abetted the first, at least in the misdemeanor crime of window breaking. *State v Gibson*, 190 SE 2d 315/NC (1972).

The phrase "in his presence" has been defined as not mere physical proximity but when the commission of the crime was apparent to the officer's senses, which include, in addition to vision, hearing and smell. A public offense may be committed within the "presence" of an officer when his auditory perception is activated by an electronic device. *People v Burgess*, 338 P 2d 524/Cal (1959).

Distinctive odor of marijuana in an automobile furnishes probable cause to arrest for a crime committed in the officer's presence (*People v Parisi*, 208 NW 2d 70/Mich–1973), as does surveillance through the use of binoculars. *State v Jones*, 193 SE 2d 314/NC (1972).

Permissible Force

Deadly force may be used if necessary to effect an arrest after the commission of a felony or when there is reasonable cause to believe, and the officer does believe, that the arrestee has committed a felony (*Reese v City of Seattle*, 503 P 2d 64/Wn–1972). But the officer has no right, absent resistance or flight, to use force or violence regardless of the crime committed; nor does an officer have the right to use a deadly weapon upon one whom he is attempting to arrest for a misdemeanor when such person does not resist but merely flees. *Carter v State*, 507 P 2d 932/Ok (1973).

Probable Cause to Arrest

"Probable cause to arrest" is defined as facts and circumstances within the knowledge of authorities of which they have reasonably trustworthy information which would warrant a man of reasonable caution to believe a suspect had committed a crime. *Com v Kenney*, 297 A 2d 794/Pa (1972).

No exact or precise formula exists to determine probable cause to believe a person has committed a felony thus justifying arrest. Each case must be decided on its own merits which include facts and circumstances surrounding the case at the time officers elected to act. *People v Ross*, 429 P 2d 606/Cal (1967).

The rule of probable cause is a practical, nontechnical concept affording the best compromise that has been found for accommodating often opposing interests, and to require more would unduly hamper law enforcement efforts; to allow less would be to leave law-abiding citizens at the mercy of the officer's whim or caprice. *Beck v Ohio*, 379 US 89/Oh (1964).

Probable cause to arrest is not to be evaluated from the remote vantage point of the library, but from the viewpoint of a prudent and cautious police officer on the scene at the time; the question raised is whether such officer, under particular circumstances, conditioned by his observations and information and guided by the whole of his police experience reasonably could have believed that some crime had been committed by the person arrested (*McWilliams v United States*, 298 A 2d 38/DC–1972). Bare suspicion is not enough to justify a warrantless arrest. *State v Whorton*, 487 SW 2d 865/Mo (1972).

In assessing probable cause to arrest, the qualification and training of the person making the arrest is pertinent. The acts of a narcotics officer in making an arrest for a narcotics violation will not be measured by the standards of an untrained citizen, nor a civilian passerby, but by a standard appropriate for the reasonable and prudent narcotics officer (*State v Poe*, 445 P 2d 196/Wn–1968). Thus, where an experienced narcotics officer—knowing that narcotics users often carry narcotics in toy balloons so that it may be swallowed when there is danger of detection—and the officer saw defendant, a known narcotics user, seized by a fit of coughing and choking, cough up a toy balloon into a handkerchief and then run for his residence, there was probable cause to arrest. *Foy v State*, 436 P 2d 811/Nev (1968).

No less is required for probable cause to arrest without a warrant than is required to justify the issuance of a warrant (*Untied States v Bosch*, 209 FS 15/Mich–1962); and the fact that officers have sufficient time prior to the arrest to obtain a warrant of arrest has no bearing on the validity of the arrest. *King v Pinto*, 256 FS 522/affirmed 376 F 2d 593/NJ (1966).

The standard which governs arrest does not require proof enough to convict, and an arrest may be valid although there is insufficient evidence of crime for the prosecutor to hold a preliminary hearing (*Von Sleichter v United States*, 472 F 2d 1244/DC–1972). Nor is it necessary that probable cause to arrest be based on evidence which would be admissible in a criminal proceeding; evidence based on hearsay alone may constitute probable cause to arrest (*People v Smith*, 323 P 2d 435/Cal–1958). The hearsay evidence rule applies only to judicial proceedings during the trial, and officers may rely on hearsay evidence in building probable cause to either search or arrest. *Brown v People*, 375 P 2d 675/Colo (1962).

The legality of an arrest depends upon the existence of probable cause to arrest which must have existed at the time of arrest, and cannot be justified by evidence uncovered in an ensuing search. *People v Garafolo*, 353 NYS 500/NY (1974).

The reputation of the accused, if known to the officer, may be taken into consideration in determining probable cause to arrest. *Leroux v State*, 207 NW 2d 589/Wis (1973).

Prompt on-the-scene confrontation of the suspect in a crime before the complaining party is not unduly suggestive and not a violation of due process. *State v Salcido,* 509 P 2d 1027/Az (1973).

Probable cause to arrest is a question of mixed law and fact; the court submits the evidence to the jury with instructions as to what facts, when proved, will amount to probable cause. The question is not whether the person arresting thought the facts constituted probable cause but whether the court thinks they did. *Director General of Railroads v Kastenbaum,* 263 US 24/NY (1923).

Examples of Probable Cause to Arrest

Usually when one tells an officer he is committing a crime the officer may assume he is telling the truth, and where an undercover officer asked the accused for heroin and the accused answered that he had some but it was for his own use, then ran from the officer, his arrest was justified. *State v Durham,* 495 P 2d 463/Az (1972).

Under a statute which made it a felony to willfully and maliciously damage property in excess of $100, officers had probable cause to arrest defendant for pouring sugar into the gas tank of another's automobile even though damage was later determined to be less than $100. *People v Roberson,* 205 NW 2d 50/Mich (1972).

Where officers found an abandoned stolen vehicle and followed fresh bootprints in the snow to defendant's house and were admitted by defendant's mother, they had probable cause to arrest defendant who was asleep in the basement; his boots beside his bed and evidence found in an incident search was admissible. *State v Lewis,* 201 NW 2d 397/SD (1972).

A police officer was justified in arresting a customer in a tavern where the bartender had stated to police that she wanted to sign a complaint against the customer for disorderly conduct, and thereupon pointed him out to the officers. *People v Foss,* 309 NE 2d 677/Ill (1974).

Misdemeanor Arrests

Most jurisdictions restrict a peace officer's powers of arrest for a misdemeanor to occasions where the crime was perceived by the officer or he has reasonable cause to believe he perceived the crime, and if officers arrive at the scene of an accident not having seen defendant driving prior thereto, they cannot legally arrest him for driving while intoxicated. However, if officers did arrest defendant illegally, evidence obtained in the investigation, if otherwise admissible, is not rendered inadmissible merely because defendant was arrested illegally. Furthermore, had the circumstances warranted the conclusion that defendant was drunk in public view he could have been arrested on that charge if committed in the presence of the officers. *Farnsworth v State,* 343 P 2d 744/Ok (1959).

As a rule, a police officer may make a warrantless arrest for a misdemeanor only when there is reasonable cause to believe the crime "*is being committed in his presence*" (*Com v Reeves,* 297 A 2d 142/Pa–1972), but this restriction, if it exists, is a statutory restriction only, there being no constitutional prohibition against such arrests. *Street v Surdyka,* 492 F 2d 368/Md (1974).

Suspicion that a misdemeanor has been or is about to be committed does not justify an arrest. *State v Thomas,* 203 SE 2d 445/W Va (1974).

Flight

The flight of one upon observing the approach of officers is a factor in establishing probable cause for arrest (*Green v State,* 194 SE 2d 678/Ga–1972), and may indicate a consciousness of guilt, but flight alone is not sufficient probable cause to arrest. *Com v Pegram,* 301 A 2d 695/Pa (1973).

Although flight combined with other facts may provide probable cause for arrest, if flight was a direct response to unlawful police action it becomes "tainted" and cannot be used. *In re V,* 517 P 2d 1145/Cal (1974).

A beat officer, upon observing what he suspected of being a transfer of narcotics from defendant to another, walked toward defendant and called out, "I would like to talk to you a minute," in response to which defendant, within the hearing of pedestrians, shouted a four-letter expletive and ran; the officer had probable cause to arrest defendant for disorderly conduct, and the ensuing search for weapons which produced a bag of heroin was lawful. *Von Sleichter v United States,* 472 F 2d 1244/DC (1972).

Police officers who saw defendant running and heard a bystander "hollering, 'stop, thief,'" had probable cause to arrest the defendant at that time, and it was not necessary that officers first locate the victim of the theft. *State v Franklin,* 452 P 2d 498/Az (1969).

Official Information Sources

Information upon which an arrest may be predicated is "reasonably trustworthy" when arresting officers receive such information through official police sources (*State v Williams,* 452 P 2d 112/Az–1969); an official police communication such as an all-points bulletin provides probable cause to arrest provided the communication was based on probable cause. *State v Deschamps,* 495 P 2d 18/Id (1972).

Kansas officers had probable cause to arrest defendant upon information received via an all-points bulletin sent by Colorado officers alleging robbery and describing the escape vehicle used by the robber. *People v Duncan,* 500 P 2d 137/Colo (1972).

Where an officer who received by radio a description of an armed suspect sitting in a booth in a restaurant, entered the restaurant and observed the described suspect, he was justified in placing his own gun at suspect's side and seizing suspect's gun from beneath his coat. *Murphy v United States,* 293 A 2d 849/DC (1972).

Information From Other Officers

In determining probable cause for arrest, an officer may act upon information received from another officer who is working with him, or a police radio broadcast (*People v Wrona,* 286 NE 2d 370/Ill–1972), the test being the information known to the officer who requests a second officer to make the arrest. *Piper v State,* 484 SW 2d 776/Tex (1972).

Where one officer arrests upon the direction of another, and the officer arresting lacks sufficient probable cause to arrest, the state must show evidence upon which the directing officer acted. *Collins v State,* 302 A 2d 693/Md (1973).

In a large metropolitan police department the collective knowledge of the organization as a whole can be imputed to an individual officer for the purpose of establishing probable cause when he is requested or authorized by superiors or associates to make an arrest. *United States v Canieso,* 470 F 2d 1224/NY (1972).

Voluntary Admissions

Where defendant voluntarily made incriminating statements at a police station which were not in response to questions by the police, the statements were admissible although defendant had not been advised of his constitutional rights (*Burns v State,* 495 P 2d 602/Nev–1972), and an in-custody statement does not become a product of in-custody interrogation simply because an officer asks arrestee to explain a statement which had been made voluntarily. *State v Haddock,* 190 SE 2d 208/NC (1972).

Defendant's statement, voluntarily made as he entered a police car, that he "can't afford this pinch," was no less voluntary because he was in custody. *People v Valiquet,* 293 NE 2d 670/Ill (1973).

Where defendant approached two officers in a bar and said, "I'm wanted by the FBI in California for bank robbery; I want to give myself up," such statement was not inadmissible on the theory that it was made while in custody and before he had been advised of his constitutional rights. *United States v Katzman,* 461 F 2d 655/Cal (1972).

The defendant, in a statement to police voluntarily made, was designed to exculpate another, was not vitiated by the fact that the statement incriminated him nor was the voluntariness of the statement affected thereby. *United States v Adams,* 470 F 2d 249/Ok (1972).

A confession by one participant in a robbery-murder implicating his coprincipal, establishes sufficient probable cause to arrest the coprincipal. *Com v Kenney,* 297 A 2d 794/Pa (1972).

Admissions by silence or tacit admissions during custodial periods are inadmissible for the purpose of showing guilt as defendant is under no obligation to deny an accusation made by a peace officer (*State v Greer*, 492 P 2d 36/Az–1971). However, if an accusation is made by one other than an administrator of justice, or if, after advisement of constitutional rights and a waiver thereof, tacit admissions are made, they may be admissible. Thus, where arrestee had been advised of his constitutional rights and he thereafter initiated a conversation with a police officer in an attempt to exculpate himself, his admission by silence when confronted with a $100 bill which he had allegedly stolen was admissible against him. *State v O'Dell*, 492 P 2d 1160/Az (1972).

Mistake in Arrest or Booking

When police have probable cause to arrest one person but through an honest mistake of identification they arrest another, and an incident search of the arrestee's apartment discloses incriminating evidence, such arrest is lawful and evidence thus seized is admissible. *People v Hill*, 446 P 2d 521/Cal (1968).

An arrest is not unlawful merely because the arresting officer named a crime for which he had insufficient probable cause to arrest, when he, in fact, was in possession of information which would justify arrest on another charge. *United States v Story*, 463 F 2d 326/Mo (1972).

Knock and Announce and Forcible Entry

A statute which *permits* an officer, in effecting arrest, to break open any outer or inner door or window of any dwelling house or building after notice and purpose has been announced and admittance refused, does not, under the Fourth and Fourteenth Amendments, *require* forcible breaking to enter. *State v Miller*, 499 P 2d 241/Wn (1972).

Notice of authority and purpose are prerequisite to the breaking of a door or window to effect a warrantless arrest, except that an officer may be excused when to knock and announce would (1) increase the officer's peril (2) permit escape, or (3) permit destruction of evidence. Also, it has been held that an officer need not declare his purpose when his purpose is known to the occupant and such announcement would be a useless gesture. *United States v Wylie*, 462 F 2d 1178/DC (1972); *Parsley v Superior Court*, 104 CR 643/Cal (1972); *Ker v California*, 374 US 23 (1963).

The "knock and announce" rule need not be followed where officers are in possession of information which leads them to believe that defendant is armed and dangerous. *State v Petite*, 495 P 2d 785/Or (1972).

A statute which permits officers after "knocking and announcing" to break open any door or window in the execution of a search warrant, also applies to a warrantless arrest. *United States v Bradley*, 455 F 2d 1181/Mas (1972).

Noncompliance With Knock and Announce Rule

Under the knock and announce rule, an officer is not exempted by the fact that the door was open—he must still knock and announce, identify himself, state his mission and demand admittance; and upon being denied admittance he may force entry, or, if the door is open, enter. *People v Buckner,* 111 CR 32/Cal (1973).

Where an officer knocked on the door of an apartment and falsely stated that he was investigating a gas leak, and when the door was opened he saw a plastic bag containing what appeared to be marijuana, seizure of the marijuana was violative of arrestee's constitutional rights and should have been suppressed. *People v Jefferson,* 350 NYS 2d 3/NY (1973).

Arrests of Automobile Drivers

There is contention between legal authorities that a traffic citation does not constitute an arrest, but rather a detention only. Let us examine these two procedures: an *arrest* is the taking of a person into custody for the purpose of holding him or detaining him to answer to a criminal charge *(Black's Law Dictionary)*; *detention* is the brief stopping of an individual to ask him questions, but without sufficient cause to take him into custody. The United States Circuit Court has ruled that brief detention of citizens for investigation is not *ipso facto* unconstitutional, for when the totality of the circumstances warrant the belief that brief detention is necessary to the public safety, such detention will have judicial sanction (*Gilbert v United States,* 366 F 2d 923/Cal–1966). In the first instance the person is taken into custody to answer to a criminal charge; in the second instance he is stopped briefly for the purpose of asking him questions. To stop one for the purpose of issuing a traffic citation contains all the ingredients of arrest, but in most instances he is released upon his written promise to appear—the equivalent of a personal recognizance release. In view of the procedures involved in the issuance of a traffic citation—that the subject has committed an act denounced by law as a crime; that he is deprived of his liberty and charged with a crime to which is annexed a penalty—it seems clear that the issuance of a traffic citation constitutes an arrest which necessarily includes detention.

When the driver of an automobile is stopped for a traffic violation and there are other occupants in the vehicle, although their progress may be interrupted, they are not under arrest and may not be required to remain at the scene absent additional facts warranting such restraint. *Harper v State,* 440 P 2d 893/Nev (1967).

A statute which authorizes a peace officer to issue a summons in lieu of arrest for a misdemeanor, is lawful and enforceable and does not contravene the Constitution. *State v Perry,* 315 A 2d 60/RI (1974).

Delay in Arrest

Usually an arrest must be made forthwith after the commission of crime when an officer has sufficient cause and an opportunity, but when good and sufficient cause exists to delay the arrest and the delay is not unreasonable, the legality of the arrest will not be vitiated by mere delay. *State v McCune*, 201 NW 2d 852/Neb (1972); *State v Hawkins*, 502 P 2d 464/Wn (1972).

Where appellant prosecuted his appeal on the grounds that he was denied due process in not being arrested until seven months after the commission of the crime, the court held in affirming conviction that due to the nature of the investigation—that of narcotics and drug sales and use on a widespread basis—and the fact that to have arrested sooner would have almost certainly frustrated other investigations then in progress, the delay was permissible; that since defendant and others were arrested immediately upon conclusion of the investigation the delay was for a valid police purpose and defendant was not denied due process. *Wilson v United States*, 409 F 2d 184/certiorari denied 395 US 983/Wn (1968).

A six-month delay in the arrest of defendant who sold heroin to a narcotics officer was not shown to be prejudicial to defendant. *Salazar v State*, 492 SW 2d 949/Tex (1973).

A delay in the arrest of a person may constitute grounds for dismissal of action where the delay is unreasonable and without cause; and where officers, though having grounds for arrest, procrastinate for other than good and sufficient reasons, their arrest will be unlawful. Thus, where officers were in possession for several days of sufficient facts to warrant the arrest of defendant for receiving stolen property, and they went to his house and waited until midnight, knocked on his door and placed him under arrest without a warrant, the arrest was unlawful; lottery tickets observed while officers were unlawfully on the premises were unlawfully seized and should have been suppressed in a prosecution for their unlawful possession. *Perez v State*, 267 S 2d 33/Fla (1972).

Fresh Pursuit

Police may enter premises without a warrant when in hot pursuit of an offender, and once inside officers may search any place on the premises where the offender may be hiding. *Erickson v State*, 507 P 2d 508/Alk (1973).

Where three robbers robbed a liquor store in Kansas City, Kansas, and fled across the river (also the state line) into Kansas City, Missouri, and were followed by a citizen witness and Kansas City, Kansas, police officers and arrested in Missouri by Kansas officers about 90 minutes after the robbery, the arrest was lawfully made according to the terms of the Uniform Law on Fresh Pursuit, both states being signatory thereto. *State v Tillman*, 494 P 2d 1178/Kan (1972).

Arrests Outside Bailiwick

As a general rule a peace officer may not make a peace officer's arrest, i.e., in his official capacity, outside the territorial boundary of the state, county, city or bailiwick in which he is elected or appointed to serve (*Irwin v Department of Motor Vehicles,* 517 P 2d 619/Wn–1973); (*State v McCarthy,* 303 A 2d 626/NJ–1973); Pennsylvania has held that absent legislation to the contrary, township officers cannot go into another township in fresh pursuit of a misdemeanant and arrest as peace officers but must communicate with officers of the asylum township and request their assistance. *Com v Troutman,* 302 A 2d 430/Pa (1973).

Under Texas law a city police officer is a peace officer and, as such, is authorized to make arrests outside the city limits where he serves (*Green v State,* 490 SW 2d 826/Tex–1973). But see *People v Martin,* 36 CR 942/Cal (1964), where the California Court of Appeals held that an officer arresting outside his bailiwick is restricted to the laws of arrest provided for private persons. Thus, as a general principle, well-established in most jurisdictions though not specifically held in any controlling decisions in California, a public officer for a particular county or municipality has no power to arrest offenders beyond the boundaries of the county or district for which he is appointed; and when acting beyond the limits of the geographical unit by which he is appointed, his powers of arrest become that which is conferred upon a private citizen in the same circumstances. *People v Martin, supra.*

Advisement of Constitutional Rights—When

The United States Supreme Court has ruled that when a person is taken into custody, or is otherwise deprived of his liberty in any significant way, and before he is asked any question designed to elicit incriminating information, he must be advised of the following constitutional rights to: (1) silence, (2) knowledge that if he does divulge any incriminating information it may be subsequently used against him in a criminal proceeding, and (3) the services of an attorney—retained if desired or appointed if indigent—prior to any questioning. Notwithstanding the advisement of these rights, arrestee may not yet be asked incriminating questions until it is ascertained by the arresting officer that he understood these rights and has voluntarily and knowingly waived such rights (*Miranda v Arizona,* 384 US 436–1966). The Supreme Court did rule that all arrestees must be advised of their constitutional rights, only when the officer intended to ask incriminating questions. Nor is it incumbent upon an officer to interrupt a voluntary admission against interests and advise the speaker of his rights. Id.

The advisement of *Miranda* rights does not have to follow a ritualistic formula of words which are to be uttered without deviation; it is only necessary that arrestee be advised in words which he understands of his right to silence, that any information he imparts is admissible against him and of his right to an attorney, retained or appointed. *People v Gilmer*, 511 P 2d 494/Colo (1973).

When Advisement Not Required

The mandate pronounced in *Miranda v Arizona, supra*, that defendant must be advised of his constitutional rights prior to any custodial interrogation, does not require police to interrupt a suspect who is talking freely and in the process of making a spontaneous statement, in order to advise him of his constitutional rights; and any statement made by a suspect in the absence of any questioning is not inadmissible by virtue of a failure to give such advice. *Rogers v State*, 268 S 2d 859/Ala (1972).

Repeated and continued *Miranda* warnings are not required prior to each series of questions put to arrestee unless there has been a substantial time lapse since the last series of questions, and a one-half hour time lapse between questions would not normally require a second warning (*People v Luick*, 101 CR 252/Cal–1972), nor even where questioning was resumed a few hours after the arrest (*People v Rosario*, 281 NE 2d 714/Ill–1972); nor were officers required to readvise arrestees of their *Miranda* rights where they were first interrogated on August 19, and so advised and again interrogated on August 20. *State v Carlton*, 495 P 2d 1091/NM (1972).

The arrest of defendant was lawful even though he was not advised of his right to silence and to counsel where no statement or action had been made or undertaken by him; for an arrest to be void for failure to advise arrestee of his rights, there must be evidence that such failure was detrimental to arrestee. *Jones v State*, 198 SE 2d 336/Ga (1973).

Under the *Miranda* warning, defendant is not entitled to be advised that at any time during interrogation he can, if he desires, stop answering questions. *State v Jones*, 196 NW 2d 606/Min (1972); *Flannagin v State*, 266 S 2d 637/Ala (1971).

The rule postulated in *Miranda v Arizona*, 384 US 436/Az (1966), that the arrestee be advised of certain constitutional rights, is not required antecedent to chemical tests for blood alcohol content under the implied consent law. *State v Mastaler*, 285 A 2d 776/Vt (1971).

Where an officer arrived at the scene of a shooting and upon seeing several persons standing around and upon recognizing defendant asked him, "What happened," defendant's answer that he was shooting at birds and one of his bullets had ricocheted and hit a man was admissible against him absent an advisement of his constitutional rights as defendant was not a suspect at the time and the matter was still at the "investigatory," not the "accusatory" stage. *State v Smith*, 193 SE 2d 318/NC (1972).

Where defendant was arrested in Juarez, Mexico, and there questioned by Mexican police without benefit of advisement of rights, the *Miranda* rule was declared to have no extraterritorial application and defendant's signed statement incriminating himself was admissible. *State v Cranford*, 491 P 2d 511/NM (1971); *United States v Dopf*, 434 F 2d 205/Tex (1970).

The California Supreme Court has ruled that once an arrestee has declined to waive his constitutional rights and discuss his crime with arresting officers, he may not be solicited at a later time to reconsider, recant and answer questions (*People v Fioritto*, 441 P 2d 625/Cal–1967). But the New York Court of Appeals ruled to the contrary in 1972, holding that no constitutional mandate prohibited an officer from making a subsequent request of defendant for a statement where the subsequent request is not made in the course of continued importunity. *People v Gary*, 334 NYS 883/NY (1972).

A refusal to sign a written waiver of rights does not render inadmissible all further statements. *United States v McDaniel*, 463 F 2d 129/Tex (1972).

Acquittal–Effect of

The right to release on *habeas corpus* or the exoneration of an arrestee in a criminal proceeding of the charge for which he was arrested, has no bearing on the legality of the arrest, as the arrestee may be entirely innocent of crime yet his arrest be legal. *Mock v Davies*, 344 US 840/Cal (1951).

The fact that defendant was acquitted in a prosecution for using vile and obscene language, had no more bearing on the legality of his arrest than would a finding of guilt in a criminal proceeding following an unlawful arrest. *People v Davenport*, 208 NW 2d 562/Mich (1973).

Unlawful Arrests

An arrest which is lawful at the outset may be unlawful if arrestee is held beyond legal limits. Thus, where arrestee manifested the objective symptoms of intoxication and was arrested on a drunk charge, his arrest was lawful, but his continued detention after being notified authoritatively that he was a diabetic and in insulin shock waxed unlawful. *Tufte v City of Tacoma*, 431 P 2d 183/Wn (1967).

An "arrest for investigation" is not a lawful arrest and an incident search is likewise unlawful and any evidence found in such search is *ipso facto* inadmissible, *Staples v United States*, 320 F 2d 817/Fla (1963).

Mere association or consorting with persons trafficking in drugs does not furnish probable cause to arrest. *United States v Lampkin*, 464 F 2d 1093/Pa (1972).

"Dragnet arrests" of members of a juvenile gang merely because other members of that gang had been involved in a street fight in which persons were killed, is not an arrest based on probable cause and is thus condemned, especially when the arrest is followed by several hours of involuntary confinement. *Com v Fogan*, 296 A 2d 755/Pa (1972).

An arrest cannot be justified by reason of discoveries made after the arrestee has been taken into custody, only by information known to the arresting officer at the time of the arrest. *Cutler v State*, 506 P 2d 607/Ok (1973).

Effect of Unlawful Arrest

The Fourth and Fourteenth Amendments are, *inter alia*, guarantees against unreasonable searches and seizures; the Constitution makes no guarantees against an unlawful arrest. Thus, an illegal arrest does not deprive the trial court of jurisdiction to try the defendant who is physically before the court on a criminal charge, but simply prevents the introduction of evidence seized in such arrest at the trial of the arrestee. *Richardson v State*, 511 P 2d 1127/Ok (1973).

Even though the accused was abducted in Tennessee by Alabama officers and transported back to Alabama for trial, his subsequent conviction was not vitiated by his abduction (*Taylor v Alabama*, 465 F 2d 376/Ala–1972); also, where defendant was illegally delivered into the custody of state officers by Canadian border officers, such "abduction" did not deprive the federal district court of jurisdiction to try defendant for interstate transportaton of forged checks. *United States v Hamilton*, 460 F 2d 1270/Wn (1972).

The only effect of an illegal arrest is that evidence obtained as a result thereof may be suppressed, but the court's jurisdiction over the defendant or the subject matter is not terminated nor is defendant's crime purged as a result. *De Weese v State*, 282 NE 2d 828/Ind (1972).

Privilege From Arrest

A statute exempting national guardsmen from arrest and imprisonment while under orders in active service–except for treason, felony and breach of the peace–affords no privilege from arrest for a criminal offense, because, as here used, breach of the peace includes all crimes and the privilege is from civil arrest and confinement only (*State v Murray*, 205 A 2d 29/NH–1964); citing *Williamson v United States*, 207 US 425–1907). In *Williamson*, the U.S. Supreme Court passed on this question as it applies to members of Congress– that members shall, in all cases except for treason, felony and breach of the peace, be privileged from arrest during their attendance at the session of their respective houses, and in going to and returning from the same (Section 6, Article I, U.S. Constitution). Here the Court ruled that this seeming privilege from arrest must be interpreted to mean the same as its English counterpart as it applied to members of Parliament–that a breach of the peace includes all indictable offenses and the privilege is from arrest on civil process, only. Id.

Resistance to Arrest

In most states a person being unlawfully arrested may resist such arrest by flight or by force, force which is reasonable under the circumstances; but if only his liberty is threatened he may not usually resist by the employment of deadly force. The Georgia Supreme Court has held, ". . .Every man, however guilty, has a right to shun an illegal arrest by flight. The exercise of the right should not, and would not subject him to be arrested as a fugitive." *Thomas v State*, 91 Ga 204 (1892); *State v Rousseau*, 241 P 2d 447/Wn (1952).

The right to resist an unlawful arrest which existed at common law still persists in the vast majority of jurisdictions, but this right is under attack from many sources which criticize its contemporary applicability. One theme on which this attack is based, and which has merit, is the theme that a person being arrested, knowing that he is innocent of the crime for which he is being arrested, will resist arrest confident that the arrest is unlawful; the arresting officer, on the other hand, knowing that he has probable cause to arrest, will usually overcome that resistance. Often one or both parties are injured, and to add to the woes of the injured and bewildered arrestee, he sometimes finds himself, although exonerated for the crime for which he was arrested, now facing a new charge—resisting arrest, battery, and maybe others.

Many states have adopted the rule that a person being arrested by one known to him to be a peace officer, does not have the right to resist arrest—even an illegal arrest—there being many recourses available to the aggrieved who is unlawfully arrested (*People v Gnatz*, 290 NE 2d 392/Ill—1972). Also, Alaska and California, among others, have adopted laws making resistance to a peace officer's arrest unlawful even though the arrest is unlawful.

In his majority opinion, Justice Connor of the Alaska Supreme Court has written convincingly of the new concept of arrest:

> The weight of authoritative precedent supports the right to repel an unlawful arrest with force . . . [citing cases]. This was the rule at common law. It was based on the proposition that everyone should be privileged to use reasonable force to prevent an unlawful invasion of his physical integrity and personal liberty. But certain imperfections in the functioning of the rule have brought about changes in some jurisdictions. A new principle of right conduct has been espoused. It is argued that if a peace officer in making an illegal arrest but is not using force, the remedy of the citizen should be that of suing the officer for false arrest, not resistance with force. The legality of a peaceful arrest may frequently be a close question. It is a question more properly determined by courts than by the participants in what may be a highly emotional situation. Because officers will normally overcome resistance with necessary force, the danger of escalating violence between the officer and the arrestee is great. What begins as an illegal misdemeanor arrest may culminate in serious bodily harm or death.
>
> . . .Our rules should discourage the unnecessary use of physical force between man and man. Any rule which promotes rather than inhibits violence should be reexamined.

Section 5 of the Uniform Arrest Act provides that "if a person has reasonable ground to believe he is being arrested by a peace officer, it is his duty to refrain from using force or any weapon in resisting arrest regardless of whether or not there is a legal basis for the arrest." (*Miller v State*, 462 P 2d 421/Alk–1969). Several other states, in addition to Alaska, have adopted this concept of arrest–California, Delaware, New Hampshire and Rhode Island, to name a few. Id.

Who Are Peace Officers

The term "peace officer," although variously defined by individual state laws, may be defined loosely as any officer empowered to execute a warrant of arrest or a search warrant. The term "peace officer," with full peace officer's powers, is defined in the California Penal Code by way of naming each specific type of officers. They are:

- Sheriff, undersheriff, deputy sheriff;
- Coroner, deputy coroner;
- Marshal or deputy marshal of a municipal court;
- Constable or deputy constable
- Marshal or policeman of a city or town
- Juvenile officer of a city or town
- Agents of the Department of Criminal Identification and Investigation
- Agents of the Bureau of Narcotic Enforcement
- Parole officers of the Department of Corrections and the Youth Authority

All other officers named in the statute are given only limited peace officer's powers which extends to the specific functions of their office. California Penal Code § 817; *State v Thyfault*, 297 A 2d 873/NJ (1972).

Also usually a requisite to the definition of "peace officer" is that the officer be employed full time by a public agency and paid from the public treasury.

Special Powers of Peace Officers

The legality of arrests by state officers without warrant for violations of state law is determined by state law (*Gonzales v People*, 398 P 2d 236/Colo–1968), and likewise, when an officer of the federal government makes an arrest without warrant he is bound by the laws of the state wherein the arrest was made unless there is a federal statute which is applicable. *Johnson v United States*, 333 US 10/Wn (1948).

If a federal offense is not involved, the Supreme Court looks to the law of the state to determine the legality and validity of an arrest. *State v Allen*, 194 SE 2d 9/NC (1973).

A statute limiting the time when a city police officer may be required to work does not limit the right or duty of such officer to make an arrest during hours or days when he is not on duty. *Meyers v State*, 484 SW 2d 334/Ark (1972).

The fact that a peace officer is employed and paid by a public or private agency other than one having direct responsibility for law enforcement at the time the offense is committed, neither impairs the officer's right to make an arrest or to take appropriate action to prevent crime, nor relieve him of his duty as a police officer. *Meyers v State, supra.*

The Arizona Supreme Court has held that a municipal police officer has the authority to arrest for violations of federal law (*Whitlock v Boyer*, 271 P 2d 484/Az–1954), and the federal circuit court of New York has held likewise in ruling that New York police officers may enforce federal laws (*Marsh v United States*, 29 F 2d 172/NY–1928). But the validity of an arrest must undergo the test under state standards notwithstanding that it was held to be valid under federal standards. *State v Deltenre*, 424 P 2d 782/NM (1966).

Highway patrol officers may arrest with peace officers powers within the city limits of a city as well as outside corporate limits. *Cudjoe v State*, 521 P 2d 409/Ok (1974).

USE OF INFORMANTS

In General

Before an officer can legally arrest upon information given him by another, he must have reasonable cause to believe the information is reliable–the source having been reliable. Reliability may be assumed if the information came from another officer, over a police radio, from the victim of crime, from a participant in crime who gives information against penal interest, from an eyewitness to crime or from an informant whose prior reliability has been established or whose information is corroborated from an independent source. *Moody v State*, 295 S 2d 272/Ala (1974); *State v Henderson*, 510 SW 2d 813/Mo (1974); *People v Mc Daniel*, 312 NE 2d 805/Ill (1974); *Golphin v State*, 293 S 2d 755/Fla (1974).

Probable cause to arrest on an informant's tip depends not on the accuracy of the information, but upon the reliability and credibility of the informant. *Dykes v Camp*, 333 FS 923/DC (1971).

Invasion of Privacy

Federal and state constitutions guarantee against unwarranted invasion of privacy; this guarantee is against governmental invasion and has no application where the invasion was by a private person. *Werley v State*, 271 S 2d 814/Fla (1973).

Officers were justified in arresting defendant despite claim of unlawful invasion of privacy where a service station operator had observed defendant in possession of narcotics paraphernalia through a hole in the restroom wall. *Werley v State, supra.*

Citizen Informant vs Criminal Informer

The courts have long distinguished between the citizen informant and other informers such as "stool-pigeons." Information from a known informer of unproved reliability, although relevant on the issue of probable cause, is ordinarily not enough. However, the situation in which a private citizen informs the police of criminal activities is different from that in which the information is given by the mere informer, and the California courts hold that officers may act on the observations of private citizens who report crimes committed in their presence. *People v Ziminicki*, 105 CR 614/Cal (1972).

Where an officer in making an arrest acts upon information supplied by an informer, it is not always necessary to adduce evidence of the informer's credibility; information supplied by a private citizen is not viewed by the courts with the same reservation as that from a professional informer. *People v Wayne*, 292 NE 2d 186/Ill (1972).

Reliable Informants on Arrest

"Probable cause" or "reasonable grounds" to arrest may be established by an informer whose reliability has been previously established or where the information has been independently corroborated by the officer in an independent investigation, (*People v Williams*, 306 NE 2d 678/Ill–1973), or by other facts already known to the officer. *State v Johnson*, 201 SE 2d 309/W Va (1973).

Where a reliable informant gave police detailed information regarding an automobile being used to transport narcotics and the route to be followed the next day, and such information was verified by surveillance, there was probable cause to stop the vehicle, arrest its driver and conduct incident search of the trunk of the vehicle from which the smell of marijuana emanated. *Coyne v State*, 485 SW 2d 917/Tex (1972).

The credibility of a primary informant who transmits information from a secondary informant to the police is indispensable, whether the police act without warrant or use information as a basis to procure a warrant. *Thompson v State*, 298 A 2d 458/Mo (1973).

An affidavit for a search warrant based on information from a confidential informant who had previously furnished FBI agents with information leading to five convictions and two additional arrests then pending trial, was sufficient basis for the issuance of a search warrant. *United States v Bamberger*, 456 F 2d 1119/NJ (1972).

Where an officer, having probable cause to arrest defendant, receives no response to his knock at defendant's door, he may force entry, and it is proper for him to request the landlady to unlock the door. *People v Hill*, 107 CR 791/Cal (1973).

Victim or Citizen Informant

Where the informer is a citizen who is merely a witness to or a victim of the crime, the officer may make an arrest based on information supplied by the citizen. Information coming from a private citizen is viewed in a different light from that furnished by a paid professional or an informer who is himself involved in the crime as a participant. *People v Cohn*, 106 CR 579/Cal (1973); *West v State*, 501 SW 2d 771/Ark (1973).

Probable cause to arrest may be supplied by a reliable informant when there is supplied a factual basis for the information which shows the informant's knowledge (*State v Aikins*, 503 P 2d 398/Az–1972). A citizen who purports to be the victim or a bystander who professes to have witnessed the crime, is a reliable informant although his reliability has not theretofore been established (*State v Whorton*, 487 SW 2d 865/Mo–1972). Thus, where a citizen flagged down a police car and informed the officer that he had seen three juveniles smash a store window and flee through the buildings, the officer was justified in making an arrest solely on the complaint of the citizen informant. *People v Wetzel*, 106 CR 651/Cal (1973).

Where officers received a description of a robbery vehicle and the license number from an eyewitness citizen informant, they could act on such information and it was not requisite that the informant's reliability be previously established. *People v Hubbard*, 519 P 2d 951/Colo (1974).

Untested Informants

The uncorroborated accusation by an informant whose identity is unknown and whose reliability has not been established, cannot give probable cause to arrest (*United States v Unverzagt*, 424 F 2d 396/Neb–1970), but if the officer has independent corroborative evidence of the information which would lead a reasonable and prudent person to believe a felony is being or has been committed, probable cause exists. *Sabbath v United States*, 380 F 2d 108/reversed on another point 391 US 585/Cal (1968).

In order that information given by an untested informant be acted upon by arrest, search or seizure, it must be corroborated in essential respects by other facts, sources or circumstances (*People v Ballassy*, 106 CR 46/Cal–1973); information from one untested informant may be corroborated by information from another untested informant if they were interviewed independently at different times and places. Id.

In a case of pressing emergency an arrest may be based solely on information from an untested informant who is not a victim or an eyewitness. *People v Braun*, 106 CR 56/Cal (1973).

Anonymous Informants

Arrest and search based on the tip of an anonymous informant have been previously upheld where the police first corroborated much of the information. *Harris v United States*, 293 A 2d 851/DC (1972).

An anonymous informant giving information on criminal activity where officers corroborated specific details of the information by surveillance and by observing that suspects were not conducting themselves in the manner of typical tourists, furnished sufficient grounds for arrest. *United States v Horton*, 488 F 2d 374/Tex (1973).

Where an unnamed informant advised police that a stolen color television set was at a certain address, and upon being admitted into the apartment they found the stolen item, probable cause existed to arrest defendant. *People v Peterson*, 293 NE 2d 373/Ill (1973).

Corroboration of Informant

Where an informant, previously untested, provided officers with detailed information which officers were able to corroborate in almost every detail, which included the manner in which he had obtained the information, there were sufficient details furnished to justify warrantless arrest. *United States v Foster*, 478 F 2d 1001/Ind (1973).

Reliability of an informant who furnishes some information is immaterial and need not be shown where, as a result of his information, officers establish surveillance of defendant and his premises, and from the latter source acquire sufficient information to justify arrest. *United States v Dalli*, 424 F 2d 45/NY (1970).

Where officers receive information from an informer that some person has committed a felony and officers thereafter establish probable cause to arrest independently of the information received from the informer, an arrest and incident search are legal, and the privilege of nondisclosure of the identity of the informer applies. *State v Penney*, 410 P 2d 226/Or (1966); *Roviaro v United States*, 353 US 53/Ill (1957).

Identification of Suspect

Law enforcement officers may not employ methods in a pretrial line-up that are "impermissibly suggestive" as to the identity of defendant, and witnesses should not be allowed to view suspects and make identifications in the presence of each other (*State v Grierson*, 504 P 2d 1204/Id–1972); but prompt on-the-scene confrontation between suspect and victim is consistent with proper police procedures and does not offend the principles established by the U.S. Supreme Court applicable to line-up procedures. *Cole v State*, 293 S 2d 871/Ala (1974).

One-man show-up of defendant while in police custody did not deny due process to defendant where victim had ample opportunity, during the robbery, to observe the defendant. *People v McCray*, 299 NE 2d 375/Ill (1973).

The mere showing of a picture of suspect to the victim does not deny due process (*State v Jenkins*, 523 P 2d 1232/Ut–1974), nor is the showing of several photographs to the victim–one of which is the suspect–a violation of due process. *State v Smith*, 521 P 2d 1197/Wn (1974).

Disparity in dress and size of persons in a line-up did not taint in-court identification of defendant as offensive to due process. *Ramsey v State*, 205 SE 2d 286/Ga (1974).

Although the courts recognize the line-up as one of the reliable methods of identifying the accused in crime, there is no principle under which defendant is constitutionally guaranteed the right to appear in a line-up. *Hargrove v Slayton*, 349 FS 75/Va (1972).

WARRANT OF ARREST

Defined

A "warrant of arrest" is a written order from a judge for the arrest of the therein named subject and no other; it must be served forthwith by the officer to whom it is directed or his delegate, and once served it is usually exhausted, but in some rare instances–as when error is discovered after release of the arrestee–the subject may be again arrested under its authority. *Carlson v Landon*, 342 US 524/Cal (1952).

An arrest is presumed lawful in the absence of evidence to the contrary (*State v Franklin*, 268 S 2d 249/La–1972), but where an arrest is made without warrant, burden rests on the prosecution to show justification therefor. *In re C*, 105 CR 113/Cal (1972).

When considering a police officer's criteria for probable cause to effect a warrantless arrest or search, the reviewing court should apply standards no less stringent than would a magistrate as a prelude to the issuance of a warrant. *United States v Wilson*, 465 F 2d 1290/Ill (1972).

Unlike a search warrant, a warrant of arrest is not a constitutional prerequisite to a lawful arrest (*United States v Miles*, 468 F 2d 482/Pa–1972), but it is within the purview of the legislature to limit a peace officer's powers of arrest without warrant to the extent of requiring that all arrests be by warrant. *State v Cooper*, 193 SE 2d 352/NC (1972).

Who May Issue

An arrest warrant issues from a judicial officer; it is usually directed to the chief law enforcement officer of a government agency—such as the sheriff, chief of police or constable—commanding its execution. The court or issuing officer is not concerned, however, that the head law enforcement officer to whom it is directed does not make the arrest, the warrant being satisfactorily executed by any law enforcement officer of the receiving agency. A warrant of arrest cannot be executed by one other than a peace officer absent a statute to the contrary. *Black's Law Dictionary.*

Authority Under Felony Warrant

It is well settled that an officer has not only probable cause but a legal duty to arrest upon knowledge of an unexecuted felony warrant (*Crowder v Com*, 191 SE 2d 239/Va–1972), and if a felony arrest warrant is outstanding, the arresting officer need not have the warrant in his possession at the time of the arrest. *United States v Leftwich*, 461 F 2d 586/NJ (1973).

Local officers may make an arrest under the authority of a federal warrant without having the warrant in their possession. *Bowyer v Superior Court*, 111 CR 628/Cal (1973).

Misdemeanor Warrant

Many of the states now permit arrest on the authority of a misdemeanor warrant although the officer does not, at the time of arrest, have the warrant in his possession. Thus, where officers advised arrestee that he was being arrested on an outstanding traffic warrant and arrestee was shown the warrant within twenty minutes after his arrival at the jail, the arrest was lawful. *State v Singleton*, 511 P 2d 1396/Wn (1973); reversed on another point; *State v Barnett*, 512 P 2d 977/NM (1973).

Although some jurisdictions have enacted laws which permit an officer to arrest for a misdemeanor under authority of a warrant, properly issued, even though he does not have the warrant in his possession, in absence of such a statute the arrest would be unlawful. *State v Denton*, 195 SE 2d 334/NC (1973).

Civil Liability

Where an arrest is made under authority of a warrant which is regular on its face, the executing officer merely acts as an administrative arm of the court which issued the warrant and is thus immune from liability (*Miller v Stinnett*, 257 F 2d 910/NM–1958); nor will an officer, in the execution of a warrant of arrest be held civilly liable for a mistake in identity where he exercised reasonable diligence in attempting to establish identity. *Mildon v Bybee*, 375 P 2d 458/Ut (1962).

INTERSTATE COMPACT–EXTRADITION

Extradition in General

The intent and provision of the Uniform Criminal Extradition Act are that upon a proper finding the judge or magistrate in the asylum state must commit a fugitive to the county jail for such time as will enable the governor of the demanding state to forward a requisition to the governor of the asylum state; but a fugitive, under this Act, may not be committed for more than thirty days *(Com ex rel Knowles v Lester,* 321 A 2d 637/Pa–1974). And absent an adverse showing, it will be presumed that the laws of the requisitioning state are the same as the laws of the asylum state. *Ex parte Fontes,* 475 SW 2d 781/Tex (1972).

It is the duty of the governor in the asylum state to cause the arrest and delivery to officers of the demanding state, of any person charged with crime in the demanding state and who has fled from justice and is found in the asylum state. *Hill v Houck,* 195 NW 2d 692/Ia (1972).

Minors are not excluded under the Uniform Criminal Extradition Act and Florida, which sought the extradition of a fugitive for trial for the offense of murder, was not required to proceed under the Uniform Interstate Compact on Juveniles. *Ex parte Jetter,* 495 SW 2d 925/Tex (1973).

As a rule, an accused person being held on a warrant of rendition is not entitled to bail. *Belasco v State,* 289 S 2d 666/Ala (1974).

That defendant was allegedly unlawfully extradited from Tennessee to Illinois affected neither his guilt nor innocence, nor the court's jurisdiction to try him for crime (*People v Scott,* 280 NE 2d 1/Ill–1972). And this rule would apply even though defendant was forcibly abducted from without the state and transported into the state. Id.

A "John Doe" warrant with no description of the person intended so as to permit a reasonable and prudent officer to distinguish the subject from other persons is fatally defective. *Fowler v State,* 197 SE 2d 502/Ga (1973).

"Extradition" Defined

"Extradition" is a means whereby the governor of one state may assist the governor of another state in the administrative process of transporting a fugitive from an asylum state back into the demanding state to there answer to criminal charges then pending against him. *Ault v Purcell,* 519 P 2d 1285/Or (1974).

A misdemeanor is an extraditable offense under the Uniform Criminal Extradition Act; extraditable offenses thereunder are "treason, felony or other crimes" (*Graham v State,* 204 SE 2d 630/Ga–1974). But in extradition between nations, there must be a treaty provision authorizing the delivery of a person sought to be tried for crime, and in the absence of such a treaty the United

States is powerless to obtain custody of the subject. *Ryan v United States,* 360 FS 264/affirmed 478 F 2d 1397/NY (1973).

Fugitive Arrests

If a person, having been duly charged with a felony, flees into another state he may be arrested in the asylum state without warrant by a peace officer or private person (*Clemas v United States,* 382 F 2d 403/SD–1967). Where a warrant for defendant's arrest for bank robbery was issued in Alabama, his arrest in Texas by Texas officers, pursuant to a request by FBI agents, was lawful although arrested before the warrant for his arrest was received (*Gill v United States*, 421 F 2d 1353/Ala–1970). Also, where a warrant of arrest was outstanding against arrestee, the arresting officer was not required to have the warrant in his possession at the time of the arrest, and a search incident to the arrest was not invalid merely because the arresting officer did not have a copy of the warrant in his possession at the time. *United States v One Adding Machine*, 406 F 2d 1167/Tex (1969).

Extradition Hearing

Extradition is but one method in securing the presence of the defendant in the court in which he may be tried, but the proceeding is not designed to determine guilt. The responsibility for a full and fair trial on the merits rests on the demanding state. *Eathorne v Nelson,* 505 P 2d 1/Colo (1973).

At an extradition hearing the court is without jurisdiction to inquire into the guilt or innocence of the alleged fugitive *(Buckley v Russell,* 107 CR 639/Cal–1973); but to ascertain whether he was in the demanding state at the time of the crime is within the court's prerogative and does not amount to a determination of guilt or innocence. Id.

Where upon an extradition hearing in the asylum state the identity of the subject is put to issue, the burden is upon the demanding state to prove that the subject is the person named in the governor's warrant. *Ex parte Larson,* 494 SW 2d 179/Tex (1973).

Neither the present insanity of the accused nor his alleged insanity at the time the crime was committed for which he is sought, is a bar to extradition; both issues are to be determined by the court having jurisdiction of the crime in the demanding state. *Kostic v Smedley,* 522 P 2d 535/Alk (1974).

Delay in Extradition

Due process may be denied where defendant is detained in sister state and request for extradition is not made within the required time although one of the two states is not signatory to the Uniform Agreement on Detainers *(Baker v Schubin,* 339 NYS 2d 360/NY–1972), but a dismissal of an original fugitive complaint due to failure of the demanding state to obtain a warrant of rendition did not bar subsequent extradition under a newly drawn governor's warrant. *Doherty v Duggan*, 218 NW 2d 759/Min (1974).

Prisoner Triable for All Known Crimes

The trying of defendant for crimes other than those named in the extradition demand is not improper; the demanding state may upon return of accused, either by extradition or after a waiver of extradition, try him for any crime he committed prior to flight from the state. *People v Berryman*, 204 NW 2d 238/Mich (1972).

The fact that defendant was required to stand trial for a crime other than the one for which he was extradited did not deprive defendant of due process nor of equal protection under the law (*Fabian v State*, 267 S 2d 294/Mis–1972). The court quoted *Lascelles v Georgia*, 148 US 537 (1893), as having ruled, ". . . it would be a useless and idle procedure to require the state having custody of the alleged criminal to return him to the state by which he was rendered up in order to go through the formality of again demanding his extradition for the new or additional offenses on which it is desired to prosecute him." Id.

Who Is Subject to Extradition

A "fugitive from justice" is a person who, having committed or been charged with a crime in one state, has left its jurisdiction voluntarily and is found within the limits of another state and the former state seeks to subject him to criminal process in the former state. *Anderson v Roth*, 202 SE 2d 91/Ga (1973).

Appellant who left the demanding state under compulsion to complete a sentence in New York was not a fugitive from justice subject to extradition (*People ex rel Davis v Quinlan*, 330 NYS 2d 544/NY–1972), but leaving the demanding state under compulsion is not always a defense to extradition. A military serviceman who was charged with the issuance of worthless checks while stationed in Louisiana, and who was subsequently transferred to Georgia, was a fugitive and was legally arrested in Georgia for extradition to Louisiana, even though his transfer had been pursuant to orders issued by the United States Army Command. *Anderson v Roth, supra; Woody v State*, 524 P 2d 1150/Kan (1974).

Delivery of a parolee to a demanding state to there answer to criminal charges does not waive jurisdiction of the asylum state and defendant may be returned to asylum state after disposition of obligation in the demanding state. *State ex rel Hood v Purcell*, 494 P 2d 461/Or (1972).

INTERSTATE COMPACT—FRESH PURSUIT

Defined

Almost all states have adopted the Uniform Act on Fresh Pursuit which is quoted below:

> AUTHORITY OF FOREIGN PEACE OFFICER:
>
> Any member of a duly organized state, county or municipal peace unit of another state of the United States who enters this state in fresh pursuit and continues within this state in such fresh pursuit, of a person in order to arrest him on the ground that he is believed to have committed a felony in such other state, shall have the same authority to arrest and hold such person in custody as has any member of any duly organized state, county or municipal peace unit of this state, to arrest and hold in custody a person on the ground that he is believed to have committed a felony in this state. RCW 10.89.010.
>
> "FRESH PURSUIT" DEFINED
>
> The term "fresh pursuit" as used in this chapter, shall include fresh pursuit as defined by the common law, and also the pursuit of a person who has committed a felony or who reasonably is suspected of having committed a felony. It shall also include the pursuit of a person suspected of having committed a supposed felony, though no felony actually has been committed, if there is reasonable ground for believing that a felony has been committed. Fresh pursuit as used herein shall not necessarily imply instant pursuit, but pursuit without unreasonable delay. RCW 10.89.050.

Examples

Where evidence showed that appellants committed a robbery in Kansas City, Kansas, and fled across the state line into Kansas City, Missouri; where they were followed from the scene by an eyewitness who notified both city police departments when the robbers abandoned their getaway car in Missouri; and where Kansas City, Kansas, police, who were first to arrive at the abandoned car, made the arrest within 90 minutes after the crime was committed, they acted in accordance with the provisions of the Uniform Act on Fresh Pursuit, and the arrest and subsequent search of the getaway car was lawful. *State v Tillman*, 494 P 2d 178/Kan (1972).

Although officers from one state may pursue a fleeing felon into another state and there arrest and incarcerate with peace officer's powers, they may not return their arrestee to the demanding state forthwith; rather, they must take the arrestee before a magistrate in the county where the arrest was made and proceed by the laws of extradition. If, upon a hearing in the asylum state, it appears the arrestee is a fugitive from justice and that the arrest was lawful, the arrestee will be committed for a reasonable time to await extradition back to the demanding state; if it appears at the hearing that the arrest was unlawful, the arrestee will be discharged. RCW 10.89.020.

INTERSTATE COMPACT—DETAINERS

Defined

Where petitioner is serving time in state *A* he may, upon demand of state *B*, be delivered over to state *B* for adjudication of any and all actions then pending, and the question as to whether state *A* loses jurisdiction of the petitioner is for state *A* to decide—not state *B (People ex rel Johnson v Elrod*, 297 NE 2d 182/Ill—1973); a failure of state *A* to hold an extradition hearing is not relevant. Id; *Dodson v State*, 497 SW 2d 767/Ten (1973).

The Interstate Compact on Detainers is not self-executing and petitioner must comply with the statutory provisions therein contained. Upon prompt application by him, unless good cause exists for a continuance, the indictment may be dismissed if he is not brought to trial in the demanding state within 180 days. *Baker v Schubin*, 339 NYS 2d 360/NY (1972).

Failure of a state to request extradition of a prisoner being held in a sister state may constitute denial of due process, notwithstanding that one of the states is not signatory to the Uniform Agreement on Detainers; all states, whether signatories to the interstate compact or not, are constitutionally required to use good faith efforts in attempting to secure speedy trials for persons incarcerated in prisons in other jurisdictions. *Baker v Schubin, supra.*

ARRESTS BY PRIVATE PERSONS

The Common Law Rule

The common law concerning citizen's arrest was (and is, unless abrogated by state statute) that "... a private person, even, may arrest a party, if a felony has in fact been committed, and there was reasonable ground of suspicion; but, in the case of an officer, he is justified in making an arrest if no felony was in fact committed, if he acted upon information from another, on which he had reason to rely." *Smith v State*, 283 NE 2d 365/Ind (1972).

Where there is no state statute defining a private person's powers of arrest, the common law rule will undoubtedly be followed by its courts. Thus, it is well settled that when there is reasonable cause to believe that a felony has been committed and that the person arrested committed it, an arrest by a private citizen is legal. *Montiero v Howard*, 334 FS 411/RI (1971).

The common law permitted citizen's arrest, more appropriately defined as private persons' arrest, for treason, felony and breach of the peace specifically as follows:

1. To stay a breach of the peace continuing or likely to be renewed in his presence:
2. To prevent the infliction of deadly injury or the commission of treason or felony;
3. Where the felony is committed in his presence or where though not committed in his presence, he can prove its commission and his reasonable suspicion that the person arrested is guilty of that particular felony;
4. Where persons do not disperse within one hour after proclamation made under the Riot Act.[1]

The crime of treason consists of levying war against the state (the United States), adhering to its enemies giving them aid and comfort, or betraying one's country to a foreign power, and attempting by force or violence to overthrow the government to which one owes allegiance. *Black's Law Dictionary.*

"Felony," as defined under state law, is any crime punishable by death or imprisonment in a state penitentiary. Under federal law felony is divided into two types—heinous felonies and regular felonies—which are punishable by death or by imprisonment in excess of one year.

"Breach of the peace" is more comprehensive in scope and more elusive to definition; a United States court has defined it as follows:

> . . .The term "breach of the peace" has never had a precise meaning in relation to specific conduct. Yet from its early common law origin to the present it has received a fairly well defined gloss. The offense known as breach of the peace embraces a great variety of conduct destroying or menacing public order and tranquility. It includes not only violent acts but acts and words likely to produce violence in others . . . The term denotes conduct that creates consternation and alarm. It is an indecorum that incites public turbulence; yet violent conduct is not a necessary element . . . . *United States v Woodward*, 376 F 2d 136/Ill (1967).

Absent an applicable federal statute the state statute applies to federal employees, and where a postal inspector executed a citizen's arrest of a postal

---

[1] A.M. Wilshere-Berry Chedlow, *Principles of the Common Law*, 6th edition (London: Street & Maxwell, 1951).

employee in Florida, the Florida law of arrest was applicable; and there being no statutory authority for a private person's arrest in Florida the common law was applicable, and the arrest was valid even though the inspector may have obtained a warrant of arrest before taking defendant into custody. *United States v Montos*, 421 F 2d 215/certiorari denied 397 US 1022/Fla (1970).

How Executed

If the arresting person is a private person he must inform the arrestee of the reason for the arrest unless the arrestee is then engaged in the commission of a crime or arrested in flight immediately after its commission (*Allen v State*, 400 P 2d 463/Ok–1965), and any private person may summon, but may not compel, others to aid him in the arrest. *People v Campbell*, 104 CR 118/Cal (1972).

When Arrest May Be Made

A private citizen, a police officer or other public official who is in a place where he has a right to be and who then observes contraband, has a right, if not an obligation, to act against the offender. *State v Young*, 501 P 2d 1001/Or (1972).

Many of the states have enacted statutes delineating private persons' arrests. Most existing statutes are identical or similar to the California and Oklahoma statutes which state as follows:

> A private person may arrest: (1) for a crime committed or attempted in his presence; (2) when a person arrested has committed a felony although not in his presence; (3) when a felony has in fact been committed and there is reasonable cause for believing the person arrested to have committed it.

Also, a private person may take into custody one who is mentally ill to a degree that his continued liberty would likely be detrimental to himself or to society. *Allen v State*, 400 P 2d 463/Ok (1965); *Plancich v Williamson*, 357 P 2d 693/Wn (1960); California Penal Code, § 837.

Probable Cause—Felony

A private person may arrest another upon a showing that a felony has been committed and that there is reasonable cause to believe the person arrested committed it (*State v Fitz*, 490 SW 2d 30/Mo–1973). Being aware of the actual commission of a felony, a citizen may arrest the suspected perpetrator where there is probable cause to believe he is the perpetrator. And where arrestor had knowledge of a burglary of a residence and an admission from one of the principals naming defendant, there was probable cause for a citizen's arrest. *Whitaker v Com*, 479 SW 2d 592/Ky (1972); KRS 431.005 (2).

For the purpose of preserving the peace and preventing crime a peace officer or a private person may make reasonable inquiry of persons, under circumstances which reasonably suggest that a crime has been or is about to be committed (*Williams v Slate*, 373 P 2d 91/Ok–1962). Where evidence showed that defendant was attempting to arrest complainant a failure of the court to give defendant's proffered instruction to the jury, that any person has the right to arrest one who he has reasonable cause to believe has committed a felony, was reversible error. *People v Vezerian*, 193 P 2d 944/Cal (1948).

A private citizen may arrest another when circumstances exist which would lead a reasonable and prudent person to believe that a crime has been committed in his presence (*People v Burgess*, 388 P 2d 524/Cal–1959), but the citizen must act promptly and arrest without unreasonable delay, and to justify a delay there must be a continued attempt to apprehend the offender. *Ogulin v Jefferies*, 263 P 2d 75/Cal (1953).

Force Permissible in Felony Arrests

The question of how much force may be permitted in making an arrest is often critical whether the arrest was by a peace officer or a private citizen. In rejecting the rule for private persons' arrests as proposed in the Model Penal Code, the Washington Supreme Court made the following observation: "The majority of jurisdictions which have considered the question of a private person's arrest have apparently adopted the common law rule that a private citizen has the same right to use deadly force as a peace officer would have in apprehending a felon in the same situation," citing *Crawford v Commonwealth*, 44 SW 2d 286/Ky (1931) and others. *State v Clarke*, 377 P 2d 449/Wn (1962).

A private person attempting to arrest a fleeing burglar is privileged to use deadly force if such force is reasonably necessary to effect the arrest. *People v Walker*, 108 CR 548/Cal (1973).

If an officer or a private person has reasonable and just cause to believe that the person sought is on the premises of another, he may enter for the purpose of arresting one who is accused of felony or breach of the peace or misdemeanor committed in his presence. However, the arresting person usually must knock and announce and be denied entry before he may forcibly enter. *Livingston v Browder*, 285 S 2d 923/Ala (1973).

Peace Officers Outside Bailiwick

Where an officer in his official capacity had received information from a reliable source that petitioner would return to the state with narcotics in his possession, the officer, though in a city outside his bailiwick at an airport, upon seeing petitioner walk through the gate, had reasonable cause to believe he was committing a felony, i.e., possession of contraband narcotics, and he had the authority to arrest and detain petitioner as a private citizen. *Monteiro v Howard*, 334 FS 411/RI (1971).

Colorado officers, irrespective of their official status in Arizona, were authorized to arrest as private persons for a felony committed in their presence. *State v McCullar*, 520 P 2d 299/Az (1974).

Airline Searches

An airline freight agent's search on his own initiative of a package left for shipment was a lawful private inspection; in finding the package to contain dangerous drugs, he notified officers who arrested the receiver of the package at its destination, and contents of the package were untainted by unlawful seizure and thus admissible. *People v Hively*, 480 P 2d 558/Colo (1971).

Where a deputy United States marshal had reason to believe defendant was attempting to smuggle a weapon hidden in his boot into a commercial aircraft, he could properly detain and search; when the resultant search disclosed contraband, a felony under California law, he could properly seize the contraband and arrest defendant despite defendant's claim on appeal that the marshal's authority to arrest as an officer was only for federal misdemeanors, otherwise his power to arrest was that of a private citizen. *People v Lacey*, 105 CR 72/Cal (1973).

Detention by Security Guards

Where a private security guard at an industrial plant took an employee to the plant guard station allegedly for possession of a hallucinogen, there was no arrest. *State v Lamb*, 299 NE 2d 317/Oh (1973).

A member of a university campus security force, his status being essentially that of a private person, upon observing defendant on private property of the university at night without visible or lawful business and in an area of high incidence of thefts from automobiles, had reasonable cause to detain defendant for investigation and to arrest him for disorderly conduct which included loitering upon the private property of another without lawful business. *People v Wilkins*, 104 CR 89/Cal (1972).

Misdemeanor Arrests

The term "public offense" in a statute permitting a private person to make an arrest for a public offense committed or attempted in his presence, includes misdemeanors (*People v Campbell*, 104 CR 118/Cal–1972), but neither a peace officer nor a private person, except under statutory authority, has the authority to arrest for a misdemeanor unless committed within his presence. *People v Robinson*, 194 NW 2d 537/Mich (1971).

A private person has the right to arrest another for petty theft, a misdemeanor, when he observes the theft of his own property or the property of another over which he has custodial responsibility (*State v De Santi*, 443 P 2d 439/Az–1968). A storekeeper seeing what appears to him to be a theft of goods may pursue the thief and place him under arrest. *Ira v Columbia Food Co*, 360 P 2d 622/Or (1966).

A bus driver was authorized, as a private citizen, to detain another who was operating a motor vehicle in a manner indicating he was under the influence of intoxicating liquor (*Oklahoma Railway Co v Sanford*, 258 P 2d 604/Ok–1953). A private person may arrest a prowler thought to be a "peeping tom" when found on his neighbor's property. *Wingfield v State*, 160 P 2d 945/Ok (1945).

A private person, unlike a peace officer, may not arrest solely on reasonable cause to believe a public offense has been committed in his presence; nor may a private person arrest only on the reasonable belief that the person arrested has committed a felony. In each case, however, a police officer may arrest, and if it develops that no crime was actually committed, the police officer's position is unaltered. *People v Martin*, 36 CR 924/Cal (1964).

Crime Must Have Occurred

A private person's position is much less tenable then that of a peace officer when making a misdemeanor arrest. When a private person makes a misdemeanor arrest, three conditions must exist which do not usually exist in an arrest by an officer. They are:

1. The misdemeanor must have been actually committed;
2. The arresting person may not violate a law with impunity in effecting the arrest;
3. Resistance to the arrest is not forbidden by statute.

Generally, an arrest by a private person is unlawful unless the person arrested actually committed the crime for which he was arrested. *Jacques v Sears Roebuck & Co Inc*, 334 NYS 2d 632/NY (1972).

The validity of an arrest by a private person here for petty larceny, a misdemeanor, depends on the guilt of the person arrested, and no other consideration–such as reasonableness of the arresting person's belief–is of any significance (*Hoffay v Stanley Dept Stores Inc*, 328 NYS 2d 798/NY–1972). But the guilt of the arrestee when arrested by an officer is not relevant, only that probable cause existed at the time of the arrest. *People v Martin, supra.*

The Washington Supreme Court in stating the common law rule applicable to private person's arrest held: "Should the one arrested not be proved guilty, the private person will not be justified unless an offense has been committed by someone; while the officer is justified though no offense had been committed; yet both must have had reasonable cause to suspect the one apprehended." *State v Symes*, 55 P 626/Wn (1899).

Disposition of Arrestee

A private person who makes a private person's arrest must, without unnecessary delay, deliver the person arrested to a peace officer or take him before a magistrate. *Smith v State*, 510 P 2d 962/Ok (1973).

The responsibility of a private citizen who makes an arrest for a misdemeanor committed in his presence ends with the delivery of the arrestee to a peace officer; if thereafter there is an unreasonable delay in taking the arrested person before a magistrate, culpability would lie elsewhere than with the arresting person. *Sima v Skaggs Payless Drug Center Inc*, 353 P 2d 1085/Id (1960).

DETENTION FOR INVESTIGATION

In General

Detention for questioning is an invasion of privacy but is nevertheless permissible where the officer can point to specific and articulable facts which taken together reasonably warrant the intrusion. *People v Siegenthaler*, 499 P 2d 499/Cal (1972).

Circumstances short of probable cause to arrest may justify an officer's approach to a person for the purpose of investigating possible criminal behavior and may warrant temporary detention, but before detention may be undertaken there must be an objectively reasonable suspicion that something out of the ordinary has taken place, that the activity is related to crime and that the defendant is connected with the activity (*People v Junious*, 106 CR 344/Cal–1973). And assuming a valid stop, a limited search of a suspect for weapons is justified if a reasonably prudent man under the circumstances would be warranted in the belief that his safety or the safety of others was in danger. *People v Watson*, 292 NE 2d 457/Ill (1972).

The Pennsylvania Supreme Court observed that street encounters between police and citizens are incredibly rich in diversity and each case involving detention for questioning must be viewed under its own unique facts and circumstances in order to determine validity of the detention. *Com v Mackie*, 320 A 2d 842/Pa (1974).

An investigatory detention, although a seizure of the person, may be based upon circumstances falling short of probable cause to arrest. *Racine v State*, 286 S 2d 890/Ala (1973).

Seeking of Interviews

Officers, in the performance of their duties, will receive judicial sanction in the seeking of interviews of persons out at night, and it is possible under some circumstances that even a refusal to answer proper questions, in light of surrounding circumstances, may constitute grounds for arrest (*State v Chronister*, 353 P 2d 493/Ok–1960). Also, police have the right to seek interviews of persons in their homes (*People v Martin*, 290 P 2d 855/Cal–1955), but this does not include the right to walk into one's house uninvited (*People v Hoven*, 381 P 2d 927/Cal–1963), nor to demand that a person open his door for such interview. A suspect has no obligation or duty to cooperate with officers in securing evidence against himself. *People v Shelton*, 388 P 2d 655/Cal (1964).

Where customs officers went to the home of defendant merely to seek an interview and in response to their knock at his door defendant's eight-year-old daughter invited them in whereupon they observed marijuana in plain sight, defendant's arrest and seizure of the evidence were lawful. *Davis v United States*, 327 F 2d 301/Cal (1940).

Local police officers usually possess broader powers of arrest and detention than do federal officers; thus, local officers, being guardians of the peace, may make vehicular stops in the pursuit of that activity whereas a federal officer may not, being restricted to the enforcement of specific federal laws. *United States v Ward*, 488 F 2d 162/Wn (1973).

When Persons May Be Detained

When an automobile is lawfully stopped for an interview of an occupant, the occupant may be required to produce evidence of his identity as a proper and necessary part of law enforcement (*United States v Lincoln*, 494 F 2d 833/Cal–1974), and temporary detention in order to determine the verity of the subject's answers by radio is not unreasonable. *State v Sinclair*, 523 P 2d 1209/Wn (1974).

Circumstances short of probable cause to arrest will justify an investigation by officers and should the investigation disclose additional evidence, in this instance a shotgun used in the commission of a robbery, such evidence may be considered in establishing probable cause to arrest. *State v Gunter*, 414 P 2d 734/Az (1966).

The applicable constitutional provisions do not require a policeman who lacks the precise level of information necessary for probable cause to arrest, simply to shrug his shoulders and allow crime to occur or a criminal to escape. The United States Supreme Court in *Terry v Ohio*, 392 US 1 (1968), permits brief stops, though forcible, of a suspicious individual for momentary maintenance of the *status quo* while obtaining more information, if the officer's discretionary decision is reasonable in light of the facts known to him at the time. *Bays v Com*, 486 SW 2d 706/Ky (1972).

Extent of Investigation

A peace officer is authorized to stop any person in a public place who he reasonably suspects is committing, has committed or is about to commit a crime, and may, in the interest of community security, demand of the suspect his name, address and an explanation for his actions. *State v McCune,* 201 NW 2d 852/Neb (1972).

Even without probable cause to arrest, an officer has the right under appropriate circumstances to stop a person and interview him for purposes of investigation. Where officers had a right to conduct a "pat-down" search of a suspect whom they were interviewing, they were justified in arresting him for unlawfully carrying a concealed pistol, and a subsequent search of arrestee at the police station, which produced heroin, was lawful being incident to a lawful arrest. *Hurst v United States,* 425 F 2d 177/Wn (1970).

An officer has the right to detain persons for questioning who are out late at night. Where an officer observed defendant in a deserted area in the early morning hours and observed a bulge under his shirt, he had the right to make a "weapons search," and in feeling a metal object had the right to determine what the metal object was; burglary tools thus discovered are not illegally seized. *State v Streeter,* 193 SE 2d 347/NC (1972).

Grounds for Detention

Where an officer entertains a well-founded suspicion not amounting to probable cause to arrest, he may stop the suspected person and require that he give an accounting of his activity. Under such circumstances the suspect has not been arrested within the legal meaning of the word, but has been detained, only. *State v Gluck,* 518 P 2d 703/Wn (1974).

Where police had probable cause to detain, and did detain a suspect for investigation, the fact that police called the detention an "arrest" rather than a "stop" was not controlling, and marijuana thus discovered was admissible. *People v Amick,* 111 CR 280/Cal (1973).

Police officers had the right to stop a vehicle being driven slowly and erratically, to investigate a possible curfew violation upon observing a female passenger in the front seat who appeared to be either very small or slouched down. *State v Wicklund,* 205 NW 2d 509/Min (1973).

Officers, in observing an automobile occupied by four males being driven around in a residential area at night, had the right to inquire as to their presence; burglary tools thrown from their vehicle was abandoned property and properly seized by the officers along with contraband in the vehicle in plain view. *Com v Tatro,* 297 A 2d 139/Pa (1972).

An officer who was searching a neighborhood for a Negro rape suspect driving a named make of automobile, did not need probable cause to arrest in order to detain a Negro suspect driving the named automobile. *Lee v Wainwright,* 488 F 2d 140/Fla (1973).

Police officers who observed a person of Mexican descent in an area where there were no Mexicans acted reasonably in stopping him for interrogation; and upon observing a yellow balloon under the subject's tongue which officers were unable to recover because the subject swallowed it, his subsequent arrest and search which produced a marijuana cigarette was lawful. *State v Ruiz*, 504 P 2d 1307/Az (1973).

A "detention" of a type depriving one of freedom does not exist where police officers drive alongside a pedestrian and ask him questions as he walks along. *People v Juarez*, 110 CR 865/Cal (1973).

Limits on Detention Investigations

Police encounters with citizens which limit personal freedom but do not amount to arrests, such as "stops" or "frisks," are constitutional even in the absence of probable cause to arrest so long as they satisfy the test of reasonableness; but the mere fact that a stop was reasonable does not necessarily imply that a frisk, or otherwise placing of hands upon the subject, is also reasonable. Thus, the testimony of an officer that he was always in fear that someone may be armed, although properly reflecting a police attitude to be prepared for any contingency, did not support a claim of routine authority to conduct a pat-down search of any and all citizens stopped for interview. *United States v Coates*, 495 F 2d 160/DC (1974).

Chapter VIII

Automobile Searches

In General

A search warrant is not necessary prior to the search of an automobile in motion, after hot pursuit, in the area where a lawful arrest is made, for things obvious to the senses, for property that has been abandoned and where consented to. *State v Duvernoy*, 195 SE 2d 631/W Va (1973).

The rule governing searches and seizures is that a warrant based on probable cause must be obtained before a search may be conducted; the exception is that a search may be made on probable cause without a warrant under exceptional or exigent circumstances. An example would be in the search of vehicles which can be readily moved; suspects may take flight, or evidence or contraband may be removed therefrom or destroyed. *City of Milwaukee v Cohen*, 203 NW 2d 633/Wis (1973).

The rules for searching a motor vehicle are not the same as those permitting the search of a fixed structure such as a residence (*State v Romonto*, 212 NW 2d 641/Neb–1973), and if there is probable cause to search an automobile, such search need not be "incident to" or "contemporaneous with" an arrest; it may be searched wholly independent of an arrest or whether or not there was an arrest. *State v McCollum*, 507 P 2d 196/Kan (1973).

There is no requirement that an officer have probable cause to search an automobile before asking the driver's consent to search (*State v Burns*, 516 P 2d 479/Or–1973), and a person in control of an automobile may consent to a search of the automobile, although the search may incriminate himself or another passenger or one who is not a passenger. *State v Herhal*, 307 A 2d 553/Del (1973).

Passengers in an automobile had no right to object to search of that automobile which was found to contain implements and tools of a burglary (*State v Hamilton*, 141 SE 2d 506/NC–1965), but a police informant acting in concert with police who did not object when his vehicle was stopped and searched, could not consent to an invasion of the rights of his two passengers. *People v Robles*, 104 CR 907/Cal (1972).

The validity of a search without a warrant and incident to a lawful arrest depends, not upon the practicability of procuring a search warrant, but upon the reasonableness of the search (*State v McCoy*, 437 P 2d 734/Or–1968). The search, "though remote in time and place from the arrest, may be constitutional where the officers have taken lawful custody of the automobile for a purpose immediately connected with the crime for which the arrest is made." *Cooper v California*, 386 US 58 (1967).

Under the authority of a warrant, officers searched defendant's house, but they were not authorized under the warrant to search defendant's automobile; however, due to the mobility of an automobile, officers were authorized to search the automobile under the "emergency" doctrine. *People v Dumas*, 109 CR 304/Cal (1973).

An automobile may be searched without a warrant under circumstances wherein the search of a building or a house would require a warrant (*State v McMillin*, 476 P 2d 612/Kan–1970). The circumscription announced in *Chimel v California*, 395 US 752 (1969), related to the search of a residence and in no manner affected previous rules for automobile searches. *State v Darst*, 399 P 2d 618/Wn (1965).

The inspection of an automobile so as to obtain the serial number in order to identify it is not a search under the Fourth Amendment. *People v Shutter*, 310 NE 2d 694/Ill (1974).

Probable Cause Stop

Officers may stop an automobile for legitimate investigation and interrogate the occupants if there is probable cause for such action even though there is no probable cause to arrest at the time; if previous knowledge of officers coupled with further evidence obtained in the investigation supplies probable cause to arrest, then an incident search is justified. *Robertson v State*, 445 P 2d 352/Nev (1968).

Police officers having reasonable cause to believe an automobile which they have stopped contains contraband or evidence of a crime, may search the vehicle without a warrant. *Orricer v Erickson*, 471 F 2d 1204/SD (1973).

Observing the same automobile stop at a bar three times within five hours, the driver remaining only a few minutes each time, gave officers probable cause to stop the driver upon his third departure and ask for identification; upon seeing the driver place mismatched gloves on the floor of his vehicle, officers had probable cause to examine the gloves; and upon finding heroin in one of the gloves, officers had probable cause to conduct a warrantless search of the trunk compartment and to seize the gun found therein. *State v Gray*, 285 A 2d 1/NJ (1971).

Where defendant, upon being stopped for interrogation by a narcotics agent, abandoned his vehicle while it was still moving and fled, and the agent jumped into the car to apply the brakes and in so doing smelled marijuana emanating from inside the car, he was justified in searching the vehicle and seizing marijuana. *United States v Barron*, 472 F 2d 1215/Cal (1973).

Reasonable cause to believe that the driver was intoxicated created reasonable cause to stop the vehicle, and finding the driver to be intoxicated furnished further reasonable cause to search the vehicle for intoxicants or drugs. *State v Gustafson*, 258 S 2d 1/Fla (1972).

Stop for Traffic Violation

When an officer stops a motorist for a traffic violation, not as a pretext or excuse for stopping the driver, and observes a crime being committed, such as the illegal possession of a firearm, he may arrest for such crime. *State v Hanawahine*, 443 P 2d 149/Haw (1968).

Upon stopping an automobile at night for not having a left rear taillight, the officer shined his flashlight into the rear seat and observed and recognized items on the seat to have been taken in a theft from a local address; he knew the occupants were strangers in the area and knew the license plate had been changed since he first observed the automobile about five minutes previously; he thus had probable cause to arrest for a felony. *State v Regan*, 457 P 2d 1016/Wn (1969).

Where defendant was stopped for a traffic violation and upon request of the officer was unable to produce a registration certificate and the officer looked inside the vehicle for the certificate and saw a plastic bag which he believed to contain marijuana, there was probable cause to arrest, and a contemporaneous search of the vehicle was proper. *Marquez v People*, 450 P 2d 349/Colo (1969).

Where defendant's vehicle had been involved in a hit-and-run accident, officers had the right to search the vehicle to establish the *corpus delicti* and identity of the driver, and a shopping plate, a driver's license and a quantity of marijuana observed inadvertantly were subject to seizure under the plain view doctrine. *Nasiriddin v State*, 298 A 2d 490/Md (1973).

Probable Cause to Search Vehicle

Probable cause for searching a motor vehicle is to be determined in view of its mobility and by a practical rather than technical standard, and differs from that required to search a fixed structure. *State v Connor*, 202 NW 2d 172/Neb (1972).

An officer may rely on his senses in determining whether contraband is present in a vehicle. If contraband is seen or smelled, the officer is not required to close his eyes or nostrils, walk away, and leave the contraband undisturbed. *State v Romonto*, 212 NW 2d 641/Neb (1973).

Search Incident to Arrest

After properly stopping a vehicle and frisking a passenger, who was found to be carrying a loaded pistol, police officers had probable cause to infer that some joint criminal enterprise was planned and a warrantless search of the vehicle and the seizure of a revolver under the driver's seat were proper. *Jeffreys v United States*, 312 A 2d 308/DC (1973).

The U.S. Supreme Court has mandated a change in the concept of search when defendant is under arrest for a minor traffic violation. In *United States v Robinson*, 94 SC 467/DC (1973), defendant was under arrest for driving while his license was suspended, and a full search was conducted of his person which disclosed fourteen capsules of heroin. Also, in *Gustafson v Florida*, 94 SC 488/Fla (1973), the court observed that the arresting officer had the right to conduct a full-scale body search of arrestee, which disclosed marijuana, although he was under arrest for driving without an operator's license in his possession and the officer, pursuant to such arrest, was not required to have the arrestee in custody preparatory to incarceration. Id.

Removal of Vehicle From Scene

Most jurisdictions require that an automobile searched incident to a lawful arrest, must be searched contemporaneously and at the place of the arrest, but if it is not practical to search at the time and place of arrest, the vehicle may be moved and searched. Where an officer observed a suspect vehicle proceeding away from the scene of a robbery, he was justified in transporting the vehicle to the police station and there to conduct a thorough search rather than attempt the search in the cold and darkness of a December evening and on a busy street (*King v State*, 298 A 2d 446/Md–1972). Also, the courts have approved the search of an automobile at the police station some distance away from the place of arrest because the street on which the arrest was made was narrow and congested and at the time a light drizzle was falling (*Leffler v United States*, 409 F 2d 44/Mo–1969). And where a search was begun at the scene immediately after the arrest and continued at the police station a short time later (*Crone v United States*, 411 F 2d 251/Ga–1969); or where darkness fell preventing an effective search of the automobile used in a robbery and it was removed to the police station where the search could be resumed under more favorable conditions (*Chambers v Maroney*, 396 US 900/Pa–1968); or where there was a search for fingerprints of a vehicle used in a rape, one hour after its removal to a garage, where such removal was for the purpose of preserving possible fingerprints—the courts approved the searches. *McCoy v Cupp*, 298 FS 329/Or (1969).

Insofar as federal constitutional principles apply, an automobile may be searched at a time and place remote from the arrest and incident to the arrest provided: (1) the police have lawful custody of the automobile, (2) the arrest is valid, and (3) the search is made for the fruits of the crime or evidence relating to the crime for which the accused is arrested. *State v Houchin*, 428 P 2d 971/Mont (1967).

Where police had probable cause to search defendant's automobile at the time of his arrest, and exigent circumstances were present which would have justified immediate on-the-scene search—which search was conducted as soon as the automobile was removed to the police station—a warrantless search was valid *(Gomez v Beto*, 471 F 2d 774/Tex–1973). Also, where officers who had probable cause to conduct incident search of an automobile at the time and place of arrest, they could search the trunk a few minutes later after the automobile was moved to the police station. *State v Hornbeck*, 492 SW 2d 802/Mo (1973).

When police lawfully seize an automobile which is itself evidence of the crime rather than a mere container of incriminating articles, they may postpone the search until the vehicle is removed to a place where and at a time when examination can be made in accordance with sound investigative principles. *People v Braun*, 106 CR 56/Cal (1973).

Once the warrantless search of an automobile is justified, there is no prohibition against deferring the search until the vehicle is moved to a more convenient location, such as the police station, and the obtaining of a search warrant thereafter is superfluous. *Com v Barnes*, 312 NE 2d 575/Mas (1974).

Search of Parked Vehicles

It is not only practicable but mandatory that a search warrant be obtained authorizing the search of a parked unoccupied automobile, except under exigent circumstances. *State v C*, 520 P 2d 773/Mont (1974).

When there is probable cause to believe an automobile parked on the highway contains contraband or evidence of crime, or was itself an instrumentality of the commission of crime, law enforcement officers need not obtain a search warrant before searching the vehicle as there is no distinction of constitutional proportion between the immediate search on probable cause and immobilizing the vehicle until a warrant can be secured. *People v Laursen*, 501 P 2d 1145/Cal (1972).

Police officers who observed what they thought to be marijuana on the floor of a parked and unattended vehicle were justified in searching the vehicle and seizing marijuana found in the search. *Com v Dobkin*, 302 A 2d 457/Pa (1973).

An officer was justified and no "search" was involved where he observed a vehicle parked in a carport, which matched the description of one used in a bank robbery, and he raised the hood to determine if the engine was warm. *United States v Jones*, 352 FS 369/Ga (1972).

Where an officer found an out-of-state vehicle parked on the road in an unpopulated area with a flat tire, and in his "innocent investigation" to ascertain if the vehicle was stolen or if the owner needed help or to protect property from theft, he discovered property later determined to be stolen, his search and seizure was justified under the "exigent circumstances" rule, and property thus seized was admissible against the accused in a subsequent prosecution. *State v Bright*, 493 P 2d 757/Or (1972).

Border Searches

A search conducted at the international border under authority of the Immigration and Nationality Act, does not require antecedent probable cause to search (*State v Gagnon*, 207 NW 2d 260/ND–1973), and where, in a good faith search for aliens, officers find contraband or other evidence of crime they may seize it. *United States v Foerster*, 455 F 2d 981/Cal (1972).

Officers may properly delay the search of a suspect vehicle crossing the border, although probable cause exists upon entry, for the purpose of tracing the vehicle to its destination and sweeping up all guilty parties along with the contraband. *United States v Caraway*, 474 F 2d 25/Fla (1973).

Searches conducted approximately 55 miles north of the Mexican border can be justified as a border search as it was well within the 100-mile limit, and border patrol officers may properly stop and investigate vehicles for concealed aliens without the rigid requirement of probable cause, but they do not have the authority to search bags, containers and compartments too small to conceal a human being. *United States v Thompson*, 475 F 2d 1359/Tex (1973).

Consent Searches

Officers are not required to tell the driver of an automobile that he does not have to consent to a search of his automobile when asked or that he could demand a search warrant, and where the driver was asked for permission to search and without vocal response handed officers her keys, she thereby gave valid consent to the search. *United States v Mallory*, 460 F 2d 243/Kan (1972).

Plain View Doctrine Relative to Vehicle Searches

When officers are legally on the premises of another or on public property and see the fruits of a crime in plain view, they may arrest with probable cause and conduct an incident search (*State v Brown*, 426 P 2d 129/Kan–1967). This rule is equally applicable where officers stop an automobile for a traffic violation and see contraband or fruits of a crime in the vehicle (*State v Hanawahine*, 443 P 2d 149/Haw–1968), and if the incident occurs at night officers may shine a light into the passenger compartments of a legally stopped automobile to aid in visual inspection (*Sharkey v State*, 459 P 2d 769/Nev–1969). Thus, where the officer from outside of the vehicle directs the beam of a flashlight inside a vehicle in search of a weapon and sees "green stuff" which appears to be marijuana, it may be seized under the plain view doctrine. *Armour v Trotty*, 486 SW 2d 537/Ten (1972).

If police, under authority of a statute to stop automobiles upon the highway to inspect drivers' licenses and registrations, observe contraband narcotics in plain view in the vehicle, all such contraband is subject to seizure. *State v Garcia*, 192 SE 2d 2/NC (1972).

Where an officer stopped a driver for speeding and discovered the license plate to be stolen and observed a pistol lying on the front seat in plain view, he was justified in searching the vehicle, its occupants and their effects. *State v Walker*, 490 SW 2d 332/Mo (1973).

Vehicle Inventory

The term "police inventory" as used in the impoundment of an automobile is susceptible to only one meaning–that the inventory be conducted by an officer of the law, preferably the arresting officer, for the purpose of protecting the contents and for the protection of the officer should he be later sued for the misappropriation of the contents thereof. *Gonzales v State*, 507 P 2d 1277/Ok (1973).

Before police may justify an inventory of the property in a vehicle, the vehicle must be in lawful custody, and if the inventory is pursuant to the arrest of an occupant, the arrest must have been lawful. *City of St Paul v Myles*, 218 NW 2d 697/Min (1974).

Police have the authority to inspect and inventory all articles of personal property in plain sight within a disabled vehicle and, if necessary, to lock property in the trunk of the vehicle, or to transfer it to some other place for safekeeping, and if, in the course of such inventory, police discover contraband or other incriminatory evidence, they may seize it and use it in a prosecution of one responsible for its presence. *In re One 1965 Econoline*, 511 P 2d 168/Az (1973).

A vehicle inventory by police, initiated and supervised by a federal agent, was proper and the discovery of a check-writing machine fell within the plain view doctrine and could be seized; the seizure did not fall within the ambit of the so-called "silver-platter" doctrine, wherein the officers of one jurisdiction seize evidence illegally and turn it over to officers of another jurisdiction. *Capps v State*, 505 SW 2d 727/Ten (1974).

Where a vehicle was lawfully impounded, the officer conducting an inventory search was justified in seizing a matchbox containing LSD which was lying on the floor of the rear compartment. *Lee v State*, 198 SE 2d 720/Ga (1973).

Although police have the right to inventory and to secure arrestee's vehicle when he is arrested for driving while intoxicated, they have no right to conduct a general exploratory search for evidence. *People v Rivera*, 339 NYS 2d 82/NY (1972).

Improper Searches

If the arrest or stopping of a driver is a sham, made as an excuse to search the vehicle, any evidence found as a result thereof will not be admissible (*United States v One Cadillac Hardtop*, 224 FS 210/Wis–1963). Thus where Tacoma police held a misdemeanor warrant for the arrest of defendant for the possession of gambling equipment, and believing him to be northbound from Tacoma toward the Canadian border, they notified King County sheriffs of the warrant. Shortly thereafter a King County patrol unit observed defendant northbound fail to signal his intention to turn and stopped him allegedly for that reason, but for the real purpose of searching his truck for gambling equipment which they found. The court held in reversing conviction that the search was unlawful not being incident to the traffic arrest. *State v Michaels*, 374 P 2d 989/Wn (1962).

Probable cause to search a passenger in the back seat does not exist; where a driver was stopped for speeding during a rush hour and the only basis for the search was a movement of the passenger's right arm and shoulder "as if to hide something," a gun and heroin found in a subsequent search should have been suppressed. *United States v Page*, 298 A 2d 233/DC (1972).

Although defendant was properly arrested on an enclosed automobile storage lot for tampering with an automobile, the warrantless search of his personal automobile parked some distance away on the street was improper (*Martin v State*, 305 A 2d 197/Md–1973). Nor was a search of arrestee's automobile a proper incident search where the automobile was not under the immediate control of arrestee and he could not have obtained a weapon of offense or destructible evidence therefrom. *People v Dumas*, 512 P 2d 120/Cal (1973).

The warrantless search of defendant's home and his vehicle after his arrest on a warrant and his transfer to the police station, was not justified by exigent circumstances, nor was the search incident to a lawful arrest as defendant was arrested in his home and incident search must be made in the immediate vicinity of the arrest to be valid. *Com v Heard*, 301 A 2d 870/Pa (1973).

Where defendant first refused a trooper's request for consent to search the trunk of his automobile and reluctantly produced a key after some equivocation, consent was not freely given but rather acquiescence, and narcotics found therein should be been repressed. *Vaughn v State*, 477 SW 2d 260/Ten (1971).

While police may take note of any personal property in plain sight within an automobile being taken into custody, only objects which are plainly visible without probing may be listed in the inventory or other police report, and a search into a closed suitcase, or a package or bag, constitutes an unreasonable search. *People v Landa,* 106 CR 329/Cal–1973); *State v Gwinn,* 301 A 2d 291/Del (1972).

The warrantless search of an impounded automobile on the day following the arrest of its occupants could not be justified as being incident to arrest and the evidence thus seized was improperly admitted into evidence. *People v Hill,* 107 CR 791/Cal (1973).

An error committed in conducting a second search where nothing was seized has no bearing on the validity of a previous search. *State v McGown,* 203 NW 2d 445/Neb (1973).

Vehicle Forfeiture

A statute declaring forfeiture of any automobile *or other vehicle* usedor intended to be used to conceal, carry or transport drugs illegally, included within the definition an airplane and its forefeiture to the state was proper. *McReynolds v Municipal Court,* 207 NW 2d 792/Ia (1973).

A proceeding for the forfeiture of an automobile or other vehicle illegally used to transport or facilitate the sale of contraband drugs or narcotics, is a civil proceeding and the state need prove its case only by a preponderance of evidence, and there is no constitutional objection to placing the burden upon its owner to prove that he is entitled to recovery of his vehicle as falling within one of the exceptions to the law. *Fell v Armour,* 355 FS 1319/Ten (1972).

Absent exigent circumstances, an automobile may not be seized on the theory that it is an instrumentality of the crime and in plain view; as a rule, such seizure must be authorized by a search warrant. *Lewis v Cardwell,* 354 FS 26/Oh (1972).

Chapter IX

Search and Seizure—General

"Search" Defined

A "search," in the constitutional sense, is an examination of a man's house, buildings, premises or person for the purpose of discovering some evidence of his guilt to be used in a prosecution of him for a crime for which he is, or may be charged; it implies a prying into hidden places for that which is concealed, an exploratory investigation or an invasion and quest. *State v Cundy*, 201 NW 2d 236/SD (1972); *Bielicki v Superior Court*, 371 P 2d 288/Cal (1962).

"Curtilage," which is protected by the Fourth Amendment against unreasonable searches and seizures, includes a small sector of land, which may be enclosed but need not be, around a dwelling house and generally includes incidental buildings used for domestic purposes. *United States v Wolfe*, 375 FS 949/DC (1974).

The careful exploration of the outer surface of a person's clothing or a "pat-down" (*State v Ramey*, 282 NE 2d 65/Oh–1972), the use of electronic devices to intercept conversation of others (*United States v Hall*, 488 F 2d 193/Az–1973), and the taking of blood from the veins of one suspected of driving while under the influence of alcohol, are searches within the meaning of the Fourth Amendment. *State v Brunner*, 507 P 2d 233/Kan (1973).

A "stop" is a "seizure" of the person and a "frisk" is a "search" within the contemplation of the Fourth Amendment. *Gibbs v State*, 306 A 2d 587/Md (1973).

A Louisiana court held that where an officer grabbed a suspicious package from defendant, which was in plain view, there was only a seizure, since that which is in plain view is not the subject of a search. *State v Jackson*, 269 S 2d 465/La (1972).

In General

At common law and throughout the history of American jurisprudence, the courts have held that an officer, in the execution of a lawful arrest, may conduct an incident search of the *immediate vicinity* for the fruits of the crime, means used to commit the crime, evidence of the crime, and, if warranted, for weapons or potential weapons which may be used to launch an attack upon the officer or to effect an escape. "Immediate vicinity," prior to 1969, in most jurisdictions meant search of an entire residence, attached garage, etc., to which the arrestee had access. In 1969, in *Chimel v California,* 395 US 752, the traditional "immediate vicinity" was redefined by the U.S. Supreme Court and more narrowly circumscribed to include that area virtually within the reach of arrestee, thus overruling centuries of tradition. The Constitution had not changed; the law had not changed; men privileged to interpret the Constitution *had* changed.

Searches and seizures by law enforcement officers are governed by the Fourth and Fourteenth Amendments to the United States Constitution:

> *Article IV.* The right of the people to be secure in their persons, houses, papers, and effects, against unreasonable searches and seizures, shall not be violated, and no warrants shall issue, but upon probable cause, supported by oath or affirmation, and particularly describing the place to be searched, and the persons or things to be seized.
>
> *Article XIV. Section 1.* All persons born or naturalized in the United States and subject to the jurisdiction thereof, are citizens of the United States and of the State wherein they reside. No State shall make or enforce any law which shall abridge the privileges or immunities of the citizens of the United States; nor shall any State deprive any person of life, liberty, or property, without due process of law; nor deny to any person within its jurisdiction the equal protection of the laws.

A search without a warrant is, *per se,* unreasonable unless it falls within one of the narrowly defined exceptions to the warrant requirement. The exceptions are basically four in number. They are:

1. Incident to a lawful arrest: arrestee's person and the immediate vicinity to which he has access;
2. Exigent circumstances: when police are in hot pursuit; they may enter premises and may search therein anywhere the suspect may be hiding;
3. Imminent destruction of known evidence: when police are privy to the existence of evidence and they have reasonable cause to believe it is about to be destroyed;
4. With consent: consent must be voluntary, intelligently given,

unequivocal and uncontaminated by duress or coercion. *Erickson v State*, 507 P 2d 508/Alk (1973).

There is no known statute under any law which requires one to cooperate with police in producing or discovering evidence to be used against him in his prosecution; conversely, there is no constitutional right nor right under any statute to destroy evidence; indeed, it is a crime in most jurisdictions to destroy evidence. Thus, where officers armed with an arrest warrant observed defendant attempt to swallow ten heroin capsules, their act of grabbing him by the throat to prevent swallowing was not undue force nor brutal. *United States v Harrison*, 432 F 2d 1328/DC (1970).

Although there is a presumption that an official duty is lawfully performed, when the defendant upon trial raises the issue that he was searched or arrested without warrant, the arrest or search, as a rule, is then presumed unlawful and the burden is upon the state to prove the lawfulness of the police action. *Greene v State*, 508 P 2d 1095/Ok (1973); *State v Branch*, 508 P 2d 254/Or (1973).

In the vast majority of jurisdictions the state has the burden of proving that a warrantless search was reasonable, or that a consent search was freely and voluntarily given (*Flournoy v State*, 205 SE 2d 473/Ga–1974); (*State v York*, 521 P 2d 950/Wn–1974), but a few states hold to the contrary–here Montana and Illinois–that the defendant must prove the unlawfulness of the search. *State v Tritz*, 522 P 2d 603/Mont (1974); *People v Rogers*, 310 NE 2d 854/Ill (1974).

Different rules apply to the search of an automobile from those applicable to the search of a home or an office (*Scillion v Com*, 508 SW 2d 307/Ky–1974), and this same principal applies if a search warrant is sought. *Cardwell v Lewis*, 94 SC 2464/Oh (1974).

An "inventory search" may be conducted of the person as well as an automobile or premises; an inventory search of the person is conducted when the person is under arrest and is made preparatory to placing him in detention either by thrusting the hands into the pockets and clothing of the arrestee or by ordering him to empty his pockets. *People v Dixon*, 205 NW 2d 852/Mich (1973).

Absent unusual circumstances, a house may not be seized as evidence. *People v Hill*, 107 CR 791/Cal (1973).

When Authorized

Police are authorized to conduct a search and seizure by authority of a search warrant, by consent of one who has an interest in the place and property which is the subject of search and seizure, when made contemporaneously with a legal arrest (*People v Neulist*, 338 NYS 2d 794/NY–1972), and under exigent circumstances which compel an officer to act swiftly and which make the application for a warrant impractical (*United States v Kahan*, 350 FS 784/NY–1972). Also, there are certain circumstances under which a suspect may be searched and property seized without an arrest, such as an automobile in motion, searches made in hot pursuit, searches made around the area where an arrest is made, things that are obvious to the senses, property that has been abandoned, and searches under consent. *State v Duvernoy*, 195 SE 2d 631/W Va (1973).

During the booking process, defendant not only *may* be searched, but it also is the duty of the jailor to search him, and evidence found on his person, including inside his wallet, may be seized. *People v Balassy*, 106 CR 461/Cal (1973).

One arrested for public drunkenness may be detained and searched incident to a lawful arrest irrespective of the place of confinement or whether held in jail or at a detoxification facility. *People v Superior Court*, 105 CR 695/Cal (1972).

When "Frisk" or "Pat-Down" Search May Be Made

The law differentiates between a "search" and a "frisk." The latter has attained legal status in recent years describing a police activity whereby a police officer, not having probable cause to arrest, does have probable cause to detain and does have probable cause to believe that suspect may be armed and dangerous. When these circumstances exist the officer may conduct a "cursory" or a "pat-down" search but only for weapons or objects which may be so employed. He is not usually justified in removing small or soft objects from a suspect's person (*People v Bremmer*, 106 CR 797/Cal–1973); (*Terry v Ohio*, 392 US 1/Oh–1967), and feeling a soft object in a suspect's shirt pocket during the course of a pat-down search for weapons would not justify further intrusion into that pocket for the purpose of self-protection. *People v Taylor*, 501 P 2d 918/Cal (1972).

A protective frisk for weapons may evolve into a full search if suspicions of the searching officer are properly aroused, otherwise a frisking officer may not remove any object from the suspect's pockets unless he reasonably believes the object to be a weapon. *United States v Robinson*, 471 F 2d 1082/DC (1972).

Actual fear by a policeman for his own safety or the safety of others is not a prerequisite to reasonableness of a protective search; the test is whether he had sufficient cause, as a reasonable and prudent man, to experience fear for himself or others under the circumstances. *Nash v State*, 295 A 2d 715/Del (1972).

Defendant's conviction of unlawfully carrying a concealed weapon was sustained where his conduct and that of two associates, gave an officer reasonable cause to believe that the three were about to commit a robbery and a pat-down search of defendant prior to interview disclosed the illegally concealed weapon. *Terry v Ohio*, 392 US 1/Oh (1968).

Restrictions on the right of a policeman to stop and frisk individuals suspected of criminal activity are: (1) that the stop itself be justified by specific and articulable facts which, when taken together with rational inferences, warrant the intrusion; (2) assuming a valid stop, a limited search of suspects for weapons is justified only if there are reasonable grounds for the apprehension of danger; and (3) the search be confined to the scope of the intrusion reasonably designed to discover objects capable of use as weapons. *People v Watson*, 292 NE 2d 457/Ill (1972).

Search Incident to Arrest

A search of the immediate vicinity incident to a lawful arrest was permitted under the common law of England and has been permitted under the common law rules in the United States unless modified by statute. But that area subject to incident search was materially narrowed by redefinition in *Chimel v California*, 395 US 752 (1969), to that area to which the arrestee had immediate control from which he may have seized and destroyed evidence or seized a weapon. Since *Chimel* involved the search of a residence, it affected fixed locations and had little or no application to the search of an automobile. *Chambers v Maroney*, 399 US 42/Pa (1970).

An incident search beyond the reach of arrestee is not prohibited if circumstances of the arrest are such that the arresting officer is justified in believing that an expanded search is necessary for his protection. *Simpson v State*, 486 SW 2d 807/Tex (1972).

State statutes and state appellate court rulings holding that one may not be searched incident to an arrest for a traffic violation by a police officer were overruled by the U.S. Supreme Court in *United States v Robinson*, 94 SC 467/DC (1973). However, notwithstanding the Supreme Court declaration that a full-scale search of an arrestee under lawful arrest for whatever cause, may be made, the individual states are not mandated to follow this ruling but may more narrowly circumscribe the lawful limits of incident search by restricting the search of one arrested for a traffic offense to evidence pertinent to that arrest. *People v Kelly*, 353 NYS 2d 111/NY (1974)

Where state police had reason to believe arrestees were participating in illegal gambling, they were justified in incident searches pursuant to a gambling raid in seizing money found on the person of each arrestee. *People v Di Lorenzo*, 338 NYS 2d 293/NY (1972).

The Washington Supreme Court has ruled: "The law is . . . clear that a search without a warrant may be made incident to an otherwise lawful arrest without a warrant where the arresting officers had reasonable grounds to believe that a felony had been, was being or *was about to be committed* by the person arrested" (emphasis added) (*State v Darst*, 399 P 2d 618–1965). Further, "The search, even assuming it occurred prior to the arrest, was incident to the arrest and the alleged stolen property was lawfully seized" (*People v Torres*, 366 P 2d

823/Cal–1961). The legality of a search made prior to a lawful arrest which is substantially contemporaneous and incident thereto, is not altered by the flight of the accused and the search may continue in his absence. *People v Terry*, 454 P 2d 36/Cal (1969); *Sizemore v State*, 308 NE 2d 400/Ind (1974).

An officer's right to incident search before or after a lawful arrest applies in felony arrests and in misdemeanor arrests as well (*State v Park*, 439 P 2d 212/Haw–1968), and the arrest being lawful, the officer not only has the right, but also the duty, to search the arrestee and seize any incriminating article which is connected with the crime. *State v Little*, 439 P 2d 387/Kan (1968); *Italiano v Com*, 200 SE 2d 526/Va (1973).

A warrantless search incident to a lawful arrest and the seizure of incriminating articles is justified either on the grounds of security to the officer or to prevent its destruction or concealment by gathering the fruits and implements of the crime. *State v Elkins*, 422 P 2d 250/Or (1966).

A search warrant is not necessary to the seizure of allegedly obscene motion picture films where the seizure is incident to a lawful arrest. *Good v State*, 195 SE 2d 264/Ga (1972).

Before a search incident to arrest can be deemed lawful, it must first be established that the arrest was lawful (*State v Fitz*, 490 SW 2d 30/Mo–1973), and officers should search incident to arrest and not arrest incident to a search. *United States v Failla*, 343 FS 831/NY (1972).

An officer may make an arrest for a misdemeanor committed in his presence, and incident thereto he may search the arrestee's person and his immediate environs for evidence of the crime or tools which would aid in the arrestee's escape, but the officer must be searching for specific articles (not a general exploratory search) (*Roybal v People*, 444 P 2d 875/Colo–1968), and a search of defendant at the city jail prior to incarceration is lawful. *State v Ivey*, 439 P 2d 974/Wn (1968).

Nontestimonial Evidence

The search incident to arrest must be reasonably related to the crime, and where defendant was arrested for assault with intent to commit rape, a benzidine test for the presence of blood on his penis by a trained police technician shortly after defendant's arrest was not constitutionally proscribed. *United States v Smith*, 470 F 2d 377/DC (1972).

Where defendant, who was suspected of murdering his wife, voluntarily went to a police station and, although not under arrest there was probable cause for arrest, and he refused to allow police to take a sample of fingernail scrapings, there was justification for the warrantless taking of scrapings without his consent and against his will. *Cupp v Murphy*, 93 SC 2000/Or (1973), justices Douglas and Brennan dissenting.

The Taking of Blood for Analysis

The Fourth Amendment to the Constitution does not forbid the compulsory seizure of a person's blood, without a warrant, to be analyzed for blood-alcohol content, provided the blood is taken in a medically approved manner, incident to a lawful arrest, and based on the reasonable belief that the arrestee is intoxicated (*Schmerber v California*, 384 US 757/Cal–1966), but where the subject is not under arrest, even though there is justification therefor, and the arrest is a mere formality, the forcible seizure of one's blood for evidence is an unlawful intrusion into his body and the result of an analysis of blood thus seized is inadmissible (*People v Superior Court*, 493 P 2d 1145/Cal–1972). Any seizure over the objection of the subject for analysis to determine intoxication is permissible provided it meets a three-pronged test: (1) the blood must be extracted in a medically approved manner; (2) the subject must be under arrest; and (3) the seizure must be based on the reasonable belief that the subject is intoxicated. *People v Superior Court, supra.*

The taking of blood from the driver of an automobile over his objections or without consent requires that the subject be under arrest, and the prospect of rapid dissipation of alcohol in the body of one involved in a fatal accident is not justification for a deviation from the rule especially when the subject was available for arrest and his arrest would have consumed little or no additional time. *People v Superior Court, supra.*

While the taking of a blood sample from the veins of a driver without his consent is permissible if taken incident to a lawful arrest (*State v Hausen*, 206 NW 2d 352/Min–1973), the taking of blood samples otherwise is unlawful. *Com v Brown*, 302 A 2d 475/Pa (1973).

In a prosecution for manslaughter in the driving of a motor vehicle, defendant's consent or nonconsent to a blood test is irrelevant where the test was made pursuant to a valid arrest; moreover, his consent is implied from the fact of his driving. *State v Spry*, 207 NW 2d 504/SD (1973).

Where defendant, because of the nature of his injuries and semiconscious condition, is incapable of refusing to submit to a blood test for alcohol content, the result thereof, taken without his consent, is nevertheless admissible against him in a criminal prosecution. *Morrow v State*, 303 A 2d 633/Del (1973).

States which have adopted the Uniform Motor Vehicle Act have, as a part of that act, what is popularly referred to as the "implied consent" law. This means that anyone licensed under the state law to operate a motor vehicle has given implied consent, by the application for and the acceptance of a driver's license, to the giving of either blood, breath or urine, when *he has been arrested* as a result of the driving of a motor vehicle for the violation of some law and there is reason to believe that he was operating such motor vehicle while under the influence of an intoxicating beverage. Under the aegis of this Act, the driver (if conscious) is advised by the arresting officer that he has a right to refuse to cooperate in this test but if he does refuse his license will or may be suspended for a specified period of time. It appears that the subject's "right" to refuse is a fallacy, for when one may be deprived of life, liberty, property or privilege for exercising a right, the so-called right is non-existent.

A breathalyzer test constitutes a search of the person and its validity depends on the lawfulness of the preceding arrest (*State v McCarthy*, 303 A 2d 626/NJ–1973), and where one is under arrest for driving while under the influence of intoxicating liquor and is requested by the arresting officer to submit to a breathalyzer test and refuses, such refusal is admissible against him as showing a consciousness of guilt. *People v McGinnis*, 123 Cal App 2d 138/Cal (1954).

Even though defendant did not consent to a breathalyzer test, where there was probable cause to arrest him for driving while under the influence of intoxicating liquor, the administering of the test to defendant while he was in custody was reasonable and the results thereof admissible. *State v Osburn*, 508 P 2d 837/Or (1973).

Perception by Smell

Trained investigators may rely on their sense of smell to establish probable cause just as they may rely on their senses of sight, hearing, touch and taste (*Waugh v State*, 318 A 2d 204/Md–1974). Thus, reasonable cause exists to search a package if the officer senses an odor emanating therefrom and if the odor suggests contraband (*People v Bleile*, 108 CR 682/Cal–1973). Where an officer smelled the odor of marijuana emanating from a parked automobile readily movable on a parking lot (*People v Gale*, 511 P 2d 1204/Cal–1973), or where the officer detected the odor of marijuana emanating from a truck stopped for a traffic violation, the arresting officer had probable cause to search the vehicle and marijuana found in the search was admissible in a prosecution for its unlawful possession. *People v Laird*, 296 NE 2d 864/Ill (1973).

Experienced customs officers, upon information from a freight office employee familiar with the odor of marijuana that he had detected that odor emanating from certain suitcases, had probable cause to conduct a warrantless search of the suitcases. *United States v Valen*, 348 FS 1163/Pa (1972).

Consent Searches

A permissive search by the owner is not an unreasonable search (*State v Manning*, 490 SW 2d 512/Ten–1972), but officers may not arbitrarily ask consent to search; first there must be justification for such request. *People v Hyde*, 108 CR 785/Cal (1973).

If there is a valid consent a warrantless search may be conducted, though consent, in order to be voluntary, must be unequivocal, specific, and intelligently given, uncontaminated by duress or coercion. *Erickson v State*, 507 P 2d 508/Alk (1973).

Mere persuasion, however, is not the same as coercion in a request for consent to search, and where subject first refused consent and was then advised by officers that they could easily obtain a warrant to search–when in fact officers did not know exactly what they were looking for and would not have been able to obtain a search warrant–whereupon subject withdrew her refusal and gave consent, subsequent search was held to be with valid consent. *State v Murray*, 509 P 2d 1003/Wn (1973).

The burden is upon the state to establish the validity of a warrantless search and seizure, and where defendant is under arrest at the time he gives consent to search the burden increases (*Com v Burgos*, 299 A 2d 34/Pa–1972). But the mere fact that defendant is under arrest does not negate his rights under the Fourth Amendment to consent and he may consent or decline as he chooses (*United States v Candella*, 469 F 2d 173/NY–1972), and the fact that defendant was under arrest at the time he consented to search of his home is of no consequence if consent was voluntarily and freely given. *Ribble v State*, 503 SW 2d 551/Tex (1974).

A landlord may not give police consent to search a tenant's room or apartment (*People v Hill*, 107 CR 791/Cal–1973), but when police announce themselves at the door of a place of residence and a person responds to the knock, there is a demonstration of apparent authority to search. However, the governing rule to consent search is that if made with the consent of a cooccupant under circumstances that give officers good reason to believe the person consenting has the authority to give consent, the search will be permissible, and valid consent may be extended by actions as well as words. *People v Superior Court*, 107 CR 756/Cal (1973).

The owner of a house may consent to search that portion of the house common to all members only, and that portion specifically set aside for a particular member may not be searched. *United States v Jones*, 352 FS 369/Ga (1972).

A landlord cannot give consent to police to search rented rooms but he can permit the search of hallways, washrooms and other areas commonly shared by tenants. (*State v Person*, 298 NE 2d 922/Oh–1973), and a hotel clerk or manager cannot give consent to search a guest's room until the guest's time expires and he vacates the room. *State v Dougherty*, 493 P 2d 1383/Or (1972).

Whether a consent search was voluntary or was a product of duress or coercion, or express or implied, is a fact to be determined by the totality of the circumstances (*Schneckloth v Bustamonte*, 93 SC 2041/Cal–1973), and where there is conflicting evidence as to whether a party consented to a search, the trial court is in a better position than the court of appeals to determine consent or lack thereof. *Jones v State*, 272 S 2d 910/Ala (1973).

Joint Occupancy of Premises

It is a well-settled rule that where premises are occupied by two or more persons, a search of that portion jointly possessed is reasonable if consent is granted by one of the joint occupants who is present at the time of the search, and seizure of evidence belonging to another joint occupant is lawful whether or not its owner is present or consents to the search or present and not asked. Here the wife consented to the seizure of her husband's clothing which he was believed to have worn at the time of the murder. *People v Meneley,* 105 CR 432/Cal (1972); *State v Thibodeau,* 317 A 2d 172/Me (1974).

Consent to search premises over objection is valid if given by one of multiple cooccupants whose occupancy is at least equal to any other cooccupant challenging the legality of the search (*United States v Gargiso,* 456 F 2d 584/NY–1972), but permission to search by an occupant who is not present is annulled by the objection of a cooccupant who is present. *Tompkins v Superior Court,* 378 P 2d 113/Cal (1963).

A wife, having equal right to access and occupancy of premises with her husband, may give consent to officers to search and the right of her accused husband is not violated (*McCravy v Moore,* 476 F 2d 281/Ten–1973). But a federal district court in Pennsylvania has held that a wife may give consent to search only that portion of the premises under mutual control. *United States ex rel Cook v Cliff,* 341 FS 1038/Pa (1972).

Defendant's wife had joint control over an automobile which her husband had borrowed and had parked in the family yard, and in the absence of her husband she could give consent for its search, and evidence of a bank robbery found therein was admissible in the subsequent prosecution of her husband. *United States v Hayles,* 492 F 2d 125/Tex (1974).

A joint occupant may not give consent to the search of another's private room. *People v Douglas,* 213 NW 2d 291/Mich (1973).

Advisement of Rights Not Required

A small number of jurisdictions have held that a consent search is invalid unless at the time consent to search is sought, defendant was effectively advised of his right to refuse (*United States v Menke,* 339 FS 1023/Pa–1972); but defendant is not entitled to an advisement of his constitutional rights relating to arrest before being asked for consent to search. *Dickhaut v State,* 493 SW 2d 223/Tex (1973); *Schneckloth v Bustamonte,* 93 SC 2041/Cal (1973).

Where defendant consented to a search, inviting officers to "come into my apartment, take a look around, I have nothing to hide," whereupon the officers entered and saw incriminating evidence in plain view, they could legally seize it, and defendant's attempt to rescind consent retroactively was unenforceable as rescission of consent starts at the time an officer is given notice. *United States v Young,* 471 F 2d 109/Ill (1972).

The "Knock and Announce" Rule

Where a state statute requires that officers, before entry into a structure to arrest or search, identify themselves, state their purpose and demand entry, such requirement may be suspended where officers act in reasonable good faith in the belief based upon specific information that compliance with the statute would (1) increase their peril, (2) frustrate the arrest, or (3) permit the destruction of evidence (*Ker v California*, 374 US 47–1962); (*Parsley v Superior Court*, 104 CR 643/Cal–1972). Also, officers may execute a forced entry if, after having complied with any statutory "knock-notice" rule, admittance is denied. *State v Collier*, 270 S 2d 451/Fla (1972).

Forcible Entry

Absent exigent circumstances, an announcement by officers of their identity and purpose must precede entry, and any occupant on the premises must be given a reasonable time whereby to surrender his privacy before a forced entry may be made. *Com v Cerulla*, 296 A 2d 858/Pa (1972).

Under a statute which provides in essence that an officer, after having made demand for admittance and been refused admittance, may break open any door or window in order to execute a search or a search warrant, the officer reasonably complies with the statute when he merely opens an unlocked door and he is not required to "break" the door down (*United States v Bustamente-Gamez*, 488 F 2d 4/Cal–1973). A nonconsensual entry for the purpose of a search or an arrest is a "breaking" (*People v Bennetto*, 517 P 2d 163/Cal–1974), and the unauthorized entry by use of a passkey is a forcible entry. *Com v Cerulla, supra.*

A statute permitting officers to break open any door or window to search, if after giving notice of identity and purpose admittance is refused, governs warrantless searches as well as warrant searches, even though not mentioned in the statute. *United States v Glassel*, 488 F 2d 143/Az (1973).

Officers need not, in all cases, knock, identify, demand admittance and wait until admittance is denied before they may force entry. Where officers went to defendant's apartment upon information from a reliable informant that defendant was in possession of heroin, looked through an eye-level hole in the door, and observed defendant in the act of injecting possible heroin into his arm, and upon knocking they heard rapid retreating footsteps, they could immediately force entry and pursue defendant. *Johnson v State*, 299 NE 2d 194/Ind (1973).

Where several city police and federal narcotics agents, armed with a search warrant, knocked on defendant's door and shouted "police," and inside they heard screaming and scurrying feet, their forcible entry was justified to prevent destruction of evidence, and narcotics seized in the search was admissible. *State v Young*, 455 P 2d 595/Wn (1970).

A police officer who received a telephone call from defendant's father-in-law informing him that defendant had shot his wife and was going to kill himself had probable cause to force entry into defendant's home without a search warrant, arrest defendant and seize evidence relating to the killing. *State v Corbin,* 516 P 2d 1314/Or (1973).

Exigent Circumstances

Under the "exigent circumstances" rule a reasonable search might be quite broad in scope, as where an armed robber, having demonstrated a pronounced proclivity for shooting people, sought refuge in an apartment building containing eight to twelve units; a systematic search by police in hot pursuit of all units for the suspect and weapons, although admittedly an invasion of privacy, was permissible as being reasonable under the circumstances. *People v Bradford*, 104 CR 852/Cal (1972).

An officer may search without a warrant when, *inter alia,* exigent circumstances exist, and the mere taking of the occupants of a vehicle into custody does not remove the exigency of the circumstances. *Bailey v State,* 294 A 2d 123/Md (1972).

A warrantless search is permissible if there is danger of imminent destruction of known evidence (*Erickson v State,* 507 P 2d 508/Alk–1973), but threatened destruction of evidence upon which a warrantless search is sought to be justified, must appear to be "imminent" destruction. *United States v Brewer,* 343 FS 468/Haw (1972).

Once probable cause is established to take blood from a driver for a blood-alcohol test, exigent circumstances exist because of the medical fact that alcohol in the blood dissipates with the passing of time. *State v Osburn,* 508 P 2d 837/Or (1973).

Open Field Searches

A search is not necessarily unlawful merely because the searching officers were trespassing at the time (*Dinkens v State,* 291 S 2d 122/Fla–1974), and the fact that officers were trespassers on defendant's neighbor's yard did not require suppression of evidence against defendant thus obtained. *People v Superior Court,* 112 CR 764/Cal (1974).

A search may be made in an open field without warrant and without probable cause, and that which is discovered either on or in the ground is not repressible by reason that it was obtained through trespass. *Conrad v State,* 218 NW 2d 252/Wis (1974).

The "Open Fields Doctrine," contrary to the Fourth Amendment which teaches that special protection be accorded to people in their persons, houses, papers and effects, does not extend to open fields. Where defendant buried a suitcase containing the "bait" money from a robbery in a chicken coop in an open field and then abandoned the suitcase and contents, police, acting on information filtering to an FBI agent, were justified in seizing and opening the suitcase without warrant, and contents were admissible against defendant in a robbery prosecution (*United States v Brown*, 473 F 2d 952/La–1953). Likewise, the search by police of a stone quarry, in an open field and adjacent to a wooded area, did not violate defendant's constitutional rights under the Fourth Amendment. *Corman v State*, 294 NE 2d 812/Ind (1973).

Discarded or Abandoned Property

The U.S. Supreme Court in *Katz v United States*, 389 US 347 (1967), ruled that "the Fourth Amendment protects people, not places," and wherever an individual may harbor "a reasonable expectation of privacy" he is entitled to be free from unreasonable governmental intrusion. Thus, where defendant attempted to burn stolen articles and abandoned their remnants in a trash barrel at the rear of his house, his apparent abandonment was a revocable decision which would not be irrevocable until he either vacated the premises or placed the barrel and contents in public view. *Ball v State*, 205 NW 2d 353/Wis (1973).

Articles abandoned in a wastebasket in a government office still retained their status as private property as the person who placed them there intended that they be destroyed (*United States v Kahan*, 350 FS 784/NY–1972). Also, the warrantless search of a trash can within a few feet of the back door of defendant's home and on defendant's property was held unlawful (*People v Edwards*, 458 P 2d 713/Cal–1969). But the search by police officers of a garbage can located in an alley adjacent to where defendant was arrested and the seizure of evidence found therein did not violate defendant's Fourth Amendment rights. *State v Fassler*, 503 P 2d 807/Az (1972).

When an article is dropped, thrown or placed away from the person of the accused in a public place, the recovery thereof does not involve a search and any evidence which is discovered thereby is admissible; accordingly, a paper bag thrown over a six-foot block wall upon the approach of police was subject to recovery by police and heroin therein was admissible against defendant. *Gomez v State*, 486 SW 2d 338/Tex (1972).

Where, upon the approach of officers, defendant threw a suitcase over a wall, the act of detaining suspect while one officer looked into the suitcase was reasonable as detention in order to obtain a search warrant would have been protracted while immediate search could have dispelled suspicion and terminated detention. *People v Orr*, 103 CR 266/Cal (1972).

Where officers upon approaching a suspect ordered him to remove his hands from his pockets and in so doing he removed a cigarette package and discarded it, a subsequent inspection of the contents by officers did not amount to a search. *People v Stafford*, 104 CR 754/Cal (1972).

Although evidence abandoned is usually admissible against defendant, where defendant pushed a wooden box containing narcotics overboard into the water it could not be recovered and used against him where the "abandonment" was a consequence of an illegal search. *Earnest v State*, 293 S 2d 111/Fla (1974).

The "Plain View" Doctrine–In General

The legal principle underlying the "plain view" doctrine is that a police officer is entitled to seize evidence of a crime which he recognizes as such, provided that he has a right to be in the place where he is when he observes the evidence (*State v Sagner*, 506 P 2d 510/Or–1973); but where police, while standing on defendant's property in the middle of the night, looked through the window of a storage trailer, property they saw did not come within the principle of the plain view doctrine. *Ball v State*, 205 NW 353/Wis (1973).

An officer does not have the right to seize any and all objects for examination in order to determine if the object has evidential value; its discovery must be inadvertent and its evidential value readily apparent (*State v Meichel*, 290 S 2d 878/La–1974), and where officers expect to find evidence in a particular place, the plain view doctrine does not apply. *State V Person*, 298 NE 2d 922/Oh (1973).

The plain view doctrine applies, not only in the seizure of that which is visible, but to that which is detected through the sense of smell. Where defendant was lawfully stopped while driving with defective brake lights, and upon approaching the driver the officer smelled the distinctive odor of marijuana emanating from the vehicle, probable cause to search arose under the plain view doctrine and exigent circumstances existed justifying a warrantless search of the vehicle. *Rose v City of Enterprise*, 293 S 2d 862/Ala (1974).

The Michigan Supreme Court has observed of the plain view rule, "[It] does not slink away at sunset to emerge again at the break of day," and such rule, permitting seizure of objects within plain view of an officer lawfully in place, could be applied even if "view" was obtained solely with aid of an officer's flashlight. *State v Stark*, 506 SW 2d 1/Mo (1974); *People v Whalen*, 213 NW 2d 116/Mich (1973).

Eavesdropping and surrepitious observation through a keyhole into a private room, even though the officer was standing in a common passageway in a rooming house, was a "search" within the meaning of constitutional proscription and a violation of the occupant's reasonable expectation of privacy (*State v Person*, 298 NE 2d 922/Oh–1973). But the Federal Circuit Court of New York has held that what can be heard by the naked ear or seen by the naked eye, even through a keyhole, is not protected by the Fourth Amendment. *United States v Ortega*, 471 F 2d 1350/NY (1972).

Narcotics paraphernalia which was in plain view to officers when the door was opened in response to their knock, was subject to seizure under the plain view doctrine (*Wheeler v United States*, 300 A 2d 713/DC–1973). Also, when the thing observed is in a building and officers, while standing in a place where they have a right to be which is open to the public, see through an open door into a back room where there is paraphernalia peculiar to the operation of a lottery, they have reasonable cause to enter, search and arrest. *Fisher v United States*, 205 F 702/DC (1953); *People v Bennetto*, 517 P 2d 1163/Cal (1974).

An officer who had a right to be in defendant's house and who looked toward an open closet to ascertain if someone was hiding therein, was justified, when he saw what he thought to be marijuana debris on the closet floor, in walking closer and using his flashlight for a closer inspection of the debris, and he was further justified in seizing the marijuana and secobarbital capsules which were in plain view. *People v Shepard*, 109 CR 388/Cal (1973).

Where officers, with permission of the owner, stood on his porch in order to see into the adjacent yard, stood on their toes and leaned around a partition and stood on a box, their observations were subject to the plain view doctrine. *United States v McMillon*, 350 FS 593/DC (1972).

Where officers had probable cause to arrest defendant for a felony, here grand larceny, they could enter his hotel room without a warrant; and once inside legally, the officers had the right to seize a stolen stereo set they observed in plain view. *State v Hackett*, 481 P 2d 466/Wn (1971).

Where an officer bought a deck of allegedly obscene playing cards from defendant, there was no "seizure" involved and the cards were admissible as evidence. *State v Hughes*, 508 NW 2d 6/Mo (1974).

Plain View Evidence Following Entry to Arrest

Although a search of a residence cannot be made for evidence except under well-defined circumstances, a search may be made for a suspect. Thus, where police had been informed that five men, all armed, were involved in a kidnap and robbery, and the officers, upon entry of the apartment, observed only four, they were justified in searching the apartment for the fifth man and all evidence found inadvertantly in the search was admissible. *Com v Flowers*, 298 NE 2d 898/Mas (1973).

Where officers were lawfully on the premises to arrest defendant and another person unknown to officers ran up defendant's stairs, officers were justified in following as a protective measure and were lawfully in the bathroom when they observed heroin in plain view providing right of seizure. *Simpson v State*, 486 SW 2d 807/Tex (1972).

Officers, upon arresting defendant in his residence, had the right to walk through the house and conduct a cursory examination prior to securing the premises to ascertain if anyone else was present to threaten their safety or destroy evidence prior to their return with a search warrant to conduct a thorough search, but in the cursory search articles of evidence in plain view were subject to seizure. *United States v Christophe*, 470 F 2d 865/NY (1972).

Where defendant furnished informant a quantity of wine-soaked marijuana thus giving officers probable cause to arrest, and officers knocked on defendant's door and demanded admittance, and when their demands were ignored, they properly entered his house forcibly. In searching through defendant's house for defendant, one officer passed a closet with the door ajar; he opened the door wider and looked inside, saw a paper bag on the floor, smelled the strong odor of wine-soaked marijuana; he opened the bag and found it to contain marijuana. In finding a rear window open and the premises vacant, officers staked out and arrested defendant upon his return. The appellate court observed in reversing conviction that officers were justified in forcibly entering in search of defendant, and could properly search the premises including the closet for *defendant*, but could not search the paper bag. *People v Marshall*, 442 P 2d 665/Cal (1968).

Wrongful Employment of Plain View Doctrine

The "plain view" doctrine is operable where the thing viewed is recognizable to the officer and not usually otherwise. Thus, a brown paper bag containing money taken from behind a water heater by police, was not properly a "plain view" seizure when all that was visible was the brown paper bag and the paper bag did not constitute evidence and was not a fruit nor an instrumentality of the crime. *United States v Shye*, 473 F 2d 1061/Ten (1973).

The plain view doctrine does not apply to a sealed package whose appearance is not indicative of its illicit contents. *State v Matthews*, 216 NW 2d 90/ND (1974).

Where under a wrongful assertion of authority defendant opened her apartment door for officers, they could not rely on what they had seen in plain view to justify her arrest and search incident thereto. *People v Shelton*, 388 P 2d 665/Cal (1964).

Narcotics officers, acting on a tip from an informant, went to a designated address and as a ruse to induce occupant at the address where a "pot party" was in session to open the door, one officer advised occupant that he had hit an automobile parked on the street. Upon being thus advised, defendant opened the outer door at which time officers detected the distinctive odor of burning marijuana. The officers entered and observed narcotics and paraphernalia in plain view. It was held that the officers did not act improperly and evidence thus obtained was admissible. *People v Troy*, 334 NYS 2d 953/NY (1972).

Search of Body Cavities

The fact that users and sellers of contraband narcotics often conceal the substance in moisture-proof wrappings inside body cavities justifies a strip-search and a visual scrutiny of the rectal area to assist in providing a clear indication of the necessity of a subsequent cavity search and probe. *United States v Holtz*, 479 F 2d 89/Az (1973).

As part of a strip-search the subject may be required to spread his buttocks for visual scrutiny of the rectal area and evidence thus discovered may justify anal and/or vaginal probe for hidden contraband. *United States v Holtz, supra.*

Where an X-ray revealed an object in the rectum of a prisoner when he reentered the prison after an outside-the-wall assignment, and he refused to submit to an enema and was placed under surveillance in a maximum security cell with the water to the commode turned off, prison officials did not violate any right of the prisoner when they entered the cell after prisoner used the toilet and retrieved a prophylactic containing marijuana. *Larkin v People*, 493 P 2d 1/Colo (1972).

Evidence concealed within the body of the defendant—here, a bullet fired by the murder victim—may under proper circumstances be removed where there is no danger to life or limb of the defendant. The extraction of the bullet, to be used as evidence in defendant's prosecution for murder, does not violate defendant's right against self-incrimination nor does it constitute an unreasonable search and seizure. *Creamer v State* 192 SE 2d 350/Ga (1972).

Mere suspicion will not justify a skin search or the search of body cavities; rather, a "real suspicion" supported by objective and articulable facts is necessary. *Shorter v United States*, 469 F 2d 61/Haw (1972).

Student Searches by School Officials

High school officials are not government officials within the meaning of the Fourth Amendment in its guarantee against unreasonable searches and seizures; furthermore, the doctrine of *in loco parentis* (in place of parents) expands to high school officials in their exercise of responsibility and control over students (*In re W*, 105 CR 775/Cal—1973), and the opening of a student's locker with a master key to verify another student's report that the locker contained marijuana, was reasonable. Id.

When one is the owner and in possession of premises and contraband is found thereon, the owner is presumed to be in constructive possession of the contraband. *Neves v State*, 268 S 2d 890/Mis (1970).

Entry to Render Emergency Aid

Police officers may enter a dwelling without a warrant to render emergency aid and assistance to a person whom they reasonably believe to be in distress and in need of assistance, and where officers were summoned to a named address to assist one there whom the emergency operator believed to need assistance, and officers could see a man inside standing and swaying who did not respond to repeated knocks on the door, their entry without warrant or invitation was justified and evidence of a homicide including the dead body thus discovered was lawful. *State v Sanders*, 506 P 2d 892/Wn (1973).

An officer investigating a reportedly abandoned car who knocked on defendant's door and was informed by a five-year-old girl that she and her two-year-old brother were at home alone, had reasonable cause to believe that the children may be endangered and to enter the premises, and a loaded pistol and a plastic bag of marijuana brought to the officer by the little girl were not the product of an unlawful search. *People v Somas,* 327 NYS 779/NY (1972).

Examples of Probable Cause to Search

Information upon which probable cause to arrest or search may be based is practically endless. Any reasonable stimulant which raises in the mind of an ordinary prudent person that facts exist justifying arrest or search, will be recognized and condoned by the courts. Ultimately, however, informed and deliberate determination of probable cause for a search is to be made by a neutral and detached magistrate rather than by a police officer. *Slate v Bastida,* 271 S 2d 854/La (1973).

If one officer has probable cause to search a suspect and he directs another to conduct a search of the suspect's person, the search is valid even though the searching officer has no information which would justify the search. *State v Smith,* 517 P 2d 83/Az (1973).

Where officers received a call from their dispatcher to investigate a "pot party" at a given address, it was their right and duty to investigate; and since while standing at a place where they had a right to be (at the front door) they observed through parted drapes defendant trying to light what appeared to be a marijuana cigarette, their subsequent arrest and seizure of evidence was lawful. *People v Buttoroff,* 500 P 2d 979/Colo (1972).

Evidence of a trained dog's high level of performance and great degree of accuracy in detecting marijuana odors by scratching, barking and biting, justified reliance on the dog's reaction as corroboration of an informant's tip. The court observed, "We are aware of no reported cases involving the use of dogs as marijuana detectors [but] their use in tracking fugitives has long been admissible in evidence to show an accused was the perpetrator of a criminal act." *People v Furman,* 106 CR 366/Cal (1973).

Where defendant entered an apartment and upon observing an officer in the act of arresting an occupant, turned and ran, the officer was justified in pursuing and searching defendant and evidence thus discovered was admissible. *Martinez v State,* 504 SW 2d 897/Tex (1974).

The transfer of suspects from their motel room to another adjacent to investigating officers which had connecting doors thus facilitating eavesdropping by the police—all with the cooperation of the motel manager—was not repugnant to the Fourth Amendment as violating an expectation of privacy, and conversation thus heard was admissible against defendants. *United States v Perry,* 339 FS 209/Cal (1972); *United States v Sin Nagh Fong,* 490 F 2d 527/Or (1974).

Where an officer reponded to a call to a bus depot and found a man lying unconsious on the floor of the rest room, objective facts dictated right and duty to search the subject's person for identification and evidence of his comatose condition. *State v Miller,* 486 SW 2d 435/Mo (1972).

Where an informant had been obviously beaten and approached an officer stating he had been robbed and pointed out the alleged robber, the officer was justified in arresting the suspect and the defendant's subsequent acquittal of the charge had no effect on the lawfulness of his arrest. *State v Eckman,* 515 P 2d 837/Wn (1973).

Information from a reliable informant may constitute probable cause and justify a warrantless search for contraband even though the information is hearsay. *In re One Peterbilt Tractor,* 506 P 2d 1199/NM (1973).

The general test to determine whether an illegal search has occurred is whether the person whose privacy was invaded had a reasonable expectation of privacy (*People v Dajnowicz,* 204 NW 2d 231/Mich–1972). The facts of every case must be examined in light of the "reasonable expectation of privacy" test and only after it is determined that the aggrieved party did not have such expectation do traditional consent tests come into play. *Braddock v State,* 194 SE 2d 317/Ga (1972).

Defendant enjoyed no reasonable expectation of privacy where he stored stolen automobile parts in his backyard surrounded by an opaque fence and officers made observations into his backyard from a neighbor's yard and from a helicopter, and seizure of the goods thus observed was lawful. *People v Superior Court,* 112 CR 764/Cal (1974).

Defendants who had permission to use a neighbor's trash can enjoyed no reasonable expectation of privacy, and an officer's act of retrieving a bag of narcotics therefrom did not violate the owner's expectation of privacy as she was innocent of crime. *People v Superior Court,* 100 CR 604/Cal (1972).

Challenge of Legality of Search

The first essential prerequisite in challenging incriminating evidence seized in a search alleged to be unlawful, is that the challenger must have "standing" to raise the question (*State v Hornbeck,* 492 SW 2d 802/Mo–1973). Thus, defendant had no standing to object to the introducton of evidence taken from an automobile which did not belong to him (*State v Gallagher,* 509 P 2d 852/Mont–1973), nor did defendant have standing to challenge incriminating conversation obtained in a wiretap where he did not claim to be a party to any conversation or against whom the interception was directed, nor that the wiretap occurred on his premises. *United States v Ceraso,* 355 FS 126/Pa (1973).

One does have standing to challenge the legality of a search of his automobile even though he disclaims ownership or knowledge of items seized (*Cash v Williams,* 455 F 2d 1227/Ten–1972), but he does not have standing to complain of the search of an automobile and seizure of articles therefrom when he denies ownership of the automobile. *Russell v State*, 259 S 2d 298/Ala (1972).

One charged with a narcotics violation has no standing to challenge the legality of the search of a body cavity of his accomplice. *United States v Johnson*, 454 F 2d 700/Cal (1972).

A lawfully arrested person has no reasonable expectation of privacy while being transported in a police vehicle, and where defendant abandoned counterfeit bills therein, he had no standing to challenge the legality of the search of the police vehicle and the recovery of the hidden and abandoned bills. *United States v Maryland*, 479 F 2d 566/Pa (1973); *Alvarez v State*, 508 SW 2d 100/Tex (1974).

One has no standing to object to a search when privacy has not been invaded (*United States v Colbert*, 474 F 2d 174/Ala–1973), or to the seizure by police of property which has been abandoned (Id), or to the search of a motel room after the subject has checked out (*Lamer v State*, 508 P 2d 665/Ok–1973). Nor does defendant have standing to challenge the legality of a search of his wife's purse. *United States v Ramirez*, 480 F 2d 76/Cal (1973).

Where marijuana plants which were seized by police came not from defendant's property but from property adjacent to his, they were admissible against defendant and he had no standing to complain of an illegal search of the property from which the plants were taken. *Freeland v State*, 285 S 2d 895/Mis (1973).

Contraband

"Contraband" is property such as counterfeit coin, narcotics, or machine guns, which may not be lawfully possessed except by the state and need not be returned to the possessor (*Sullivan v Grupposo*, 355 NYS 2d 55/NY–1974). The right to have contraband returned is not governed by the law of search and seizure, but by the law of contraband. *Stroupe v Tidwell*, 510 SW 2d 77/Ten (1974).

An officer, in conducting an anti-skyjacking search for weapons and explosives, is not required to return to the owner such articles as counterfeit money, drugs or narcotics, when he does not discover items for which the search was made. *People v Lopez*, 342 NYS 2d 420/NY (1973).

UNLAWFUL SEARCHES

In General

Police may not escape the proscription of the Fourth Amendment by directing a private citizen to conduct a search which they cannot lawfully conduct, for in so doing the private citizen becomes the agent of police and the Fourth Amendment rules of search and seizure apply equally to him (*United States v West*, 453 F 2d 1351/Del–1972); but a private citizen not acting in concert with nor at the direction of police in conducting a search, is not acting in violation of the Fourth Amendment and any evidence thus discovered is admissible. *Cash v Williams*, 455 F 2d 1227/Ten (1972); *Burdeau v McDowell*, 41 SC 574/Pa (1921).

Where officers illegally entered a residence through the front door, the finding and seizure of growing marijuana plants in the backyard was tainted by the illegal entry and inadmissible in a prosecution for its unlawful cultivation and possession. *People v Abdon*, 106 CR 879/Cal (1973).

Where police officers knocked on the door of an apartment and falsely stated they were investigating a gas leak, and when the apartment door was opened they saw a clear plastic bag containing what appeared to be marijuana, the search and arrest were violative of defendant's constitutional rights and evidence should have been suppressed. *People v Jefferson*, 350 NYS 2d 3/NY (1973).

Where police went onto the premises of a dwelling house and one of the officers entered the back of a truck parked in the driveway, and from this vantage point looked through a window of the dwelling, such acts constituted an "invasion of privacy," and evidence thus discovered should have been repressed. *United States v Langley*, 466 F 2d 27/Mich (1972).

Suspicion of the commission of crimes in a public rest room, permits officers to enter as any member of the public, and if they observe crime in plain view they may arrest. But where an officer entered a plumbing access room to observe clandestinely the interior of the rest room and observed defendant committing an act of oral copulation (sodomy) on another man, his conviction was improper and was reversed on the ground that the state based its case on the intangible fruit of an illegal search. *People v Triggs*, 506 P 2d 232/Cal (1973).

An entry by authority of a void process is an illegal entry, and where officers gained entry into defendant's residence by means of a void search warrant, the subsequent search and seizure of marijuana was unlawful. *State v Langan*, 445 P 2d 465/Mont (1968); *United States v Merritt*, 293 F 2d 742/Pa (1961).

Where one of the attending officers suggested the possibility of kicking defendant's door in if they were refused admission, consent to a subsequent search was tainted by coercive tactics and heroin found in the search should have been suppressed. *Lightfoot v State*, 520 P 2d 955/Nev (1974).

Without more, officers may not search two suspects who they see exchange unidentified objects, even if the exchange occurs in an area of high narcotic incidence. *Filitti v Superior Court*, 100 CR 583/Cal (1972).

Victims of illegal searches and seizures may sue officers to obtain civil damages, but defendant officer may offer by way of rebuttal his good faith belief in the validity of his search or arrest and the manner in which it was conducted. *United States v Artieri*, 491 F 2d 440/Con (1970).

Search or Arrest on Hunch

The inarticulate hunch, suspicion or good faith of the arresting officer is insufficient to constitute probable cause for an arrest, a search, or even a temporary detention. *Tolbert v State*, 489 SW 2d 309/Tex (1973).

An unlawful search cannot justify an arrest (*Johnson v United States*, 333 US 10/Wn–1947), but rather, what is known by officers at the time of the search or arrest. Nor does the validity of the arrest depend on the actual guilt of the arrestee, only that there was reasonable cause to believe the person arrested had committed a felony. *State v Loyd*, 435 P 2d 797/Id (1967).

The finding of marijuana concealed beneath the shirt of one illegally searched does not justify his arrest as it is well established that an arrest cannot be justified on what is found in a subsequent search. *Rios v United States*, 364 US 253/Cal (1960).

Arrest at One Place—Search of Another

The warrantless search of arrestee's bedroom following his arrest in the kitchen was unlawful and the doctrine of plain view provided no independent justification for the seizure of an unregistered firearm found in plain view in his bedroom in a "sweep search." *United States v Gamble*, 473 F 2d 1274/Ill (1973).

Although officers had probable cause to arrest defendant in a residence, they were not entitled to delay the formal arrest, transport defendant to his hotel room and there place him under formal arrest for the purpose of conducting a search of his hotel room incident to the arrest (*People v Haven*, 381 P 2d 927/Cal–1963), and when defendant raises the issue at his trial that he was arrested or searched without a warrant he establishes *prima facie* that the arrest or search was illegal and the burden devolves upon the prosecution to show proper justification. Id.

Where city police officers without warrant searched defendant's hotel room in another city and found a gun and a pair of sunglasses used in a robbery in their city, the seizure of such articles was unlawful and could not be justified on the grounds that the search was with permission of the hotel clerk, nor could it be justified as incident to arrest as the defendant was not arrested until two days later and in another state. The court further observed in reversing conviction that at least twice previously the Supreme Court had refused to permit police searches of hotel rooms based on permission from a hotel manager or proprietor. *Stoner v California*, 84 S Ct 889 (1964).

It is not improper to delay search of the arrestee until he has been taken to the police station, and a search under such circumstances is a proper incident search. *People v Howell*, 105 CR 748/Cal (1973).

Lawful Arrest—Unlawful Search

Where officers entered defendant's apartment with probable cause to arrest and found defendant gone, and thereupon conducted a search finding incriminating evidence and arresting defendant upon his return, their search was not incident to the arrest and evidence found and seized was inadmissible. *Mosco v United States*, 301 F 2d 180/Cal (1962).

Although officers had probable cause to enter defendant's house forcibly to arrest him for possession of marijuana, they had no right to search for the evidence known to be in the house even when an officer smelled the odor of wine-soaked marijuana emanating from a closet partially open (*People v Marshall*, 442 P 2d 665/Cal–1968), but evidence illegally seized did not invalidate the arrest. *United States v Artieri*, 491 F 2d 440/Con (1974).

Arrestee, thought to be a runaway juvenile, was properly taken into custody for the purpose of proving identification and age, but such custody was not an arrest and could not provide justification for the search of the subject's purse and the seizure of marijuana found therein. *State v Hough*, 516 P 2d 613/Mont (1973).

Fruit of the Poison Tree

Information or evidence illegally obtained as a result of an unlawful search by government officers or their agents, is not admissible in any court in a criminal prosecution (*Mapp v Ohio*, 367 US 643–1961); also, any derivative information or evidence uncovered as a result of the original unlawful search is likewise inadmissible as "fruit of the poison tree." *Silverthorne Lumber Co v United States*, 251 US 383/NY (1920); *United States ex rel Chennault v Smith*, 366 FS 717/NY (1973).

In order for the fruit of the poison tree doctrine to be applicable, the seizure of the evidence in the first instance must have been illegal. *State v Rendel*, 509 P 2d 247/Az (1973); *Wong Sun v United States*, 371 US 471 (1963).

If the police use illegally seized evidence to induce or trigger a confession, the confession is inadmissible as fruit of the poison tree (*McCloud v Bounds*, 474 F 2d 968/NC (1973). This doctrine forbids the use of such evidence whether verbal or tangible. Id.

Where information upon which a search warrant was based was derived from a conversation illegally intercepted, the search warrant was a nullity and any evidence seized thereunder was fruit of the poisonous tree and should have been repressed. *People v Sturgis*, 352 NYS 2d 942/NY (1973).

A second search of defendant's residence, although made under authority of a warrant, was illegal when information on which the warrant was issued was gained in a prior unlawful search, and LSD thus discovered and seized was tainted by the prior unlawful search. *Michaud v State*, 505 P 2d 1399/Ok (1973).

INFORMANTS

Credibility—How Established

The credibility of an informant can be established by a showing that he had previously furnished information which led to conviction, that he was an eyewitness with personal knowledge or that the information imparted by the informant was against his penal interests, but these methods are not exclusive. Thus, where several informants are furnishing information—each unknown to the others—and information from one is corroborated by information from another, reliability in all is enhanced thereby. *Huff v Com*, 194 SE 690/Va (1973).

The New Mexico Supreme Court has held that the identity of a reliable informant need not be disclosed in order that information provided by him be used as a basis for a warrantless search; credibility of an informant may be established by the testimony of an officer who has received reliable information from the informant in the past. *In re One Peterbilt Tractor*, 506 P 2d 1199/NM (1973).

Victim Informants and Eyewitnesses

Although an arrest or search cannot be based solely on information received from an informant whose reliability as a witness is unknown, this rule does not apply to the victim of crime who makes hue and cry. Thus, where a seventeen-year-old girl told officers that defendant, after giving her narcotics, had sexual intercourse with her, the officers had reason to believe defendant had committed the crime of statutory rape, a felony, and they could then lawfully arrest defendant without a warrant (*Pendleton v Nelson*, 404 F 2d 1074/Cal–1968). Also, where information was furnished by a citizen who claimed to be the victim of robbery or assault, such information constituted grounds for arrest even though the citizen was unknown to police and untested as an informant. *People v Hogan*, 457 P 2d 868/Cal (1969).

The requirement of prior reliability does not apply where information leading to arrest is supplied by ordinary citizens (*People v Vanable*, 298 NE 2d 299/Ill–1973), and in the absence of exceptional circumstances, an informant who advises an officer that he was an eyewitness to a crime may be deemed reliable. *State v Vineyard*, 497 SW 2d 821/Mo (1973).

Anonymous Informants

As a rule anonymous information received by telephone or otherwise does no more than point the finger of suspicion, and before an arrest can be made as a result of such information, probable cause independently thereof must be obtained. *Cali v United States*, 388 F 2d 974/Mas (1964).

Where there is no emergency an officer cannot arrest solely on information received from an anonymous source, but such information is relevant in establishing probable cause to arrest (*Willson v Superior Court*, 294 P 2d 36/Cal–1956). Courts have held, in rare instances however, that an arrest may be made solely on information furnished by an anonymous informant where his voice is known to the officer and he has previously furnished information regarding criminal activity which was verified; such informant achieves the status of "tested informant" and is therefore reliable. *People v Prewitt*, 341 P 2d 1/Cal (1959).

SEARCH WARRANTS

In General

No search warrant will issue but on probable cause shown by affidavit naming or describing the person to be arrested and describing the property and place to be searched. *State v Wright*, 503 P 2d 514/Or (1972).

A "search" implies some exploratory investigation or an invasion and quest, a looking for or seeking out, a prying into hidden places for that which is concealed or intentionally put out of the way. *People v Monson*, 105 CR 92/Cal (1972).

A search without a warrant is *per se* unreasonable unless it falls within one of the narrowly defined exceptions to warrant requirements. *Erickson v State*, 507 P 2d 508/Alk (1973).

A search warrant may be served only by a peace officer. An exception to this rule exists when a peace officer requires assistance from a private person and the peace officer remains present and supervises the execution of the warrant. *State v Meidinger*, 502 P 2d 58/Mont (1972).

A search warrant directed to "any peace officer in the state" is not defective where a statute provides that any peace officer in the direction of the warrant could serve it. Id.

Recording a conversation is a seizure cognizable under the Fourth Amendment. *People v Hill*, 107 CR 791/Cal (1973).

That portion of the Fourth Amendment to the U.S. Constitution regulating searches and seizures states in part:

> The right of the people to be secure in their persons, houses, papers, and effects, against unreasonable searches and seizures, shall not be violated, and no Warrants shall issue, but upon probable cause, supported by Oath or affirmation, and particularly describing the place to be searched and the persons or things to be seized.

The Amendment does not outlaw all searches, only those that are unreasonable. *State v Sainz*, 501 P 2d 1199/Az (1972).

The phrase of the Fourth Amendment requiring that a warrant particularly describe the place to be searched and the thing to be seized, is met in a warrant authorizing the seizure of "narcotic drugs" where heroin is found and seized, and a warrant thus worded is not a general search warrant within the Fourth Amendment proscription. *State v Foye*, 188 SE 2d 67/NC (1972).

Whether public school authorities are considered to be government officers for purposes of the Fourth Amendment to the U.S. Constitution, depends on the view taken by the individual states (*Interest of C*, 296 A 2d 102/NJ–1972). But this rule has no application where the school official is acting in the capacity of a private person. Id.

The search of clothing currently worn is within the ambit of a personal search and outside the scope of a search warrant authorizing the search of premises. *United States v Micheli*, 487 F 2d 429/Mas (1973).

The reviewing court cannot validate a warrant by determining that probable cause did in fact exist; independent determination by a neutral authority must be made *before* the warrant is issued, not afterward (*Com v McCants*, 299 A 2d 283/Pa–1973). The same probable cause standards apply to both federal and state warrants. *Collins v State*, 302 A 2d 693/Md (1973).

The Nature of the Warrant

The filing of an affidavit is vital to the issuance of a search warrant whether or not the issuing magistrate presides over a court of record. *Holtel v State*, 290 NE 2d 775/Ind (1972).

Search warrants must describe with particularity the place to be searched and the things to be seized (*State v Moreau*, 306 A 2d 764/NH–1973), and when the place is described with sufficient particularity so that it cannot reasonably be mistaken for another place, the wrong apartment number included in the description will not vitiate an otherwise valid warrant (*State v Gallo*, 279 S 2d 71/Fla–1973). But a warrant which authorized seizure of an "undetermined amount of United States currency" and a firearm which was merely described as a "weapon," did not describe articles with sufficient particularity and their seizure thereunder was invalid. *People v Holmes*, 312 NE 2d 748/Ill (1974).

Where a warrant authorized the search of a dwelling and the curtilage, and there were three automobiles parked within the curtilage, the search of defendant's vehicle—when at the time it was not known if it belonged to him—was improper. *Dunn v State*, 292 S 2d 435/Fla (1974).

The Nature of the Affidavit

Affidavits of probable cause for the issuance of search warrants are based on much less rigorous standards than those governing the admissibility of evidence at a trial (*Lomax v State*, 298 A 2d 454/Md–1973), and the fact that the affidavit in support of a search warrant contained some hearsay and even some triple hearsay, or hearsay on hearsay, did not of itself render the affidavit insufficient. *United States v McCoy*, 478 F 2d 176/Ut (1973); *People v Cohn*, 106 CR 579/Cal (1973).

An opinion or conclusion of the affiant alone is insufficient as a basis for the issuance of a search warrant, and a statement such as "affiant further believes that there is probable cause to believe that there is other contraband contained on the premises," is surplusage if not supported by facts. *United States v Hatcher*, 473 F 2d 321/Oh (1973).

Some jurisdictions hold that the issuing magistrate must base the issuance of a warrant solely on the information contained in the affidavit; others hold that the magistrate may consider not only that information contained in the affidavit, but any additional information furnished by the affiant. Thus, Maryland, Oregon and Texas, among others, have held that in determining the sufficiency of the affidavit, consideration for the issuance of a search warrant must be based solely on information in the affidavit and restricted to the four corners thereof (*Hegdal v State*, 488 SW 2d 782/Tex–1972), and matters which were privy to the affiant officer but not put before the magistrate in the affidavit cannot weigh in the equation (*State v Sagner*, 506 P 2d 510/Or–1973); (*Collins v State*, 302 A 2d 693/Md–1973). But Pennsylvania, citing the U.S. Supreme Court, and New Hampshire have held that the issuing magistrate may properly issue a warrant based on supplementary oral information from the affiant and all information employed as a basis for its issuance need not be included in the affidavit or the warrant. *Com v Fisher*, 296 A 2d 848/Pa (1972); citing *Spinelli v United States*, 393 US 410 (1969); *State v Moreau*, 306 A 2d 764/NH (1973).

The "jurat," that is, the magistrate's certification that the affidavit was subscribed by the affiant, is not a part of the affidavit; it is simply evidence that probable cause was supported by oath (*Huff v Com*, 194 SE 2d 690/Va–1973), and multiple warrants may properly issue from a single affidavit so long as the affidavit supports probable cause for such multiple issuance. Id.

Reliable Informants

Information received from a reliable confidential informant that one person was operating a lottery and bookmaking office at a stated address and was assisted by one other person, and the informant's information was corroborated by the officer's observation as to movements of one of the suspects, probable cause existed to issue a search warrant and thus seizure of evidence was proper. *Kates v State*, 284 A 2d 651/Md (1971).

Where a reliable informer advised officers that defendant lived at the address described in the application for a search warrant, the police were not required prior to acting on the information to corroborate such information by interviewing occupants of the dwelling. *People v Webb*, 111 CR 524/Cal (1973).

Where a search warrant is issued upon information furnished by informants, reliability of the informants must be shown (*Miller v State*, 191 SE 2d 883/Ga–1972), and where the information was furnished by an air force base police officer such showing was inherent as official information is presumed to be authentic. *Neves v State*, 268 S 2d 890/Mis (1972).

Under normal circumstances the statement of the victim of crime alone would be sufficient basis on which to issue a search warrant. *Com v Mamon*, 297 A 2d 471/Pa (1972).

Where officers received information from an informer that narcotics was being dispensed at a named address, officer's subsequent surveillance and identification of seven known users of narcotics entering and leaving the premises owned by a woman previously convicted of possession of narcotics, gave substantial support to an application for a search warrant. *State v Ebron*, 294 A 2d 1/NJ (1972).

Where an unknown informant furnishes an abundance of details, this fact alone supplies some basis on which to assess the reliability of the informant (*State v Collins*, 298 A 2d 742/NH–1972), and where officers are able to substantiate much of the information thus furnished, there may exist probable cause for the issuance of a search warrant. Id.

The validity of a search warrant depends not on whether the informer was in fact reliable, but on whether facts sworn to by the officer from his personal knowledge were sufficient to support a determination that the informer was reliable and that the information was probably accurate. *State v Salem*, 193 SE 2d 755/NC (1973).

Where the only source of information is an anonymous informant, the reasons for assessing his reliability must be included in the affidavit. *Miller v State*, 191 SE 2d 883/Ga (1972).

Telephonic Warrants

A statute authorizing a telephonic search warrant is constitutional (*People v Peck*, 113 CR 806/Cal–1974), and an officer's sworn telephonic declarations in conversation with a magistrate constituted an "affidavit" sufficient to support the issuance of a search warrant despite the magistrate's delay in certifying the transcript plus the fact that the officer did not sign the written affidavit until the following day. *Bowyer v Superior Court*, 111 CR 628/Cal (1974).

Time Lapse Between Information and Search

The lapse of time alone will not negate probable cause for the issuance of a search warrant, but it will incite closer scrutiny by the magistrate and stale information cannot be considered as constituting probable cause for the issuance of a search warrant. *United States v Harruff*, 352 FS 224/Mich (1972).

Where an informant's tip reveals that contraband was at a certain place at a certain time, the likelihood that such contraband will remain there diminishes with the passing of time, and thus time is relevant in the determination if probable cause presently exists for the issuance of a search warrant. *State v Hutton*, 505 P 2d 263/Az (1973).

A five-day delay in the execution of a search warrant, where probable cause still existed, was not unreasonable and met the "forthwith" requirement of federal rules of criminal procedure, where the delay was occasioned by a shortage of personnel. *United States v Rael*, 467 F 2d 333/NM (1972).

Where there is an unreasonable lapse of time after the search warrant was issued and before execution, here 15 days, it is mandatory that police return to the issuing magistrate for a redetermination of probable cause. *Com v McCants*, 299 A 2d 283/Pa (1973).

"Knock and Announce" and Forcible Entry

The statutory "knock and announce" requirement was violated where officers, in the execution of a search warrant, opened a screen door and turned the knob of the primary door, opened it, stepped inside defendant's house, then announced their presence and purpose. The knock and announce rule requires, absent exigent circumstances, that officers in the execution of a warrant, in a dwelling house or other structure, must knock at the door, ring the doorbell or otherwise announce their presence, then orally identify themselves, state their purpose and demand admittance. If admittance is denied or delayed while evidence is being destroyed or there is good reason to believe evidence is about to be destroyed, entry may be made by opening or breaking a door or window. *State v Kelly*, 260 S 2d 903/Fla (1972); *McCary v State*, 477 SW 2d 624/Tex (1972).

The laws requiring that an officer, before forcing entry into a building to serve a warrant, announce his presence at the door, identify himself and state his purpose, do not prescribe any particular time he must wait for compliance before forcing entry; the answer will depend on the circumstances of each case. *United States v Phelps*, 490 F 2d 644/Cal (1974).

Compliance with a statute requiring officer to knock and announce will be overlooked if compliance would increase the officer's peril or if the conduct of the defendant is such as to lead the officer to believe that he is aware of the officer's presence and may attempt escape (*Rodriguez v Jones*, 473 F 2d 599/Tex—1973), or where the evidence is small and readily disposable and the officer reasonably believes that to knock and announce would incite destruction or disposal of the evidence. *State v Brothers*, 507 P 2d 398/Or (1973).

A homeowner has no right to deny admittance to officers armed with a search warrant; in knocking and announcing officers are not asking permission to enter but announcing right to enter thus giving the homeowner the prerogative of opening the door. *United States v Bustamente-Gamez*, 488 F 2d 4/Cal (1973).

A police officer's mistaken belief that in the execution of a warrant he was authorized to make an entry unannounced, did not justify such entry. *People v Mecca*, 342 NYS 2d 677/NY (1973).

As a rule, in the execution of a search warrant an officer, before entering a residence, must attempt to call to the attention of anyone within, his presence outside, by knocking or by other reasonable means and must announce his authority and purpose for being there (*State v Collier*, 270 S 2d 451/Fla–1972); if, after a reasonable lapse of time, the officer is not voluntarily admitted he may force entry. *State v Valentine*, 504 P 2d 84/Or (1972).

If police are in possession of facts which they believe warrant the dispensing of the knock and announce rule—in other words a forced entry—these facts should be brought to the attention of the issuing magistrate to be included on the search warrant; if the magistrate refuses to waive the knock-notice rule, a subsequent forced entry may, nevertheless, be permissible if at the time of entry officers are in possession of information not known at the time of making the affidavit which would justify forced entry. *Parsley v Superior Court*, 104 CR 643/Cal (1972).

Officers were justified in disregarding the knock and announce rule where they knocked on defendant's door, identified themselves to a woman who appeared in an upstairs window and who stated she was alone and her husband was in jail, and could justifiably force entry when they heard a man and a woman's voice emanating from the apartment, under the assumption that evidence was being destroyed. *Com v Pugh*, 296 A 2d 864/Pa (1972).

Where officers, under authority of a search warrant, twice stated their purpose at the door and heard unintelligible conversation inside but received no response, they were justified in effecting a forced entry. *United States v Cox*, 462 F 2d 1293/Mo (1972).

Evidence Not Described in the Warrant

Some jurisdictions have previously held that the searching officer could seize only that property which was described in the warrant, except that contraband narcotics could be seized when found whether or not included in the warrant. It is now the accepted rule in virtually all jurisdictions that property constituting evidence of crime, not named or described in the warrant, may be seized under the plain view doctrine. And this is true even though no property sought is discovered. *United States v Various Gambling Devices,* 478 F 2d 1194/Mis (1973); *United States v Forlano*, 358 FS 56/NY (1973).

Officers armed with a search warrant which authorized the seizure of gambling paraphernalia were justified in seizing telephones in an apartment which had the bell subdued and the number discs and earpieces removed, since these instruments thus modified are often used in receiving and transmitting bets and gaming information. *Com v Todisco*, 294 NE 2d 860/Mas (1973).

Where officers were armed with a search warrant authorizing the seizure of three weapons, they could properly seize other illegal weapons found on the premises. *State v Lewis*, 350 FS 813/affirmed 469 F 2d 291/Pa (1972).

The execution of a search warrant naming and describing a particular contraband narcotic, permits a reasonable search for that narcotic, and when in the search therefor officers discover a different type of narcotic not named in the warrant, its seizure is permissible. *State v Davenport*, 516 P 2d 65/Haw (1973).

A search warrant which authorized a search for and seizure of cocaine and heroin, also authorized the seizure of paraphernalia used in cutting and preparing the narcotics into individual doses. *United States v Smith*, 462 F 2d 456/Min (1972).

An officer in the execution of a search warrant for stolen items, after finding several items described in the warrant, could properly seize an item not therein described but known to be stolen—here, a stereo—plus other items scattered about the house and not in use. *State v Turner*, 504 P 2d 168/Kan (1972).

Where police were searching premises for narcotics and observed a prohibited sawed-off shotgun, the shotgun was lawfully seized (*United States v Barno*, 340 FS 1326/DC—1972); (*People v Senkir*, 103 CR 138/Cal—1972), and conversly, under a search warrant authorizing the search for and the seizure of a portable welder, marijuana which was discovered in the search was lawfully seized as being tangible evidence of crime. *Bradley v State*, 205 SE 2d 463/Ga (1974).

Contraband—Seizure of

The seizure of articles not named or described in the search warrant is permissible if contraband or, as a rule, if there is evidence of other crimes. A 38-caliber shell casing was properly seized under a search warrant naming and describing a 38-caliber revolver, the court holding that the seizure of articles other than those described in the warrant is lawful if there is a relationship between the item seized and the crime and if there is reasonable cause to believe the item is relevant to or an integral part of, or an instrumentality of the crime. *State v Fields*, 279 NE 2d 616/Oh (1971); *People v Hill*, 107 CR 791/Cal (1973).

Officers in the execution of a search warrant for narcotics, who during their search observed a pistol with an obliterated serial number, were justified in seizing the pistol as contraband (*Com v Pellier*, 289 NE 2d 892/Mas—1972); likewise, officers were justified in seizing marijuana and LSD under a search warrant describing and naming heroin. *State v Wright*, 503 P 2d 514/Or (1972).

Marijuana is defined as a "narcotic drug" constituting a "contraband article" and subject to seizure and forfeiture. *United States v McCormick*, 468 F 2d 68/NM (1972).

SEARCH OF PAROLEES AND PROBATIONERS

Parolees

The rules relating to the searches of parolees and probationers are virtually the same. In both instances the subject is a prisoner-at-large serving his sentence outside prison walls, the difference being, as a rule, that the parolee has served a portion of his sentence and is supervised while on parole by state parole officers; probation, on the other hand, is granted by the court having jurisdiction, the subject having served none of his sentence and supervision while on probation being furnished by county probation officers. *Black's Law Dictionary*.

The rules of search and seizure under the Fourth Amendment, applicable under ordinary circumstances, are not applicable to parolees on parole. Persons convicted of crime and released conditionally into society may have a reduced expectation of privacy thereby rendering certain intrusions by government agents reasonable, which under traditional concepts would be unlawful. *Himmage v State*, 496 P 2d 763/Nev (1972).

Due to the high risk of recidivism, especially in the early months of parole, and until readjustment is effectuated to an appreciable degree, the department of parole may subject the parolee to periodic searches, including his home, without probable cause or warrant. By accepting the privilege of parole the prisoner accepts the terms thereof which include broad visitorial powers by his parole supervisor.

A parolee may be rearrested and returned to prison for a violation of parole, which violation may or may not have been a violation of a substantive law. Upon being returned to custody the parolee is not entitled to bail nor a judicial hearing; however, he is entitled to a hearing before the prison board upon the merits of the recommendation for revocation submitted by his parole supervisor. *People v Hernandez*, 229 CA 2d 143/Cal (1967); *Pierce v Smith*, 195 P 2d 112/Wn (1948).

Prisoners released on parole are presumed to have accepted the favor of parole subject to the degree of surveillance and search required under the circumstances for the effective supervision of the parolee and the protection of the public. Although physically no longer behind walls, a prisoner released on parole is not free; he is at all times in *custodia legis* and still a prisoner. *State v Williams*, 486 SW 2d 468/Mo (1972).

A warrantless search of a parolee's residence may be conducted under circumstances which amount to less than the traditional probable cause, but a parole officer must have a valid reason to believe that the terms of parole have been violated. Also, if the search is justified, a parole officer may enlist the aid of police officers in conducting the search. *State v Simms*, 516 P 2d 1088/Wn (1973).

Inmates and their cells and quarters may be subjected to intense surveillance and search unimpeded by Fourth Amendment barriers. *State v Williams, supra.*

Probationers

Although parolees and probationers are entitled to constitutional protection under the Fourth Amendment against unreasonable searches and seizures, what is unreasonable in the case of a free citizen is not the same as in the case of a prisoner-at-large who is in legal custody and under continuing supervision (*People v Adams*, 336 NYS 2d 533/NY–1972). Thus, the warrantless search of a probationer's apartment by his parole officer was authorized as a condition of his probation after conviction of possession of marijuana, and hashish and marijuana found in the search were admissible in probationer's probation revocation hearing. *State v Schlosser*, 202 NW 2d 136/ND (1972).

Normally, the warrantless search of a probationer by or at the direction of his probation officer acting under a general search order imposed as a condition of probation is reasonable, but unrestricted search by law enforcement officers at their whim and caprice and at any time is a form of harassment proscribed by the Fourth Amendment. *People v Bremmer*, 106 CR 797/Cal (1973).

SEARCH AND SEIZURE BY PRIVATE PERSONS

In General

Protection against unreasonable searches and seizures applies in cases involving governmental action only, and does not apply to searches and seizures made by private individuals (*Bernovich v State*, 272 S 2d 505/Fla–1973, citing *Burdeau v McDowell*, 256 US 465–1921); (*People v Topp*, 114 CR 856/Cal–1974), and evidence seized by a private person, not in collaboration with police, is not within the exclusionary protection of the Fourth Amendment (*State v Becich*, 509 P 2d 1232/Or–1973). However, one who is a private citizen may taint an otherwise admissible search by him by the participation of government officials or by becoming an agent of the police. *Aikens v Gomes*, 367 FS 401/Az (1972).

A search incident to a lawful arrest may be made either by a peace officer or a private person, and evidence seized in the search is admissible against defendant whether it consists of fruits of the crime for which defendant was arrested, the means used to commit that crime or evidence of an unrelated crime (*United States v Biddle*, 39 FS 203/Pa–1941). But a private person cannot, in an arrest for breach of the peace, invade the home or office of the arrestee and conduct an incident search. *United States v Chodak*, 68 FS 455/Md (1946).

Examples

Where a private citizen illegally removed a package from the garage of defendant, but without the knowledge or cooperation of police, state action in opening the package was not improper where there was probable cause to believe the package contained marijuana (*People v Cohn*, 106 CR 579/Cal–1973), and the subsequent warrantless arrest of four persons upon information received from an anonymous informant was justified when it appeared that defendants were loading the marijuana into an automobile preparatory to flight. *People v Cohn, supra.*

The search and seizure of obscene materials by a private person, not acting in collusion with federal officers, was not unlawfully seized and was thus admissible in a prosecution for importation of obscene materials. *United States v Harding*, 475 F 2d 480/Colo (1973).

Hotel security officers are not peace officers and were not acting in conjunction with state officers in detaining, searching and questioning petitioner in a Nevada hotel and were not subject to the search and seizure restrictions as are governmental officers. *Emslie v State Bar*, 520 P 2d 991/Cal (1974).

Documents stolen by private persons and subsequently delivered to federal officers, may be used in a criminal prosecution of the owner of the documents if government agents did not participate in the procurement of the documents. *Philadelphia Resistance v Mitchell*, 58 FRD 139/Pa (1973).

Physical Searches at Air Terminals

It is not necessary that an airline employee have probable cause to search a passenger's baggage unless he is acting as a police agent. *State v Fellows*, 511 P 2d 636/Az (1973); *Bell v State*, 519 P 2d 804/Alk (1974).

An air freight company's legal inspection of bags, disclosing marijuana, in effect placed the marijuana in plain view of a California officer permitting seizure; and his marking of the suitcase and allowing it to be shipped to New York by air freight did not change its status as "seized" contraband and New York officers, therefore, could reassert custody of the marijuana after it reached its destination and was placed in the back seat of an automobile by defendant. *United States v De Berry*, 487 F 2d 448/NY (1973).

Airline authorities have an absolute right, as a condition of boarding a plane, to require a passenger to submit to search, both person and baggage, but the passenger must be aware of his option under the Fourth Amendment to avoid search by declining to go aboard (*United States v Allen*, 349 FS 749/Cal–1972). However, defendant who was *otherwise* subject to pat-down and subsequent search when he entered an airport boarding area, did not have the right to avoid search by requesting an opportunity to return his ticket and leave without boarding. *State v Adams*, 312 A 2d 642/NJ (1973).

Where airline employees detected the odor of marijuana emanating from suitcases and notified police who in turn identified the odor as marijuana, there was probable cause for a warrantless search of the suitcases. *Hattersley v State*, 487 SW 2d 354/Tex (1972).

Seizure of obscene materials by an air freight employee not acting in collusion with federal officers was not tainted by seizure and was admissible against defendant in a prosecution for the importation of obscene materials.

United States v Harding, 475 F 2d 480/Colo (1973); *Burdeau v McDowell*, 256 US 465 (1921).

Magnetometer Searches

The use of a magnetometer by customs agents at airline embarkation points to detect metallic objects is a "search," the Arizona court holding: "We can see no difference between an intrusion into the defendant's handbag by means of an electronic device rather than an actual physical intrusion by opening the handbag and conducting a physical search." But the Constitution does not forbid all searches and seizures, only those that are unreasonable and the magnetometer is justified under the "exigent circumstances" doctrine. *State v Damon*, 502 P 2d 1360/Az (1972).

The exposure of airline passengers to a magnetometer is not unreasonable due to the threat of air piracy (*United States v Epperson*, 454 F 2d 769/Va—1972); and the anti-hijacking system employed at major air terminals which consists of (1) profile selection, (2) magnetometer detection and (3) stop and frisk, is constitutional. *United States v Bell*, 335 FS 797/NY (1971).

An airport marshal was justified in opening a flight bag which triggered a high reading on the magnetometer, and in opening the bag and smelling the odor of marijuana, he was not required to search only for metal, a safety razor, but could also search for the marijuana. *People v Bleile*, 108 CR 682/Cal (1973).

A marshal did not have the legal duty, before opening the flight bag of the accused which had precipitated an acute reaction of the magnetometer, to advise the accused that he had the option of permitting search of the bag or leaving without boarding the plane. *People v Bleile, supra.*

EAVESDROPPING

In General

As a general rule police officers may not conduct electronic surveillance, wiretap, or record any telephone conversations between private persons except upon order by a magistrate, but a magistrate's order is not necessary under federal law where *any* party to the conversation consents to interception and recordation, either by police officers, their agents or others. *People v Patrick*, 208 NW 2d 604/Mich (1973); *Title 18 US Code*, § 2511 (2) (C).

A state law authorizing the interception of a telephonic conversation and setting forth the circumstances under which the interception may be made, although conforming to state law, may be unconstitutional unless it conforms essentially to the federal Omnibus Crime Control and Safe Streets Act. *United States v Tortorello*, 480 F 2d 764/NY (1973).

One who is not a participant in a wiretapped conversation has no standing to object to its interception by government agents. *United States v Hall*, 488 F 2d 193/Az (1973).

Face-to-Face Conversations Intercepted

The recording of defendant's conversation with a coconspirator who had withdrawn from the conspiracy and had been granted immunity, was admissible in a subsequent prosecution of the remaining members of the conspiracy, notwithstanding that the withdrawn member was then a police agent. *State v Mickell*, 185 SE 2d 814/SC (1971).

Testimony by a police officer of statements he overheard in a conversation between defendant and a police informer who carried an electronic recording device, was admissible. *People v Sims*, 195 NW 2d 766/Mich (1972); *United States v White*, 91 SC 1122/Ill (1971).

The recording and transcription of a congressman's conversation with the consent of the other party did not violate the constitutional principle of separation of powers. *United States v Dowdy*, 479 F 2d 213/Md (1973).

Monitor or Wiretap With Permission

It is well-established that where one party to a conversation gives consent to an officer to listen to conversation on an extension, there is no violation of defendant's rights under the Fourth Amendment. *United States v Black*, 472 F 2d 130/Ky (1972).

Each party to a conversation, telephonic or otherwise, takes the risk that the other party may divulge the contents of that conversation, and should this occur there is no violation of the right to privacy. *Smith v Cincinnati Post and Times-Star*, 475 F 2d 740/Oh (1973).

Although a party in a telephone conversation with one or more other persons generally does not expect revelation of information he may give connecting him with crime, he has no justifiable expectation that another party thereto will not reveal the contents of the conversation or consent to governmental interception of the conversation. *United States v Bonanno*, 487 F 2d 654/NY (1963).

Where one party to a conversation consented to surreptitious electronic surveillance of his telephone, the conversation was admissible against the second party despite his nonconsent to the intrusion (*United States v Palazzo*, 488 F 2d 942/Tex–1974). Likewise, incriminating tapes of private conversation between defendants and a government informer who was equipped with a recording and broadcasting device provided by FBI agents, were not obtained in violation of defendant's constitutional rights as any party to a conversation, under federal law, may permit its interception. *United States v Kline*, 366 FS 994/DC (1973).

A "telephone trap" placed on the receiver of a woman who was allegedly receiving obscene telephone calls was lawful and was sufficient to sustain conviction against the caller. *Hall v State*, 498 P 2d 415/Ok (1972).

In some jurisdictions a police officer may not monitor nor record a telephone conversation without the consent of all parties concerned; in some other jurisdictions consent of the sender is necessary before one may monitor or record, but the majority of jurisdictions, including federal, hold that one may monitor or record a telephone conversation with the permission of *any* party thereto. Thus where federal narcotics officers listened to a two-way conversation between defendant and an informant on an extension telephone, with knowledge and consent of the informant, they could use information gained thereby to establish probable cause to arrest. *United States v Hickman*, 426 F 2d 515/ Ind (1971).

Wiretap by Warrant

To allow police to indiscriminately place "bugs" on telephones without first obtaining warrants would be as much a violation of individual rights as to allow officers to arbitrarily enter homes without obtaining prior judicial approval. *Tollett v State*, 272 S 2d 490/Fla (1972).

The reasons for the requirement that a search warrant be obtained prior to surreptitious surveillance of a conversation between persons exhibiting a reasonable expectation of privacy, were intended to protect such persons from an uninvited ear and not from a breach of trust of parties to the conversation. *People v Murphy*, 503 P 2d 594/Cal (1972).

Conversations Between Prisoners and Visitors

The electronic surveillance of conversations between jail inmates and their visitors (provided their visitor is not their attorney) does not transgress constitutional prohibition against unreasonable searches and seizures. *People v Santos*, 101 CR 517/Cal (1972).

A tape recording of conversation between defendant and codefendant secured by the placing of a microphone in the police interrogation room at the police station and without the knowledge of either party, shortly after codefendant had confessed, was not fruit of an illegal search and seizure since the protection under the Fourth Amendment extends to "places," not "persons," and an interrogation room at a police station bears none of the attributes of the privacy of a home, automobile, office or hotel room. *Williams v Nelson*, 457 F 2d 376/Cal (1972).

PART III

CRIMES AGAINST MORALS, ORDER AND JUSTICE

Chapter X

Crimes Against Morality

GAMING

"Wagering" or "Betting" Defined

Whether the pari-mutuel system of betting on horses is a game of skill as some believe, or a game of chance as many have learned, it provides a legal method of separating the bettor from his money. The licensed track sells tickets and acts as custodian of the funds that accumulate from bets placed on horses to win, place or show. From this pool of funds the track takes two shares—one for itself and one for the state; from the residue holders of winning tickets are paid. *Mattson v Hollywood Turf Club*, 225 P 2d 276/Cal (1950).

The Idaho Supreme Court has ruled that horse racing, where the pari-mutuel system of wagering is used, does not determine winners on the basis of chance alone, and is therefore not a lottery and does not contravene the Constitution in the prohibition of lotteries. *Oneida County Fair Bd v Smylie*, 386 P 2d 374/Id (1963).

The offense of "wagering" is complete when the bet is offered and accepted and it is immaterial whether or not the horse on which the wager was placed ran in the race. *State v Decter*, 242 P 2d 551/Az (1952).

In General

There are two basic methods of gambling: (1) betting or wagering and (2) lottery. Gambling by "wager" or "bet" differs from a "prize" or a "premium" in that in the latter case the person posting has no chance of gaining back the thing posted if he abides by the rules; whereas, in the case of the former, both the offerer and his counter-participant have a chance to win and each stands the risk of losing. *Las Vegas Hacienda v Gibson*, 359 P 2d 85/Nev (1961).

The playing of any game for money was not a crime at common law and is not now a crime unless proscribed by statute. *Monterey Club v Superior Court*, 119 P 2d 349/Cal (1941).

Any participant in the operation of an illegal gambling business, except customers and persons placing bets, are guilty of conducting gambling, and this includes runners, telephone clerks, salesmen and watchmen. *United States v Thaggard*, 477 F 2d 626/Ala (1973); *United States v Kohne*, 358 FS 1053/Pa (1973).

The government is not required to prove, in a prosecution for gambling, that defendant knowingly violated the gambling law; rather, it need only prove that defendant intended to do all of the acts proscribed in the gambling statute. *United States v Thaggard, supra*.

Money seized in a gambling raid cannot be forfeited to a government entity by administrative or executive action; such money must first be declared to be contraband in a judicial proceeding. *City of Chicago v United States*, 372 FS 178/Ill (1974).

Bookmaking

"Bookmaking" is committed when one accepts money or other consideration as a wager on the outcome of a contest between men or beasts at a place other than a pari-mutuel office; but where one individual accepts money from another for placement, in a lawful contest at a pari-mutuel race track, and such individual acts as a mere conduit and gains no benefit from the transaction, he is not guilty of bookmaking within statutory proscription. *State v Andreano*, 285 A 2d 299/NJ (1971).

Giving of information on the betting line and taking of bets are facts within the concept of conducting a bookmaking operation under Pennsylvania law. *United States v Cerase*, 467 F 2d 652/Pa (1972).

Maintaining Premises for Gambling

As a rule, the owner of the premises where gambling is carried on, may be convicted as keeper of a gaming place if knowledge of gambling is proved. *State v George*, 313 A 2d 401/NH (1973).

Although premises allegedly were not maintained for the purpose of gambling, where the owner allows gambling to be conducted and participates therein, he may be convicted of keeping a place for the purpose of gambling. *State v George, supra*.

"Professional gambling" under an Indiana statute was established where evidence showed that defendant owned the premises where poker games were conducted, that he provided free drinks to players, was present during the entire course of the game, counted out chips to an undercover officer who was participating, and had dealers collect a share of each pot not kept by them. *State v Stone*, 311 NE 2d 446/Ind (1974).

Illegal Gambling Devices

The phrase "coin-operated gaming devices" has been interpreted to include machines other than the so-called "one-armed bandit" type machine. And a machine, the object of which was for players to select winning poker hands from five rotating wheels, was a gaming device—the element of chance being present—despite possibility of the development of skill by experience and experimentation. *United States v "Dealer's Choice" Machines*, 341 FS 1147/DC (1972).

A Montana statute prohibiting the possession of gambling implements was violated notwithstanding defendant's claim that he had implements in his possession solely for the purpose of repair work prior to shipping articles to Nevada where such implements were legal. *State v Wilson*, 503 P 2d 522/Mont (1972).

The federal Gambling Device Act, which prohibits interstate transportation of gambling devices, and a statute which denounces the use of facilities in interstate commerce with intent to facilitate illegal gambling enterprises are complimentary to and not in conflict with each other; they are aimed at the eradication of that aspect of organized crime that is nourished on illegal gambling profits. *United States v Bally Mfg Corp*, 345 FS 410/La (1972).

Nonenforceability of Gambling Contracts

One cannot lawfully place a bet through an agent and recover winnings from the agent at a place other than at a pari-mutuel betting enclosure. *Schnoor v Griffin*, 439 P 2d 922/NM (1968).

At common law no action could be maintained for the recovery of money lost at gambling. Many states have statutes prohibiting gambling and, in addition, will also lend their civil processes to the recovery of losses sustained in gambling; for instance, under New York law any person losing $25 and upward in a dice game may, any time within three months after payment and delivery, sue the winner to recover his loss. *Cross v Sam Katz Distinctive Tours Ltd*, 338 NYS 2d 717/NY (1972).

Under Nevada law (which follows the general rule), gambling debts are unenforceable in the courts; also, such proscription applies to enforcement of a loan made with the intent or understanding that the money would be used in gambling. *Dunes Hotel v Mayo*, 354 NYS 2d 52/NY (1974).

The rule that courts will not recognize an illegal betting contract and will leave the parties as it finds them, applies even though the winner wins by fraud or deceit. *Bradley v Doherty*, 106 CR 725/Cal (1973).

"Lottery" Defined

To constitute a lottery three elements must be present: (1) consideration, (2) chance and (3) prize. If one is absent there is no lottery regardless of the purpose of the scheme; if all elements are present the scheme is a lottery regardless of the purpose of its sponsor. *Morrow v State*, 511 P 2d 127/Alk (1973).

The consideration, which is an essential element of the *corpus delicti* of all lotteries, need not actually be extended, as a promise thereof completes the crime. *People v Postma*, 160 P 2d 221/Cal (1945).

Any skill or judgment indulged in by a participant or by another in his behalf, removes the enterprise from the category of a lottery. *Braddock v Family Finance Corp*, 506 P 2d 824/Id (1973).

In General

Conduct which is proscribed by the lottery statute is determinative of whether the game comes within the statutory proscription, and this determination is not based on whether the game is deemed to be or called a lottery, a scheme, a plan or other name (*State v Netto*, 486 SW 2d 725/Ten–1972). The court will inquire not into the name but into the game, however skillfully disguised, in order to ascertain if it is prohibited or if it has the element of chance. Id.

The question as to whether a game is one of chance or one of skill depends on which factor predominates and is a question of fact for the jury. *Cossack v City of Los Angeles*, 523 P 2d 260/Cal (1973).

Constitutional Prohibition Against Lottery

Where lottery is forbidden by the state constitution, any effort to legalize, authorize or license lotteries is unconstitutional; likewise, the legislature is prohibited from indirectly doing so by way of exemption of gambling from criminal prosecution (*Tussey v State*, 494 SW 2d 866/Tex–1973). A statutory amendment to the state constitution allowing lotteries at fairs, churches, religious societies and veterans' organizations, was unconstitutional. Id.

A constitutional provision that the legislature shall have no power to authorize lotteries for any purpose and shall pass laws to prohibit the sale of lottery tickets within the state is a blanket prohibition against lotteries. *State v Netto, supra*.

A statute attempting to legalize bingo or the use or possession of slot-machines, when inconsistent with constitutional prohibition against lotteries, cannot stand; to allow a legislative act permitting lotteries requires a constitutional amendment. *State v Nelson*, 502 P 2d 841/Kan (1972).

A constitutional provision forbidding the legislature to enact any law authorizing any lottery, was self-executing and mandatory and not only prohibited the state from conducting a lottery, but banned any form of lottery from being conducted within the state. *State v Reader's Digest Assn Inc*, 501 P 2d 290/Wn (1972).

Lottery Devices

The name of a device does not determine its character as to whether it is a gambling device; this fact is to be determined by the manner and result of its operation. *Antrim v State*, 220 P 2d 846/Ok (1950).

A pinball machine—operated by placing a nickel in a coin slot and pushing the slot forward to release a metal ball, and then by releasing a plunger against the ball which was propelled into the playing area, the ball would cause automatic release of designated nickels by landing in certain designated slots—was deemed a gambling device subject to confiscation. *People v Headrick*, 128 P 2d 757/Id (1942).

A slot machine, under Oklahoma law, is a machine, instrument, mechanism or device that operates or may be operated or played mechanically, electrically, automatically or manually by inserting a coin or other thing of value therein, by which play or operation by skill or chance or a combination of the two, one stands to win or lose a thing of value. *Delano v State*, 168 P 2d 659/Ok (1946).

A device designed to be attached to a regular cigarette vending machine, its function being to occasionally and by chance activate a mechanism in the machine causing the delivery of a free package of cigarettes in addition to the one the customer purchased, is a gambling device and subject to forfeiture. *United States v 11 Star-Pack Cigarette Merchandiser Machines*, 248 FS 933/Pa (1966).

A game having a board containing eighty numbered squares, in the operation of which twenty numbers from one through eighty were drawn by lot, and which paid a predetermined sum of money to players who had selected five or more of the numbers drawn, was a lottery. *State ex rel Olsen v Crown Cigar Store*, 220 P 2d 1029/Mont (1950).

A football forecasting contest conducted by a newspaper for its readers was prohibited as a lottery but not as a gambling game. *Seattle Times Co v Tielsch*, 495 P 2d 1366/Wn (1972).

Slot machines, like other gambling devices, are not property, but are contraband subject to seizure and summary destruction, and money found therein is subject to seizure. *State v Nichols*, 117 P 2d 468/Id (1941).

The Arizona Supreme Court has observed philosophically "that gambling is a social evil that eats at the very heart of public welfare and destroys moral and financial stability, does not authorize executive officers nor the judiciary to order the destruction of [gambling] devices . . . unless authorized by legislative act." *In re Twenty-one Slot Machines*, 236 P 2d 733/Az (1951).

Examples of Lottery Schemes

A weekly drawing held on Wednesday in a parking lot adjacent to a grocery store had the following requirements for participation: (1) appear at the grocery store and register, (2) appear again during the week (except on Wednesday) to have a coupon validated, and (3) be personally present at the drawing. According to the Oregon Supreme Court this was not a lottery notwithstanding that some of the participants may have made purchases during their personal appearances (*Cudd v Aschenbrenner*, 377 P 2d 150/Or–1962). The California Supreme Court held similarly that the mere requirement of a personal appearance of a participant is not a "necessary consideration" paid or promised and to hold otherwise would be stretching the statute to the breaking point. *California Gasoline Retailers v Regal Petroleum Corp*, 330 P 2d 778/Cal (1958).

Where defendant distributed coupons to potential customers on which was written, "This coupon is distributed and accepted with the distinct understanding that it is neither a wagering contest nor a lottery, but simply an advertising medium," the medium nevertheless constituted a lottery. The scheme was called a "suit club" whose membership cost $1.50 per month, members being entitled to a suit of clothes valued at $49.50 after making 32 monthly payments; also, the advertising coupon entitled a member to a free suit of clothes whenever the last three numbers in the United States Treasury receipts corresponded with the coupon number. All of the elements of lottery were present: (1) payment of a valuable consideration, (2) prize, and (3) chance. *Bills v People*, 157 P 2d 139/Colo (1945).

A promotional contest sponsored by an oil company whereby the company's service station dealers distributed small cards, the object of the contest being to acquire a group of cards which in combination would comprise one of the company's advertising slogans, constituted a lottery. *Geis v Continental Oil Co*, 511 P 2d 725/Ut (1973).

A "cash night" drawing at a theater which required participants to pay an entrance fee was a lottery notwithstanding that participants paid the same price on cash night as they were required to pay on other nights when a more popular play was presented. *People v Gonzales*, 144 P 2d 605/Cal (1944).

Chain referral or pyramid-selling scheme under which a sponsoring participant gambled for the recovery of his investment on the motivation, success and efforts of each of his recruits over whom he had no control constituted a lottery. *Wesware Inc v State*, 488 SW 2d 844/Tex (1972).

A coin-operated miniature crane was deemed a gambling device where a player attempted to pick up metal figurines with a boom and claw apparatus from a bed of candy, as the element of chance clearly predominates over skill insofar as the average person or general public was concerned. *Boies v Bartell*, 310 P 2d 834/Az (1957).

Punchboards on which there were tokens, tickets and slips of paper containing numbers and which evidenced the right of the holder to a chance to receive a thing of value at a drawing by lot, and for which he had been required to pay a valuable consideration, were gambling devices (*State v Brown*, 244 P 2d 1190/Kan—1952). A punchboard is, in reality, a series of lottery tickets. Id.

What Constitutes a Prize

The states differ in ruling on the question of a "prize" consisting of additional games on the machine or device. The California courts held that a pinball machine programmed to allow a free game upon the attainment of a designated high score, and which automatically released the coin slot without an additional deposit, was not merchandise, money or tokens redeemable for a thing of value, and the machine was not subject to seizure and destruction as a gambling device (*Gayer v Whelan*, 138 P 2d 763/Cal—1943); but the Idaho courts have held that a pinball machine constructed to permit five shots for five cents and when the player was successful in hitting a certain knob he would receive five free plays, the free plays were representative of value in amusement and the machine was therefore subject to seizure and destruction. *Thamart v Moline*, 156 P 2d 187/Id (1945); *State v Wassick*, 191 SE 2d 283/W Va (1972).

Where One Element Is Missing

The gratuitous distribution of property by lot or chance where no consideration is paid, either directly or indirectly, is not a lottery (*Bills v People*, 157 P 2d 139/Colo—1945). A television give-away program known as "dialing for dollars," wherein persons whose telephone numbers picked from a directory were called and if the person knew the code number and amount of the jackpot he won a prize, was not a lottery as persons were not required to advance a valuable consideration (*State ex rel Frizzel v Highwood Service Inc*, 473 P 2d 97/Kan—1970); a selling plan under which the seller offered the buyer a specified sum of money to secure another person to make a purchase did not constitute a lottery. *A A Murphy Inc v Taylor*, 383 P 2d 648/Ok (1963).

No chance was involved to bring the act within the purview of the lottery statute where the owner of a golf course offered $5,000 to any person who could shoot a hole-in-one upon a requirement of an entry fee of 50 cents (*Las Vegas Hacienda Inc v Gibson*, 359 P 2d 85/Nev—1961); nor where the buyer of a number of cattle agreed with the seller thereof to set the price of the cattle by the flip of a coin, as this was merely a method of negotiation, and enforcement of the contract through court action was permissible. *Savage v Moore*, 119 P 2d 535/Kan (1941).

Where at a "bank night" drawing at a theater the defendant, in pretending to draw the winning ticket from a drum, already had a ticket palmed and made no selection from the drum, there was no lottery but larceny by bunco since the element of chance had been removed as the winner was predetermined. *People v Carpenter*, 297 P 2d 498/Cal (1956).

Nonactionable Nature of Lottery Contracts

A wagering contract is unenforceable in most states (*Ferris & Hardgrove v Buff*, 146 P 2d 331/Wn–1944). The courts will not recognize an illegal contract and will not aid the parties thereto, but will leave them where it finds them. *Kyne v Kyne*, 106 P 2d 620/Cal (1940).

A party who lends money to another with the understanding that the money will be used in illegal gambling or who participates and shares in gambling transaction thus promoted, by his conduct becomes *particeps criminis* and cannot recover in a court action money thus advanced (*Rose v Nelson*, 180 P 2d 749/Cal–1947); but the lending of money which is subsequently used for the purpose of gambling is not, *per se*, illegal where the lender has no knowledge of the unlawful purpose for which the money was borrowed. *Leite v Deitz*, 212 P 2d 265/Cal (1950).

DRUGS AND NARCOTICS

"Narcotic" Defined

A "narcotic drug" is one which induces sleep and makes one insensitive to pain; *cannabis* (marijuana) is not a narcotic drug, but rather a mild hallucinogenic having alternate effects on the central nervous system—first a stimulant and ultimately a depressant. *State v Zornes*, 475 P 2d 109/Wn (1970).

The states are divided in the classification of marijuana as is illustrated, *infra*, by the Colorado and Illinois courts: The classification of marijuana as a narcotic, the possession of which is a felony under Colorado law, rather than as a hallucinogenic or dangerous drug, the possession of which is a misdemeanor, is not arbitrary nor unreasonable and does not deny equal protection (*People v Summit*, 517 P 2d 850/Colo–1974). But the Illinois courts have held, contrary to the majority opinion, that the classification of marijuana as a narcotic under the Narcotic Drug Act was arbitrary, and a denial of equal protection and conviction under that act of the sale of marijuana—a narcotic—could not stand. *People v McCaffrey*, 277 NE 2d 153/Ill (1971).

The number of substances classified either as a narcotic or drug presently exceed one hundred and are growing, so no attempt will be made to list them; however, some of the basic narcotic substances from which are extracted compounds, salts or other derivatives are: opium, coca leaves, marijuana, pethidine, methadone, lophophora. Some basic drugs are: acetyluria, barbituric acid, lysergic acid diethylamide and amphetamines. *California Health and Safety Code*, § § 11001, 11901; *La Duron v State*, 299 NE 2d 227/Ind (1973).

Dangerous drugs and narcotic drugs are of a different nature and their possession is usually proscribed under separate statute, the possession of narcotic drugs being the more serious of the two crimes. *Frazier v State*, 480 SW 2d 37/Tex (1972).

To establish the unlawful possession of drugs, the state must establish not only actual or constructive possession, as possession alone is not criminal; in addition, it must prove that defendant intentionally and with knowledge of the nature of the substance unlawfully possessed a dangerous drug or narcotic (*Buono v Com*, 193 SE 2d 798/Va–1973), and once the state has proved possession with knowledge, it devolves upon the defendant to explain, excuse or justify his possession. *State v Dodd*, 505 P 2d 830/Wn (1973).

Under Illinois law the offering to sell a narcotic drug followed by the selling of a nonnarcotic substance constitutes larceny by false pretenses–a separate and distinct offense from the selling of a narcotic drug. *People v Robinson*, 288 NE 2d 484/Ill (1972).

Possession–General

"Actual possession" of narcotic drugs describes physical possession, while "constructive possession" denotes possession by dominion or control over either the substance or the premises where the substance is located (*State v Perry*, 516 P 2d 1104/Wn–1973). And it is not a characteristic of possession of a controlled substance that it be exclusive, for it may be possessed jointly by two or more persons. *Italiano v Com*, 200 SE 2d 526/Va (1973).

The crime of possession of a dangerous drug requires proof of physical or constructive possession with knowledge of the nature of the substance (*People v Patello*, 344 NYS 2d 33/NY–1973), and mere knowledge of its presence and proximity does not establish possession or control. *Com v Sungenis*, 303 A 2d 524/Pa (1973).

A statute forbidding the possession of heroin includes possession by addicts or for one's own use, notwithstanding defendant's appeal on the grounds that the legislature did not intend to deny possession to addicts. *State v Gibson*, 312 A 2d 662/NJ (1973).

Federal statutory provision permits the jury to infer unlawful importation into the United States from unlawful possession not satisfactorily explained when the narcotic is heroin, and an instruction to the jury to this effect accurately states the law. *Turner v United States*, 396 US 398/NJ (1970).

Joint Possession

Possession of narcotics need not be exclusive for one may be convicted of possession when he was in "joint" possession with another (*Simpson v State*, 486 SW 2d 807/Tex–1972), but joint possession cannot be established against one who was or had been in the company of another having physical possession of the substance, absent other inculpating circumstances tending to link him with one in physical possession. *Petty v People*, 477 P 2d 217/Colo (1968).

Where the accused drove an accomplice to a meeting place with a narcotics peddler for the purpose of obtaining heroin, the accused was guilty of unlawful possession of heroin by aiding and abetting his accomplice. *People v Henderson*, 264 P 2d 225/Cal (1953).

Possession Under Prescription

Under Arizona law, the possession of a dangerous drug is criminal although sold under a valid prescription and in its original container, if the drug was prescribed for another and unidentified person. *State v Moore*, 507 P 2d 1014/Az (1973).

In a prosecution under a statute forbidding the possession of certain narcotics without a prescription, the burden is on the defendant to prove that he had a prescription (*People v Harmon*, 200 P 2d 32/Cal–1948), and the burden is not on the state to prove that possession was not within one of the exceptions included in the Uniform Narcotic Drug Act, as proof of exception, mitigation or other defense privy only to the defendant, is upon him. *State v Boggs*, 358 P 2d 124/Wn (1961).

Fleeting or Incidental Possession

The incidental handling of contraband narcotics for the sole purpose of disposal does not constitute "possession" within the meaning of a statute forbidding possession of narcotics (*People v Mijares*, 491 P 2d 1115/Cal–1971); but where defendant held a hashish pipe in his hands and took two puffs from the pipe knowing that it contained marijuana in hashish form, he had possession of marijuana within the meaning of the statute. *State v Hogue*, 486 P 2d 403/Haw (1971).

"Fleeting possession" of contraband drugs may be of sufficient duration to warrant conviction of possession where attendant circumstances clearly indicate criminal possession, as where police, armed with a search warrant, knocked on defendant's door and demanded admittance and shortly thereafter defendant opened a window and tossed a brown paper bag containing marijuana outside which an officer caught; possession, although fleeting, was of such a nature as to warrant conviction of its unlawful possession. *Watson v State*, 306 A 2d 599/Md (1973).

Constructive Possession

In a prosecution for the unlawful possession of narcotics the law has developed the policy that a person in exclusive control of premises will be deemed to have possession and control of any drugs found on the premises. *State v Funk*, 490 SW 2d 354/Mo (1973).

Where evidence showed that defendant placed a quantity of narcotics in the jacket pocket of another without his permission or knowledge, defendant's conviction for constructive possession would lie. *People v Newman*, 273 P 2d 917/Cal (1954).

In a prosecution for possession of marijuana growing in clay pots, proof of residence was offered in the form of an empty envelope, a postal card, and a hospital bill found in the apartment and addressed to defendant at the address where the marijuana was found. *State v Weller*, 496 P 2d 735/Or (1972).

Where a prisoner asked the jailor to get his coat from his locked automobile and gave the keys to the jailor for that purpose, the jailor could infer possession of amphetamine capsules found in the coat pocket to the prisoner, and conviction of the unlawful possession of a dangerous drug was proper. *State v Brandon*, 197 SE 2d 53/NC (1973).

Defendant was convicted for constructive possession of marijuana where he furnished undercover narcotics agents with a map and thereon indicated the location of a hidden cache of hashish and agents found the cache under a bush at the designated location, conviction being sustained on the theory that defendant had constructive possession of the substance and the power to exercise dominion or control over it (*United States v Capelis*, 426 F 2d 134/Cal–1970). The fact that one occupant of an automobile dropped a container of heroin from the automobile in which he was riding would not preclude the conviction of a second occupant of joint possession of the drug. (*Agobian v United States*, 323 F 2d 693/Cal–1963). The power to produce upon request, and the power to dispose of, a narcotic is evidence of control sufficient to establish constructive or joint possession. *Bass v United States*, 326 F 2d 884/Mo (1964).

In some states the mere possession of narcotic paraphernalia used in the illegal injection of narcotics, such as a hypodermic needle or syringe, is a crime. *People v Neal*, 299 NE 2d 532/Ill (1973).

Possession by Clinicians

Where defendant claimed a defense to possession in that he was a registered pharmacist, the burden of proving this defense was upon him, and the state was under no obligation to prove that he was not a pharmacist. *State v Culp*, 288 NE 2d 308/Oh (1971).

A licensed practical nurse who had charge of the narcotics cabinet at a hospital and who removed drugs therefrom and retained them for her own use, did not record their removal and refilled the units with another substance, was properly convicted of obtaining narcotics by fraud or deceit (*Forbes v Ingraham*, 338 NYS 2d 955/NY–1972); likewise, physicians are not exempt from prosecution for unlawful possession of narcotics obtained through deceit or subterfuge. *State v Jacobs*, 503 P 2d 826/Az (1972).

A medical doctor may be convicted of dispensing a controlled substance if his prescription is not for a legitimate medical purpose issued in the usual course of his professional practice. *United States v Leigh*, 487 F 2d 206/rehearing denied 488 F 2d 1055/Tex (1973).

Where defendant-pharmacist testified that he had received a telephone call from a doctor instructing him to sell morphine to a named person without a prescription, which he did, his defense was not tenable. *People v Gelardi*, 175 P 2d 855/Cal (1946).

"Usable" Amount

In a prosecution for possession of narcotics, the states are divided as to what constitutes sufficient evidence for conviction. To name a few in the minority holding, California, Arizona, Idaho, Texas and the District of Columbia have formulated the rule that minimum evidence for a conviction of possession requires proof of possession of a *usable* amount of the drug; while Wisconsin, Washington, Utah, Oregon, North Carolina, New Jersey, Missouri, Maryland, Colorado and Alabama, have held that a conviction for possession may be based on proof of possession of *any* quantity sufficient for identification *(State v Goetz*, 491 P 2d 220/Or–1972). Since the *Goetz* decision many jurisdictions have followed the Oregon ruling. Id.

In order to establish that defendant possessed a usable amount of marijuana, the state could rely on circumstantial evidence and need not produce in court a usable amount as evidence (*State v Goetz*, supra/certiorari denied 92 SC 2510/Or–1971); also, identity of a drug in a possession or distribution case may be established by circumstantial evidence. *State v Hutton*, 502 P 2d 1037/Wn (1972).

The usability rule of possession of narcotics applies to dangerous drugs as well, i.e., for a possessor to be guilty of a violation of a statute forbidding possession, he must be in possession of a usable quantity. *State v McGuire*, 493 P 2d 513/Az (1972).

Attempt to Possess Narcotics

The California court has held that one may be convicted of an attempt to possess a narcotic where the actor clearly manifests an intent coupled with a direct ineffectual act toward that end. Thus, where defendant, a deputy sheriff, solicited a "large supply of heroin" from a fellow deputy assigned to the narcotics detail, who advised his superiors of the solicitation and was advised to feign complicity in the scheme, defendent-deputy's arrest and conviction were sustained for attempt to possess heroin when the narcotics officer furnished him talcum powder and he received it thinking it to be heroin. *People v Siu*, 271 P 2d 575/Cal (1954).

Possession for Distribution

As a rule, possession of a drug or narcotic with intent to distribute is a more serious crime than possession for personal use, and where the amount possessed is substantial, possession with intent to distribute may be inferred; thus, the possession of 188 pounds of hashish raised an inference of possession with intent to distribute (*United States v Perry*, 480 F 2d 147/Fla–1973). A statute providing that possession of more than five grams of marijuana raised a presumption of possession with intent to distribute, merely sets forth a rule of evidence in establishing a *prima facie* case. *State v McGee*, 197 SE 2d 63/NC (1973).

In a prosecution for possession with intent to sell, the state may prove the possessor is a nonuser of the drug from which fact the jury may logically infer possession with intent to sell. *State v Villavicencio*, 502 P 2d 1337/Az (1972).

Possession is one crime and sale or distribution is another and defendant may be convicted and punished for either or both (*People v Stewart*, 207 NW 2d 907/Mich–1973); (*State v Thornton*, 196 SE 2d 701/NC–1973). It is no defense that the drug was sold to an undercover officer or his agent. *People v Meyers*, 510 P 2d 430/Colo (1973).

Furnishing

A deputy sheriff who directed a minor to purchase a "lid" of marijuana with a marked $10 bill was not guilty of a violation of narcotics laws by furnishing marijuana to a minor when, without the knowledge of the deputy, the minor took advantage of the opportunity and bought a second lid with his own money. *State v Chudy*, 492 P 2d 402/Az (1972).

The simultaneous possession of two different types of contraband narcotics constitutes but one offense (*Jones v State*, 482 SW 2d 194/Tex–1972), but where the accused was found to have furnished narcotics to a minor on four consecutive days, his conviction of four separate offenses of furnishing could be sustained, not one count only, of a continuing nature. *People v Tipton*, 268 P 2d 196/Cal (1954).

A go-between in the sale or transfer of narcotics is equally guilty with principal perpetrator if he has knowledge of the item he is transferring. *State v Robinson*, 503 P 2d 817/Az (1972).

Sale of Controlled Substances

Guilty knowledge is an essential element of the possession or sale of dangerous drugs; i.e., that the possessor had knowledge of the narcotic nature of the substance. *State v Clouatre*, 264 S 2d 595/La (1972); *State v Anderson*, 498 P 2d 295/Mont (1972).

Although some states have adopted the rule that unlawful *possession* of a dangerous drug or narcotic imparts the possession of a usable amount of the substance, no such rule has been applied where the crime is one of *sale* and any amount sold violates the act. *Carter v State*, 480 SW 2d 735/Tex (1972).

A statute which forbids the distribution of controlled substances is violated when the substance is placed in the U.S. mail, the effect being the equivalent of turning the substance over to an agent for delivery (*State v McHorse*, 517 P 2d 75/NM–1973). Also, sale to a government informant constitutes distribution. *United States v Pruitt*, 487 F 2d 1241/Mo (1973).

Where defendant sold a substance to undercover narcotics officers which he claimed was marijuana but which contained only a minuscule amount of marijuana insufficient to produce a narcotic effect, his conviction of sale of marijuana was nevertheless valid. *State v Grady*, 201 NW 2d 493/Ia (1972).

The proffered testimony that the smoking of hashish or marijuana is not harmful to the health, was not relevant to any issue in a prosecution for possession of a dangerous drug for the purpose of sale, nor in the consideration in assessing the degree of punishment, and the exclusion of such testimony did not deny defendant any right guaranteed under the Constitution. *Kuhl v Com*, 497 SW 2d 710/Ky (1973).

Where a person is asked by an undercover narcotics officer where he might be able to obtain marijuana, and the person gives the officer a name and address, the person furnishing such information cannot be convicted of criminal facilitation because of lack of intent. *People v Gordon*, 343 NYS 2d 103/NY (1973).

Marijuana

The statutory classification of marijuana as a "narcotic drug" rather than as a "dangerous drug" is not arbitrary and unreasonable and did not deprive petitioner of due process and equal protection under the law. *Tracey v Janco*, 351 FS 836/Va (1972); *Gaskin v State*, 490 SW 2d 521/Ten (1973).

The finding of nine marijuana seeds weighing .19 gram on the floor of defendant's automobile which was occupied by him and others was an insufficient quantity under Texas law to sustain a charge of unlawful possession of marijuana. *Taylor v State*, 505 SW 2d 927/Tex (1974).

Where appellant contended on appeal that marijuana was a "beneficial herb," his defense was untenable even if true, as a beneficial herb may be declared contraband, and a law proscribing possession of marijuana is not unconstitutional. *People v Mistrill*, 241 P 2d 1050/Cal (1952).

Use of Narcotics in Religious Ceremonies

In a prosecution for the possession of peyote it is a defense that the peyote was being used in a *bona fide* pursuit of religious belief, that it was an integral part of the religious exercise, and that it was used in a manner that was not dangerous to public health, safety or morals. *State v Whittingham*, 504 P 2d 950/Az (1973).

The state, pursuant to its police power, may proscribe the use of peyote even though technically a hallucinogen rather than a narcotic, but when such proscription imposes a burden on the free exercise of religion observed by the Navajo Indian tribes who use peyote as a sacramental symbol similar to the bread and wine used in the Christian churches, it violates free exercise of religion guaranteed by the First Amendment of the U.S. Constitution (*State ex rel Offerdahl*, 481 P 2d 338/Mont–1971): (*People v Woody*, 394 P 2d 813/Cal–1964). Such exemption did not deny equal protection to defendant, who was a member of the Neo-American Church, which embraced the indefensible principle that marijuana and LSD are the true host and are sacramental foods to be partaken of by members on regular occasions. *United States v Kuch*, 288 FS 439/DC (1968).

Addiction

The characteristics of the process of addiction to the use of narcotics are (1) "emotional dependence on the drug," (2) "increasing tolerance to its effects," (3) "physical dependence," characterized by withdrawal symptoms upon sudden termination of drug intake. *People v O'Neil*, 401 P 2d 928/Cal (1965).

A state law which denounced the "status" of narcotic addiction and declared such status punishable by not less than 90 days in the county jail and triable at any time before the addict reformed, inflicted "cruel and unusual punishment" in violation of the Fourteenth Amendment and was thus unconstitutional. *Robinson v California*, 370 US 660 (1962).

In *Robinson v California, supra*, the U.S. Supreme Court started the trend of dealing with narcotic addiction as an affliction or disease. The addict's cure and rehabilitation are paramount, although he is incarcerated and isolated. The philosophy behind his incarceration is treatment not punishment. The California Supreme Court ruled in essence that in the enactment of a statute permitting commitment and corrective treatment of narcotic addicts (which is essentially a quarantine), the legislature intended to create a new program for confinement, treatment and rehabilitation of narcotic addicts. *California WIC*, § 3000 *et seq.*

A provision of the Narcotic Addict Rehabilitation Act, making one previously convicted of a crime of violence ineligible to treatment as a narcotic addict in lieu of penal incarceration, does not deny equal protection (*United States v Krehbiel*, 493 F 2d 497/Cal–1974). Also, where one has been twice previously convicted of a felony, he is not entitled to treatment under this Act, and such denial does not violate due process nor deny equal protection. *Neria v United States*, 493 F 2d 913/Tex (1974).

Commitment to a drug rehabilitation program for narcotics addicts is not voluntary and is not dependent upon defendant's motivation or his desire to participate in the program. And under California law the court is required to commit the defendant to a drug rehabilitation center, but continued refusal to cooperate in the program may be basis for the return of the addict to the court to stand trial for a criminal offense. *People v Barajas*, 103 CR 405/Cal (1972).

OBSCENITY

In General

The U.S. Supreme Court in *United States v Roth*, 354 US 476 (1956), declared rules by which obscenity was to be assessed. In 1973, in *Paris Adult Theater I v Slaton*, 93 SC 2628, the same court under different complexion held that obscene material has no protection under the First Amendment, that the States have a legitimate interest in regulating commerce in obscene material and in regulating the exhibition of obscene material in places of public accommodation, including the so-called "adult" theaters. In light of this premise nothing precludes the state of Georgia from the regulation of the allegedly obscene materials exhibited in the Paris Adult Theater I, provided the applicable Georgia law meets the First Amendment standards set forth in *Miller v California*, 93 SC at 2614-16. In other words, the individual states or political subdivisions thereof may, under this Supreme Court ruling, proscribe obscenity under community standards which are not national in scope.

The scope given freedom of speech and freedom of expression depends materially on the personal moral philosophy of the individual members of the appellate court viewing the question of obscenity. Thus, the California courts have held that a dance by male and female performers in a night club, which included the simulation of an act of sexual intercourse between the two and which performance also consisted of the male bringing his mouth in physical contact with the female's vagina, was a method of expression constitutionally protected and could not constitute a basis for denial of a permit for cafe entertainment (*Sanita v Bd of Police Commissioners*, 104 CR 380/Cal–1972). And in another California case, an injunction against a bar featuring live entertainment wherein the performers' genetalia and anuses were exposed was likewise held to be an invalid restraint on free expression (*People ex rel Hicks v "Sarong Gals,"* 103 CR 414/Cal–1972). But the Ohio courts ruled adversely, holding that a regulation prohibiting dancing or entertainment by females with insufficient attire did not violate First Amendment guarantee of freedom of expression. *A B Jac Inc v Liquor Control Commission*, 285 NE 2d 763/Oh (1972).

Obscene materials are not protected by the First Amendment and nothing therein contained requires the trier of fact to consider hypothetical and unascertainable national standards when attempting to determine whether certain materials are obscene. *State v J–R Distributors Inc*, 512 P 2d 1049/Wn (1973).

Obscene and pornographic films do not acquire constitutional immunity from state regulation simply because they are exhibited to consenting adults, only. *Paris Adult Theater I v Slaton*, 93 SC 2628/Ga (1973).

The constitutional right to privacy does not include any fundamental right to watch obscene moving pictures in a place of public accommodation (*Paris*

Adult Theater I, supra), nor does the right of privacy in marriage extend to intercourse on a public street corner or a theater stage. Id.

The government has the right to punish those who pander to the perverted sexual engrossment of a minority by supplying them materials for a price; the government through its laws, make the suppliers run the risk of punishment if caught. *State v Shapiro*, 300 A 2d 595/NJ (1973).

"Obscenity" Defined

In 1957, the U.S. Supreme Court annulled obscenity statutes in most of the states establishing itself as guardians of the conscience of the "community," the community being the United States and its territories. *Roth v United States*, 354 US 476 (1957).

Under the Roth test three elements were required: (1) that the dominant theme of the material taken as a whole appeal to a prurient interest in sex; (2) that the material be patently offensive as affronting contemporary community standards; and (3) that the material be utterly without redeeming social value. *Visual Educators Inc v Koeppel*, 268 S 2d 22/Ala (1972).

In 1973 the U.S. Supreme Court reviewed the question of obscenity and made two significant changes as set forth in *Roth, supra*: (1) that the "community" was not the entire United States but rather the state or local community, and (2) that instead of a finding that the material be utterly without redeeming social value, the state only need prove that the material be without serious literary value. *Miller v California*, 93 SC 2607 (1973); *Roth v United States, supra.*

"Sexual conduct," within the definition of obscenity, consists of acts of sexual intercourse between humans, normal or perverted, actual or simulated; acts of masturbation; fellatio and cunnilingus; acts of excretory function; lewd exhibition of the genitals—especially in a stimulated condition; and sexual relations between humans and animals. *State ex rel Chobot v Circuit Court*, 212 NW 690/Wis (1973).

"Community" Defined

The U.S. Constitution does not require that juries in a state obscenity prosecution be instructed to apply standards of a hypothetical statewide community; such instructions may, but need not be given. Instructions may be given to the effect that community standards be applied without specifying what community to apply. *Jenkins v Georgia*, 94 SC 2750/Ga (1974).

"Community" by whose contemporary standards the issue of obscenity is to be determined, need not be the state as a whole; rather, it is constitutionally permissible to apply the contemporary community standards of a county, though not necessarily the whole county. *Davison v State*, 288 S 2d 483/Fla (1973); *Price v Com*, 201 SE 2d 798/Va (1974).

Mere Nudity

Nudity alone is not obscene in most jurisdictions, and a statute which makes criminal the operation of a nudist camp or the engagement in nudist practices is vague and indefinite so as to offend due process and therefore unconstitutional (*Roberts v Clement*, 252 FS 835/Ten–1966). And likewise, a magazine whose theme is the advocation and promotion of nudism is not obscene. *United States v 1,000 Copies of "Solis,"* 254 FS 595/Md (1966).

Nudity in the privacy of a home is not a legitimate object of state interest, but nudity on a crowded street, although exercised without lewd intent, is a matter of government concern since it may constitute a threat to peace, or may be thrust upon unwilling observers or may constitute a traffic hazard. *Yauch v State*, 505 P 2d 1066/Az (1973).

Mere nudity does not constitute indecent exposure. For a conviction of this crime the state must prove not only that the defendant exposed himself, but also that he intended by his conduct to direct public attention to his genitals for sexual arousal, gratification or affront. Under California law, one who simply sunbathes in the nude on an isolated beach does not lewdly expose his privates within the meaning of the statute. *In re Smith*, 497 P 2d 807/Cal (1972).

Indecent exposure under New York law has four elements: (1) exposure of private or intimate parts of the body; (2) intentional exposure; (3) lewd exposure; (4) exposure in a public place (*People v Gilbert*, 338 NYS 2d 457/NY–1972). Mere nudity in a public place, without regard to motives, intentions or actions, does not constitute public lewdness. Id.

Partially Nude Waitresses

"Topless" and "bottomless" ordinances were invalid as unduly restrictive in the freedom of expression in the performance of dances and plays in Arizona but were valid in their requirement of clothing for persons serving food and drink. *Yauch v State, supra.*

A city ordinance prohibiting bar and tavern owners and managers from allowing female employees to appear with one or both breasts or her lower torso exposed or substantially exposed to public view was not violative of the Constitution in Washington nor discriminative against the female sex. *Seattle v Hinkley*, 517 P 2d 592/Wn (1973).

Indecent Exposure—Public Places

The offense of indecent exposure of the person does not depend on the number of persons present who are or may be offended thereby, as such exposure viewed by only one person is just as much a violation as an act viewed by many. Thus, where defendant was viewed in his own garage by a female neighbor from her backyard the statute was violated. *Davison v State*, 281 P 2d 196/Ok (1955).

"Skinnydipping" or nude bathing and sunbathing by defendants in a national forest near a public camp ground with other people being in the immediate vicinity and in an area of concentrated recreation use, there being signs posted prohibiting public nudity, constituted indecent conduct defined in a state statute. *United States v Hymans*, 463 F 2d 615/Colo (1972).

Where defendant took sunbaths in the nude on a beach which was popular for fishermen, was used by the public in general and accessible to the public by a well-worn path and was at a place so publicly inhabited that the trier of fact could infer that defendant wanted to be seen, his conviction for indecent exposure was warranted. *State v Rocker*, 475 P 2d 684/Haw (1970).

Obscene Stage Performances

The legislature may proscribe nude dancing in the public streets, since the state may limit time, place and the manner of expression under the First Amendment. *Yauch v State*, 505 P 2d 1066/Az (1973).

An indecent exposure statute as was applied to females who danced on a stage clad only in "briefs" covering the lower part of their bodies, was not unconstitutionally discriminatory on the theory that males appearing in public wearing trunks and bare from the waist up were not prosecuted. *Robinson v State*, 489 SW 2d 503/Ark (1973).

A stage performance in which female performers exposed their private parts to an all-male adult audience was obscene *per se* and no opinion evidence was necessary to support a determination of obscenity (*City of Seattle v Marshall*), 512 P 2d 693/Wn–1974). And one who aided and abetted several females in a stage performance wherein they exposed their private parts to an audience of about 75 males in a public place, could be properly convicted of indecent exposure by aiding and abetting. *State v King*, 204 SE 2d 667/NC (1974).

In appealing from a conviction of oral copulation in a stage play in front of an audience, appellant urged that oral copulation was a form of expression and therefore constitutionally protected. The California Supreme Court in affirming conviction held:

> . . . appellants make the fantastic contention that oral copulation is merely a method of expression and is a form of speech protected by the First Amendment. Such contention would also apply to such crimes as sodomy, incest, rape, and crimes against nature, if committed during a stage performance. Appellants are not charged with "a constitutionally protected demonstration" but with a criminal act. *People v Drolet*, 105 CR 824/Cal (1973).

Obscene Films

Films which contained little, if any, plot or story and which were occupied fully with scene-after-scene of sexual intercourse, lesbianism, cunnilingus, fellatio, sodomy and masturbation were obscene and defendant corporation was guilty of knowingly circulating and publishing obscene movie films. *State v Little Art Corp*, 204 NW 2d 574/Neb (1973).

Motion picture films showing "deviate sexual intercourse"—defined as sexual conduct consisting of contact between the penis and the anus, the penis and the mouth, the vulva and the mouth—constitutes "hard-core pornography" and is not constitutionally protected, and an officer viewing such film may seize a film as an incident to a lawful arrest. *People v Wrench*, 341 NYS 2d 985/NY (1973).

A motion picture film entitled "Beauty and the Boxer," showing sex acts between a female human being and a dog, was hard-core pornography and obscene *per se*. *State v Valchar*, 295 NE 2d 424/Oh (1973).

A film entitled "The Art of Marriage," which portrayed actual and implicit heterosexual intercourse between nude males and females, was obscene under constitutional standards and constituted hard-core pornography; a prosecution for its exhibition to the general public, though adult, was permissible as such obscene expression is not protected by the First Amendment. *State v Lebewitz*, 202 NW 2d 648/Min (1972).

A film depicting, *inter alia*, a woman masturbating and two other women performing acts of lesbianism including a close-up of each scene, was obscene (*State v Shackman*, 278 NE 2d 61/Oh–1971), and the fact that the film was exhibited exclusively to consenting adults was no defense to a subsequent prosecution for its exhibition. Id.

Slides which depicted a nude man seated or lying on his side facing the camera holding his erected penis, and others depicting two nude males in an act of fellatio, was held to be hard-core pornography and thus obscene (*United States v Wild*, 422 F 2d 34/NY–1969). Further, a film that portrayed young women being spanked, slapped, or otherwise struck on the buttocks with the open hand, a paddle, a cane or a bullwhip reflected a revolting desecration of the human body. *Ratner v Weddle*, 307 FS 471/affirmed 420 F 2d 1382/Cal (1968).

Where defendant showed lurid, sexually deviant behavior on an outdoor screen visible to an unwilling audience, his defense that local residents could have drawn their shades and passing motorists could have averted their eyes, was not tenable. *State v Rabe*, 484 P 2d 917/Wn (1971).

An obscene film trailer which followed the featured film and was exhibited without warning as a coming attraction to an entire theater audience, and was so obtrusive as to offend persons within the audience, was obscene, not being constitutionally protected. *State v Boyd*, 300 NE 2d 752/Oh (1972).

Photographs and Pictures

Not all photographs of nude women are obscene, even though attention is focused on the breasts or pubic area, or where the female has assumed a kneeling, sitting or reclining position if such position is not lewd or enticing; nor does the inclusion of nude men in the photograph with a nude female constitute obscenity unless some type of sexual activity is depicted or suggested. *United States v 25,000 Magazines Entitled "Revue,"* 254 FS 1014/affirmed 381 F 2d 821/Md (1966).

Photographs depicting nude females posing singly and illustrating no form of sexual activity were not obscene (*In re Ponchot*, 448 P 2d 385/Cal–1968), nor was a nudist magazine obscene in a constitutional sense wherein numerous photographs of nude adults proclaimed the alleged virtues of nudity as a way of life (*People v Noroff*, 433 P 2d 479/Cal–1967). A state statute which denounced the display of a nude woman, man, boy or girl in a public place except an art gallery was overbroad and unconstitutional. *Delta Book Distributors Inc v Cronvich*, 304 FS 662/La (1969).

Photographs, pictures and drawings which portrayed in a patently offensive manner sexual conduct which was normal and perverse, actual and simulated, and which depicted acts of masturbation, fellatio, cunnilingus, lewd exhibitions of the genitalia, and sexual acts between humans and animals, were obscene and when taken as a whole had no serious literary, artistic, political or scientific value. *State v J–R Distributors Inc*, 512 P 2d 1049/Wn (1973).

Magazines and Other Publications

Publications containing photographs of nudes posed so that the camera was focused directly at the genital organs were not obscene within the meaning of the law when distributed to adults. *State v Oregon Bookmark Corp*, 492 P 2d 504/Or (1972), citing *Burgin v South Carolina*, 404 US 806 (1971).

A magazine consisting primarily of photographs which depicted the genitalia of both sexes alone or in juxtaposition with persons or objects, bearing captions designed to be humorous though ribald, but not suggesting sexual conduct, was not obscene. *Chicago v Geraci* 294 NE 2d 725/Ill (1973).

A magazine composed almost exclusively of photographs of nude males and females, although not coupled in sexual activity, posed so as to focus attention on their genitals and in many instances sexual activity was suggested and imminent, was declared to be obscene (*People v Melander*, 295 NE 2d 20/Ill–1973). And books which were each a collection of chronicles of sexual intercourse, masturbation, flagellation, fellatio, cunnilingus, lesbianism, rape and murder, purely for their prurient appeal, held together by the merest modicum of a story or plot, were obscene. Id.

A magazine entitled "Whiplash Lovers" containing 48 pages—40 pages of which consisted of nude males and females engaged in sex acts and the remaining 8 pages devoted to pornographic articles—was obscene. *Gronto v McDougall*, 336 FS 1372/Ga (1972).

What Constitutes Obscenity in Books

For a conviction under a statute denouncing the possession of obscene literature with intent to sell, distribute or otherwise dispose of, the state must prove that the possessor had knowledge of the nature of the literature, or—if the material is a film, or the alleged obscenity is an act, play or exhibition—that the person responsible for its exhibition had knowledge thereof. Under a prosecution for selling obscene literature where the seller sold an undercover police officer a book which gave no indication of the contents on the cover, evidence of possession for sale, without more, was insufficient for conviction. *People v Wepplo*, 178 P 2d 853/Cal (1947); *State v Jackson*, 356 P 2d 495/Or (1960).

Where the alleged obscenity is contained between the covers of a book, the total work is the criterion by which the book will be judged, and where there are isolated words or phrases therein which when taken by themselves are obnoxious and offensive, obscenity is not necessarily established (*People v Wepplo, supra*). Remote scenes, passages or components may not be plucked from the whole of the work for the purpose of judging the totality of the work. *Zenith International Film Corp v City of Chicago*, 291 F 2d 785/Ill (1961).

Books textually advocating incest between all members of the family regardless of age, and also advocating homosexuality and lesbianism, and depicting every form of sexual intercourse including oral copulation, were obscene and subject to forfeiture under statutory provision (*United States v Four (4) Books*, 289 FS 972/Cal—1968); films depicting a near-nude female model moving and undulating, clearly indicative of sexual activity, and simulating intercourse and invitations to engage therein, violated the state obscenity statute. *Schackman v Arnebergh*, 258 FS 983/appeal dismissed 387 US 427/Cal (1966).

Possession for Sale

In a prosecution for the sale of, or for possession for the purpose of sale of, obscene literature, *scienter* is an essential element and must be proved beyond a reasonable doubt (*State v Blair*, 291 NE 2d 451/Oh—1972). *Scienter* within the meaning of the statute means knowledge of the contents of the publication. *State v Richardson*, 506 SW 2d 488/Mo (1974).

Scienter was established by proof that the entrance to defendant's bookstore was marked "Adults Only"; that the store contained only magazines alleged to be obscene; and at defendants' trial they did not testify as to their lack of knowledge of the nature of the material. *Cherokee News & Arcade Inc v State*, 509 P 2d 917/Ok (1973).

In a prosecution for possession for sale of obscene literature, it is not necessary to prove defendant knew the material was obscene, only that he knew the nature of the matter, leaving legal ruling to the court. *United States v Gundlach*, 345 FS 709/Pa–1972); *State v J–R Distributors Inc*, 512 P 2d 1049/Wn (1973).

Where a police officer entered a bookstore and told defendant that he wanted to get something that showed everything and that he wanted to see the actual acts, and defendant responded by pointing to certain magazines and saying, "Those magazines will show you everything," there was sufficient evidence of *scienter* to support a finding of guilty of selling obscene matter. *State v Richardson, supra.*

Obscene Devices

A nude figurine may be obscene because of its position or pose, or because of its position in relation to another figurine depicting the same or the opposite sex. *United States v Baranov*, 293 FS 610/Cal (1968).

Rubber devices known as "extensions" which were composed of a thin outer layer of rubber and having a large thick rubber end simulating an erected penis of exaggerated size, were objects of "indecent character" whose interstate transportation was properly condemned (*United States v Gentile*, 211 FS 383/Md–1962), but devices known as "French ticklers" which were similar to an ordinary contraceptive condom except that the device had small bits of rubber attached to the outside, were not "goods of an indecent character." Id.

Adversary Hearing

The states are in disagreement as to whether a judicially supervised adversary hearing is necessary before police may seize allegedly obscene material antecedent to arrest and prosecution. In *City News Center Inc v Carson*, 310 FS 1018/Fla (1970), the federal court held: "Due process of law requires prior adversary, judicially-supervised hearing before seizure of allegedly obscene material, since, without such threshhold protection, evanescent freedom of unintimidated expression becomes meaningless."

An adversary hearing antecedent to seizure of allegedly obscene matter, requires that an exhibitor or speaker have a fair opportunity to present reasons why the material should not be seized. *West v State*, 489 SW 2d 597/Tex (1972).

A prior adversary hearing to determine obscenity is not a constitutional prerequisite in Georgia to the seizure of allegedly obscene materials to be used in a criminal prosecution (*Good v State*, 195 SE 2d 264/Ga–1972). But see *Com v Amick*, 298 A 2d 905/Pa (1972), wherein the Pennsylvania court held that no committing magistrate, without an adversary hearing, can constitutionally issue a search warrant authorizing the seizure of obscene literature.

A preseizure adversary hearing is not required before seizure of an allegedly obscene motion picture film for evidence, but an order of seizure and destruction of allegedly obscene prints and articles may be ordered only after an adversary hearing and a judicial determination of obscenity. *Julian v City of Las Vegas*, 493 P 2d 1037/Nev (1972).

Although an officer may legally arrest one for exhibiting obscene films—a misdemeanor committed in his presence—he must view the film in its entirety (*Hosey v City of Jackson*, 309 FS 527/Mis—1970), and to this end he may seize the film for evidence, but he may not estop production nor the showing of duplicate films. However, the state may explicitly halt the dissemination of alleged obscene matter, such as films, books, and magazines, but only for a judicial determination in an adversary proceeding. *Astro Cinema Corp v Mackell*, 305 FS 863/reversed in part 422 F 2d 293/NY (1969).

Expert Testimony

Expert testimony is not necessary to a conviction of obscenity as the jury may so find by inferences adduced from other evidence (*People v Enskat*, 109 CR 433/Cal—1973); (*Papp v State*, 281 S 2d 600/Fla—1973); (*Richards v State*, 497 SW 2d 770/Tex/1973). Furthermore, an instruction to the jury that expert testimony may be totally disregarded if they find to the contrary, is proper instruction. *People v Enskat, supra*; *United States v One Reel of Film*, 360 FS 1067/Mas (1973).

The Oregon court has ruled that expert testimony on the issue of appeal to prurient interest in sex, is not essential to conviction where the material in question is so patently and exclusively sexual that the average trier of fact is capable of recognizing its prurient appeal to arouse lustful desires and lascivious thoughts in the average person. *State v Childs*, 447 P 2d 304/certiorari denied 394 US 931/Or (1968).

Shipment in Interstate Commerce

There is no correlative right to ship obscene materials through the medium of interstate commerce merely because possession of such materials in the home is constitutionally protected (*United States v Caeser*, 368 FS 328/Wis—1974), and similarly, merely because consensual acts of sexual intercourse in the privacy of the home are lawful does not mean that interstate transportation of females for the purpose of prostitution is likewise lawful. Id.

What Is Not Obscene

What constitutes lewdness in one community may not constitute lewdness in another. Sophistication and/or morality are significant determinants. Thus, in New York where defendant in her late twenties, while on a public beach removed her bathing suit and during a 90-minute period was observed to play with a ball, swim, wave at a passing boat, slowly apply suntan lotion to the front of her body down to her pubic hair, lay on a blanket, legs spread apart 12 to 18 inches, her conduct could *not* be considered lewd beyond a reasonable doubt. *People v Gilbert*, 338 NYS 2d 457/NY (1972).

Where a professional dancer performed nude in a nightclub whose audience was screened as to age and whose patrons were warned by a large sign that there would be a nude performance inside, and there was no evidence that anyone was offended except two officers who were present in their official capacity, the performance was not a violation of the indecent exposure statute. *Haines v State*, 512 P 2d 820/Ok (1973).

Magazines containing photographs portraying females in the nude and showing some physical contact with males, although uncouth and tawdry, were not obscene where there was no portrayal of sexual activity. *Thacker v State*, 490 SW 2d 854/Tex (1973).

A political cartoon depicting policemen raping the Statue of Liberty and the Goddess of Justice was not constitutionally obscene, so ruled the U.S. Supreme Court in *Papish v Board of Curators of the University of Missouri*, 93 SC 1197/Mo (1973).

A deck of cards depicting a man and a woman engaged in sexual intercourse on the back of each card, and illustrating various positions, was found by a jury not to be obscene. *United States v Palladino*, 475 F 2d 65/Mas (1973).

A key chain which depicted a male and a female in an act of sexual intercourse was not obscene. *People v Nawodylo*, 297 NE 2d 388/Ill (1973).

Mere Possession

Preparation and possession of obscene material without intent to distribute do not violate the obscenity statute (*In re Klor*, 415 P 2d 791/Cal—1966), but the ruling by the U.S. Supreme Court to the effect that the individual states may not proscribe the private possession by one of obscene materials for his personal pleasure, would not prevent a prosecution of the author, director, actor or actress contributing to the production of an obscene play. *Rephael v Hogan*, 305 FS 749/NY (1969).

ABORTION

In General

Women have at least two fundamental rights: the right to life and the right to choose whether to bear children. *People v Barksdale*, 503 P 2d 257/Cal (1972).

The U.S. Supreme Court held:

> [The right of privacy] is broad enough to encompass a woman's decision whether or not to terminate her pregnancy . . . . Maternity, or additional offspring, may force upon the woman a distressful life and future. Mental

> and physical health may be taxed by child care. There is also the distress, for all concerned, associated with the unwanted child . . . . In other cases, as in this one, the additional difficulties and continuing stigma of unwed motherhood may be involved. *Roe v Wade*, 93 SC 705/Tex (1973).

The initial decision to terminate pregnancy is one that is purely personal to the pregnant woman and a matter between her and her physician, and any unreasonable governmental interference must yield to the woman's right to privacy (*Jones v Smith*, 278 S 2d 339/Fla–1973); the consent of the putative father is not included within the terms of the Florida abortion law. Id.

First Trimester of Pregnancy

A South Carolina abortion statute making it a crime to terminate pregnancy in the first trimester, that is, within the first three months of pregnancy, was unconstitutional under a U.S. Supreme Court ruling in *Roe v Wade, supra. State v Lawrence*, 198 SE 2d 253/SC (1973).

A woman's right to terminate pregnancy is included in her constitutional right to privacy, but this right ends at the termination of the first trimester of pregnancy. *Jones v Smith, supra.*

Pregnancy–Clinical Termination

A state may not require that abortions prior to the end of the first trimester be performed in a hospital (*Doe v Bolton*, 93 SC 739/Ga–1973), and a statute declaring criminal the termination of pregnancy in a place other than an accredited hospital licensed by the state is unconstitutional (*State v Ingel*, 308 A 2d 223/Md–1973); any clinic or hospital having appropriate facilities may terminate such pregnancy. *Doe v Bolton, supra.*

Second and Third Trimesters

The state may curtail a woman's due process right to terminate pregnancy in the second trimester by laws reasonably related to maternal health, and in the third trimester by laws recognizing the state's interest in the potentiality of human life, but such laws must be tailored to accommodate the conflicting rights of pregnant women and the interests of the state. *Doe v Woodahl*, 360 FS 20/Mont (1973).

PROSTITUTION

In General

Acts of prostitution are not forbidden by federal law (except interstate and federal enclaves), and are not usually forbidden by state law, being a type of activity which is usually proscribed at the county and city level. *State v Bittner*, 196 NW 2d 186/Neb (1972).

The word "fee" or a cognate—which is usually an essential element of prostitution and which is used in a statute providing that a person is guilty of prostitution when such person engages or offers or agrees to engage in sexual conduct with another person in return for a fee—means payment in return for professional services rendered (NY Penal Law 1965 § 230.00); (*People v Block*, 337 NYS 2d 153/NY—1972). The term "sexual conduct" as here used means and includes masturbation, homosexuality, sexual intercourse, or physical contact of a person's clothed or unclothed genitals, pubic area, buttocks, and, if such person be a female, the breasts. Id. It is recognized that the New York definition of prostitution would not be applicable in all jurisdictions since homosexuality as mentioned in the statute is a felony in many jurisdictions and not dealt with as an act of prostitution, which is almost always a misdemeanor.

Testimony of a vice officer that defendant had agreed to engage in "French" and "around the world" with him was sufficient to show that defendant intended to engage in deviant sexual conduct for money. *State v Ward*, 517 P 2d 1069/Or (1974).

A statute which forbids living in a house of ill fame is not unconstitutional as being imprecise and not adequately informing one of conduct which is denounced. *Sumpter v State*, 306 NE 2d 95/Ind (1974).

Pimping

"Pimping" consists of accepting all or part of the earnings of a prostitute and was committed where complaining witness was introduced to a female with whom he had sexual relations and upon payment of money to the prostitute she transferred it to defendant. *State v Emerson*, 517 P 2d 245/Wn (1973).

Where defendant's participation in the crime of prostitution consisted of furnishing a motel room and knowingly receiving money from the prostitute's earnings as a prostitute, there was sufficient participation to sustain conviction. *Minor v Com*, 191 SE 2d 825/Va (1972).

Pandering

"Pandering" consists of the procuring of a woman for prostitution, and transporting her into or out of the state for such purpose is not an element under state law (*Taylor v State*, 516 P 2d 1351/Ok—1973). If the female is transported interstate for such purpose, even though consensual, the federal Mann Act applies (*United States v Caeser*, 368 FS 328/Wis—1974). Although females, only, may be the subject of interstate transportation for prostitution, the Mann Act may be violated by either sex. Id.

The crime of pandering was proved when evidence was introduced by testimony of a state's witness that she turned over to the defendant $125 which she had received through prostitution. *Kleinrichert v State*, 297 NE 2d 822/Ind (1973).

Under a statute which prohibits solicitation or procuring for prostitution, lewdness or assignation, the act solicited must be criminal and the crime is complete upon solicitation. Response by the person solicited is not an element. *Cherry v State*, 306 A 2d 634/Md (1973).

Defendant theater owner was guilty of promoting prostitution where he paid a male and a female to engage in an act of sexual intercourse on stage before a live audience in his theater. *State v Kravitz*, 511 P 2d 844/Or (1973).

Solicitation to Commit

Under the rules of entrapment the government officer or his agent may not induce or incite an innocent person to commit crime which the person had no intention of committing absent such inducement (*State v McDonald*, 289 NE 2d 583/Oh–1972), but an officer may actually solicit another to commit a crime which the person intends to commit should the opportunity present itself (*United States v Hill*, 469 F 2d 673/Ok–1972). Notwithstanding the general rule of entrapment, the courts generally hold that to convict for prostitution the officer or agent may do no more than present himself as a prospective customer and the prostitute must make the offer.

Chapter XI

Perversion of Justice

BRIBERY

Defined

"Bribery" is an attempt, whether successful or not, to influence a public officer, *de jure* or *de facto*, in the discharge of his official duties either in the executive, legislative or judicial branches of government, by the offer of a reward or other pecuniary consideration. That an officer's status was *de facto* would not relieve the defendant of criminal responsibility. *State v London*, 78 P 2d 548/Wn (1938).

Bribery is committed where it is found that benefit is conferred or offered to one public official in exchange for his efforts to influence the judgment or actions of other public officials. *People v Mitchell*, 338 NYS 2d 313/NY (1972).

The Nature of Bribery

Bribery is of two types: that of the corruptor wherein the bribe is offered, promised or given, and that of the corrupt, wherein the bribe is solicited or received—but in either event the intent is to pervert justice. *Black's Law Dictionary*.

Where the crime is one of offering a bribe, there is imposed upon the state the burden of proving an agreement or understanding between two or more persons, but where the crime is one of asking for or receiving a bribe, no such understanding need be proved. *State v Emmanuel*, 253 P 2d 836/Wn (1953).

"Bribery" and "Extortion" Distinguished

The difference between extortion and bribery is at times subtle, but as a rule, if the gratuity or reward was advanced under threat or coercion, the crime is extortion; if delivered under persuasion, the crime is bribery. Where defendants obtained money from a physician for the stated purpose of bribing federal narcotics agents, and had no intention of using the money for that purpose, and nothing was given, offered or promised, neither bribery nor attempt bribery was committed. *United States v Teed*, 185 F 2d 561/Wn (1950).

The essence of the crime of bribery is that both parties to the agreement and transaction act voluntarily, while in extortion one acts under duress. *United States v Addonizio*, 451 F 2d 49/NJ (1971).

"Public Officer" Defined

A "public office" must have been created by constitutional or legislative authority; duties and powers must be defined by law; duties must be performed independently and free from control of a superior power and be endowed with some degree of permanency and continuity (*Vander Lynden v Crews*, 205 NW 2d 686/Ia–1973). Indicia of a public officer as opposed to a public employee are to be found in the nature, functions and duties to be performed and tenure of the office holder (*Haller v Carlson*, 346 NYS 2d 108/NY–1973). The holder must possess authority to perform public duty which constitutes an aspect of governmental sovereignty whether legislative, judicial or executive. *Kirk v Flournoy*, 111 CR 674/Cal (1974).

The following public employees have been held to be public officers on appeal from bribery convictions: a highway patrolman, a city police officer, a deputy prosecuting attorney, the secretary of a board of land commissioners, a sheriff, a member of a board of education, a governor's secretary, a judicial officer, a state legislator, a state food inspector, a school teacher, a city councilman. *State v White*, 500 P 2d 1242/Wn (1972).

Pretender to Office

Under Oklahoma law one accepting a thing of value may be convicted of bribery although he is not a public officer. The law states in part: "every. . . public officer, or any person assuming to act as such officer . . ." who corruptly accepts or asks any gift, gratuity or reward with the understanding that his behavior or conduct in office will be influenced thereby, is guilty of bribery. This statute, or one of a similar nature, would apparently apply to one who, although not a public officer but pretending to be, asks, receives or agrees to receive any emolument, gratuity or reward in his assumed position. *Finley v State*, 181 P 2d 489/Ok (1947).

Official Capacity

Official duties include not only those duties prescribed by statute, but duties which in the ordinary course of business may be assigned to such officer by his superiors or by customary office practice. *State v Emmanuel*, 253 P 2d 386/Wn (1953).

A police officer regularly appointed is a public officer within the proscription of bribery, and where a police officer accepted money with the understanding that he would get a larceny case "kicked out of court," bribery was complete even though the officer had completed his investigation and submitted all reports to the prosecuting attorney. *State v Austin*, 400 P 2d 603/Wn (1965).

The agreement by a public officer requisite to the crime of bribery must be an agreement to do an official act connected with his office, or to refrain from doing such act, and it is immaterial whether he actually had such authority, only that he presumed or pretended to have such authority. *State v Martin*, 245 P 2d 411/Az (1952); *State v Austin, supra.*

"One who asks or receives a bribe to influence his official acts, can avail himself nothing by the defense that he intended to do them anyway . . ." so ruled the Washington Supreme Court. *State v Lyskoski*, 287 P 2d 114/Wn (1955).

Acts which constitute official capacity of course, must be considered in relation to the public officer involved, for that which would amount to official capacity when considered in relation to one public officer might not be official capacity or official duty in relation to another. Following are instances of official capacity: a sheriff who asked and received money from a woman pursuant to an agreement that he would not interfere with her operation of a house of assignation (*State v Martin*, 245 P 2d 411/Az–1952); that the testimony of a witness will be influenced either by giving false testimony or by withholding true testimony (*State v Ferraro*, 198 P 2d 120/Az–1948); a pawnbroker who offered a chief of police $3,000 for the privilege of operating a gambling house and a house of prostitution within the city (*People v Finkelstein*, 220 P 2d 934/Cal–1950); a city commissioner who asked a reward of ten per cent of gaming proceeds to vote favorably for a gaming license (*Peccole v McNamee*, 267 P 2d 243/Nev–1954); a police officer who received a bribe for the release of a prisoner (*State v Cooney*, 161 P 2d 442/Wn–1945); a constable who received $40 in advance, and a pint of whiskey and $10 a week thereafter to refrain from raiding the premises of a bootlegger (*Finley v State*, 181 P 2d 849/Ok–1947); a sheriff who was offered a reward to permit defendant to operate a wholesale liquor business within the county (*Handley v State*, 102 P 2d 947/Ok–1940); a county commissioner who received $100 to use his influence in rezoning a district for use as an airfield (*State v Whetstone*, 191 P 2d

818/certiorari denied 335 US 858/Wn–1948); municipal plaster inspectors who agreed to receive bribes to approve condemned work (*People v Walsh*, 301 P 2d 247/Cal–1956); a cannery president who offered a bribe to a cannery inspector to release quarantined tomato paste (*People v Zerillo*, 223 P 2d 223/Cal–1950); a police officer who accepted a bribe to permit bookmaking. *People v Hicks*, 145 P 2d 689/Cal (1944).

Third Party Intermediary

Bribery of a public official prohibits indirect as well as direct bribes, and where defendant gave money to an intermediary with directions that it be given to the official whose influence was sought to be perverted, bribery was complete. *United States v Rosner*, 352 FS 915/NY (1972).

Where one solicits a third party to offer a bribe to a potential juror the act is not insulated by a failure of, or a lack of intent of, the party solicited to make the approach; the corrupt endeavor to influence is the criterion by which the act is judged (*United States v Osborn*, 350 F 2d 497/affirmed 385 US 323–1965). Where a third party is involved as an intermediary, the bribe is complete as soon as the bribe leaves the hands of the offering party with instructions to the intermediary that it be given or offered to a public officer. Id.

Examples of Bribery

In a prosecution of a police officer whose defense was feigned complicity to secure evidence for a prosecution of a cafe owner for offering a bribe, whether the officer intended to use the money to protect the cafe owner in a pending prosecution or as evidence against him in a subsequent prosecution for bribery, was a question of fact for the jury. Conviction was reversed, however, due to improper instruction of the jury on another point. *People v Skaggs*, 181 P 2d 390/Cal (1947).

Although the actual decision to *nol pros* (*nolle prosequi*) rests with the prosecuting attorney, the right of a police officer in the county where an action is pending to recommend *nol pros* was implicitly authorized by custom and practice, and where an officer received money from a traffic violator to recommend a *nolle prosequi* such act was within the purview of the bribery statute. *Kable v State*, 299 A 2d 493/Md (1973).

A conviction of bribery was sustained against an investigator of the California Board of Architectural Examiners for soliciting and receiving a bribe to release answers to questions in the examination for architect's license, when the secrecy of the examination was required and it was the duty of the investigator to maintain secrecy. *People v Silver*, 197 P 2d 90/Cal (1948).

A conviction was sustained against defendant where evidence showed that he accepted a gratuity of $50 with the understanding that he would select and hire a particular person as a teacher in a public school. *Stone v State*, 157 P 2d 468/Ok (1945).

Most, if not all, states include within their criminal codes an interdiction against the bribery of participants in sporting events and athletic contests, such as horse racing, boxing, football, baseball and basketball. Usually the statute will forbid a player or a participant to accept corruptly or agree to accept anything of value with the understanding that such player or participant will put forth less than his best effort to win. *State v Yoshida*, 361 P 2d 1032/Haw (1961); *People v Phillips*, 173 P 2d 392/Cal (1946).

Corruption of Witnesses

A statute making it a crime to corruptly influence a witness does not require that an action or proceeding be then pending, nor is action restricted to one then under subpoena. A corrupt attempt to influence a person who could reasonably expect to be subpoenaed falls within the purview of the statute. *State v Reed*, 516 P 2d 913/Kan (1973).

A corrupt endeavor to influence a witness constitutes obstruction of justice and the success or failure of the endeavor is immaterial (*Roberts v United States*, 239 F 2d 467/Cal–1957). Where one is a probable witness and expects to be called as a witness–here, before a Senate committee–he is a witness for purposes of a prosecution for corruptly attempting to influence a witness, and the furnishing of a false story to a prospective witness to be told to that committee completed the crime. *Stein v United States*, 337 F 2d 14/Cal (1964).

Although a witness violates no law by exercising the privilege against self-incrimination, one who bribes, coerces or otherwise induces him to exercise such privilege with corrupt motive, obstructs the administration of justice. *United States v Cioffi*, 493 F 2d 1111/NY (1974).

At common law embracery was defined as the corrupt attempt to influence a juror by promises, persuasion, entreaty, entertainment or money, and the crime was complete as soon as the attempt was made. 18 *Am Jur*–Embracery.

In every bribery or attempt to bribe a juror, there is also included the common law crime of embracery, but embracery may be committed where there is no bribery. An essential element of bribery is the giving, offering or promising of a thing of value or advantage; the crime of embracery can be committed by the corrupt attempt to sway or persuade a juror, and reward or consideration is not an element.

In some jurisdictions the crime of embracery is defined as the corrupt attempt to influence a judge, juror or witness; in other jurisdictions the crime may be more narrowly defined including either one or two of the foregoing. However it is defined, it often constitutes bribery also.

Acts Falling Short of Bribery

The acceptance of a gratuity is not sufficient of itself to support a charge of bribery. *People v Jordan*, 304 NE 2d 713/Ill (1973).

Where defendants paid a county commissioner $1,000 to influence his granting of a permit to dig a canal, there was no bribery as no permit was required for the proposed canal. *Nell v State*, 277 S 2d 1/Fla (1973).

A councilman elect, who had not yet been sworn into office, was not a "member" or "officer" within the meaning of the bribery statute and was not, therefore, guilty of bribery when he solicited a reward for his vote as a councilman. *State v Penta*, 316 A 2d 733/NJ (1974).

PERJURY

Defined

"Perjury" in New York is the willful, knowing and false swearing in a matter material to the issue in a judicial proceeding by a person to whom a lawful oath or affirmation has been administered (*Walther v O'Connell*, 339 NYS 2d 386/NY–1972), but every self-contradiction a witness utters in the heat of a contested trial is not perjury. *People v McCoun*, 201 NW 2d 345/Mich (1972).

Perjury may be committed by the willful and false swearing to the:

1. Existence of a fact known to be nonexistent;
2. Nonexistence of a fact known to exist;
3. Existence or nonexistence of a fact whose existence or nonexistence is not known to the witness.

An unqualified statement of that which one does not know to be true is the equivalent of a statement of that which one knows to be false. *People v Dixon*, 221 P 2d 198/Cal (1950).

In General

An attorney owes no duty to his client to offer or allow false testimony in his behalf, and an attorney who attempts to benefit his client through perjured testimony may be subject to criminal prosecution for subornation of perjury as well as other disciplinary action. *In re Branch*, 449 P 2d 174/Cal (1969).

Immunity afforded a witness by constitutional guarantee against self-incrimination relates to the past and does not endow the witness with license to commit perjury. *United States v Malnik*, 348 FS 1273/Fla (1972).

A prisoner under sentence in a penal institution who is subpoenaed into court to testify is bound by the same rules as freemen, and false testimony offered by him subjects him to prosecution for perjury. *Credille v United States*, 354 F 2d 625/Ok (1965).

The Nature of Perjury

Crucial to the question of perjury is the belief of the witness in the verity of his sworn statement; if he believes his statement to be true and offers it in good faith, it is not perjury (*United States v Winter*, 348 F 2d 204/NY–1965). Thus, knowledge of the falsity of a statement at the time it is uttered is an essential element of perjury. *People v Taylor*, 236 NE 2d 122/Ill (1972).

The offense of perjury can be committed only by the use of words; the words used are not only a means by which the offense is committed, but the only means. *People v Aud*, 288 NE 2d 453/Ill (1972).

The statement on which a prosecution for perjury is predicated must be knowingly false, and since the actual state of mind of the defendant cannot be proved by direct evidence, knowledge of the falsity of his statement is a question of fact for the jury. *People v Dixon*, 221 P 2d 198/Cal (1950).

In any prosecution for perjury where the alleged perjury was committed in a judicial proceeding, it is essential that the court have jurisdiction of the matter, and the crime of perjury cannot be assigned on false testimony given in the course of a trial or before a tribunal where the court is without jurisdiction of the offense charged. *Bennett v District Court*, 162 P 2d 561/Ok (1935).

Perjury, subornation of perjury, attempt to suborn perjury, solicitation of perjury, false swearing or conspiracy to commit any of the aforementioned—being public offenses—are offenses against the sovereignty only, and in the absence of a statute to the contrary no action will lie to recover damages in a civil proceeding for such offenses whether committed in connection with a civil or a criminal action, or whether the offender was a witness in, or a party to, an action. *Platts v Platts*, 438 P 2d 687/Wn (1968); *Graham v Morgan*, 129 FS 199/Ok (1955).

The Oath

"Oath" shall include affirmation and all forms of attestation by which a party signifies that he is bound in conscience to perform an act faithfully and truly. *Black's Law Dictionary*.

It is essential to a prosecution of perjury that the government establish that an oath was administered to the defendant and that the person administering had the legal authority to do so. *Harrell v United States*, 220 F 2d 516/Ala (1955).

Although reluctantly and with reservations, appellate courts have held that it is not essential to a conviction of perjury when the affiant is a peace officer, in his application for a warrant, that he be formally sworn by the raising of his hand and the invocation of the deity. Where it is obvious that the officer knows the nature of the warrant and the affidavit therefor, and he affixes his signature thereto followed by the jurat of the judicial officer, the document is of legal efficacy and if information therein contained is knowingly false the affiant is liable to prosecution for perjury. *State v Douglas*, 428 P 2d 535/Wn (1967); *Atwood v State*, 111 S 865/Mis (1927); *Cole v State*, 223 P 2d 155/Ok (1950).

False Affidavits

One can be guilty of perjury without giving false testimony at a trial, as the making of a false affidavit or deposition may also be perjury. *State v Howard*, 158 P 104/Wn (1916).

An affidavit required by law can be made the basis for a charge of perjury when it was made before a notary public as well as a judicial officer (*United States v Cook*, 17 FRD 412/Tex–1955).

An officer who swore falsely to an affidavit for a search warrant (*State v Douglas*, 428 P 2d 535–1967), and an elector who, in swearing to an affidavit of registration as an elector, gave a false name and a false place of birth, such statement being material, were subject to a prosecution for perjury. *People v Darcy*, 139 P 2d 118/Cal (1943).

"Affidavit" and "Deposition" Distinguished

Although the words "affidavit" and "deposition" are often used interchangeably, there is a distinction. Both are sworn statements made under oath administered by one having authority to administer such oath, and regarding matters required or permitted by law, the difference being that the affidavit is *ex parte*—on behalf of one party only—while a deposition is adversary—there being two or more parties concerned in the matter and the adverse party, being present, may cross-examine the deponent. *Black's Law Dictionary*.

The false making of a deposition, affidavit or certificate is deemed complete when it is subscribed and sworn to or affirmed by the maker with intent that it be delivered to another to be published, but actual publication is immaterial (*People v Pierce*, 423 P 2d 969/Cal–1967). If the false statement is a writing, the crime of perjury is not complete until the verified false statement leaves the hands of its author. *People v Agnew*, 176 P 2d 724/Cal (1947).

Extrajudicial Perjury

False testimony given before a grand jury may be the subject of a prosecution for perjury (*State v Bell*, 368 P 2d 177/Wn–1962), but the testimony must be given regarding a matter which the grand jury had the power to investigate (*Bennett v District Court*, 162 P 2d 561/Ok–1945). The oath taken before the grand jury is binding not only on the day of the original appearance of the witness, but on subsequent days in giving testimony concerning the same matter, and the witness need not be resworn each day. *People v Sagehorn*, 294 P 2d 1062/Cal (1956).

It is not necessary to inform one appearing as a witness before the grand jury of his constitutional rights, and a failure to so advise does not preclude prosecution for perjury of one giving false testimony (*Stassi v United States*, 401 F 2d 259/vacated on another point 394 US 310/Fla–1968), and this is true even though the proceeding is accusatory in nature. *United States v De Giovanni*, 397 F 2d 409/Ill (1968).

A governmental efficiency and economy committee composed of members of the state's lower house of the legislature, which was investigating garbage and rubbish collection in greater Los Angeles, had the power to administer the oath, and false testimony before that committee constituted perjury. *Matula v Superior Court*, 303 P 2d 871/Cal (1956).

Materiality

The test of materiality is whether the false testimony was capable of influencing the tribunal on the issue before it, not whether in fact it did; and as a rule, every question propounded on cross-examination is said to be material for the purposes of a prosecution for perjury. *Barnes v United States*, 378 F 2d/Tex (1967).

Where materiality is of essence to a prosecution for perjury it is no defense that the witness did not know of the materiality of his testimony, nor that the proceeding was not, in fact, affected by the false testimony but only that it might have affected the outcome of the matter, and the question of materiality is one of law to be resolved by the court, not the jury. *State v Ingels*, 104 P 2d 944/Wn (1940).

The materiality of the false statement under oath must be proved by the state wherein materiality is an element, but it is not necessary that the state prove the witness knew the materiality of the testimony (*State v Bell*, 368 P 2d 177/Wn–1962). In this case defendant appealed, citing 123 alleged errors which must be a near record but which availed the appellant nothing as conviction was affirmed. Id.

In an investigaton before a grand jury or at defendant's trial, materiality as an element of perjury refers to the time the witness made the statement before the grand jury as affecting the grand jury's objective at the time and it cannot vanish at the trial even though at that time it has ceased to be material. *United States v McFarland*, 371 F 2d 701/NY (1966); *United States v Gremillion*, 464 F 2d 901/La (1972).

Whether or not testimony offered by a witness was material is a question of law for the court to decide; but whether the witness gave that testimony, and if he did do so willfully and corruptly, are questions entirely within the purview of the jury. *State v Ingels, supra; Vitello v United States*, 425 F 2d 416/Cal (1970).

In some states perjury is divided into degrees—first and second degree.

First degree is the false swearing to a material matter and second degree is the false swearing to any matter. *State v Dodge*, 425 P 2d 781/Ut (1967).

Where a witness gave expert testimony as a technologist in an abortion case, his qualification as an expert was material; when he testified that he had obtained a B.S. degree at one university and had completed two years of medical training at another, and the registrars of both universities testified that there was no record of his enrollment at either university, his testimony was material and warranted conviction for perjury. *State v Elder*, 433 P 2d 462/Kan (1967).

Under the statutes of some states, materiality of testimony is an essential element of the statute and nonmaterial matter, unless included in the statute, is noncriminal. Thus, under the statute proscribing false testimony before a grand jury, materiality was an indispensable element. *United States v Wesson*, 478 F 2d 1180/Ind (1973).

Under Florida law where the allegedly false testimony was not material to the issue wherein such testimony was given, there could be no conviction of perjury for having given such testimony (*Wolfe v State*, 271 S 2d 132/Fla–1972). But under Washington law where purjury is divided into first and second degree, "Every person who . . . shall knowingly swear falsely concerning any matter whatsoever, shall be guilty of perjury in the second degree . . ." a felony. RCW 9.72.030.

Proof Requisite to Conviction

The crime of perjury requires a higher measure of proof than any other crime known to law, treason alone excepted (*State v Wallis*, 311 P 2d 659/Wn–1967). Unlike most crimes, perjury cannot be proved by circumstantial evidence alone, but must be established by the testimony of two witnesses or one witness and corroborating circumstances, and failure of the court to so instruct the jury is reversible error irrespective of the number of witnesses testifying (*Sparth v United States*, 232 F 2d 776/Oh–1956). This rule existed under the common law; it is the rule followed by the United States courts (*Weiler v United States*, 323 US 606–1945), and is the rule of most, if not all. of the states. For a conviction of perjury in the federal courts, if there is only one witness to the perjury, there must be corroborative evidence no matter how persuasive the witness. *Sigmen v United States*, 320 F 2d 176/Wn (1963); *Gebhard v United States*, 422 F 2d 281/Cal (1970).

Although the question of the materiality of a matter is within the exclusive province of the court (*State v Ingels*, 104 P 2d 944/Wn–1940), corroboration is within the exclusive province of the jury, and in a perjury prosecution it is the function of the jury to interpret the attitude, conduct and testimony of the accused in order to determine whether the necessary corroboration has been supplied (*Pisher v State*, 418 P 2d 983/Alk–1966). Corroborating circumstances may come from the defendant's own testimony when he testifies in his own behalf. *People v Sagehorn*, 294 P 2d 1062/Cal (1956); *Broadway v State*, 291 S 2d 338/Ala (1974).

The "two witnesses" or "one witness and corroborating circumstances" rule does not, in light of present rulings, require that a witness be a living witness, especially where the defendant's own acts, correspondence and documents show that his oath was false (*United States v Rose*, 215 F 2d 617/Pa–1955). Also, the rule requiring corroborating circumstances has no application where the accused admits in open court that he gave false testimony. *State v Johnson*, 374 P 2d 504/Mont (1962).

All of a witness's false statements may be embraced in one count of perjury and proof of any one of the alleged false statements proves perjury (*United States v Edmondson*, 410 F 2d 670/Alk–1969), but perjury may not be compounded by the repetitious propounding of the same questions as there is but one offense whether the perjured statement was made once or repeated. *Masinia v United States*, 296 F 2d 871/Mo (1961).

In a perjury prosecution under Michigan law, the opinion of a polygraph examiner based on a properly conducted polygraph examination is more than character evidence; it is direct evidence on the point of truthfulness of the defendant and may be offered by either side regardless of whether defendant takes the stand or puts his character at issue. *United States v Ridling*, 350 FS 90/Mich (1972).

Where there are multiple assignments of perjury, and only one witness testifies, his testimony must be corroborated concerning the assignment or assignments about which he testifies; if corroborative evidence applies to an assignment other than one about which he testifies, his testimony is not corroborated and conviction will not lie. *Cameron v State*, 365 P 2d 576/Ok (1961).

Under the federal statute proscribing false declarations before a grand jury or court, the two witness rule is abolished as this rule is not a constitutional requirement and thus may be abrogated by statute. *United States v Ceccerelli*, 350 FS 475/Pa (1972); *United States v Hamilton*, 348 FS 749/Pa (1972).

The rule requiring corroboration of the testimony of a single witness does not apply in a prosecution for attempt to suborn perjury, as here the testimony of one witness, uncorroborated, is legally sufficient for a conviction. *State v Williams*, 300 A 2d 578/NJ (1973).

Corroboration is a procedural device required in order to prove the crime of perjury and does not change the material elements of the crime (*In re Ruggiero*, 338 NYS 2d 749/NY–1972). Corroborative evidence is additional evidence of a different character but to the same point. *People v Tolmachoff*, 138 P 2d 61/Cal (1943).

Effect of False Testimony Immaterial

The false testimony of a witness is not purged by the acquittal of defendant in whose case the testimony is given nor is a prosecution therefor barred. *Wheatley v United States*, 286 F 2d 519/Ok (1961).

Where defendant was charged with careless driving and was acquitted on the basis of false testimony of codefendant who testified that defendant was driving at the time of the infraction, would not, under the concept of double jeopardy or *res judicata*, preclude a prosecution of defendant for conspiracy to pervert justice nor a subsequent prosecution of codefendant for perjury. *State v Redinger*, 312 A 2d 129/NJ (1973).

Examples

Where defendant testified at his trial for possession of heroin that he had never before seen the automobile in which the heroin was found until it was loaned to him—refuted by the testimony of a highway patrolman that one week prior he had cited defendant while driving the car plus the finding of the citation in the glove compartment of the car—the minimum requirement of one witness and corroborating evidence necessary to sustain conviction for perjury was met. *United States v De Leon*, 474 F 2d 790/Tex (1973).

A juror who, on *voir dire* examination, gave a false answer to a question put to him as to his employment of plaintiff's council, was subject to prosecution for perjury. *Kerby v Heisterman*, 178 P 2d 194/Kan (1947).

In a grand jury investigation of the collection of and the accounting for campaign funds, defendant falsely testified that he did not receive contributions from particular persons; he thereby laid the groundwork for his conviction of perjury. *State v Ingels*, 104 P 2d 944/Wn (1940).

In response to questions before a grand jury a captain of a sheriff's department denied that he had written a letter to an assistant chief of police advising city police to stay out of the county; such testimony warranted conviction of perjury after a finding that he had, in fact, written the letter. *People v Guasti*, 243 P 2d 59/Cal (1972).

Where a woman testified at a preliminary hearing that her husband had struck her and had dragged her through the house by her hair, and at her husband's trial for battery she denied all previous allegations, such conflict in testimony warranted a finding that her denial of her earlier allegations was false and thus perjury. *People v Chiuminatta*, 318 P 2d 753/Cal (1957).

Where a witness at a preliminary examination denied that he had been previously convicted of perjury, after which it was established that he had been so convicted, his testimony, being material, warranted his subsequent conviction of perjury. *State v Carpenter*, 225 P 654/Wn (1924).

Recantation or Retraction—Effect of

A false statement made by a witness while testifying is not perjury if the false statement is corrected before submission to the jury (*State v Ledford*, 81 P 2d 830/Wn–1938). This holding by the Washington Supreme Court reflects the exception rather than the rule, for perjury once committed cannot usually be purged by a retraction. Id.

If a witness intentionally lies to a grand jury, his later recantation does not vitiate the perjury, but willingness to correct the statement is relevant to the issue of intent. *United States v Lococo*, 450 F 2d 1196/Cal (1971); *United States v Kahn*, 472 F 2d 272/NY (1973).

The prosecutor is under no obligation to seek recantation of a false statement, and a failure of the state to show that the witness was given an opportunity to recant is not an element of the offense of perjury. *United States v Gill*, 490 F 2d 233/Ill (1974).

Mere Variance or Conflict in Testimony

A mere variance in the testimony of a witness at a second trial to his testimony at a previous trial is not, *per se*, perjury (*Tyler v State*, 501 SW 2d 189/Mo–1973), nor will prior inconsistent statements alone support a perjury conviction. But where a witness, while under oath, denied making the prior inconsistent statements when in fact he had made such statements, groundwork was laid for a perjury prosecution. *United States v Letchos*, 316 F 2d 481/Ill (1963).

Testimony which conflicts with an affidavit alone, does not establish perjury, and where it is impossible to distinguish which of defendant's statements were false—his testimony as a witness in the prosecution of another, or his affidavit and contradictory statements—there is sufficient evidence to sustain conviction. *State v Wallis*, 311 P 2d 659/Wn (1957).

SUBORNATION OF PERJURY

Defined

The crime of "subornation of perjury" consists of two elements: (1) the actual commission of perjury by the person solicited and (2) the willful procurement of such perjury by the suborner (*State v McBride*, 190 SE 2d 658/NC–1972). Being relevant in a prosecution for subornation of perjury, it must be established that perjury has already been committed; in other words, the guilt of both the suborned and the suborner must be proved beyond a reasonable doubt. *State v McBride, supra.*

If the person solicited does not commit perjury then subornation is incomplete, but under an appropriate statute the would-be suborner may be prosecuted for solicitation of or attempt to suborn perjury. Since an essential element of the crime is that the person solicited commit perjury, it is incumbent upon the state to allege and prove that subsequent to the solicitation perjury was committed. *State v Bixby*, 177 P 2d 689/Wn (1947); *United States v Petite*, 147 FS 791/Md (1957).

Nature of the Offense

Although a witness has the constitutional right to refuse to testify before a grand jury, a right which he may exercise or waive, the person being investigated may not by threat or intimidation attempt to persuade the witness to exercise that right. And defendant's claim that his conviction should be reversed on the ground that he only urged a witness to do that which he had a right to do, was without merit; the sacred right to guard against self-incrimination is no more negotiable than is virtue. *Cole v United States*, 329 F 2d 437/Cal (1964).

Under federal law perjury and subornation of perjury are separate and distinct offenses, and the suborned witness is not the accomplice of one on trial for perjury. *Segal v United States*, 246 F 2d 814/Min (1957).

Solicitation of Perjury

Where the person solicited declines, refuses or fails for any reason to bear false witness the crime is, under appropriate statute, either attempt to suborn perjury or solicitation of perjury. Where defendant solicited another to testify to a nonexistent traffic accident, he could be convicted, under California law, of solicitation of perjury since perjury was not committed. *People v Haley*, 227 P 2d 48/Cal (1951).

Solicitation by defendant, an attorney, of a 14-year-old girl to testify falsely—that she did not have sexual intercourse with his client, amounted to an attempt to suborn perjury, which resulted, *inter alia*, in defendant's disbarment. *In re Caffry*, 429 P 2d 880/Wn (1967).

Attempted Subornation

Where defendant instructed an intermediary to advise a juror to vote not guilty and to "Tell her there might be a reward in the future," and the intermediary refused part of the request but did ask the juror to vote not guilty, there was insufficient evidence to establish an attempted bribery. But the court added, "Any contact with the jury by or on behalf of a litigent is reprehensible and the court is not to be understood as implying the defendant's conduct was lawful or that he may not be guilty of another offense" (*Smith v State*, 279 S 2d 652/Mis–1973). The conduct depicted here amounted to embracery under the common law.

Defendant was guilty of obstructing justice where he offered compensation to a witness to withhold testimony in a criminal case then pending against defendant, and the fact that the preliminary hearing had been erroneously scheduled for Sunday did not vitiate the information. *Fox v State*, 477 P 2d 591/Nev (1970).

Obstruction of justice is complete when the attempt at corruption is made, and the success or failure of the endeavor is immaterial. *Roberts v United States*, 239 F 2d 467/Cal (1957).

Who Is Subject to Subornation

It is not necessary to a prosecution for subornation of perjury that the suborned witness be under subpoena, as one who can reasonably expect subpoena because of his knowledge of material facts in a matter then pending is subject to subornation. Thus, where the potential witness was not then under subpoena but anticipated subpoena to testify before a Senate committee, and was solicited to testify falsely, he was a witness for the purpose of a prosecution of his solicitor for subornation of perjury. *Stein v United States*, 337 F 2d 14/Cal (1964).

Attorney-Client Relationship

An attorney may not knowingly permit a witness to testify falsely, and an attorney who attempts to benefit his client through the use of perjured testimony may be subject to criminal prosecution for offering false evidence, or subornation of perjury, as well as severe disciplinary action imposed in disbarment proceedings. *In re Branch*, 449 P 2d 174/Cal (1969).

"Subornation" Distinguished From "Conspiracy"

The difference between subornation of perjury and conspiracy to commit perjury is that in the former it is essential that some person actually commit perjury at the instance of another, while in conspiracy there must be an agreement between two or more persons to the effect that one or more of the coconspirators commit perjury and an overt act done toward that end. *People v Sharpe*, 216 P 2d 519/Cal (1950).

RESISTANCE OF PUBLIC OFFICERS

"Public Officer" Defined

The term "public officer" is not necessarily synonymous to "public employee"; a public officer is in an office of greater importance, a more independent position, is bonded, is of more durable tenure, must execute an oath of office and his duties are prescribed by law. A public officer holds his position as a tenured member of a public corporation whose office was created by statute, is performing a public function for public benefit and is vested with the exercise of some sovereign powers. *Leymel v Johnson*, 288 P 858/Cal (1930).

Generally, a peace officer is a person employed by a governmental agency—whether city, county, state or federal—whose duty it is to enforce substantive law, preserve the peace, arrest and witness against violators, and who is paid for his services from public monies. He may have plenary peace officer's powers or he may be restricted by the law of the state to less than full peace officer's powers in certain areas outside his specialty.

Peace officer is defined in most states by statute, and where this is the case there is less room for doubt as to who are peace officers. *Black's Law Dictionary* offers no definition for the term, but rather names specific officers who are embraced by the term. They are: city police officers, sheriffs and their deputies, constables, marshals and other officers whose duty it is to enforce laws and preserve the public peace. Id.

Under Arkansas law a police officer is a "ministerial officer" within the meaning of a statute proscribing obstruction or resistance of a ministerial officer in the discharge of his official duty. *Meyers v State*, 484 SW 2d 334/Ark (1972).

To be guilty of obstructing and delaying an officer, it is essential that the person obstructed to be a *bona fide* public officer, and where *de facto* deputy sheriffs carried identification cards defining their status and they were covered by false arrest insurance in the county of employment, these facts were not sufficient to establish them as public officers. *State v Owens*, 442 P 2d 719/Az (1967).

In General

Peace officers are often heard to say that they are on duty 24 hours a day and are thus peace officers at all times, and absent a statute to the contrary, this is true, but one is a peace officer only in the bailiwick which employs him. But suppose a city police officer, while not specifically on duty in the city, accepts employment from a private employer within the city and he has the occasion to arrest. Is he a peace officer? Is he entitled to false arrest insurance coverage? If he is severely injured, is he entitled to hospitalization at city expense or to a disability pension? The Arizona Supreme Court ruled that duly appointed police officers of the Phoenix Police Department were peace officers within the meaning of the law relating to resisting, obstructing or delaying a peace officer, even though at the time privately employed if the instant task was one of "vindication of public right and justice" as opposed to one of personal service to his private employer. Here, three Phoenix police officers in uniform were working off-duty in a ballroom, their duties being to maintain order, and were being paid from private funds; one of the three officers placed defendant under arrest for the use of obscene language in the presence of women, and a second defendant attempted to liberate the first and a fight ensued between defendants and officers. The court held that notwithstanding their off-duty status, the officers were public officers within the meaning of the statute proscribing the obstructing and delaying of a public officer in the performance of his duty. *State v Kurtz*, 278 P 2d 406/Az (1954).

The Concept of No Resistance to Arrest

An increasing number of states have abolished the right to resist an illegal arrest (*State v Koonce*, 214 A 2d 428/NJ–1969); (*People v Curtis*, 450 P 2d 33/Cal–1969); (*Miller v State*, 462 P 2d 421/Alk–1969), New Jersey, California and Alaska, being three of this group. In those states the law reads in essence that if a person has knowledge, or by the exercise of reasonable care should have knowledge, that he is being arrested by a peace officer, it is his duty to refrain from using force or any weapon to resist such arrest (*State v Koonce, supra*). Nor may a third person interfere, the court holding that the safe and sufficient course to follow is to turn to the courts rather than engage in a combat in which one or the other will surely be wrong. *State v Madden*, 294 A 2d 609/NJ (1972).

In ruling on the emerging concept that resistance, even to an illegal arrest, should be proscribed, the Alaska Supreme Court has ruled:

> The weight of authoritative precedent supports the right to repel an unlawful arrest with force . . . . This was the rule at common law. It was based upon the proposition that everyone should be privileged to use reasonable force to prevent an unlawful invasion of his physical integrity and personal liberty. . . . Our rules should discourage the unnecessary use of physical force between man and man. Any rule which promotes rather than inhibits violence should be reexamined.
>
> Section 5 of the Uniform Arrest Act provides: "if a person has reasonable ground to believe he is being arrested by a peace officer, it is his duty to refrain from using force or any weapon in resisting arrest regardless of whether or not there is a legal basis for the arrest." *Miller v State*, 462 P 2d 421/Alk (1969).

Under a statute prohibiting the use of force to resist an arrest—legal or illegal—defendant's act of seizing the arresting officer's arm constituted hinderance or obstruction of an officer. *City of St Louis v Treece*, 502 SW 2d 432/Mo (1973).

Conventional Laws on Resistance

In jurisdictions which still permit the resistance of an unlawful arrest, the person sought to be arrested may exercise his right of self-defense, but in exercising that right he may not use any more force than is reasonably necessary. *Carter v State*, 507 P 2d 932/Ok (1973).

The offense of resisting arrest, under the laws of most jurisdictions, presupposes a lawful arrest, and it is axiomatic that every person has the right to resist an unlawful arrest (*State v Jefferies*, 193 SE 2d 388/NC–1972), but when an arrest is being lawfully made there is a duty imposed on the person being arrested to submit to the arrest, and *intent* to resist is not vital to a conviction for resisting arrest. *City of St Joseph v Blakley*, 486 SW 2d 511/Mo (1972).

The crime of resisting arrest can only be committed in the resistance of a peace officer (*People v Rivera*, 341 NYS 2d 157/NY–1973), and a special patrolman is not a peace officer. Also, where defendant's arrest was predicated upon an illegal search and seizure, the arrest was unlawful thereby nullifying a subsequent charge against defendant of resisting an officer in line of duty. *Kishel v State*, 287 S 2d 414/Fla (1974).

Verbal Obstruction

Speech alone, not accompanied by physical force, is punishable only when it is substantially equivalent to force; that is, when it is intended to, and does, incite an unlawful resistance by another to the discharge of an official duty, or when the speech itself, by its very volume and intensity, interferes substantially with the carrying out of an official duty. *State v Tages*, 457 P 2d 289/Az (1969).

Defendant, who threatened to kill the officer who had arrested him for disturbing the peace, in such a manner as to make the officer "think twice" about persisting in the arrest or releasing defendant, amounted to an attempt to prevent or deter an executive officer from performing a legal duty. *State v Wozniak*, 486 P 2d 1025/Id (1971).

Police Officers Outside Bailiwick

The question often arises as to whether a police officer of a city or county has peace officer's powers outside his bailiwick. In relation to this question the California Court of Appeal ruled in 1964 as follows: Two officers of the Los Angeles Police Department were investigating narcotic activity which took them to the nearby city of Alhambra. Assuming at that time that their power of arrest as peace officers was state-wide, they arrested defendant for narcotic addiction, a misdemeanor. The court reversed, holding that the officers being outside their bailiwick and divested of their peace officer's power, exceeded their power of arrest as private persons, this being their status outside the city limits of Los Angeles (*People v Martin*, 36 CR 924/Cal–1964). But where city police officers pursued a motorist across the city line for speeding, they were clothed with the authority of sheriff and justified in acting in his arrest as peace officers; defendant's resistance to the arrest constituted resisting an officer although outside the city limits. *Delude v Raasaka*, 215 NW 2d 685/Mich (1974).

Refusal to Obey Lawful Command

In most jurisdictions it is a violation of law to refuse to assist an officer in the lawful performance of his duties when so requested or commanded. Where an officer sought to serve a misdemeanor warrant for shoplifting to a woman at her residence and asked defendants to inform him if she left by the back door—defendants being advised at the time that refusal to assist was a violation of the law—their refusal to assist was, in fact, a violation of the law (*Williams v State*, 490 SW 2d 117/Ark—1973). And the claim that the statute was unconstitutional in that it required involuntary servitude by requiring citizens to perform police work without compensation and other benefits of employment was without merit. Id.

The unlawful parking of a vehicle in an intersection was a separate and distinct offense from refusal to obey the lawful command of a police officer who ordered the driver to remove it, and a conviction of both offenses was valid. *State ex rel Scott v Berberian*, 284 A 2d 590/RI (1971).

Examples of Obstruction, Delay and Resistance

The driving at a speed of 90 miles per hour in an attempt to elude a state highway patrolman and physical resistance to arrest therefor constituted resisting a public officer, a highway patrolman being a public officer under the statute. *Tomaris v State*, 224 P 2d 209/Az (1950).

A game warden is a public officer when resisted in the performance of his duties. Where defendant, while fishing with bait suspected to be illegal, refused to allow inspection by moving the fishing pole around, and when a struggle ensued for control of the pole and the game warden fell into the water and was assaulted by defendant, resistance to a public officer had been committed. *State v Sandman*, 286 P 2d 1060/Ut (1965).

The object used in an assault is always admissible under the *res gestae* rule. Thus, a rolling pin used by defendant's sister to assault an FBI agent was admissible as evidence of "what was going on", although defendant claimed her actions were in response to the agent's unprovoked attack on her brother; but the agent testified that defendant kicked him after he had been "floored" by defendant's sister with the rolling pin. *United States v James*, 453 F 2d 27/Or (1971).

Where a deputy sheriff and a special deputy sheriff, each wearing regulation uniforms and working in an unmarked police car but displaying a flashing red light, pursued defendant after he ran a stop sign until he stopped at his home, it was of little consequence in a prosecution for resisting arrest that defendant was not told at the time he ran the stop sign that he was under arrest. *Yeley v State*, 286 NE 2d 183/Ind (1972).

A uniformed police officer hired by the manager of a dance hall to work during off-duty hours, acted in his official capacity as a peace officer in seizing a firearm from the handbag of a patron. *State v Williams,* 297 S 2d 52/Fla (1974).

Mere Failure to Cooperate

To be an obstruction of justice, the act or failure to act must be one which is forbidden or commanded by law, and not a mere failure to cooperate with an officer. Thus, the failure of one to open his door upon demand by a peace officer is not obstructing or delaying and this is so even though the officer is armed with a search warrant. *People v Cressey,* 471 P 2d 19/Cal (1970).

The refusal to state his occupation on demand and the retrieving of his driver's license from the citing officer before the officer was ready to return it but after the officer had obtained all the information he needed and had completed the citation, did not constitute resisting an officer in the line of duty. *Seattle v Nave,* 383 P 2d 491/Wn (1963).

FALSE IMPRISONMENT

Defined

"False imprisonment" is the unlawful restraint of a person's freedom of locomotion and may be committed by the requiring of a person to go where he does not wish to go, or to remain where he does not wish to remain (*CJS* False Imprisonment, Volume 35). The person must be detained against his will and that detention must be unlawful. The true test is not the extent or means of the restraint, but the unlawfulness thereof. Id.

False imprisonment may be committed by words alone, by acts alone, or by both; it may be committed by merely operating on the will of another, or by personal violence, or by both. It is not necessary that the offended be confined in prison, or within walls; nor that he be assaulted or even touched. It is not necessary that there be injury done to his person, character or reputation. It is not necessary that the wrongful act be committed with malice, ill-will, or even any wrongful intent. Nor is it necessary that the act be under color of legal or judicial proceeding. *Munsell v Ideal Food Stores,* 494 P 2d 1063/Kan (1972); *Sturgeon v Holtan,* 486 SW 2d 209/Mo (1972).

The word "false," as used in conjunction with false arrest and false imprisonment, must be interpreted to mean "unlawful." *Burlington Transportation Co v Josephson,* 153 FS 372/SD (1946).

The Nature of False Imprisonment

Public officials are presumed to discharge their duties honestly and in accordance with reason and rules of law (*O'Hare v Malcolm*, 356 NYS 2d 525/NY–1974), and this presumption exists when an officer makes a warrantless arrest for a crime committed in his presence. However, upon a showing in a judicial preceeding that an arrest was made without a warrant of arrest, the presumption reverses, the presumption then being that the arrest was unlawful and the burden devolves upon the arresting officer or the prosecuting attorney to prove that the arrest was lawful. *Smith v Nassau County*, 355 NYS 2d 349/NY (1974).

In all cases of false arrest there is also false imprisonment as the two are indistinguishable as causes of action since both consist of an unlawful restraint of the personal liberty of another. But false imprisonment may be committed exclusive of false arrest; in other words, false arrest necessarily includes false imprisonment but false imprisonment does not necessarily include false arrest. *Holland v Lutz*, 401 P 2d 1015/Kan (1965); *Harrier v Montgomery Ward & Co*, 221 P 2d 428/Mont (1950).

A person who is falsely arrested is at the same time falsely imprisoned, and an unlawful arrest may give rise to a cause of action for either false arrest or false imprisonment. *Sturgeon v Holtan, supra.*

False imprisonment is tortious in addition to criminal and is actionable both civilly and criminally. The law does not provide a precise rule for the ascertainment of damages for false imprisonment, only that which will fairly compensate the offended party for his humiliation, disgrace and mental anguish. *Waters v Brand*, 497 P 2d 875/Wyo (1972).

False imprisonment is a continuing offense and continues as long as the victim's personal liberty is violated. *Baldwin v State*, 215 NW 2d 541/Wis (1974).

"Restraint" Defined

A person is "restrained" or "imprisoned" for purposes of false imprisonment when he is deprived of either his liberty of movement or freedom to remain in a place of his lawful choice and such restraint or imprisonment is accomplished by physical force, threat of force, or by conduct reasonably implying that force will be used to accomplish such purpose (*Kilcup v McManus*, 394 P 2d 375/Wn–1964). The unlawful arrest of plaintiff without a warrant who was neither suspected of having committed a felony nor observed to have committed a misdemeanor, constituted actionable false imprisonment. Id.

Some restraint, whether constructive or actual, is an essential element of false imprisonment. In addition, the subject must be deprived of his liberty by force, or threats of force (*People v Zilbauer*, 279 P 2d 534/Cal–1955). The threat of force may be express or implied. It is express by words; it is implied by words, acts or conduct which the victim fears to ignore. *Parrott v Bank of America*, 217 P 2d 89/Cal (1940).

"False Imprisonment" Distinguished From "Malicious Prosecution"

False imprisonment differs from malicious prosecution in that a false imprisonment is the unlawful detention or violation of the personal liberty of another (*Black's Law Dictionary*), while malicious prosecution consists of (1) a criminal proceeding instituted against defendant, (2) an adjudication of the proceeding in favor of the accused, (3) absence of probable cause for the proceeding, and (4) malice, or motive other than bringing the offended before the bar. *Brewer v Mele*, 298 A 2d 156/Md (1972); *Singleton v Perry*, 289 P 2d 794/Cal (1955).

The essential difference between malicious prosecution and false imprisonment is that in the former the perpetrator is acting with malice but under due process of law, while in the latter the detention is without color of legal authority. *Robinson v Chicago Great Western Ry Co*, 144 FS 713/Mo (1956).

"False Imprisonment" Distinguished From Kidnap

Under the rules of common law false imprisonment was necessarily included in the offense of kidnap (*State v Evans*, 243 P 2d 975/Id–1952), but the mere confinement or restraint of another person aganst his will is not kidnaping but rather imprisonment, and if done without justification it is false imprisonment (*State v Clark*, 455 P 2d 844/NM–1969); it is not the duration of the restraint or confinement that is controlling, but the fact of such action. *Lukas v J C Penney Co*, 378 P 2d 717/Or (1963).

The remedy available to one who is abducted from an asylum state by police officers and transported into the demanding state without benefit of extradition, is an action for false imprisonment (*Johnson v Buie*, 312 FS 1349/Mo–1970). However, despite defendant's seizure in the asylum state and removal to the demanding state by false imprisonment or even kidnap, he may, nevertheless, be tried for the crime for which he was sought. *United States v Vicars*, 467 F 2d 452/Tex (1972); *Davis v Rhay*, 413 P 2d 654/Wn (1966).

Kidnap is nothing more than aggravated false imprisonment, the principal difference being in the intent of the perpetrator. If it is the intent of the perpetrator secretly to confine his victim by removing him to another location, then the crime is kidnap. *CJS* 35, False Imprisonment.

Lawful Arrest—Unlawful Imprisonment

Even though lawfully arrested, one may have a cause of action if not taken before a magistrate without unreasonable delay (*Luttrell v Freeman*, 444 P 2d 857/Ok–1968), and one unlawfully arrested, or illegally detained after a lawful arrest, is entitled to immediate relief by *habeas corpus*, and, in addition, may maintain a civil action for damages. *State v Maldonado*, 373 P 2d 583/Az (1962).

To hold one in prison under confinement for drunkenness by one who knows or should know under the prevailing circumstances that the person is not drunk, constitutes actionable false imprisonment, and this is true even though there was probable cause for the arrest. *Tufte v City of Tacoma*, 431 P 2d 183/Wn (1967).

Principal and Agent

A principal is liable for a false imprisonment committed by his agent when the agent is acting within the scope of his instructions from the principal (*Kaufman v Brown*, 209 P 2d 156/Cal–1949); but in the case of an agent who is a regularly appointed police officer working temporarily for a private concern and while so employed makes an arrest as an agent of the state, the arrest cannot be ratified so as to render his temporary employer liable. *Wheatley v Washington Jockey Club* 234 P 2d 878/Wn (1951).

Where an agent's employer had instructed his agent never to arrest for nor to accuse a customer of theft, but the agent thereafter followed a customer a block from his place of business, summoned police and upon their arrival accused the customer of theft causing his arrest, the agent was not acting within the scope of his employment and his principal (employer) was not liable for false arrest. *Rogers v Sears Roebuck & Co*, 297 P 2d 250/Wn (1956).

Examples of False Imprisonment

The mortgagee of an automobile is entitled to repossess the automobile from the mortgagor when the terms of the contract are violated such as by a default in payment, but in repossession he is not entitled to use force against the person of the mortgagor which would amount to assault, battery or false imprisonment. *Westerman v Oregon Automobile Credit Corp*, 122 P 2d 435/Or (1972).

Where an employee of a corporation started to drive an automobile away from a garage where a repairman held a lien for repairs, and in an attempt to prevent the action the repairman jumped into the vehicle as it was being driven out of the garage and the driver drove into the corporation compound whereupon another employee immediately closed and locked the gate and the repairman was required to find his way to the administrative office in order to free himself from the locked enclosure, his recourse was an action for false imprisonment. *Sanchez v Securities Acceptance Corp*, 260 P 2d 703/NM (1953).

A deputy sheriff was liable for false imprisonment when he wrongfully denied to a prisoner opportunity to give bond. *Missouri ex rel v Fidelity Casualty Co*, 107 F 2d 343/Mo (1940).

Where city vice officers forcibly entered the hotel room of a married couple under the mistaken belief that the two were engaged in an act of prostitution, and detained them for questioning, such intrusion constituted false imprisonment, notwithstanding officer's good faith belief supported by some evidence to justify such belief. *Ware v Dunn*, 183 P 2d 128/Cal (1947).

If an arrest by a policeman is unlawful, all other policemen who assist in the arrest are responsible for the entire damage caused the plaintiff, although they had no knowledge of the unlawfulness of the arrest and intended to act only in the strict discharge of their duties. *Delude v Raasaka*, 202 NW 2d 508/Mich (1972).

Defenses—Peace Officer

Where an arrest is effected under a proper warrant of arrest, an action for false arrest will not lie (*Brewer v Mele*, 298 A 2d 156/Md—1972), nor will an action lie where the arrest is followed by conviction regardless of the validity of the arrest when made. *Menard v Mitchell*, 430 F 2d 486/DC (1970).

The trial and conviction of appellant of the crime for which he was arrested establishes probable cause for such arrest and prosecution and is a complete defense to a charge of false arrest or malicious prosecution absent a showing of a conviction by fraud or perjury (*Hill v Day*, 215 P 2d 219/Kan—1950). Also, the holding to answer of defendant at his preliminary hearing is likewise a defense. *James v Southwestern Ins Co*, 354 P 2d 408/Ok (1960).

A peace officer, in arresting without a warrant, is protected when he acts under a reasonable mistake of fact, but he is not protected—however reasonable his conduct—if he acts under a mistake of law other than a mistake as to the validity of the law or an ordinance. *Cambist Films v Duggan*, 475 F 2d 887/Pa (1973).

A police officer incurs no liability for false imprisonment where he acts under authority of a state statute which he reasonably believes to be valid but which is later held to be unconstitutional. *Pierson v Ray*, 386 US 547/Mis (1967); *Anderson v Reynolds*, 476 F 2d 665/Ut (1973).

Where police officers are charged with false arrest, their good faith and reasonable belief in the validity of the arrest is a defense. *Galella v Onassis*, 487 F 2d 986/NY (1973).

Whether a sheriff had the authority to arrest his deputy for being intoxicated was a question for the jury to determine from conflicting evidence as to whether the deputy was in fact intoxicated. *State v Mills*, 203 SE 2d 362/W Va (1974).

An insurmountable obstacle in a civil action for false imprisonment is that plaintiff committed the crime for which he was arrested—a complete defense. *Lathon v Jefferson Parish*, 358 FS 558/La (1973).

Defenses—Private Person

A private person does not become liable to suit for false arrest where he furnishes information—even though erroneous—to police who thereafter arrest on the basis of the information. But one who knowingly gives false information to an officer thus precipitating another's arrest, would be liable. *Fletcher v Capital Milk Producers Co-Operative Inc*, 321 A 2d 821/Md (1974); *Newton v Spence*, 316 A 2d 837/Md (1974).

A merchant may detain a customer only when he has probable cause to believe the customer has wrongfully taken or has actual possession of or is wrongfully about to take merchandise. *Gaszak v Zayre of Illinois Inc*, 305 NE 2d 704/Ill (1973).

Where there are reasonable grounds to believe his property is being stolen, one may be justified in detaining the suspected thief in order to conduct an investigation—a privilege which existed at common law—and if properly exercised, his action is defensible against false imprisonment. *Jacobson v State*, 510 P 2d 856/Nev (1973).

Where one of two sisters stole a dress under circumstances which would lead a person of ordinary prudence to believe that the other sister was *particeps criminis*, and during the detention and booking of one the other never protested her innocence, and only one of the two was convicted of the theft, the other had no cause of action against the store for false arrest. *Davis v Zions Co-op Merchantile Inst*, 509 P 2d 362/Ut (1973).

CONTEMPT

Defined

"Criminal contempt" is defined as any conduct which is calculated to embarrass, hinder or obstruct a court in the administration of justice, or derogate from its authority or dignity thereby bringing the administration of law into disrepute (*People v Jaravas*, 281 NE 670/Ill–1972); the definition includes one who willfully disobeys any lawful order of a court or fails to comply with any undertaking which has been given. *Black's Law Dictionary.*

Contempts of court are classified as direct or constructive, or direct and indirect, and civil or criminal. *Roll v State*, 288 A 2d 605/Md (1972).

Civil Contempt

"Civil contempt" consists of failing to do something ordered to be done by the court in a civil action for the benefit of the opposing party therein. *Ex parte Woods*, 494 SW 2d 264/Tex (1973).

Contempt may be proscribed by statute just as any other substantive offense (*United States v Ryan*, 455 F 2d 728/Cal–1971), but whether or not it is statutorily proscribed, it is punishable under the court's inherent power (*People v Javaras, supra*), and a statute to that effect is not necessary. *In re Perrello*, 291 NE 2d 698/Ind (1973).

Reliance on the advice of an attorney to disobey a court order is no defense (*United States v Seavers*, 472 F 2d 607/Oh–1973), and one who defies a court order does so at his peril. However, when the court acts in excess of its authority in issuing an order, noncompliance is not punishable as a contempt. *In re Banks*, 306 A 2d 270/DC (1973).

Disobedience to, or contemptuous conduct before, subordinate officers appointed by the court—such as commissioners and referees—or before a grand jury, as a rule, may be punished only by the appointing court, the contempt being regarded as a contempt of the appointing authority. *Marcus v Workmen's Compensation Board*, 111 CR 101/Cal (1973).

The legislature may authorize the trial for contempt of legislature in the courts and such authorization is not a violation of the principle of separation of powers. *Joint Legislative Committee v Strain*, 268 S 2d 629/La (1972).

The crime of contempt is a misdemeanor. *Roselle v State*, 503 P 2d 1293/Ok (1972).

Criminal Contempt

A "criminal contempt" is conduct directed against the majesty of law or the dignity and authority of the court, whereas a civil contempt ordinarily consists of failing or refusing to carry out an order of the court directed for the benefit of an adversary. *Sullivan v Sullivan*, 306 NE 2d 604/Ill (1973).

A criminal contempt proceeding should conform as nearly as possible to other criminal proceedings. *Planning and Zoning Commission of Middlefield v Zemel Bros Inc*, 292 A 2d 267/Con (1971).

Criminal contempt is distinguished from civil contempt in that criminal contempt involves a fixed penalty for the misdeed, while civil contempt is merely a means of compelling compliance with lawful orders of the court. *Joint Legislative Committee v Strain*, 268 S 2d 629/La (1972).

A trial for criminal contempt is a quasi-criminal proceeding; thus, the ordinary rules of evidence apply and the accused must be proved guilty beyond a reasonable doubt. *Browning v Jarrell*, 192 SE 2d 493/W Va (1972).

Direct Contempt

"Direct contempt" is contempt committed in the presence and immediate view of the court. *In re Rosen*, 106 CR 757/Cal (1973).

Although, as a rule, contempt constitutes offensive conduct within the presence of the court, failure to appear after proper subpoena was held to constitute contempt under the premise that the act of being absent after having been subpoenaed was within the presence of the court and thus a subject for a contempt finding. *Waterhouse v Celli*, 336 NYS 2d 960/NY (1972).

Defendant's attorney was guilty of contempt where during a criminal trial he shouted objections, employed a strident tone and sarcastic language, engaged in unnecessary argument and misstated the law, and responded in scatological terminology when told by the judge to sit down. *In re Cohen*, 370 FS 1166/NY (1973).

Where a lawyer, in willful disregard of a court order, appears at a designated location two hours after the appointed hour for a scheduled hearing, he subjects himself to discipline pursuant to a court's inherent power to punish summarily for contempt committed within the presence of the court. *In re Niblack*, 476 F 2d 930/DC (1973).

Where defendants entered the courtroom wearing judicial robes to which were attached stars of David, and upon leaving the courtroom removed the robes thus exposing a policeman's shirt which one defendant was wearing, and one defendant placed his robe on the floor and walked on it, their conduct constituted direct contempt although there was no disruption of judicial proceedings. *In re Dellinger et al*, 370 FS 1304/Ill (1973).

Reversal of convictions under the federal Anti-Riot Act of five defendants who were cited for contempt of court during that trial, furnished no grounds for a reversal of the contempt charges. *In re Dellinger, supra.*

Examples of conduct which have been held to be criminally contemptuous are: the refusal of defendant to rise when the judge entered the courtroom (*In re Chase*, 468 F 2d 128/Ill–1972); defendant's response to a witness' answer on cross-examination with the charge "You're a goddamn liar" (*Robinson v State*, 503 P 2d 582/Ok–1972); the arrival in court of the state's attorney 20 minutes late after a previous warning by the judge and without sufficient excuse (*People v Magnes*, 290 NE 2d 378/Ill–1972).

Summary Contempt

The elements of summary contempt are intentional misbehavior causing actual and material disruption or obstruction of the administration of justice within the presence of the court, which also constitutes direct contempt. *United States ex rel Robson v Oliver*, 470 F 2d 10/Ill (1972).

Direct contempt is usually dealt with summarily while indirect contempt is treated as any other statutory violation. *City of Cincinnati v District Council, 51*, AFL-CIO, 299 NE 2d 686/Oh (1973).

Summary contempt proceedings are proper only in cases where the conduct of the contemnor is a serious threat to orderly criminal procedure and immediate vindication of the dignity of the court is necessary. *State v Roll*, 298 A 2d 867/Md (1973).

Summary contempt proceedings before a trial judge may be justified by the policy of preserving the peace and order of the courtroom or on the theory that it would be a waste of judicial resources to hold a hearing before another judge when the contemptuous conduct has occurred before the trial judge in open court (*United States v Meyer*, 462 F 2d 827/DC–1972). But any factor which requires disqualification of a trial judge, such as where the judge becomes personally embroiled with the contemnor, would require an adversary, rather than summary disposition. Id.

A witness who refused to testify after repeated warnings that continued refusal would amount to contempt, was not denied due process when summarily held in contempt as a hearing was unnecessary. Refusal to testify when called as a witness is a direct contempt as one being committed in the presence of the court. *People v Clinton*, 346 NYS 2d 345/NY (1973).

In a proceeding involving direct criminal contempt, no formal charge is filed, and no plea, issue or trial is required. *People v Thor*, 286 NE 2d 769/Ill (1972).

Indirect or Constructive Contempt

Any contempt which does not occur in the immediate presence of the court, witnessed by the judge, is an "indirect contempt" and the contemnor may not be punished summarily but must be proceeded against as in any other crime (*Losavio v District Court*, 512 P 2d 266/Colo–1973)–which includes notice of the charge, right to counsel, a hearing, right to call and to confront witnesses and a specific finding by the court (Id). An indirect contempt is essentially synonymous to a "constructive" contempt. *Ex parte Caldwell*, 280 S 2d 558/Ala (1973).

A court has no power to summarily punish a contempt which occurred outside the presence of that court. *Ex parte Arnold*, 503 SW 2d 529/Tex (1974).

Acts Falling Short of Contempt

Symbolic acts of refusing to stand when a court convenes or adjourns may not necessarily rise to the level of actual and material obstruction of the judicial process so as to constitute contempt. *In re Dellinger*, 461 F 2d 389/Ill (1972).

Any person on the street may take photographs of any other person on the street; also a photograph may be taken of a public officer in a public building–here, an undercover agent in a hallway outside the courtroom where there was no interference with justice and no violation of a court order to the contrary. *Ex parte Arnold*, 503 SW 2d 529/Tex (1974).

An attorney may not be held in contempt for the misconduct of others in the courtroom unless his own conduct is disruptive, nor is he under any obligation to assist in maintaining order even where his own client is contumacious and disruptive. *In re Dellinger, supra.*

False testimony alone does not amount to a contempt of court. *United States v Campbell,* 350 FS 213/Pa (1972).

Chapter XII

Disturbance of Public Order

BREACH OF THE PEACE

Defined

"Breach of the peace" is a disturbance of public tranquility or order and may be created by any act which molests other persons in the enjoyment of peace and quiet or which excites disquietude or fear, but fear is not an element of the crime. *State v Cleveland*, 469 P 2d 251/Kan (1970).

The phrases "disturb the peace" and "breach of the peace" are substantially synonymous and are taken to mean disruption of public order by acts which are themselves violent or which tend to incite others to violence. *In re Bushman*, 463 P 2d 727/Cal (1970); *Flores v City and County of Denver*, 220 P 2d 373/Colo (1950).

A breach of the peace occurs when one maliciously and willfully disturbs the peace or quiet of a neighborhood, family or person by loud or unusual noise; tumultuous or offensive conduct; threatening, traducing, quarreling, challenging to fight or fighting; or directing any violent, abusive or obscene epithets toward another. *State v Gotarez*, 442 P 2d 842/Az (1968).

The Texas Criminal Court of Appeal defines breach of the peace thus:

> The term "breach of the peace" is generic, and includes all violations of the public peace and order, or decorum; in other words, it signifies the offense of disturbing the public peace or tranquility enjoyed by the citizens of a community; a disturbance of the public tranquility by any act or conduct inciting to violence or tending to provoke or incite others to

break the peace; a disturbance of the public order by an act of violence, or by an act likely to produce violence, or which, by causing consternation and alarm, disturbs the peace and quiet of the community . . . . Breach of the peace is a common law offense . . . . The offense may consist of acts of public turbulence or indecorum in violation of the common peace and quiet of an invasion of the security and protection which the laws afford to every citizen, or of acts such as tend to excite violent resentment or to provoke others to break the peace. Actual or threatened violence is an essential element of a breach of the peace. Either one is sufficient to constitute the offense. Accordingly, where means cause disquiet and disorder and which threaten danger and disaster to the community are used, it amounts to a breach of the peace, although no actual personal violence is employed. Where the incitement of terror or fear of personal violence is a necessary element, the conduct or language of the wrongdoer must be of a character to induce such condition in a person of ordinary firmness. *Head v State*, 96 SW 2d 981/Tex (1936).

Breach of the peace, although varying in definition in some jurisdictions, includes the following types of behavior:

- Assaulting or striking another;
- Creating a hazardous or physically offensive condition;
- Publicly exhibiting, distributing, posting or advertising any offensive, indecent or abusive matter concerning any person;
- Using abusive or obscene language or making any obscene gesture in a public place;
- Threatening to commit any crime against another or his property;
- Behaving violently, tumultuously or threatingly in a public place;
- Engaging in fighting;
- Annoying or interfering with another by the use of offensive or disorderly conduct;
- Making any unreasonable noise where there are others to be offended;
- Disturbing a lawful meeting or assembly;
- Obstructing vehicular or pedestrian traffic unlawfully;
- Congregating with others in a public place and defying a reasonable dispersal order by a public official. *State v Anonymous* (1972-74), 298 A 2d 52/Con (1972).

Acts constituting breach of the peace embrace a variety of conduct which menace the public order, and may be verbal or physical; if verbal it may be obscene or indecent, or possessing neither quality; it may be provocative or aspersive, such as a profane indictment of the President or the U.S. Marine

Corps (*State v Rollins,* 469 P 2d 255/Kan–1970); or soliciting school girls to get into an automobile with defendant (*State v Stroble,* 217 P 2d 1073/Kan–1950); or where a disciple of a religious order went from door to door in a rooming house knocking on doors and entering rooms while occupants were asleep and playing a victrola, after having been requested by the landlady to desist (*City of Ft Scott v Arbuckle,* 187 P 2d 348/Kan–1947); inciting another to commit an assault (*Ricketts v State,* 202 P 2d 431/Ok–1959); profane language directed to another calculated to arouse anger (reversed on another point). *Weitz v State,* 104 P 2d 445/Ok (1940).

"Fighting Words" Breach of the Peace

The doctrine of "fighting words," as employed in defining breach of the peace, has its roots in *Cantwell v Connecticut,* 310 US 296 (1940). There members of one religious group, attempting to gain converts to their religious philosophy, played phonograph records which were provocative and insulting to another religious group, and in affirming conviction of Cantwell, Mr. Justice Murphy alluded to the term "fighting words." *City of Cincinnati v Karlan,* 298 NE 2d 573/Oh (1973).

Epithets used in a public place and directed toward police officers and which were likely to provoke the average person to retaliatory breach of the peace, were fighting words and utterance thereof was punishable as criminal even though arresting officers were assertedly unmoved thereby. *City of Cincinnati v Karlan, supra.*

Obscene and Indecent Language

Lewd and indecent language which referred to motherhood in a most obscene and shocking manner, and profane and perverted language addressed to a branch of the armed forces, the Flag and the President of the United States—all in a loud voice—did disturb the security and tranquility of young men and women in the lobby of a student union building and constituted a breach of the peace. *State v Cleveland,* 469 P 2d 251/Kan (1970).

The wanton cursing, reviling, or the use of obscene or opprobrious language directed toward a peace officer while in the performance of his duty is a breach of the peace. *New Orleans v Lewis,* 269 S 2d 450/La (1972).

An officer, upon hearing defendant and his wife cursing each other in a public place, had the right to arrest defendant for disturbing the peace. *Hatch v State,* 509 P 2d 1396/Ok (1972).

Where defendant, while in a public place with several females present, directed toward police officers the words "mother-fucking fascist pig cops," his conduct amounted to the uttering of obscene language. It is interesting to note that, on appeal, defendant admitted that the words were "filthy, vile, reprehensible, vulgar and obnoxious"—but not obscene. Conviction affirmed. *Brown v State,* 492 P 2d 1106/Ok (1972).

Acts Amounting to Breach of the Peace

Examples of breach of the peace are: prowling around the house of another during the early morning hours causing a commotion to the disturbance of the inhabitants; a clergyman who declared in a sermon, "Some men will stand around . . . street corners and watch the women pass, and size them up, the foot, the ankle, the form and they would . . . give five dollars for the fork"; the wanton discharge of a firearm on the public streets; the contemptuous address of a policeman as "boy scout"; the words "goddamn sons-of-bitches" directed to others; the calling of a city marshal a "damned racketeer" and a "damned Fascist"; an assault or battery; the deliberate breaking of a glass bottle or jar in the driveway of another; the challenging or provoking to fight; the reckless flourishing of a pistol in a public place while intoxicated; unlawful assemblies; riots and affrays. Vol 5A *Words and Phrases*, Breach of the Peace.

Where a House Committee on Un-American Activities was conducting a hearing and defendant created a disturbance and when requested by a deputy marshal to leave the hearing room he fell limp on the floor, such disruptive behavior was so unreasonable as to constitute disorderly conduct. *United States v Woodward*, 376 F 2d 136/Ill (1967).

Where defendant slapped his pistol against his leg several times in an agitated manner, withdrew the weapon, pointed it at a witness and threatened to shoot him and spat on witness' automobile as he drove away, his actions amounted to a breach of the peace. *State v Turley*, 521 P 2d 690/Mont (1974).

The disturbance of a public meeting was committed where basketball players and spectators had gathered in anticipation of a basketball game starting at 8:05 p.m., but due to rubbish and liquids thrown on the playing surface by defendants the game was delayed 35 to 40 minutes. *State v Orzen*, 493 P 2d 768/NM (1972).

The wearing of a T-shirt bearing the word "FUCK" in bold red letters across the front in the cafeteria of a state university violated a statute which prohibited the outrage of public decency. *Patty v State*, 491 P 2d 300/Ok (1971).

Where defendants shouted at plaintiff and threatened her and intentionally and unreasonably subjected her to severe mental distress and fright with the result that plaintiff suffered an acute upset of the glandular system causing nervousness and unstable pulse, heartbeat and blood pressure, their behavior gave plaintiff a cause of action. *Emden v Vitz*, 198 P 2d 696/Cal (1948).

Conduct Falling Short of Breach of the Peace

A complaint charging breach of the peace, which alleged that defendant used language so vile and obscene as would offend common decency to describe it in the complaint, and that defendant refused to leave a service station to the annoyance of customers and the owner, did not adequately and sufficiently charge disorderly conduct. Sufficiency of the complaint would be met only if the specific language used by the defendant was set forth in the complaint. *State v Good,* 308 A 2d 576/Me (1973).

A mere allegation in a complaint that defendant's conduct was boisterous and otherwise disorderly was insufficient, since it did not include how defendant was boisterous and disorderly. *State v Elson,* 208 NW 2d 363/Wis (1973).

Loud shouting or cheering which is designed to and does disrupt, rather than communicate, is not necessarily a breach of the peace; it is a breach of the peace only when there is clear and present danger of imminent violence and where such conduct is a guise to disrupt lawful endeavors rather than to communicate. *In re Brown,* 510 P 2d 1017/Cal (1973).

The making of a telephone call to a state trooper berating him by the use of obscene and profane language did not amount to a breach of the peace. *Aniniskette v State,* 489 P 2d 1012/Alk (1971).

A member of a religious order, in response to a question posed by a member of an audience, who answered that he believed in no man-made law and that he did not respect and would not salute the United States Flag was not guilty of a breach of the peace. *Miller v State,* 133 P 2d 223/Ok (1943).

DISORDERLY CONDUCT

In General

Breach of the peace and disorderly conduct are virtually synonymous and are treated as such in most jurisdictions. Any difference, if it exists, is made so by statutes of the individual states. One who commits a breach of the peace is also guilty of disorderly conduct, but not all disorderly conduct is a breach of the peace *(Seattle v Franklin,* 70 P 2d 1049/Wn–1934). However, in deference to jurisdictions differentiating between the two concepts, they are distinguished in this text.

Disorderly conduct is not an offense known at common law, and a conviction for disorderly conduct must be based on some offense prohibited by substantive law. *State v Taylor,* 297 A 2d 216/NJ (1972).

Fighting Words—Disorderly Conduct

Fighting words, although not obscene, may constitute disorderly conduct, but for obscene words to amount to disorderly conduct the language used is subject to the contemporary community standards rule, which means the words must be so grossly offensive to members of the public who actually overhear it as to amount to a nuisance. *Von Sleichter v United States,* 472 F 2d 1244/DC (1972).

Under a statute forbidding harrassment, defendants' conduct in addressing an officer who had cited one of their number for a traffic violation, using such invectives as "you stupid bastard" and "you son-of-a-bitch," was within the proscription of the statute. *People v Cuomo*, 335 NYS 2d 219/NY (1972).

At a meeting of the board of education where defendant addressed a city police officer by saying, "I'll kick the s--- out of you, you m----- f-----; remember you work for me—you take that badge off and I'll kill you," such invectives constituted fighting words in that they were likely to incite another to violence. *State v Brown*, 303 A 2d 886/NJ (1973).

Examples of Disorderly Conduct

A statute defining disorderly conduct as that exemplified by one who loiters or wanders upon the streets or from place to place without apparent reason or business and who refuses to identify himself and account for his presence when requested so to do by any peace officer—if surrounding circumstances are such as to indicate to a reasonable man that the public safety demands such identification—is not unconstitutional for vagueness. *People v Solomon*, 108 CR 867/Cal (1973).

Where loud and boisterous group conduct committed at a public high school disturbed and disrupted studies therein, and where defendant was identified as a member of that group by a witness who testified that his mouth was moving, there was sufficient evidence to sustain conviction. *Hicks v State*, 294 NE 2d 613/Ind (1973).

Disorderly conduct was committed where defendants refused to leave an administrative office of a high school upon request and thereafter inflicted damage in the office. *State v Woods*, 205 SE 2d 578/NC (1974).

Where a group of demonstrators were in the street blocking vehicular traffic and police were also in the street attempting to restore order, and defendant addressed the demonstrators in a loud voice soliciting them to repeat illegal acts of blocking traffic, his arrest for disorderly conduct was warranted. *Hess v State*, 297 NE 2d 413/Ind (1973).

A statute declaring every lewd, disorderly, or dissolute person to be a vagrant, and providing a punishment not to exceed six months in the county jail or a fine of not more than $500, satisfies constitutional standards for precision and clarity. *State v Jones*, 511 P 2d 74/Wn (1973).

The malicious activating of a fire alarm when there was no fire was disorderly conduct. *State v Moretti*, 319 A 2d 342/RI (1974).

Conduct Not Disorderly

Merely talking back to a police officer does not constitute disorderly conduct. *Von Sleichter v United States*, 472 F 2d 1244/DC (1972).

It was not disorderly conduct where defendant placed himself within the field of vision of approaching motorists, displaying a sign which read "RADAR AHEAD." *State v Taylor*, 297 A 2d 216/NJ (1972).

The burning of the flag of another country (Israel), did not amount to disorderly conduct absent a showing that defendants intended to cause public inconvenience, annoyance or alarm, and recklessly create a risk thereof. *People v Mehdi,* 327 NYS 2d 659/NY (1971).

UNLAWFUL ASSEMBLY

Defined

"Unlawful assembly," at common law, consisted of the gathering together of three or more persons in such a manner as to disturb the public peace and for the purpose of a violent and forcible execution of some enterprise, and the crime was complete upon assembly; if the persons so assembled took steps or advanced toward the accomplishment of their enterprise, their act became a "rout"; and if they put their design into effect it was a "riot."

In General

The intent for which persons are assembled is the very essence of an unlawful assembly, and in many instances intent can only be determined by acts, language, conduct of members, and other circumstances stimulating the members to assemble. *Lair v State,* 316 P 2d 225/Ok (1957).

Unless abrogated or modified by statute, the common law applies and the minimum number of persons requisite to the formation of an unlawful assembly is three; they must have a common interest or purpose to commit an unlawful act against the person or property of another. *State v Martinez,* 210 P 2d 620/NM (1949).

A statute which prohibits three or more persons from assembling with intent to disturb the public peace, or after assembling to attempt or threaten acts which produce a breach of the peace, does not limit, abridge nor vitiate freedom of speech nor the right to assemble; and that portion of the statute which declares that "every person participating therein by his presence, aid or instigation shall be guilty" is not unconstitutional on the theory that innocent bystanders or passersby could be caught up in the crowd and found guilty simply by being there. The court, in affirming conviction observed:

> . . . there is hardly a criminal statute in the books which cannot in one degree or another be analyzed into absurdity. Apply enough sophistry to the statute, collate its convolutional genesis, envelope it with sufficient rhetoric, stretch the internal logic of the law far enough, and most any part of the criminal code can—specifically, at least—be made to appear

indefinite, uncertain, overbroad or downright unintelligible .... *State v Dixon*, 479 P 2d 931/Wn (1971).

Refusal to Disperse

In the giving of a dispersal order, police are not required to set a time limit within which to disperse before any arrest may be made. *State v Johnson*, 500 P 2d 788/Wn (1972).

Under a statute denouncing failure to disperse from the place of an unlawful meeting, no exception is made for the innocent bystander, and one who refuses to disperse upon lawful order may be found guilty if by his presence he participates, aids or instigates, whether or not he has physically participated in any act of violence. *State v Johnson, supra.*

Criminal Trespass

Members of a group who remained on public school premises after having been ordered to leave were guilty of criminal trespass and were not denied freedom of speech or assembly, nor the right to petition for redress of grievances. *Daniel v State*, 201 SE 2d 393/Ga (1973).

Defendants who sat in a selective service office and read poetry, read off names of persons killed in action and sang religious and protest songs were engaged in a type of conduct calculated to interfere with business carried on in the office and were properly found guilty of unlawful interference with the use of a public building. *Quinn v State*, 281 NE 2d 478/Ind (1972).

What Is Not Unlawful Assembly

Although where three or more persons assembled indulge in violent or boisterous conduct—a requisite of the crime of unlawful assembly—not every such gathering of people wherein such conduct is characterized by three or more persons is an unlawful assembly. *Shenfield v City Court*, 443 P 2d 443/Az (1968).

Persons who assemble for a lawful purpose are not guilty of unlawful assembly by virtue of the unlawful acts of others; when the assembly becomes unlawful, those who disassociate themselves from the assemblage as soon as it becomes unlawful, do not fall within the purview of the common law definition of unlawful assembly. *Abby v City Court*, 439 P 2d 302/Az (1968); *Lair v State*, 316 P 2d 225/Ok (1957).

A statute forbidding unlawful assemblies proscribes only those assemblies which are violent or which pose a clear and present danger of imminent violence. *In re Bozorg*, 510 P 2d 1017/Cal (1973).

An unlawful assembly statute is limited to the regulation of criminal conduct, not peaceful protests, general obnoxiousness or deviant life styles. *State v Hipp*, 213 NW 2d 610/Min (1973).

RIOT

Defined

A "riot," under Florida law, is a tumultuous disturbance of the peace by three or more persons, assembled together of their own volition with the intent to assist each other mutually against any who shall oppose them in the execution of some enterprise of a private nature; the execution of the plan or enterprise is in a violent and turbulent manner to the terror of the people, whether the act intended was of itself lawful or unlawful. *Daytona Beach v Brown*, 273 S 2d 124/Fla (1973).

In General

Unlawful assembly is a necessary element of rioting. The minimum number of persons necessary to constitute a riot is stated in the statute of each of the states; in some states the minimum number is three (*Whaley v State*, 496 SW 2d 109/Tex–1973), or it may be two. California Penal Code, § 404; *State v Albers*, 303 A 2d 197/NH (1973).

Although every riot is preceded by an unlawful assembly, if only by moments, riot may be charged and secured without either alleging or proving the antecedent unlawful assembly from which the riot emerged. *Schoolcraft v State*, 178 P 2d 641/Ok (1947).

Where four persons entered a bar together, were loud and boisterous, threw furniture, and beat and kicked the manager, a reasonable inference was raised that they were acting together (*State v Biddlecome*, 481 P 2d 533/Az–1971). However, unless specifically included in the statute as a part of the *corpus delicti*, neither concert of action, conspiracy nor previous agreement are elements of riot and need not be shown. *Trujillo v People*, 178 P 2d 942/Colo (1947); *United States v Jeffries*, 45 FRD 119/DC (1968).

Failure to Disperse Upon Order

At common law it was the duty of the magistrate, sheriff or constable, in case of riot or tumultuous assembly, to go to the scene and amongst the rioters, read them the Riot Act, and command them in the name of the people immediately to disperse. *Annala v McLeod*, 206 P 2d 811/Mont (1949).

After a dispersal order is given to the rioters no one can maintain the status of innocent bystander, and anyone remaining present not lending aid in suppressing the riot will be deemed a rioter, and it is immaterial that his conduct was not turbulent nor his language violent. *State v Moe*, 24 P 2d 638/Wn (1933).

Examples

Where 25 to 30 strikers at a lumber mill attacked nonunion workers who were operating the lumber mill and threw rocks—some of which stuck and injured workers while others damaged vehicles and property—conviction of felony assault and rioting against two of the rioters was warranted. And in the trial of defendants some of the rocks thrown were admitted into evidence against both defendants without proof as to who threw the rocks. *People v Bundte*, 197 P 2d 823/Cal (1938).

The commission of larceny by a number of people through force and violence makes all persons participating chargeable with larceny and riot, notwithstanding that some participants took property without the use of force. *State v Moe, supra.*

Where four defendants who were acting in concert with other striking associates encouraged all strikers present to assault nonunion workmen, and assaults were committed pursuant thereto, in a manner likely to produce great bodily injury, defendants were guilty as principals whether or not they were actually identified as having thrown rocks at nonunion workers. *People v Moore*, 197 P 2d 835/Cal (1948).

DANGEROUS OR DEADLY WEAPONS

Constitutional Rights—As Modified—to Bear Arms

Under the U.S. Constitution, Amendment II, citizens have the right to keep and bear arms and use them in defense of person, habitation and property (*State v Nickerson*, 247 P 2d 188/Mont—1952), but such constitutional guarantee is subject to reasonable regulation under the police power of the state (*State v Krantz*, 164 P 2d 453/Wn—1945). The proscription against ownership or possession of a concealable firearm by anyone who has been convicted of a felony is within the realm of the state's police power. Id; *People v Garcia*, 218 P 2d 837/Cal (1950).

Under the state's legitimate interest in public welfare and safety, it may enact laws prohibiting certain classes of persons from possessing firearms and may require others to obtain licenses to carry concealable firearms. *State v Storms*, 308 A 2d 463/RI (1973).

The constitutional right to bear arms does not include the right to possess a sawed-off shotgun in violation of the Federal Firearms Act (*United States v Casson*, 288 FS 86/Del—1968); nor does it assure convicted felons the right to possess a sawed-off shotgun or a 22-caliber semiautomatic rifle (*United States v Wiley*, 309 FS 147/Min—1970), and particularly it does not assure a convicted felon the right to bear arms while he is serving a sentence in the state prison. *People v Wells*, 156 P 2d 979/Cal (1945).

There is no absolute right under the Constitution of an individual to possess a firearm (*United States v Day*, 476 F 2d 562/Ky—1973). If this were true under the Constitution, infants, ex-felons, and even prisoners serving sentences in prison would have that right.

The finding of two pistols in different locations in a search of an alien's residence constitutes but one offense under California law (*People v Puppilo*, 280 P 2d 545/Cal—1929), but under the federal law the possession of five unregistered firearms simultaneously constitutes five offenses. *United States v Tarrant*, 460 F 2d 701/Tex (1972).

A felony, as it relates to the National Firearms Act, is an offense punishable by a term of imprisonment exceeding one year, but does not include any offense classified as a misdemeanor under a state law, the punishment for which is two years or less. *United States v Glasgow*, 478 F 2d 850/Min (1973).

Weapons in General

Weapons are either dangerous or deadly—as declared by statute or by the courts—based upon the manner in which they are used. Some weapons which are dangerous by statutory declaration as a result of their design are guns, daggers, spring-blade knives, slung shots, sand clubs, blackjacks, and metal knuckles. Some weapons, under particular circumstances, are so clearly lethal that a court may declare them to be lethal as a matter of law, such weapons being designed or designated as weapons; other objects are lethal or not, depending on their capabilities and the manner in which they are used, and whether they are capable of producing death or great bodily injury is a question for the trier of fact. *State v Spurlock*, 371 P 2d 739/Ok (1962).

Most states have enacted statutes forbidding certain types of weapons as contraband, some of which may be possessed by peace officers as part of their equipment, while others may not be possessed except when taken as evidence to be used in a prosecution of the possessor. As a rule a blackjack, often called a "sap," may not be possessed by one other than a peace officer or a business enterprise involved in its manufacture or sale. *People v Norris*, 198 NW 2d 430/Mich (1972).

The legislature did not intend to restrict the definition of weapons to those which are store-bought, but the test is whether the instrumentality can be used to injure or kill and whether it has been thus used sufficiently to set a pattern of criminal conduct so that the courts must take cognizance thereof. *Beeler v State*, 334 P 2d 799/Ok (1959).

A statute making the possession of certain kinds of weapons or instruments a crime, embraces instruments other than those specifically created or manufactured for criminal purposes; where defendant detached a table leg and possessed it at night at the scene of a riot, such instrument was clearly within the statutory proscription (*People v Grubb*, 408 P 2d 100/Cal—1965). A small modified baseball bat taped at the handle and carried in an automobile and not used in playing baseball, was held to be a billy and unlawful. Id.

Some instruments which have been held to be dangerous or deadly but which are not designed as weapons are fingernail files, razors, beer bottles, chains, automobiles, shoes while being worn, air guns, chairs, clocks, rocks.[1]

Dangerous Weapons

A "dangerous instrumentality" and a "deadly instrument" are not synonymous; all deadly instruments are dangerous but all dangerous instruments are not deadly. *Hopkins v State*, 286 S 2d 920/Ala (1973).

A pocket knife with a blade three and one-half inches long is not a dangerous knife if the blade is closed and the knife is in the pocket of the possessor *(State v Edwards*, 293 A 2d 234/NJ–1972), but a knife with a blade three and one-fourth inches long is a deadly or dangerous weapon when one carries it concealed in the boarding of an aircraft (*United States v Margraf*, 347 FS 230/Pa–1972). A blackjack is a dangerous weapon. *State v Hart*, 157, P 2d 72/Id (1945).

Deadly Weapons

A "deadly weapon" is one likely to produce death or great bodily injury, and the determination is a question of fact, not law. *People v Moran*, 109 CR 287/Cal (1973).

A statute proscribing possession of a dirk, dagger or dangerous knife does not limit the design of the instrument to one intended to be used as a weapon, nor does it mean that a dangerous knife must have similar characteristics to a dirk or dagger, or have a fixed or locked blade. An ordinary pocket knife of the folding type is not a dangerous knife *per se*, but if possessed to be used as a weapon it may fall within the interdiction of the statute. *State v Green*, 303 A 2d 312/NJ (1973).

"Dagger" is a generic term designating stabbing-type weapons which includes dirk, stiletto, poniard, etc. *People v Thomas*, 337 NYS 2d 850/NY (1972); People v Syed Shah, 205 P 2d 108/Cal (1949).

A statute enumerating deadly weapons included a knife having a blade longer than three inches making such intrument a deadly weapon as a matter of law, but whether a pen knife having a blade of one and one-half inches, with which victim was assaulted, raised a question for the jury and here they so declared. *State v Sorenson*, 492 P 2d 233/Wn (1972).

A pocket knife with a two-inch blade was a deadly weapon as used by defendant to stab victim in the back thus precluding an instruction on simple assault and requiring a verdict of felony assault or not guilty. *United States v Enos*, 453 F 2d 342/Az (1973).

A straight razor is not a deadly weapon *per se* since it is a domestic tool

[1] Jesse R. Pistole, *Washington Criminal Law*, 2nd edition (Lynnwood, Wa.: Snyder Publications, 1974), p. 225.

designed to shave hair from the face or other parts of the body, but it must be included in the generic term of "knife" as defined by statute. *State v Howard,* 308 A 2d 366/NJ (1973).

A sawed-off shotgun with a barrel twelve and one-fourth inches long, although not a concealable firearm within the defining statute, is nevertheless a deadly weapon. *State v Clipston,* 473 P 2d 682/Or (1969).

An operable rifle, that is, one capable of being loaded and fired, is a deadly weapon or instrument whether or not loaded. *People v Lay,* 334 NYS 2d 398/NY (1972).

While an automobile is not a deadly weapon *per se,* justifying a presumption of intent to kill by the use of an automobile as the instrumentality, such intent may be shown from all of the circumstances surrounding the killing. *Palafax v State,* 484 SW 2d 739/Tex (1972).

A wooden shaft twenty-six by one and one-half inches with a leather thong attached to one end was a policemen's club and fits any standard definition of a billy, and was thus unlawful. *People v Schoonmaker,* 339 NYS 2d 338/NY (1972).

A heavy metal chain wrapped with tape and looped to provide a handle constituted a bludgeon or a blackjack within the meaning of a statute forbidding the unlawful use of a weapon. *People v Collins,* 286 NE 2d 117/Ill (1972).

The human fist is not a deadly weapon within the meaning of a statute defining assault with a deadly weapon, but defendant may nevertheless be found guilty of a deadly assault where only the fists were used, depending on the manner in which they were used. *Quarles v State,* 204 SE 2d 467/Ga (1974).

"Firearms" Under the National Firearms Act

"Firearms," as defined and proscribed by the National Firearms Act are: (1) a shotgun with a barrel less than 18 inches; (2) a rifle or shotgun modified to less than 26 inches; (3) a rifle with a barrel less than 16 inches; (4) a machine gun; (5) a firearm muffler or silencer; (6) a destructive device or (7) any other weapon capable of being concealed on the person and capable of expelling a missile by explosive energy, *except* ordinary pistols, revolvers, rifles and shotguns. Title 18 USCA, § 5845.

The word firearm includes handguns, rifles and shotguns. The National Firearms Act defines firearm as being any device designed to expel a missile through the medium of explosive energy. *United States v Thompson,* 202 FS 503/Cal (1952).

A "destructive device" includes bombs, which are fragmentary, incendiary or gaseous; grenades; rockets with a propellant charge of more than four ounces; mines; other similar convertible or converted devices. Title 18 USCA, § 5845 (f).

In 1962 the United States District Court of California, Northern District, ruled that a shotgun without a firing pin was not a firearm within the meaning of the National Firearms Act (*United States v Thompson, supra*), but in 1965 the United States District Court of Louisiana ruled the reverse where the gun was a sawed-off shotgun, the court holding that "even though the firing pin was missing from a sawed-off shotgun it was a firearm under the National Firearms Act inasmuch as an ordinary wire nail, accessible and available to almost anyone, could be effectively substituted for the firing pin." *United States v Cosey*, 244 FS 100/La (1965).

The possession of a sawed-off shotgun which is inoperable but which is of such a nature that it may be readily restored to operating condition, is a violation of the National Firearms Act. *United States v Barno*, 340 FS 1326/DC (1972); 26 USCA § § 5845 (d), 5861 (d), 5801.

Specific Weapons Defined

The National Firearms Act defines "machine gun" by whatever name as having the following characteristics:

1. Separable mechanical device or reservoir in which ammunition may be loaded;
2. Capable of firing five or more shots per second; and
3. Designed to fire continuously with a single pull of the trigger. Title 18 USCA, § 5845 (b).

A "pistol" is defined as a firearm which is capable of discharging a projectile with lethal force by a chemical explosion of gas, gunpowder or rocket propulsion. A carbon dioxide gas-powered air pistol is not a firearm within the meaning of a statute forbidding felons from carrying firearms. *Thompson v State*, 488 P 2d 944/Ok (1971).

"Possession" Defined

"Possession" may be actual or constructive; it is actual when a person knowingly has direct physical control over an object at a given time; it is constructive when one knowingly has dominion or control over a thing either directly or through the agency of another. *United States ex rel England v Anderson*, 347 FS 115/Del (1972).

Where a pistol was laying on the console between driver and passenger of an automobile, constructive possession was placed in the passenger where a search of his person disclosed cartridges for the pistol. *Jones v United States*, 299 A 2d 538/DC (1973).

A statute forbidding possession of a concealed firearm is not concerned with the ownership of the weapon, and possession may be constructive or physical, individual or joint; thus, two or more persons may be in possession of a single weapon. *State v Kelley*, 507 P 2d 837/Or (1973).

To limit firearm possession by those who have demonstrated by their past conduct an unfitness to bear arms, is in the interest of public health, safety and welfare and clearly within the scope of the police power of the state. *People v Trujillo,* 497 P 2d 1/Colo (1972).

"Concealed" Firearms

"Concealable firearms" as a rule, include pistols and revolvers having a barrel of less than twelve inches in length. *Mena v State,* 504 SW 2d 410/Tex (1974).

A weapon is concealed, within the meaning of a statute forbidding the carrying of a weapon concealed, when it is hidden from ordinary observation and need not be invisible to others to fall within the purview of the statute (*McKee v State,* 488 P 2d 1039/Alk–1971). Unlawful possession may be proved by any circumstantial evidence inconsistent with innocence. *State v Karney,* 494 P 2d 1204/Kan (1972).

A weapon need not be completely concealed in order to qualify as a concealed weapon; if it is concealed from ordinary view, although partially visible through an opening in the pocket of the possessor, it is concealed within the meaning of the concealed weapons law (*State v Sellers,* 281 S 2d 397/Fla–1973). The same rule applies when the weapon is carried in a vehicle at night and only the butt of the weapon is visible. *Smith v State,* 308 A 2d 442/Md (1973).

Unless specifically exempted by statute, private detectives, members of detective associations and special police officers fall within the purview of a statute forbidding the carrying of a concealed weapon without a permit. *State v Nicol,* 295 A 2d 25/NJ (1972); *Franklin v United States,* 458 F 2d 861/DC (1972).

In a prosecution for carrying a pistol without a license, the government need not prove that defendant owned, customarily carried or intended to use the pistol. *United States v Freeman,* 462 F 2d 290/DC (1972).

The purpose or intent existing concomitant with the carrying of a concealed weapon is not an element of the offense and is immaterial in a prosecution for a violation of the statute. *People v Johnson,* 209 NW 2d 868/Mich (1973).

It is no defense to a prosecution for unlawfully carrying a concealed weapon that the defendant was a nonresident, or an out-of-state traveler. *Garcia v State,* 292 NE 2d 810/Ind (1973).

A statute forbidding the carrying of a concealed weapon is violated whether or not the gun is loaded. *State v Boyd,* 492 SW 2d 787/Mo (1973).

Under Pennsylvania law intent to do bodily harm may be inferred solely from the fact that defendant carries a deadly weapon upon his person. *Com v Spriggs,* 302 A 2d 442/Pa (1973).

Evidence supported conviction for unlawfully carrying a concealed weapon where a police officer testified that he saw defendant draw the weapon from his pocket where it had been entirely concealed prior to withdrawal. *State v Colomb*, 260 S 2d 619/La (1972).

Concealed in an Automobile

Under a statute prohibiting the carrying of a pistol concealed in a vehicle, the statute is violated although a portion of the pistol is visible. Where an officer stopped defendant for a traffic violation and observed what he thought to be a portion of the butt of a revolver, which, when recovered, was found to be a 357-magnum revolver, the revolver was concealed within the meaning of the statute. *People v Zazzetti*, 286 NE 2d 745/Ill (1972).

In a prosecution for carrying a concealed weapon in a vehicle, the burden does not fall on the people to prove that defendant did not have a permit to carry such weapon. When, upon discovery of the weapon in a proper search, defendant does not produce a permit or otherwise justify or excuse possession, the people have proved their case *prima facie* and the burden of proceeding or producing evidence reverts to the accused. *People v Henderson*, 206 NW 2d 771/Mich (1973).

A weapon is concealed when it is so placed as not to be visible to ordinary observation (*State v Williams*, 481 SW 2d 1/Mo–1972). Darkness may well be a factor in making a determination of concealment (Id), and where defendants were carrying a shotgun in their automobile at night, not visible to officers until defendants exited the vehicle, the weapon was concealed within the meaning of the statute. *People v Latson*, 284 NE 2d 236/Ill (1972).

Accessibility of a weapon is not an element of a statute prohibiting the carrying of a concealed firearm within a vehicle. *People v Zazzetti, supra.*

Possession of Firearms by Ex-Felons

Possession of firearms by ex-cons is usually forbidden by individual state statutes and the weapon, as a rule, may be any firearm and is not restricted to pistols or concealable firearms. *United States v Pleasant*, 469 F 2d 1121/Mo (1972).

A statute declaring it a felony for a previously convicted felon to own or possess a pistol applies equally to persons who have been convicted in another state. *State v Krantz*, 164 P 2d 453/Wn (1945).

Defendant's plea of guilty to attempted grand larceny in Washington, followed by an order deferring the imposition of sentence and placing defendant on probation, was deemed a prior felony conviction in Oregon for purposes of a statute forbidding possession of a concealable firearm by an ex-con (*State v Tipple*, 517 P 2d 1063/Or–1973).

A statute making unlawful the possession of a firearm by one having been previously convicted of a felony is violated notwithstanding that defendant was granted a full pardon after conviction; pardon does not obliterate a prior felony conviction (*Jones v State*, 509 P 2d 924/Ok–1973), absent a showing that the pardon expurgated defendant's record of all disabilities. *Kellogg v State*, 504 P 2d 440/Ok (1972).

Where defendant had been convicted of a crime punishable by imprisonment in either the state prison or the county jail, and judgment had not been pronounced, and probation had been granted and had expired, defendant was a convicted felon within the meaning of a statute forbidding the possession of a revolver by an ex-felon. *People v Banks*, 348 P 2d 102/Cal (1960).

Probation accompanied by a suspension of sentence is a conviction within the meaning of a statute forbidding the possession of firearms, and it is not necessary that defendant shall have served time to attain the status of ex-felon. *State v Cartwright*, 418 P 2d 822/Or (1966).

The state is not required to prove that a firearm, apparently in good working order, is operable when such weapon is entered into evidence. *State v Cartwright, supra.*

The carrying of a firearm in the home by defendant who was an ex-felon, was a criminal offense under the statute proscribing the carrying on his person or in any vehicle a dangerous or deadly weapon easily concealable. *Roark v State*, 465 P 2d 480/Ok (1970).

The rule against ex-felons carrying firearms is strictly statutory, and the carrying of a 22 rifle in an automobile, not being specifically proscribed, was not within the ambit of the statute. *Marr v State*, 513 P 2d 324/Ok (1973).

Possession by Aliens

Statutory prohibition against an alien *owning or possessing* a concealable firearm has been declared unconstitutional by the California Court of Appeals, as constituting a denial of equal protection under the law–a violation of the Fourteenth Amendment to the U.S. Constitution (*People v Rappard*, 104 CR 535/Cal–1972), but a statute prohibiting a felon from *carrying* a firearm in Oklahoma is not a denial of the equal protection clause and is a reasonable classification. *Roberson v State*, 502 P 2d 351/Ok (1972).

PART IV

CRIMES AGAINST THE PERSON

Chapter XIII

Assaults

BATTERY AND MISDEMEANOR ASSAULTS

In General

The term "assault" is often defined as an unlawful attempt coupled with the present ability to commit a violent injury on the person of another, but this definition is not precise. A better definition has been held to be an attempt with unlawful force to inflict bodily injury on the person of another accompanied by *apparent* present ability to give effect to the attempt (*Howell v Winters*, 108 P 1077/Wn–1910). Also, the California Supreme Court has ruled in an earlier decision that the assailant need not be within striking distance of the victim but only sufficiently near to warrant the conclusion in the mind of the victim that he will be struck unless he immediately defends or flees. *People v Islas*, 27 Cal 630 (1885).

The oldest conception of assault held that an attempt but unaccomplished battery was an assault without regard to whether the victim was put in fear. The shooting at another and missing, even if the victim is unaware of the attempt is an assault; indeed, the victim may even be asleep and yet be the subject of assault. *Com v Richards*, 293 NE 854/Mas (1973).

"Simple" Assault Defined

Although few if any of the states have statutes which define "simple" assault, the term simple is often used in conjunction with the crime of misdemeanor or a lesser assault to distinguish between misdemeanor and felony assault. Also, where the crime is not aggravated, distinction is made between assault and battery. Assault may be committed exclusive of battery but battery cannot be committed exclusive of assault, assault being the unlawful attempt coupled with the apparent present ability to commit a violent injury on the person of another and battery being the unlawful application of the force.

"Assault" and "Battery" Distinguished

An "assault" is an offer to show violence to another without striking him, whereas a "battery" is the carrying of the threat into effect by the infliction of the blow, it being without consent of the person on whom the offer of violence was made or on whom the blow was inflicted. *Ormond v Crampton*, 191 SE 2d 405/NC (1972).

Assault is one crime and battery is another; therefore, there is no single crime called assault and battery. When the term is used to denote the actual application of force upon the person of another, the crime is battery and the word assault is superfluous (*Woods v State*, 288 A 2d 215/Md–1972). Assault is an inchoate battery and battery is a consummated assault. *State v Worrey*, 322 A 2d 73/Me (1974).

Nature of the Offenses

One sometimes hears a remark to the effect that some assaults and/or batteries are permissible or lawful. This belief is fallacious and a statement to that effect is untrue. *Neither assault nor battery is ever lawful.* The force applied by one upon another in contact sports, such as boxing or football, if the rules of the games are followed, is neither assault nor battery. The corporal punishment of a child by his parent or guardian, and usually his teacher, is likewise neither assault nor battery.

The word assault is deceptive in that when used to define aggravated or felonious assaults it may include battery, but not necessarily so. Thus, to point even an empty pistol at another menacingly when within range is a felony assault under the laws of most states (*State v Matthewson*, 472 P 2d 638/Id–1970); also, where defendant pointed a loaded revolver at another pulling the trigger three times, he committed an assault with a deadly weapon—a felony—even though the revolver misfired three times. *State v Gotarez*, 442 P 2d 842/Az (1968).

The question as to whether an assault has been committed in a particular case depends more upon the apprehension created in the mind of the assailed than upon the undisclosed intention of the assailant. *State v Murphy*, 500 P 2d 1276/Wn (1972).

One who starts a fight but suffers the greater pain and injury is in no position to claim damage from assault and battery unless his adversary subjects him to a clearly excessive beating. *Lanahan v Taylor*, 290 NE 2d 340/Ill (1972).

As a rule, provocation is not justification for an assault. *United States v Ramirez*, 460 F 2d 1322/Colo (1972).

Attempted Assault

A novel offense is illustrated in a Colorado case whrein officers stopped defendant's automobile and defendant reached under the seat for his gun and was thereupon arrested. At his trial for attempted assault he defended on the ground that he was reaching for the weapon to hide it, not to use it against the officers. On appeal the court observed in reversing: an assault is nothing more than an attempted battery; therefore defendant's conviction of attempted assault was the equivalent to an attempted attempt and no such crime exists under Colorado law *(Allen v People*, 485 P 2d 886/Colo–1971). But compare *Allen* to *In re M, infra*, where the California court observed that although under common law there was no such crime as attempted assault, under California statutory law a person could be properly charged with and convicted of attempted assault, and the crime occurred when battery was attempted and was unsuccessful and the actor lacked the present ability to consummate it. *In re M*, 105 CR 809/Cal (1972).

"Violence" Defined

The term "violence" as used in conjunction with assault and battery bears no relationship to the severity of an attack nor to the extent of resultant injury; here, "violence" is synonymous with "force," and includes any application of force. Nor is pain a necessarily included ingredient, as the type of force is immaterial and any unlawful touching of the person of another is a battery. *State v Smith*, 306 A 2d 5/Me (1973).

The Hands As a Weapon

There exists in the minds of many laymen and no small number of police officers the illusion that the hands of a professional boxer or karate expert are, *per se*, deadly weapons. If this were true the slightest contact of such a person's hand upon the person of another, or even an attempt to make such contact would be an assault with a deadly weapon—a felony in most jurisdictions—unless such action was consented to or condoned. To further illustrate the fallacy of this illusion, assume that such a person were observed by an officer to insert his hand in his pocket; would the officer be justified in arresting the subject for carrying a concealed weapon? A negative answer seems obvious.

The hands of a professional boxer or a karate expert are not deadly weapons and, as a rule, would be regarded in the light ordinarily applied to assault by the use of hands. The applicable rule being that when one is assaulted viciously with the hands thus causing great bodily injury, the assault may be felonious or aggravated whether or not the hands belong to a vigorous professional or a debilitated layman. The Oklahoma court has ruled that the question as to whether hands and fists are dangerous weapons within the meaning of the statute depends on the circumstances of the case and is a matter for resolution by the trier of fact. *Pettigrew v State*, 430 P 2d 808/Ok (1967).

Acts of Force by Peace Officers

An officer, as keeper of the peace, cannot suffer himself to be overcome by opprobrium, insolence and abusive language from an arrestee; he cannot while acting as minister of the law and while armed with legal power, chastise his prisoner for insults; he cannot yield to passion and undertake the administration of punishment into his own hands. *Rutherford v State*, 258 S 2d 65/Ala (1972).

In states where an arrestee is permitted to resist an unlawful arrest, or to resist a lawful arrest where excessive force is used, he has the right of self-defense but may not use any more force than is reasonably necessary to resist such arrest. *Carter v State*, 507 P 2d 932/Ok (1973).

An officer must not inflict unnecessary bodily harm or death on a fleeing misdemeanant. *Havier v Partin*, 492 P 2d 761/Az (1972).

Examples

In an early Georgia case the court ruled, in defining assault:

> "If to put the arm, though tenderly, about the neck of another man's wife, against her will, is not an assault and battery then what is it? Surely, the matrons of the land are not exposed to such an indignity at the pleasure of every libertine . . . . To touch a virtuous wife in the way of an illicit love is a far greater outrage than to touch in anger and equally a breach of the peace. It is violence proceeding from lust, instead of violence proceeding from range." *Goodrum v Georgia*, 60 Ga 509 (1898).

Although victim, a female, consented to a hypodermic injection which caused unconsciousness, defendant's acts of placing his hands on her, removing her clothing and climbing on top of her, amounted to assault and battery. *Avery v State*, 292 A 2d 728/Md (1972).

An unauthorized surgical operation constitutes assault and battery and the surgeon performing the surgery is liable civilly for damages resulting therefrom (*Shetter v Rochelle*, 409 P 2d 74/Az–1969). Also, where an operation is authorized and an inadvertant operation is performed on a patient's right leg when the operation was planned and intended for the left leg, there is an assault and battery plus civil liability. *Moos v United States*, 225 F 2d 705/Min (1955).

An officer was acting in the lawful discharge of his duty even though he was off duty and engaged in directing traffic from a private lot onto a public highway for a private concern at the time he was assaulted, and the assault was one upon an officer in line of duty (*Wood v State*, 486 SW 2d 771/Tex–1972). Alleging that the officer was not working for the Dallas Police Department at the time was based on a faulty premise. Id.

Evidence that defendant touched victim on the shoulders and sides and held her hands was sufficient to sustain conviction of aggravated assault of a sexual nature upon the person of a female less than 15 years of age. *State v Carrillo*, 502 P 2d 1342/Az (1972).

Mere Words and Menaces

Words of abuse, reproach and scorn addressed to a person, or uttered to another concerning him, however opprobrious or insulting they may be, will not justify assault upon the speaker (*People v Mears*, 298 P 2d 40/Cal–1956); (*State v Jones*, 173 P 2d 960/Or–1946). It must be remembered, however, that in most, if not all, states, personal invectives directed toward or about another would amount to a violation of some law such as breach of the peace, intimidation, threats, slander, etc.

Inflammatory remarks or insulting words do not justify an assault (*Merriman v State*, 499 P 2d 477/Ok–1972); nor do mere words constituting threats in a menacing manner amount to an assault (*In re DWJ, Jr*, 293 A 2d 268/DC–1972); rather, there must be an effort to carry the intention into execution. *Anstedt v State*, 509 P 2d 968/Nev (1973).

The rule that mere words will not justify an assault and battery in criminal law is not applicable to civil cases (*Fontenot v Walls*, 269 S 2d 272/La–1972), and where there was evidence in a civil action that plaintiff called defendant "a dirty son-of-a-bitch," there was sufficient evidence of provocation by plaintiff. Id; *Morneau v American Oil Co*, 272 S 2d 313/La (1973).

Consent As a Defense

An assault may be committed upon a child irrespective of the child's consent or assent, and it is no defense that the hand of the child touched the body of the defendant; here the hand of the child touched the sexual organ of defendant at his suggestion thus reversing the ordinary fact situation of an assault. *Beausoliel v United States*, 107 F 2d 292/DC (1940).

Consent to assault is a defense in some instances where the consentor is competent, as where plaintiff voluntarily engaged in horseplay with other persons and was accidently injured. *Hellriegel v Tholl*, 417 P 2d 362/Wn (1966).

The state will not ordinarily dismiss a charge of assault made in good faith where the victim has had a change of heart. Thus, testimony by the victim that she did not blame defendant and that his attack upon her was justified, was irrelevant. An assault is a crime against the state as well as against a victim and does not disappear upon forgiveness. *State v Brown*, 447 P 2d 82/Wn (1968).

What Are Not Assaults

A conviction of battery could not stand where evidence showed that the injury to complainant was accidentally inflicted. *McDonald v Sheriff of Carson City*, 512 P 2d 774/Nev (1973).

An indictment charging aggravated battery was fatally defective and could not stand where it alleged conduct of an insulting and provoking nature but did not allege physical contact. *People v Latham*, 299 NE 2d 808/Ill (1973).

Neither a menace nor a conditional offer of violence is an assault; an assault is any attempt by force or violence to offer corporal hurt to another coupled with present ability to carry attempt into effect. *Bryant v State*, 272 S 2d 286/Ala (1972).

FELONY ASSAULTS

In General

Under a prosecution for a felonious assault, the crime is complete whether or not a battery has been committed, and as such there can be no conviction of an *attempted* felonious assault. *People v Banks*, 216 NW 2d 461/Mich (1974).

Unlike the crime of voluntary manslaughter, one who acts in the heat of passion in the assault of another commits no lesser assault because of that fact, and an aggravated assault and battery would not be reduced by one so acting. *Com v Rife*, 312 A 2d 406/Pa (1973).

Where evidence clearly shows a serious crime, the court may refuse to instruct the jury on a lesser offense and require a finding of either guilty or not guilty on the greater crime. Thus in a prosecution for assault with intent to commit rape, where both victim and defendant testified that defendant struck victim, the court properly refused to instruct the jury on simple assault. *Com v McKay*, 294 NE 2d 213/Mas (1973).

Intent Relevant to Felony Assault

Assault with force likely to produce great bodily harm is a crime of general intent—specific intent not being an element of the crime. *People v Martinez*, 107 CR 284/Cal (1973); *People v Johnson*, 202 NW 2d 340/Mich (1972).

When an act inherently dangerous to others is committed with conscious disregard of human life and safety, the act transcends recklessness, and intent to commit battery is presumed. *People v Jathus*, 110 CR 921/Cal (1973).

Assault with intent to commit a particular crime is, by its very definition, a specific intent crime and always includes an attempt to commit that crime. Although "assault with intent to commit" necessarily includes an attempt, the reverse is not true; there may be an attempt without assault. *Graves v Young*, 420 P 2d 618/Nev (1966).

What Constitutes Great Bodily Harm

Usually the difference between an aggravated assault (or felony assault) and a simple assault is that in the former the assault is made with a dangerous or deadly weapon, or in a manner likely to cause death or great bodily injury, or with intent to commit a felony. "Great bodily harm" or "grievous bodily injury" is not always clear and is a matter of fact, as a rule, to be decided by the jury.

A skull fracture and concussion resulting in loss of memory constitutes grievous bodily harm as referred to in the statute. *Com v Rife*, 312 A 2d 406/Pa (1973).

Where testimony of a physician established that victim had to be put to sleep, his cheek opened by surgery and the broken fragments of his jawbone wired together, the injury constituted great bodily harm (*Anderson v State*, 291 NE 2d 579/Ind–1973). Where defendant interrupted a party by loud and boisterous contention and when ushered from the premises by a guest he stabbed the guest, he was properly convicted of aggravated assault (*State v Land*, 203 NW 2d 541/Min–1973). Injury to the face of victim by an unknown hard dark object which necessitated the removal of an eye was an aggravated assault and battery (*Priola v State*, 292 NE 2d 604/Ind–1973). Where defendant with knife in hand took a menacing step toward officers, one of whom had his gun drawn, defendant nevertheless had the means of carrying out his threat. *People v Roberson*, 205 NW 2d 50/Mich (1972).

Examples of Dangerous and Deadly Weapons

Articles, although innocent in design, which have been held to be dangerous weapons are a wine bottle, shoes, a rake, a thrown club, a brick, a chair leg. It is not necessarily the object's latent capabilities, but this factor, plus the manner in which the object is used, are determinative of the nature of the object. *United States v Daulton*, 488 F 2d 524/Ga (1973).

"Dangerous instrumentality" and "deadly instrument" are not synonymous; although all deadly instruments are dangerous, all dangerous instruments are not deadly. *Hopkins v State*, 286 S 2d 920/Ala (1973).

A deadly weapon is not only a weapon which is designed to kill or one which may readily effect death, but also any instrument which may produce death by the manner in which it is used—such as a file used to inflict deep stab wounds. *Matthews v State*, 286 S 2d 91/Ala (1973).

Examples of Assault With a Deadly Weapon

Requisite intent of assault with a deadly weapon is intent to commit battery, but battery is not a lesser and necessarily included offense of assault with a deadly weapon. *People v Lathus*, 110 CR 921/Cal (1973).

In an affray where defendant, who was wearing boots, kicked his victim about the head and face, such assault constituted an assault with a dangerous weapon, and the fact that no serious injury resulted was not controlling (*Berfield v State*, 458 P 2d 1008/Alk–1969). And an assault upon a federal officer with a shoe also constituted an assault with a dangerous weapon although a shoe, as a matter of law, is not a dangerous weapon. *United States v Barber*, 297 FS 917/Del (1969).

Where the driver of one vehicle pursued another with intent to frighten and terrify the occupants thereof, the pursuer was guilty of an assault with a dangerous instrument. *Vaughn v Baxter*, 488 P 2d 123/Ok (1971).

Where assault with a deadly weapon is shown and assault with intent to kill is sought to be shown, the question of intent resolves itself into whether defendant was motivated by malice or passion: if by passion, the crime is assault with a deadly weapon, only; if by malice, the crime is assault with intent to kill. *Farley v State*, 187 SE 2d 558/Ga (1972).

The fact that it was not shown whether the gun was loaded did not preclude conviction of an assault upon a federal officer with a dangerous weapon; the jury was justified in inferring that one who draws a gun would not do so were he not in a position to use it. *United States v Maynard*, 452 F 2d 1087/Mas (1971).

Where defendant threatened to kill an officer and grabbed the officer's gun in its holster with both hands, although unable to withdraw it, the jury was warranted in finding that defendant had control of the weapon sufficient to warrant conviction of assault with a deadly weapon. *People v Gordon*, 498 P 2d 341/Colo (1972).

The crime of assault with a deadly weapon does not require a battery as an element. Where defendant fired a shotgun at an occupied automobile striking the left front door below the window, there was an assault with a deadly weapon though the metal was not pierced. *State v Snipes*, 192 SE 2d 62/NC (1972).

Even if the arrest of defendant after pursuit in a police car was unlawful, defendant was not justified in resisting arrest by the use of a pistol or other deadly weapon. *Potter v State*, 507 P 2d 1282/Ok (1973).

Lesser Included Offenses—When Not Considered

Although simple assault is a lesser included offense of assault with a deadly weapon, it is not incumbent upon the court to instruct the jury on the crime of simple assault when the assault is clearly of an aggravated nature and no other interpretation is reasonably applicable, or when it is clear by the evidence that the defendant is either guilty of the crime charged or not guilty (*People v McCoy*, 153 P 2d 315/Cal–1945). Thus, instruction on a lesser included offense of assault was properly refused in a prosecution for maiming where defendant shot his victim in the right arm with a shotgun (*State v Lytle*, 280 P 2d 924/Kan–1955); in the crime of kidnaping—assault and battery not being an included offense (*State v Dryan*, 113 P 2d 1052/Kan–1941); in the prosecution of a son for the murder of his father where evidence showed that the son beat his father about the head with a shotgun and then set fire to the building in which his father was lying (*Fields v State*, 322 P 2d 431/Ok–1958; in a prosecution for the rape of a twelve-year-old girl (*State v Griffin*, 166 P 2d 580/Kan–1946); where defendant fired five shots point-blank at victim (*Holland v State*, 414 P 2d 590/Nev–1966); where defendant shot and seriously wounded a sheriff who was driving an automobile, defendant being a passenger in the rear seat (*State v Bloomer*, 390 P 2d 29/Kan–1954); where defendant stabbed his estranged wife in the back with a pocket knife, piercing her lung. *State v Ireland*, 447 P 2d 170/Wn (1968).

Aggravated Battery

The material element of an aggravated assault and battery is intentional and unlawful infliction of great bodily harm or disfigurement upon another, and identification of the instrument used in the assault is not a necessary element. *Priola v State*, 192 NE 2d 604/Ind (1973).

Under a charge of aggravated battery there must be a showing of physical harm to complainant; a mere showing that a deadly weapon was used in a battery and identification of the perpetrator would be insufficient. *People v Johnson*, 278 NE 2d 177/Ill (1971).

Under the laws of most states, aggravated or felonious assault is not necessarily a specific intent crime (*State v Bitting*, 291 A 2d 240/Con–1971). Where the means used is likely to or does cause great bodily injury, such as assault by fire, or where a dangerous or deadly weapon is used, the assault is "aggravated" regardless of the intent of the assailant. *State v Matthewson*, 498 P 2d 575/Az (1972); *State v Hayden*, 267 S 2d 551/La (1972).

Assault With Hands or Feet

Hands and feet are not deadly weapons, but one may be convicted of a felonious assault where either the feet or hands were used and serious injury was inflicted or where they were used in a manner calculated to produce death or great bodily injury. *State v Clark*, 521 P 2d 298/Kan (1974); *State v Wraggs*, 496 SW 2d 38/Mo (1973).

Assault With Firearms

If one who is within shooting distance menacingly points a gun at another, he commits as assault whether or not the gun is loaded. *State v Murphy*, 500 P 2d 1276/Wn (1972).

Although apprehension in the mind of the assailed is not an element of assault (*State v Wigley*, 488 P 2d 766/Wn–1971), apprehension may be inferred when one points a revolver at another *unless the victim knows the gun to be unloaded* (*State v Miller*, 426 P 2d 986/Wn–1967), and malice may be inferred where one fires point-blank at the head of another. *Gonzales v People*, 452 P 2d 46/Colo (1969).

Defendant was found guilty of second degree assault—a felony—where he withdrew a pistol from his belt and angrily ordered air pollution control officers off his property and officers testified that defendant pointed the gun at them. *State v Murphy*, 500 P 2d 1276/Wn (1972).

Under a statute forbidding the pointing of a gun at another except under described circumstances, defendant's act of pointing a pistol at a friend in a fast-draw demonstration amounted to an assault. *State v Blanton*, 200 SE 2d 425/NC (1973).

A statute prohibiting the pointing of a "gun, pistol or other firearm" authorized conviction of defendant for pointing a B-B gun at another. *Com v Lowary*, 313 A 2d 317/Pa (1973).

Where, after a robbery was accomplished through fear by the pointing of a gun at victims, and after the robbery was complete defendant forced victims to lie on the floor where he again pointed the gun at them, there was a separate and distinct assault which did not merge with the robbery and defendant could be properly convicted of both robbery and assault with a deadly weapon. *State v Gregory*, 501 P 2d 387/Az (1972).

Defendant's conviction of assault on a peace officer was sustained where he claimed he thought the officer was his wife's suitor and he hid in a closet and looked at the uniformed officer through an opening in the door; upon being commanded by the officer to come out, he emerged with a loaded pistol in his hand "somewhat leveled" at the officer and refused to drop it upon command of the officer. *People v Prante*, 493 P 2d 1083/Colo (1972).

The shooting of or shooting at another without legal reason is an aggravated or felonious assault and/or battery, and defendant cannot defend on the theory of consent—even where victim procured a pistol, handed it to defendant and said, "Go ahead and shoot me if you want to," whereupon defendant picked up the pistol, put the muzzle against victim's head and pulled the trigger—wounding victim seriously. *State v Fransua*, 510 P 2d 106/NM (1973).

Under a statute which forbade firing at or into a dwelling house, defendant could be properly convicted although he was physically inside the house at the time he fired a shot into the floor. *Gaines v Com*, 505 SW 2d 174/Ky (1974).

"Assault With Intent to Murder" Defined

The elements of assault and battery with intent to kill under Indiana law are: the unlawful touching of another human being in a rude, insolent or angry manner with intent to kill (*Allison v State*, 299 NE 2d 618/Ind–1973). Intent to kill may be inferred where defendant employed a deadly weapon in a manner likely to produce death (*Chandle v State*, 198 SE 2d 289/Ga–1973). Under Texas law, in a prosecution for assault with intent to commit murder, the state must prove the assault and a specific intent to kill (*Boazman v State*, 501 SW 2d 894/Tex—1973). But compare this definition with the following: the California courts have held that proof of intent to kill is not the same as proof of intent to murder; thus, proof of an assault with intent to commit murder requires proof beyond a mere assault with intent to kill. The state must prove the assault, the specific intent to take the life of another, under circumstances which would have been murder had the actor succeeded. But the state need not prove which degree the murder would have been had the act been accomplished (*People v Heffington*, 107 CR 859/Cal—1973); (*Bremer v State*, 307 A 2d 503/Md—1973). There may be an assault with intent to kill under circumstances in which the killing, if accomplished, would only amount to voluntary manslaughter. *People v Heffington, supra; Lay v State*, 501 SW 2d 820/Ten (1973).

Assault with intent to commit murder and attempted murder are not identical offenses; although the assault contains all the elements of an attempt, the reverse is not true. *People v Provencher*, 108 CR 792/Cal (1973).

Examples of Assault to Commit Murder

Defendant's conviction of assault with intent to commit murder was sustained where evidence showed that he assaulted his cell mate with a club made from three bars of soap wrapped in a towel, and another towel which he used in an attempt to strangle his victim. *United States v Daulton*, 488 F 2d 524/Ga (1973).

Where evidence showed that defendant and a companion entered a service station at 2:30 a.m., and defendant pointed a pistol at victim stating, "This is a stick-up," then "chuckled" and shot victim at point-blank range, there was sufficient evidence to warrant the conclusion that defendent intended to commit murder. *People v Hammonds*, 297 NE 2d 743/Ill (1973).

A criminal who demands under threat of death and possessing the power of execution, that a security guard or a police officer assist him to escape, is guilty of assault with intent to commit murder. *Gavin v State*, 259 S 2d 544/Fla (1972).

Where defendant, a police captain, placed an explosive device in the engine compartment of the automobile of a newspaper reporter, wired so as to detonate upon activation of the ignition, and the bomb did explode injuring the reporter, a conviction of assault with intent to commit murder was warranted. *People v Kynette*, 104 P 2d 794/certiorari denied *Kynette v California*, 312 US 703/Cal (1940).

Examples of Assault to Commit Rape

Assault with intent to commit rape requies: (1) an assault and (2) the intent, not merely to have sexual intercourse, but to have sexual intercourse against the will and without the consent of the victim. The mere vigorous handling of the female against her will with the intent and hope of arousing desire within the female which would lead to her acquiescence in the sex act, although an indecent assault, would not sustain conviction of assault with intent to commit rape (*United States v Bryant*, 420 F 2d 1327/DC–1969); (*Bass v State*, 263 S 2d 611/Fla–1972). And where the state proves assault with intent to have sexual intercourse only, it has fallen short of proving assault with intent to commit rape. *Bass v State, supra.*

In a prosecution for assault with intent to commit rape, evidence of lack of chastity of the prosecutrix is admissible as relevant to the issue of consent, the theory being that a female of unchaste character is more likely to consent to the act (*State v Simmons*, 368 P 2d 378/Wn–1962). Also, previous consensual acts of sexual intercourse between defendant and prosecutrix are admissible as bearing on possible consent of the prosecutrix and intent of defendant. *Smiloff v State*, 439 P 2d 772/Alk (1968).

Under Texas law where the prosecution is for the crime of rape by force, it is not necessary to allege that the injured female is not the wife of defendant. *Craig v State*, 478 SW 2d 86/Tex (1972).

In a prosecution for assault and battery with intent to commit rape where it is alleged that the victim is under the age of legal consent, it is only necessary that the state establish a touching of the person of the female child with intent to have sexual intercourse with her. *Kelly v State*, 280 NE 2d 55/Ind (1972).

Intent to rape was properly inferred from defendant's conduct of pushing victim against a wall, placing a knife against her neck, kissing her and fondling her vagina with his finger and by telling her if she screamed again he would kill her. *People v Williams*, 299 NE 2d 500/Ill (1973).

Although assault with intent to commit rape is a specific intent crime, testimony by the prosecutrix that defendant "was so drunk he did not even know his name," did not establish, as a matter of law, that defendant was incapable of forming the requisite intent (*State v Gailey*, 204 P 2d 254/Id–1969). And where defendant tore away victim's clothing, fractured her maxillary bone and inflicted other lesser injuries, the fact that he was impotent because of his intoxicated condition and could not effect penetration, did not act to negate his intent. *United States v Contreras*, 422 F 2d 828/Nev (1970).

Where the suspect, a murder parolee, who was naked from the waist down, in the early morning hours entered the bedroom of his victim who was bedridden and in an institution and climbed atop prosecutrix holding her arms and threatening to choke her, desisting only after she screamed, the conclusion that he intended to have sexual intercourse with her against her will and without her consent was warranted, thus sustaining conviction of assault with intent to commit rape. *State v LaVine*, 411 P 2d 436/Wn (1966).

Administering Poison

"Administering poison" with intent to kill means more than presenting or offering the poison to another to be ingested into the body. Thus, where evidence showed that defendant sent poisoned candy through the U.S. mail to a family intending that they eat it but instead the candy was thrown away, there was no administering under the statute. *People v Gaither*, 343 P 2d 799/Cal (1959).

Threats Made Criminal by Statute

Threats against the life of the President of the United States are made criminal under federal law, and lack of intent to carry out the threat or that the threat was made in jest is immaterial. *Watts v United States*, 394 US 705/DC (1969); Title 18, § 871 (a).

Where defendant threatened to bomb a public school, his intent to bomb or not to bomb was irrelevant, the crime being complete when the threat was made (*State v Young*, 523 P 2d 934/Wn–1974), and a refusal of proffered instruction to the contrary was not error. *United States v Nusz*, 462 F 2d 617/Az (1972).

Assaults Upon Peace Officers

A state may constitutionally view a deliberate attack upon an officer in his line of duty as a greater social evil than a similar attack on a private citizen (*People v Hanson*, 289 NE 2d 611/Ill–1972), but it is incumbent upon the state to prove that the assailant knew or should have known that the assailed was a peace officer. *Celmer v Quarberg*, 203 NW 2d 45/Wis (1973).

Under the laws of many states a simple battery knowingly committed upon a police officer in the line of duty thus becomes an aggravated battery—a felony. *People v Brown*, 310 NE 2d 498/Ill (1974).

MAYHEM

Defined

Every person who shall unlawfully and maliciously deprive another of a member of his body, or who shall disable, disfigure or render the member useless, or who shall cut or disable the tongue, put out an eye or slit the ear, nose or lip, shall be guilty of mayhem. California Penal Code, § 203.

In General

A statute making it an offense to commit mayhem or maliciously disfigure another requires permanance of injury or disfigurement in some appreciable form. "Disfigure," as here used, is to make less complete, perfect or beautiful in appearance or character; "disfigurement," in law as in common acceptation, may well be something less than total and irreversible deterioration of a bodily organ. *United States v Cook*, 462 F 2d 301/DC (1972).

It is not necessary that the body member be destroyed by the direct act of defendant as destruction or diminution of vigor may result indirectly. Thus, where defendant willfully and maliciously bit the finger of victim, necessitating its subsequent amputation due to infection, defendant was guilty of mayhem. *People v Montes*, 204 P 2d 659/Cal (1949).

Cosmetic effects of scarring may be sufficiently severe to bring the assault within the ambit of a statute prohibiting malicious disfigurement. *United States v Cook, supra.*

Examples of Mayhem

Where defendant-physician, with the aid of three accomplices, kidnaped the suspected paramour of defendant's wife and transported him to an isolated area and there whipped and beat him; then defendant obtained a scalpel from his medical kit declaring his intention to emasculate victim but was stayed by one of his accomplices, whereupon defendant obtained a pair of pliers from his vehicle using them to beat victim in the area of the privates, finally tearing away the foreskin from victim's penis with the pliers, defendant's prosecution, *inter alia*, for mayhem was warranted. However, under the statute proscribing mayhem, substantial recovery at the time of the trial, prevented a conviction of mayhem but did support conviction of felony assault, first degree kidnap and medical disbarment. *State v Berry*, 93 P 2d 782/Wn (1939).

A malicious injury, such as a deliberate battery, inflicted upon another resulting in the loss of an eye is mayhem (*State v Hatley*, 484 P 2d 252/NM–1963); likewise, the malicious throwing of lye water into the eyes of another resulting in near total blindness is mayhem. *People v Crooms*, 152 P 2d 533/Cal (1944); *United States v Cook*, 462 F 2d 301/DC (1972).

Defendant's conviction of mayhem was sustained where evidence showed both that he burned the leg of a three-year-old child causing disfigurement and that the burns were maliciously inflicted. *People v Strohm*, 523 P 2d 973/Colo (1973).

Under a statute declaring the malicious slitting of the ear to be mayhem, the method of slitting is immaterial; where two women engaged in a fight and one bit out a section of the other's ear, the act was mayhem. *Lamb v Cree*, 466 P 2d 660/Nev (1970).

Although there was evidence that defendant cut off part of the hair from victim's head and her pubic area, hit and kicked her, whipped her with a branch, cut her wrist with a knife, and burned her with a lighted cigarette and the cigarette lighter from a car, it failed to support a charge of mayhem. *United States v Stone*, 472 F 2d 909/Ga (1973).

Chapter XIV

Sex Offenses

RAPE

Defined

"Rape" at common law consisted of carnal knowledge with a female over the age of ten years, forcibly without her consent and against her will, or with a female under the age of ten years whether or not with consent. *CJS*–Rape, at 75.

The term "ravish" means more than mere sexual intercourse; it implies force, and means carnal knowledge with a woman by force and against her will and without her consent. "Ravish" is synonymous with "rape." *State v Abron*, 492 SW 2d 387/Mo (1973).

Under the laws of most states rape is an act of sexual intercourse with a female who is not the wife of the actor, under any of the following circumstances:

1. When she is under the legal age of consent;
2. When the act is committed forcibly against her will and without her consent;
3. When committed without her consent and against her will, and her resistance is prevented through threat of great bodily injury and such injury appears imminent;
4. When the act is accomplished without the consent of the female through the administration of a drug, narcotic or anesthetic which renders her incapable of resisting;

5. Where the female is prevented through lunacy or other unsoundness of mind of giving legal consent;
6. When the female is unconscious as to the nature of the act and this is known to the accused;
7. When the accused has perpetrated a counterfeit marriage through hoax and pretense and the female believes she is legally married. California Penal Code, § 261.

Under subparagraph 1, *supra*, an act of sexual intercourse is rape whether or not committed with the consent of the female. This type of rape is usually referred to as "statutory rape," but under the laws of some states the act is called "carnal knowledge" and includes the sex act committed upon a child of either sex (Kentucky and Washington, among others, punish this act as carnal knowledge). KRS 435.100; RCW 9.79.020.

In General

Most jurisdictions view rape as a complaint easily made, hard to prove and harder to defend; consequently, courts exercise great care and vigilance to assure that a conviction therefor is based on competent evidence and is not a result of passion and prejudice or inspired by a malicious contriver. *State v Atkinson*, 209 NW 2d 154/Neb (1973).

Assault and battery are necessarily included offenses of forcible rape. *State v Worrey*, 322 A 2d 73/Me (1974).

A verdict of assault with intent to commit rape was not defective notwithstanding that rape was actually committed. *State v Banks*, 213 NW 2d 483/Ia (1973).

Rape requires no specific intent, and voluntary intoxication is neither an excuse nor a justification. *State v Ramirez*, 500 P 2d 451/NM (1972).

Two acts of sexual intercourse within a short period of time under circumstances amounting to rape are considered but one act of rape. *Turnbow v State*, 454 P 2d 674/Ok (1969).

Complaint of the Prosecutrix

The first person to whom the prosecutrix complains after the attack usually may testify to the fact of complaint, physical appearance and emotional condition of complainant, but may not testify as to details of her complaint such as naming her assailant, unless her statement was made under circumstances making it admissible under the *res gestae* rule of evidence as an "excited utterance." *State v Finley*, 338 P 2d 790/Az (1959). *State v Blake*, 495 P 2d 1208/Or (1972).

Although it is a universal rule that the complaint of the prosecutrix made soon after rape is admissible to show her state of mind, failure to make timely complaint is admissible on behalf of the defendant as a circumstance tending to discredit her testimony (*Padilla v People*, 397 P 2d 741/Colo–1964). It should be understood, however, that where the complaint is delayed for an undue length of time, prosecution of defendant is not thereby foreclosed; it merely means that the first person to whom the victim complained may not testify to the fact of complaint or to the physical and emotional condition of the prosecutrix. The prosecutrix, however, may testify in any case to all pertinent facts surrounding the case.

When rape appears probable to the prosecutrix and she does not flee when opportunity presents itself, does not complain of the attack at the first opportunity nor offer a satisfactory explanation for her behavior, there is a strong presumption against the truth of her complaint. *Gullat v State*, 158 P 2d 353/Ok (1945).

Testimony offered by a third person of a complaint of rape by the prosecutrix, is not an exception to the hearsay rule, as victim's complaint is not offered to prove the truth of the complaint, but rather the fact of complaint and the physical and emotional condition of prosecutrix at the time of complaint. *People v Brown*, 100 CR 854/Cal (1973).

Corroboration of the Prosecutrix

At common law, the testimony of the prosecutrix in the trial of all offenses against the chastity of women was alone sufficient to support a conviction, and corroborating evidence or circumstances were not necessary. *State v Fisher*, 212 NW 2d 568/Neb (1973).

Although a few jurisdictions require corroboration of the testimony of the prosecutrix to sustain conviction–Arizona, Georgia, Nebraska, New York, the District of Columbia, to name a few–the vast majority of jurisdictions hold to the contrary where the complaint of the prosecutrix is timely made and is not inherently improbable. Corroboration is proof of a different nature but to the same point. *State v Navarro*, 367 P 2d 227/Az (1961); *Morgan v State*, 192 SE 2d 338/Ga (1972).

Case law is replete with decisions negating the requirement of corroboration of the prosecutrix. But where there is delay in making the complaint, or where there are inconsistencies in statements made by the prosecutrix, or a conflict in the evidence, the appellate courts will scrutinize the record closely for abuses of discretion and misconduct which may have prejudiced the defendant. *Gullat v State, supra.*

Under a statute requiring corroboration of the testimony of the prosecutrix, prompt complaint by the prosecutrix may furnish sufficient corroboration (*State v Ferguson*, 196 NW 2d 374/Neb–1972), or corroboration may be established wholly by circumstantial evidence. *People v Bercume*, 329 NYS 2d 862/NY (1972).

Under Indiana law, which characterizes the majority rule, conviction of rape may be sustained on the sole uncorroborated testimony of the prosecutrix whether the charge is statutory rape or forcible rape. *Maul v State*, 300 NE 2d 678/Ind (1973).

Penetration—When Complete

Sexual intercourse occurs when there is any penetration, however slight, of the female organ by the male organ (*People v Polk*, 294 NE 2d 113/Ill—1973), and the fact that the victim does not resist at that instant does not deprive the sex act of its forceful and violent character. *People v Adkins*, 508 P 2d 377/Colo (1973).

Proof of emission is never essential to a conviction for rape, incest, sodomy, adultery or carnal knowledge. *State v Haston*, 166 P 2d 141/Az (1946).

Defendant's conviction of forcible rape upon a five-month-old infant was reversed on the grounds that the state did not prove penetration of the female organ by the male organ beyond a reasonable doubt. Although penetration of the vagina of the infant was proved, proof that penetration was made by the insertion of defendant's penis was inconclusive. *People v Borders*, 195 NW 2d 331/Mich (1972).

Although penetration to the slightest degree completes the crime of rape—other elements being present—this fact must be proved beyond a reasonable doubt (*Nilsson v State*, 477 SW 2d 592/Tex—1972). But testimony to the fact of pentration by the prosecutrix is not essential, as where she is rendered unconscious by the accused; penetration then may be established by circumstantial evidence. Id.

Effect of Consent

If the conduct of the prosecutrix toward the defendant at the time of the alleged sex act, was such as to create in the mind of the accused an honest and reasonable belief that the prosecutrix had consented or was willing for defendant to have connection with her, defendant should be acquitted. *Rhoden v State*, 274 S 2d 630/Ala (1973).

Consent induced through fear of personal violence is not consent though a man lay no hands on a woman; yet if, by an array of physical force, he so overpowers her mind that she does not resist, he is guilty of rape if sexual intercourse follows. *State v Walker*, 484 SW 2d 284/Mo (1972).

Where the complaining witness is under the age of consent, defendant's act of sexual commerce with her is rape even though she gives her consent and cooperates in the act with defendant in every way. *State v Klein*, 200 NW 2d 288/ND (1972).

Reluctant submission to the sex act does not imply consent (*State v Thomas*, 510 P 2d 1137/Wn—1973). Consent is an act of free will exercised by the female, and it is synonymous with the absence of resistance in the face of actual or threatened force. *Com v Hayden*, 307 A 2d 389/Pa (1973).

When defendant's defense to rape is consent, the reputation of the prosecutrix for unchastity is admissible to show probability of consent, but if defendant denies intercourse then prosecutrix' reputation is irrelevent. *Brown v State,* 280 S 2d 177/Ala (1973).

Effect of Chastity

In a prosecution for rape the reputation of the prosecutrix for chastity in the community in which she lives has substantial probative value in judging the likelihood for her consent, but specific acts of sexual intercourse with one other than the defendant are usually not admissible to establish reputation for chastity. *Hicks v Hiatt,* 64 FS 238/Pa (1946).

A woman who is "chaste" is one who has never had an unlawful act of sexual intercourse, and an act of sexual intercourse without her consent and against her will, if she is capable of consent, does not destroy her chastity. But where the female consented to sexual intercourse with one member of a group who told her that it was either him or the whole group, her chastity was not destroyed for purposes of prosecution of the remaining members for rape. *State v Brionez,* 197 NW 2d 639/Neb (1972).

Although under Nebraska law chastity is defined as a virtue in a woman who has never had an act of unlawful intercourse, a better definition would appear to be where the woman has never had an act of sexual intercourse outside wedlock. Consensual sexual intercourse between unmarried adults is legal in most states and under the Nebraska definition a woman could be legally chaste but morally promiscuous. *State v Brionez, supra.*

Degree of Resistance Required

The rule at common law which required the victim of an attack to resist to her utmost, is obsolete in virtually all jurisdictions, not being included in the substantive law of today. Rather, the amount of resistance required to show the victim's nonconsent varies with the circumstances, such as the relative ages, sizes and strengths of the parties. *State v Dizon,* 390 P 2d 759/Haw (1964).

If the type of rape alleged is forcible rape, the state must prove not only rape, but also that the acts performed were forcible and against the will of the prosecutrix, and the degree of force exerted by the defendant and the amount of resistance required by the female depend on facts of the individual case. *People v Smith,* 288 NE 2d 694/Ill (1972).

Under a charge of forcible rape the state need not show that the female fought to the last ditch as threats of bodily harm coupled with some degree of force constitute the crime; as where the defendant seized the victim in a park, twisted her arm behind her back, forced her to the ground and, while lying on top of her, told her three times with increasing menace, "Take your clothes off and I won't hurt you." *Laughlin v United States*, 368 F 2d 558/Wn (1966).

In a prosecution for rape of the first degree under New York law, contrary to the general rule, the state must prove that the victim opposed the man's advances to the utmost limits of her power, and resistance must be genuine and active. *People v Hughes*, 343 NYS 2d 240/NY (1973).

When Committed Under Threat

Resistance was not an element of rape where the accused told the prosecutrix he had a knife and would not hesitate to use it if she resisted, whereupon he effected penetration without resistance (*State v Kidwell*, 475 P 2d 241/Az–1970). It is not incumbent on the state to offer evidence of resistance when there is evidence that the female was deterred by threats of imminent and great bodily harm. *Cortez v People*, 394 P 2d 346/Colo (1964).

One may be guilty of rape although the female offers no resistance—for example, where she is prevented from resisting through fear of physical violence to herself or to her children—and it is immaterial that the threat of violence comes from one other than the perpetrator if such threat was with the knowledge of the accused. *State v Gray*, 497 SW 2d 545/Mo (1973).

Apparent acquiescence of the victim after the rape provides no defense to the accused. Thus, where after the rape the defendant offered five dollars to the victim and she accepted it, the rape was not purged thereby nor was defendant absolved of any aspect of criminal responsibility. *State v Fowler*, 89 P 757/Id (1907).

Where the Female Is of Unsound Mind

Where the female is incapable through lunacy or other unsoundness of mind of giving legal consent, an act of sexual intercourse with her, even though consensual, is rape. Such denouncement, of course, presupposes that she is incapable of understanding the nature and possible consequences of the sex act, but the mere fact that the female is retarded and has a mental age of less than fourteen years would not necessarily make the act rape. *Hacker v State*, 118 P 2d 408/Ok (1941).

Sexual intercourse with a mentally retarded woman having the equivalent of the mind of a two-year-old is rape. Here, the victim was retarded to the extent that she could not talk or feed herself and her only means of locomotion was to "scoot" around. *Bradford v State*, 477 SW 2d 544/Tex 1972). But where defendant was charged with the rape of a mentally diseased woman and evidence showed that her diseases was interspersed with lucid intervals during which times she could appear normal, and there was no evidence as to defendant's knowledge of the victim's mental incapacity, his conviction of rape could not stand. *Harris v State*, 474 SW 2d 706/Tex (1972).

Unconsciousness or Deceit

The courts have consistently held that resistance is not an element when the victim was unconscious (*State v Hashimoto*, 339 P 2d 146/Haw–1963), or asleep (*State v Stroud*, 240 SW 2d 111/Mo–1951), or mentally retarded (*People v Boggs*, 290 P 2d 618/Cal–1930), or under the age of consent (*State v Nab*, 421 P 2d 388/Or–1966), or under heavy sedation (*Rhine v State*, 336 P 2d 913/Ok–1959). Also, the courts have held that an act of sexual intercourse was rape where the female was deceived into thinking she was receiving a digital genital examination or massage from a physician. *State v Ely*, 194 P 988/Wn (1921).

Where defendant, a physician, administered nembutal to his intended victims by injection thus destroying their will to resist, although conscious, he was guilty of rape notwithstanding that prosecutrix delayed nearly a year before making complaint. *Rhine v State, supra; People v Ing*, 422 P 2d 590/Cal (1967).

The word "unconscious," as used to describe the condition of a rape victim—such as "unconscious as to the nature of the act"—does not necessarily mean a comatose condition or a state of insensibility, and includes sexual intercourse with the woman while she is asleep. *Ex parte Childers*, 310 P 2d 776/Ok (1957).

Rape by Aiding and Abetting

One of the elements of rape is penetration; thus, the crime can only be committed by a male. However, a female who was an accessory before the fact in rape committed by a male, may be prosecuted and convicted as a principal of a crime impossible for her to commit if acting alone (*Green v State*, 270 S 2d 695/Mis–1972). Rape by aiding and abetting may be summed up as follows: the *corpus delicti* of rape being proved—that one had sexual intercourse with a female against her will and without her consent—it is possible to convict one woman of raping another, here the victim's mother aided and abetted in the debauchery of her daughter (*People v Haywood*, 280 P 2d 180/Cal–1955); and likewise, a husband may be convicted of the rape of his wife where he counsels and encourages another to have sexual intercourse with her by force while he remains in the background, declining to interfere (*State v Blackwell*, 407 P 2d 617/Or–1965); (*Cody v State*, 376 P 2d 625/Ok–1962). The North Carolina court has ruled that "The husband who aids and abets another to ravish his wife . . . may be convicted as if he were a stranger . . . . Though in marriage she has given up her body to her husband, she is not to be by him prostituted to another . . . ." *State v Martin*, 194 SE 2d 60/NC (1973).

Acquittal of the man who actually ravished the victim did not preclude conviction of her husband for rape of his own wife where he held her while the other man raped her. *Rozell v State*, 502 SW 2d 16/Tex (1973).

Where defendant disrobed the victim he could be convicted of rape as an accessory before the fact even though he left the premises prior to the time codefendant had sexual intercourse with victim. *People v Gomez*, 519 P 2d 1191/Colo (1974).

Circumstantial Proof

Rape may be established by circumstantial evidence where testimony of the victim is not available; here, a two-year-old girl was the victim of rape which was established by blood on defendant's shorts, opportunity to commit the crime, and testimony by an examining physician that victim's vagina was torn almost to her rectum. *Scott v State*, 492 SW 2d 902/Ark (1973).

Sex Acts Not Amounting to Rape

Where there was evidence that prosecutrix had made no serious effort to resist defendant's advances, had kissed defendant, had ridden with her arm around defendant to the place where she was allegedly raped, could not remember whether she or the defendant had removed her clothes and she failed to make timely complaint after the incident, a reasonable doubt as to defendant's guilt was created, thus warranting acquittal. *People v Bain*, 283 NE 2d 701/Ill (1972).

Under a statute proscribing rape by force, force is implied when sexual intercourse or deviate sex acts are accomplished under the pretext of medical examination or treatment and the female is unaware of the perpetrator's intent and purpose. But where she became aware that defendant had applied his mouth to her vulva, after which he inserted his sex organ into her vagina, she must have been aware of his intent and it then became her duty to resist further acts and her failure to resist was the equivalent of implied consent—deviate sexual assault affirmed, rape reversed. *People v Borok*, 301 NE 2d 1/Ill (1973).

Where evidence showed that defendant had sexual intercourse with his victim after having kidnaped and asported her some five to ten miles, conviction of rape was reversed upon the basis of defendant's testimony that before he engaged in the sex act with her he shot her through the head and her death was virtually instantaneous. There can be no rape unless the victim is alive at the instant of penetration. *People v Stanworth*, 522 P 2d 1058/Cal (1974).

STATUTORY RAPE

Defined

In a prosecution for carnal knowledge the state must prove that (1) defendant carnally knew and abused the female; (2) that she was at the time under the age of consent; and (3) she was not the wife of the perpetrator. Chastity of the female is not pertinent to the issue and is usually inadmissible except in rare cases and then only for limited purposes. *State v Linton,* 216 P 2d 761/Wn (1950); *People v Harper,* 204 NW 2d 263/Mich (1972).

In General

"Sexual intercourse" and "carnal knowledge" have been held to be synonymous as has "rape" and "carnal knowledge," but the definitions are not comparable in all states. In those jurisdictions where there exists a statute forbidding carnal knowledge, it is not synonymous with sexual intercourse, for sexual intercourse may be lawful and carnal knowledge is criminal. *State v Flippin,* 186 SE 2d 917/NC (1972).

Any sexual penetration, however slight, satisfies a statute forbidding either carnal knowledge, statutory rape or forcible rape (*State v Ray,* 286 P 2d 423/Wn–1963). "Penetration" means the slightest penetration of the body of the female by the sexual organ of the male and can only be accomplished by "penial" not "digital" penetration. *State v Hughes,* 456 P 2d 393/Az (1969).

Where the victim was under the age of 18 years and married to another although sexual intercourse was consensual, defendant was guilty of statutory rape (*People v Courtney,* 4 CR 274/Cal–1960), or carnal knowledge, depending on the wording of the denouncing statute. *State v Huntsman,* 204 P 2d 448/Ut (1949).

Where a female is under the age of consent, in most states 18 years, and has consensual sexual intercourse with a male over the age of 18 years, not her husband, such act is criminal but the name of the crime may vary. It may be second degree rape, as in Arizona (*State v White,* 398 P 2d 903/Az–1965), or statutory rape as in Idaho (*State v Gee,* 470 P 2d 296/Id–1970), or carnal knowledge, as in Utah. *State v Hodges,* 381 P 2d 81/Ut (1963).

The various jurisdictions are not in agreement as to the right of defendant to cross-examine the female in a prosecution for carnal knowledge as to previous acts of unchastity. The Alabama Criminal Court of Appeals has ruled that to allow such cross-examination is illogical and contrary to the weight of authority in the courts of last resort in the United States, and declared that defendant had no such right. *State v Linton,* 216 P 2d 761/Wn (1950); *Gandy v State,* 269 S 2d 141/Ala (1972).

Proof of Age

Failure to allege the age of the female in an information charging rape is a fatal error where the charge is statutory rape as proof of age of the accused is necessary to determine the grade of the offense and the punishment to be imposed. *Thomas v Sheriff of Clark County,* 504 P 2d 1313/Nev (1973).

How Proved

In a prosecution for carnal knowledge the pregnancy of the female is relevant to show she had previously had sexual intercourse with someone (*State v Hodges*, 381 P 2d 81/Ut–1963). Likewise, where the victim's doctor testified that victim's vagina was infested with fresh gonorrhea germs, the exclusion of testimony of defendant's doctor that defendant was free from veneral disease for the purpose of showing that prosecutrix had had sexual intercourse with an unknown man prior to the act with defendant, was proper as such prior or subsequent act with another would in no way absolve defendant of criminal responsibility. *State v Atkinson*, 209 NW 2d 154/Neb (1973).

The law does not permit a child under the statutory age of consent to consent to sexual intercourse. Accordingly, it was immaterial that victim told defendant that she was over the statutory age and likewise immaterial that defendant believed her. *Hughes v State*, 198 NW 2d 348/Wis (1972).

Prior acts of consensual sexual intercourse between defendant and the prosecutrix are not admissible if offered by the defendant, but are admissible when offered by the state to show the relation of the parties as corroboration of the testimony of the prosecutrix (*State v Gee*, 470 P 2d 296/Id–1970), or to show the lustful disposition of the defendant toward the prosecutrix. *State v Harold*, 275 P 2d 895/Wn (1954).

Delay in making a complaint of rape may have the effect of diminishing the value of the complaint but does not affect its competency. *State v Tirone*, 308 A 2d 38/NJ (1973).

Principal or Accessory to Statutory Rape

Under the rules of principality in crime it is not necessary to a conviction to show that defendant personally had sexual intercourse with the female. Thus, where defendant encouraged two minors—the boy 18 and the girl 16—to engage in an act of sexual intercourse while he photographed their activity, he became a principal by advising and encouraging the crime (*People v Lewis*, 248 P 2d 416/Cal–1952). Likewise, where defendant, a motel manager, rented a room to a male and a female with knowledge that the room was to be used for sexual intercourse and that the girl was below the age of consent, his conviction of statutory rape was warranted, notwithstanding that the actual perpetrator was allowed to give evidence for the state and was never tried for the rape. *People v Wood*, 205 P 2d 698/Cal (1922).

Consent—No Defense

Virtually all jurisdictions hold that consent of the prosecutrix is no defense and this is true even though she solicits the embraces of the male; resistance of the female is not an element. *State v Stevens*, 172 P 2d 299/Mont (1946).

Where the sex act is with a female under the age of consent, the only remaining element of the *corpus delicti* is penetration, for when a child under the age of consent is the victim the law conclusively presumes force and the question of consent is immaterial. *United States v Jones*, 477 F 2d 1213/DC (1973).

Good Faith Belief of Age of Consent

In a charge of statutory rape it has been traditionally held that defendant's good faith belief that prosecutrix was of the age of consent, even though induced by the female's deceit as to her age, is inadmissible. In 1964 the California courts overruled this concept observing that defendant's good faith belief in the majority of the female *was* relevant and should be admitted into evidence (*People v Hernandez*, 393 P 2d 373/Cal–1964). In reviewing this issue in 1971, the Hawaii Supreme Court ruled that in the seven years following the Hernandez decision, not one other state had elected to follow the California ruling and that court did not choose to do so then. *State v Silva*, 491 P 2d 1216/Haw (1971).

CHILD MOLESTATION

Defined

This crime–variously described as lewdness, child molestation or indecent liberties–consists of three elements: (1) a lewd or lascivious act upon any part of the body (2) of a child as defined under local law (3) with intent to arouse or gratify the passions of either the child or the perpetrator. But is is not necessary that the passion of either be aroused. California Penal Code, § 288.

"Private parts" include not only the reproductive organs but the surrounding area. Where defendant lowered the pants of an eleven-year-old girl and fondled her bare buttocks the jury was justified in finding that he fondled her private parts. *State v Blount*, 286 A 2d 36/NJ (1972).

Examples

Defendant's conviction of rape and child molestation was sustained where evidence showed that defendant had first had sexual intercourse with his adopted daughter when she was nine years old, had had sexual intercourse with her over a period of five years, had requested permission from his wife to have sexual intercourse with the daughter, had taken obscene photos of her, had practiced nudism for some time and refused to allow members of the family to close the bathroom door when using its facilities. *State v Finley*, 501 P 2d 4/Az (1972).

Where defendant's conduct consisted of standing nude in the doorway of his home and attracting the attention of three passing high school girls by saying, "Hi, girls," there was sufficient evidence to warrant conviction for indecent exposure. *State v Prince*, 206 NW 2d 660/Min (1973).

Reaching under the dress of a 13-year-old girl and touching her abdomen was indecent within the purview of a statute denouncing indecent assault. *State v Beaulieu*, 290 A 2d 850/RI (1972).

Sexual intercourse between husband and wife in the presence of their son who was under the age of 14 years for the alleged purpose of demonstrating the method of procreation by the human race, was a lewd and lascivious act in violation of the statute. *Chesebrough v State*, 255 S 2d 675/Fla (1971).

The testimony of defendant's ten-year-old daughter disclosing defendant's commission of unnatural lascivious acts upon her body, which consisted of placing his hands and his private parts on her private parts, was sufficient to prove lewdness and contributing to the delinquency of a minor. *People v Lett*, 160 P 2d 112/Cal (1945).

The masturbation of a 12-year-old boy by a 54-year-old man constituted indecent liberties contributing to the sexual delinquency of a child. *People v Keegan*, 286 NE 2d 345/Ill (1971).

Proof

As a rule the complaint of the prosecutrix to a third party may be related on the witness stand by the third party, but may not include details such as the naming of the defendant. The Washington courts have gone one step further: Two subjects, females, six years old, were victims of indecent exposure. Later one of the girls "burst into her home with a 'funny' look on her face," and in response to her mother's question related the incident. The mother informed the other girl's mother of the incident, and her daughter in response to questions stated that a man "had his pants open." Although the complaints of the two girls were not excited utterances and were made not spontaneously, but in response to questions, their mothers were permitted to testify to the complaints. Deviation from the rule was, no doubt, due to the tender ages of the victims. *State v Canida*, 480 P 2d 800/Wn (1971).

INCEST

"Incest" Defined

The essence of "incest" is marriage or sexual intercourse by two persons of the opposite sex who are related within the forbidden degrees of consanguinity. *Henley v State*, 489 SW 2d 53/Ten (1972).

"Consanguinity" Defined

In order to make out a *prima facie* case of incest the state must prove consanguinity. *People v Hawk*, 193 NW 2d 177/Mich (1971).

"Consanguinity" means relationship by blood. It is computed by two methods: linear, and lateral or collateral. Some jurisdictions dispense with this method by lumping all ancestors and decendants into the first degree followed by the lateral degrees. More specifically, consanguinity as it applies to incest, is computed as follows:

- Linear consanguinity:
  First degree—father-daughter/mother-son;
  Second degree—grandfather-granddaughter/grandmother-grandson
- Lateral consanguinity:
  First degree—siblings
  Second degree—uncle-neice/aunt-nephew
  Third degree—first cousins

Incest was not a common law crime in England and punishment therefor was left solely to the ecclesiastical courts. *People v Baker*, 447 P 2d 675/Cal (1968).

Virtually all jurisdictions forbid intermarriage or sexual intercourse between members of the first two degrees of either linear or lateral consanguinity and some jurisdictions include the third degree of either within its statutory proscription.

For the sex act to amount to incest the participants must be related by consanguinity and sexual intercourse with one related by affinity is not forbidden. Thus, where a stepfather had sexual intercourse with his stepdaughter there was no incest as the relationship was by affinity. *State v Bielman*, 150 P 1194/Wn (1915).

Whenever two persons are related within the forbidden degrees of consanguinity and engage in an act of sexual intercourse, the act is incest whether the relationship is legitimate or illegitimate. Thus, where defendant had sexual intercourse with his illegitimate daughter, the act was nevertheless incest. *State v Williams*, 213 P 921/Wn (1923).

Where the female is under the age of consent she is not an accomplice and not guilty of incest (*People v Hamilton*, 198 P 2d 907/Cal—1946). If the act of sexual intercourse amounted also to rape or carnal knowledge, it is no less incest and defendant would be guilty of both crimes. *People v Stratton*, 75 P 166/Cal (1904).

The chastity of the prosecutrix in a proceeding for incest is immaterial. *Hill v State*, 480 SW 2d 670/Tex (1972).

Necessary Proof

The states are not in agreement as to proof of incest. In some states defendant may be convicted solely on the uncorroborated testimony of the prosecutrix, as in Maine, where the testimony of defendant's 15-year-old daughter, although corroborated, would have been sufficient alone (*State v Frost*, 315 A 2d 198/Me–1974). However, under Texas law defendant's daughter, although only 13 years old, was held to be an accomplice in acts of sexual intercourse with her father, and under the law he could not be convicted solely on the testimony of an accomplice. *Bolin v State*, 505 SW 2d 912/Tex (1974).

Testimony of a daughter as to previous acts of sexual intercourse with her father and testimony of two other daughters to many previous acts of sexual intercourse, were admissible in a prosecution of the father for incest under two theories as an exception to the nonadmissibility of prior crimes: evidence relating to a general scheme or plan, and proof of motive or intent. *Hendrickson v State*, 212 NW 2d 481/Wis (1973); *Summit v State*, 285 S 2d 670/Fla (1973).

SEDUCTION

Defined

"Seduction" signifies a leading astray of a female of previously chaste character by inducing her to yield to an act of sexual commerce by any of a variety of artifices calculated to have that effect. *Hirschy v Coodley*, 253 P 2d 93/Cal (1953).

In General

Where an action was brought against defendant by the female's husband for the seduction of his 20-year-old wife, the court ruled: when a married woman freely engages in an act of unlawful sexual intercourse the act cannot be seduction. ". . . Only an unmarried female can be seduced. . . . Likewise, she must be chaste. . ." *Hirschy v Coodley, supra.*

Female Must Be Chaste

Where the female is seduced and submits to sexual intercourse under promise of marriage, the promise need not be expressed in any particular language; it is sufficient if the language used was calculated to, and did, convey a promise of marriage. *Ricky v State*, 126 P 2d 753/Ok (1942).

A female may be of "previously chaste character" for the purposes of seduction even though she is of mature years and has borne children, provided of course the children were not conceived outside wedlock. *Rockwell v Day*, 172 P 754/Wn (1918).

In a prosecution for seduction the chastity of the prosecutrix is presumed as is the innocence of the defendant. Although these presumptions are in conflict, there is no inconsistency in the dual application of both principles; both presumptions are rebuttable and, as in other cases of conflict, resolution is for the jury. *State v Jones*, 142 P 35/Wn (1914).

Proof of Unchastity

The defendant, in order to rebut the presumption of chastity of the prosecutrix, may properly introduce acts of lewdness and unchastity committed with other men (*State v Kellog*, 158 P 344 91 Wn 665 (1916), but prior acts of sexual intercourse between defendant and prosecutrix cannot be considered in assessing chastity at the time of the seduction. *State v Storrs*, 192 P 984/Wn (1920).

The chastity of the prosecutrix is presumed until the contrary is shown, and the burden of proving unchastity, where it is employed as an affirmative defense, is upon the defendant. A woman having been previously seduced, under Idaho law, although of unchaste character at the time, may refrain from other acts of debauchery and thus reformed again be the subject of seduction. *Fulgham v Gotfield*, 241 P 2d 824/Id (1952).

SODOMY

Defined

The phrase "crime against nature" is a euphemism for particular acts that constitute sodomy at common law. In its narrower sense, sodomy is carnal copulation between two human beings per anum, or copulation of a human being in any manner with a beast; in its broader sense sodomy means carnal copulation by human beings with each other against nature or with beast, in which sense it includes all acts of unnatural copulation. *Stephens v State* 489 SW 2d 542/Ten (1972).

Sodomy per anum is sometimes called buggery, the infamous crime, the crime against nature. Forty-eight *Am Jur*–Sodomy, § § 1–7.

In Nevada the sodomy statute includes not only the common law crime of sodomy, but also includes fellatio and all other unnatural acts of carnal copulation (*Hogan v State*, 441 P 2d 620/Nev–1968), and in Colorado cunnilingus has been specifically declared to come within the ambit of the sodomy statute. *Gilmore v People*, 467 P 2d 828/Colo (1970).

Under state laws differentiating between sodomy and oral copulation, defendant–who forced prosecutrix into a hotel room and there compelled her to submit to sexual intercourse, anal sodomy and fellatio–could be convicted of three crimes: rape, sodomy and sex perversion. *People v Battilana*, 126 P 2d 923/Cal (1942).

The common law definition of sodomy still endures in some states but has been declared void on its face in Florida for vagueness and uncertainty. It reads: "Whoever commits the abominable and detestable crime against nature, either with mankind or with beast, shall be punished by imprisonment in the state prison. . ." *Franklin v State*, 257 S 2d 21/Fla (1971).

Penetration Essential

Most jurisdictions hold, just as in rape or carnal knowledge, that penetration is essential to the crime of sodomy. A California court has held that the mere application of the mouth of one person to the sex organ of another, either to "kiss" or "lick" the organ, does not constitute copulation, a requisite element of the statute. *People v Angier*, 112 P 2d 659/Cal (1941).

Where evidence showed that defendant, a physiotherapist, hypnotized two girls who visited his office and the 17-year-old prosecutrix was placed upon a table and defendant attempted to insert his penis into her mouth, but because he was unable to pry her teeth apart he was unable to penetrate past her lips, his act was nevertheless sex perversion and conviction was sustained notwithstanding that prosecutrix did not make complaint until 21 months later. *People v Hickok*, 216 P 2d 140/Cal (1950).

Solicitation to Commit Sodomy

A statute which proscribes solicitation for the purpose of sodomy does not deny equal protection by prohibiting such acts between two men or a man and a woman but not between two women. *United States v Cozart*, 321 A 2d 342/DC (1972).

A statute prohibiting the solicitation to commit sodomy is within the domain of state power and such statute does not offend the First Amendment protection of freedom of speech. *Riley v United States*, 298 A 2d 288/DC (1972); *Lowe v City of Eugene*, 463 P 2d 360/Or (1969).

Acts Committed in Private

The question of whether a sodomy statute invaded the right to privacy was not before the appellate court when the offense was committed not in privacy, but upon a 14-year-old boy in an automobile on a public road adjacent to an interstate highway. *Connor v State*, 490 SW 2d 114/Ark (1973).

The Georgia courts have declared that acts of indecency committed within the privacy of one's home do not constitute crime. *Horne v State*, 186 SE 2d 542/Ga (1971).

Examples

In the crime of sodomy it is usually necessary that the sex organ of at least one participant be involved by penetration into an unnatural body cavity. Where evidence showed that an unknown "blunt object" was inserted into the anus of the prosecutrix and tore through the wall of the lower bowel into the vagina, the jury could reasonably infer that the blunt object was the sex organ of the defendant, thus warranting conviction under an Oregon statute of sexual perversity (*State v Anthony*, 169 P 2d 587/Or–1946). But the Maryland court has held that the fact that defendant penetrated victim's rectum with a mop handle or a broomstick rather than his sex organ did not render defendant's act any less an "unnatural or perverted sexual practice" within the laws of Maryland. *Edmonds v State*, 305 A 2d 205/Md (1973).

An act of oral sodomy committed during a stage performance was not a method of expression nor a form of speech protected by the First Amendment. *People v Drolet*, 105 CR 824/Cal (1973).

Where a state's witness testified to defendant's act of sexual intercourse with an animal but could not distinguish whether penetration was vaginal or anal, the court held the act to be sodomy as sexual intercourse between man and beast is sodomy whether penetration is vaginal or anal. *People v Smith*, 256 P 2d 586/Cal (1953).

Where defendant manifested his intent by declaring he was going to "screw" victim, a minor male, then violently attacked victim and disrobed him in an automobile, though victim was able to escape clad only in socks, defendant's act was clearly an attempt to commit sodomy. *State v Trejo*, 494 P 2d 173/NM (1972).

The act of masturbation of one adult male by another adult male is "an act committed in an unnatural manner" within the meaning of the statute denouncing lewd and lascivious conduct, but does not amount to sodomy. *State v Mortimer*, 467 P 2d 60/Az (1970).

Constitutionality of Sodomy Statutes

A sodomy statute which does not include within its prohibition the conduct of married couples, is constitutionally valid although consenting unmarried couples are included; if the couples are unmarried, consent is no defense (*State v Lair*, 301 A 2d 748/NJ–1973). Included within the statutory proscription are both heterosexual and homosexual acts. Id.

The sodomy statute does not violate the First Amendment on the grounds that those holding a majority belief have imposed their ethics on the minority who follow homosexual practices. *State v Rhinehart*, 424 P 2d 906/Wn (1967).

A statute which prohibits the infamous crime against nature either with mankind or animal, is neither ambiguous nor vague to the extent of being unenforceable, especially since the statute has been the subject of judicial construction for 58 years. *State v Carringer*, 523 P 2d 532/Id (1974).

A statute proscribing the crime against nature is not ambiguous and had a definite meaning at common law and is synonymous with sodomy. *Jellum v Cupp*, 475 F 2d 829/Or (1973).

Chapter XV

Kidnaping

Defined

The elements of kidnaping under federal law are: (1) the transportation across a state line (2) of a nonconsenting person (3) knowingly and willfully (4) for the purpose of ransom, reward or otherwise (*Hattaway v United States*, 399 F 2d 431/Fla–1968), and the purpose of the kidnaping need not be for reward or pecuniary gain (*Bailey v United States*, 410 F 2d 1209/Kan–1969), nor is harm to the victim an element of the *corpus delicti*, harm being relevant only when imposing sentence. *DeHerrera v United States*, 339 F 2d 587/NM (1964).

Kidnaping under state law is the unlawful taking and carrying away of a human being against his will by force, threats or fraud. *State v Tilley*, 196 SE 2d 818/NC (1973).

In General

Kidnaping is a type of crime which is rarely, if ever, an ultimate goal. It is employed as a means to an end, such as for the purpose of extortion, rape, robbery, air piracy, assault.

The gravamen of kidnaping is the use of compulsion in some form, but such compulsion need not consist of physical force or express threats. A taking is by force when it is accomplished as a result of orders from the accused, and the victim feels compelled under the circumstances to obey under fear of injury from the accused. *People v Dagampat*, 334 P 2d 581/Cal (1959).

Kidnaping under the common law contained all of the elements of false imprisonment and most jurisdictions view false imprisonment as a lesser included offense of kidnaping. *State v Evans*, 243 P 2d 975/Id (1952).

Definition of Force

Under the common law definition of kidnaping, the taking away of a person by the employment of fraud, threats or intimidation is the equivalent of the use of force. *State v Hudson*, 187 SE 2d 756/NC (1972).

Kidnaping is forcible when it is accomplished by the giving of orders which the victim feels compelled to obey for fear of harm or injury and such apprehension is not unreasonable under the circumstances. *People v Stephenson*, 517 P 2d 820/Cal (1974).

Movement of the Victim

Unless specifically required by the statute defining kidnaping, movement of the victim is not necessary. Thus, under a statute which forbids seizure or detention with intent to extort or obtain money by extortion, ransom, robbery or "otherwise," one would be guilty of kidnaping though the victim is not moved. *State v Taylor*, 312 P 2d 162/Az (1957).

Under some forms of kidnaping movement of the victim is necessary, but where movement is an element the distance moved is immaterial as it is the fact of, not the distance of, movement which completes the act (*Jensen v Sheriff*, 508 P 2d 4/Nev–1973). The forcing of an unwilling female into an automobile where she was restrained a short time, constituted kidnaping although she was moved only a few feet (*State v Padilla*, 474 P 2d 821/Az–1970), and the asportation of a female 11 feet for the purpose of rape was held to be sufficient asportation to violate the statute. *State v Ayers*, 426 P 2d 21/Kan (1967); *State v Hudson, supra.*

California holds, contrary to the weight of authority, that where the crime is essentially rape or robbery, to amount to kidnaping also, movement of the victim incidental thereto must substantially increase the risk of harm to the victim. Thus, in a kidnaping for the purpose of robbery, there must be proof that the asportation involved was not solely to facilitate robbery, or, if it was, that the movement of the victim substantially increased the risk of harm over and above that necessarily present in the crime of robbery itself (*People v Henderson*, 101 CR 129/Cal–1972). And asportation of the victim of kidnap "into another part of the same county" did not occur within the meaning of the kidnaping statute where victim was seized and raped, the entire incident occurring within a single room of a laundromat (*People v Thornton*, 523 P 2d 267/Cal–1974); nor was the asporting of victim from within her house to a place about 75 feet outside her house kidnaping, the court holding that such movement was trivial. *People v Stanworth*, 522 P 2d 1058/Cal (1974).

What Constitutes Bodily Harm

Where bodily harm is an element of kidnaping or of first degree kidnaping, it has been held that rape and forcible fellatio upon a female amount to bodily harm even though the victim may have felt no pain. In this case defendant was convicted of kidnaping with injury—a capital crime—and sentenced to death and sentence was ultimately executed after numerous appeals, eleven and one-half years later. *People v Chessman*, 238 P 2d 1001/Cal (1951).

Kidnap for the Purpose of Robbery

When robbery occurs during the process of a kidnaping, the crime then becomes a kidnaping for the purpose of robbery from the beginning, regardless of the intent of the kidnaper at the beginning (*In re Ward*, 414 P 2d 400/Cal—1966). Also, when a kidnaping occurs after a robbery is complete and for the purpose of facilitating the robbery or escape thereafter, the kidnaping is nevertheless a kidnap for the purpose of robbery. *People v Bean*, 198 P 2d 379/Cal (1939); *People v Laursen*, 501 P 2d 1145/Cal (1972).

Where defendant and codefendants seized victim and drove him several miles into the Arizona desert before robbing him, the restraint employed was far beyond the minimum restraint necessary incidental to robbery and such restraint was sufficient to support a conviction of both robbery and kidnaping for the purpose of robbery. *State v Soders*, 417 P 2d 275/Az (1970).

Kidnap to Commit Rape

Defendant may be convicted of kidnap with intent to commit rape although rape was not committed, if the circumstances surrounding the kidnap show a clear intent to rape at the time of the kidnaping. *State v Adrian*, 522 P 2d 1091/Az (1974).

Testimony of the complaining witness plus other evidence warranted a conviction of kidnaping where it was shown that defendant tied victim and transported her in the trunk of a car and sexually attacked her, such acts clearly violating a statute which denounced kidnaping for the purpose of extorting a thing of value or advantage. *Householder v State*, 501 P 2d 1112/Or (1972).

Where the prosecutrix was driven some distance from her home and there raped, and detained a total period of 45 minutes, a conviction of aggravated kidnaping, in addition to rape, was warranted. *People v Canale*, 285 NE 2d 133/Ill (1972).

Child Stealing or Second Degree Kidnaping

Under a statute forbidding child stealing and declaring the *corpus delicti* to be the malicious, forcible or fraudulent removal of a child from the legal custody of its custodian with intent to unlawfully detain or conceal it, consent of the child to accompany its abductor is no defense. *State v Randall*, 193 NW 2d 766/Neb (1972).

Defendant's relationship with a 13-year-old girl during a two-and-one-half month period which started in Los Angeles and terminated in Seattle, warranted the conclusion that defendant led, enticed or detained her and supported a second degree kidnaping charge despite defendant's claim, even if true, that victim consented during the entire episode. *State v Griffin*, 491 P 2d 1320/Wn (1971).

Air Piracy

It is not essential to kidnaping that the victim be forced to go to a place where he does not wish to go. For example, defendant and his son, while in flight from Phoenix to El Paso and while over New Mexico, each brandished a gun, menaced the crew and commanded that the destination of the aircraft be rerouted to Cuba via Monterrey, Mexico. Upon being convinced by the captain that the plane had insufficient fuel to fly to Monterrey, defendants then ordered the captain to land the craft at El Paso, there to refuel and continue to Cuba via Monterrey. At El Paso, however, defendants were taken into custody, prosecuted and convicted of multiple counts of kidnaping although neither destination, course, nor time of arrival were altered. *Bearden v United States*, 304 F 2d 532/NM (1962).

The federal statute proscribing air piracy applies only when the aircraft is in flight when seized, and the attempted piracy by a female of an airplane parked at an air terminal was a state offense, only, and triable in the state court. *United States v Pliskow*, 354 FS 369/Mich (1973).

Examples

When one, without lawful authority, boards the automobile of another and menaces the driver with a pistol, forcing the driver to take him to a named destination, he is guilty of kidnaping (*Pittser v State*, 461 P 2d 1015/Ok–1969). Likewise, where a fugitive from justice entered a taxicab in Seattle and ordered the driver at knife point to drive him to Portland, perpetrator was guilty of kidnaping although transported only a short distance before the cab driver escaped. *State v Andre*, 80 P 2d/Wn (1936).

Where the suspect was observed dragging a child from a playground toward a building and was frustrated by the intervention of an outraged father, his act was no less kidnaping because he was prevented from dragging the child into the building. *State v Roberts*, 197 SE 2d 54/NC (1973).

Chapter XVI

Homicide

Corpus Delicti

The *corpus delicti* of a criminal homicide consists of two elements: (1) the death of a human being and (2) the criminal act of another causing death. If the homicide was infanticide the state must prove that the child was born alive, and for this purpose an independent blood circulation is necessary; it is not necessary to prove that the child breathed, nor is proof that the child breathed for a moment conclusive proof that the child was born alive. *State v Collington*, 192 SE 2d 856/SC (1972); *Biddy v State*, 277 S 2d 115/Mis (1973).

In General

Some specific types of homicides are designated as the killing of:

- A brother by his sister or vice versa—fratricide;
- Husband by his wife—mariticide
- Wife by her husband—uxoricide
- One's mother—matricide
- One's father—patricide
- A baby—infanticide

Deaths of human beings may be listed under four general headings: homicide, suicide, natural and accidental. Likewise, homicide may be divided into three general types: criminal, justifiable and excusable.

Homicide is not necessarily a crime; it is a necessary ingredient of criminal homicide, i.e., murder and manslaughter, but there are other types of homicide which are noncriminal. *Black's Law Dictionary*.

The generally accepted definition for the term "homicide" is simply the killing of one human being by another human being. Homicide may be lawful as well as unlawful, intentional or unintentional, felonious or nonfelonious. *Corpus Juris Secundum*—HOMICIDE; *Com v Redline*, 137 A 2d 472/Pa (1958).

An accidental or unintentional death may be murder of either degree (*Com v Fostar*, 317 A 2d 188/Pa–1974), while a deliberate killing may amount to voluntary manslaughter (*People v Towers*, 308 NE 2d 223/Ill–1974), or justifiable homicide. *People v Beyea*, 113 CR 254/Cal (1974).

An accidental killing may be murder, manslaughter or no crime (*Thomas v United States*, 419 F 2d 1203/DC–1969). It may be murder of either degree if the killing occurs in the commission of a felony; the felony committed or attempted will determine the degree of murder.

As long as there is life in a human being, the extinguishment thereof by another is homicide (*State v Bebee*, 195 P 2d 746/Ut–1948). And the fact that defendant was worthless and deserved to die does not affect guilt or innocence of defendant, but may be a consideration in assessing punishment. *State v Goettina*, 158 P 2d 865/Wyo (1945).

Once the killing has been established the law presumes the killing to be second degree murder (*Shanklin v State*, 491 SW 2d 97/Ten–1972); to reduce the degree of the homicide below second degree murder, the defendant must prove absence of malice; to raise the killing to first degree, the state must prove premeditation. Id.

The gravamen of both first degree murder and voluntary manslaughter is the intentional, inexcusable and unjustified killing of a human being. Both crimes require the finding of a specific intent to kill and are thereby distinguished from second degree murder. They are distinguished from each other by the presence of malice in murder, and passion and provocation in voluntary manslaughter. *Com v Butcher*, 304 A 2d 150/Pa (1973).

Under California law one who sets a spring-gun to prevent entry into premises by burglars does so at his peril; if the device kills a mere trespasser, the killing is a criminal homicide; if one is seriously injured, the injury may amount to a felonious assault, but if it kills one who entered with intent to commit burglary, and the device was reasonably necessary to prevent burglary, no crime has been committed (*People v Ceballos*, 108 CR 538/Cal–1973). The mere setting of such a trap or device under the laws of some states is criminal, and if one—anyone—is injured or killed thereby, the magnitude of the crime is intensified. RCW 9.41.180.

The unlawful sale of heroin to victim who dies as a result of injection, does not amount to homicide under New York law, and the seller of the heroin is not criminally liable. *People v Pickney*, 328 NYS 2d 550/NY (1972).

Evidence of a diseased mind to the extent of legal insanity does not act to reduce the degree of a homicide but is a complete defense (*State v Sturdivan*, 497 SW 2d 139/Mo–1973). Also, excuse or justification in the commission of a homicide is not a mitigating circumstance but a complete defense. *State v Clarke*, 406 P 2d 772/Wn (1962).

Common Law on Homicide

There were no degrees of murder at common law and all criminal homicides were viewed as equally repugnant (*United States v Millette*, 299 A 2d 150/NH–1972). But there were two types of criminal homicide: a killing with malice–murder–and a killing without malice–manslaughter. The subdivisions and refinements have been added by substantive laws of the various states (*State v Jensen*, 417 P 2d 273/Kan–1966). Pennsylvania was the first state to divide murder into degrees. *Com v Redline*, 137 A 2d 472/Pa (1958).

When a Fetus Becomes a Human Being

The courts are often called upon to determine when a fetus becomes a human being subject to homicide. The rule followed by the majority of the states is that the child must have been born completely and alive. Evidence of the child's independent existence may be established by proof of breathing and independent circulation. Not all jurisdictions agree, however, on the requirement that the umbilical cord shall have been severed.

A presumption exists that a fetus is not viable within the first trimester of pregnancy, but its viability after that period is a question of fact concerning which expert and lay witnesses may give evidence. *Larkin v Cahalan*, 208 NW 2d 176/Mich (1973).

Under the common law an infant could not be the subject of homicide unless the state could prove that it had been born alive. The California courts have held that a viable fetus in the process of being born is a human being within the meaning of the homicide statute (*Keeler v Superior Court*, 470 P 2d 617/Cal–1970). But under the Michigan law the killing of an unborn quick child by abortion is manslaughter. A "child" under this statute is a viable fetus within its mother's womb capable of surviving the trauma of birth with the aid of ordinary medical care. *Larkin v Cahalan, supra.*

Transferred Intent

Under the doctrine of transferred intent a person who attempts to kill one person but by mistake or inadvertence kills another instead, is guilty of the same offense as he would have been had he accomplished his purpose. *People v Carlson*, 112 CR 321/Cal (1974).

If *A*, in the exercise of lawful self-defense and without criminal intent, shoots at *B* but misses and hits *C*, no criminal intent exists as to *C*. The inquiry must be whether the killing would have been justifiable had the accused killed the person he intended to kill, as the unintended act derives its character from the intended act. *State v Pinkney*, 290 NE 2d 923/Oh (1972); *Napier v State*, 298 NE 2d 427/Ind (1973).

The Use of a Deadly Weapon

In a killing wherein the perpetrator uses a deadly weapon, a rebuttable presumption of malice attaches making the killing murder, and if done with premeditation it is first degree murder. *State v Barrett*, 201 SE 2d 553/NC (1974).

Homicide may be presumed malicious by the intentional use of a deadly weapon in a manner calculated or likely to produce death (*Napier v State, supra*). A pistol is a deadly weapon per se. *Ortiz v State*, 490 SW 2d 594/Tex (1973).

If one who provokes a conflict thereafter withdraws in good faith and informs his adversary by words or actions of his desire to end the conflict, and he is thereafter pursued, he is justified in using deadly force to save himself from death or serious bodily injury. *State v Haakenson*, 213 NW 2d 394/ND (1973).

Essential Elements—How Proved

In virtually all, if not all, the United States and territories death may be established by circumstantial evidence. For example, defendant claimed that when he went to get a jacket from his closet, his loaded and cocked rifle fell to the floor discharging and killing his estranged wife, and in panic he thereafter loaded her body into a delivery truck and dumped it into a river and it was never found. Defendant's appeal was based on the ground that since the body was never found, the *corpus delicti* had not been established. In affirming conviction of second degree murder, the court held: ' . . . Is the body or some part thereof required to establish the 'fact of death' element of the *corpus delicti*? We think not. To require direct proof of the killing or the production of the body . . . would be manifestly unreasonable and would lead to absurdity and injustice." *State v Lung*, 423 P 2d 72/Wn (1967).

A criminal homicide may be proved by any evidence that is competent and relevant unless excluded under some specific rule such as the probative value being outweighed by its inflammatory nature. A dying declaration is competent and, if made under specific conditions, relevant. The declaration must have been made *in extremis*, that is, under a sense of impending death; it must have described events causing declarant to be in his dying condition; and declarant must die. *Wilson v State*, 468 P 2d 346/Nev (1970).

Time Limit Within Which Victim Must Die

Under common law the "year and a day" rule was applicable to all homicides: if the decedent lived more than a year and a day after the injury was inflicted it was conslusively presumed that death was not caused by the injury; on the other hand, if death occurred within a year and a day the assailant could be tried for the homicide at any time during his life. This rule still applies in many states. In some, however, it has been modified by statute (*State v Brown*, 318 A 2d 257/Md–1974) and extended to three years and a day. *People v Snipe*, 102 CR 6/Cal (1972); *Elliott v Mills*, 335 P 2d 1104/Ok (1959); RCW 9.48.010.

Where defendant and codefendant were convicted of child beating as a result of beating defendant's three-year-old daughter, they could be further prosecuted for a felonious homicide when the child died 21 months later, notwithstanding that the law of death after the fatal blow had been increased from one year and a day to three years and a day, after the fatal assault. Here *ex post facto* is not applicable, being a bar, only, to acts made criminal retroactively and where increased punishment after the crime is committed. *People v Snipe, supra.*

Extraneous Contributory Cause of Death

Where assailant unlawfully strikes another and inflicts injury, not of itself fatal but by so doing he starts a chain of causation leading to death, he is guilty of a criminal homicide although deceased contributed to or accelerated his own death by negligence or by failing to take proper care and treatment. *United States v Hamilton*, 182 FS 548/DC (1960).

Once the blow has been struck, although not immediately fatal, it is no defense that the victim left the hospital prematurely and contrary to a physician's orders, thereby probably accelerating victim's death (*State v Myers*, 125 P 2d 441/Az–1942), or that the doctor who treated the wound was negligent. *People v Freudenberg*, 263 P 2d 875/Cal (1953).

In a prosecution for criminal homicide it would be immaterial whether cause of death was a blow on the head or from the head striking the sidewalk if defendant's blow caused deceased to collapse and strike his head on the sidewalk. *Com v Robinson*, 299 A 2d 220/Pa (1973).

Conviction should be sustained where there is a causal connection between the injury inflicted by defendant and death of the victim. Where defendant inflicted a shotgun wound not necessarily fatal upon victim, and victim initially recovered from the wound but an autopsy examination showed cause of death to be serum hepatitis contracted from a blood transfusion administered as a result of the wound, there was insufficient intervening cause of death and defendant was liable. *People v Flenon*, 202 NW 2d 471/Mich (1972).

Disease or Enfeeblement As a Contributory Cause

Where the decedent prior to his death was enfeebled with terminal disease or injury, and the unlawful act of defendant hastened his death, notwithstanding defendant's ignorance of decedent's condition, defendant is responsible for the homicide even though the assault probably would not have been fatal to one physically sound. *Chase v State*, 382 P 2d 457/certiorari denied 375 US 979/Ok (1963).

That death may have resulted from the combined effects of disease or a preexisting condition and a wound or blow inflicted by defendant, does not relieve defendant of criminal responsibility (*Armstrong v State*, 502 P 2d 440/Alk–1972); nor is it a defense that the victim's wound was improperly treated by unskilled hands of attending physicians or surgeons. *People v Stamps*, 291 NE 2d 274/Ill (1972).

Notwithstanding advanced state of lung cancer in decedent, nonexpert testimony was sufficient to permit a finding that stab wounds were in fact the cause of death, and the fact that decedent was likely soon to expire from his cancerous condition did not relieve defendant of any criminal responsibility. *State v Decello*, 523 P 2d 74/Az (1974).

Principality to Criminal Homicide

Under New Jersey law where there are multiple participants to a criminal homicide, parties may be guilty of homicide in varying degrees depending on their respective participation and intent. Thus, if two should attack one victim and one intends a simple assault and battery and he is unaware of the intent of the other to use deadly force, each would be guilty according to his own intent and wrong (*State v Madden*, 294 A 2d 609/NJ–1972). This case does not express a prevailing rule, for it is the general rule that one who willfully participates in a crime with others is equally guilty with all. *Com v Yuknavich*, 295 A 2d 290/Pa (1972).

Venue of Homicide

In a prosecution for manslaughter resulting from a battery the time of the offense is fixed at the time the fatal blow was inflicted (*State v Hare*, 208 NW 2d 264/Neb–1973). And where the fatal blow is struck in one state and the victim dies in another state, Arizona has ruled that venue is in the county in which the fatal blow was inflicted. *Collins v State*, 294 P 625/Az (1930).

MALICE

Defined

"Malice," as it applies to murder, may be "express" or "implied": it is express when there is manifest by external circumstances capable of proof, a deliberate intent to take away the life of a fellow creature (*Walker v People*, 489 P 2d 58/Colo–1971); it is implied when no considerable provocation appears or when the circumstances attending the killing show an abandoned and malignant heart. *State v Coward*, 496 P 2d 131/Az (1972).

Malice, an essential element of all murder and assaults with intent to commit murder, exists in the doing of an intentional cruel act (*Howard v State*, 303 A 2d 653/Del–1973). Malice is not only hatred, ill will or spite, as it is ordinarily understood; it also includes that condition of the mind which prompts one person to take the life of another intentionally and without just cause, excuse or justification. *State v Tilley*, 196 SE 2d 816/NC (1973).

Malice is a state of mind deliberately bent on mischief and showing a heart that is without regard for social duty or the life and safety of others (*United States v Hinkle*, 487 F 2d 1205/DC–1973), and ill will toward or hatred of the victim are not requisites of malice as that term is used to define murder (*People v Sedeno*, 518 P 2d 913/Cal–1974). One who commits euthanasia bears no ill will toward his victim and believes his act morally justified, but nevertheless he who kills in euthanasia acts with presumed malice regardless of his personal belief. *People v Conley*, 411 P 2d 911/Cal (1966).

"Malice Aforethought" Defined

"Malice aforethought" is an unjustifiable, inexcusable and unmitigated man-dangering state of mind which involves every attitude of mind including (1) an intent to kill, (2) an intent to inflict great bodily injury, (3) an intent to do an act in wanton and willful disregard of an unreasonable human risk, or (4) an intent to perpetrate a dangerous felony; malice is an indispensable element of murder. *State v Millette*, 299 A 2d 150/NH (1972).

In General

Malice consists either of an express intention to kill or inflict great bodily harm, or of a wickedness of disposition, hardness of heart, cruelty, recklessness of consequence, a mind regardless of social duty and extreme indifference to the value of human life. *Com v Paquette*, 301 A 2d 839/Pa (1972).

Malice and, therefore, murder in the first degree was proved where evidence showed that deceased, a mute with the mind of a five-year-old child, had been subjected to torture by the burning of her pubic hair and the inside of her thighs, and the burning and tearing out of the hair from her head. *State v Gonzales*, 523 P 2d 66/Az (1974).

If malice is proved in a criminal homicide prosecution beyond a reasonable doubt and no affirmative defense applies, defendant is guilty of murder; if there is no malice the killing is manslaughter. *United States v Alexander*, 471 F 2d 923/DC (1972).

When Malice Presumed

Malice is presumed, under Alabama law, from the use of a deadly weapon unless the circumstances surrounding the killing disprove it (*Knight v State*, 276 S 2d 624/Ala–1973), but under Pennsylvania law such act only raises an inference of malice. *Com v Robinson*, 305 A 2d 354/Pa (1973).

Malice is implied whenever the killing is accomplished with a deadly weapon and no circumstances of mitigation, justification or excuse appear at the time of the killing (*Erby v State*, 487 SW 2d 266/Ark–1972). And a killing with malice is murder and may be of either degree. *State v Barrett*, 201 SE 2d 553/NC (1974).

MURDER–FIRST DEGREE

Defined

"Murder in the first degree" is the willful, deliberate, premeditated and malicious killing of one human being by another. *Luck v State*, 278 S 2d 772/Ala (1973).

The *mens rea* of first degree murder is characterized as malice aforethought, and is found in (1) an intent to kill, (2) the intentional commission of an act dangerous to life without a specific intent to kill, or (3) the commission of a dangerous felony. *People v Williams*, 114 CR 522/Cal (1974).

Malice aforethought is an essential ingredient of first degree murder, and malice may be express or implied. *Wilbur v Robbins*, 349 FS 149/Me (1972).

"Aforethought," as used in the definition of homicide, means thought of beforehand for any length of time, however short. *State v Wraggs*, 496 SW 2d 38/Mo (1973).

In General

First degree murder statutes of the several states do not all define the crime in the same manner. Usually murder will be defined as a premeditated design to effect death, or a willful deliberate and premeditated killing, or any killing with malice aforethought. These definitions are along the lines of the definition at common law. By statute the definition of the act constituting the crime has been refined, redefined and broadened in scope in some jurisdictions to include all killings by poison, torture or lying in wait. And added to the array of acts amounting to first degree murder is the statutory first degree murder rule–that one who kills in the commission of or attempt to commit certain specified felonies is also guilty of first degree murder.

A killing wherein the perpetrator intends to cause pain and suffering is not of itself a killing by torture and thus first degree. But where there is manifest in the nature of the killing an intent to cause extreme pain and cruel suffering for the purpose of revenge, extortion, persuasion, or some other untoward propensity, the killing is first degree murder and it is not necessary that the assailant intend to cause death. *State v Brock*, 416 P 2d 601/Az (1966).

An accusatory pleading—whether it be indictment, information or complaint—which charges murder, permits a finding of first degree murder or any lesser included offense (*In re Walker*, 518 P 2d 1129/Cal—1974), such as murder in the second degree, but precludes a conviction of any higher degree than second degree where a mistrial is declared and defendant is again tried. *State v Kearney*, 318 A 2d 100/Con (1972).

A fatal blow administered by a fist may not be murder under most circumstances, but a great disparity in size and strength of decedent and assailant can warrant conviction of murder, such as when the blow is administered upon the person of a small child. *People v Drumheller*, 304 NE 2d 455/Ill (1973).

Since there is no limitation within which a prosecution for murder must be commenced, the time of the killing is not material except that the state must prove that deceased died within the common law limit—a year and a day. *Flannagin v State*, 266 S 2d 637/Ala (1971). (Note: several states have, by statute, extended the time limit of one year and a day to three years and a day.)

"Murder" Distinguished From "Voluntary Manslaughter"

In some states, the crime of voluntary manslaughter is not recognized (Texas and Washington, to name two), and any voluntary or intentional killing, unless justifiable, is murder. *Brazile v State*, 497 SW 2d 302/Tex (1973).

The gravamen of both first degree murder and voluntary manslaughter is the intentional, inexcusable and unjustified killing of a human being. Both types require a specific intent to kill and are thereby distinguished from second degree murder. *Com v Butcher*, 304 A 2d 150/Pa (1973).

The distinguishing feature between murder and voluntary manslaughter is the presence or absence of premeditation. As a rule, a killing in the heat of passion is voluntary manslaughter, but if the killing was premeditated, it would be murder despite the presence of passion. *Baxter v State*, 503 SW 2d 226/Ten (1973).

"Premeditation" Defined

"Premeditation" means thought of beforehand for any length of time, however short (*State v Smart*, 485 SW 2d 90/Mo—1972). Elements of premeditation are not ordinarily susceptible to direct proof but are inferred from various circumstances such as ill will, previous difficulty between assailant and deceased, or evidence that the killing was committed in a vicious and brutal manner. *State v Fountain*, 191 SE 2d 674/NC (1972).

Where premeditation is an element, the law requires only that some appreciable time elapse during which necessary premeditation could take place (*United States v Mack*, 466 F 2d 333/DC–1972), and it may be formed in a mere instant (*Miller v State*, 523 P 2d 1118/Ok–1974). However, premeditation or deliberation need not be present in a killing under a felony-murder statute. *State v Miniefield*, 522 P 2d 25/Az (1974).

Purpose to kill may be formed a moment before execution, or an hour, or a day (*State v Palen*, 178 P 2d 862/Mont–1947), and there may be deliberation and premeditation where there is only sufficient time for one thought to follow another. *Hammil v People*, 361 P 2d 117/Colo (1961); *Aubrey v State*, 307 NE 2d 67/Ind (1974).

Premeditation may be shown by direct or circumstantial evidence, such as defendant's act of placing a loaded shotgun in his automobile before he followed victim to her home where he shot her incident to an argument which he had provoked (*State v Koho*, 423 P 2d 1004/Id–1967), or where defendant pointed a loaded pistol at his wife and asked, "Shall I pull the trigger now?" which he did. *Opie v State*, 389 P 2d 684/Wyo (1964).

Examples of Premeditation

A grotesque example of premeditation is shown where defendant, upon being struck by a woman, deliberately opened his pocket knife, cut the woman's throat, then hacked and cut her until she was dead and his energy was expended. *State v Snowden*, 313 P 2d 706/Id (1957).

Although defendant's motive, as expressed by him, was to have his victim die happy, he could still be found guilty of a willful, deliberate and premeditated killing, and thus first degree murder. *People v Dessaur*, 241 P 2d 238/Cal (1952).

Where evidence showed that defendant stood over his prostrate wife and at point-blank range fired six shots into her body with a pistol, he could not be heard to claim the killing was without design to effect death. *State v Gray*, 369 P 2d 330/Kan (1962).

A finding of premeditation, and thus first degree murder, was warranted where evidence showed that decedent was killed with a 22-caliber bullet filed to a flat nose or "dum-dum," and defendant stated to officers that he had shot his father, the person he wanted to kill, and was glad he had done so. *People v Corsa*, 213 NW 2d 579/Mich (1973).

Proof of premeditation was conclusively established, as opposed to appellant's claim of killing in the heat of passion, where appellant armed himself with a single-shot shotgun, sought out deceased at his place of employment, and methodically shot him four times reloading after each shot (the last two of which were fired into the victim's prostrate body while he lay helpless on the ground begging for life). *Baxter v State*, 503 SW 2d 226/Ten (1973).

A most diabolical example of deliberation is exemplified where defendant attempted an act of sex perversion upon a six-year-old female and when she protested and started to scream he choked her with his hands, then tied his necktie tightly around her neck, struck her twice on the temple with a hammer, inflicted three stab wounds in her chest and back with an ice pick, inflicted six skull fractures with a poleax, and finally cut her spinal cord with a knife. The court held that such killing was murder in the first degree under two theories: (1) willful, deliberate and premeditated killing and (2) killing by torture. *People v Stroble*, 226 P 2d 330/Cal (1951).

Failure of the court to instruct the jury on manslaughter was not error where evidence showed that defendant was ejected from a restaurant and he thereupon stole a shotgun (after being unable to borrow one), test-fired it, and returned to the restaurant after a lapse of about 45 minutes, and without a word shot decedent who was standing in the doorway to the restaurant. Defendant's conviction of first degree murder was sustained. *State v Burgess*, 477 SW 2d 105/Mo (1972).

In a prosecution for murder, especially first degree murder, wherein premeditation and malice are factors, prior disputes and quarrels between decedent and accused are generally admissible (*State v Davis*, 108 P 2d 641/Wn–1940). Thus, where defendant was under prosecution for uxoricide, evidence of a quarrel with his wife ten days previous to her death was admissible to show motive. *State v Spangler*, 159 P 785/Wn (1916).

Lying in Wait

The elements of "lying in wait" are the placing of oneself in concealment or in a place of vantage and watching and waiting with an intent to kill at a time appropriate and advantageous to the perpetrator (*State v Brooks*, 445 P 2d 831/Az–1968). Lying in wait is one of the methods by which first degree murder may be committed. *People v Ward*, 103 CR 671/Cal (1972).

The fact of lying in wait is not affected where the actor falls asleep while he is waiting, nor is the character of the killing modified thereby (*People v Gibson*, 206 P 2d 375/Cal–1949). And where the state proves that a murder was committed by one who was lying in wait, such proof establishes the murder as first degree and obviates the necessity of proving deliberation and premeditation. *People v McNeal*, 325 P 2d 166/Cal (1958).

Eyewitness testimony that defendant was sitting on a car fender when deceased emerged from a building and that defendant shot him several times, warranted the conclusion that defendant was lying in wait and the killing was deliberate and premeditated. *Virgin Islands v Lanclos*, 477 F 2d 603/VI (1973).

Malice aforethought was established by evidence which showed that defendant lay in wait in anticipation of killing a presidential candidate, and by the assassination of that candidate when he appeared. *People v Sirhan*, 497 P 2d 1121/Cal (1972).

Intent to Kill

Except in the case of felony-murder, a specific intent to kill implies first degree murder, not second degree. *People v Heffington*, 107 CR 859/Cal (1973).

Homicide committed with a design to effect death is murder, and no less so because the perpetrator was at the time intoxicated. However, "intent to effect death," being an element of first degree murder, may not exist in the mind of one so intoxicated that he is unable to form the requisite intent, in which case the crime would be manslaughter. *Williams v State*, 513 P 2d 335/Ok (1973).

When one intends to kill a certain person with a deadly weapon but by mistake or inadvertence he kills another, in the eyes of the law his intent is transferred from the first object of his assault to the person he actually kills; he is deemed guilty of the crime he originally intended to commit just as if he had originally intended to kill the person he actually killed. *Napier v State*, 298 NE 2d 427/Ind (1973); *Tolen v State*, 272 S 2d 279/Ala (1972).

The "Felony-Murder Rule" Defined

Under the felony-murder rule of most jurisdictions, the killing of a human being while in the commission of or while in withdrawing from the scene of one of the enumerated felonies, although accidental, is nevertheless, first degree murder. Michigan holds that when the homicide occurs in the perpetration of or attempt to perpetrate one of the statutory felonies, it may be manslaughter, and mere proof of the homicide does not establish first degree murder (*People v Wimbush*, 205 NW 2d 890/Mich–1973). New York holds that the purpose of the felony-murder rule is to reduce the number of accidental killings which occur during the commission of designated felonies, by punishing the person responsible for the homicide for murder rather than manslaughter (*People v Miller*, 344 NYS 2d 342/NY–1973). Although of doubtful value in general application, the felony-murder doctrine did not apply in the death of an intended rape victim where death occurred during acts of preparation by defendants and before their acts had gone far enough to amount to an attempt to commit rape. *People v Streiff*, 342 NYS 2d 543/NY (1973).

The felony-murder laws vary in many states, therefore it is necessary that the reader know the specific felonies named in the felony-murder statute of his state. As a rule, the killing of a human being in the commission of or in the attempt to commit one of the named felonies, even though accidental, is first degree murder; a killing which results from the commission of any other felony is usually second degree murder. *Witman v People*, 420 P 2d 416/Colo (1966); *People v Mitchell*, 392 P 2d 526/Cal (1964); *State v Thomas*, 400 P 2d 549/Or (1965).

Most states wherein the felony-murder rule is employed have agreed that a killing in the commission of arson, rape, robbery and burglary which are felonies makes the killing murder in the first degree; other felonies named in most statutes vary to include mayhem, kidnaping, larceny. *State v Millette*, 299 A 2d 150/NH (1972).

Under the felony-murder rule, a killing in the course of robbery or an attempted robbery is first degree murder, whether the killing is willful, deliberate or premeditated, or whether accidental or unintentional, and whether or not the killing is planned in conjunction with the robbery. *People v Johnson*, 104 CR 807/Cal (1972).

A single act can be both a premeditated killing and a killing under the felony-murder rule and thus first degree murder. *Gray v State*, 463 P 2d 879/Alk (1970).

The felony-murder doctrine applies whether a statutory requirement is "malice aforethought" (*People v Johnson*, 104 CR 807/Cal–1972), or "premeditated design to effect death." *State v Shuler*, 486 SW 2d 505/Mo (1972).

One who aided and abetted in the commission of a burglary wherein a person was killed, could be convicted of murder even though he was not at the immediate scene but waiting in an automobile to drive participants away after the burglary. *Com v Dankel*, 301 A 2d 365/Pa (1973).

In a prosecution under the felony-murder rule, the state is under no obligation to indict for, and convict defendant of, the underlying felony in order to sustain a felony-murder conviction for first degree murder. *Mumford v State*, 313 A 2d 563/Md (1974).

Robbery-Murder

When in the commission of robbery a human being is killed, not by one of the robbers but by the victim who misses the robbers and shoots an innocent bystander, malice aforethought may not be imputed to the robber as it may not be inferred either that the killing was a risk reasonably to be foreseen or that the robbery was the proximate cause of death (*People v Washington*, 402 P 2d 130/Cal–1965). In this incident it should be noted that the robbers did not shoot nor make any threats of imminent bodily harm and the third person was killed while the robbers were fleeing the scene. The principal difference between this case and *Taylor* (*Taylor v Superior Court*, 477 P 2d 131/Cal–1970), is that in *Taylor* one of the robbers was highly nervous and made several threats of immediate execution precipitating the ensuing gun battle between defendants and victims.

Where two or more persons enter into a conspiracy to commit robbery and one of the members kills a human being in the perpetration thereof, all members are equally guilty of first degree murder even though they did not participate in the killing, did not intend that life should be taken, had forbidden other coconspirators to kill and regretted the killing (*People v Romero*, 223 P 2d 511/Cal–1950). And the result would have been the same had the killing been accidental, if it had occurred in furtherance of the object crime or to facilitate escape thereafter. *People v Schrader*, 401 P 2d 665/Cal (1965); *State v Refuge*, 270 S 2d 842/La (1972).

Defendant's conviction of first degree murder under the felony-murder rule was sustained where, during the commission of a robbery, he shot at the victim who was struggling with his accomplice, but missed the victim and killed his accomplice. *People v Warren*, 205 NW 2d 599/Mich (1973).

In a prosecution for the murder of a policeman during a robbery in Pennsylvania, the court properly charged the jury that under the law of the state it was immaterial whether the defendant or one of his companions or the widow of the policeman fired the fatal shot. The offense was nonetheless a killing in the commission of robbery and, as such, first degree murder. *United States ex rel Almeida v Baldi*, 195 F 2d 815/Pa (1952).

Defendant who participated in the planning and execution of an attempted robbery could be convicted of the murder of a police officer whether the shot was fired by him or by an accomplice or by another police officer in resisting the robbery. *People v Allen*, 309 NE 2d 544/Ill (1974).

Where defendant and codefendant killed a human being during the commission of robbery, defendant's conviction of first degree murder would lie even though codefendant actually did the killing and had been found not guilty by reason of insanity. *People v Jones*, 518 P 2d 819/Colo (1974).

First degree felony-murder in the commission of robbery was sustained against defendant who walked into victim's hotel room with a loaded pistol and picked up victim's wallet, and when victim objected to his presence defendant shot and killed him. *State v Boyland*, 495 P 2d 315/Ut (1972).

Even though there is evidence which would raise the inference that a killing was accidental, the defendant is not entitled to have the jury instructed on involuntary manslaughter if the killing was committed in the perpetration of robbery. *People v Clark*, 402 P 2d 856/Cal (1965).

Where defendant was tried for first degree murder—a killing in the commission of robbery—it was no defense that the statute of limitations had expired on the robbery, or that defendant was not charged with robbery (*People v Risenhoover*, 477 P 2d 925/Cal–1968). Nor is it necessary that defendant personally remove a thing of value from the victim, for when two or more persons commit robbery through concerted action, all are equally guilty. *Burton v State*, 292 NE 2d 790/Ind (1973).

Burglary-Murder

The killing of a detective by a fellow officer while attempting to frustrate the escape of defendants immediately after the commission of a burglary, constitutes felony-first degree murder by defendants notwithstanding that defendants did not fire a weapon. When a killing occurs immediately after a burglary during an attempt to escape, the killing becomes one in the commission of burglary and thus first degree murder. *People v Hickman*, 297 NE 2d 582/Ill (1973).

Defendant was shown to have entered the apartment of deceased female at 2:30 a.m., a stranger to him, and when she awakened he told her to put a pillow over her head and that he was going to kill her. He attempted to do so, but she managed to jump from her third-floor apartment window in an attempt to escape, as a result of which she died. The court properly found that defendant's entry constituted burglary and that in the commission thereof he proximately caused the death of a human being—though by her own act, her death was precipitated by the unlawful acts of defendant and under the law of Illinois the felony-murder rule applied. Murder and burglary were affirmed. *People v Smith*, 307 NE 2d 353/Ill (1974).

The state may prove burglary against the accused even though incidental, and where the facts showed that defendant's primary purpose for entering the structure was to kill his wife and her male companion, a killing pursuant to such entry was statutory first degree murder. *State v Morris*, 405 P 2d 369/Or (1965).

Arson-Murder

Where defendant enters into a conspiracy to commit arson and arson is committed, and as a result thereof a human being is killed, the killing is murder in the first degree under the felony-murder rule notwithstanding that the deceased was one of the conspirators; defendant is equally guilty of murder though not present at the killing nor assenting thereto. *State v Morran*, 306 P 2d 679/Mont (1957).

Evidence that defendant and two codefendants were ejected from a beer tavern and apparently in a spirit of revenge returned a short time later, emptied a five-gallon can of gasoline on the floor and ignited it, causing the death of six patrons, warranted convictions of each participant of six counts of first degree murder on two theories: killing by torture and killing in the perpetration of arson. *People v Chavez*, 329 P 2d 907/Cal (1958).

Killing in Flight From the Scene

A killing is perpetrated in the commission of robbery even though committed during pursuit of the robber after the loot is taken or while the robber is in flight from the scene and has not yet won a place of temporary safety. *People v Salas*, 500 P 2d 7/Cal (1972).

The killing of a deputy sheriff about six or seven minutes after a robbery, while defendant was in flight therefrom in an automobile, constituted first degree murder under the felony-murder rule *even if the killing was accidental or unintentional. People v Salas, supra.*

Where defendants were fleeing from the scene of a burglary and an officer shot and killed one who was carrying a handgun and who was later discovered to be a detective, defendants were guilty of first degree murder of the detective notwithstanding that he was shot by another officer. *People v Hickman*, 297 NE 2d 582/Ill (1973).

Where defendant had committed a robbery 48 minutes earlier and was stopped en route away from the scene by a police officer whom he shot and killed, the court was correct in finding that defendant was still in flight from the scene of the robbery which was not yet at end and that the killing was murder in the commission of robbery. *People v Kendrick*, 363 P 2d 13/Cal (1961).

Where in his flight from the scene of a robbery in a high-speed automobile chase by police, defendant's get-away car collided with another vehicle and killed three occupants, his flight could constitute a continuation of the robbery and hence be a sufficient basis for sustaining a first degree murder conviction. *State v Jasper*, 486 SW 2d 268/Mo (1972).

Jury Instruction on First Degree Only

At times the evidence offered in a murder prosecution is evidence of first degree murder only, and under such circumstances the judge will instruct the jury on first degree only, thus requiring a verdict of guilty as charged or not guilty. Where defendant committed homicide in the perpetration of robbery or burglary, proof of which was conclusive, an instruction on second degree murder and manslaughter was properly refused (*People v Sanford*, 203 P 2d 534/Cal–1949); and an instruction to the jury that if they found that deceased was killed by poison, torture or lying in wait, they had no alternative but to find defendant guilty of first degree murder, was a proper instruction (*People v Thomas*, 261 P 2d 1/Cal–1953). Also where decedent was killed by the medium of arson (*Green v United States*, 218 F 2d 856/DC–1955), or where, as a result of a fight with decedent, defendant held him and shot him at least three times then emptied his revolver into decedent's prostrate body (*State v Hicks*, 448 P 2d 930/Wn–1968), the court's instruction precluding a finding of guilty of any lesser offense than first degree murder was proper.

In a prosecution where defendant admitted the killing and evidence of premeditation was conclusive, being established by defendant's own testimony, the killing "was either first degree murder or nothing"; the court properly instructed the jury that as a matter of law the killing was neither justifiable nor excusable, and instruction on second degree murder was error and should not have been given. But since the error was to the advantage of defendant, it was not reversible error. *State v Biondic*, 288 P 2d 845/Wn (1955).

Where defendant, after shooting her husband, claimed she "blacked out" and thus could not have formed the intent to murder, the court held: an epileptic seizure or blackout occurring after the homicide was committed, if it occurred at all, would have no bearing on the issue of intent. Further, the trial court properly refused to instruct the jury on manslaughter, as the evidence showed the killing to be murder—either first or second degree, depending on the presence or absence of premeditation, or whether accidental—and a conviction of first degree murder was sustained. *State v Huff*, 458 P 2d 180/Wn (1969).

Involuntary manslaughter, being an unintentional killing through negligence or in the commission of a misdemeanor, would preclude instruction to the jury on involuntary manslaughter where the evidence showed an intentional shooting. *State v Briggs*, 201 SE 2d 580/NC (1974).

Failure to feed a child causing death from malnutrition is first degree murder if defendant harbors a specific will to withhold nourishment to the extent that death result therefrom. *People v Lynch*, 208 NW 2d 656/Mich (1973).

In the robbery of a liquor store where one of three principals waited outside in the getaway car while his two coprincipals went inside to commit robbery, the felony-murder rule was applicable. Evidence showed that victim's wife was armed and standing on a ladder inside the store, and upon hearing the robbers' demands and threats to execute her husband, she opened fire on the robbers, wounding one (who later died); the husband then armed himself with an available pistol and joined his wife in a gun battle with the two robbers. The third robber, upon hearing shots inside, left the scene abandoning his two accomplices but was later apprehended as was the other surviving principal. The court observed in affirming conviction of felony-murder against both defendants: "When the defendant or his accomplice, with a conscious disregard, intentionally commits an act that is likely to cause death, and his victim or a police officer kills in reasonable response to such act, the defendant is guilty of murder." *Taylor v Superior Court*, 477 P 2d 131/Cal (1970).

Where the state's witness testified that she knocked on the door of the defendant, the paramour of the victim's mother, and receiving no response went to a window and looked in and saw defendant carrying the 22-month-old victim downstairs by the ears and then slam the baby's head against the stair railing, and defendant, upon seeing witness, told her not to say anything or he would kill her children, this warranted a conviction of first degree murder. *State v Gee*, 498 P 2d 662/Ut (1972).

Homicide committed in the theft of an automobile is first degree murder in states which name larceny in the felony-murder statute. *State v Ortega*, 419 P 2d 219/NM (1966); *State v Daniels*, 205 P 1054/Wn (1922).

Where defendant attempted to coerce victim into an act of sexual intercourse with him and, failing, killed her in order to accomplish his goal, he was guilty of statutory first degree murder. *People v Goodridge*, 452 P 2d 637/Cal (1969).

MURDER–SECOND DEGREE

Defined

Second degree murder is the unlawful killing of a human being with malice but without premeditation or deliberation. *State v Cannady*, 192 SE 2d 677/NC (1972); *People v Bryant*, 204 NW 2d 246/Mich (1972).

Malice, an essential element of murder, may be inferred from the use of a deadly weapon at close range. *Estes v State*, 507 SW 2d 216/Tex (1974).

Second Degree Presumed

Once the fact of a killing has been established, the law presumes the killing to be murder of the second degree. To reduce the degree of the homicide the defendant must prove an absence of malice; to raise the degree of the homicide to first degree murder, the state must prove premeditation, deliberation or some other ingredient peculiar to first degree. *Shanklin v State*, 491 SW 2d 97/Ten (1972); *State ex rel Duncan v Brierly*, 277 FS 751/Pa (1968).

Requisite Intent in Murder

If it be shown that the accused, on trial for murder of the first degree, was so drunk at the time he committed the homicide that he was utterly incapable of forming a deliberate and premeditated purpose to kill—an essential element of first degree—then first degree murder is not proved and the crime is murder in the second degree. *State v Bunn*, 196 SE 2d 777/NC (1973).

One is presumed to intend the natural and probable consequences of his voluntary acts, and intent to commit murder may be inferred from an act of shooting into a crowd of people. *Blackburn v State*, 291 NE 2d 686/Ind (1973).

Imminently Dangerous Act

Where defendant was charged with and convicted of second degree murder only, and appealed from conviction thereof, the court in affirming conviction observed that one who points a revolver at a group of persons and declares, "I'm going to kill all of you sons-of-bitches," whereupon he fires into the group killing one person, is fortunate not to have been tried for first degree murder in an act imminently dangerous to others evincing a depraved mind. *State v Harris*, 421 P 2d 662/Wn (1966).

The unlawful and forceful striking of another in anger with a loaded pistol, resulting in the discharge of that weapon killing the victim, constitutes an "act imminently dangerous to another" and "evincing a depraved mind regardless of human life," within the definition of the second degree murder statute. *State v Bryan*, 287 S 2d 73/Fla (1973).

Defendant who fired two rifle shots into an inhabited apartment living room killing a person, such act being imminently dangerous evincing a depraved mind regardless of human life, was properly found guilty of second degree murder although he claimed no injury was intended (*State v Gill* 474 P 2d 23/Ok–1970). Likewise, defendant's act of firing a gun into a crowded room where a person was operating a dice game, thereby killing deceased, supported a charge of second degree murder for the same reasons stated in *Gill, supra. State v Thompson*, 170 P 2d 153/Ut (1946).

If a person commits or attempts to commit a felony *malum in se*, not one enumerated in the first degree felony-murder statute, and in so doing proximately causes the death of any person, malice may be implied and the killing is usually second degree murder. But if the felony committed or attempted is one of a type not inherently dangerous to human life, the killing may constitute manslaughter, only. *People v Carter*, 197 NW 2d 57/Mich (1972); *State v Jasper*, 486 SW 2d 268/Mo (1972).

Furnishing, selling or administering a narcotic drug to another is a felony, and if death ensues from the commission of such felony, it constitutes murder in the second degree. It is immaterial whether the furnisher or another administered the narcotic in a prosecution of the furnisher; under California law his crime is second degree murder in either event (*People v Wong*, 111 CR 314/Cal–1973). But compare *Wong* to *Dixon*, which follows: The sole act of selling heroin to a user who voluntarily and without the presence or assistance of the seller, injects a lethal quantity of heroin into his body, does not constitute second degree murder under the Arizona law. *State v Dixon*, 511 P 2d 623/Az (1973).

Instruction to the Jury

An advisory instruction to the jury that the law "presumes that in the absence of justification, excuse or some other circumstances of mitigation, all homicides are committed with malice and thereby constitute murder in the second degree," did not deny defendant his constitutional right to due process. *Burko v State*, 313 A 2d 864/Md (1974).

If, after diligently weighing all the evidence, the jury is convinced defendant is guilty of murder but is uncertain as to the degree, it should find the defendant guilty of the lesser degree. *State v Jones*, 179 P 2d 1001/NM (1947).

Examples of Second Degree Murder

Where two persons voluntarily enter into combat with deadly weapons by previous agreement, self-defense is not tenable for either unless one in good faith attempts to withdraw from the affray and his intentions are brought home to his adversary. If the one attempting to withdraw is thereafter pressed or pursued and it appears that he is in danger of death or great bodily injury, he may then exercise the right of self-defense. *Freeman v State*, 262 P 2d 713/Ok (1953).

In most states a killing in the fighting of a duel is murder in the second degree by statute. If no statute regarding such killing exists, the death may well be classified as one with malice aforethought or with a premeditated design to effect death and, thus, first degree murder.

Testimony that defendant assisted in holding the victim down and beating him for about one hour, then collaborated with another in refusing victim medical care, was sufficient to show defendant's malice in the subsequent death of victim. *People v Moran*, 114 CR 413/Cal (1974).

Shortly after killing a Greek, a dog snapped at defendant; he asked a witness whether or not the dog was Greek or Irish, and threatened to kill it if it was Greek. His statement concerning the dog was admissible at his trial as tending to show malice toward Greeks. *State v Stone*, 13 P 2d 427/Wn (1932).

Defendant was found guilty of second degree murder where evidence showed that he was the only person in the hotel room with victim, owned the gun which killed her, and was heard by a witness to cry out after a shot was fired, "Oh my God, I killed her..." despite defendant's claim of unconsciousness due to drug use. *State v Caruthers*, 495 P 2d 1319/Az (1972).

MANSLAUGHTER–GENERAL

Defined

"Manslaughter" is the unlawful killing of a human being without malice, deliberation or premeditation (*State v Burn*, 196 SE 2d 777/NC–1973). A killing in the heat of passion is manslaughter and not murder. Id; *United States v Alexander*, 471 F 2d 923/DC (1972).

Characteristics of Manslaughter

Manslaughter is the most subdivided of the homicides. In California there are four subdivisions: (1) voluntary; (2) involuntary; and in the driving of a vehicle (3) with gross negligence, and (4) without gross negligence. In Washington there is only involuntary manslaughter and negligent homicide. Many of the states subdivide into degrees such as first, second and third degree. However, despite the numerous degrees or subclassifications in existence in criminal jurisprudence, there are only two basic types: voluntary and involuntary.

Some jurisdictions distinguish between manslaughter intentionally committed and that which was accidental or unintentional, by classifying the two types of killings as first and second degree manslaughter, while other jurisdictions classify them as voluntary and involuntary manslaughter. *Fulghum v State*, 277 S 2d 886/Ala (1973); *Chiles v State*, 508 P 2d 1108/Ok (1973).

Requisite to a conviction of voluntary manslaughter, involuntary manslaughter or negligent homicide in the operation of a vehicle, is wanton indifference to the value of human life, or reckless conduct according to standard conduct of a reasonable man, or negligent operation of a vehicle. *Owens v Com*, 487 SW 2d 897/Ky (1972).

Mere words alone are insufficient provocation for manslaughter. *People v Felton*, 298 NE 2d 372/Ill (1973).

"Voluntary" and "Involuntary" Distinguished

The common law differientiated between voluntary and involuntary manslaughter in the following manner: involuntary manslaughter was characterized as an unlawful homicide not intentionally done but resulting from an act that constituted such disregard of probable harmful consequences to another as to amount to wanton or reckless conduct; voluntary manslaughter was characterized by an existing design and purpose to kill but without malice. *Com v Hinckley*, 294 NE 562/Mas (1973).

Mutual Combat—Responsibility of Participants

One who voluntarily participates in mutual combat for purposes other than protection, cannot justify or excuse the killing of his adversary on the grounds of self-defense, regardless of what extremity or imminent peril he may have been reduced to in the progress of the combat. However, he may justify it if before the homicide is committed he withdraws and endeavors in good faith to decline further conflict and, either by word or act, makes this fact known to his adversary. *State v Graham*, 196 SE 2d 495/SC (1973).

Jury Instruction

In a prosecution for murder of either degree wherein any evidence is offered which if believed by the jury would warrant a conviction of manslaughter, the court must instruct the jury on the issue of manslaughter, and to refuse to give such instruction is reversible error. *Laymon v State*, 513 P 2d 883/Ok (1973).

VOLUNTARY MANSLAUGHTER

Defined

"Voluntary manslaughter" is the unlawful killing of a human being without malice, premeditation or deliberation (*State v Davis*, 197 SE 2d 6/NC–1973), and intent to kill is not a necessary ingredient. *Burton v State*, 495 SW 2d 841/Ark (1973).

Manslaughter is voluntary when the killing is in "sudden heat" and without malice. If the element of sudden heat is not present, the killing is murder, and if malice—a necessary element of murder—was premeditated, the killing is first degree murder. *Ellis v State*, 304 NE 2d 546/Ind (1973); *State v Quila*, 502 P 2d 525/Az (1972).

In General

Provocation, in order to be sufficient to reduce an offense from second degree murder to manslaughter, must be such as might induce a reasonable man in the passion of the moment to lose self-control and commit the act on impulse and without reflection; a blow or other personal violence may constitute adequate provocation, but trivial or slight provocation, entirely disproportionate to the violence of the retaliation, is not adequate provocation to reduce second degree murder to manslaughter. *United States v Alexander*, 471 F 2d 923/DC (1973).

Voluntary manslaughter is committed when one kills another without lawful justification while acting under a sudden and intense passion resulting from serious provocation which may have been incited by the decedent or another (*People v Curse*, 308 NE 2d 270/Ill—1974). If there is sufficient interval between provocation and homicide for reason to prevail, the killing will be murder and not manslaughter. *English v People*, 497 P 2d 691/Colo (1972).

A manslaughter statute allows mitigation to manslaughter of a killing which would otherwise be murder, where some unexpected and provocative event triggers the actor into the commission of homicide. *State v Berry*, 503 P 2d 505/Or (1972).

Intent to kill is not necessarily an element of voluntary manslaughter; it is only necessary that death result from an act intentionally committed which is dangerous to life. *People v Williams*, 114 CR 522/Cal (1974).

"Heat of Passion" Defined

"Heat of passion" will not reduce an intentional killing to manslaughter unless it was engendered by adequate provocation; if the element of provocation is either lacking or legally insufficient, the crime is murder. *State v Ross*, 501 P 2d 632/Ut (1972).

Heat of passion includes rage, resentment, anger, terror and fear. Heat of passion may be produced by fear as well as rage. *United States v Alexander*, *supra.*

Mere words alone are not sufficient to constitute provocation such as is required to reduce murder to the crime of voluntary manslaughter. *People v Clark*, 305 NE 2d 218/Ill (1973).

Intoxication As Affecting Homicide

The jurisdictions are not in unanimous agreement as to the effect of voluntary intoxication in a deliberate killing of a human being. The Iowa courts have held that voluntary drug intoxication does not permit a jury to reduce a homicide to manslaughter (*State v Hall*, 214 NW 2d 205/Ia–1974), but the Kentucky courts have held that intoxication by liquor or drugs may be shown in evidence and considered by the jury in a homicide case, and such evidence may operate to reduce the crime from murder to voluntary manslaughter. *Geary v Com*, 503 SW 2d 505/Ky (1972).

The Killing of a Quick Child

A "quick child" is a viable fetus within its mother's womb, capable of surviving birth with the aid of ordinary medical care. The killing of a quick child by means of an unlawful abortion is manslaughter. *Larkin v Cahalan*, 208 NW 2d 176/Mich (1973).

In a prosecution for infanticide death may be established by circumstantial evidence, as in any homicide prosecution. Where an autopsy showed that the infant's mouth and throat had been packed tightly with toilet tissue or kleenex before it was dumped in a trash bin on a college campus, the fact of life and death by a criminal agency were circumstantially established and a manslaughter conviction was sustained. *State v Collington*, 192 SE 2d 856/SC (1972).

INVOLUNTARY MANSLAUGHTER

Defined

"Involuntary manslaughter" is the unlawful killing of a human being without malice, premeditation or deliberation, and without the intention to kill or inflict serious bodily injury on the deceased. *State v Davis*, 190 SE 2d 434/NC (1972).

Involuntary manslaughter may result from the commission of a lawful act as well as an unlawful act, and where the killing was accomplished through the medium of a lawful act but done in an unlawful manner or without due caution and circumspection, the killing is involuntary manslaughter. *State v Grubbs*, 512 P 2d 693/NM (1973).

The killing of another must be without design and without malice while engaged in the doing of an unlawful act not amounting to a felony and not tending toward great bodily harm. *Hallowell v State*, 298 A 2d 330/Del (1972).

Under Texas law negligent homicide is distinguished from an accidental killing by the fact that negligent homicide results from an act intentionally done, while accidental homicide results from an act unintentionally done (*Palafox v State*, 484 SW 2d 739/Tex–1972); the only difference between first and second degree negligent homicide is whether the negligence occurred during the commission of a lawful or unlawful act. Id.

In General

Involuntary manslaughter is committed when it plainly appears that neither death nor great bodily injury was intended, but that death was accidentally caused by an unlawful act, or an act not unlawful per se but done in an unlawful manner or without due caution and circumspection. *United States ex rel Powell v Pennsylvania*, 294 FS 849/Pa (1968).

Involuntary manslaughter may flow as a result of the commission of both lawful and unlawful acts: if in the commission of an unlawful act, the unlawful act must be a lesser crime than a felony; if in the commission of a lawful act, the defendant must have acted without due caution and circumspection. *State v Grubbs*, 512 P 2d 693/NM (1973); *State v Betts*, 519 P 2d 655/Kan (1974).

As a rule, there is no justification for reversal or other disturbance on appeal where defendant is tried for murder and found guilty of manslaughter only, although evidence would have sustained a conviction of murder (*Smith v State*, 175 P 2d 348/Ok–1946). And where defendant was convicted of manslaughter he could not complain that the evidence showed him to be guilty of second degree murder, if anything. *State v Griego*, 294 P 2d 282/NM (1956).

The term "without due caution and circumspection," as it applies to involuntary manslaughter, is virtually the equivalent of "negligence" (*State v Wojahn*, 282 P 2d 675/Or–1955). Failure to secure medical aid by one whose duty it is to secure such aid, the proximate result of which is death, constitutes involuntary manslaughter. *State v Mally*, 366 P 2d 868/Mont (1961).

Under the "diminished capacity" doctrine, as adopted by California, a claim of either a defense or a mitigation due to the voluntary ingestion of alcohol, may permit a finding all the way from first degree murder to involuntary manslaughter. *People v Garcia*, 104 CR 69/Cal (1972).

Death Due to an Overdose of Narcotics

Under California law the injection or use of heroin is a misdemeanor, and defendant who acted as a lookout while an associate injected heroin into his body, from which he died, became a principal to a misdemeanor and constituted involuntary manslaughter. *People v Hopkins*, 226 P 2d 74/Cal (1951).

In a prosecution of defendant who sold three packets of heroin to deceased, a 21-year-old narcotic addict who died of an overdose of heroin, a question of fact as to defendant's culpability of involuntary manslaughter was presented to the jury. *State v Thomas*, 288 A 2d 32/NJ (1972).

Death From Child Neglect

A person who has care and custody of a child and causes the death of the child by willfully failing to procure medical aid when such aid is needed, is guilty of either manslaughter (*State v Crawford*, 196 NW 2d 915/Neb–1972) or criminally negligent homicide depending on the wording of the statute violated. *People v Henson*, 349 NYS 2d 657/NY (1973).

Where defendant's three-year-old child died of malnutrition weighing 19 pounds, and during its last year of life it became steadily thinner, and defendant did not seek medical attention for the child, there was sufficient evidence to sustain conviction for manslaughter. *Nozza v State*, 288 S 2d 560/Fla (1974).

Examples of Voluntary Manslaughter

To sustain a conviction for involuntary manslaughter, the action of the defendant must have been a direct cause of the death in issue. However, there can be more than one proximate cause of death just as there can be more than one direct cause of death (*Com v Skufea*, 294 A 2d 787/Pa–1972). For example, a mother who locked her two children in her apartment unattended while she went out at night, one child being three and one-half years old and the other 22 months, was guilty of involuntary manslaughter by fire and suffocation when the apartment building caught on fire and volunteers could not effect entry to save the children when they were heard crying. Id.

The killing of an unwelcome guest in an attempt to expel him is manslaughter, absent any other provocative factors (*State v Sill*, 289 P 2d 720/Wn–1955). Nor can one employ deadly force to prevent trespass or to eject a trespasser, and where defendant fired a gun into a wooded area where he believed trespassers to be and killed one of the trespassers, he was guilty of manslaughter. *State v Williams*, 216 P 2d 1630/Ut (1950).

Any careless and reckless use of a loaded gun which jeopardizes the life of another is unlawful, and if death results therefrom the crime is manslaughter. Here, defendant was shooting at some birds in a field and a ricocheting bullet killed deceased who was concealed from defendant's view by a junked automobile. *State v Smith*, 193 SE 2d 318/NC (1972).

Where defendant was attempting a fast-draw trick with a friend and he unintentionally shot and killed the friend, the killing was involuntary manslaughter. *State v Blanton*, 200 SE 2d 425/NC (1973).

Defendant was guilty of involuntary manslaughter where evidence showed that while under the influence of LSD, he entered the apartment of strangers, pushed and struggled with the husband and knocked the wife down, and the husband, while attempting to pull defendant away from his wife, collapsed and died of a heart attack. *Phillips v State*, 289 S 2d 447/Fla (1974).

Where defendant was the aggressor in an argument which progressed into a fist fight, and defendant struck the deceased on the chin causing him to fall and strike his head resulting in fatal injuries, defendant was guilty of manslaughter though no undue advantage was taken, no dangerous weapon was used, and notwithstanding that deceased left the hospital prematurely against the doctor's orders and thereby accelerated an otherwise unlikely death. *State v Myers*, 125 P 2d 441/Az (1942).

JUSTIFIABLE HOMICIDE

In General

Justifiable homicide is similar in some respects to deliberate premeditated murder and voluntary manslaughter. In all three instances the actor deliberately employs deadly force upon the person of another causing death. The differences between the three types of homicide lie in the intent of the actor and the presence or absence of premeditation, provocation or justification. In murder the actor without provocation, justification or excuse and with malice aforethought, kills a human being, in voluntary manslaughter the actor deliberately kills a human being but while impassioned by some event which obscured reason; justifiable homicide is the deliberate killing of a human being, or the deliberate employment of deadly force which effects death but which is justifiable under the circumstances because of misdeeds of the decedent.

In justifiable homicide defendant is entitled to act upon appearances, and if the conduct of decedent was such as to incite in the mind of the reasonable man under all circumstances then existing, fear or belief that death or great bodily injury was about to be inflicted upon him by decedent, it is immaterial whether danger was real or apparent (*Hood v State*, 106 P 2d 271/Ok–1940). And an assault of sufficient magnitude to justify homicide need not be accompanied by a battery (*Haines v State*, 275 P 2d 347/Ok–1954), nor is a killing which is justified by the circumstances surrounding the killing made criminal by the subsequent criminal conduct of the accused. *People v Sanchez*, 184 P 2d 673/Cal (1947).

In order to justify a killing it must be done in good faith and under an honest belief that a felony is about to be committed and that the killing is necessary to prevent accomplishment. Although actual necessity for taking life need not be shown, it is necessary that it appear to the slayer under circumstances which would incite such belief in the mind of the reasonable and prudent person that actual necessity existed. *Gray v State*, 463 P 2d 897/Alk (1970).

Justifiable homicide is homicide committed under circumstances which justify the killing although it may be deliberate and intentional, and the actual state of the mind of the slayer has little relevancy, for his act will be judged on the scale of the reasonable and prudent person. *State v Clark*, 337 P 2d 449/Wn (1962).

If the killing of one person by another would have been justifiable or excusable homicide under all circumstances of self-defense, then the unintended killing of an innocent bystander by a random shot fired in proper and prudent self-defense would be justifiable or excusable. *Pittman v State*, 272 P 2d 458/Ok (1954); *People v Mason*, 165 P 2d 481/Cal (1946).

When Justified

Homicide is justifiable when defendant kills because he reasonably believes such force is necessary to prevent great bodily injury. *Williams v State*, 191 SE 2d 100/Ga (1972).

Felonies which will justify the killing of an aggressor, and then only if necessary, are crimes of violence and surprise such as murder, robbery, burglary, arson, breaking into a house with intent to commit sodomy or rape; or crimes in defense of self or others or the defender's property, against one who manifestly intends or endeavors to commit one or more of the aforementioned crimes. *State v Nyland*, 287 P 2d 345/Wn (1955).

One is privileged to defend a third person on the same basis he is privileged to defend himself, provided his belief is reasonable that the third person would be privileged to act in self-defense and that his intervention is necessary for such person's protection. *Thomas v State*, 192 NW 2d 864/Wis (1972).

When Not Justified

Not all felonies are of sufficient gravity and turpitude to warrant deadly force in their prevention or in the arrest of one after their commission. Where defendant allegedly killed deceased because deceased attempted fellatio on him while he was asleep and defendant tried to prevent its recurrence, the court in affirming conviction of manslaughter observed: there was no reasonable grounds to believe that defendant was in imminent danger of death or great bodily injury, but rather a battery was all that was intended. *State v Milbrandt*, 415 P 2d 2/Wn (1966).

The general rule is that, "neither insulting words nor insulting conduct or epithets, nor assaults previously made, had and done, to the defendant at other and different places than the scene of the homicide, no matter how opprobrious, will justify or mitigate a homicide." *Burroughs v State*, 158 P 2d 723/Ok (1945).

Adultery—a felony in some states—not being a crime of violence or one imperiling life or threatening the safety of the offended spouse, is not a type of felony which will justify the killing of an adulteror; neither is a wife's adulterous conduct an excuse for uxoricide nor a mitigating circumstance in the assessment of the husband's punishment. *Honda v People*, 141 P 2d 178/Colo (1943).

The shooting of an army deserter while in flight by a town marshal in an attempt to arrest him, was not a justifiable killing and warranted a conviction of the marshal for voluntary manslaughter. *Storer v State*, 180 P 2d 202/Ok (1947).

EXCUSABLE HOMICIDE

Defined

To be excusable there must exist in the commission of the homicide the following four elements: (1) the homicide must have been committed by accident or misfortune; (2) it must have occurred in the doing of a lawful act by lawful means; (3) ordinary caution must have been observed by the actor, and (4) the killing must have been done without any unlawful intent. If any one of these four elements is absent the killing will not fall within the ambit of excusable homicide. *State v Hedges*, 113 P 2d 530/Wn (1941).

In General

Homicide is excusable when committed under a mistake of fact which disproves any criminal intent or when committed through accident or misfortune when there is no evil design or criminal negligence (*Somers v Superior Court*, 108 CR 630/Cal–1973): or when it was inadvertent and the defendant's negligence, if any, was not of sufficient magnitude to warrant a conviction of involuntary manslaughter (*United States v Alexander*, 471 F 2d 923/DC–1972), but homicide cannot be excusable when it is the result of an unlawful act. *State v Reynolds*, 505 P 2d 1050/Az (1973).

PART V

CRIMES AGAINST PROPERTY

Chapter XVII

Arson

Corpus Delicti

The *corpus delicti* of arson is complete when the state proves that defendant (1) willfully and maliciously set fire to a building and (2) there was a burning of the building. It is not necessary that the building be consumed; the charring of a wooden portion of one restroom and smoke damage to another within the same building was a "burning" within the contemplation of the statute. *List v State*, 308 A 2d 451/Md (1973).

In establishing the *corpus delicti* of arson the state must prove not only the fact of fire but also that the fire was maliciously set, and it is not essential to the *corpus delicti* that defendant's culpability be established. However, to convict for the crime of arson it is axiomatic that defendant's culpability be established beyond a reasonable doubt. *Smith v State*, 318 A 2d 568/Md (1974).

In General

At common law the crime of arson consisted only of the willful and malicious burning of the dwelling house of another, but this definition has been amplified by statute in most states to include not only the dwelling house of another, but the house of the arsonist as well as other structures, usually buildings which are inhabitated for commercial use. *Ex parte Bramble*, 187 P 2d 411/certiorari denied in *Bramble v California*, 377 US 960 (1949).

Where the evidence shows that a structure burned, the law assumes that the fire resulted from accident or some providential cause rather than by criminal design, and for a conviction of arson or unlawful burning, it is incumbent upon the state to prove that the fire was incendiary (*State v Schleigh*, 310 P 2d 341/Or–1957). Evidence that the burning was caused by multiple fires on the premises (*People v Hays*, 225 P 2d 600/Cal–1950), or evidence showing the presence of petroleum residue in burned portions of the building, there being two distinct fires and the proprietor being present at the time, may be sufficient to rebut the presumption of accident or providential cause and thus establish the *corpus delicti* of arson. *O'Briant v State*, 395 P 2d 396/Nev (1956).

Arson is a type of crime that rarely lends itself to proof by direct evidence, its very nature dictating the necessity of proof by circumstantial evidence (*People v Horowitz*, 194 NW 2d 375/Mich–1971). Evidence showing that defendant was indebted for construction materials and supplies, that liens had been filed, that fire insurance obtained by the owner was in excess of the value of the house and that a questionable mortgage and note had been executed, was admissible as proof of motive for arson. *State v Murdock*, 500 P 2d 387/Mont (1972).

The fire, which is an essential element of arson, need not necessarily be set on the building itself, and where defendant piled clothes on a bed and ignited them, the resultant fire was arson. *Crump v State*, 287 NE 2d 342/Ind (1972).

As a rule, arson of the first degree may be committed by the burning of a dwelling house, whether occupied or unoccupied or whether the property of the perpetrator or another. *Tukes v State*, 189 SE 2d 135/Ga (1972).

To establish murder under the arson-murder rule, the state must prove that the fire was of incendiary origin and that the fire proximately caused the death of a human being. *Com v May*, 301 A 2d 368/Pa (1973).

"Burning" Defined

"Burning," which is a requisite element of arson, is accomplished whenever some portion of a building, however small, is wasted, charred or destroyed, as distinguished from being smoked or discolored (*Gonzales v Virgin Islands*, 109 F 2d 215/VI–1940); (*People v Simpson*, 50 Cal 304–1875). The charring of accoustical tile attached to the ceiling of a room fulfilled the requirement of the statute. *State v Nielson*, 474 P 2d 725/Ut (1970).

Examples

The charring of a wooden partition in one restroom and smoke damage to another restroom adjacent to the dining area of a restaurant, constituted sufficient burning to complete the *corpus delicti* of arson. *List v State*, 308 A 2d 451/Md (1973).

Where evidence disproved accidental ignition of a fire which destroyed defendant's home on which he had recently increased fire insurance coverage, and showed that defendant was in his house alone ten to twenty minutes prior to the start of the fire, and that defendant falsely claimed destruction of his clothing by the fire, there was sufficient proof to sustain defendant's conviction for arson with intent to defraud his insurance company. *People v Bailey*, 202 NW 2d 557/Mich (1972).

Attempted Arson

Attempt to commit arson under the statutes of some states is unique in that acts of preparation plus intent complete the attempt. In no other known circumstances under contemporary substantive law do these two elements alone amount to an attempt (RCW 9.09.060); (Cal PC § 451a); (*People v Archibald*, 331 P 2d 69/Cal–1958). In *Archibald*, defendant placed crumpled newspapers and gasoline-soaked towels on the floor of a ladies' restroom and was thereafter seen with a handful of papers upraised toward a vent which opened into the restroom, and he gave conflicting reasons as to why he was there. Thus, conviction of attempted arson was warranted. Id.

Where an officer observed defendant throw an object through the window of a building and flee when the officer ordered him to halt, plus the fact that a pool of liquid amidst broken glass smelled like gasoline, plus evidence of gasoline on defendant's person, arrest and conviction of attempted arson and possession of a fire bomb were warranted. *Gedicks v State*, 214 NW 2d 569/Wis (1974).

Chapter XVIII

Burglary

FIXED STRUCTURES

Defined

"Burglary," under statute, is the unlawful breaking and entering of a building with intent to steal any property therein or to commit a felony (*Henson v State*, 500 P 2d 859/Ok–1972). Under the laws of some states breaking is not an element in the definition, the *corpus delicti* being entry with intent to commit theft or felony, and burglary is committed by one who, during business hours, enters a merchantile establishment along with customers, if he, upon entry, harbors an intent to commit theft or felony therein. California Penal Code § 459.

The essential ingredient of burglary in Nevada (as is the case in most jurisdictions) is the entry of a building with intent to commit petit or grand larceny or any felony. *Clark County v Hicks*, 506 P 2d 766/Nev (1973).

In General

The law of burglary follows two general themes: (1) in some states the burglary statute requires the entry of a structure with the intent to commit larceny or any felony; (2) in other states the entry with intent to commit any crime consummates the burglary. Also, in some states it is an essential element of the *corpus delicti* that there be a "breaking and entering" and this element is especially applicable if the subject of the attack is a commercial structure. Thus, the entry during regular business hours of a commercial building which is open to the general public, with intent to commit theft or felony is burglary in

Illinois, while such an entry with nothing more constitutes no crime in the state of Washington. It is essential that the reader know the elements of burglary in his state in order to apply pertinent cases alluded to in this chapter.

At common law burglary consisted of the breaking and entering of a dwelling house in the nighttime with intent to commit a felony (*State v Cookson*, 293 A 2d 780/Me–1972), but the scope of burglary has been broadened by most, if not all, states to include a variety of structures and object crimes. Burglary under statutory definition is never the goal or object crime but an incidental crime committed in pursuit of the actor's goal.

Under the burglary statutes of most states the entry of any structure named in the statute with intent to commit theft or felony constitutes burglary, and it is immaterial whether the perpetrator walked in through an open door of a vacant or empty building, or through the open door of a merchantile establishment wherein the public was invited by implication, or whether he broke and entered a locked structure. Thus, the fact that a supermarket was a public place did not preclude it as a building subject to burglary, as "entry without authority," an element of the offense, is present since patrons are not authorized to enter for the purpose of stealing merchandise. *McLain v House-Wright*, 293 NE 2d 911/Ill (1973).

Where defendant broke and entered a building and subsequently reentered with a coconspirator, his second entry did not constitute a second burglary but a continuing offense–that of the first burglary Nor is it necessary that entry be made at the time of or substantially contemporaneous to the breaking; the breaking may occur at one time and the entry at a later time, both elements being essential to burglary. *Knight v State*, 280 S 2d 163/Ala (1973).

Theft is not an essential element of burglary (*State v Miller*, 501 P 2d 383/Az–1972). And if the object of attack is an automobile, under a state law making an automobile the subject of burglary, this rule also applies. *Jones v State*, 482 SW 2d 634/Tex (1972).

A burglar who steals an unloaded pistol as part of the loot does not by this fact alone "arm" himself with a deadly weapon within the meaning of the statute declaring "armed" burglary to be first degree. *People v Ford*, 388 P 2d 892/certiorari denied 377 US 940/Cal (1940).

No Merger of Burglary With Object Crime

The object crime does not merge with the burglary as the burglary is complete the instant of entry, and where defendant entered victim's apartment with intent to commit rape, his conviction of both the burglary and the rape was proper (*People v Alexander*, 298 NE 2d 355/Ill–1973); and larceny committed during burglary is a separate and distinct offense, permitting conviction of defendant for burglary of a private dwelling house at night and a subsequent prosecution for larceny after a conviction of burglary. *Garcia v Veto*, 348 FS 884/Tex (1972).

"Breaking" Defined

The element of "breaking" plays a varied role in the burglary statutes of the several states. At times it is not an element; at other times it is an element of first degree, only, or of second degree, only, or of both. Breaking means making an opening into a building by treaspass and it occurs when the intruder removes or puts aside some part of the structure relied on as an obstruction to intrusion. The mere opening of a door is a breaking within the meaning of the term as it applies to burglary. *State v Hougland*, 197 NW 2d 364/Ia (1972).

When breaking is an element of burglary it may be effected by the exertion of only a slight degree of force to remove any obstacle or barrier (*Gable v State*, 424 P 2d 433/Ok–1967), such as raising a window which was already partly open (*State v Kohlfuss*, 211 A 2d 143/Con–1965); or lifting a door latch or turning a door knob (*Fondrew v State*, 175 S 2d 628/Mis–1965), or opening wider a door that is partially closed. *Rayburn v Com*, 474 SW 2d 405/Ky (1971); *People v Hill*, 193 NW 2d 909/Mich (1971).

The Fifth Circuit of the U.S. Court of Appeals has held that breaking under a Georgia statute is committed by the mere opening of a door which is closed and held shut by friction, or the pushing open of a screen door held shut by spring hinges, or the turning of a door knob thus retracting the bolt from the bolt recess and pushing the door open; it is not necessary to a breaking that splinters fly. *United States v Evans*, 415 F 2d 340/Ga (1969).

Under a burglary statute requiring that entry be accomplished by breaking, the *corpus delicti* was complete where three men were found hiding behind stacks of lumber in a fenced-in lumberyard in possession of burglary tools during the early morning hours, the breaking being accomplished by the bending down of a barbed wire stretched across the top of the gate. *Stanley v State*, 512 P 2d 829/Ok (1973).

"Entry" Defined

"Entry" is accomplished if any part of the body or an arm, hand, finger, foot or an instrument is inserted into the building. *State v Wilbely*, 300 A 2d 860/NJ (1973).

Where two or more persons are working in concert in the commission of burglary, it is only necessary that one enter the structure to constitute burglary, and where one person is acting alone his entire body need not be admitted. Thus where defendant broke the glass in the door of a building and reached his hand through in an attempt to unlock the door, burglary was complete when his hand entered, notwithstanding that the door could not be opened without a key and the closest property to the door was eight feet away. *Thompson v State*, 477 SW 2d 469/Ark (1972).

Where defendant was seen by a police officer with his leg inserted in a hole in the door of a grocery store, entry—and therefore burglary—was complete. *Hendrix v State*, 474 SW 2d 230/Tex (1971).

It is not necessary that the thief intend to steal from the building entered if entry is made to facilitate a theft nearby. For example, where the burglar entered a building to turn on lights at the gas pumps in order to steal gasoline, his conduct is one continuous transaction and thus burglary. *People v Vance*, 102 CR 266/Cal (1972).

To convict for burglary there must be proof of entry by at least a part of the body of the actor or by the insertion of an instrument with intent to take property from the building, but entry of the instrument used to effect the break-in is not an entry requisite to burglary (*Tanner v State*, 473 SW 2d 936/Tex–1971). Nor is the discharging of a firearm into a dwelling with intent to injure, an "entry" within the meaning of the word as it pertains to burglary and, thus, would not be burglary. *Williams v State*, 505 SW 2d 838/Tex (1974).

Consent to Enter–Effect of

Under the laws of some states, consent to enter, express or implied, purges the burglary even though the actor, at the time of entry, harbored the intent to commit theft or felony therein. Under similar laws the courts of other states have held that even though the actor enters upon invitation, his entry is trespassory if he harbors intent to commit crime after entry, and his entry is thus burglary.

Consent to enter a structure may be a defense to burglary, but where one has permission to enter or be in a building at a certain time only, and he enters at a time outside the scope of permission, his entry would be trespassory and, thus, burglary. *State v Keys*, 419 P 2d 943/Or (1966).

Authority or implied invitation to enter a business building or other building open to the public extends only to those who enter with a purpose consistent with the reason for the building being open. Accordingly, a burglar's entry of a car wash was without authority, notwithstanding that the car wash was a public place. *People v Blair*, 288 NE 2d 443/Ill (1972).

A janitor who was lawfully in a building and had keys to third floor offices and had instructions to clean such offices in the nighttime, could not be convicted of burglary when he stole articles from one of the offices. *People v Woods*, 510 P 2d 435/Colo (1973).

Breaking and Entering

The offense of "breaking and entering," like burglary, is complete upon entry, and the larceny of personal property thereafter constitutes a separate offense each distinct in its *corpus delicti*, and a conviction of both offenses does not amount to double jeopardy. *State v Coldwell*, 190 SE 2d 371/NC (1972).

Where both breaking and entering are essential elements of the burglary statute, they need not occur simultaneously; the breaking may occur at one time and the entry some time later. *Knight v State*, 280 S 2d 163/Ala (1973).

The size of the hole is not a determinative factor in a breaking, but rather whether or not entry was made, if by instrument, for the purpose of committing a felony. *People v Davis*, 279 NE 2d 179/Ill (1972).

Presumption or Not Upon Unlawful Entry

As to whether the unauthorized breaking and entering raises an inference of guilt, a presumption of guilt, or neither, depends on state law and how viewed by the courts of the subject state. The essential difference between these two concepts is how they are to be viewed by the trier of fact; a presumption is a deduction *required* by law, while an inference is a deduction *permitted* by law. *Hinds v John Hancock Mut Life Ins Co*, 155 A 2d 721/Me (1959).

Mere proof of breaking and entering, under Florida law, does not warrant the inference that the accused intended to commit a felony (*Griffin v State*, 276 S 2d 842/Fla–1973), but under the laws of most states, intent upon entry to commit petty larceny—a misdemeanor—as well as entry with intent to commit a felony, completes the crime of burglary.

Where Suspect Is Hiding Inside Building

Under the burglary statute of some jurisdictions it is not necessary that the perpetrator break into the structure, and under the Georgia statute defendant was guilty of burglary where he was found hiding in a shop and when questioned he admitted he had entered with intent to steal. *Smith v State*, 203 SE 2d 375/Ga (1973); *Thommen v State*, 505 SW 2d 900/Tex (1974).

When one is found inside premises where he has no right to be and there is evidence of breaking and entering, the jury may infer by the mere presence of the intruder that he entered with intent to steal. *Young v State*, 286 S 2d 76/Ala (1973).

Both the entry of a tavern at a time when it was open for business and defendant's concealment in the attic where he was later discovered, presented a question as to whether defendant intended to steal upon entry or formed the intent after entry; here defendant was convicted of burglary. *People v Terry*, 321 P 2d 709/Cal (1957).

Requisite Intent to Burglary

Although the statutes defining burglary vary from state to state, they all have one element in common—specific intent to commit some crime inside the building. Under some statutes the object crime is restricted to larceny; under others the object crime may be larceny or any felony; under still others the object crime may be any crime—felony or misdemeanor.

As a rule the state of mind of the perpetrator upon entry of the structure is the very essence of the crime of burglary. If the actor intends to commit the forbidden crime when he enters, his crime is burglary; if he forms the intent to, and does, commit the crime after his entry, his crime is not burglary. He could, however, be guilty of breaking and entering or trespass plus the object crime. Of course, one enters and steals at his peril and he may not be believed when he alleges that his intent to commit the object crime was not formed until after the entry was made. Thus, where defendant claimed, and was believed, that he entered an office to find the key to the restroom and decided to take the secretary's wallet from her purse after entry, burglary conviction could not stand. *Hutton v People*, 494 P 2d 822/Colo (1972).

Proof of defendant's intent upon entry may be inferred from facts surrounding the case such as entry without invitation, being a stranger to occupants, ransacking or disarranging articles of property, threatening violence to or committing violence upon any person when discovered (*Eby v State*, 290 NE 2d 89/Ind–1972). That defendant commits an act of violence upon any person after breaking and entering the dwelling house of another raises no presumption in law, but rather a reasonable inference that such intent existed upon entry. Id.

Where larceny is actually committed after entry, intent to steal is more readily apparent, but a failure to steal after an entry with intent to steal is no defense to a charge of burglary. *State v Balduin*, 509 P 2d 350/Ut (1973).

Trespass As It Relates to Burglary

A trespasser is defined as "one who enters the premises of another without invitation or permission, express or implied but goes, rather, for his own purposes or convenience, and not in the performance of a duty to the one in possession of the premises" (*Schock v Ringling Bros and Barnum & Bailey Combined Shows*, 105 P 2d 838/Wn–1940). One who enters the premises of another as a trespasser does so at his peril. The owner owes the trespasser no duty except to refrain from willfully or wantonly injuring him. *Winter v Mackner*, 416 P 2d 453/Wn (1966).

The California courts hold that trespass is not an essential element of burglary, for one may enter premises upon invitation and commit burglary therein (*People v Talbot*, 414 P 2d 633/Cal–1966), but Oregon and Colorado courts hold to the contrary that all burglaries are trespassory, actual or constructive (*Macias v People*, 421 P 2d 116/Colo–1966); (*State v Keys*, 419 P 2d 943/Or–1966). All three states achieve the same results, i.e., that although one enters premises upon invitation, he is guilty of burglary if he enters with intent to commit theft or felony.

Structures Subject to Burglary

Burglary, under some statutory definitions, cannot be committed by entry into a building which is a mercantile business and at the time open to the public, as entry thereinto is not an "unauthorized entry" within the meaning of the burglary statute. *State v Dunn*, 267 S 2d 193/La (1972).

The Oklahoma court ruled that a lumberyard compound entirely surrounded either by walls or a fence was a "structure" within the meaning of the burglary statute, and where three suspects were arrested inside the compound after being discovered hidden, and having in their possession burglary tools and a walkie-talkie radio, their entry constituted burglary. In this instance the breaking, a requisite to second degree burglary, was committed by bending a wire stretched across the top of a gate. *Stanley v State*, 512 P 2d 829/Ok (1973).

Watercraft or aircraft may be the subject of burglary if named in the burglary statute (*State v Gonzales*, 430 P 2d 376/NM–1966), as well as a service station office (*State v Torres*, 435 P 2d 216/NM–1967), or a mine–here defendant entered a mine with intent to steal silica (*People v Silver*, 108 P 2d 4/Cal–1940), or a boxcar wherein defendant "was caught red-handed helping himself to brass and copper scraps and placing them in a gunny sack." *Panion v People*, 331 P 2d 501/Colo (1958).

A garage which was under the same roof as the remainder of the house and which was surrounded on three sides by rooms occupied by the family, was properly the subject of first degree burglary-dwelling house where a bicycle was stolen from the garage. *State v Haas*, 510 P 2d 852/Or (1973); *People v Gargano*, 295 NE 2d 342/Ill (1973).

A carport included within the frame of the roof of a house, fenced to prevent entry, was a "structure" within the meaning of the Louisiana burglary statute whether it be regarded as part of the dwelling or as an independent structure. *State v Baggett*, 292 S 2d 201/La (1974).

The entry of a laundromat with intent to commit theft is burglary in some states notwithstanding that it is open to the public, but here the courts hold that the public is invited only for the purpose of legitimate business and entry with intent to commit theft is trespassory. *State v Zumwalt*, 439 P 2d 511/Az (1968).

Although not the rule in all states, a metal telephone booth bolted to a concrete floor and having glass windows was a "building" within the definition contained in the burglary statute of Illinois. *People v Embry*, 297 NE 2d 604/Ill (1963).

"Inhabitation" Defined

It is not essential to the crime of aggravated burglary of an "inhabited" dwelling that a human being be present at the time (*State v Hicks*, 286 S 2d 331/La–1973). However, where the statute expressly states ". . . in which there shall be at the time a human being," then it is requisite to first degree or aggravated burglary that a person other than the burglar be physically present at the time of the burglary. RCW 9.19.010.

As a rule, the burglary of an inhabited dwelling house in the nighttime is first degree burglary without any additional element. Inhabitance may exist even though no human being is in the house at the time of the burglary due to temporary absence of the occupants (*People v Loggins*, 282 P 2d 961/Cal–

1955). The length of the absence of the occupants is not of great importance, as a rule, as long as there exists *animo revertendi* (intent to return). Here victim's house was held to be an "inhabited dwelling" within the meaning of the burglary statute although the occupants had been away for several weeks. *State v Lisiewski*, 252 NE 2d 168/Oh (1969).

For a burglarized house to be a dwelling, it is sufficient that the house is occasionally occupied for residential purposes, and any such lawful occupant has a superior right as against burglars for purposes of a burglary indictment. *Montgomery v State*, 195 SE 2d 784/Ga (1973).

Under an Indiana statute the fact that a breaking and entering of a dwelling house occurred in the daytime while the occupants were away did not preclude a finding of first degree burglary. *Newman v State*, 290 NE 2d 133/Ind (1972).

Conviction of first degree burglary, which consisted in breaking into an inhabitated dwelling house, was erroneous where the building at the critical time was neither occupied nor inhabited. *Territory of Guam v Camacho*, 470 F 2d 919/Guam (1972).

Possession of Recently Stolen Property

Possession of recently stolen goods raises an inference that the possessor stole them, but in most states this inference alone, even without explanation by the possessor, is not sufficient to warrant conviction of either larceny or burglary. Of course, almost invariably corroborating circumstances will be present, such as failure to explain possession, equivocation, deceit, attempt to flee, no knowledge of brand names of the loot, or suspect's contention that he was given the property by an anonymous benefactor. It must be remembered by the officer, however, that the possessor is not obliged to explain possession; he may elect to remain silent and no adverse inference may be drawn therefrom. *People v Conerly*, 342 P 2d 305/Cal (1959); *State v Deeds*, 243 P 2d 314/Mont (1952).

Exclusive, unexplained possession of recently stolen goods is evidence of theft, and if at the time the goods were stolen burglary was committed, such possession is also evidence of burglary. *People v Jefferies*, 285 NE 2d 592/Ill (1972); *Engebrecht v State*, 268 S 2d 507/Mis (1972).

Where defendant at the time of arrest had sole possession—that is, conscious dominion or control over recently stolen goods—such possession supported a presumption or inference of guilt and warranted both larceny and burglary convictions (*Laubacher v State*, 306 A 2d 728/Del—1973). Had the stolen property been found at a place to which another had access as well as the accused, then sole or exclusive possession would not have existed, and an inference of guilt would not have been warranted. *People v Bynum*, 299 NE 2d 150/Ill (1973).

Where one is found in possession of recently stolen property taken in a burglary, the state is not required to prove the falsity of every explanation made by him as to how he came into possession of the stolen property, but only the explanation, if any, he offered at his first opportunity to explain. *Simmons v State*, 493 SW 2d 937/Tex (1973).

Defendant under prosecution for burglary can explain possession of recently stolen property by testimony, by calling another to testify in his behalf, or by the introduction of other types of evidence; if he does not explain by any of the enumerated methods, such possession may be properly considered by the jury in arriving at a verdict. *State v Lane*, 506 P 2d 446/Mont (1973).

As to what constitutes "recently stolen" goods presents a question for the jury and may vary from a few minutes to as long as two years, depending on the nature of the property and other circumstances. *Rueda v People*, 348 P 2d 958/Colo. (1960).

"Nighttime" Burglary Defined

"Nighttime," at common law and as a rule by statute, often is an element which will increase the magnitude of burglary from second degree to first degree, and particularly if the object of attack is a dwelling house. Nighttime is that period between sunset and sunrise. Nighttime is not to be confused with "hours of darkness," which is that period starting 30 minutes after sunset to 30 minutes before sunrise. Hours of darkness is usually restricted in application to the vehicle code as a time period during which vehicle lights must be turned on. *People v Helsley*, 108 P 2d 97/Cal (1940).

The time of entry is usually significant if the subject building is an inhabited dwelling house. Some jurisdictions declare any burglary of an inhabited dwelling in the nighttime to be burglary of the first degree. In other jurisdictions the burglary of an inhabited dwelling house in the nighttime is second degree unless there are additional factors, such as the house being then occupied, or the burglar being armed or committing an assault.

Burglary by Aiding and Abetting

One who acts as a lookout while an accomplice actually breaks and enters in violation of the burglary statute, is equally guilty of breaking and entering. *State v Jackson*, 317 A 2d 814/Me (1974).

The dismissal of burglary charges against one party so that he could testify against his accomplices was not an acquittal on the merits; therefore, possession of a pistol by the discharged accomplice at the time of the burglary could be imputed to his confederates, warranting conviction of burglary while armed with a deadly weapon. *People v Hadden*, 180 P 2d 371/Cal (1947).

Where defendant knew his accomplice intended to break and enter a certain structure and drove him to the scene so that he could do so, he was an aider and abettor in the crime with equal responsibility. *People v Sparks*, 198 NW 2d 900/Mich (1972).

Value of Property Relative to Burglary

The value of the goods the burglar intends to steal is not an element of burglary and is of no aid in establishing the degree of the crime, nor is the crime mitigated because nothing was stolen. *Ware v State*, 284 NE 2d 543/Ind (1972).

Under a statute requiring property of value to be in the place entered, a storage room containing empty pop bottles and trash containers, contained property having value. *State v Stead*, 473 SW 2d 714/Mo (1971).

Examples

Under a burglary statute which requires, as an element, intent to steal upon entry and since state of mind is not subject to direct proof, the state had met its obligation where it offered proof of unlawful entry into a schoolhouse by defendant at 1:00 a.m., a place containing personal property, and upon being discovered by the school custodian defendant viciously assaulted him and fled from the scene in an effort to escape. In affirming conviction for burglary the court observed, ". . . the inference [of intent to steal upon entry is] grounded in human experience which justifies the assumption that the unlawful entry was not purposeless, and, in the absence of other proof, indicates theft as the most likely purpose." *People v Polansky*, 287 NE 2d 747/Ill (1972).

Where defendant was found at 7:00 a.m., stuck in a ventilator shaft, his head, shoulders and arms sticking out, and when asked to explain his predicament, he first stated that he had fallen two stories from the top of an adjacent building and had landed feet-first in an uncovered shaft; when asked to explain how his jacket, cigarettes, the ventilator cover and four screws were lying a few feet away out of reach, he then explained he had fallen onto the roof and had attempted to complete his descent via the ventilator shaft. Nevertheless, the entry having been made and explanations inconsistent with the facts established requisite intent. *State v Holden*, 451 P 2d 666/Wn (1969).

Evidence sustained conviction of breaking and entering with intent to commit larceny where, while in possession of a hammer, pliers, knife and flashlight, the defendant was caught by a private guard reaching into a building and was handcuffed to the door. *People v Burton*, 207 NW 2d 415/Mich (1973).

That defendant, a stranger, was found in an apartment without permission of the owner and was carrying a flashlight, a leather glove and a rubber glove, sustained conviction of burglary notwithstanding defendant's testimony that he had entered the apartment to use the restroom (*People v Konetzke*, 308 NE 2d 649/Ill–1974). Likewise, defendant's conviction was sustained where he explained that he had entered burglarized premises to investigate and had "scared" two people out the back door. *Thomas v State*, 291 S 2d 744/Mis (1974).

That defendant broke into the wrong building intending to break into the building next-door and steal property therefrom, made him no less guilty of burglary of the building he actually entered. *Shipp v State*, 482 SW 2d 870/Tex (1972).

Where defendant broke into a motel room and assaulted a male and female occupant, then pointed a revolver at them, whereupon the male occupant struggled with the defendant who then fled without ever having spoken, under Oklahoma law he could be convicted of either burglary, attempted robbery or felonious assault, but not all three. *Menthen v State*, 492 P 2d 351/Ok (1971).

Whether defendant possessed the requisite intent to steal was for the jury to decide from the following facts: defendant and codefendant approached by jumping from tree to tree, stealthly entered a garage attached to a house, at night, armed with a revolver and without invitation. *People v Gargano*, 295 NE 2d 342/Ill (1973).

Under a statute declaring entry of a dwelling with intent to commit theft or felony to be burglary, one would be in violation of the statute if he entered with intent to commit murder but found his intended victim gone, even though he left the premises without having committed any crime. *Duchac v State*, 505 SW 2d 237/Ten (1973).

It is not necessary, absent a statute to the contrary, that anything of value be inside the place entered, and if the potential thief finds himself in an empty building, the abortion of his plan was caused by physical impossibility. It is legal impossibility, not physical impossibility that is a defense to crime. *State v Sufferin*, 32 P 1021/Wn (1893).

Proof of Theft Alone

Proof of the crime of larceny does not, in itself, establish the burglary in which the goods were stolen. The crime of burglary requires, *inter alia*, a breaking or an entry without breaking, and the prosecution must establish this as part of the *corpus delicti* before an inference from the possession of recently stolen property may be properly indulged. While possession of recently stolen goods gives rise to an inference that the possessor stole the goods, it is not ordinarily proof or even *prima facie* evidence of burglary. *White v United States*, 300 A 2d 716/DC (1973).

BURGLARY FROM MOTOR VEHICLE

In General

Many of the states have, by statutory provision, made an automobile the subject of burglary. A usual requisite to burglary from a motor vehicle is that the doors be locked and the windows rolled up thus requiring a breaking to enter (*Hammons v People*, 385 P 2d 592/Colo–1963). Likewise, the breaking into the locked trunk of a motor vehicle with intent to commit theft is burglary (*People *v Toomes*, 306 P 2d 953/Cal–1957). The Oklahoma court has held that where victim's automobile contained a television set in the trunk, and since the trunk lid could not be closed (the victim had secured it with a nylon cord), defendant's breaking of the cord amounted to a breaking and his reaching in to extract the television set constituted an entry and thus burglary (*Houchin v State*, 473 P 2d 925/Ok–1970). In Montana the wrongful entry into the enclosed engine compartment of an automobile with the requisite intent is an "entry" within the meaning of the statute and a burglary, and a "breaking" to enter is not an element. *State v Richter*, 451 P 2d 833/Mont (1969).

The rules of burglary in regard to fixed structures are applicable; thus, the offense of breaking and entering is complete when the vehicle is broken into and entry is made. *Chavez v State*, 479 SW 2d 687/Tex (1972).

Examples

Evidence that defendant forcibly opened the door of a locked vehicle and was in the act of entering when apprehended, sustained a conviction for entering a motor vehicle with intent to commit a felony although nothing was stolen. *Com v Hooks*, 301 A 2d 827/Pa (1973).

A carton of cigarettes in defendant's possession which was locked in a truck in a garage, was admissible against defendant to prove he broke and entered the truck and the state was not required to prove that defendant also broke into the garage. *State v Mays*, 204 NW 2d 862/Ia (1973).

Where evidence shows that an automobile has been burglarized, defendant's unexplained possession of some or all of the property stolen therefrom is sufficient evidence to sustain his conviction for the burglary. *Martinez v State*, 484 SW 2d 706/Tex (1972).

POSSESSION OF BURGLARY TOOLS

Corpus Delicti

The elements of the crime of possession of burglary tools are: (1) adaptation and design of the tool or implement for breaking and entering, (2) possession of such tools with knowledge of their character, and (3) intent to use them for the purpose of breaking and entering. *Pamphlet v State*, 271 S 2d 403/Mis (1972); *People v Spencer*, 294 NE 2d 17/Ill (1973).

In General

As a rule, two offenses may be separately prosecuted if each requires proof of an element which the other does not (*United States v Hunter*, 478 F 2d 1019/Ind–1973). Burglary and the possession of burglary tools are separate and distinct and each has elements not inlcuded in the other. Therefore, defendant may, under Georgia law, be convicted of both offenses although they are committed in the same transaction (*Smith v Ault,* 197 SE 2d 348/Ga–1973). Yet the Illinois courts have held that defendant may not be convicted of the possession of burglary tools where he was convicted of burglary by the use of those same tools in a single transaction. *People v Garnes,* 298 NE 2d 399/Ill (1973).

Burglary tools need not be of any specific design or type nor need they be sophisticated, and where defendant was in possession of a concrete block which could be used to break a window, and a tapered iron bar which could be used to pry open a drawer, he was properly convicted of possession of burglary tools. *State v Cockrum,* 512 P 2d 1373/Or (1973).

Whether an implement is a burglary tool depends somewhat on its capability, but it depends more on the purpose for which the possessor intends to employ it; whether or not an instrument is a burglary tool is a jury question. *State v Smith,* 446 P 2d 4/Az (1968).

Burglary tools may be ordinary tools innocent in design but possessed by one who intends to use them in the commission of burglary. Crowbars, hammers, flashlights, screwdrivers, wrenches, goggles, cutting torches, etc., have honest and legitimate uses in themselves; however, finding them in combination, without explanation, at 4:00 a.m., in an automobile which has just been driven behind closed businesses by defendant, warrants the conclusion that defendant intended to use them to commit burglary. *State v Gibson,* 188 SE 2d 526/NC (1972).

Requisite Intent

When the tools possessed were of a type which could be used in burglary and equally in innocent employment, the question of the possessor's intent must be the controlling factor and must be shown. *People v Spencer,* 294 NE 2d 17/Ill (1973).

Illinois has held that possession of burglary tools is not a specific intent crime, that proof of intent to burglarize some structure or some vehicle is all that is required (*People v Ray,* 278 NE 2d 170/Ill–1972). This holding seems to contain an inherent inconsistency and does not represent the majority rule. Intent to burglarize some structure or vehicle *is* specific intent.

Proof Necessary to Conviction

In order to convict one of possession of burglary tools, the state must prove possession under circumstances which evince an intent to employ such tools to commit burglary, such as the recent commission of other burglaries (*State v Olsen,* 263 P 2d 824/Wn–1953). Thus, where two or more persons are acting in concert all may be in joint possession or constructive possession of the tools (*State v McDonald,* 445 P 2d 345/Wn–1968). Where defendant had burglary tools in an adjoining room of his house, he had dominion or control over, and thus constructive possession of, burglary tools. *State v Palmer*, 487 P 2d 249/Wn (1971).

It is not necessary that the state prove that defendant possessed tools with intent to commit any particular burglary, only that they were possessed with intent to commit burglary (*State v Caldrone*, 451 P 2d 205/Kan–1969), and ownership of the tools is not an element in a prosecution for their illegal possession. *State v McDonald, supra.*

Examples

A burglary alarm jumper found in defendant's apartment (*Salisbury v State*, 293 S 2d 434/Mis–1974), a three-pound hammer and a five-eights inch punch when possessed with intent to commit burglary (*Schutz v United States*, 395 F 2d 225/Ok–1968), and a piece of concrete block which could be used to break a window and an iron bar tapered at one end which could be used to force open drawers were "burglary tools" within the contemplation of the statute forbidding their possession. *State v Cockrum*, 512 P 2d 1373/Or (1973).

Chapter XIX

Theft—General

Corpus Delicti

"Larceny" is the wrongful taking and carrying away, i.e., asportation, of the personal property of another with fraudulent intent to deprive him thereof (*United States v Barlow*, 470 F 2d 1245/DC–1972), and there must exist in the mind of the perpetrator, intent to permanently deprive the owner of his property. *State v McKeough*, 300 A 2d 755/Me (1973).

One who, knowing he has no right to do so, takes and carries away the property of another with the intent to deprive the owner of his property permanently and to convert it to his own use is surely guilty of larceny. However, he is no less guilty if, when he took the property, his intention was to convert it to the use of another or to destroy it so that no one could use it. *State v Lee*, 193 SE 2d 705/NC (1973).

"Theft" and "Larceny" Defined

The words "theft" and "larceny" are often used interchangeably and their meanings are essentially synonymous. *Black's Law Dictionary* defines theft, *inter alia*, as "a popular name for larceny." Although some states distinguish between these two concepts, this text treats them as synonymous.

The Fifth Circuit of the U.S. Court of Appeals observes that "theft" is not, as is "larceny," a technical word of art whose meaning is narrowly defined but is, on the contrary, a word of general and broad connotation, covering all types of criminal appropriation and including in particular the crimes of swindling, embezzlement, false pretenses or any other taking of property by guile (*Edwards v Bromberg*, 232 F 2d 107/Ill–1956). And in another case the Fifth Circuit has observed that some states regard "theft" as a synoptic concept embracing numerous methods of unlawfully depriving another of his property—such as false pretenses, trick or device, embezzlement—but these same varieties and others may be included in a statute defining larceny (*Cameron v Hauck*, 383 F 2d 966/Tex–1967). If there is a marked difference in the meaning of the two words within a jurisdiction it will be the result of legislative preference and court interpretation in that state.

Under Oregon law the larceny or theft statute defines one single concept of theft, not several. *State v Jim*, 508 P 2d 462/Or (1973).

The Nature of Theft

Larceny is an offense against possession rather than an offense against ownership; therefore ownership of the property in most jurisdictions is immaterial (*Levin v United States*, 338 F 2d 265/DC–1964), and one who steals property from another who has himself stolen it may, nevertheless, be convicted of larceny. Id.

The Colorado courts hold that one means of committing theft is by threats or extortion (*People v Moore*, 518 P 2d 944/Colo–1974), but the California law does not treat property taken by extortion as stolen property since it is obtained with the consent of the victim. California Penal Code, §§ 496, 518.

Where appellants attempted to justify larceny by showing that poverty and want existed among the unemployed and this was their motive and purpose for taking merchandise from a store, the court responded, in affirming conviction, that economic necessity has never been an acceptable defense to larceny; that if it were ever countenanced it would leave to individuals the right to take the law in their own hands. *State v Moe*, 24 P 2d 638/Wn (1933).

Consent to the taking of property is a complete defense to a prosecution for theft provided the consentor is competent and the consent is genuine. However, the act of an undercover police officer, feigning drunkenness in the front seat of his car and turning over so as to expose the pocket which contained his wallet, did not amount to consent to its taking. *Odom v Sheriff*, 497 P 2d 906/Nev (1972).

"Steal" Defined

According to *Corpus Juris Secundum*:

> The word "steal" has a fixed and well-defined meaning, a uniform signification, in common, as well as in legal, parlence . . .
>
> The word "steal" itself imparts a wrongful taking and appropriation of the property of another to the taker's own benefit, and thus is defined as meaning to take and carry away feloniously; to take without right or leave, and with intent to keep or make use of wrongfully; to take and

> carry away property of another with the felonious intent to deprive the owner thereof . . . the felonious taking and carrying away personal goods of another . . . . *Corpus Juris Secundum* Vol 82–Steal.

The word "steal" has no common law definition to restrict its meaning, but it is commonly used to denote any dishonest transaction whereby one person obtains that which rightfully belongs to another and deprives the owner of the rights and benefits of ownership, but it does not necessarily include the element of stealth as does the word "purloin." *United States v Handler,* 142 F 2d 351/NY (1944).

"Property" Subject to Theft

"Property" is a thing of value and capable of ownership, a thing having value whether tangible or intangible, corporeal or incorporeal, visible or invisible, real or personal. *Black's Law Dictionary.*

The Oregon Court of Appeals has declared property to be, but not limited to, a blank check, drivers' licenses, draft cards, a hospital association card, Boy Scout card, Social Security card, union card, a hunting and fishing license. The receipt and concealment of such articles, knowing them to have been stolen, will support a conviction of receiving stolen property (*State v Hardesty,* 493 P 2d 56/Or–1972). Other articles or things which constitute property are a contraband slot machine (*People v Gonzales,* 144 P 2d 605/Cal–1944), personal service such as lodging and hotel accommodations (*State v Higgins,* 406 P 2d 784/Wn–1965), gas and electricity. *Selman v State,* 406 P 2d 181/Alk (1965).

A blank check or a document containing a compilation of information can be the subject of theft. *State v Alden,* 495 P 2d 302/Or (1972); *People v Kunkin,* 100 CR 895/Cal (1972).

A woman's chastity or virtue, although a "thing" of value or advantage for the purpose of kidnap (*Householder v Raney,* 485 P 2d 247/Ok–1971), has not been declared to be a thing of value capable of being stolen.

Theft of Lost Property

A statute proscribing theft of lost property, or of property mislaid or delivered by mistake, is merely a refined description of acts forbidden in the larceny statute more generally described as taking, appropriating, obtaining or withholding from the owner with intent to defraud the owner thereof. *State v Jim,* 508 P 2d 462/Or (1973).

A failure to take reasonable steps to restore property to its owner is an essential element of the offense of theft of lost property. *People v Hines,* 299 NE 2d 581/Ill (1973).

Where defendant, by his own testimony, was handed two checks by a stranger on the sidewalk and he, suspecting that something was wrong with the checks, put them in a litter basket, he was guilty of theft of found property; it is no defense that he derived no benefit from the property. *People v Hines, supra.*

Ownership of Property—Proof of

In a prosecution for theft in some jurisdictions the state must allege and prove either ownership or some form of superior possessory interest in the property in one other than the accused (*People v Ruiz*, 305 NE 2d 653/Ill—1973). The reason for proving ownership is twofold: to obviate consent to the taking, and to identify the occasion to foreclose double jeopardy (*White v State*, 288 S 2d 175/Ala—1974). An accusatory pleading charging theft must name the owner of the property stolen, and the state must so prove for conviction (*People v Barrett*, 312 NE 2d 653/Ill—1974). Louisiana represents the alternative concept holding that proof of ownership is not an element of proof of the crime of theft; the state is required only to prove that the property belonged to a person other than the defendant. *State v Rossi*, 273 S 2d 265/La (1973).

A person who holds property as collateral for a debt is the "owner" of that property as it relates to larceny. *Cabell v State*, 312 NE 2d 142/Ind (1974).

Ordinarily one could not be convicted of stealing his own property, but when the personalty is in the possession of another by virtue of some special right or title and is taken by the owner with intent to deprive the possessor of his right to possession, or to charge him for the value of the chattel, then a conviction of larceny will lie. *Trevathan v Mutual Life Ins Co of New York*, 113 P 2d 261/Or (1941).

Intent to Steal

Intent to steal—intent to permanently deprive the owner of his property—and *animus furandi* are phrases essentially synonymous and a requisite element of larceny (*State v Leicht*, 305 A 2d 78/NJ—1973).

To constitute larceny the felonious intent to steal must exist at the time of the taking, and if defendant had no such intent he would not be guilty of larceny even though he subsequently formed such intent to, and did, retain possession of the property. *State v Hopple*, 357 P 2d 656/Id (1960); *Gibson v State*, 328 P 2d 718/Ok (1958).

Intent to permanently deprive the rightful owner of his property is proved when it is shown that defendant, after taking the property, sold it to a third party. *State v McClanahan*, 262 S 2d 499/La (1972).

If defendant harbored the requisite intent to steal property at the time of the taking, it is immaterial that he later formed the intent to restore it (*State v Black*, 1 P 2d 206/Wn—1931); nor would a partial or even a complete restoration of property once stolen purge the thief of criminal responsibility. *Kelly v People*, 443 P 2d 734/Colo (1968).

Intent to deprive the owner of his property can be inferred where property is taken and subsequently abandoned (*State v Langis*, 444 P 2d 959/Or–1967), such as throwing the victim's shoes into a field and disposing of her purse where larceny by criminal conversion was established (*State v Golladay*, 470 P 2d 191/Wn–1970). And where the property is taken and destroyed, the requisite intent is manifested and it is immaterial that the taker did not benefit therefrom or, if so, that he benefited in a pecuniary manner. *Farrington v State*, 489 SW 2d 607/Tex (1972); *State v Lee*, 193 SE 2d 705/NC (1973).

The deliberate smashing of the victim's eyeglasses "permanently deprived" the owner thereof and justified conviction of larceny rather than malicious mischief. *People v Bell*, 292 NE 2d 291/Ill (1972).

Asportation

An early California case demonstrates the element of asportation. A merchant hung an overcoat on a "clothing dummy" outside his store in the city of Los Angeles. Defendant attempted to steal the coat by removing it from the dummy but discovered that a chain ran through one of the sleeves and was fixed to the building. Defendant was arrested, tried and convicted of theft; he appealed. In reversing, the court held that although the coat was removed from the dummy, defendant did not have dominion or control over the coat and, thus, asportation was lacking. *People v Myer*, 17 P 431/Cal (1888).

"Asportation" has been defined as gaining dominion or control over, and movement of, a person or a thing (*Tucker v State*, 279 S 2d 576/Ala–1973). But this definition is not applicable in a self-service store, for here asportation of an article of property is not complete until the actor passes a check-out stand without paying for the article. *State v Hauck*, 209 NW 2d 580/Neb (1973).

It is not necessary in all cases that the property be removed from the building in which the property is located. The concealment of articles beneath clothing (*Hutchison v State*, 427 P 2d 112/Ok–1967), or the removal of articles to another location on the premises, has been held to be sufficient asportation to complete larceny (*State v Hill*, 486 P 2d 1398/Kan–1971). The element of asportation, a requisite of both larceny and robbery, is sufficiently established when there is shown the least removal of the thing from its place of rest with intent to steal it (*Rutkowski v United States*, 149 F 2d 481/Mich–1945). Thus, asportation was deemed complete where evidence showed that a heavy valve weighing about 175 pounds had been moved two or three feet from its original position and defendant was apprehended leaving the scene. *Baker v State*, 511 SW 2d 272/Tex (1974).

Theft Through Agent

One who uses an agent to procure property under circumstances which make the taking larceny, is guilty as a principal of larceny, and the agent may or may not be guilty of larceny depending on the presence or absence of *animo furandi. United States v Pauldino*, 487 F 2d 127/Colo (1973).

Where defendant employed an agent to steal an automobile for him, the defendant was as guilty of theft as though he personally stole the automobile. And if the agent was unaware of the nature of the taking, he would be innocent of any wrongdoing for lack of criminal intent. *United States v Pauldino, supra.*

When Separate Thefts May Be Segregated

Each taking of property, if the result of a separate, independent impulse or intent, is a distinct crime, but when the successive takings are the result of a single continuing impulse, and are pursuant to a single larcenous scheme or plan, such successive takings constitute but a single larceny regardless of the time lapse between successive takings (*State v Vining*, 472 P 2d 564/Wn–1970). This rule applies to all types of larceny. Thus, a public officer charged with the safekeeping and disbursement of public moneys may, by a series of small appropriations from such funds, be liable to prosecution for the embezzlement of the gross amount taken as constituting but one offense (*Geymen v State*, 192 P 2d 707/Ok–1948). But where one person steals property from different persons at different times, the total may not be aggregated so as to make two misdemeanor thefts into one felony theft. *State v Pena*, 516 P 2d 761/Or (1973).

Shoplifting

Shoplifting, in those states having a shoplifting statute, denounces the taking of a commodity which is offered for sale in a commercial business. Under a burglary statute which does not require a breaking but declares "entry with intent to commit larceny" to be burglary, shoplifting may amount to burglary. It is difficult, of course, to prove intent to commit larceny at the time of entry. Shoplifting is a necessarily included offense of larceny. *State v Ponton*, 399 P 2d 30/certiorari denied 382 US 1014/Or (1965).

In larceny by shoplifting, it is not essential to a conviction that the thief be allowed to leave the premises before he is arrested. Thus, where defendant entered a drugstore and placed a bottle of pills in his coat pocket and went to the check-out counter using a lane where he could go directly out of the store and was arrested as he was leaving the check-out lane, still in possession of the pills, not paid for (*People v Thompson*, 299 NE 2d 76/Ill–1973); or, where defendant took a box with him into a department store and placed therein 63 pairs of men's shorts and 13 sport shirts, and abandoned the box and contents inside the store and ran when discovered (*People v Tyerina*, 459 P 2d 680/Cal–1969); or where defendant removed a television set from its place in a warehouse and placed it in his automobile—conviction for larceny was not circumvented though the property was not moved from the premises. *State v Crowe*, 414 P 2d 50/Kan (1966).

Theft From the Person

Under a statute denouncing larceny from the person, it is requisite that the property shall have been contained in or on clothing being worn, or was being carried in the hand or in some type of a receptacle. Where evidence showed that defendant took gambling tokens valued at $250 from a table beside victim in a gambling casino, his conviction of grand theft-person could not stand. *Terral v State*, 422 P 2d 465/Nev (1968).

Under South Dakota law, however, the taking of a thing of value may be grand larceny if taken by stealth from the person or from the *immediate presence* of the victim. *State v Aschmeller*, 209 NW 2d 369/SD (1973).

Larceny from the person may be compounded by a slight degree of force over and above that necessary to extract the property from its owner and thus become a robbery. All robbery wherein the property taken was in the physical possession of the victim, necessarily includes larceny from the person; however, if the property taken was not from the physical possession of the victim, but from his immediate presence instead, and if taken by force or fear the taking would be robbery but not larceny from the person. *Cannon v State*, 107 P 2d 809/Ok (1940).

Crossing State Lines With Stolen Property

As a rule, the stealing of property in one state and transporting it into a second state is made larceny in the second state by statute on the theory of continuing larceny. *Clewley v State*, 288 A 2d 468/Me (1972); *Hamilton v State*, 288 A 2d 885/Md (1972).

A person committing larceny in one state and transporting the stolen property into another state is liable to prosecution in the latter state as well as the former as the offense is one of a continuing nature and the crime follows the thing stolen (*State v Johnson*, 2 Or 15–1864), but defendant may not be tried in both states as this would constitute being twice placed in jeopardy for the same offense—a violation of the Fifth Amendment to the U.S. Constitution. *People v Case*, 313 P 2d 840/Cal (1957).

Federal law supplements state law where the thing stolen is valued at $5,000 or more and transported across a state line. An exception to the $5,000 value exists if the thing stolen was forged securities, tax stamps or tools used in their production (United States Code, Title 18, § 13); (*United States v Hassel*, 341 F 2d 427/Va–1965). "Securities" as used in Title 18, includes money orders (*Nelson v United States*, 406 F 2d 1136/Fla–1969), stolen blank traveler's checks filled in and cashed (*United States v Brown*, 417 F 2d 1068/Fla–1969) and forged checks in the amount of $20 or less. *Argent v United States*, 325 F 2d 162/Fla (1963).

Proof of Theft

Although obviously of probative value, the introduction of the stolen property or a partion thereof is not necessary to a conviction, and direct testimony describing the thing stolen is usually sufficient especially if the thing stolen was of such a nature as to make its production in court impractical. *State v Newman*, 412 P 2d 515/Wn (1966).

Examples

Where defendants took a trailer loaded with goods, moved it several miles then broke the lock to gain entry, and found FBI agents inside, their act was no less a larceny because of the fact that the trailer had been under constant surveillance. *United States v Douver*, 472 F 2d 472/Cal (1973).

Where an officer placed handcuffs on arrestee, the officer merely relinquished custody of the handcuffs—title and possession remaining with him—and arrestee's taking of the handcuffs through the process of escape constituted theft. *Dedmon v State*, 478 SW 2d 486/Tex (1972).

Where an undercover officer gave money to defendant in an offer to purchase heroin and defendant ran away with the money, larceny had been committed. *Com v Coplin*, 313 A 2d 349/Pa (1973).

Defendants who were sisters, 13 and 14 years of age, were convicted of robbery where the evidence showed that they approached their victim, an 84-year-old man, and "punched" him about the trunk of the body allegedly to "bring him luck," and while "bringing him luck" one stealthily removed a $757 roll of bills from his pocket while an older brother of the girls looked on from an automobile parked a short distance away. Conviction was reversed, however, and remanded for sentence for larceny due to the apparent absence of fear and the insufficient force employed. *Marks v State*, 102 P 2d 955/Ok (1940).

Grand Theft

Except when the property stolen is from the person or as designated by other statutory exceptions, value of property is significant in distinguishing between grand and petty larceny. The value line distinguishing grand larceny starts as low as $20 in Oklahoma to as high as $200 in California, and these figures may not designate the two extremes. To correlate the case law herein contained to the crime of theft (larceny), it is necessary that one know the value line between grand and petty larceny as defined by the laws of his state.

Under a statute declaring the larceny of livestock regardless of value to be a felony, defendant was as guilty of grand larceny—a felony—where he killed a cow, then hauled away its carcass as though he had stolen the live cow. *State v Crossman*, 63 P 2d 934/Wn (1936); *State v Breville*, 270 S 2d 852/La (1972).

The value of personal property stolen is not an element of the crime of theft from the person, as the theft of anything of value from the person is grand theft. *State v Mallory*, 504 P 2d 556/Az (1972).

What Is Not Theft

The mere taking of the property of another absent *animus furandi* is not larceny. Although intent to steal ordinarily may be inferred by the taking, proof of a state of mind incompatible with such intent precludes a finding of guilty pursuant to a charge of either robbery or larceny. *People v Butler*, 421 P 2d 703/Cal (1967).

A charge of larceny will not lie where one takes openly and avowedly under a claim of title preferred in good faith even though such claim is untenable (*People v Photo*, 114 P 2d 71/Cal—1941). Intent to collect a secure debt negates *animus furandi*, but such claim was emasculated where defendant took more money than was due him. *State v Trujillo*, 489 P 2d 977/Or (1971).

Larceny is not committed when the actor takes the property from its owner with the intent of borrowing it and returning it later (*Fredericks v United States*, 306 A 2d 268/DC—1973), as intent to steal must exist at the time of the taking. *State v Puga*, 510 P 2d 1075/NM (1973).

It has been held that partnership funds belong equally to all partners, and a member who absconds with all of the funds is not guilty of either larceny or embezzlement (*Dethlefsen v Stull*, 195 P 2d 56/Cal—1948); (*State v Elsbury*, 175 P 2d 430/Nev—1946). But in a later California case the court has ruled that partnership property may be the subject of embezzlement. *People v Sobiek*, 106 CR 519/Cal (1973).

A good faith attempt to recover money lost in an illegal wager is neither theft nor attempted theft. *People v Littleton*, 101 CR 489/Cal (1972).

"Larceny," "Embezzlement" and "False Pretenses" Distinguished

The crimes of larceny and embezzlement are inconsistent. Embezzlement presupposes lawful possession at the time the thing of value was converted, while theft is predicated upon an unlawful taking. *United States v Trevino*, 491 F 2d 74/Tex (1974).

The primary distinctions among larceny, embezzlement and obtaining property under false pretenses have been clearly delineated in *Com v Barry*, 124 Mas 325 (1878), as follows:

> If a person honestly receives the possession of the goods, chattels or money of another upon any trust, express or implied, and, after receiving them, fraudulently converts them to his own use, he may be guilty of the crime of embezzlement . . . . If the possession of such property is obtained by fraud, and the owner of it intends to part with his title as well as his possession, the offense is that of obtaining property by false pretenses . . . . If the possession is fraudulently obtained, with intent on the part of the person obtaining it, at the time he receives it, to convert the same to his own use, and the person parting with it intends to part with his possession merely, and not with his title to the property, the offense is larceny. *State v Jesser*, 501 P 2d 727/Id (1972).

EMBEZZLEMENT

Defined

The terms "embezzle" and "fraudulently convent" are synonymous (*State v Tauscher*, 360 P 2d 764/Or–1961), and they define a type of larceny having a unique characteristic–that of fiduciary relationship. Specifically, embezzlement is larceny by a clerk, servant or agent, and consists in appropriating for himself that which he receives from another in trust. *Livingston v State*, 441 P 2d 681/Nev (1968).

The Nature of Embezzlement

Historically, larceny and embezzlement are of different origins: larceny is a common law crime and embezzlement is a creature of statute. The gravamen of embezzlement is breach of trust. *State v Schofield*, 438 P 2d 776/Az (1968).

A "fiduciary relationship" is one founded on trust or confidence by one person in the integrity and fidelity of another. *Mobil Oil Corp v Rubenfeld*, 339 NYS 2d 623/NY (1972).

The fundamental nature of embezzlement is the coming into possession of property honestly and by virtue of trust, and the conversion of the property to one's own use or to some other purpose not within the terms of his employment (*State v Taylor*, 378 P 2d 352/Ut–1963), or the lawful acquisition and the unlawful appropriation of property (*State v Konop*, 384 P 2d 385/Wn–1963). Concealment is not an element of embezzlement and neither mitigates nor increments the crime. *State v McCormick*, 442 P 2d 134/vacated and remanded on another point 448 P 2d 74/Az (1968).

Actual possession of the property embezzled is not necessary to conviction, as where defendant was the vice-president of a bank and he ordered a check deposited to his benefit though he never physically possessed the money, instead appropriating by constructive possession only. *State v Larson*, 216 P 28/Wn (1923).

A demand by the bailee for the return of the embezzled property is not a necessary antecedent to conviction (*State v Lyon*, 452 P 2d 838/Kan–1969). If this were the case the embezzler could retain the money until discovered and until demand was made for its return. Under such a system public funds would fall prey to plunderers. *State v Larson, supra.*

Effect of Intent–When Formed

It is not fatal to a conviction of embezzlement resting on entrustment that fraudulent intent to appropriate money existed at the time of, or was formed coincidentally with, receipt of the money (*State v Konviser*, 259 P 2d 785/NM–1953). But if the defendant's state of mind at the time of receipt of the property can be ascertained, the crime then may be fixed with certainty as either embezzlement or larceny by trick. *Gibson v State*, 328 P 2d 718/Ok (1958).

Intent to permanently deprive the owner of his property, a requisite of other types of larceny, is not a necessary element of embezzlement, and the trial court's instruction to the jury that such intent was a necessary element of embezzlement was error but favorable to defendant and adverse to the state and thus, not reversible error. *State v Lilopulos*, 10 P 2d 564/Wn (1932).

Contrary to the general rule pertaining to larceny, intent to return the property at some future date is no defense once the property has been appropriated (*State v Schofield*, 438 P 2d 776/Az–1968), as neither intent to return property once embezzled nor its actual return to the owner, nor intent to make restitution by some other means relieves the perpetrator of criminal responsibility (*United States v Powell*, 294 FS 1353/Va–1968). Further, the fact that defendant intended to return the property not only is no defense but it also is not grounds for mitigation of punishment; however, if restoration is made before the filing of an accusatory pleading, such fact may be considered under appropriate statute in the fixing of sentence. *M K & O Coach Lines v Meister*, 330 P 2d 579/Ok (1958).

Public Monies

The embezzlement of public money in some states is a felony regardless of the value of the property taken. A city councilman who used city-owned stationery furnished him to be used in his official capacity as councilman, was guilty of embezzlement when he used the stationery to promote his campaign for reelection (*People v Nathanson*, 284 P 2d 975/Cal–1955); a police officer whose duty it was to receive and transmit bail money and who unlawfully took $150 of that money and converted it to his personal use, was guilty of embezzlement. *People v Best*, 342 P 2d 314/Cal (1959).

Defendant's possession of public monies plus a failure to account for it in court records, together with a false entry in a prisoner's file that he had received the equivalent of $79 in jail-time credit, when in fact he had paid a fine, amounted to embezzlement of public monies. *State v Stiltner*, 479 P 2d 103/Wn (1971).

Examples

Money collected by one person while in the employ of, and for, another, is rightfully due the latter, and failure to transfer such monies as required amounts to "conversion," a necessary element of embezzlement. *Hucal v People*, 493 P 2d 23/Colo (1971).

Where defendant received an automobile from a dealer "for a trial run" and took it to a second dealer and represented it as his own and attempted to trade it for another, there was evidence of fraudulent conversion from which the trier of fact could infer intent to deprive the owner of his property. *Valencia v State*, 502 SW 2d 125/Tex (1973).

A bailee who accepted a check in payment of a vehicle, and then refused to deliver the vehicle making it necessary for the purchaser to again pay for the vehicle, was guilty of embezzlement. *State v Ahl*, 371 P 2d 7/Mont (1962).

Evidence that defendant sold a motorcycle to complainant and thereafter borrowed it from him and sold it to another, substantially established the crime of embezzlement. *State v Gregg*, 492 P 2d 1260/NM (1972).

Where defendant accepted a combination radio-phonograph under an agreement to repair it and return it within three days and under a pretense that he needed it to procure parts, induced the victim who could not read English to sign a bill of sale, his deception constituted embezzlement. *State v King*, 182 P 2d 915/Az (1967).

Where a city fireman removed property from the area of a brush fire to prevent its destruction by fire, he was thus bailee of the property; but when he continued to withhold the property from its owner and converted it to his own use he was guilty of embezzlement. *People v Coon*, 101 P 2d 565/Cal (1940).

A civilian manager of an Army post exchange who took cigarettes off the post and sold them in excess of the government sale price and retained the excess for his own use, was guilty of embezzlement notwithstanding that he returned to the government the regular price of the cigarettes. *United States v Titus*, 64 FS 55/NJ (1946).

An informant who accepted money from an undercover narcotics officer with instructions to use it to purchase narcotics but who then failed to use the money as instructed and converted it to his own use, was guilty of embezzlement. *Ex parte Pickerill*, 44 FS 714/Tex (1942).

By false representations defendant obtained money from a union official which the official had himself embezzled from the union. The accused defended on the grounds that he could not be convicted for taking stolen money from a thief. The circuit court, in affirming his conviction, held that larceny is a crime against possession and not necessarily against ownership. *Levin v United States*, 338 F 2d 265/DC (1964).

The taking of a television set from a motel room which defendant had rented amounted to embezzlement under Kansas law (*State v Taylor*, 512 P 2d 449/Kan–1973). But the Oregon courts hold that a motel guest does not have possession of property in his room in a fiduciary capacity, and the unlawful taking of property therefrom is larceny and not embezzlement. *State v Lewis*, 433 P 2d 617/Or (1967).

"Embezzlement," "False Pretenses" and "Bunco" Distinguished

Embezzlement differs from obtaining money by false pretenses and larceny by trick or bunco in the original acquisition of the money. In embezzlement the accused enjoys a position of trust or a fiduciary relationship with the victim, and by virtue of that trust receives money or other property in trust; after receipt thereof and contrary to his trust, he converts the property either to his personal use or to some other purpose not contemplated in the trust. *State v Seefeldt*, 212 P 2d 1053/NM (1949).

Where defendant received machines under an agreement to sell them, a refusal to turn over the proceeds therefrom constituted larceny. Had defendant intended unlawful conversion at the time he received the machines the specific crime would have been larceny by trick or device; had he formed the intent after receiving the machines, the crime would have been embezzlement. *People v Martin*, 314 P 2d 493/Cal (1957).

Where the taker formed the intent to steal certain property before he received it, and employed trick and deception in obtaining it, the crime could not be embezzlement, for one cannot embezzle that which he has already stolen. *State v Taylor*, 378 P 2d 352/Ut (1963).

The custody and control of property requisite to embezzlement must be more than bare custody. Thus where defendant, a hired hand on a farm, was directed to drive a truck from a field to the owner's house, and the hired hand thereafter loaded the truck with various articles of the owner's property and drove away, he was properly charged with and convicted of larceny and not embezzlement, as his act constituted a separate and independent venture. *State v James*, 143 P 2d 642/Kan (1943).

FALSE PRETENSES

Defined

Material to an allegation of obtaining money or other property by "false pretenses" are: (1) intent to defraud; (2) a false pretense or representation based on an existing or past fact; (3) knowledge by the accused of the falsity of the representation; (4) reliance on the fraud by the victim; and (5) accomplishment of that fraud by the victim's parting title and possession of his property to the swindler. *State v Warren*, 212 NW 2d 509/Ia (1973); *State v Parsons*, 201 NW 2d 895/ND (1972).

The crime of false pretenses is committed when a person, by making a false representation of a past or existing fact with intent to defraud and having knowledge of the falsity of the representation, obtains any chattel, money or valuable security from another who relies on the false representation to his detriment. *Maloney v State*, 304 A 2d 260/Md (1973).

In General

Theft by false pretext is but another form of theft and the element of "appropriation" is merely evidentiary in relation to the taking. *Smith v State*, 502 SW 2d 133/Tex (1973).

The crime of false pretenses may be consummated where the perpetrator actually obtains ownership, although fraudulently, of the property and not mere possession. *Shope v State*, 307 A 2d 730/Md (1973).

The crime of false pretenses requires not only that there be a misrepresentation, but that such representation be made by defendant with full knowledge that it is false and with specific intent to cheat or defraud. *State v Thyfault*, 297 A 2d 873/NJ (1972).

A conviction of false pretenses in some jurisdictions cannot be sustained on the testimony of only one witness but requires corroboration; such corroboration may be in the form of a false token or writing employed in the commission of the crime, or it may be supplied by two witnesses or one witness and corroborating circumstances. *People v Randono*, 108 CR 326/Cal (1973); *Bradshaw v State*, 510 P 2d 972/Ok (1973).

Nature of the Pretense

A false pretense may consist of any, act, word, symbol or token calculated to deceive; it may be express or implied, and if express, it may be oral or written (*State v Larsen*, 286 P 2d 646/Id—1955); or the fraud may be perpetrated by the silence of the actor when an honest disclosure of pertinent circumstances are required (*Balleine v District Court*, 153 P 2d 265/Ut—1944); or it may be perpetrated by silence, gestures, or conduct such as where defendant presents a false or forged document for payment but says nothing. *State v Moore*, 66 P 2d 836/Wn (1937); *People v Randono, supra.*

False Pretense Must Be Based on Present or Past Fact

As a rule larceny by false pretenses must be predicated on an existing or past fact; however, a conviction will lie where there is a promise made to perform in the future and there is no intent to perform (*Lamascus v State*, 516 P 2d 279/Ok—1973); (*United States v 1557.28 Acres of Land*, 486 F 2d 445/Kan—1973). Thus, where defendant falsely declared his intention to assist victim in attaining a designated position in a social organization—having no intention to carry out his promise and making the declaration to induce victim to part with money to the defendant which was the result—larceny by false pretenses based on a future event was committed. *Com v Moreau*, 304 NE 2d 198/Mas (1973).

Statements of mere opinion cannot form a basis for a prosecution for fraud. *United States v 1557.28 Acres of Land, supra.*

Victim Must Rely on the Pretense

The false representation made by the actor need not be the sole cause which induces the victim to part with his property; it is sufficient for the victim to rely on the representation to a degree that it influences his decision. A false representation alone is not criminal, the three elements being a false representation, reliance thereon and defrauding the victim of property (*State v Brown*, 400 P 2d 111/Az–1965). Nor must the state prove that the victim had a right to rely on the representation made by the accused, and defendant is not purged by the fact that the victim was gullible or credulous. The court cannot instruct the jury to weigh a false pretense or inducement to action of any scale other than its effect on the victim. *State v Cooke*, 371 P 2d 39/Wn (1962).

The purpose of the false pretenses statute is to punish cheats, but this cannot be accomplished when the victim has knowledge that the cheating is about to occur (*People v Wilde*, 202 NW 2d 542/Mich–1972); and when the owner is aware of the false pretense and places no reliance thereon, the crime is not committed (*State v Hauck*, 209 NW 2d 580/Neb–1973). But lack of proof of reliance by the victim upon the false pretense does not exculpate defendant of crime, for his act would still fall within the inchoate area of attempt to commit crime. *People v Wilde, supra.*

Financial Loss Not Essential

The Montana Supreme Court has ruled that although there is authority that pecuniary loss is essential to a conviction for larceny by false pretenses (*Daniel v State*, 10 SE 2d 80/Ga–1940), the better rule does not require loss to the victim and a conviction of false pretenses is valid whether or not the victim suffered loss so long as he parted with his property (*State v Johnson*, 367 P 2d 891/Mont–1962). Therefore, that no loss was suffered, or, if suffered, that restitution was made is no defense. *State v Mills*, 396 P 2d 5/Az (1964).

In determining the degree of the theft the amount of money received by the defendant, and not the loss to the victim, is the proper determinant (*People v Ross*, 100 CR 703/Cal–1972), and that the victim can recoup his loss by civil action neither nullifies nor abates the magnitude of the false representation. *Foor v State*, 413 P 2d 719/Kan (1966).

The fact that the property was worth the consideration paid is no defense if evidence shows that the accused knowingly made false and fraudulent representations of existing facts (*People v Raines*, 153 P 2d 424/Cal–1944). And victim's ultimate financial loss or even gain is immaterial as the victim is merely a witness in a criminal action and the state is the plaintiff. *People v Talbott*, 151 P 2d 317/certiorari denied 324 US 845/Cal (1944).

Automobile Larceny

There is a conflict of authority as to the type of larceny committed when the object of the larceny is an automobile. The California courts hold that where the accused obtains possession of an automobile but not title thereto, the crime is not larceny by false pretenses but rather larceny by trick or device (*People v Pillsbury*, 138 P 2d 320/Cal–1943). But the Montana Supreme Court has held that where the property obtained is a motor vehicle it is not necessary to prove that title actually did pass to the defendant (*State v Love,* 440 P 2d 275/Mont–1968). And the Oregon courts have likewise held that when the property taken is an automobile, passage of title may be accomplished within the meaning of false pretenses without full compliance with the motor vehicle registration statute. *State v Alden*, 495 P 2d 302/Or (1972).

Larceny by Spurious Check

Although forgery, the issuance of a check without sufficient funds to redeem the check upon presentation, and the fraudulent use of another's credit card are usually prosecuted under specific statutes, each act also amounts to obtaining property by false pretenses or representations. *State v Koester,* 209 NW 2d 172/Neb–1973); *Worton v State,* 492 SW 2d 519/Tex (1973).

If at the time of a sale, the seller agrees to hold the purchaser's check until a later time, a debtor-creditor relationship is established and the buyer is not guilty of false pretenses when the bank fails to honor the check because of insufficient funds. *People v Cundiff,* 305 NE 2d 735/Ill (1973).

Welfare Fraud

Absent a specific statute proscribing welfare fraud, such frauds may be prosecuted as a larceny by false pretenses. Thus, where defendant made application for county welfare and falsified her application by failing to include the salary of a man living in her house and contributing to her support and to the support of her children, and she thereafter received welfare checks as a result of such application, she was guilty of larceny by false pretenses (*People v Shirley,* 360 P 2d 33/Cal–1961). Also, where defendant made application for welfare assistance and thereon certified that she had not received any income during the twelve-month period immediately preceding, when in fact she had received $7,000 during that period from a theretofore undisclosed source, her receipt of welfare checks thereafter was larceny by false pretenses. *State v Morgan,* 393 P 2d 180/Or (1964).

Examples of Frauds

A misdemeanor vehicle code statute forbidding the turning back of the odometer of an automobile to show less mileage than the vehicle has actually traveled in order to promote automobile sales, did not preclude the prosecution of defendant-automobile dealer for grand theft by false pretenses under a penal code statute in the sale of automobiles on which the odometer had been turned back. *People v Ross,* 100 CR 703/Cal (1972).

Where defendant sold two watches bearing price tags of $150.00 but received a check of $40 therefor, the usual price of similar watches being from

$5 to $7, a question of false representations was presented for the jury who found adverse to defendant. *Colaluca v State*, 494 SW 2d 885/Tex (1973).

The selling of a parcel in a cardboard box to victim who was assured the parcel was worth $5,000, when in fact the accused knew it was worth only $5, was larceny by false pretenses. *State v So*, 231 P 2d 734/Id (1951).

A claim by defendant that she was an internationally known psychologist and could cure victim's son of his suicidal tendencies for a sum of $500, when in fact she had no such qualifications and the claims were made with intent to defraud, sufficiently established the offense of obtaining money by false pretenses. *Randle v United States*, 113 F 2d 945/DC (1940).

Where a chiropractor represented that he could cure cancer without surgery and thus caused the removal of a cancer victim from a hospital allegedly to undergo cancer cure, he committed larceny by false pretenses. *People v Phillips*, 414 P 2d 353/Cal (1966).

Defendant's false declaration as to the nature of his employment, whereupon he was granted a credit card with a $50 limitation and he thereafter ran up a bill of $637—none of which he paid—constituted grand larceny and not petty larceny. The theft is for the total amount of all purchases and not a separate offense for each purchase although purchases were made over a period of several days. *People v Robertson*, 334 P 2d 938/Cal (1959).

A representation that certain specified lumber was number two grade and would meet FHA requirements, though in fact when used it did not meet minimum standards of FHA and this fact was known to the accused, was a false representation of a present fact and not a future promise and thus violative of the statute. *State v Freeman*, 279 P 2d 443/Az (1955).

The rule of *caveat emptor* (let the buyer beware) has no application in a charge of larceny by fraud and where defendant represented two zircons to be genuine diamonds larceny by false pretenses was complete as soon as the victim parted with his property. *State v Bellew*, 203 P 2d 822/Cal (1949).

Where desert lands were sold to naive victims under the claim that there were oil deposits underlying the area, when defendants knew or had good reason to believe that the lands were outside the perimeter of the oil deposits at least in commercial quantities, a finding of guilty of larceny by false pretenses was warranted. *People v Gordon*, 163 P 2d 110/Cal (1945).

Although only one case in point could be found on "blockbusting," it is of sufficient importance to appear here. Blockbusting is a method of exploiting property owners and exciting hostility by the practice of inducing a property owner to sell his property because of actual or rumored advent into the neighborhood of a member or members of a particular racial, ethnic or religious group, and obtaining property by this method may amount to larceny by false pretenses. *State v Wagner*, 291 A 2d 161/Md (1972).

"False Pretenses" Distinguished From "Bunco"

Obtaining money by false pretenses differs from larceny by trick, device or bunco in that in false pretenses the victim, relying upon the false pretense or representation, turns over to the swindler *both title* to *and possession* of his property, while in bunco the victim relinquishes *possession, only*, to the swindler, never intending that title shall pass to the accused. The victim in a bunco scheme, in parting possession of his property, indicates to the thief how the money or property is to be used while the thief, pretending to agree to use the money as directed, intends to use it as he pleases and not to the victim's benefit. In short, the distinguishing element between the two swindles lies in the intent of the *victim* not the swindler. If the victim, in parting with his property, intends that both title and possession shall pass, then the theft is by false pretenses; if the victim intends that possession, only, shall pass and he has "strings attached" to the title, then the theft is larceny by trick, device or bunco. *People v Santora,* 125 P 2d 606/Cal (1942); *Abbott v State,* 149 P 2d 514/Ok (1944).

LARCENY BY TRICK OR DEVICE OR BUNCO

Defined

"Larceny by trick or device" occurs when the victim parts with possession of his property but does not intend to pass complete title to the defendant and intends that the defendant apply the property to a specific purpose; the defendant, on the other hand, intends upon receipt of the property to convert it to his own use. *People v Lafka,* 344 P 2d 619/Cal (1959).

One who obtains money from another upon the representation that he will perform certain specified services for that person with the money but who intends at the time to convert the money to his own use and actually does so, commits larceny by trick, device or bunco.

In General

Larceny by trick or device, also known as larceny by fraud and larceny by bunco, has a common characteristic with embezzlement: in each case the victim intends that possession shall pass to the defendant for a specific purpose and that title shall not pass to the defendant (*People v Gould,* 270 P 2d 551/Cal–1954). The essential difference between these two crimes is that in embezzlement there is a fiduciary relationship between victim and accused, usually by virtue of the defendant's employment, while in trick or device there is no such relationship.

A vital element of trick or device is that the owner retains title to his property although relinquishing possession, only, to the taker; if the owner intends to part both title and possession to the perpetrator of the fraud, the larceny is one by false pretenses, not by trick or device. *United States v Mangus*, 33 FS 596/Ind (1940).

At times a fraud is perpetrated which may constitute a larceny by either trick or device or by false pretenses. Where defendant obtained various sums of money from numerous victims allegedly to bet on a fixed horse race, which in fact was not fixed at least to the knowledge of defendant, his conviction could be sustained on either the theory of trick and device or false pretenses. Here, defendant's conviction of 14 counts of grand theft by trick and device and 17 counts of bookmaking was sustained. *People v Owens*, 255 P 2d 114/Cal (1953).

Examples

Where defendant took property from victim on consignment but after selling the property he kept the proceeds therefrom contrary to agreement, he was guilty of larceny. If defendant had formed the fraudulent intent before he received the property the crime would have been larceny by trick; if he had formed the intent after receipt of the property the crime would have been embezzlement. *People v Martin*, 314 P 2d 493/Cal (1957).

A coin-matching scheme where two confederates induced their victim to join them in a three-handed coin-matching game and thereby bilked victim of a sum of money, was larceny by trick and not false pretenses. It is important in some jurisdictions to distinguish between these two types of larceny because a conviction for false pretenses cannot stand on the testimony of one witness only, i.e., the victim, as his testimony must be corroborated, while corroboration is not necessary to a conviction for larceny by trick, device or bunco. *State v Scott*, 175 P 2d 1016/Ut (1946); *People v Reinschreiber*, 297 P 2d 658/Cal (1956).

Defendant, who anticipated the privilege of drawing the winning ticket at a theater bank night drawing, conspired with a confederate to "palm" the confederate's ticket; upon pretending to draw a ticket from the drum, he presented the palmed ticket instead and divided the prize money with the confederate. He thus was guilty of conspiracy and grand theft on the grounds that the element of chance, a requisite element of lottery, was eliminated by the fraudulent scheme employed, and the crime was instead larceny by trick or device. *People v Carpenter*, 297 P 2d 498/Cal (1956).

Where defendant-attorney advised an alien client who had applied for citizenship, that in order to square a recent arrest it would cost him \$2,200–\$200 for attorney fee and \$2,000 to pay a policeman off–his act was larceny by trick notwithstanding his claim that his client gave him both possession and title to the money. *Graham v United States*, 187 F 2d 87/DC (1950).

A conviction of larceny by false pretenses was reversed and remanded where the accused led his victim to believe he could change the denomination of currency and was induced to furnish the accused $3,000 for that purpose under the agreement that the money would be returned plus $500 for the use thereof, but defendant kept the $3,000. The court in reversing held that the larceny was one by fraud (bunco) and not by false pretenses. *Welch v State,* 146 P 2d 141/Ok (1944).

A bootlegger who accepted money from victim with the understanding that the money was in payment for whiskey which the bootlegger never produced, though he kept the money, was guilty of larceny by fraud. *Bourbonaise v State,* 248 P 2d 640/Ok (1952).

RECEIVING STOLEN PROPERTY

Defined

The elements of the crime of "receiving stolen property" require more than mere receiving. They are: (1) receipt of, actual or constructive, (2) property that has been stolen, (3) with knowledge of the status of the property and (4) intentional concealment or withholding from the rightful owner (*State v Carter,* 196 NW 2d 607/Min—1972); (*State v Myers,* 406 P 2d 623/Wn—1965). It may be committed by any of four methods: buying, procuring, receiving or concealing. Any singular method coupled with *scienter* completes the offense. *State v Carlton,* 484 P 2d 757/NM (1971).

In General

A few of the states hold that possession of recently stolen property raises neither inference nor presumption that the possessor stole it (*Smith v State,* 278 S 2d 408/Mis—1973), yet the vast majority hold that unexplained possession of recently stolen property raises either an inference or presumption of the larceny or burglary in which the property was stolen, and will sustain conviction if not satisfactorily explained by the accused (*Huff v State,* 492 SW 2d 532/Tex—1973). The explanation made at the time the accused is found in possession of the stolen goods controls, not the explanation made at the time of the trial. *Sirabella v State,* 492 SW 571/Tex (1973).

It is not necessary to a charge of receiving stolen property that the property shall have been received from the thief or any other particular person (*Kirby v United States,* 174 US 47/SD—1898), and if, pursuant to an agreement between the thief and the receiver, the thief delivers the property to a place owned or controlled by the receiver, the receiver is guilty of receiving stolen property upon delivery. *State v Elias,* 249 P 2d 941/Az (1952).

A person is guilty of receiving stolen property if at the time he received the property he knew it was stolen, and he is equally guilty if upon receiving the property he was unaware it was stolen but subsequently concealed it after learning it was stolen. *McBride v State*, 490 SW 2d 560/Tex (1973).

One who possesses and retains stolen property intending to return it to the rightful owner only if a reward is offered, has the prerequisite guilty intent of receiving stolen property. *State v Simonson*, 214 NW 2d 679/Min (1974).

Unexplained Possession of Recently Stolen Property

Unexplained or unsatisfactorily explained possession of recently stolen property permits an inference that the possessor stole it. *White v United States*, 300 A 2d 716/DC (1973).

The federal circuit courts are in agreement that unexplained exclusive possession of recently stolen property raises an inference of guilt from which the jury may properly find guilty knowledge or participation in the crime in which the property was stolen. *Lee v United States*, 363 F 2d 469/Mo (1966).

Although an arrestee may remain silent when arrested and is under no obligation to give evidence against himself, it would still be his duty to explain how he came into possession of the property in order to vitiate the adverse inference or presumption; if he refuses or declines, or gives an illogical or false account of possession, or if he fled or attempted flight when discovered, such conduct would be corroborative evidence of criminal possession and would warrant submission of the matter to the jury. *State v Kirkman*, 432 P 2d 638/Ut (1967); *State v Hunter*, 433 P 2d 22/Az (1967); *Thomas v State*, 490 P 2d 1374/Ok (1971).

Possession of recently stolen goods, when not satisfactorily explained, would permit the fact finder to draw an inference that the possessor is the thief; if the property was taken in a robbery, an inference is likewise justified that the possessor is the robber (*King v State*, 298 A 2d 446/Md–1972); if the goods were stolen in a burglary, possession will also support an inference of guilt of the burglary. *Holtel v State*, 290 NE 2d 775/Ind (1972).

Explanation as to the possession of recently stolen property must withstand the reasonable man standard, that is, a logical and credible explanation which would lead the reasonable man to believe that possession is not criminal (*State v Hatch*, 483 P 2d 864/Wn–1971). Where defendant, when arrested for possession of recently stolen property, offered no explanation justifying possession, he could not complain that he was not asked to give an explanation. *State v Martinez*, 442 P 2d 943/Ut (1968).

Presumption or Inference Raised by Possession

In some states the law permits the attaching of a presumption of guilt from the unexplained possession of recently stolen property, while other states permit only an inference to be drawn therefrom. South Dakota, which represents a minority, permits a presumption (*State v Larkin*, 202 NW 2d 862/ND–1972), while Maryland, representing the majority, permits an inference. *Davis v State*, 297 A 2d 320/Md (1972).

A "presumption" and an "inference" are not the same thing: a presumption is a deduction which the law requires the trier of fact to make, while an inference is a deduction which the trier of fact may or may not make. A presumption is mandatory, an inference is permissible, *Black's Law Dictionary*, Fourth Edition at 917.

Whether or not the law of a state allows the drawing of an inference or a presumption of guilt from the unexplained possession of recently stolen property, the result is usually the same; that is, if believed by the trier of fact, such fact alone will support conviction.

Bare Possession

Receipt of stolen property, without more, is not criminal; it is the knowledge that it is stolen and the withholding it from its rightful owner that makes the act criminal (*State v Thompson*, 413 P 2d 951/Wn–1966); or, receipt coupled with an explanation that was later rebutted or an explanation that could neither be affirmed nor rebutted but which the trier of fact considered improbable, would sustain conviction. *State v Douglas*, 423 P 2d 535/Wn (1967).

Even though one comes into possession of property not knowing it to have been stolen, but thereafter learning of its larcenous appropriation withholds and conceals it from its rightful owner, he becomes *particeps criminis* and thus culpable. *People v Scaggs*, 314 P 2d 793/Cal (1957).

Even though stolen goods are found on the premises of defendant, the state must usually prove that defendant knew of their presence and their stolen character. *State v Motyka*, 298 A 2d 793/RI (1973).

Exclusive Possession

Exclusive, unexplained possession of recently stolen goods is evidence of theft, and if at the time the articles were stolen burglary was committed, such possession is also evidence of burglary. *People v Jefferies*, 285 NE 2d 592/Ill (1972).

"Exclusive possession" of recently stolen property does not imply solitary possession, for two or more persons may have exclusive possession of the property. *Hudson v State*, 193 SE 2d 919/Ga (1972).

It is the rule that defendant is found in exclusive possession of recently stolen property and he attempts to explain it, he must give a reasonable explanation or be judged by its improbabilities. *People v Punyka*, 293 NE 2d 672/Ill (1973).

The Thief As Receiver

The receiver of stolen property must be one other than the thief who stole it (*State v Silva,* 292 A 2d 228/RI–1972), but no doubt the reverse is often the case. Since unexplained possession of recently stolen property raises an inference that the possessor stole it, the thief may be in possession when discovered and apprehended which would likely result in his conviction of receiving if unexplained (*Nunley v State,* 479 SW 2d 836/Ten–1972). And testimony, even if true, that defendant stole the very property he is charged with receiving and concealing, would not preclude conviction for receiving stolen property (*Walls v State*, 491 P 2d 320/Ok–1971). The state need not prove that one other than the defendant stole the property he is on trial for receiving. *State v Watkins*, 481 P 2d 689/Mont (1971); *State v Carter*, 196 NW 2d 607/Min (1973).

The thief who stole the property may be convicted of larceny and feloniously receiving that property where he disposes of it and subsequently thereto he again comes into possession of it in a new transaction (*People v Kot*, 339 P 2d 899/Cal–1959). Also, where a conspiracy exists between the thief and the fence, or receiver, that the thief steal and the receiver receive, each may be convicted of both crimes–larceny and receiving stolen property. *United States v Stephenson*, 110 FS 623/Alk (1953); *Williams v Superior Court*, 458 P 2d 987/Cal (1969).

Proof of Knowledge

Scienter is an essential element of receiving stolen property; it cannot be proved, as a rule, by direct evidence. But where the defendant, of mature age and experienced in business negotiations, was approached in the middle of the night by a stranger and made no inquiry as to the stranger's identity, bought meat at a price substantially below the going rate, paid cash, and neither a bill of lading nor a receipt was asked or given, it could be reasonably inferred that defendant knew the meat was stolen. *State v Abraham,* 205 NW 2d 342/Neb (1973).

Where defendant, when shown a search warrant preparatory to the search of his premises, stated that he would "get" the person that finked on him, plus the fact that he fled without shoes or shirt and was apprehended two months later in the state of Colorado, knowledge was sufficiently established to sustain conviction. *State v Redeman,* 496 P 2d 230/Or (1972).

Corroboration

Corroboration may be furnished by circumstantial, as well as direct, evidence, such as where possessor purchased the property at a price well below its fair market value (*State v Butler,* 450 P 2d 128/Az–1969); or where property was stored in an unusual place, such as automobile tires, transmission and a console stored under a bed or in a clothes closet (*State v Grujalva,* 445 P 2d 88/Az–1970); where the receiver directed that the check for payment exclude his name (*State v Zarafonetis*, 472 P 2d 388/NM–1970); or where the receiver used a fictitious name in the transaction (*State v Tollet*, 431 P 2d 168/Wn–1967); or where serial numbers had been cut from automobile tires and the tires were concealed by the side of the road and delivery was made at night. *Lewis v State*, 162 P 2d 201/Ok (1945).

Flight is usually sufficient corroboration to warrant conviction. Where defendant's truck was found to contain property stolen about thirty minutes earlier from an automobile parked beside the truck and upon being accused defendant jumped a fence and disappeared, his act of possession had been sufficiently corroborated to warrant conviction (*State v Brooks*, 126 P 2d 1044/Ut–1942). And where defendant was found upon an Indian reservation in possession of recently stolen property and when accused of burglary he broke from custody, and fled, his possession was sufficiently corroborated to justify conviction. *United States v Kinney*, 437 F 2d 407/Az (1970).

Examples

Where defendant was found in possession of stolen lumber and he explained that he had obtained most of the lumber from a "hippy" whom he had paid one dollar per piece and that he did not know where the hippy had gotten the lumber, his knowledge of the stolen character of the lumber could be inferred beyond a reasonable doubt. *State v Casey*, 300 A 2d 325/NJ (1973).

Where defendant, with knowledge that motors were stolen, found a buyer and arranged a meeting between the thief and the buyer, assisted the thief in transferring one motor from the thief's automobile to that of the buyer and received $25 for his assistance in the transaction, he was properly charged with and convicted of receiving stolen property. *State v Doster*, 427 P 2d 413/Or (1967).

When stolen property discovered in the hands of the thief who is bent upon delivering it to a receiver and who is allowed to do so, it loses its character. For example, where defendants believed goods delivered to them were stolen, they were guilty of an attempt, only, to receive stolen goods as the goods were no longer "stolen" goods but "recovered" goods. *People v Rojas*, 358 P 2d 921/Cal (1960).

THEFT OF AUTOMOBILE

In General

The value of the thing stolen is not significant when the thing stolen is an automobile in driveable condition, as value may be inferred (*People v Sparks*, 292 NE 2d 447/Ill–1972). In most states, and under federal law, the stealing of an automobile is grand larceny—a felony—regardless of its value (*Loader v Hand*, 208 FS 915/Kan–1962), but Colorado offers an exception to this rule, for there the automobile's value must exceed $100 before its taking would amount to grand larceny. *People v Austin,* 523 P 2d 989/Colo (1974).

The mere showing that defendant was a passenger in a stolen vehicle without a showing that he was acting in concert with the driver, does not sufficiently show joint possession of the automobile to warrant his conviction also. *State v Franklin,* 192 SE 2d 626/NC (1972).

Taking Without Owner's Consent

With the liberation of youth a new crime has evolved—that of taking another's automobile without his consent and driving it for a short period of time and abandoning it never intending to permanently deprive the owner thereof. More than 90% of all cars taken without the owner's consent are found within a few days or even a few hours, wrecked, stripped or partially stripped, or, if the owner is lucky, simply used, abused and abandoned. Virtually all states have enacted statutes forbidding this type of activity, sometimes referred to as "joy-riding."

While the crime of larceny requires that the thief harbor the specific intent to deprive the owner of his property permanently, no such intent is requisite in the taking and driving away of a motor vehicle without consent, and intent to deprive temporarily is all that is necessary (*Robinson v State*, 302 A 2d 659/Md–1973). But where defendant attempted to register a motor vehicle three days after its theft by the use of a false name and a spurious bill of sale, his conviction of the theft of a motor vehicle was justified. *State v Rendell,* 509 P 2d 247/Az (1973).

Distinction Between "Auto Theft" and "Joy-Riding"

Under a joy-riding statute, the taking of another's motor vehicle without permission is not to be treated as a theft, but rather as a criminal trespass (*People v Woods,* 308 NE 2d 856/Ill–1974). The essential difference between joy-riding and grand theft-vehicle lies in the intent of the taker; if he intends merely to use the vehicle temporarily the crime is joy-riding; if he intends to permanently deprive the owner thereof, the crime is grand theft-auto. *State v O'Brien,* 317 A 2d 783/NH (1973).

The Supreme Court of Maine has held that even if defendant actually intended only to use an automobile temporarily in order to effect escape from police, such fact would not necessarily negate larceny of the automobile as a matter of law where the automobile was taken at gun point through fear. *State v Gordon,* 321 A 2d 352/Me (1974).

Examples of Auto Theft

The leasing of an automobile from an automobile rental agency by the use of a false name and a stolen credit card, although amounting to obtaining property under false pretenses, does not amount to larceny by false pretenses as that crime requires that the thief obtain both possession and title. It was abundantly clear that when the Hertz agency rented the automobile to defendant they had no intention that title should pass. *Shope v State*, 307 A 2d 730/Md (1973).

Evidence which established, *inter alia*, that 20 days after the theft of an automobile defendant was found asleep in the backseat with the key in the ignition and the motor running, and that defendant was seen standing near the stolen vehicle on the day it was stolen, proved intent to deprive and defraud owner of his automobile. *Shank v State*, 289 NE 2d 315/Ind (1972).

Once the thief or the joy-rider takes the automobile of another his crime is complete and the subsequent retaking of the vehicle, although the actor had abandoned it, does not amount to a new crime. *State v Diebold*, 277 P 394/Wn (1929).

VALUE

In General

"Value" is important in pleading a grand larceny, but in most jurisdictions the value of the property taken in a robbery is irrelevant. Thus, where defendants in attempting to take victim's property by force succeeded only in ripping off his trouser pocket and carrying it away, they deprived him of a thing of value satisfying the robbery statute (*People v Graham*, 455 P 2d 153/Cal–1969). Also, the felonious taking of the wallet from another which was immediately discarded upon finding it to be empty was, nevertheless, robbery. *People v Carroll*, 463 P 2d 400/Cal (1970).

The retail price of stolen property is relevant to show the value of the property taken and to establish jurisdiction by establishing the degree of the theft. *Clinton v State*, 502 P 2d 852/Kan–1972); *People v Fuzi*, 208 NW 2d 47/Mich (1973).

In a grand larceny prosecution the jury cannot be allowed to speculate as to the value of property merely on appearances, and unless the state has proved the value to be sufficient to warrant a conviction for grand larceny, the jury is justified in returning a conviction for petty larceny, only, or a verdict of not guilty. *Boone v United States*, 296 A 2d 449/DC (1972).

Substantial discrepancy between fair market value of an item and the price actually paid for the item may tend to prove guilty knowledge, and evidence thereof is relevant to the issue of a charge of receiving a stolen vehicle. *State v Hanks*, 517 P 2d 750/NM (1973).

The value of property stolen refers not to its value after having been damaged or demolished by the taker, but to its value at the inception of the taking. *State v Cope*, 438 P 2d 442/Az (1968).

What May Have Value

The Oregon courts have ruled the following to be property capable of ownership and thus having value: blank checks, drivers' licenses, draft cards, a hospital association card, Boy Scout card, Social Security card, union membership card, a hunting and fishing license (*State v Hardesty*, 493 P 2d 56/Or–1972), a contraband slot machine (*People v Gonzales*, 144 P 2d 605/Cal–1944), personal service such as lodging and hotel accommodations (*State v Higgins*, 406 P 2d 784/Wn–1965), and gas and electricity. *Selman v State*, 406 P 2d 181/Alk (1965).

A roster of undercover narcotic agents had value and was thus subject to receipt in violation of a statute denouncing receiving stolen property, its value being established under four theories: (1) merely as sheets of paper; (2) as "paper in place," reflecting the cost of its preparation, assembly and distribution; (3) as a tangible compilation of information; and (4) as a thing wanted by defendants themselves and the offering of $20 therefor (*People v Kunkin*, 100 CR 845/Cal–1972).

If a document is removed from the files of another, photocopied by the use of his equipment and the copy then delivered to a third person, the third person has received stolen property; or, if the document is removed from the office of another, photocopied outside and returned to its place in file, and the copy is delivered to a third person, the third person has received stolen property, since the status of the document as stolen property is fixed as soon as it is taken from the office of its owner, and its subsequent transmutation in form does not alter its character. *People v Kunkin, supra.*

"Fair Market Value" Defined

To make out a *prima facie* case in a prosecution for the felonious receipt of stolen goods, it is incumbent upon the people to present complete evidence of the reasonable market value of the goods at the time of the alleged offense. *People v Paris*, 511 P 2d 893/Colo (1973).

The fair market value is ". . . neither a panic price, auction value, speculative value, nor a value fixed by depressed or inflated prices. We have defined it as the amount of money which a purchaser is willing, but not obliged . . . to pay for the property to an owner willing, but not obligated, to sell it, taking into consideration all uses to which the property is adapted and might in reason be applied . . . ." *Donaldson v Greenwood*, 242 P 2d 1038/Wn (1952).

The price received for stolen tools has no relevance in establishing market value of property for the purpose of determining grand or petty larceny. *State v Dees*, 187 SE 2d 433/NC (1972).

The value of a stolen check is its face value for purposes of larceny although a stop payment order is issued subsequent to the larceny or even though the thief sold the check to another at less than face value. *State v Easton*, 422 P 2d 7/Wn (1966); *United States v Lee*, 454 F 2d 190/Cal (1972).

How Established

If the value of property becomes an issue in a criminal prosecution, it is the reasonable cash market value at the time and place stolen and in its condition upon appropriation; if it has no value there, then its value would be that which it would cost to replace it. *Wise v State*, 494 SW 2d 921/Tex (1973).

The actual cost price of an article stolen is admissible as being one factor among others the jury may consider in establishing fair market value. *Williams v State*, 482 SW 2d 810/Ark (1972).

A retail store owner's testimony that one of two stolen coats was priced for sale at $54.95 and the other at $59.95, established their value as being in excess of $100.00, and proof of their cost to the retailer was not necessary. *Keel v State*, 304 NE 2d 304/Ind (1973).

Testimony of an expert as to the street value of heroin was admissible to show that possession was not inadvertent, and since expert opinion as to market value is always based on hearsay, testimony was not rendered inadmissible thereby. *State v Liles*, 521 P 2d 973/Wn (1974).

Where stolen aircraft pump parts were discarded as having been worn out and were to be disposed of as scrap metal, their cost price was irrelevant and did not constitute proof that the combined total value of the articles stolen exceeded the minimum value requisite of grand theft. *United States v Cutterbuck*, 421 F 2d 485/Cal (1970).

When Precise Value Is Necessary

It is not necessary that the state prove the actual market value of the property stolen where the defendant is charged with petty larceny, only, the rule being that the state merely show that the thing taken has value (*State v Paramo*, 376 P 2d 554/Az—1962); (*Boone v United States*, 296 A 2d 449/DC—1972). Nor is proof of the value of the thing stolen essential when the taking was from the person of another, for regardless of its value this type of theft is grand theft (*People v McIntosh*, 369 P 2d 987/Colo—1962). But where the larceny is divided into degrees, which are relevant to both jurisdiction and punishment, it is essential that the value of the property taken be alleged and proved. *Robinson v United States*, 333 F 2d 323/Mo (1964).

Value of Contraband Narcotics

The value of contraband narcotics is not a necessary ingredient of its possession and in a prosecution therefor the state is not required to, but may, prove value so as to shed light on other circumstances which may be helpful to the jury (*Williams v State*, 198 SE 2d 683/Ga—1973). Thus, where the accused was found in possession of a box containing a large amount of various narcotics and he claimed to be keeping it for a friend and was unaware of its contents, the fact that its value was approximately $2500 was relevant to refute defendant's claim and to assist the jury in the placing of due credibility on defendant's testimony

(*People v Lotrean*, 261 P 2d 543/Cal–1953). Also, where marijuana cigarettes were found on the person of defendant and he claimed to be unaware of their presence, their value was relevant to rebut the suspicion that someone placed them in his pocket without his knowledge or gave them to him. *People v Mac Cagnan*, 276 P 2d 679/Cal (1954).

Chapter XX

Robbery—General

Defined

Three elements are included in the crime of robbery: (1) force or fear employed on the victim, (2) felonious intent to steal and (3) taking the property of another from his person or from his presence (*Anderson v State*, 285 S 2d 748/Mis—1973). It will be noted that the taking need not be from the person of the victim as a taking from his presence, the other elements being present also amounts to robbery. Essential, also, to the crime of robbery is larceny—the taking of the property with intent to permanently deprive the owner thereof. *State v Gover*, 298 A 2d 378/Md (1973).

The Nature of Robbery

The word "robbery" describes an aggravated form of larceny or theft, the aggravation consisting of the use of actual or constructive violence against the person of the victim or the use of force or fear to accomplish the taking of property from the possessor. There can be no robbery without violence, and no larceny with it, this being the principal distinction between larceny and robbery. *Corpus Juris Secundum*, Vol 52A—Larceny.

Robbery is a larceny compounded by force or fear, and in an escape where one of two prisoners took the jail keys after locking the deputy sheriff inside, only for the purpose of delaying pursuit and to facilitate escape there was lacking the specific larcenous intent for a conviction of robbery and a conviction of escape, only, was sustained. *Young v State*, 487 SW 2d 305/Ten (1972).

While larceny remains an offense against possession, robbery is basically a crime against the person. *United States v Dixon*, 469 F 2d 940/DC (1972).

"Possession," as used in robbery statutes, does not mean that the possessor must own the property taken from him, as "custody or control" is all that is required. *United States v Dixon, supra.*

The federal courts take the position, as do numerous states, that robbery is a crime against the person while larceny is a crime against possession (*Neufield v United States,* 118 F 2d 375/DC–1941); however, this proposition leaves room for argument as the goals in both crimes are identical—to steal the property of another. A further argument against this proposition is that burglary is considered to be a crime against property, yet burglary can be committed exclusive of larceny and robbery cannot be; robbery is a compound larceny. *CJS* 52A–Larceny.

Although the possessor of a thing of value may not be able to establish legal right at law to its possession, such as a slot machine, one without claim of right may not mutilate such article or take it from the possessor by stealth, trick, threat or force (*City of Bremerton v Smith,* 199 P 2d 95/Wn–1948). Likewise, stolen money may be the subject of robbery as in larceny and one who has the right of possession as against the thief is, so far as the thief is concerned, the owner, and ownership may be laid to the possessor in an indictment even though he himself is a thief and came into possession of the money by larceny. *State v Pokini,* 367 P 2d 449/Haw (1962).

A statute making the taking from the presence of the victim a robbery as well as a taking from his person, designates "an area with no metes and bounds" but close at hand, and the extent of the area depends on the circumstances of the taking. *People v Risenhoover,* 447 P 2d 925/Cal (1968).

Where robbery has been committed the robber cannot absolve himself of blame by returning the property to the victim, as such generosity neither vitiates the crime nor entitles the robber to any special consideration. *People v Tipton,* 216 P 2d 570/Cal (1950).

When the loot is seized under threat, force or fear the robbery is not at end no matter how far from the scene the robber has traveled nor how much time has elapsed if the robber has not won his way to a place of safety even though momentary. *People v Salas,* 500 P 2d 7/Cal (1972).

How Accomplished

Robbery may be committed by any of three means: force, violence or fear of injury, but the employing of all three means does not make three acts of robbery; *State v Carlson,* 310 P 2d 867/Wn (1957).

Force or fear, being elements of robbery, may be exerted against a victim to either obtain possession or to retain possession otherwise obtained. *Hood v State,* 175 P 2d 918/Ok (1945).

Intent to steal (*United States v Robinson,* 475 F 2d 376/DC–1973), and either force or fear, but not both, must be proved in every prosecution for robbery (*People v Thomas*, 509 P 2d 592/Colo–1973). But the degree or amount of force employed is immaterial as long as it was sufficient to induce the victim to part with his property. *State v Parsons*, 87 P 349/Wn (1906).

To amount to robbery, the property must be taken from the person of the victim or from within his area of control (*Com v Johnson*, 294 NE 2d 492/Mas–1973). "Area of control" is substantially synonymous to "immediate presence." (California Penal Code § 211), and "immediate possession," as defined in *United States v Dixon*, 469 F 2d 940/DC (1972), means an area within which the victim could reasonably be expected to exercise some physical control over his property.

Actual testimony of the victim that he parted with his property induced by fear is not necessary. The use or display of a pistol upon demand of the money and compliance by the victim furnish adequate circumstantial evidence that victim's compliance was actuated by fear. (*State v Spencer*, 513 P 2d 140/Az–1973); the prosecution is not bound by the victim's claim that he was not fearful under the menace of the robber's weapon where there is other evidence that he acted in fear and it can be reasonably inferred that he would not have disgorged the contents of his employer's till had he not been in fear. *People v Renteria*, 393 P 2d 413/Cal (1964).

Force, which is one means of obtaining property in a robbery, must be such that one is deprived of and the offender gains possession of property (*Anderson v State*, 285 S 2d 748/Mis–1973); if fear is employed, it must be fear of such a magnitude that the victim feels compelled to part with his property. Id.

Intent

Indiana holds that robbery is not a specific intent crime (*Snipes v State*, 298 NE 2d 503/Ind–1973). This premise is supported by New Mexico law, apparently distinguishing between the wrongdoing of the act and the taking of the property, holding: the intent necessary for robbery includes the *general* criminal intent of conscious wrongdoing plus the *specific* intent to steal (*State v Puga*, 510 P 2d 1075/NM–1973). Iowa holds with the majority that *animus furandi* is essential to robbery as in theft, and must exist at the time of the taking (*State v Campbell*, 214 NW 2d 195/Ia–1974). Thus, where defendant contended that his commission of acts inside a residence which were interpreted to be robbery, was a prank, even if true it could not have been robbery, nor theft, nor attempted theft, as *animus furandi* was lacking, and a failure of the judge to so instruct the jury under the stated circumstances would have been reversible error. *State v Stoneberg*, 517 P 2d 333/Or (1973).

"Felonious taking," a phrase used in some robbery statutes, means the taking with specific intent to permanently deprive the owner of his property. *People v Belcher*, 106 CR 807/Cal (1973).

Asportation—When Complete

Proof of a carrying away or removal of the victim's property, by the robber, is not required to establish asportation; asportation has occurred when the robber transfers the property from the victim's control to his control, and it is immaterial whether the transfer is made by the robber himself, or by a third person, or even by the victim acting under orders from the robber. *Com v Flowers*, 298 NE 2d 898/Mas (1973).

"Robbery" and "Theft From the Person" Distinguished

The use of only that amount of force necessary to remove the property from the person of another is not robbery, but if, during its removal, the victim, here a female, is jostled or dragged causing her to fall down, there is sufficient force to constitute robbery. The evidence showed that victim's purse was in a shopping bag and in defendant's and victim's contention for possession of the shopping bag the victim fell to the ground, thus, defendant's force was sufficient to sustain conviction of robbery. *State v Segura*, 472 P 2d 387/NM (1970).

The distinction between robbery and theft from the person may be very close, but there is a distinction in that in robbery the taking must be by force or fear (*Cannon v State*, 107 P 2d 809/Ok–1940). Also, there can be no larceny from the person when the property is taken from close proximity of the victim but not from his person, yet such a taking by force or fear would amount to robbery. *Terral v State*, 422 P 2d 465/Nev (1968).

The secret and stealthy purloining of property from the person of another or the sudden seizure of property held in his hand, when no additional element is present, constitutes larceny from the person and not robbery; but additional force in the taking, such as the striking of the victim on the jaw at the time the property is seized, constitutes robbery. *State v Stuard*, 452 P 2d 98/Az (1969).

"Robbery" and "Extortion" Distinguished

In distinguishing robbery and extortion, or robbery and blackmail, one need answer three questions: Does the taking amount to larceny? Was delivery made immediately? Was the taking by force?

If the taking was by force from the person of the victim, the taking is larceny and the crime is robbery; if accomplished by fear and delivery is made immediately, the crime is robbery; if the taking was without the consent of the victim it is larceny, a necessarily included offense of robbery, and thus robbery. On the other hand, if the property was delivered to the perpetrator willingly and with consent, although reluctantly as the least undesirable of the alternatives, the taking is not larceny and thus amounts to extortion; if delivery is to be made at a substantially later time and by choice of the victim, the crime is extortion; if the property is extracted under color of authority or official right, the crime is extortion. Thirty-five *CJS*—Extortion; Seventy-seven *CJS*—Robbery.

Under the robbery statute of Florida the court has declared that every armed robbery will give rise to a change of extortion, since the joint offenses anticipate the use of force, threats or violence to force another to do or not to do something against his will (*Davis v State*, 277 S 2d 300/Fla–1973); however, all jurisdictions do not hold to the Florida rule. California does not view property obtained by extortion to be stolen property, a necessary ingredient of robbery. Under California law property extorted is received with the consent, although reluctantly, of the victim, while in robbery the property is taken without consent. California Penal Code § § 496 and 519.

When Assault Is Distinct From Robbery

Where defendant beat victim and took his wallet and left, then later returned and beat him again, defendant could properly be convicted of robbery and assault with intent to commit murder (*State v Blazak*, 516 P 2d 575/Az–1973). Likewise, where defendant after having robbed victim, put a pistol to victim's head and threatened to blow his brains out, he could be properly convicted of robbery and aggravated assault as the assault occurred after the robbery was completed. *Griffin v State*, 286 S 2d 220/Fla (1973).

Exception to "Possession or Immediate Presence" Rule

An exception to the rule that the taking be from the person or immediate presence exists where the victim, by the employment of force or fear, has been removed or prevented from approaching the place from which the property was taken. In this instance employees were locked in a vegetable produce cooler. *State v McDonald*, 443 P 2d 651/Wn (1968).

Where victim was induced under the menace of a gun to disclose the location of certain property which was in an automobile parked outside the building, and was then required to enter a refrigeration vault inside the building, the subsequent taking of the property from the automobile by the assailant was held to be a taking from the presence of the victim and, thus, robbery. *Fields v State*, 364 P 2d 723/Ok (1961).

When Taking From a Corpse Is Robbery

A dead man is a "person" within the meaning of the robbery statute and robbery may be committed though the taking was from a corpse. *United States v Butler*, 455 F 2d 1338/DC (1971).

Where evidence showed that defendant stabbed the victim and she was probably dead at the time property was taken from her body, she was nevertheless a "person" within the meaning of the robbery statute and properly the subject of robbery, and the case would not have been altered had defendant formed the intent to take her property after her death (*Carey v United States*, 296 F 2d 422/DC–1961). Also, where defendant and a coprincipal killed a motorist and immediately thereafter took property from his clothing being worn, the court observed that the robbery commenced with the first overt act; that the robbery and homicide were so interwoven with one another as to be inseparable, thus warranting conviction of robbery and statutory first degree murder. *State v Coe*, 208 P 2d 863/Wn (1949).

The taking of property from the person of one whom the perpetrator has knocked unconscious is robbery (*State v Larson*, 376 P 2d 537/Wn–1962), but the taking of property from the person of one who is unconscious from some extrinsic cause is not robbery but grand theft-person. *Mitchell v State*, 408 P 2d 566/Ok (1965).

Multiple Takings

The taking of cash from each of four bank tellers at the same time and place constituted but a single robbery, not four (*United States v Canty*, 469 F 2d 114/DC–1972). Also, where the robber forced victim to part with both his personal money from his billfold and money from victim's desk which belonged to his employer, there was but one robbery. *Com v Lockhart*, 296 A 2d 883/Pa (1972). But where defendant and coparticipants forced a tavern owner to open his cash register from which they took money, and thereafter they robbed two patrons of the tavern, they could be convicted of three separate robberies notwithstanding that all robberies occurred essentially at the same time and place (*People v Lewis*, 308 NE 2d 59/Ill–1974). Also, where defendant entered a store with two companions and pointed a gun at and robbed one victim while his two companions robbed a second victim, each could be convicted only of the robbery he alone committed. *Booker v State*, 203 SE 2d 194/Ga (1974).

Kidnaping for the Purpose of Robbery

When robbery is committed the crime does not terminate until the robber reaches a place of temporary safety. Where after an attempted robbery two suspects, unable to start their getaway car, commandeered another car forcing the driver to drive them away from the scene, the kidnaping of the driver was properly held to be a kidnaping for the purpose of robbery even though the robbery amounted only to an attempt and all acts of the attempt were complete before the kidnaping was committed. *People v Laursen*, 501 P 2d 1145/Cal (1972).

Where defendant kidnaped two women at gunpoint and took them to a motel where he committed sexually deviate acts on each and thereafter took the purse and automobile of one and the purse and a ring from another, he could properly be convicted of two counts of kidnaping and two counts of robbery, sodomy not being charged in the indictment. *People v Ellington*, 286 NE 2d 367/Ill (1972).

Taking Under Claim of Title

Where one takes money from the person or presence of another by force or fear, it is no defense that the money was owed to the taker (*State v Martin*, 516 P 2d 753/Or—1973). The majority opinion, *infra*, holds that the good faith taking of property from another under claim of title and right of ownership is not robbery even though taken by force or fear as the requisite intent to steal is lacking (*State v Hardin*, 406 P 2d 406/Az—1965), and the bona fide belief, though mistakenly held, that the actor has a claim to the property negates criminal intent requisite to robbery (*People v Butler*, 421 P 2d 703/Cal—1967). Taking property under such circumstances, however, is fraught with potentially dangerous consequences as the trier of fact may not believe the testimony of the witness. Thus, where defendant took money by force from victim with whom he claimed to have been drinking insisting that victim owed him an amount of money for drinks purchased during their social spree, defendant's conviction for robbery was warranted. *State v Austin*, 373 P 2d 137/Wn (1962).

Principal to Robbery

Where several persons participate in a robbery it is immaterial which takes the property (*Gibson v State*, 268 S 2d 49/Ala—1972), and likewise, where one of two suspects held a knife at victim's throat while the other removed his wallet, both could be convicted of armed robbery. *Shows v State*, 267 S 2d 811/Mis (1972).

Where one passenger in an automobile robbed a second passenger while a third passenger did nothing to assist or prevent the robbery, the third passenger would not necessarily be guiltless as his mere presence may have aided and abetted in the robbery. *State v Cummings*, 423 P 2d 438/Haw (1967), citing *State v O'Keefe*, 43 P 918/Nev (1896).

The driving of the getaway car without otherwise participating makes one guilty of robbery as a principal. *United States v Duran*, 461 F 2d 1096/Cal (1972).

Examples

It is not the case in larceny, and likewise in robbery, that the robber actually takes the property into physical custody. Where two defendants ordered victim to get out of his car with his hands up, which he did upon seeing a pistol pointed at him, and when ordered he threw his wallet on the ground stating that there was nothing in it, and then defendant ordered victim to pick up his wallet and show them it was empty, which he did, and upon seeing that the wallet was empty, defendant ordered victim to "get in that car and get out of here" there was sufficient evidence for a finding of robbery on the grounds that defendants secured dominion over the wallet when it was thrown upon the ground, asportation then being complete. *People v Quinn*, 176 P 2d 404/Cal (1947).

A, *B*, and *C*, intent on robbery, drove to the Bank of America in La Mesa, California. *A* drove the getaway car and remained in the car; *B* and *C* entered the bank to execute the plan by forcing three bank employees to lie on the floor while *C* scooped the money from a teller's drawer into a bag and then ordered an employee to open the vault. He stuffed about $5,000 into the bag and moved approximately 30 feet toward the door when he tripped and fell spilling part of the money, and before he could regain his footing and money he was assailed by bank employees and knocked unconscious. Simultaneously at another teller's window a female patron, upon observing *B* standing behind her with a gun, screamed and slapped his face; he responded by striking her over the head with the revolver and running from the bank. Having heard the commotion, *A* fled in the getaway car abandoning *B* and *C*. From subsequent conviction defendants appealed on the grounds that their crime was at most an attempt as asportation was not accomplished. The court in affirming conviction of armed robbery held that *C* had obtained dominion or control over the money and the 30-foot movement of the money, although never having been taken from the bank premises, was asportation. *People v Beal et al*, 39 P 2d 504/Cal (1934).

Where the accused entered a retail store intending to commit larceny, under California law he had committed burglary even though he entered during business hours along with customers, and breaking was not an element. When he pointed a gun at a clerk and demanded money, in addition to burglary he had committed attempted robbery; and when the clerk denied having any money and the accused bludgeoned him over the head with a pistol, he had committed a felony assault. The accused was properly convicted of and sentenced on all three counts against his contention on appeal that he had only committed one crime—that of attempt robbery. *People v White*, 253 P 2d 108/Cal (1953).

Evidence which showed that victim was struck from behind and knocked down and her purse snatched from her hand, supported conviction of robbery by assault as distinguished from theft from the person. *Ashford v State*, 502 SW 2d 27/Tex (1973).

Where victim was carrying a strongbox under his arm and defendant struck the box knocking it from his grasp but the victim caught it before it struck the ground, whereupon defendant again struck the box and again knocked it from the victim's grasp and on the second occasion caught the box himself and ran but was pursued and apprehended, his force in acquiring possession of the box was sufficient to sustain robbery. *People v Clayton*, 264 P 1105/Cal (1928).

A conviction of robbery by force was sustained where defendant inserted his hand in the cash drawer in a cleaning shop in an attempt to extract money therefrom, and when the clerk closed the drawer on his hand he shoved her aside with such force that she fell and lacerated her knees and he then jerked the tray from its recess onto the floor, removed the money and fled. *State v Blunt*, 193 NW 2d 434/Neb (1972).

Even though defendants' motive for slugging the chief of police may have been for the purpose of escape, they were guilty of robbery when they took the chief's pistol, car keys and parking meter keys. *Slavens v Com*, 481 SW 2d 650/Ky (1972).

Attempted Robbery

Robbery was attempted where defendant walked into a savings and loan association, handed the teller a handprinted note which read, "This is a holdup, close door. Lock doors . . . " at which time another teller approached whom defendant recognized as his sister's neighbor, whereupon defendant took back the note and stated he was just kidding and walked out of the building. Intent to commit the robbery was present, the teller was imbued with fear, and demand for the property was made; that defendant abandoned his purpose after the attempt was complete was no defense. *State v Hoover*, 187 SE 2d 453/NC (1972).

Where defendant entered a grocery store and displaying a toy pistol stated, "This is a hold-up" whereupon the female victim gave defendant the paper currency from the cash register, saying to her oppressor, "Please don't shoot me," that defendant looked at victim a minute, returned the money, saying that it was all an April fool's joke and left, was no defense to a prosecution for attempted robbery (*People v Crittle*, 195 NW 2d 799/Mich–1972). Defendant was fortunate not to have been prosecuted for completed robbery as he secured dominion and control over the money, which has been held in other jurisdictions to be a completed robbery. *People v Wellman*, 296 P 2d 82/Cal (1956).

ARMED ROBBERY

Defined

"Armed Robbery" is that type of robbery consummated while the perpetrator is armed with a weapon. It is not necessary that the weapon be a weapon *per se*, nor is it necessary that the weapon be used or that the victim know of its presence. An ice pick is a dangerous weapon within the meaning of the statute denouncing armed robbery. *People v Klimek*, 341 P 2d 722/Cal (1959).

To be "armed" within the meaning of the robbery statute, the weapon must be carried on the person or placed close at hand in a position of readiness for use at the robber's whim, but where two conspirators committed robbery while unarmed, the element of being armed cannot be imputed to them merely because a third conspirator, unknown to them, had a revolver in his glove compartment some distance away. *People v Calderone*, 191 P 2d 75/Cal (1948).

In General

The U.S. Circuit Court of Appeals for Washington, D.C., has held that under an indictment for robbery, the government must prove both larceny and assault

(*United States v McGill*, 487 F 2d 1208/DC–1973). It is not the law in most jurisdictions necessarily to include assault in the crime of robbery. Thus, where perpetrator advises the teller at a bank that he will blow up the bank unless money is delivered over, or where perpetrator demands money under threat of burning victim's house, the circumstances would certainly amount to robbery if the victim was fearful and as a result parted with property to the perpetrator, yet there is no assault in either case. California Penal Code, § 211.

In a robbery accomplished by the use of a firearm, it is immaterial that at no time during the robbery was the gun pointed at victim (*State v Shaw*, 372 P 2d 777/Or–1962); nor is it necessary that the state prove the gun was loaded, as a pistol, even a short one, is a dangerous weapon when used as a bludgeon. *Hutton v People*, 398 P 2d 973/Colo (1965).

When one takes the property of another under circumstances amounting to larceny, and then displays a weapon so as to overcome or prevent resistance, the larceny is then elevated to robbery. *Burko v State*, 313 A 2d 864/Md (1974).

Where defendant committed robbery while armed with a stiletto-type knife, his robbery was first degree as the device was a dangerous weapon. *People v Thomas*, 337 NYS 2d 850/NY (1972).

Where the Weapon Used Was a Toy Pistol

Armed robbery may be committed by the perpetrator being armed with a toy pistol. Thus, a toy pistol resembling a 32-automatic, six and one-half inches long and weighing about eight ounces, which defendant claimed to have used in the robbery to intimidate victim, and which could have been used as a bludgeon, was a dangerous weapon making the crime armed robbery (*People v Ward*, 190 P 2d 971/Cal–1948). But if under a statute a toy pistol does not qualify as a dangerous or deadly weapon, and defendant alleges that the gun used in a robbery was only a toy, the burden of proving such fact is upon the defendant. *Powell v State*, 489 SW 2d 538/Ten (1972).

In order to convict of robbery with firearms, the instrument used, as a rule, must meet the definition of "firearm" as defined in the Firearms Act. But where the instrument used in the robbery of a grocery store was a starter pistol or cap pistol, and was incapable of firing a projectile but had the appearance of a pistol, it was a firearm within the meaning of the Firearms Act and defendant's conviction was affirmed. *Smith v State*, 378 P 2d 790/Ok (1972).

When Assault Does Not Merge With Robbery

As a rule, defendant may not be convicted of both robbery and assault with a deadly weapon where a gun was pointed at victim to facilitate the robbery, but where the assault or battery is excessive, or where committed after the robbery is complete, defendant may be convicted of both. *State v Horton*, 492 P 2d 395/Az (1972).

Although the question is not always clear, normally if a battery immediately precedes a robbery, it will be held to be a component of the robbery, but if it follows the robbery it is usually regarded as an offense distinct from the robbery (*People v Ashford*, 308 NE 2d 271/Ill–1974). But where defendant shot victim in the stomach as he approached, then bent over his prostrate form and took $200 from his pocket, a conviction of both aggravated assault and robbery was proper even though the assault was committed before the robbery. *People v Gilford*, 308 NE 2d 55/Ill (1974).

Defendant could not be convicted of both armed robbery and assault with a deadly weapon where his accomplice merely drew a revolver and pointed it at victim to facilitate the robbery (*State v Jernigan*, 492 P 2d 1204/Az–1972), but where in the commission of an armed robbery the robber seriously injures the victim, the assault becomes a separate and distinct offense and defendant may be convicted of both crimes (*State v Stepney*, 185 SE 2d 844/NC–1972). Also, a rape committed upon the victim of robbery pursuant thereto never becomes a part of the robbery nor merges therewith, and defendant may be convicted of both the rape and the robbery. *Collins v State*, 492 P 2d 1133/Ok (1972).

Where, after the robbery was accomplished through fear by the pointing of a gun at victims, and thereafter perpetrator forced victims to lie on the floor while he pointed the gun at them, there was a separate and distinct assault–the first assault, only, merging with the robbery, and defendant was properly convicted of both the robbery and assault with a deadly weapon. *State v Gregory*, 501 P 2d 387/Az (1972).

Where the force used in an aggravated assault was only that sufficient to subdue his victim and to accomplish robbery, and defendant was convicted of both robbery and aggravated assault, the conviction of aggravated assault could not stand. *State v Jorgenson*, 502 P 2d 158/Az (1972).

Principality in Robbery

To convict for armed robbery by means of a dangerous or deadly weapon, it is only necessary that the state show that defendant was present and participated; it is not necessary to show that defendant personally took money or wielded the gun. *State v Young*, 490 SW 2d 28/Mo (1973).

The question of who holds the gun in an armed robbery committed by two or more persons is immaterial, and where defendant and codefendant commit robbery–codefendant holding the gun–both are guilty of armed robbery. *People v Tallent*, 200 P 2d 214/Cal (1948).

Examples of Armed Robbery

Where defendant took money from a Salvation Army employee at a store where defendant was also employed, and which owed him money, by threatening victim with a knife and taking all the money from the cash register except coins without counting it and taking more than was due him, evinced an intent not to limit his taking to the amount owed him and thus warranted a conviction of robbery. *State v Trujillo*, 489 P 2d 977/Or (1971).

Robbery was sustained against defendant where evidence showed that he entered a tavern and ordered the bartender at gunpoint to put all the money from the cash register upon the bar, and as the bartender placed the money on the bar as ordered, a patron struck the defendant on the head with a metal shuffleboard disc rendering him unconscious and then sat upon him until the arrival of an ambulance. Here, the court ruled that when the bills were placed on the counter they then came under the constructive possession of defendant and thus completed asportation. *People v Wellman* 296 P 2d 82/Cal (1956).

It was logical to infer that defendant and codefendant, while in the act of larceny, and upon being surprised by deceased, modified their intent to commit larceny to intent to commit robbery by overcoming resistance of the deceased, and a homicide committed in the commission of the robbery made the killing a statutory first degree murder. *Durham v Com*, 198 SE 2d 603/Va (1973).

Evidence that defendant "laid a pistol beside the register" then took the money from the register saying nothing, supported a conviction of armed robbery by fear. *Burko v State*, 313 A 2d 864/Md (1974).

Where the victim of rape told her assailant that she would give him money if he would leave her alone, whereupon defendant forced victim at gunpoint to go about the house searching for money, a conviction of armed robbery was warranted, *inter alia*, despite defendant's claim that victim first mentioned the money and offered to give it to him as a gift. *Whitaker v State*, 281 NE 2d 809/Ind (1972).

Where defendant threatened victim with death and thereafter raped her twice, then slit her throat and abdomen and left her to the elements to die, also taking her money, ring and wristwatch, he was guilty of three distinct crimes—rape, robbery and attempted murder—and was sentenced to serve consecutive sentences of 100, 100 and 20 years respectively. *People v Walker*, 279 NE 2d 23/Ill (1971).

When Forceful Taking Is Not Robbery

The retaking of money lost in an illegal gambling game, even by force or fear, does not constitute robbery on the theory that the money still belongs to the loser, but where the loser takes an amount of money from a fellow gambler over and above that which he has lost, such taking is robbery. *State v Hardin*, 406 P 2d 406/Az (1965).

Where U.S. Treasury agents assisted in the search of private premises under the authority of a warrant which was technically defective and exceeded the authority inherent in the warrant, the taking of property thereunder, although illegally seized, did not amount to robbery. *In re Lewis*, 83 F 159/Wn (1897).

The forcible taking of a gun from one who unlawfully pointed it at victim and ordering him to leave the immediate area, was justified and thus not robbery. *State v Campbell* 214 NW 2d 195/Ia (1974).

EXTORTION

Defined

The crime of "extortion," within the meaning of federal law, is defined as the obtaining of the property of another with his consent but induced by the wrongful use of fear or under color of official right. Extortion may be committed by the employment of either method and both fear and official right need not be exerted. *United States v Kenny*, 462 F 2d 1205/NJ (1972).

In General

To constitute extortion the victim must consent, albiet under coercion and intimidation, to part with his property. The victim has a choice: either to part title and possession to designated property, or to relinquish some advantage, or to suffer the consequences of the alternative. If the victim submits to the demands of the perpetrator as a preference to an alternative, the crime is extortion; if he submits not actuated by fear but for the purpose of obtaining evidence against the would-be extortionist, or if he elects to suffer the consequences instead, then the crime is only attempted extortion. *State v Reinoche*, 218 P 2d 865/Id (1950).

Although extortion is not viewed as larceny in some jurisdictions, it may be so designated by statute and treated as a form of larceny. *State v Jim*, 508 P 2d 462/Or (1973).

Blackmail

The word "blackmail" is a word of common parlance and is often used interchangeably with extortion. *Greenspun v Grandolfo*, 320 P 2d 628/Nev (1958).

Blackmail is the equivalent of extortion and is defined as the extraction of money for the performance of a duty, the prevention of injury, or the exercise of influence; the wrongful extraction of money; the extortion of money from a person by threats of accusation or exposure; obtaining a valuable thing from a person as a condition of refraining from making an accusation against him or disclosing some secret calculated to operate to his prejudice; a bribe to maintain silence. *Corpus Juris Secundum*, 35–Extortion.

Extortionate Threats

Threats that constitute extortion include the following but are not necessarily limited thereto; a threat to:

1. Accuse one of crime, or
2. Injure another or a member of his family or his property, or
3. Publish any libel concerning him, or
4. Expose or impute to him any deformity or disgrace, or
5. Publicize any secret adversely affecting him. *California Penal Code,* § 519.

A threat against the President of the United States, to be criminal, must be more than idle talk or jest or mere words uttered in a political agrument, but must be a serious threat, and the full context in which the words were spoken should be considered (*United States v Rogers,* 488 F 2d 512/La–1974). But where the threat was against the President of the United States, the prosecution is not required to prove that defendant intended to carry out the threat. Id.

Threats sufficient to constitute extortion may be made to victim's wife, using her as a conduit through which to funnel threats for the purpose of frightening and intimidating victim. *United States v Zito,* 467 F 2d 1401/NY (1972).

A threat to effect economic loss which excites fear is fear which will support a charge of extortion. *United States v Jacobs,* 451 F 2d 530/Fla (1971).

A threat to do that which a person has a legal right to do without demanding or extracting from another a thing of value or advantage, is not extortion. *McKey v Local Union No. 1067,* 106 P 2d 373/Cal (1940).

"Fear" As Employed in Extortion

"Fear," as used in a statute defining extortion, includes not only fear of physical violence but fear of economic harm; it is not necessary that fear be the consequences of a direct threat, only that the circumstances surrounding the alleged extortion render the victim's fear reasonable. *United States v De Met,* 486 F 2d 816/Ill (1973).

The Hobbs Act

The Hobbs Act is a federal extension of state extortion laws and consists of the following elements: (1) the inducement of one to part with his property (2) by the wrongful use of fear (3) which adversely affects interstate commerce. If the act committed by defendant has no reasonable expectation of affecting interstate commerce, the Hobbs Act is not violated and the state law on extortion must be utilized. *United States v Addonizio,* 451 F 2d 49/NJ (1971).

The Hobbs Act, under federal law, not only forbids extortion which *interferes* with interstate commerce but also forbids extortion which *affects* interstate commerce. U S C A § 1951; *United States v Gill,* 490 F 2d 233/Ill (1973).

Where defendant threatened a tavern owner with closure by the department of liquor control unless he allowed coin-operated machines to be placed in his tavern and to share in the profits, evidence was sufficient for prosecution for extortion under the Hobbs Act. *United States v Howe,* 353 FS 419/Mo (1973).

Under federal law, the Hobbs Act forbids the obstruction of interstate commerce by robbery or extortion. However, it did not apply where union members employed the wrongful use of violence during a strike to achieve legitimate objectives, for here, there was no wrongful taking of the employer's property; however, the Act did apply where union officials used threatened force or violence against employer to obtain personal payoffs and to extract wage payments in return for imposed, unwanted, superfluous and fictitious services. *United States v Emmons* 93 SC 100/35 LE 2d 379/La (1973).

"Extortion" Distinguished From "Robbery"

Robbery and extortion are distinguished by two and sometimes three characteristics:

1. In extortion the victim has a choice to either meet the demands made upon him or suffer the consequences. In robbery the victim has no choice;
2. In extortion the taking in some jurisdictions does not amount to larceny;
3. In extortion the transfer of property or the execution of some act is done at a later time, while response to the robber's demands must be immediate.

Examples of Extortion

Where defendant telephoned victim and threatened him and his family by the planting of a bomb in victim's building unless victim paid him a stated sum of money to be placed along a road beside a sign at a particular time, and defendant drove his automobile to the spot, looked all about then picked up the bag of money, there was sufficient evidence to warrant conviction for intimidation and attempt theft. *People v Babic,* 287 NE 2d 24/Ill (1972).

Where defendant went into victim's home with intent to commit a felony and thereafter stole a camera and its accessories and also attempted while posing as a police officer to extract money from the victim under the threat of charging him with a crime, such acts supported convictions of burglary, grand theft and attempted extortion. *People v Goodman*, 323 P 2d 536/Cal (1958).

Defendant, while posing as a vice officer, declared to a female victim, "I am going to spread your name and his all over the front page of the paper" (regarding presumed indiscretions), then took $42 from victim's hand and demanded $3,000 more for his silence. Defendant committed extortion if victim agreed to the taking of the $42, and grand theft-person if she did not—a determination to be made by the jury. *People v Goldstein*, 191 P 2d 102/Cal (1948).

Although defendant-officer had made prior decisions not to arrest minors who purchased intoxicating beverages, his acceptance of $300 under an agreement not to cite a liquor store owner for selling such beverages to minors, had no relation to previous decisions. Such decisions were irrelevant to the fact at issue and defendant's act amounted to extortion, not bribery, as victim paid the $300 under fear of losing his liquor license. *United States v Gill*, 490 F 2d 233/Ill (1973).

Where a business agent of a labor union forcibly prevented a truck driver from unloading his truck and demanded that he employ a member of the agent's local union to unload the truck paying the prescribed wage, he was guilty of extortion. *United States v Kemble*, 198 F 2d 889/NJ (1952).

Threats to one person, breaking of a camera store window and assault upon another had all the earmarks of a design to instill fear in both victims so as to support conviction under the Hobbs Act. *United States v Nadaline*, 471 F 2d 340/Fla (1973).

Where defendant contacted his ex-common law wife and threatened to distribute certain lewd photographs of her which he had taken during their cohabitation unless she delivered certain named property, his demand was criminal, but when defendant was arrested prior to the delivery of the property his conduct amounted to attempted extortion, only. *Yoder v State*, 493 P 2d 1141/Ok (1972).

An indictment alleging that an employee of the Internal Revenue Service under the color and pretense of authority, demanded that a named individual permit the IRS employee to perform homosexual acts upon him, failed to allege a crime under the statute forbidding extortion as money or other thing of value extracted or demanded by defendant. *United States v Provinzano*, 50 FRD 361/Wis (1970).

Chapter XXI

Forgery

The Elements of Forgery

The elements of forgery are: (1) knowledge that the instrument is false, (2) representation of the instrument to be genuine, and (3) intent to defraud (*Dodson v State*, 497 SW 2d 767/Ten–1973). Some jurisdictions by statute enlarge on this fundamental definition to include an intent to either deceive, injure or defraud, but in no jurisdiction, when the forgery is for the purpose of unlawfully obtaining narcotics or drugs, is there a requirement that there be an intent to defraud.

The false making or material alteration of an instrument in writing which is of apparent legal efficacy with intent to defraud is forgery. *State v Bauguess*, 186 SE 2d 185/NC (1972).

Intent Requisite to Forgery

In the crime of forgery there is manifest in the perpetrator an intent to defraud another of his property through the medium of a false writing or instrument in whole or in part, or by the alteration of a material part thereof by fabrication, counterfeit, addition or erasure. *State v McFall*, 439 P 2d 805/Az (1968).

Intent to defraud (in most instances) is an essential element of the crime of forgery and such intent must be charged in the indictment. *United States v Bates*, 468 F 2d 1252/La (1972).

Defendant's guilt of forgery depends not on whether the check was payable on demand or whether postdated, but on the maker's specific intent to defraud as evidenced by his conduct. *State v Etheridge*, 443 P 2d 536/Wn (1968).

Alterations

Forgery is committed when any instrument is altered or any addition is made with intent to defraud, and a deed (*Harding v Ja Laur Corp*, 315 A 2d 132/Md–1974), and a will have been held to be "instruments" subject to forgery where there have been material alterations with intent to defraud. *People v Horowitz*, 161 P 2d 833/Cal (1945).

It is not essential to a forgery that the entire instrument be false; a material addition or alteration made with intent to injure or defraud is just as much a forgery as where the entire instrument was counterfeit. Thus, where defendant typed the number "12" in front of the number "107.89," and typed the word "Enterprises" after the name "Lee Thompson," the check then being for $12,107.89 drawn on Lee Thompson Enterprises, whereupon defendant uttered the check and deposited the proceeds into her private account, actionable forgery was committed. *State v Barnett*, 423 P 2d 527/Wn (1967).

Where defendant came into possession of a check which had been signed by the maker but on which the amount and the payee's name had not been entered, the filling in of the amount and the signing of his own name as payee, without authority, constituted a material alteration and thus came within the purview of the forgery statute. *State v Rovin*, 518 P 2d 579/Az (1974).

Signing the Name of Another

When one knowingly passes a check on the account of another without his consent, the crime is complete upon presentation of the instrument, as intent to defraud is inferred by the very act of passing the check. *People v Wing*, 107 CR 836/Cal (1973).

Where the forgery is that of the name of another, the state must prove that defendant signed the name of another and that he had no authority to do so. *Lewis v Com*, 191 SE 2d 232/Va (1972).

In a forgery where defendant knowingly passes a forged instrument on the account of another without his consent, it is the general rule that subsequent restitution or repayment to the victim is irrelevant to the question of intent to defraud. *People v Wing, supra.*

Conviction for forgery was sustained where evidence showed that defendant tied his 80-year-old father to a chair, removed his social security check from the mailbox, signed his father's name thereto and presented the check for payment. *State v Hunt*, 188 SE 2d 546/NC (1972).

Signing a Fictitious Name

The mere signing of a fictitious name is not a forgery unless there is an intent that such signature will be taken as the genuine signature of another coupled with intent to defraud. (*Rapp v State*, 274 S 2d 18/Fla–1973). And if the forgery is one of a fictitious name the state must prove that no such person existed in the area where the check was passed. *State v Willard,* 279 P 2d 914/Ut (1974).

Generally a forgery conviction will not lie where the maker signs his true name; however, if the name of the accused is identical to that of another person, and an instrument is uttered not in his own name but in the name of the other person, he has committed forgery. *State v Lutes*, 230 P 2d 786/Wn (1951).

What Constitutes "Uttering"

The word "utter" as it is used in conjunction with forgery, means to offer for payment a forged instrument, with an indication by words or actions that the instrument is genuine. And the fact that the check was refused and nothing of value was received therefor has no effect on the utterance (*State v Eubanks,* 383 P 2d 342/Id–1963). "Uttering" is synonymous to "publishing." *State v Singh,* 419 P 2d 403/Az (1966).

A forged instrument is uttered not only when it is put into circulation, but also when there is an offer to so do by its possessor. *People v Harris,* 114 CR 892/Cal (1974).

Although in principal any crime may be attempted, and in a few instances such as escape the attempt is punishable to the same extent as an escape, for practical purposes the crime of attempted forgery does not exist. If one utters a forgery and the instrument is refused, forgery has been committed although the actor's attempt to obtain money by the utterance was aborted. Where defendant was charged by information with "attempt to utter a forged check . . . with intent to defraud," his guilty plea was upheld on appeal (*Dill v Cranor,* 235 P 2d 1006/Wn–1951); but see *Ponds v State ex rel Eyman,* 438 P 2d 423/Az (1968), where the Arizona Supreme Court held that a conviction of "attempt to pass a forged instrument" was a conviction of forgery, not of an attempt.

Under a statute forbidding the uttering or delivering of a check when the drawer has insufficient funds in, or credit with the drawee bank, with intent to defraud, the crime is complete upon presentation of the check, i.e., utterance, and it is not necessary for the state to allege or prove that the accused received anything of value therefor (*State v Roderick,* 375 P 2d 1005/Id–1962). Notice of nonpayment to the maker of the check is not a necessary antecedent to the commencement of action. *State v Johnston,* 267 P 2d 891/Mont (1962).

Pecuniary Loss Not an Element

Pecuniary loss to the victim is not an element of forgery. *Aldridge v State,* 492 SW 2d 477/Tex (1973).

As a rule it is not necessary that any person be defrauded. Under the laws of some states the mere making of an instrument with intent to defraud is forgery. In virtually all jurisdictions the uttering of a forgery, i.e., the presenting of an instrument for payment, constitutes forgery. *State v Peeples*, 129 P 108/Wn (1912); *People v Weitz*, 267 P 2d 295/Cal (1954).

That defendant received no benefit from the forgery does not purge the transaction. Where defendant crudely altered a check for $19 to $2,919, and the bank accepted the check on deposit without withdrawal privileges, the utterance, nevertheless, was forgery. *United States v Jenkins*, 347 F 2d 345/Va (1965); reversed and remanded on another point.

Possession With Intent to Utter

One may be convicted under the statutes of some jurisdictions for the crime of forgery when he possesses a forged instrument with intent to utter and defraud. Defendant's conviction of possession of a forged instrument with intent to utter and defraud was sustained where physical possession was actually with another, but there was abundant evidence that appellant was acting in concert with a coconspirator in a common criminal design and therefore possession by one is the possession of another. *State v Andrews*, 127 P 1102/Wn (1912).

Possession of a forged instrument by one who utters or seeks to utter it or in any way realize a profit by it, without a reasonable explanation of how it came into defendant's possession, warrants an inference that the possessor himself committed the forgery or was *particeps criminis* to its commission. *State v Massey*, 492 SW 2d 48/Mo (1973).

Forgery of a Credit Card

Defendant who unlawfully utilized the credit card of another to defraud and in the course thereof forged the signature of the card owner on a charge slip for the purpose of obtaining goods or services, could be prosecuted under the general forgery statute. *State v McCurdy*, 257 S 2d 92/Fla (1972).

Where defendant presented the credit card of another in an attempt to purchase stereo tapes and thereafter signed the name of the owner of the credit card on a sales slip, but left the store without his purchase, he could, nevertheless, be prosecuted for the forgery of the name of another with intent to defraud. *State v Ulmer*, 519 P 2d 867/Az (1974).

Postdated Checks

As a rule a postdated check is not the subject of forgery, being rather a form of promissory note; however, this rule assumes that the receiver knew the instrument to be postdated. Where the receiver is so advised such notice warrants the inference that the receiver was put on notice that the instrument was not, at the time of the making, a liquid instrument and would not be such until the arrival of the date appearing thereon (*People v Lane*, 300 P 2d 321/Cal–1957). But postdating alone does not vitiate intent to defraud, and defendant's guilt would necessarily depend on such intent (*State v Eichman*, 418 P 2d

418/Wn–1966). The fact that a check was postdated one year merely defers negotiability and does not negate its efficacy nor render it void as an enforceable obligation. *Gentry v People*, 441 P 2d 675/Colo (1968).

In a prosecution for passing a forged instrument as true, the state must prove that the accused passed or attempted to pass the instrument, that it was a forgery, and that the accused had knowledge of the forgery at the time of utterance. *Rice v State*, 484 SW 2d 589/Tex (1972).

Although there may be expert testimony as to whether, in the opinion of the handwriting expert, the accused indited the instrument, the question is one of fact to be decided by the jury by visual comparison of the questioned instrument with the handwriting exemplar of the accused. *State v Maxwell*, 102 P 2d 109/Kan (1940).

Forgery of a Narcotic Prescription

Delivery of a forged prescription for the purpose of obtaining a narcotic drug may usually be prosecuted under the forgery statute of the criminal code, obtaining property by false pretenses under the crimimal code, or under the Uniform Narcotic Drug Act governing acquisition of drugs by fraud or deceit (*People v Merchant*, 283 NE 2d 724/Ill–1972). And in a prosecution for forgery of a narcotic prescription the state is not required to prove an intent to defraud, as defrauding in this type of forgery is not an element (*State v Osborn*, 494 P 2d 773/Az–1972). A statue prohibiting the obtaining of narcotics by a forged prescription is not aimed at protection of persons from being defrauded of property, but at the misuse of narcotic drugs and the usual elements of forgery are not included. *State v McFall*, 428 P 2d 101/vacated on another point 439 P 2d 805/Az (1968).

Insufficient Funds

Notification to the payee by the maker that there was then insufficient funds to cover the check purges the transaction of its criminal character, the element of intent to defraud being absent equates the transaction to an extension of credit. *State v Eikelberger*, 239 P 2d 1069/Id (1951).

In a prosecution for uttering a check on an insufficient fund account, the crime is complete when the check is presented for payment with knowledge of its insufficiency and with intent to defraud. Reliance upon the authenticity of the check by the victim, although an element under false pretenses, is not an element hereunder; nor is it necessary that any person be defrauded. *State v Koester*, 209 NW 2d 172/Neb (1973).

In a prosecution for the uttering of a check without sufficient funds, the state is not required to prove that the victim actually parted with any property, nor is it necessary that there be any reliance upon the false representation of the defendant. *State v Koester, supra.*

Forgery to Pay Preexisting Debt

Where defendant and plaintiff together with others were engaged in an illegal gambling game and defendant lost steadily securing his losses with a total of seven I.O.U.'s, and at the end of the game he wrote plaintiff a check for $2,750, the total amount represented by the I.O.U.'s, and the check was returned unpaid, there was no crime as an illegal gambling debt is unenforceable in the courts (*Rose v Nelson,* 180 P 2d 759/Cal—1947). Also, intent to defraud cannot be inferred where a worthless check is uttered solely as purported payment on account or in the discharge of an existing debt where no present benefit is contemplated. *State v Blasi,* 312 A 2d 135/NJ (1973); *Hoye v Hoffman,* 416 P 2d 232/Nev (1966).

Glossary of Words and Phrases

Abet: applied to a principal or an accessory before the fact; to assist, advise or encourage a coprincipal in crime with knowledge of his wrongful purpose.

Adulterine bastard: one begotten as a result of his mother's adulterous sexual intercourse.

Amicus curiae: friend of the court; one who gives information to the court, but is not a witness; advises on points of law or order.

Animo furandi: intent to steal.

Animo revertendi: intent to return.

Asportation: the gaining of dominion or control over, plus movement, however slight, of property or of a person.

Bill of attainder: a legislative act which inflicts punishment without a judicial trial; at common law a bill of attainder was a decree of a punishment of death with an "attaint" of bloodline and a forfeiture to the state of all property.

Bill of particulars: a detailed statement of criminal charges which is or may be supplementary to an indictment.

Caveat emptor: let the buyer beware; a concept wherein the buyer of a thing assumes all risk for imperfections or faults.

Certiorari, writ of: often referred to as a writ of review; is employed when no other remedy is available and is usually issued by a superior or an appellate court and when used as a writ of review it is directed to a lower court, ordering cretain records sent up for review.

Chattel: an article or item of personal property; it is distinguished from the word "goods" in that chattel is more comprehensive and includes inanimate as well as animate objects. Goods includes only inanimate objects.

Commitment: a warrant, order or process by which a court or magistrate directs a ministerial officer to take a person to jail or prison and to there detain him.

Competency: competent evidence is admissible evidence, not excluded by some rule; a competent witness is one who understands the nature of his oath and his obligation to testify truly, or one who is not excluded by privileged communication or some other rule; a competent defendant is one who is not mentally diseased and is possessed of sufficient intelligence to understand the nature of the charge and to assist in his defense.

Conviction: a plea of guilty or a finding of guilt by either a jury or by a judge sitting without jury.

Corpus delicti: the elements of the crime; every crime has a *corpus delicti;* a human corpse or cadaver is not a *corpus delicti.*

Crime or public offense: an act committed or omitted in violation of a law forbidding or commanding it for which is provided upon conviction a prescribed punishment.

Darkness, hours of: as used in conjunction with motor vehicle laws, is that period of time starting 30 minutes after sunset and extending to 30 minutes before sunrise.

De facto: in fact; existing without legal sanction.

De jure: by lawful right; right by law.

De novo: anew; to occur again; said of a new trial; such as "a trial *de novo*."

Duces tecum: bring with you; a subpoena *duces tecum* is a command to a witness to appear and bring named documents.

Ejusdem generis: of the same kind or origin.

Escheat: the reversion or forfeiture of property, real or personal, to the state upon death of the owner when there is no known heir and no will.

Ex parte: on the part of one party, only; not adversary in nature.

Ex post facto: a law having retroactive effect; or, in its relation to an offense or its consequences, it alters conditions to the disadvantage of a party; or, impairs or deprives the party of a defense which the law has provided; or, a law which declares an act to be criminal which was not criminal at the time it was committed, or which increases the punishment.

Felonious intent: does not necessarily mean intent to commit a felony, but rather intent to commit crime; however, it is defined more specifically according to the terms of the crime to which it relates.

Felony: a crime punishable by death or imprisonment in the state penitentiary; under federal definition, any crime punishable by death or more than one year imprisonment.

Fiduciary relationship: a position of trust or confidence as exists between employer and employee wherein the employee receives company funds and disburses and distributes them according to the terms of his employment.

Furnish: to provide or supply and connotes a transfer of possession.

Habeas corpus, writ of: you have the body; a writ setting bail for an arrestee or otherwise ordering his release.

In banc (also bank, banque): the reviewing of cases on appeal by the entire panel of judges or justices of a supreme court. As a rule, they may sit in "department," three to a department, or in "banc," the entire panel.

In absentia: in his absence; a matter adjudicated in the absence of one or more parties.

Incorporeal: without substance; not tangible or physical.

In extremis: at the point of death; under a sense of impending death; said of a dying declaration.

In propria persona: in person; personally.

Inter alia: among other things.

Knowingly: an act or omission was intentional; it is not necessary that the actor intended to break the law, only that he intended to commit the act.

Lex communis: common law.

Magistrate: a judicial officer having the power to issue a warrant of arrest.

Mala (malem) in se: wrong of itself; morally wrong.

Mala prohibita (prohibitum): wrong by law; declared illegal by statute.

Malice: an absence of all elements of justification, excuse or recognized mitigation; actual intent to cause harm which is produced; the wanton and willful doing of an act with knowledge of a strong likelihood that such harm may result.

Materiality: evidence of substantial importance or weight; that evidence which is or may be essential to the fact at issue.

Mens rea: guilty intent.

Modus operandi: method of operation; habit acquired in work or performance.

Mootness or a moot question: one which has lost its character in controversy when it reaches an appellate court and the appellant has received relief from another source or the alleged wrong has ceased to exist, such as a decision as to the legality of the Viet Nam war after hostilities terminated.

Nighttime: that period of time between sunset and sunrise.

Nisi prius: jury trial, trial of the issue of fact.

Nolo contendere: I will not contest it; the equivalent of a guilty plea except that it may not be used against defendant in any subsequent civil proceeding.

Nolle prosequi: I will not prosecute; an entry on the record in a civil case by the plaintiff or in a criminal case by the prosecutor; in effect a dismissal of the pending charge or litigation, but does not bar a future prosecution.

Non compos mentis: not of sound mind; insane.

Nunc pro tunc: now for then; an act done with retroactive effect.

Obiter dictum: an opinion collateral to the issue before the court: an opinion not necessary to a ruling in the instant case.

Onus probandi: burden of proof; the duty to prove guilt beyond a reasonable doubt.

Pari delicto: of equal guilt; equally guilty.

Particeps criminis: an accomplice; a party to crime; a coprincipal.

Passion: used in conjunction with voluntary manslaughter, includes anger and terror, provided such emotions reach a degree of intensity sufficient to obscure reason.

Pleading: a written allegation of what is affirmed by one party or denied by another; an "accusatory pleading" is employed exclusively in criminal proceedings and includes indictment, information, complaint or any other means by which one accused of crime is brought to bar.

Possession: physical control; care and management of a thing; constructive possession is accomplished when one has dominion or control over a thing or the premises on which the thing is located.

Prima facie: at first sight; on the first appearance; presumably; a fact established prima facie is presumed to be true unless and until controverted by competent evidence.

Probable cause, sufficient cause, and reasonable cause: essentially synonymous, mean such a state of facts as would lead a man of ordinary caution or prudence to believe and conscientiously entertain a strong suspicion of the guilt of the accused.

Quid pro quo: what for what; the giving of one valuable thing for another; a trade of objects or things, tangible or intangible.

Ravish: synonymous with the word rape; forcible sexual intercourse with a female against her will and consent.

Relevancy: a tendency to prove the fact at issue; something material, more or less probable in the light of logic; experience and accepted assumptions concerning human behavior.

Res gestae: literally means things done, but as a rule for the admissibility of evidence it means all things done or said immediately antecedent to, during or subsequent to the crime to which it relates, by a participant or victim; it includes excited utterances, spontaneous declarations, acts performed and physical objects. Admissibility does not depend as much on immediacy as on spontaneity.

Res ipsa loquitur: the thing speaks for itself.

Res judicata: a matter adjudicated; a judicial decision; a thing or matter settled by a judgment.

Scienter: knowledge; knowlingly.

Search: a quest by the use of force, either actual or constructive; an invasion; a probing or exploration for something that is concealed from the searcher.

Seize and seizure: the forcible or secretive dispossession of one's property against his will; to grasp or snatch and assume possession of.

Solicitor: as used in this text means an attorney at law and particularly the prosecuting attorney or the district attorney.

Stare decisis: to abide by; the rule of following precedent in cases previously adjudicated; the rule of prior decision.

Sua sponte: of his own will; action taken by a judge although no motion is made.

Swear: a solemn invocation of the Deity renouncing mercy and imprecating the vengeance of Heaven if the witness does not speak the truth.

Tort: a legal wrong not involving contract; an act or omission of one in violation of a duty from which injury to another accrues. A tortious act or omission may be criminal or noncriminal.

Ultra vires: without authority; beyond powers; beyond the scope of a corporate charter.

Utter: as used in forgery means to present for payment; to deliver for payment an instrument such as a check representing value.

Venire: the jury panel; twelve good and lawful men of the county.

Voir dire: literally means to speak the truth; in law it is a preliminary examination which a witness or a juror may be given to determine competency or bias.

Waiver: an intentional and knowing relinquishment of a constitutional or other lawful right.

Index